D1600410

# HANDBOOK OF CRITICAL INFORMATION SYSTEMS RESEARCH

# Handbook of Critical Information Systems Research

Theory and Application

*Edited by*

Debra Howcroft

*Manchester Business School, University of Manchester, UK*

Eileen M. Trauth

*School of Information Sciences and Technology, Pennsylvania State University, USA*

**Edward Elgar**

Cheltenham, UK • Northampton, MA, USA

658.4038
H2363

Published by
Edward Elgar Publishing Limited
Glensanda House
Montpellier Parade
Cheltenham
Glos GL50 1UA
UK

Edward Elgar Publishing, Inc.
136 West Street
Suite 202
Northampton
Massachusetts 01060
USA

A catalogue record for this book
is available from the British Library

ISBN 1 84376 478 4 (cased)

Printed and bound in Great Britain by MPG Books Ltd, Bodmin, Cornwall

# Contents

## PART II THEORY AND APPLICATION

# Figures

# Tables

# Contributors

**Alison Adam** is Professor of Information Systems at the Information Systems Institute, University of Salford, UK. Her research interests are in gender and technology, computer ethics and critical information systems.

**Rosio Alvarez** has concurrent appointments as faculty of information systems at the University of Massachusetts Boston and director of the information technology (IT) division at the University of Massachusetts Amherst. She has worked as a systems engineer and IT professional for a number of years. Her research focuses on language and socio-cultural issues of technology implementations.

**Chrisanthi Avgerou** is Professor of Information Systems at the London School of Economics and Political Science. Her main research interests concern the relationship of information technology to organizational change, and the role of IT in socio-economic development. She is chair of the International Federation for Information Processing (IFIP) Technical Committee 9 on social implications of IT, and past chair of IFIP WG 9.4 on computers in developing countries. Among her latest publications are *Information Systems and Global Diversity* (Oxford University Press, 2002) and *The Social Study of Information and Communication Technology* (Oxford University Press, 2004).

**Dubravka Cecez-Kecmanovic** is Professor of Information Systems at the Faculty of Commerce and Economics, University of New South Wales (UNSW), Sydney, Australia. She earned her BS in Electrical Engineering at the University of Sarajevo, MS in System Sciences and Information Systems at the University of Belgrade and PhD in Information Systems at the University of Ljubljana. Until 1992 she was with the Informatics Department, Faculty of Electrical Engineering, University of Sarajevo. She has published in the field of social systems of information and government information systems (IS), decision support systems, Web-enhanced cooperative learning and teaching, and electronically mediated work and communication. Her recent research interests include a sensemaking theory of knowledge in organizations and the co-emergence of IS and organizations. Many of her empirical studies have been informed by critical theory, focusing especially on IS impacts on increasing rationalization and control in organizations, as well as domination, power and emancipation. She has initiated and co-chaired a critical IS research mini-track at Americas Conference on Information Systems (AMCIS) and is currently involved in co-editing special issues of *Critical Sociology* (on critical management studies) and the *Information Systems Journal* (on critical IS research).

**Bill Doolin** is Professor of eBusiness at Auckland University of Technology, New Zealand. His research focuses on the processes that shape the adoption and use of information technologies in organizations. This has involved work on information systems in the public health sector and electronic commerce applications and strategies. He has over 30 refereed publications in international conferences and journals such as *Information Systems Journal*, the *Journal of Information Technology*, *Accounting, Management and Information Technologies, Organization* and *Organization Studies*.

**Anita Greenhill** is a lecturer in information systems and technology management at Manchester Business School. Anita's research interests include social, cultural and organizational aspects of information systems. Adopting social shaping and critical approaches to IS research, she researches a diversity of topics including information and communication technology (ICT) enabled work practices, space, virtuality, Web information systems development, and gender.

**Christopher Grey** is a reader in organizational theory at the University of Cambridge and Fellow of Wolfson College, Cambridge, having previously held posts at the universities of Leeds and Manchester, from where he gained his PhD, and visiting posts at Stockholm University, Sweden. He has published widely in diverse areas of organization theory and management studies and is editor-in-chief of *Management Learning*, European co-editor of the *Journal of Management Inquiry* and an editorial board member of numerous journals including the *Journal of Management Studies*, *Organization* and the *British Journal of Management*.

**Dagfinn Hertzberg** holds a Masters degree from the Norwegian University of Science and Technology (NTNU). He is finishing his PhD based on a study of organizational transformation of global business organizations. He has worked within the externally funded project Næringslivets idefond (Business prospects) at NTNU.

**Debra Howcroft** is a senior lecturer in information systems at Manchester Business School, University of Manchester. Her research interests are concerned with the social and organizational aspects of information systems.

**Ela Klecun** is a lecturer in information systems at the London School of Economics and Political Science (LSE). She holds a PhD in information systems from the LSE. Her research interests include health information systems, evaluation of information systems, and the application of critical theory and actor-network theory in the field of information systems.

**Lynette Kvasny** is Assistant Professor of Information Sciences and Technology, and a founding member of the Center of the Information Society at the Pennsylvania State University. She earned a PhD in Computer Information Systems from Georgia State University where she was a KPMG Doctoral Scholar. She has also received the National Science Foundation's Faculty Early Career Development Grant (2003–08). Her research interests include digital divide, IT diversity, and community informatics. Her research has appeared in publications including the *Data Base for Advances in Information Systems*, and the *International Journal of Technology and Human Interaction*.

**Kathy McGrath** is a lecturer in information systems at Brunel University in West London. She has extensive experience as an IS practitioner, including eight years as an IS and management consultant in the public and private sectors. More recently, she gained an MSc and a PhD in information systems from the London School of Economics and Political Science. Her teaching and research interests focus on IS implementation and management, and the relationship between IT and organizational change.

**Laurie McLeod** is currently a PhD candidate at Auckland University of Technology, New Zealand. After working for a number of years as a research scientist, she is now undertaking interpretive research into the detailed processes of interaction that occur in and around IS development. Recently, she has worked as a usability engineer at the University of Waikato, New Zealand. Her usability work has been presented at international computer science conferences.

**Shirin Madon** is a senior lecturer in information systems at the London School of Economics and Political Science. Her main research interest is studying the impact of information systems on planning and administration in developing countries and she has carried out extensive fieldwork in India on several funded research projects. More recently, she has extended her field of intellectual inquiry beyond IT in the government sector to broader issues of e-governance and development and she continues to be engaged in long-term fieldwork through support from a succession of small grants from various research funding bodies.

**Nathalie N. Mitev** is a lecturer at the London School of Economics and has held positions at Salford University and City University. She has French postgraduate degrees, an MBA and a PhD. Her research career initially concentrated on information retrieval and human-computer interaction and has moved to IS and organizations. She has published on implementation issues in small businesses, and the health, travel and construction industries. Her theoretical inclinations are towards the social construction and history of technology and she has applied actor-network theory to analysing IS failures.

**Eric Monteiro** is Professor of Information Systems at the Department of Computer and Information Systems at NTNU. He is broadly interested in organizational transformations and ICT in general, and issues of globalization in particular. His publication outlets include: *MIS Quarterly*, the *Journal of Computer-Supported Cooperative Work, Science, Technology and Human Values, Information and Organization, Methods of Information in Medicine, The Information Society* and the *Scandinavian Journal of Information Systems*.

**Helen Richardson** joined the University of Salford in 1998 after a varied career including working in the field of social care and running a research and training unit promoting positive action for women at work. Her research interests reside in the field of critical research in information systems, especially cultures of consumption and gender issues in IS.

**Leiser O. Silva** is Assistant Professor in the Decision and Information Sciences Department at the C.T. Bauer College of Business, University of Houston. He holds a PhD in information systems from the London School of Economics and Political Science. His current research examines issues of power and politics in the adoption and implementation of information systems. In addition, he is looking at managerial aspects of information systems, specifically, contextual and institutional factors. His work has been published in journals such as the *Journal of the Association for Information Systems, Communications of the Association for Information Systems, The Information Society* and *Information Technology and People*.

**James Stewart** is Senior Research fellow in the Research Centre for Social Sciences/Institute for Studies of Science, Technology and Innovation at the University of Edinburgh.

**Eileen M. Trauth** is Professor of Information Sciences and Technology at the Pennsylvania State University and Director of the Center for the Information Society. Her research interests are at the intersection of socio-cultural and organizational influences on IS and the IS profession. In 2003 she was the recipient of an E.T.S. Walton Distinguished Visitor Award from Science Foundation Ireland to continue her research on socio-cultural aspects of Ireland's information economy. Her original work is chronicled in *The Culture of an Information Economy: Influences and Impacts in the Republic of Ireland* (Idea Group Publishing, 2001). In 2002, she received a grant from the National Science Foundation to examine socio-cultural influences on gender in the American IS profession. She has been a visiting scholar in several countries where she has conducted research on socio-cultural influences and impacts. She has also published papers on qualitative research methods and is the editor of *Qualitative Research in IS: Issues and Trends*. She serves on the editorial boards of several international journals.

**Geoff Walsham** is Professor of Management Studies at the Judge Institute of Management, Cambridge University, UK. His teaching and research is centred on the social and management aspects of the design and use of information and communication technologies, in the context of both industrialized and developing countries. His publications include *Interpreting Information Systems in Organizations* (Wiley, 1993), and *Making a World of Difference: IT in a Global Context* (Wiley, 2001).

**Chris Westrup** is a senior lecturer at the Manchester Business School in the University of Manchester. He is interested in the processes of recognizing, communicating, and codifying management knowledge in both 'developed' and 'developing' countries.

**Robin Williams** is Professor of Social Research on Technology and Director of the Research Centre for Social Sciences/Institute for Studies of Science, Technology and Innovation at the University of Edinburgh.

**Melanie Wilson** is a lecturer in information systems and technology management at Manchester Business School. Generally her research interests lie in the area of social and organizational aspects of information systems. Adopting social shaping and critical approaches to IS research, specific topics include gender success/failure and ICT-enabled work practices.

**Lakshman Yapa** is Professor of Geography at the Pennsylvania State University. He earned a PhD in Geography from Syracuse University. His research combines theories of economic development, postmodern discourse theory, and geographical information systems (GIS). He served as a consultant on economic development with several international agencies including the US Agency for International Development, the World Bank, and the United Nations Development Programme. His research has appeared in *Futures, Annals of the Association of American Geographers* and the *Bulletin of Science, Technology, and Society.*

# 1 Choosing critical IS research
*Debra Howcroft and Eileen M. Trauth*

**Introduction**

This handbook presents a collection of reflections on key themes and emergent issues in critical information systems (IS) research. Written by specialists in their respective fields, it draws together a variety of contributions to the study of information systems. Common to the contributions is a shared concern with challenging what is seen by some as the current orthodoxy about IS theory and research. Since the publication of the seminal paper by Orlikowski and Baroudi (1991) which noted the dearth of critical IS research, there has been a considerable shift in the research landscape. The last few years have witnessed a more explicit focus on such research, as evidenced in an increasing number of publications, conference streams, special issues and academic electronic networks concerned with discussing critical IS.[1] Continuing in that vein, this handbook adopts an inclusive approach to consider alternative insights that can arise from critical IS research. We do not attempt to cover all varieties of this research, but rather incorporate some of its most influential currents. In this introduction we begin by considering the motivation to engage in critical IS research. We then go on to describe the organization of the book. Included in this is a brief overview of each of the chapters.

**The evolution of critical IS research**

Accompanying the development and diffusion of information technologies (IT) throughout organizations and society, comes the research challenge to examine the relationship between IS and the organizations/societies within which they are embedded. The social nature of activities associated with the development, implementation and use of IS, and the management of people who carry out these activities, naturally leads to considerations of social and political power. As the field of IS matures, it is fitting that consideration be given to the ways in which such an examination is carried out. Thus, there is a need to consider the research approaches that are used to carry out these assessments.[2]

It is worth noting that the meaning of the term 'critical' is not self-evident and is often subject to various interpretations. In the social sciences, the term is used to describe a range of related approaches, including critical theory

*1*

(Horkheimer 1976), critical operational research (Mingers 1992), critical accounting (Critical Perspectives on Accounting), critical ethnography (Forester 1992) and critical management studies (Alvesson and Willmott 1996). Each of these is subject to its own disciplinary connotations (Mingers 2000). However, a commonality across all of these various understandings of the term is that they are generally informed by the critical theory of the Frankfurt school (Hammersley 1995), for example, Theodor Adorno, Max Horkheimer, Herbert Marcuse and Jürgen Habermas.

Yet, despite such commonality, there are some fairly distinct styles in the way research is performed (geographically, institutionally and disciplinarily), resulting in a diversity of intellectual activity, some of which is indeed oppositional (for example, realism versus relativism,[3] class politics versus gender politics[4]). Hence, there exists a broad range of epistemological/ontological positions, which fall under the 'critical' umbrella and which draw upon a variety of social theories and social thinkers. These include, for example, the Frankfurt school of critical theory (Horkheimer 1976), actor-network theory (Latour 1991), Marxism (Marx [1867] 1974), feminist theory (Wajcman 1991), and the work of Bourdieu (1990), Dooyeweerd (1973), Foucault (1979) and Heidegger (1953).

In contrast to the diversity within the social sciences, critical IS research was initially guided by the Frankfurt school generally (Brooke 2002a), and more particularly, the work of Jürgen Habermas (Ngwenyama 1991; Doolin and Lowe 2002) with a core of authors committed to this area (Lyytinen and Klein 1985; Lyytinen and Hirschheim 1988, 1989; Ngwenyama 1991; Lyytinen 1992; Klein and Hirschheim 1993; Hirschheim and Klein 1994; Ngwenyama and Lee 1997; Cecez-Kecmanovic et al. 1999; Cecez-Kecmanovic 2001). As a result, some authors have argued that the relative dominance of the Habermasian approach is unnecessarily limiting (Doolin and Lowe 2002) and have called for enrolling other critical social theorists whose work could be of relevance to IS (Brooke 2002b).

In editing this handbook we are addressing this need. We do so, first and foremost, by producing a reference book in which insights into the conduct of critical IS research are provided by established scholars who write from a basis of experience with the theory and practice of critical research. We also address this need by the diversity of contributing chapters. This handbook reflects a broad range of critical approaches, thereby enriching our understanding of critical IS research.

In order to help the reader make sense of this evolving and rich area of study we identify five key themes or foci which shape a critical epistemology. These themes emanate in part from the critical management studies (CMS) literature, an area of critical research that has resonance with the IS research community, and is well developed with an increasing proliferation of sources.

It is not our intention here to put forth an exhaustive, comprehensive, or definitive set of criteria for what constitutes critical IS research. Rather, we note these elements as a way of illustrating the breadth of definition that is possible, and to use this structure to explain our strategy of inclusion for the handbook.

The first theme – emancipation – is fundamental in a range of critical intellectual traditions be it Habermasian, feminist or Marxist research (Alvesson and Willmott 1992). A thread running through all of these perspectives is a commitment to freeing individuals from power relations around which social and organizational life are woven (Fournier and Grey 2000). Often portrayed as the central objective of critical research, the intention is to focus on 'the oppositions, conflicts and contradictions in contemporary society, and to be emancipatory in that it should help to eliminate the causes of alienation and domination' (Myers and Avison 2002: 7). Despite this common interest in emancipation, the ways in which power relations are theorized, resisted and overthrown are seriously contested within the various intellectual traditions. The emancipatory discourse has been described as merely another form of domination that is in itself totalizing (Wilson 1997). As noted by Land (2004), one person's emancipation could be another person's enslavement. To adopt unitary and simplistic views of emancipation is necessarily limiting and will do little to further the critical project. Thus, more research and reflection are needed to investigate this issue further.

The second theme, critique of tradition, seeks to disrupt rather than reproduce the status quo. Whereas mainstream accounts seek to justify organizational and technological imperatives as natural and/or unavoidable, critical research challenges rather than confirms that which is established, and encourages dissent rather than acceptance of surface consensus. This critique of tradition (Mingers 2000) endeavours to upset existing patterns of power and authority. Critical research questions and deconstructs the taken-for-granted assumptions inherent in the status quo, and interprets organizational activity (including information systems) by recourse to a wider social, political, historical, economic and ideological context (Doolin 1998). Described as the sharing among critical researchers of oppositional tendencies (Grey, Chapter 9 this volume) this manifests as 'oppositional to established power and ideology; to managerial privilege; to hierarchy and its abuse; to, to put it at its most generic, not only the established order but the proposition that the established order is immutable' (pp. 186–7). As IS researchers we could add opposition to the ideas of progress that are aligned with technological development. Although there are problems with building a research stream that is based only on oppositional tendencies and negation, this does not by implication deny our choice to suggest an alternative and radically different view of the world, one which emphasizes change but in a more positive way. This highlights the areas of commonality that draw critical researchers together and underlines critical research as a political project.

The third theme, non-performative intent (Fournier and Grey 2000), concerns the rejection of the provision of tools to support and assist managerial efficiency through re-engineering minimum inputs for maximum outputs. It rejects a view of action that is guided only by economic efficiency as opposed to a concern for social relations and all that is associated with this. This notion of anti-performativity stands in contrast to non-critical research, which aims to develop knowledge that contributes to the production of maximum output for minimum input (means–ends calculation). Similar claims are made on behalf of technology in general and information systems in particular, which are seen as augmenting the power of managerial decision making.

The fourth theme, critique of technological determinism, challenges the discourse surrounding socio-economic change – be it post-industrial society, information society, or globalization – which assumes that technological development is autonomous and that societal development is determined by the technology (Bijker 1995). It disrupts the inner logic of technology as a given, something that is assumed to provide an effective and reliable vehicle for social and organizational change (Williams and Edge 1996). The concern of critical researchers is not with the effectiveness of information systems, nor are they motivated by a wish to improve practice. Rather, the critical literature seeks to conceptualize technology development, adoption and use within the context of broader social and economic changes. Critique of the technological determinist tradition highlights both its explanatory inadequacy and its ideological function of furthering the vested interests in technical change (Russell and Williams 2002).

The final theme, reflexivity, highlights a methodological distinction between critical and more mainstream IS research. Whereas IS studies have traditionally been positivist, critical research engages in a critique of objectivity (Mingers 2000). In doing so it questions the validity of objective, value-free knowledge and information that is available, noting how this is often shaped by structures of power and interests. Like interpretive research, critical research engages in philosophical and methodological reflexivity (Fournier and Grey 2000). It provides reflections on the role of the researcher as a producer of knowledge and the mediations and negotiations that are associated with this role. In this respect, critical research is reflexive about the choice of research topic and the manner in which the research is conducted. As Kvasny (2004) has pointed out, we need to consider the extent to which we – as researchers – are implicated in mechanisms that promote suffering. The way that we select research topics for investigation and how we choose to conduct the research contains consequences. We argue that it is not a neutral process. These consequences have the potential to perpetuate global inequalities and existing power bases within society. Further, we assert that denial or ignorance of these effects does not constitute objectivity and neutrality.

Throughout the course of this book project, our guiding principle has been the desire to complement and critique mainstream IS research, not to supplant it. Thus, it is possible to take some of the ideas and theories that have emerged from for-profit research and apply these insights in the not-for-profit context (Kvasny 2004). Our goal is to encourage research that builds upon and extends the positivist and interpretive research traditions so that new avenues of research opportunity are opened up to the IS scholar.

**Organization of the book**
The objective of this book is to consider the enactment of the critical tradition in IS research and the possibilities for new insights that can arise from shifting the lens from positivist or interpretive to critical. We achieve this objective in the following way. This book is divided into two parts which broadly reflect theoretical or conceptual themes, and also the application of these theories (although these are inevitably intertwined). If read sequentially, the chapters take the reader on a journey from consideration of the nature of critical IS research to issues for reflection with respect to the future conduct of critical IS research to specific examples of the application of a critical epistemology.

*The nature of critical IS research*
Part I sets the scene by considering the nature of critical IS research. The chapters consider the origins of critical IS research, the ways in which such research differs from positivist and interpretive research, and the implications of choosing the critical epistemology.

In Chapter 2, Dubravka Cecez-Kecmanovic provides an introduction to understanding what is meant by critical enquiry. Cecez-Kecmanovic achieves this by reflecting on the fundamental assumptions and concepts that guide critical research as compared to other epistemological choices, such as positivism or interpretivism. The issues covered include the purpose and motivation of research; the role of values in research; the nature of organizations, information systems, and their relationship; and assumptions about methodology. It is intended that this chapter is part of an ongoing project to provide greater understanding and appreciation of the nature of critical research. One anticipated outcome is that this process will alert readers who are editors and reviewers to the legitimacy of this type of research. A second objective is to encourage critical IS researchers to reflect on their own assumptions and beliefs, thus continually developing and refining the critical project.

Leiser Silva, in Chapter 3, focuses on information systems and power. He considers the various theoretical approaches for studying power and discusses the challenges posed, given the technological and social aspects of information systems and the unobtrusive nature of power itself. Silva argues that theoretical frameworks with a Machiavellian view, whereby power is conceptualized in a strategic way, will enrich our understanding of the relationship between IT and organizations. He develops an integrative theoretical framework for such studies, by drawing specifically on Clegg's circuits of power and actor-network theory.

In attending to the multiple perspectives that can inform critical IS research, Nathalie Mitev, in Chapter 4, explores the issue of social contructivism and its potential contribution to the critical agenda. Constructivism, with its rejection of technological determinism and positivism, seems to have some areas of commonality with critical research. These issues are explored in the context of IS failures, which is used to highlight the differences between functionalist, interpretivist, constructivist and critical perspectives. This chapter, with recourse to an application (IS failure), advances our understanding of theory and how it can be used to inform the critical research agenda. The value of constructivism in supporting criticality is outlined, along with suggestions as to how some of the limitations of constructivism may be overcome. A case is presented that constructivist approaches, when used in such a way, have much to offer critical IS research.

In Chapter 5, Rosio Alvarez presents critical discourse analysis as an approach for understanding information systems as discursively constructed phenomena embedded within social structures. The case is made for the high proportion of IS work that entails interactional talk, thereby emphasizing the relevance of discourse analysis for IS research. This interactional talk creates and reproduces relationships of dominance, power, inequality and control. Critical discourse analysis provides IS researchers with an opportunity to examine power relations by deconstructing the language used and by giving consideration to how power is mobilized through language. Alvarez argues that this understanding paves the way towards emancipatory possibilities by 'denaturalizing' the existing social conditions and revealing alternative ways of being, explains the key elements of critical discourse analysis and provides an overview of analytical strategies that can be applied in practice. She concludes by encouraging researchers to critically examine language and consider how this level of understanding has the potential to assist both themselves as researchers and also to provide support to workers in organizations.

Alison Adam in Chapter 6 considers how ethics could be more effectively integrated into the critical wing of IS. She begins by looking to the field of computer ethics, which has some areas of commonality with critical IS, yet there is a notable absence of connection or integration. When moving on to consider the area of critical IS, Adam finds it surprising that the ethical foundations of Habermas's critical social theory has had such limited impact, especially since the focus on emancipation can be clearly cast as an ethical issue. There is much potential for further work in this area and a key question concerns how we may criticize the project of ethics yet retain and integrate it more effectively into IS. Adam argues against principles and rules of ethics and instead argues for a phenomenological, embedded nature of moral behaviour in the IS field.

In Chapter 7, Chris Westrup argues that a critical engagement with the concept of management fashions can help illuminate issues concerning similar trends within the IS field. Beginning with a thorough overview of the literature on developments in management fashions, Westrup argues that parallels can be drawn with the IS field. Some key trends are in evidence, which can be seen as waves of management fashion, as each fashion seemingly offers management new means for extracting surplus from labour. Initially, IS played a crucial role in fashions such as outsourcing, downsizing and business process re-engineering. More recently (post-1997), fashionable developments and interventions such as customer relationship management systems, e-business, and enterprise systems, are much more closely aligned with specific technologies. The chapter argues that a key difference is that IS fashions are linked to more durable technologies, rather than techniques, such as quality circles or total quality management, which can be relatively ephemeral. The rhetorics of information systems play an important role in giving different groupings (such as management, IT vendors, consultants and the business press) various ways to realign themselves. Developing and applying this argument further, Westrup then considers enterprise resource planning (ERP) systems as an example of IS-predicated management fashion.

Chapter 8 considers the issues which arise from the different critical approaches which stem from Marxism and feminism in the context of gender and information systems. Anita Greenhill and Melanie Wilson contrast the Marxist view of emancipation with that of feminists who seek reform within the existing capitalist system, and argue that the theoretical position of Marxism assists us in our understanding of both technology and women's oppression. They focus on the issue of at-home telework and present a Marxist critique of espoused benefits for women teleworkers within the traditional family. This critique questions the extent to which telework offers so-called 'liberation', given the context of home and family responsibilities, isolation and powerlessness that is often associated with most teleworking practices. The authors go on to argue that not only are these espoused benefits highly questionable, but that telework presents a regressive step for the emancipatory project. Rather than situate women in the workplace where they are arguably the strongest, telework places women back into the home where they are faced with limited opportunities for collective organizing and resistance, something that could ultimately lead to a radical change to existing society.

The last two chapters in Part I open up the focus and go beyond the realm of the IS field to consider developments within related disciplines that have had an influence on the critical IS tradition. Chapter 9 looks towards the more expansive area of critical management studies, which – arguably – is an area from which many critical IS researchers have drawn inspiration and insight. Chris Grey reflects upon the achievements and influence of CMS on mainstream business institutions and management in wider society. He discusses the limited inroads by CMS into management to date, then notes evidence of a growing authority and with it a volume of work that has increasing prominence. However, Grey argues that the development of CMS needs to be nurtured and is in jeopardy if internal debates and controversies continue at the expense of a more 'mature politics'. He suggests that CMS has the option of either developing a common front against managerialism and its related assumptions while tolerating internal differences, or engaging in endless debate about how this confrontation is to materialize. He argues that the differences among the various critical positions are less significant than the differences between critical and managerial positions. He also advocates for tolerance of internal differences while remaining uncompromising with our opponents. Within the argument that is being presented, Grey provides an overview of the context and historical development of CMS, its nature and its core propositions, a summary of the key debates that have raged within CMS and some suggestions as to how we can embark on a political project of influence.

Chapter 10, the final chapter in this part, is authored by James Stewart and Robin Williams, who challenge current thinking and common presumptions about the systems design process. Building on insights derived from the social shaping of technology perspective, Stewart and Williams propose a rich view of design processes, which has an evolutionary understanding of systems design and development, paying particular attention to social learning. They critique the conceptualization of design from early technology studies and the 'user-oriented' wing of computer science. Specifically, they argue against what they have termed 'the design fallacy' whereby it is assumed that the solution to addressing user needs lies in the collection of ever-extensive knowledge of the context and purposes of various users in the technology design process. Instead, they propose a constructivist theorization of design, which argues against the Woolgarian notion 'configuring the user', and is concerned with domestication and consumption and the ways in which users appropriate the technology. Social learning refers to the way in which properties of the technology may not be immediately apparent, but are discovered as users try to make the artefact work. This entails a collective learning process to include the interactions between actors and the processes of negotiation and struggle. The social learning framework has been elaborated and tested through a series of multiple case studies of digital experiments and trials, conducted under the European Commission's Social Learning in Multimedia (SLIM) project. A number of salient points emerged from the SLIM project, which have implications for our understanding of information and communication technology (ICT) applications as configurational technology.

*The theory and application of critical IS research*
One of the criticisms that has been levelled at critical IS research is that the theoretical ideas often fail to translate into a set of empirical studies. However, as the empirical side of critical IS research evolves and develops, this criticism is increasingly being eroded. Critical theory's strong critique of empiricism does not mean that reflective empirical work is not a worthwhile activity. To ground theories of technological determinism, bureaucracy, capitalism and managerialism in organizational contexts can only aid our understanding of these issues. Thus, Part II of the handbook provides examples of the application of critical IS research. In these chapters we can see the ways in which the research agenda, the theories guiding it, and the findings are affected by the choice of a critical approach to the topic. Closely associated with critical IS research is the ideal of representing interests and perspectives that differ from those traditionally associated with managerial power and privilege, often based within modern corporations. What can be seen in these chapters are the voices of a range of diverse groups that are often marginalized in IS studies, yet have a legitimate interest in being represented. These voices are often silenced or cannot be heard; as critical researchers we face the important task of bringing them to the fore. The chapters that follow focus attention on groups that are usually at the margin and give them prominence.

Chapter 11, by Geoff Walsham, builds on Orlikowski and Baroudi's (1991) understanding of critical research and develops this further by adding the concept of critical engagement. This is described as undertaking prolonged commitment, especially given the complexity and embeddedness of these issues within the wider society. It involves both the struggle (or battle) against the status quo and a moral duty or commitment to engage.

The notion of critical engagement is discussed in relation to the *why*, *what* and *how* of critical engagement. The 'why' is discussed in the context of the huge asymmetries of wealth and power that continue to exist. The 'what' is illustrated with an analysis of three different case studies, which concern health information systems in Africa, geographical information systems for land management in India, and digital inclusion projects in Brazil. The 'how' considers reflections on field research, publications, teaching and influence in the IS field.

Based on a critique of interpretivism, Chapter 12 by Bill Doolin and Laurie McLeod outlines how interpretivist research could add a critical edge in the form of critical interpretivism. Such an approach would draw upon the empirical richness of interpretivist research and supplement this with a reflective approach that questions and disrupts the status quo, and entertains broader considerations of power and control. Critical interpretivism is then applied to three case studies, each of which draws upon a theoretical perspective from a particular social theorist (Michel Foucault, Bruno Latour and Anthony Giddens). These multiple conceptual lenses highlight the plurality of critical approaches that are possible within critical interpretivism and also show the mutually enriching insights that emerge. This chapter shows the value of the application of appropriate critical social theories to detailed, local, situated empirical studies and reveals how this can further inform our understanding of IS research.

Chapter 13 by Helen Richardson is an ambitious endeavour that aims to deconstruct the 'post-industrial project' by its examination of the historic, political, economic and social context that frames the empirical studies. This is in the context of the relationship of technology to culture, and in particular the culture of consumption. The first illustrative case tells the stories of workers at the front line of call-centre work and draws upon the work of Pierre Bourdieu whose conceptual tools help us to understand the historical and cultural forces involved in the social relations of IS use. The second case considers home e-shopping and the domestication and consumption of ICTs within the context of the family and households, with particular consideration given to gender issues. These studies illustrate how consideration of the broader setting of history and political economy can help explain everyday life and also how technological determinism underpins the drive that persuades individuals to consume 'with a passion'. The chapter concludes with some reflections on the role of critical research in promoting radical social change.

In contrast to much of the IS literature which assumes that innovation is driven by an instrumental, universal concept of rationality, Chapter 14 argues for a recognition of multiple alternative rationalities. Chrisanthi Avgerou and Kathy McGrath draw upon Foucault's analytical perspective on power, knowledge and morality to develop an understanding of multiple rationalities and also the largely underrepresented (in the IS field) concept of emotions in IS innovation. This perspective is then used to reinterpret the example of the failed London Ambulance Service within the British National Health Service. The critical approach that they develop is informed by alternative substantive rationalities and emotions and also by the need to develop explanations interrelationally, rather than treat reason and emotion as separate entities or try to understand phenomena at different levels of analysis. They argue that this level of understanding provides a pertinent critical perspective on IS knowledge and practice. It enables the revelation of insights from the case study that are missing from previous accounts in the IS literature and, in addition, it reveals the inadequacies of the explanations provided by the predominant techno-managerial regime of truth.

Shirin Madon then considers, in Chapter 15, how to evaluate e-governance projects in India. In contrast to the majority of such projects, which measure the provision of resources and infrastructure, this chapter argues that the concepts of *value* and *process* of e-governance deserve attention. This can only be achieved by considering projects as they unfold at the micro level. In order to understand this, Madon conducted a longitudinal study in the south Indian state of Kerala with the aim of appreciating the implementations of various e-governance initiatives. This is aided by the development of a conceptual framework that is informed by the evaluation, public sector, governance and development literature, along with Amartya Sen's notion of capabilities. Accordingly, the framework evaluates e-governance projects by giving consideration to administrative and governance reform, and project effects and outcomes (in the sense of improvements in social well-being). By explication of the projects in the field, the chapter shows how evaluation should be viewed as a process with changes that occur subtly and incrementally, as opposed to a discrete activity that follows implementation. The framework has implications for future e-governance evaluation in that it encourages consideration of the three activities over time and how they can potentially support socio-economic development. Consequently, this study stands in sharp contrast to most studies, which focus primarily on return-on-investment of individual projects. Such a narrow view of these developments is necessarily limiting. When developing countries, such as India, embark on e-governance projects in the hope of promoting socio-economic development, it is crucial that we – as researchers – are able to offer a relevant contribution to understanding how these projects may be assessed and thus provide recommendations for the future. The chapter by Madon provides this level of understanding.

Chapter 16, by Lynette Kvasny and Lakshman Yapa, focuses on an area that is often neglected in much of the IS literature – that of urban poverty. The 'solution' to poverty that is often posed is one of increased investment, job creation and workforce training, which is primarily an economic discourse that sees economic investment as the answer. However, investment in areas of urban poverty is in short supply and remains so for the foreseeable future. In contrast to this economic 'solution', the authors reflect positively on the wealth of resources that exist within inner-city communities, and illustrate how these can be harnessed to improve the quality of life for citizens. They advocate an approach that goes beyond the assumption that urban poverty can be ameliorated only through jobs and higher incomes. Drawing on the work of Bourdieu they consider other forms of capital, such as social and cultural capital. This is used to analyse a case study of IT and enterprise development that involves a partnership between a university and community-based groups. The chapter provides an excellent example of how theory can be applied to practical projects. Here, academics work alongside local community groups in an attempt to alleviate some of the injustices experienced by residents in the inner-city environment and hopefully improve their quality of life.

Dagfinn Hertzberg and Eric Monteiro, in Chapter 17, explore some of the dilemmas and contradictions that face global service work, as organizations attempt to achieve economies of scale while nurturing authentic and socially embedded interactions with customers. This 'global but local' strategy is dissected in a detailed empirical study that concerns the mediated social relationships within the global organization, Rolls-Royce Marine, which spans 33 countries. During the three-year study, the disembedded nature of the relationship between the sites and the actors involved is examined. Hertzberg and Monteiro also analyse how the re-embedding actions of relationships hinges on the construction of abstract trust through processes characterized as provisional, fragile and emotional. ICT-mediated communication is deeply implicated within this process.

Chapter 18, by Ela Klecun, continues with some of the themes discussed earlier in Chapter 14, with her consideration of multiple and competing rationalities, in the context of her study of the nature and role of telehealth within the UK. Klecun argues that many of the existing studies of teleheath focus primarily on technological performance, often at the individual project level, or alternatively they fall into the hands of the futurologists who make sweeping visionary predictions regarding the transformatory potential of these systems. By contrast, her study examines key rationalities as a means of understanding the social, organizational and technological changes that are taking place within healthcare systems. This is carried out over a five-year period, whereby research reveals the underpinning rationalities in the context of national (policy), local and project levels. Consideration of the issues at the macro level necessitated an analysis of the broader, political context of UK government health policy and IS management strategy. At the mezzo level, local health authority strategies and organizations were investigated. For the micro-level analysis, a number of projects were studied over time. This layered approach illustrates how different rationalities are constructed within wider discourses and shows that, despite the predominance of a technological rationality, the presence of other rationalities are intertwined, reconstituted at different levels, and pose a serious challenge to the predominant rationality. This critical study seriously questions the construction of telehealth as the solution to all the problems associated with healthcare, and inspires us to consider alternatives to health, well-being and how technology may (or may not) support us in the pursuit of improved healthcare provision.

**Conclusion**
The commissioned chapters in this handbook speak to a number of audiences. For researchers committed to studying information systems critically, it provides an overview of research from a variety of perspectives and across a range of topics and emerging themes. For those who wish to learn more about this area, the handbook provides an accessible point of entry into a wide range of areas so that it is possible to identify what is distinctive about critical IS research. For lecturers, it provides resources concerning theory and applications of critical research that could be used to supplement more mainstream approaches to certain topics. It could also be drawn upon as a basis for advanced undergraduate and postgraduate courses in critical IS research. For practitioners, the handbook offers access to a range of perspectives and ideas that stand in contrast to the predominantly managerialist and technicist frameworks of understanding, yet offer compelling insights into current issues with IS development and use. This can provide explanatory power to aid understanding of their experiences in the field.

**Notes**
1. Examples of special issues of journals devoted to critical research include *Data Base* (2001/2002), *Journal of Information Technology* (2002) and *Information Technology and People* (forthcoming). Examples of conferences with a critical IS stream include the Critical Management Studies (CMS) conference (1999 and 2003), a Critical Research in IS (CRIS) Workshop preceding the 2001 CMS conference, and a critical stream at the Americas Conference on IS (AMCIS) since 2001.
2. See Howcroft and Trauth (2004) for an extended discussion of the choice of critical IS research.
3. Based on fundamental ontological and epistemological differences, arguments have raged between Marxists and postmodernists. Neo-Marxists have criticized relativism (postmodernism) as being politically inept, irresponsible and dangerous. For example, Parker (1992: 11) characterized postmodern writings as: 'The problems of (fictional) individuals in (mythical) organizations are safely placed behind philosophical double-

glazing and their cries are treated as interesting examples of discourse'. On the other hand, authors sympathetic to postmodernism have critiqued realism for its totalizing meta-narratives and absolutist position.
4. Vociferous debates have taken place between those who view the primacy of class politics over gender politics, with some attaching greater significance to the removal of class distinctions as opposed to gender distinctions.

## References

Alvesson, M. and Willmott, H. (1992), 'On the idea of emancipation in management and organization studies', *Academy of Management Review*, **17**(3): 432–64.
Alvesson, M. and Willmott, H. (1996), *Making Sense of Management: A Critical Introduction*, London: Sage.
Bijker, W.E. (1995), 'Sociohistorical technology studies', in T. Pinch (ed.), *Handbook of Science and Technology Studies*, Thousand Oaks, CA: Sage, pp. 229–56.
Bourdieu, P. (1990), *The Logic of Practice*, Cambridge: Polity.
Brooke, C. (2002a), 'Critical perspectives on information systems: an impression of the landscape', *Journal of Information Technology*, **17**: 271–83.
Brooke, C. (2002b), 'Editorial: critical research in information systems', *Journal of Information Technology*, **17**: 45–7.
Cecez-Kecmanovic, D. (2001), 'Doing critical IS research: the question of methodology', in Trauth (ed.), pp. 141–63.
Cecez-Kecmanovic, D., Moodie, D., Busuttil, A. and Plesman, F. (1999), 'Organisational change mediated by e-mail and intranet: an ethnographic study', *Information Technology and People*, **12**(1): 9–26.
Doolin, B. (1998), 'Information technology as disciplinary technology: being critical in interpretive research on information systems', *Journal of Information Technology*, **13**: 301–11.
Doolin, B. and Lowe, A. (2002), 'To reveal is to critique: actor-network theory and critical information systems research', *Journal of Information Technology*, **17**: 69–78.
Dooyeweerd, H. (1973), 'Introduction', *Philosophia Reformata*, **38**: 5–16.
Forester, J. (1992), 'Critical ethnography: on fieldwork in a Habermasian way', in M. Alvesson and H. Wilmott (eds), *Critical Management Studies*, London: Sage, pp. 46–65.
Foucault, M. (1979), *Discipline and Punish: The Birth of the Prison*, Harmondsworth: Penguin.
Fournier, V. and Grey, C. (2000), 'At the critical moment: conditions and prospects for critical management studies', *Human Relations*, **53**(1): 7–32.
Hammersley, M. (1995), *The Politics of Social Research*, London: Sage.
Heidegger, M. (1953), *Being and Time*, New York: State University of New York Press.
Hirschheim, R. and Klein, H.K. (1994), 'Realizing emancipatory principles in information systems development: the case for ETHICS', *MIS Quarterly*, **18**(1): 83–109.
Horkheimer, M. (1976), 'Traditional and critical theory (1937)', in P. Connerton (ed.), *Critical Sociology*, Harmondsworth: Penguin.
Howcroft, D. and Trauth, E.M. (2004), 'The choice of critical IS research', in B. Kaplan, D. Truex, D. Wastell, A.T. Wood-Harper, and J. DeGross (eds), *Relevant Theory and Informed Practice: Looking Forward from a 20-year Perspective on IS Research*, Boston, MA: Kluwer Academic, pp. 195–211.
Klein, H.K. and Hirschheim, R. (1993), 'The application of neohumanist principles in information systems development', in D. Avison, E.J. Kendall and J.I. DeGross (eds), *Human, Organizational and Social Dimensions of Information Systems Development*, Amsterdam: Elsevier Science, North-Holland, pp. 263–79.
Kvasny, L. (2004), 'On the existential problem of evil and information technology in the hotel civilization', Keynote speech, Second International CRIS Workshop: Critical Reflections on Critical Research in Information Systems, University of Salford, Manchester, UK, 14 July.

Land, F. (2004), 'Concluding remarks', IFIP WG8.2 20th Year Retrospective: Relevant Theory and Informed Practice – Looking Forward from a 20-year Perspective on IS Research, 15–17 July 2004, Manchester, UK.

Latour, B. (1991), 'Technology is society made durable', in J. Law (ed.), *A Sociology of Monsters: Essays on Power, Technology and Domination*, London: Routledge, pp. 103–31.

Lyytinen, K. (1992), 'Information systems and critical theory', in M. Alvesson and H. Wilmott (eds), *Critical Management Studies*, London: Sage, pp. 159–80.

Lyytinen, K. and Hirschheim, R. (1988), 'Information systems as rational discourse: an application of Habermas's theory of communicative action', *Scandinavian Journal of Information Systems*, **4**(1/2): 19–30.

Lyytinen, K. and Hirschheim, R. (1989), 'Information systems and emancipation: promise or threat?', in H.K. Klein and K. Kumar (eds), *Systems Development for Human Progress*, Amsterdam: Elsevier Science, North-Holland, pp. 115–39.

Lyytinen, K. and Klein, H.K. (1985), 'The critical theory of Jürgen Harbermas as a basis for a theory of information systems', in E. Mumford, R. Hirschheim, G. Fitzgerald and A.T. Wood-Harper (eds), *Research Methods in Information Systems*, Amsterdam: Elsevier Science, North-Holland, pp. 219–36.

Marx, K. ([1867] 1974), *Capital*, London: Penguin.

Mingers, J. (1992), 'Technical, practical and critical OR: past, present and future?', in M. Alvesson and H. Wilmott (eds), *Critical Management Studies*, London: Sage, pp. 90–112.

Mingers, J. (2000), 'What is it to be critical? Teaching a critical approach to management undergraduates', *Management Learning*, **31**(2): 219–37.

Myers, M.D. and Avison, D.E. (2002), *Qualitative Research in Information Systems: A Reader*, London: Sage.

Ngwenyama, O.K. (1991), 'The critical social theory approach to information systems: problems and challenges', in H.E. Nissen, H.K. Klein and R. Hirschheim (eds), *Information Systems Research: Contemporary Approaches and Emergent Traditions*, Amsterdam: Elsevier Science, North-Holland, pp. 267–80.

Ngwenyama, O.K. and Lee, A.S. (1997), 'Communication richness in electronic mail: critical social theory and the contextuality of meaning', *MIS Quarterly*, **21**(2): 145–67.

Orlikowski, W.J. and Baroudi, J.J. (1991), 'Studying IT in organizations: research approaches and assumptions', *Information Systems Research*, **2**(1): 1–28.

Parker, M. (1992), 'Postmodern organizations or postmodern organization theory', *Organization Studies*, **13**(1): 1–17.

Russell, S. and Williams, R. (2002), 'Social shaping of technology: frameworks, findings and implications for policy with glossary of social shaping concepts', in R. Williams (ed.), *Shaping Technology, Guiding Policy: Concepts, Spaces and Tools*, Edward Elgar, Cheltenham, UK and Northampton, MA, USA: Edward Elgar, pp. 37–132.

Trauth, E. (ed.) (2001) *Qualitative Research in IS: Issues and Trends*, Hershey, PA: Idea Group Publishing.

Wajcman, J. (1991), *Feminism Confronts Technology*, Cambridge: Polity.

Williams, R. and Edge, D. (1996), 'The social shaping of technology', *Research Policy*, **25**: 865–99.

Wilson, F. (1997), 'The truth is out there: the search for emancipatory principles in information systems design', *Information Technology & People*, **10**(3): 187–204.

# PART I

# THEORY

# 2 Basic assumptions of the critical research perspectives in information systems
*Dubravka Cecez-Kecmanovic*

## Introduction

Critical information systems (IS) research encompasses a wide range of diverse research endeavours with a single, yet essential identifiable thread – a critical theoretic orientation. Critical theoretic orientation, generally, means framing the purpose of research in the context of critical theoretic concerns, such as domination, power and control on the one hand, and liberation, empowerment and emancipation, on the other. Critical social research has eminently practical and essentially democratic purposes. It seeks to achieve emancipatory social change by explaining 'a social order in such a way that it becomes itself the catalyst which leads to the transformation of this social order' (Fay 1987, p. 27). Critical IS research specifically opposes technological determinism and instrumental rationality underlying IS development and seeks emancipation from unrecognized forms of domination and control enabled or supported by information systems. By framing their purpose in the context of critical theoretic concerns, critical IS researchers challenge the established regimes of truth and norms of knowledge production in both the discipline and practice of information systems. Critical IS researchers produce knowledge with the aim of revealing and explaining how information systems are (mis)used to enhance control, domination and oppression, and thereby to inform and inspire transformative social practices that realize the liberating and emancipatory potential of information systems.

IS research with such a critical social orientation has emerged as the so-called 'third path' in IS research,[1] which follows the critical tradition nurtured in philosophy, sociology, education, management, anthropology, history and so on (Habermas 1973, 1984, 1987, 1996; Friere 1976; Held 1980; McCarthy 1982; Bernstein 1983, 1994; Fay 1987; Harvey 1990; Alvesson and Willmott 1992; Morrow and Brown 1994; Alvesson and Deetz 2000; Kincheloe and McLaren 2000; Hohendahl and Fisher 2001). Compared to the long-established tradition of positivist IS research and the more recently recognized interpretive IS research, critical IS research is not yet established as a valid and legitimate option (Mingers 2003). This situation is not helped by the general lack of understanding of what 'critical' means in critical IS research. As it is not defined by the common-sense meaning of critique as a negative evaluation, the term '*critical IS* research' often causes confusion.[2] Critical IS researchers are therefore seeking both a better understanding of the nature of critical inquiry and recognition of its validity and legitimacy by the IS community. These needs motivate and determine the aims of this chapter.

While critical IS research is characterized by diversity in topics, objectives, methods and philosophical roots, there are certain basic assumptions and ideas that set the critical IS research perspective apart from those typically identified as positivist and interpretivist. Namely, research or scientific activity, like any social practice, is guided by basic beliefs and assumptions about the nature of reality (that is, ontological assumptions), the nature of (scientific) knowledge of reality, how such knowledge is acquired (epistemological assumptions), and what constitutes valid research. As Burrell and Morgan (1979, p. 37) state: 'What passes for scientific knowledge can be shown to be founded upon a set of unstated conventions, beliefs and assumptions, just as everyday, common-sense knowledge is. The difference between them lies largely in the nature of rules and the community which recognizes and subscribes to them.'

Beliefs and assumptions in the IS community about the nature of organizations, Information Technology (IT) and IT-based information systems, as well as relationships between information systems, human beings and organizations, shape how IS researchers formulate research questions and define the purpose of their research, how they design and conduct research studies and what kind of knowledge they produce. Each research approach – positivist, interpretivist or critical – is based on a distinct set of assumptions. While examination and comparison of these assumptions is a fruitful way of studying and understanding different research approaches, it is important to keep in mind that they are not fixed in concrete. They have been debated and disputed in social sciences for decades (for example, Giddens 1978; Bernstein 1983; Vatimo 1994; Habermas 1996; Lincoln and Guba 2000) and with some delay in IS as well (Hirschheim 1985; Klein and Lyytinen 1985; Orlikowski and Baroudi 1991; Walsham 1995; Lee and Baskerville 2003; Chen and Hirschheim 2004; Weber 2004). They are therefore changing and their mutual distinctions are sharpening.

The objective of this chapter is to identify and reflect on assumptions and ideas that underlie the critical IS research approach by comparing and contrasting them with assumptions and ideas characteristic of positivist and interpretivist approaches. Given that critical approach emerged as a reaction to positivist social science and in some aspects also to interpretive social science, it seems logical to start with comparing and contrasting it *vis-à-vis* positivist and interpretive approaches. Also, taking into account the relative novelty of the critical approach in IS research it seems pertinent to distinguish it from the much better known and established research approaches.

The following sections address assumptions and beliefs that underlie IS research related to: the purpose of research; values and their role in research; the nature of organizations, IS and their relationship; the nature and role of theory; and assumptions about methodology. In each section, assumptions and major ideas that characterize positivist and interpretivist approaches are first summarized, in order to contrast and compare them with those that characterize critical IS research. (A more detailed account of assumptions associated with positivist and interpretive approaches, while generally desirable, would not be appropriate for the chapter, given its focus and objective.)

## The purpose of IS research

Perhaps the very basic questions in any research are: why should one conduct scientific research and what are the motivations for conducting IS research? The three approaches provide three fundamentally different answers to these questions.

Based on the premise that there is only one science and that natural and social sciences share a common set of principles and one logic of science, positivist social science aims to discover regularities or causal laws that explain and predict phenomena in social life. The contemporary positivist spirit 'continues to adhere to a philosophy of science that attributes a radical unity to all the sciences' (Crotty 1998, p. 27). Scientific discoveries together with technological developments are seen as instruments and driving forces of progress. Following the tradition of positivist social science, the purpose of positivist IS research is scientific explanation of phenomena and discovery of objective cause–effect relationships or universal causal laws in three major domains: (a) planning, development, diffusion and implementation of IS within and across organizations, (b) operations and management of IT infrastructure, information resources and IS structure, and (c) the relationship between and the effect of IS on human beings, business processes, organizations and society. It is believed that such laws are useful for effective *control* and *prediction* of IS development and use, users' behaviour and attitudes towards IS, and ultimately systems success or failure.

In contrast to the instrumental orientation of positivist research, the purpose of interpretivist IS research is to understand information systems in their social context – how they are embedded in, how they impact on and are impacted by context. In Walsham's words (1993, p. 5):

Context is concerned with the multi-level identification of the various systems and structures within which the information system is embedded. This can include such obvious elements as the organizational department within which the system is being used, the organization as a whole, and the various sectoral, national and international contexts within which the organization is located. A more subtle set of contexts for an information system are various social structures which are present in the minds of the human participants involved with the system. Their representation of reality, their shared and contested sense of the world, create complex interacting contexts within which the information system, as a human artefact, is drawn on and used to create or reinforce meaning.

For instance, an interpretive researcher is interested in studying the processes of IS development and implementation in a particular social, organizational, political and cultural setting. The interpretive researcher not only studies and describes the observable behaviour (for example, of IS users or developers), but also aims to understand people's feelings, values, norms, interests, motivations and actions. The researcher immerses her/ himself into a field site in order to gain personal experience of how people construct meanings in natural settings and how information systems impact on subjective and intersubjective meaning creation.

While interpretive researchers aim to understand and describe multiple meanings ascribed to an information system and its impacts in a single or in different contexts, critical IS researchers:

Go further to expose inherent conflicts and contradictions, hidden structures and mechanisms accountable for these influences. Critical IS researchers aim to reveal interests and agendas of privileged groups and the way they are supported or protected by a particular information system design or use. More generally, they aim to discover and expose attempts to design and (mis)use IS to deceive, manipulate, exploit, dominate and disempower people. By doing so they aspire to help them resist these attempts, hinder such misuse of IS and promote liberating and empowering IS design and use. (Cecez-Kecmanovic 2001, p. 143)

Critical IS researchers criticize positivist IS research for being instrumentalist and for serving, often unwittingly, the interest of dominant groups. They accuse positivist IS research of defending the status quo and ultimately reinforcing power structures and strengthening managerial control over organizations and people's lives. Critical IS researchers also accuse interpretive research of accepting the status quo and being too relativist and passive; for seeking merely to understand social reality instead of 'acting upon it'. In contrast, the purpose of critical social research is to change the world – actors, information systems, organizations and society, including their dynamic, complex and emergent interrelationships. As expressed by Alvesson and Deetz (2000, p. 9):

Critical social research is ... oriented towards challenging rather than confirming that which is established, disrupting rather than reproducing cultural traditions and conventions, opening up and showing tensions in language use rather than taking surface consensus as a point of departure. The intention is thereby to contribute to emancipation, for example, to encourage rethinking and the emotional as well as cognitive working through of ideas and identities which are repressive. Alternatively and less optimistically, the enterprise may be seen as one of fuelling resistance to those powers defining who we are, what we should be and aspire to, and how we should live our lives as normal and well-adjusted persons.

The specific purpose of a critical IS research project ranges from creating knowledge as a catalyst for change, to helping and giving voice to various marginalized IS user groups or stakeholders in IS development, implementation and use, to playing an active role in transforming IS practices and IS–organization relationships, and assisting actors in emancipating themselves. This is based on the belief in the power of knowledge – in the capacity of knowledge produced by research to enlighten and engender action. It is also based on the conviction not only that it is legitimate but that it is indeed an obligation for a researcher to actively engage in the transformation of IS practices that will contribute to a more democratic workplace with greater degree of autonomy and human agency, and ultimately lead to less repressive and more equitable social relations.

For example, by revealing and explaining how an information system, supposedly implemented with the purpose to increase business processes efficiency and effectiveness, in fact increased control and decreased autonomy and human agency, IS researchers aim to assist less powerful actors in actively engaging in and affecting IS development and implementation processes. By revealing to what extent any information system design is inscribed by certain interests and values, IS researchers seek to achieve critical enlightenment regarding the value-laden and political nature of the information system. The resulting insights into the nature of an information system and how it impacts on work practices and employees' autonomy, social and power relations, and control by dominant groups, could, critical researchers believe, help employees to better understand IS-imposed or reinforced constraints and seek emancipation from them. More generally, by demonstrating how implementation of an information system is in fact a powerful agent of organizational transformation and how it implies functional/economic systems' change as well as the change in the social lifeworld of organizational members, critical IS researchers aim to expose both its dangers and its benefits and thereby introduce a 'discourse of possibility' in the IS practice (Cecez-Kecmanovic et al. 2002).

The liberatory and emancipatory purpose as a hallmark of the critical approach has, however, been disputed in IS research. Charges range from utopianism, to arrogance, to illegitimacy of research objectives, to the impossibility of achieving the desired emancipatory outcomes. Objectives such as participation of the disenfranchised in IS development; development of information systems that liberate and enhance human potential rather than repress and colonize human beings; and transformation of IS practices that will lead to reduced domination and control by the powerful and achievement of more equitable social relations, may indeed appear utopian. Nevertheless, critical IS researchers believe that such objectives are worthy of pursuit even if they are only partially achieved. The desired outcomes may not necessarily be achieved in a particular research context but the issues raised by critical research, knowledge gained and lessons learned may inform and enlighten other actors in other contexts. The personal actions of a critical researcher who, for instance, refuses to participate in legitimizing the often hidden forms of domination enabled by information systems, who feels responsible for revealing and deconstructing such forms and for producing knowledge with a liberatory and emancipatory purpose – is perhaps what ultimately matters.

Finally, critical researchers need to be cautious about conceptualizing emancipation and also to critically reflect on the emancipatory objectives. For instance, those who aimed at 'emancipating others' have justifiably been accused of arrogance. Furthermore, Kincheloe and McLaren warn us that 'no one is ever completely emancipated from the socio-political context that has produced him or her' (2000, p. 282). On the other hand, the emancipatory discourse in IS practice and research is criticized as 'totalizing in nature', as a way of establishing yet another form of domination (Wilson 1997). While such a critique may be seen as ideologically inspired and perhaps based on misinterpretation of the critical theoretic foundation, it none the less should not be simply dismissed as ill-intentioned or irrelevant. In fact, engaging in a debate and responding to critiques with argument can be seen as an obligation by critical researchers, an obligation stemming from the very nature of the critical project. Besides, self-reflection on the purpose and objectives of research and how and to what extent they are achieved or achievable is immanent in the critical approach.

**Role of values in IS research**
How do values enter into IS research? This is another question that determines the point of departure for each of the three approaches and discriminates between them from the very beginning. Lincoln and Guba (2000, p. 169) contend that values determine 'choice of the problem, choice of the paradigm to guide the problem, choice of theoretical framework, choice of major data-gathering and data-analytic methods, choice of context and treatment of values already resident within the context, and choice of

formats for presenting findings'. Values, they argue, should be a part of the basic philosophical dimensions of paradigms.

Positivist researchers generally agree that science is value neutral and objective. Most notably, they separate *fact* from *value* and are concerned with perfecting methods and techniques to collect value-free, unbiased facts. They believe that scientific knowledge is or at least aims to be objective, accurate and certain. In other words, the positivist research approach assumes the epistemology of objectivism – that 'objects in the world have meaning prior to, and independently of, any consciousness of them' (Crotty 1998, p. 27).

However, even in natural sciences (physics in particular) scientists cast doubts on such an objectivist epistemology.[3] Kuhn (1970), among others, questions the supposed objectivity of science and value neutrality of scientific discovery:

> [Kuhn] links scientific effort to the interests, and the psychology, of both the scientific community and individual scientists. Because of this, his influential line of thought constitutes a further loosening of the hold positivism has taken on scientific thought and research. The picture Kuhn paints is not a picture of objective, valid, unchallengeable findings emerging from scientists working with detachment and in a spirit of unalloyed scientific dedication. To the contrary, scientific endeavour, as Kuhn conceives it, is a very human affair. Human interests, human values, human fallibility, human foibles – all play a part. (Crotty 1998, p. 36)

As a result, a more moderate version of positivism, known as post-positivism, emerged, allowing that objectivity and certainty of results, while desirable, are not fully achievable with the best of research methods, and that they may depend on observers' standpoints, values and interests.

Neither interpretivist nor critical IS researchers believe in value-free facts. Instead they believe that values and beliefs are always involved in the production of 'facts'. Interpretive researchers specifically consider all values to be equally important, that is, no set of values is considered better or worse. Interpretive researchers need at least temporarily 'to empathize with and share in the social and political commitments or values of those [they] study' (Neuman 2003, p. 80). In their search for authentic, lived experiences, interpretivist researchers assign everyone's beliefs and values an equal status. While they consider all interpretations to be culturally and socially situated, they do not judge informants' values nor do they evaluate the epistemological status of their beliefs.

For critical IS researchers, facts can be separated neither from values nor from ideological inscriptions. This applies equally to the people studied as to the researchers. Critical IS researchers criticize both the positivist claim that their research is based on objective, value-free facts and the interpretivists' value-neutral position in presenting IS research findings. Criticalists argue that both approaches serve to passively legitimize dominant technological determinism and managerial ideology in IS practice; that value-free facts cannot and value-neutral research should not be achieved.

Basically, critical researchers believe that 'what a researcher studies, how he or she studies it, and what happens to the results involve values and morality, because knowledge has tangible effects on people's lives' (ibid., p. 86). Consequently, research, as a social activity, has a moral–political dimension that requires the researcher to commit to a value position. Critical IS researchers contend that any research project involves making moral choices. Furthermore, they believe that it is important for any research to make their value position and their moral choices explicit.

Given the place of values, the proper role of a researcher in positivist IS research is to be a 'disinterested scientist', an independent and bias-free adviser for decision and policy makers. In the interpretive approach, an IS researcher is ideally a 'passionate participant' and a facilitator of different views and voices. In the critical approach, an IS researcher is an advocate for and activist in social change and takes the role of a 'transformative intellectual' (Lincoln and Guba 2000). As transformative intellectuals, critical IS researchers are concerned with:

> How what is has come to be, whose interests are served by particular institutional arrangements, and where [researchers'] own frame of reference comes from. Facts are no longer simply 'what is'; the truth of beliefs is not simply testable by their correspondence to these facts. To engage in critical postmodern[4] research is to take part in a process of critical world making. (Kincheloe and McLaren 2000, p. 303)

In building information systems and in investigating IS practice (IS development, implementation and use) it is necessary to ask the following questions. How are 'facts' represented in an information system? Whose values are inscribed in supposedly value-free representations of organizational reality in a particular information system design? Whose interests are served by these representations? What are researchers' own values and interests that motivate and guide the research process? Explicitly addressing such questions helps critical IS researchers better understand and reflect on their own role and value position in the 'process of critical world making' through empirical IS research.

### Assumptions about the nature of social reality, technology and information systems

Every IS researcher upholds, implicitly or explicitly, basic ontological assumptions regarding the nature of social reality, the nature of human beings and organizations, as well as the nature of technology designed for and used by human beings and organizations. These ontological assumptions determine how they conceptualize the nature of IS–organization relationships and the way they study the impact of IS on human beings and organizations. The three approaches to IS research not surprisingly are based on radically different ontological assumptions, following different philosophical traditions (Orlikowski and Baroudi 1991).

Positivist IS researchers espouse a philosophy of science that proposes a unity of natural and social sciences and assumes an objective physical and social world independent of the observer. Similar to natural reality, social reality is assumed to exist 'out there' and that it can be discovered, measured and accurately represented by researchers' constructs and models. It is this objective reality of organizations and information systems that an IS researcher seeks to discover, measure and accurately represent. Understanding IS phenomena is therefore 'primarily a problem of modelling and measurement, of constructing an appropriate set of constructs and an accurate set of instruments to capture the essence of the phenomena' (ibid., p. 9). Furthermore, it is assumed that these phenomena, including IS impact on organizational processes, functioning and management, users' satisfaction with information systems or broader social implications, are patterned and exhibit regularity. Users, for instance, are assumed to interact with information systems in a patterned and orderly way. The role of scientific research is to discover these patterns and regularities and describe them in the form of cause–effect relationships and universal causal laws.

Given the objective nature of reality, scientific knowledge which describes the reality is as good as it is accurate and certain. Scientific knowledge strictly differs from opinions, beliefs, feelings and subjective experiences expressed by people in a particular context, which are considered biased, unverified and unscientific. The distinction between objective, scientifically verifiable knowledge and subjective, unverifiable knowledge parallels the distinction between value-free facts and value-laden descriptions, mentioned above, which underlies the difference between the positivist and non-positivist approaches. Contemporary IS research in the positivist tradition emphasizes validity and verifiability of scientific claims.

In contrast to the positivist philosophical tradition, non-positivist perspectives assume a fundamental difference between the social world and the world of nature. First, human beings do not create the natural world, they make sense of this world 'always already there'.[5] Second, the existence of the social world arises from human actions; thus the social world becomes meaningful 'by virtue of the very act that brings [it] into existence' (Crotty 1998, p. 56). As explained by Giddens (1976, p. 79):

The difference between the social and natural is that the latter does not constitute itself as 'meaningful'; the meanings it has are produced by men in the course of their practical life, and as a consequence of their endeavours to understand or explain it for themselves. Social life – of which these endeavours are part – on the other hand, is produced by its component actors precisely in terms of their active constitutions and reconstitution of frames of meaning whereby they organize their experience.

The interpretive approach specifically rejects the objective existence of the social reality independent of human consciousness, waiting to be discovered. Instead, interpretivist researchers assume that the social reality is intentionally created by purposeful actions of interacting human beings. In other words, through social interaction and engagement with the world they are interpreting, human beings are co-creating meanings and mutually constructing their social reality.

In addition to assumptions about organizational social reality, interpretivist IS researchers assume that information systems by their nature are social systems, only technologically realized. Information systems are intentionally created and embedded in work practices through purposeful actions by different actors – developers and users. Interpretivist IS researchers, for instance, investigate IS development and implementation processes by focusing on experiences of the actors involved. Questions of interest are as follows. How do developers experience the development process and understand users' needs and requirements? How do users experience the same process and create and co-create meaningful understanding of an IS design? How do various IS users – employees and managers in an organization and its customers or clients – make sense of the system and its implications on their work processes? How do they create and share meanings? The answers, of course, are diverse as much as the actors themselves have diverse experiences, values, interests, emotions, prejudices and so on. In order to interpret them, researchers try to make sense of individual accounts and experiences within a particular cultural, social and historic context (Walsham 1993).

The critical research approach rejects positivist assumptions of objectivism and stability relating to social reality, but also rejects the subjectivism and relativism of the interpretivist approach. The critical approach can be seen as a way of bridging the objective–subjective poles of positivist and interpretivist approaches. Critical researchers assume that social and material realities do exist independent of human consciousness, subjective perceptions and experiences. These are not mere reflections of social and material reality but are both reflections *upon* and products of this reality. There is a dialectic relationship between human beings and their concrete social and material reality. Being intentional, human consciousness is already an intervention into reality. Action and reflection upon reality cannot be separated. United in what is called *praxis*, action and reflection, 'constantly and mutually illuminating each other', transform reality (Friere 1976, p. 149).

Critical IS researchers do appreciate that social reality is subjectively experienced by actors in organizations, but they also assume that these subjective experiences are historically, socially, culturally, politically and materially conditioned and produced. To understand an information system in its organizational context it is therefore not enough to investigate the subjective experiences, meanings, values, motives and emotions of the various actors involved in or affected by its development and deployment. It is equally important to understand the historical and material conditions, social structures, power relations, conflicts and paradoxes, which shape and condition the purpose and design of the system as well as its meanings for various organizational members. For instance, to investigate problems involved in an executive IS implementation, critical researchers would not be satisfied with an explanation that employees' resistance arises from their beliefs that the system increases managers' control and centralization of decision making. Critical researchers would seek to find out how social and power relations, tensions and conflicts between management and employees, impacted on both managers' action to implement the IS and employees' action to resist it. Critical IS researchers share critical theory's dialectic concerns with social construction of human experience, in particular historical and cultural conditions, and the ways in which such experience in turn shapes human beings, their social relations, their understanding of and attitudes towards information systems, and their future choices.

Furthermore, critical researchers assume that beneath immediately observable surface reality there are dynamic, socially created layers, ideologically inscribed and historically evolving. This is why some actions and situations in IS practices cannot be explained without a deeper investigation that goes beneath the surface. For instance, users' resistance to an information system designed to improve working conditions, may at first appear incomprehensible. But an investigation of users' involvement and power conflicts during the IS development and understanding of managerial ideologies operating beneath the surface may shed more light on users' resistance. To uncover and expose the hidden layers of social reality, critical researchers need to undertake a purposefully designed inquiry. Critical social theory provides theoretical concepts for such an inquiry and serves as a map or guide to the social reality. However, it does not impose a way of seeing reality. Instead it motivates and directs the researcher to dig deeper, beyond surface appearances, and explore hidden structures, conflicts and contradictions inherent in social reality that shape and determine social actions. More specifically, critical theory assists researchers in designing strategies for exploring these deeper structures and revealing hidden social forces and inner conflicts that shape and condition subjective experiences and actions of participants (such as employees, managers and IS designers). Critical theory, as will be discussed in the following section, informs empirical inquiry and like a map helps researchers find and interpret facts.

Assumptions of social and political neutrality of IS in organizational practices are of particular concern to critical IS researchers, as are beliefs that IS development and implementation can and should be justified only in functional and economic terms, based on instrumental rationality: for instance, how much an information system contributes to cost cutting, downsizing, productivity, efficiency, effectiveness and competitiveness. These assumptions and beliefs can be criticized on several grounds. First, they reduce the problem domain of IS development and implementation to business process functioning and limit the IS goals to performance improvements. As a result, the complexity of organizational, social, political and business contexts is overlooked and a chance for deeper, systematic changes and more significant improvements is lost. Second, as performance improvements goals are taken for granted, the focus of IS design is narrowed to functional and technical aspects of IS. Consequently, wider organizational, social and political implications of IS, which may be essential for its future success or failure, are neither considered nor foreseen. Third, managers and IS experts often believe that a particular IS design or solution (for example, an enterprise resource planning (ERP) package) is the only way to achieve a given set of performance goals. Managers and IS experts together uphold the view that company progress, competitiveness and survival depend on successful application of this particular system. Not only do they omit to explore alternative IS solutions capable of achieving the same performance goals, with different and/or wider social and political implications, they also disregard other potential goals and the possible different social and political implications.

The problem is – critical researchers warn – that in such a way organizations typically overlook a range of human, social and organizational implications of IS, including fragmentation and routinization of work, loss of discretion by employees, power centralization and increased control over employees, alienation, mistrust and so on. While these dehumanizing and socially dysfunctional implications of IS are their primary concerns, critical IS researchers also reveal and point out that these may ultimately be detrimental to business performance. That is, they are likely to undermine expected performance improvements and jeopardize IS economic success. Furthermore, by focusing narrowly on cost-cutting and efficiency goals and justifying IS solutions solely based on instrumental rationality, organizations are missing the opportunity to significantly transform and improve the way they do their business through innovative development and deployment of information systems. Unlike the view that a particular IS design is inevitable, critical researchers argue that technologies, and IT in particular, are 'ambivalent', that is, malleable to different organizational and social needs (Feenberg 2002). By taking into account socially desirable outcomes in the design and implementation of IS, it has been shown that performance goals may actually be enhanced well beyond initial cost-cutting and efficiency gains (Cecez-Kecmanovic and Janson 1999).

Critical researchers argue that 'technological rationality has become political rationality' (Marcuse 1964, pp. xv–xvi) and that IS designs, deemed inevitable to achieve functional goals, conceal how values and interests of the dominant groups are inscribed in these IS designs. The dominant form of technological (instrumental) rationality stands at the intersection between managerial ideology and IS development methodology. They are brought together to control human beings in much the same way as other resources (money, raw materials or natural environment) albeit in a more subtle and covert form – through 'technical codes'. Critical researchers explore how these codes (software code, algorithms, rules and procedures) invisibly inscribe values and interests of the dominant groups and thereby reinforce power structures and hierarchies, centralize control and routinize the exercise of power. By revealing taken-for-granted assumptions behind the authoritarian appropriation of technology and by unmasking hidden agendas, interests and values of the dominant groups, critical IS researchers aim to assist all actors in an IS development/implementation process in gaining deeper insights into its broader social, organizational and political implications. More specifically, critical IS researchers aim to create or rather co-create situated knowledge to assist disadvantaged employees in their struggle for more humane working conditions, discretion and autonomy in work practices, and enhanced participation and agency.

The critical approach, it needs to be noted, assumes that human beings are creative and adaptive, and that they have the potential to think and act in novel ways in opposition to the established social structure and culture. In other words, human beings are assumed to have *agency*. However, critical researchers have long warned that the survival of agency has been among fundamental issues in technologically advanced societies and organizations. From Marcuse's warnings in *One-dimensional Man* (1964) that technologically-enabled productivity growth enslaves rather than liberates man, and Adorno's prediction of totally administered society (1970), to Habermas's exposition of colonization of the lifeworld (1984, 1987), critical theorists have identified and examined new forms of domination, control and exploitation, enabled by technological developments. They called attention to the dangers hidden in technological progress, in particular increased control and domination, loss of freedom, loss of autonomy and diminishing agency, alienation and so on.

These warnings are especially pertinent to organizational adoption and deployment of IS. Of particular concerns for critical IS researchers are increasing control, power centralization and managerial domination over employees enabled and supported by IS. By being focused on functional and technical issues, or more precisely, by being made to believe that this is what IS are all about and what they should be concerned with, employees assist in and contribute to the design and implementation of IS that work against their own interests. Employees seem to wilfully consent to increased control, domination and loss of autonomy. They are, critical researchers claim, socialized into organizational culture, subjected to managerialist ideology and technological determinism which together impose particular social meanings, representations and rituals (including IS development methodology) that produce consent to increased control and domination. Employees are thereby misled and exploited, made to act against their own interests.

How is it then at all possible to make changes? How can employees change the very conditions that shaped them and undertake actions to realize their potential? Critical researchers believe that change is possible if employees can see their illusions, understand causes of their conditions and engage with others in collective liberating actions (for instance, by taking part in critical assessment of IS implications). This is where critical IS researchers see their role and the purpose of their inquiries. By exposing assumptions and beliefs behind an IS implementation and by revealing how social forces and power structures dominate and shape consciousness, thereby producing employees' subjective experiences and acculturating them to feel comfortable in relations of domination and subordination, critical researchers aim to motivate them to (at least) question their position and assist them in undertaking transformative, liberating change processes.

**The nature and role of theory in critical IS research**
Explanation or theory in positivist social science is law-like or *nomothetic* (*nomos* in Greek means law). A theory in social science describes social phenomena in the form of formal expressions of causal relations – scientific statements similar to natural sciences. As a set of interrelated causal relations or laws, a theory in IS is developed to explain, make predictions and control IS phenomena in organizations. For instance, a causal relationship between task–technology fit (TTF) and individual performance (Goodhue and Thompson 1995) indicates to IS managers that increased performance can be achieved through improved TTF. A theory is built and repeatedly

tested by showing that it does not have logical contradictions and that it is consistent with objective facts. It is believed that progress is achieved by subjecting theories to successive tests.

By testing hypotheses against replicated observations, positivist researchers derive conclusions that support or refute causal relations. Consequently, by being subjected to potential 'falsification', scientific statements are further refined into more accurate statements (Popper [1934] 1959). Replication is vital for checking and refining scientific statements in researchers' 'unending quest' for discovering causal laws, universal across time and space. Building such causal laws requires description of the social life in the form of well-defined and precisely measured constructs, variables and their relationships. Based on the assumption of the objective and value-free science, a theory is characterized by precision in terms of the constructs, variables, axioms and theorems, as well as language used to describe them. Scientific, discipline-based language is preferred over the vague and imprecise everyday language of ordinary people (Blaikie 1993).

Being nomothetic, positivist social science is concerned with generalizability of a theory or theoretical statements. A theory is developed by employing hypothetic–deductive logic whereby a theory's propositions are tested for mutual consistency and also empirically – whether they are consistent with the objective facts from the reality. Positivism's assumption about generalizability of a theory across different settings is often taken uncritically and applied inappropriately even to non-positivist inquiries. 'A theory' – as Lee and Baskerville (2003) thoroughly explain – 'may never be scientifically generalized to a setting where it has not yet been empirically tested and confirmed' (p. 240). The only way for a researcher to properly claim that 'the theory is indeed generalizable to the new setting would be for the theory to be actually tested and confirmed in the new setting' (p. 237).

In contrast to the positivists' striving for nomothetic theories, interpretive researchers aim to develop *idiographic* theories pertaining to individuals (*idios*) in specific social settings and time periods. A theory provides detailed descriptions and interprets the experiences, values, norms, meanings, interpretive schemes and so on, of individuals and groups in their daily lives. Unlike theory in the positivist social sciences, interpretive theory does not specify universal laws holding for aggregates of people. Instead it provides in-depth insights into specific social, cultural and historical contexts within which particular events and actions are described and interpreted as grounded in the authentic experiences of the people studied. An interpretive theory of the user acceptance of a newly implemented information system would, for instance, describe and interpret processes of system introduction in a particular social and cultural context and how the users' participation in the information system design impacted on their appropriation and subsequent use of the system. While such a theory is specific to the context and applicable to a particular setting, it is still valid and legitimate. Most interpretive researchers would agree that the first aim of theory building in an interpretive study is within a particular setting: 'Generalizing within a setting stands in contrast to the positivist conception of generalizability ... Where the study of a single setting ... is an interpretive researcher's objective, generalizing within a setting is not better or worse than, but simply different from, generalizing across settings for a positivist researcher' (ibid., p. 231).

Issues of generalizability are closely related to theory development and testing. An interpretive theory developed in a particular setting is obviously first tested in the setting in which it is developed – it is judged as truthful or adequate by the people studied if it makes sense for them. A theory, however, is also tested by its capacity to convey a deep understanding of the phenomena and actors studied in a particular social setting to other actors beyond this setting. In other words, explanatory power of an interpretive theory depends on the degree to which its description and interpretation transcend a particular context and translate into a form comprehensible to readers who did not participate in the study. The more a theory provides 'thick' descriptions, that is, the more it captures colourful, vivid and authentic details from the context, the easier it becomes for the reader to achieve a deep understanding of the meanings of actions by the people involved, and get a feel for another social reality or 'form of life'. In such a way, a theory becomes meaningful to actors in other contexts.

The question of whether interpretivist theory construction can and should ultimately also try to generalize across different contexts is very controversial, and the possible methods to achieve this remain unresolved. For introductory purposes we can only point out here that Gadamer's (1975, 1977) philosophy of hermeneutics, which is one of the essential underpinnings of interpretivist research, aims at a general foundation of human understanding that is not necessarily limited to specific settings. By the same token, Heidegger wrote about the meaning of human life in general and when he addressed 'the question concerning technology' (1977), he did not limit himself to a specific setting or time period. This appears to be lending support to theoretical generalization across settings, but in different ways from positivists' formulation of laws. This position is supported by Walsham, who argues that validity of knowledge claims from individual cases does not depend on 'the representativeness of these cases in a statistical sense, but on the plausibility and cogency of the logical reasoning used in describing the results from the cases, and in drawing conclusions from them' (1993, p. 15). Furthermore, Klein and Myers (1999, p. 72) propose that empirical findings (idiographic details revealed by the data interpretation) can be generalized to theoretical, general concepts as explained by the 'principle of abstraction and generalization' (one of seven principles for interpretive field studies).

A theory in critical social research is neither an abstract, law-like representation of the social world nor a more or less thick description and explanation of it. A theory is rather seen as a map of the social world that helps in investigating and understanding it, sufficient for acting upon it and changing it. A theory in critical social research is a way of being in the world: it is accepted by a social community if it provides interesting and appropriate concepts, models and frameworks for seeing social phenomena that are useful in dealing with these phenomena. Three basic functions of a theory suggested by Alvesson and Deetz (2000, p. 41, emphasis in the original) are '*directing attention, organizing experience*, and *enabling useful responses*'. A theory directs our attention by providing a conceptual apparatus that makes certain distinctions relevant and certain differences visible. What is at issue here is not which theory is a more accurate representation of the 'real' thing, but rather the 'choice of distinctions to be used, [and] the differences that matter' (ibid., p. 42).

Critical IS researchers develop IS-specific theories by drawing from critical social theory and appropriating concepts, models and frameworks to deal with specific issues in the practice of IS development, implementation and use. Their choice and appropriation of a particular critical theory and its further development depend on its capacity to:

1. describe the relevant underlying structures of social and material conditions and explain how they shape and determine the nature and content of IS and the ways they mediate work;
2. assist in demystifying the myths of technological determinism and inevitability of particular IS designs;
3. enable exposure of taken-for-granted assumptions behind an IS design (implementation or use) and the interests and values it inscribes;
4. provide an insight into the broader social, organizational and political implications of the proposed IS; and
5. enable both researchers and the researched in seeing or envisaging the desired changes – in working conditions, business processes, decision making, organizational appropriation of IS, IS design and use and so on.

Critical IS research has *critical social theory* as its philosophical and theoretical foundation. Critical social theory is not a theory or a school of thought. The term 'critical social theory' denotes a range of critical approaches and theories.[6] It is not reducible to any fixed set of assumptions and prescriptions and it should not be treated as 'a universal grammar of revolutionary thought objectified and reduced to discrete formulaic pronouncements or strategies' (Kincheloe and McLaren 2000, p. 290). Critical IS researchers have been inspired by and have adapted and applied a diverse range of concepts, theories or theoretical frameworks from critical social theory. Typically, critical empirical IS studies appropriate a particular social theory and in applying it to specific organizational and institutional IS contexts (for instance, Ngwenyama and Lee 1997, applied Habermas's theory of communicative action, 1984) contribute to the development of the theory.

Critical theorizing in IS aims at fostering reflexivity, a capacity for change and a new basis for IS praxis in organizations, which is not only governed by instrumental rationality, managerialist ideology or technological determinism. Critical IS researchers take issue with the overdue influence of instrumental rationality and technological determinism on current management and work practices, in particular if this influence is unreflected or even purposefully concealed by ideology and vested interests. This does not mean that critical IS researchers have their own 'hidden agenda' and that they aim to impose their own values on practice (as claimed by Wilson 1997). Rather, critical researchers aim at enabling the subordinated and the disadvantaged to articulate and realize their values that have been silenced by current practices, be it by anonymous institutional pressures, which even the rulers cannot escape, or by consciously domineering elites.

Critical IS researchers reject the positivist conception of IS as tools that serve managers' goals and enable efficient control of processes and resources. They also reject the interpretivists' passive watching and 'impartial' documenting of experiences of IS practices. By avoiding value judgements and relying on informants' subjective views and experiences, coupled with the absence of historical accounts and deeper insights into the material conditions and social structures that shaped their views and experiences, the interpretivist IS researchers may inadvertently legitimate the dominant power structures and managerialist ideology embedded in IS design, implementation and use. By adopting critical social theory as its philosophical and theoretical foundation, critical IS research offers a hope for emancipatory forms of IS research (see Hirschheim and Klein 1994).

Critical IS researchers share with organization studies researchers critical theoretic concerns about dominant organizational discourses and the way they shape and legitimize particular IS designs (Parker 1992; Deetz 1997, 1998; Alvesson and Deetz 2000; Grey and Willmott 2002). Moreover, critical researchers studying contemporary organizations within different disciplines – including education, psychology, sociology, management, organization studies and IS – have become increasingly concerned with oppressive forms of power, domination of privileged over other groups, and reinforcement of oppression and domination through and by technology. The emancipatory implications of IS research may result from the researchers' ability to expose the dominant discourse in IS development and reveal how such discourse legitimizes particular representations and information structures (for example, in a database) and establishes a specific IS design as natural and inevitable (Alvesson and Willmott 1992).

Key questions for critical IS researchers include the relationship between theory and practice and how knowledge is produced and used. While the role of a critical theory in IS is to reveal distorted consciousness and hidden forms of domination and oppression achieved through or assisted by the use of information systems, the theory also derives its validity from its role in informing and actively engaging in the transformation of IS practice. The validity test for a critical IS theory is therefore in IS practice: does knowledge motivate, empower and give ammunition to actors who struggle against the domination of instrumental rationality in IS development aiming to break managerialist hold over the nature and objectives of information systems? Does (can) a theory inform or assist practical action (IS development and implementation) leading to emancipatory social change? This leads to the notion of research validity – *catalytic validity* – defined as the degree to which research informs and enlightens those it studies, assists them in gaining self-understanding and self-direction and enables them to comprehend and change the world (Lather 1993; Kincheloe and McLaren 2000).

Testing a theory should not be understood as a single, distinct phase in theory development. On the contrary, testing theory is 'a dynamic, ongoing process of applying theory and modifying it. Knowledge grows by an ongoing process of eroding ignorance and enlarging insights through action' (Neuman 2003, p. 85). Critical IS researchers have yet to demonstrate how and to what extent the knowledge they produce informs and is informed by IS practice. The lack of empirical studies – involving application, testing and modification of a critical theory through transformation of IS practice – has been identified as a major weakness of the critical IS approach (Klein 1999). Apart from the dominance of positivism in IS research (reinforced by editorial policies of major IS journals, especially in the United States[7]) and difficulties in finding sponsors for critical research, the lack of critical empirical studies in IS can be partly attributed to the problem of critical research methodology, to be discussed in the following section.

**Critical IS research methodology**
Methodology is understood here in its philosophical sense as an overall strategy of conceptualizing and conducting an inquiry, and constructing scientific knowledge. Assumptions about methodology can therefore be

examined as epistemological assumptions of methods, assumptions behind linking methods to a theory and about knowledge production. In everyday research practice they are translated into assumptions about selection of subjects/objects of study, adequacy of data collection techniques and criteria for judging good empirical evidence, the processes of deriving findings from empirical evidence and providing explanations and interpretations, as well as assumptions about correctness of explanation or plausibility of interpretation. As 'different ways of viewing the world shape different ways of researching the world' (Crotty 1998, p. 66), assumptions about methodology in positivist, interpretivist and critical approaches are significantly different.

As positivist IS research seeks to discover and test law-like theories and causal relations among constructs that describe an objectively existing reality, the key epistemological assumption underlying positivist research methodology is empirical testability of causal relations and theories. Empirical research inquiries are required to examine whether hypothesized causal relations are supported/confirmed or rejected by empirical evidence. Negative or disconfirming evidence eliminates, while supporting evidence strengthens a hypothesis of a causal relation. Theories are developed and refined over time through replicated hypothesis testing, elimination of those not supported or confirmed by empirical evidence, generation of new hypotheses and so on, thereby contributing to accumulation of scientific knowledge. It is assumed that to achieve valid and generalizable hypothesis testing a researcher needs to apply appropriate scientific methods, such as sample surveys and controlled experiments, and faithfully follow their rules and norms for research design, empirical data collection, statistical data processing and creation of findings. Furthermore, positivist researchers believe that following these sanctioned research methods 'is the only way in which valid knowledge can be obtained' (Orlikowski and Baroudi 1991, p. 10).

Research methods privileged by positivist research are based on the assumption that the measurements of empirical phenomena can be accurate and precise. It is assumed that good empirical evidence consists of objective facts that reflect reality and exist independently of personal values and biases. Objective facts are also independent of the researcher or the method used to capture or measure them. Sophisticated statistical models and techniques are developed and norms and due processes carefully applied and checked by the IS community in order to guard against value biases and guarantee a desired level of scientific rigor. Furthermore, the creation of factual knowledge results from many researchers and research studies, replicating hypothesis testing, and communicating findings. This is based on the assumption that researchers, as rational individuals, assign same (or similar) meanings to independently observable facts, that is, develop shared acknowledgement of the facts.

Assumptions behind interpretivist IS research methodologies are quite different. As evidence cannot be separated from the context and facts are not value free and objective, IS research is inevitably situated in the social practice of IS development and use (Orlikowski 1991; Walsham 1993, 1995; Klein and Myers 1999). Interpretive IS researchers believe that everyday social practices cannot be disconnected from and studied independently of socially created meaning systems and the language that actors use to describe and make sense of these practices. Interpretive researchers therefore use particular research methods, such as field studies, ethnographies, action research, discourse analysis and so on, to get inside the worlds and meaning systems of those being studied and obtain an in-depth understanding of their subjective beliefs, experiences, feelings and values. Instead of producing research findings as established facts, interpretivist researchers are offering 'findings as interpretations'. Research findings as interpretations are judged based on credibility of the research process, trustworthiness (as a parallel to objectivity) in the research design, and the ways concrete empirical material (observations, interviews, events) are analysed and interpreted. A new understanding or explanation of the phenomena studied is judged based on the richness of descriptions, internal coherence, depth and insightfulness of interpretations and plausibility of results to a reader.

As to the links between a method and a theory, interpretive researchers generally assume that people's subjective views and beliefs have primacy over the theories that may be 'imposed' on them. Interpretive researchers, however, differ among themselves in the way they interpret empirical data and derive explanations and theories. For instance, those applying *grounded theory* (first described by Glaser and Strauss 1967) approach a field study without a theoretical model or a priori concepts and derive theory inductively from data. They ground a theory in the data (see, for example, Orlikowski 1993). On the other hand, an *action* researcher may start with and apply a theoretical model and through action and learning cycles revise the model and produce empirical evidence to support it. Similarly, empirical material from ethnography can be analysed from a particular theory perspective, thus resulting in theory-informed interpretations.

Considerable ambiguity surrounds the question of empirical research methodology in critical social sciences and by implication in IS. While some research methods and techniques are closely related to the positivist approach (such as experiments, surveys and statistical equation modelling) and others to the interpretivist approach (such as interpretivist case study, ethnography and action research), this is not necessarily the case with the critical approach. It is argued that neglect of the methodological question poses a significant difficulty for critical researchers, for instance in legitimizing their claims to knowledge, and to some extent contributes to the marginalization of critical research (Morrow and Brown 1994; Klein 1999). However, there is a renewed interest among contemporary critical researchers from different disciplines in the empirical dimension of critical research and the development of critical research methodology (Crotty 1998; Klein 1999; Kincheloe and McLaren 2000). These developments emerge in two major directions simultaneously.

The first direction is based on the assumption that a distinct critical research approach needs to employ distinct critical research methods. Methods, such as *critical ethnography* (Thomas 1993; Myers 1997), *participatory action research* (Baskerville 1999) and *critical discourse analysis* (Fairclough 1992) are proposed as distinctly 'critical'. By going beyond cultural description and explanation, critical ethnography is concerned with *'cultural critique as defamiliarization* and *cultural critique as ideology critique'* (Morrow and Brown 1994, p. 255, emphasis in the original). This is achieved by grounding ethnographic work in critical hermeneutics (Thompson 1981; Vatimo 1994) and by infusing critical, social theoretic concerns into hermeneutic acts of interpretation. Participatory action research can be seen as a distinctly critical method to the degree to which it is linked to practical intervention and transformation of practice (such as IS development). Critical discourse analysis focuses on discourse and interpretations of meaning sensitive to the forms of distorted communications linked to power and ideology. As Fairclough (1992, p. 4) explains, any instance of discourse is seen simultaneously as a piece of text, an instance of discursive practice and an instance of social practice:

> The 'text' dimension attends to language analysis of texts. The 'discursive practice' dimension ... specifies the nature of the processes of text production and interpretation ... The 'social practice' dimension attends to issues of concern in social analysis such as the institutional and organizational circumstances of the discursive event and how that shapes the nature of the discursive practice.

The second direction of critical methodological developments and debate is more concerned with methodological choices, and social and political contexts in which these choices are made. A critical research programme sets an agenda and the types of explanatory substantive problems for which some methods are more appropriate than others, but the relationship is not deterministic. Critical research methodology is explicitly concerned with the choices about linking theories and research methods in any specific research context. Despite attempts to develop distinctly critical research methods, mentioned above, critical research is by no means limited to those methods perceived as critical. A critical approach to the question of research methodology is rather concerned with linking theoretical problems with the choices of methods, as Morrow and Brown (1994, p. 200) explain: 'critical theory does require critical pluralism in that it directs attention not only to how the type of theoretical problems shapes the choices of methods but also to the political and ideological contexts of methodological choices as part of the process of non-empirical argumentation'.

Galtung (1977) in particular points to the political and ideological aspect of methodological choices:

> To work with any methodology … is a political act … the choice of a methodology is implicitly the choice of an ideology, including the mystifying, monotheistic ideology that there is but one methodology – the universal one. To the extent that we are *conscious* the choice is for us to make, not to be made for us, and to the extent that we are *free* for us to enact. (p. 40, emphasis in the original)

From this perspective, critical IS researchers should be even more vitally interested in the methodological question. It is not so much the issue of distinctly critical methods (although that is also of interest) as it is the issue of a conscious methodological choice and its implications for knowledge production and use. In particular, given critical researchers' belief that all research is part of the process of social (re)production, the uniqueness of critical methodology is associated with reflexivity (especially self-reflection) and the dialectic relation between research and practice (Cecez-Kecmanovic 2001).

## Conclusions

This chapter aimed at identifying and reflecting on assumptions and ideas underlying the critical IS research approach by comparing and contrasting them with assumptions and ideas characteristic of positivist and interpretivist approaches. Identifying and reflecting on assumptions and ideas are important for the IS research community for several reasons. First, in developing an understanding of the meaning of 'critical' in critical IS inquiry and the expectations regarding its nature, purpose, method and validity. Second, by highlighting the essential characteristics and distinctiveness of critical *vis-à-vis* positivist and interpretivist research approaches, this chapter assists reviewers, editors and authors in sharpening their assessment criteria and constructing more informed and reasoned approaches towards legitimizing critical IS research, and appreciating its contributions. Third, by differentiating between the assumptions and ideas that guide the critical approach from those that guide positivist and interpretivist approaches, this chapter contributes to the visibility of the critical approach in IS research and thereby encourages critical researchers to unapologetically report their research findings, reveal the purpose and critical nature of their inquiry and reflect on their experiences. Finally, this chapter contributes to identity building of critical IS research by encouraging critical IS researchers to reflect on their own assumptions and beliefs, their social roles and responsibilities as researchers, and also to scrutinize their research questions, methodological choices and relationship with IS practice.

It is important to note here that discussion about the basic assumptions and ideas underlying the critical IS research approach and a reflective comparison with other approaches is an ongoing and progressive task, one that cannot be completed. Such a task should also be approached as a form of self-criticism and a way of questioning one's own identity (as a critical researcher). In addition, any such endeavour is ultimately a product of socio-historic developments in the IS discipline and other social sciences. This chapter therefore is inherently limited by its particular historical location and the author's critical consciousness.

Being 'critical' in IS research does not only mean commitment to a certain set of assumptions and values that determine a third path in IS research. Being 'critical' also means having a much broader historical, social and political view of the IS discipline and seeing how economic and managerial interests, ideologies and discourses, assisted by educational and research funding institutions, shape and construct IS research. Critical IS researchers are concerned with the purpose, use and misuse of IS research outcomes in organizations and society. Future critical studies are called for to investigate IS research itself as a social activity – its practice, purpose and implications – from a critical theory perspective.

Once IS researchers take critical theory seriously and consciously infuse critical theoretic concerns into their studies, interpretations and understanding, a different role of knowledge creation would be promoted; a different relation to IS practice would emerge; IS research itself would be seen as a moral and political activity and researchers as 'transformative intellectuals' and social advocates. It might then become acceptable for an IS inquiry to aspire to the name *critical* and for IS researchers 'to confront the injustice of a particular society … unafraid to consummate a relationship with emancipatory consciousness' (Kincheloe and McLaren 2000, p. 291).

**Notes**
1. Critical research has been recognized as a distinct approach or paradigm in IS, apart from positivist and interpretivist approaches, by Hirschheim (1985), Klein and Lyytinen (1985), Lyytinen and Klein (1985), Lyytinen and Hirschheim (1988), Hirschheim and Klein (1989), Orlikowski and Baroudi (1991), Lyytinen (1992), Hirschheim et al. (1996), Myers and Young (1997), Iivari et al. (1998), Klein and Myers (2001) and Mingers (2003).

2. For instance, editors (the author was one of them) of critical IS research tracks at conferences such as critical management studies (CMS) and Americas Conference on Information Systems (AMCIS) were approached by several prospective authors asking for an explanation of 'critical' in the title of the track and also received paper submissions that assumed a common-sense meaning of 'critical' in the critical IS research.
3. A number of scientific theories (from Werner Heinzenberg's and Niels Bohr's onwards) include so-called 'facts' that are theory based and not purely observable data.
4. Kincheloe and McLaren refer to 'critical postmodern' which has emerged as the 'nexus of critical theory, postcolonialism, critical pedagogy, and postmodern theory' (Boje 2001).
5. There are, however, claims that knowledge in natural sciences also results from human interpretation and is socially constructed, the discussion of which is outside the scope of this chapter.
6. Critical social theory as a term is most often related to the Frankfurt school. Namely, motivated by Karl Marx, Immanuel Kant, Georg Hegel and Max Weber, the idea of a critical theory was first outlined by the Frankfurt school theorists as a distinct form of theory – contrasted to 'traditional', metaphysical or materialist theories. The first generation of the Frankfurt school critical theorists, most notably Horkheimer ([1931] 1972, Marcuse (1964, 1968) and Adorno (1970), criticized philosophy for its blindness to the material conditions of life and social relations as well as for its inability to offer a truly critical approach to concrete social problems and the struggle of the oppressed groups to change their position. A truly critical theory, they proposed, is not restricted to pure thought and critical theorists are never satisfied with merely increasing knowledge (Horkheimer [1931] 1972). Instead, a truly critical theory is involved with the present social conditions and materializes by employing the conception of reason as a 'critical tribunal' (Marcuse 1968). Critical theory has been developed further through the works of the second-generation critical theorists, primarily Habermas (1973, 1984, 1987, 1996) and Apel (1979). Beyond the Frankfurt school, critical theorists such as Honneth (1995) in Germany and McCarthy (1982) and Benhabib (1986) in the United States, are sometimes referred to as the third generation.
7. Chen and Hirschheim (2004) found that 81 per cent of empirical research published between 1991 and 2001 in eight major IS publication outlets are positivist.

## References

Adorno, T.W. (1970), *Aesthetic Theory*, Minneapolis, MN: University of Minnesota Press.

Alvesson, M. and Deetz, S. (2000), *Doing Critical Management Research*, London: Sage.

Alvesson, M. and Willmott, H. (1992), 'On the idea of emancipation in management and organization studies', *Academy of Management Review*, **17**(3), 432–64.

Apel, K.-O. (1979), *Toward a Transformation of Philosophy*, trans. G. Adey and D. Frisby, London: Routledge & Kegan Paul.

Baskerville, R. (1999), 'Investigating information systems with action research', *CAIS* (*Communications of the Association for Information*), **2**, Article 19.

Benhabib, S. (1986), *Critique, Norm and Utopia: A Study of the Foundations of Critical Theory*, New York: Columbia University Press.

Bernstein, R.J. (1983), *Beyond Objectivism and Relativism: Science, Hermeneutics and Practice*, Philadelphia, PA: University of Pennsylvania Press.

Bernstein, R.J. (ed.) (1994), *Habermas and Modernity*, Cambridge, MA: MIT Press.

Blaikie, N. (1993), *Approaches to Social Enquiry*, Cambridge, MA: Polity.

Boje, D. (2001), 'What is critical postmodern theory?', http://cbae.nmsu.edu/~dboje/pages/what_is_critical_postmodern.htm, accessed 9 December 2002.

Burrell, G. and Morgan, G. (1979), *Sociological Paradigms and Organizational Analysis*, London: Heinemann.

Cecez-Kecmanovic, D. (2001), 'Doing critical IS research: the question of methodology', in Trauth E. (ed.), *Qualitative Research in Information Systems: Issues and Trends*, Hershey, PA: Idea Group Publishing, pp. 142–63.

Cecez-Kecmanovic, D. and Janson, M. (1999), 'Communicative action theory: an approach to understanding the application of information systems', *Proceedings of the 10th Australasian Conference on Information Systems*, Wellington, New Zealand: University of Wellington, pp. 183–95.

Cecez-Kecmanovic, D., Janson, M. and Brown, A. (2002), 'The rationality framework for a critical study of information systems', *Journal of Information Technology*, **17**, 215–27.

Chen, W. and Hirschheim, R. (2004), 'A paradigmatic and methodological examination of information systems research from 1991 to 2001', *Information Systems Journal*, **14**, 197–235.

Crotty, M. (1998), *The Foundations of Social Research: Meaning and Perspective in the Research Process*, London: Allen & Unwin.

Deetz, S.A. (1997), 'The business concept, discursive power, and managerial control in a knowledge-intensive company: a case study of discursive power', in Sypher, B.D. (ed.), *Case Studies in Organizational Communication 2*, New York: Guilford Press, pp. 183–212.

Deetz, S.A. (1998), 'Discursive formations, strategized subordination, and self-surveillance', in McKinlay, A. and Starkey, K. (eds), *Foucault, Management and Organization Theory*, London: Sage, pp. 151–72.

Fairclough, N. (1992), *Discourse and Social Change*, Cambridge, MA: Polity.

Fay, B. (1987), *Critical Social Science: Liberation and its Limits*, Ithaca, NY: Cornell University Press.

Feenberg, A. (2002), *Transforming Technology: A Critical Theory Revisited*, New York: Oxford University Press.

Friere, P. (1976), *Education: The Practice of Freedom*, London: Writers and Readers Publishing Cooperative.

Gadamer, H.-G. (1975), *Truth and Method*, rev. edn, ed. and trans. J. Weinsheimer and D.G. Marshall, New York: Crossroad.

Gadamer, H.-G. (1977), 'Theory, technology, practice: the task of the science of man', *Social Research*, **44**, 529–61.

Galtung, J. (1977), *Methodology and Ideology: Essays in Methodology*, vol. 1, Copenhagen: Christian Ejlers.

Giddens, A. (1976), *New Rules of Sociological Method: A Positive Critique of Interpretive Sociologies*, London: Hutchinson.

Giddens, A. (1978), 'Positivism and its criticism', in Bottomore, T. and Nisbet, R. (eds), *A History of Sociological Analysis*, London: Heinemann.

Glaser, B.G. and Strauss, A. (1967), *The Discovery of Grounded Theory: Strategies for Qualitative Research*, Chicago: Aldine.

Goodhue, D. and Thompson, R. (1995), 'Task-technology fit and individual performance', *MIS Quarterly*, **19**(2), 213–36.

Grey, C. and Willmott, H. (2002), 'Contexts of CMS', *Organization*, **9**(3), 411–18.

Habermas, J. (1973), *Theory and Practice*, Boston, MA: Beacon.

Habermas, J. (1984), *The Theory of Communicative Action: Reason and the Rationalisation of Society*, vol. I, Boston, MA: Beacon.

Habermas, J. (1987), *The Theory of Communicative Action: The Critique of Functionalist Reason*, vol. II, Boston, MA: Beacon.

Habermas, J. (1996), *On the Logic of the Social Sciences*, Cambridge, MA: MIT Press.

Harvey, L. (1990), *Critical Social Research*, London: Unwin Hyman.

Heidegger, M. (1977), *The Question Concerning Technology and other Essays*, trans. and introduction W. Lowitt, New York: Harper Torchbooks.

Held, D. (1980), *Introduction to Critical Theory*, Berkeley and Los Angeles, CA: University of California Press.

Hirschheim, R. (1985), 'Information systems epistemology: an historical perspective', in Mumford, E., Hirschheim, R., Fitzgerald, G. and Wood-Harper, A.T. (eds), *Research Methods in Information Systems*, Amsterdam: North-Holland, pp. 13–38.

Hirschheim, R. and Klein, H.K. (1989), 'Four paradigms of information systems development', *Communications of the ACM*, **32**(10), 1199–216.

Hirschheim, R. and Klein, H.K. (1994), 'Realizing emancipatory principles in information systems research: the case for ETHICS', *MIS Quarterly*, **18**(1), 83–109.

Hirschheim, R., Klein, H. and Lyytinen, L. (1996), 'Exploring the intellectual structures of information systems development: a social action theoretic analysis', *Accounting, Management and Information Technologies*, **6**(1/2), 1–64.

Hohendahl, P.-U. and Fisher, J. (eds) (2001), *Critical Theory: Current State and Future Prospects*, New York: Berghahn Books.

Honneth, A. (1995), *The Fragmented World of the Social. Essays in Social and Political Philosophy*, ed. C.W. Wright, Albany, NY: State University of New York Press.

Horkheimer, M. ([1931] 1972), 'Traditional and critical theory', in *Critical Theory: Selected Essays*, trans. M.J. O'Connell and others, New York: Seabury.

Iivari, J., Hirschheim, R. and Klein, H. (1998), 'A paradigmatic analysis contrasting information systems development approaches and methodologies', *Information Systems Research*, **9**(2), 164–93.

Kincheloe, L.J. and McLaren, P. (2000), 'Rethinking critical theory and qualitative research', in Denzin, N.K. and Linkoln, Y.D. (eds), *Handbook of Qualitative Research*, 2nd edn, London: Sage, pp. 279–313.

Klein, H.K. (1999), 'Knowledge and methods in IS research: from beginnings to the future', in Ngwenyama, O., Introna, L., Myers, M.D. and DeGross, J.I. (eds), *New Information Technologies in Organizational Processes: Field Studies and Theoretical Reflections on the Future of Work*, Boston, MA: Kluwer Academic, pp. 13–25.

Klein, H.K. and Lyytinen, K. (1985), 'The poverty of scientism in information systems', in Mumford, E., Hirschheim, R., Fitzgerald, G. and Wood-Harper, A.T. (eds), *Research Methods in Information Systems*, Amsterdam: North-Holland, pp. 131–62.

Klein, H.K. and Myers, M.D. (1999), 'A set of principles for conducting and evaluating interpretive field studies in information systems', *MIS Quarterly*, **23**(1), 67–93.

Klein, H.K. and Myers, M.D. (2001), 'A classification scheme for interpretive research in information systems', in E. Trauth (ed.), *Qualitative Research in Information Systems: Issues and Trends*, Hershey, PA: Idea Group Publishing, pp. 219–40.

Kuhn, T.S. (1970), *The Structure of Scientific Revolutions*, rev. edn, Chicago: University of Chicago Press.

Lather, P. (1993), 'Fertile obsession: validity after poststructuralism', *Sociological Quarterly*, **34**, 673–93.

Lee, A.S and Baskerville, R.L. (2003), 'Generalizing generalizability in information systems research', *Information Systems Research*, **14**(3), 221–43.

Lincoln, Y.S. and Guba, E.G. (2000), 'Paradigmatic controversies, contradictions, and emerging confluences', in Denzin, N.K. and Linkoln, Y.D. (eds), *Handbook of Qualitative Research*, 2nd edn, London: Sage, pp. 163–88.

Lyytinen, K. (1992), 'Information systems and critical theory', in Alvesson, M. and Willmott, H. (eds), *Critical Management Studies*, London: Sage, pp. 159–80.

Lyytinen, K. and Hirschheim, R. (1988), 'Information systems and rational discourse: an application of Habermas's theory of communicative action', *Scandinavian Journal of Management*, **4**, 19–30.

Lyytinen, K. and Klein, H. (1985), 'The critical theory of Jürgen Habermas as a basis for a theory of information systems', in Mumford, E., Hirschheim, R., Fitzgerald, G. and Wood-Harper, A.T. (eds), *Research Methods in Information Systems*, Amsterdam: North-Holland, pp. 219–36.

Marcuse, H. (1964), *One-dimensional Man*, Boston, MA: Beacon.

Marcuse, H. (1968), *Negations: Essays in Critical Theory*, Boston, MA: Beacon.

McCarthy, T. (1982), *The Critical Theory of Jürgen Habermas*, 2nd paperback edn, Cambridge, MA: MIT Press.

Mingers, J. (2003), 'The paucity of multimethod research: a review of the information systems literature', *Information Systems Journal*, **13**, 233–49.

Morrow, R.A. and Brown, D. (1994), *Critical Theory and Methodology*, London: Sage.

Myers, M.D. (1997), 'Critical ethnography in information systems', in Lee, A.S., Liebenau, J., and DeGross, J.I. (eds), *Information Systems and Qualitative Research*, London: Chapman & Hall, pp. 277–300.

Myers, M.D. and Young, L.W. (1997), 'Hidden agendas, power and managerial assumptions in information systems development: an ethnographic study', *Information Technology and People*, **10**(3), 224–40.

Neuman, W.L. (2003), *Social Research Methods: Qualitative and Quantitative Approaches*, 5th edn, London: Pearson Education.

Ngwenyama, O. and Lee, A. (1997), 'Communication richness in electronic mail: critical social theory and the contextuality of meaning', *MIS Quarterly*, **21**(2), 145–67.

Orlikowski, W.J. (1991), 'Integrated information environment or matrix of control? The contradictory implications of information technology', *Accounting, Management and Information Technologies*, **1**(1), 1–28.

Orlikowski, W.J. (1993), 'CASE tools as organizational change: investigating incremental and radical changes in systems development', *MIS Quarterly*, **17**(3), 309–40.

Orlikowski, W.J. and Baroudi, J.J. (1991), 'Studying information technology in organizations: research approaches and assumptions', *Information Systems Research*, **2**(1), 1–28.

Parker, M. (1992), 'Post-modern organizations or postmodern organization theory?', *Organization Studies*, **13**(1), 1–17.

Popper, K.R. ([1934] 1959), *The Logic of Scientific Discovery*, New York: Basic Books.

Thomas, J. (1993), *Doing Critical Ethnography*, Newbury Park, CA: Sage.

Thompson, J.B. (1981), *Critical Hermeneutics: A Study in the Thought of Paul Ricoeur and Jürgen Habermas*, Cambridge, MA: Cambridge University Press.

Vatimo, G. (1994), *Beyond Interpretation: The Meaning of Hermeneutics for Philosophy*, Stanford, CA: Stanford University Press.

Walsham, G. (1993), *Interpreting Information Systems in Organizations*, Chichester: John Wiley & Sons.

Walsham, G. (1995), 'The emergence of interpretivism in IS research', *Information Systems Research*, **6**(4), 376–94.

Weber, R. (2004), 'The rhetoric of positivism versus interpretivism: a personal view', editor's comments, *MIS Quarterly*, **28**(1), iii–xii.

Wilson, F.A. (1997), 'The truth is out there: the search for emancipatory principles in information systems design', *Information Technology and People*, **10**(3), 187–204.

# 3 Theoretical approaches for researching power and information systems: the benefit of a Machiavellian view

*Leiser O. Silva*

## Introduction

The relationship among power, politics, information systems and organizations has been the centre of several studies in the information systems (IS) field. These studies have concentrated on different power issues such as the interaction between users and designers (Kling 1991; Alvarez 2002; Davidson 2002), the possible conflict between managers and workers (Keen 1981; Markus 1983; Markus and Bjorn-Andersen 1987; Robey and Smith 1993; Newman and Sabherwal 1996), and the use of information systems as instruments of domination (Bloomfield and Coombs 1992; Hirschheim and Klein 1994; Sillince and Mouakket 1997; Griffith et al. 1998; Saravanamuthu 2002; Howcroft and Wilson 2003). Moreover, in a recent paper Jasperson et al. (2002) analysed the different theoretical approaches to studying power and its relation to information systems, by examining 82 papers. In their large sample, they found that only 13 papers took a multidimensional view of power; that is, considering information technology (IT) not only as an instrument for introducing change but also as a source of political actions. This is interesting given the benefit that integrated views would bring about for understanding a complex phenomenon such as power. In this sense, I shall argue that adopting a strategic view of power will bring into being both the instrumental and political nature of IT.

Thus, in this chapter I shall discuss distinctive theoretical approaches for studying power and IS and argue in favour of a Machiavellian stance. To develop the discussion, I shall first concentrate on the different perspectives adopted by researchers when examining power and politics in the context of information systems. Second, I shall focus on the theoretical foundations of such approaches. Third, I shall argue that a theoretical framework that deems power as strategic, that is, a Machiavellian approach, will enrich our understanding of power and politics. I conclude with a reflection on the analytical depth of those two theories.

**Making sense of power**

Power is an elusive conception which, like electricity or gravity, is only known to us through its effects while its nature remains obscure (Barnes 1988). We are all familiar with military, political and even physical power, but its nature and essence escapes us. Likewise, it is very difficult to establish whether our actions are determined by external forces. This question has been in the centre of social and political sciences debate about power (Giddens 1984). It is this double dimension of power, evident in its effects and obscure in its nature that makes power difficult to define. There are as many definitions of power as viewpoints on the subject (Russell 1938; Lukes 1974, 1986; Clegg 1975, 1979, 1989; Debnam 1984; Barnes 1986, 1988; Wrong 1995). That is why, instead of attempting the almost impossible task of defining power, I shall present an overview of the different approaches to power within the social sciences.

Before introducing our typology let us ask four questions regarding the nature and essence of power.

1. Is power a capacity?
2. Is power synonymous with influence and hegemony?
3. Can an agent or individual store power?
4. If power can be stored, what is its relationship with decision making?

These four questions point to four different approaches on power that are not necessarily contradictory. To answer these questions I have drawn on the work of Law (1991), who classifies and observes four types of power: 'power to', 'power over', 'power storage' and 'power discretion'. The examination of those four types of power will allow us to classify the works regarding power and IS and also to trace their intellectual roots.

I selected Law's classification over others, such as Lukes's (1974) three dimensions, because of the clarity of Law's categories in terms of the nature of power that each category deals with and because the categories are noticeably distinct from one another. Thus, Law's classification constitutes a distinctive and comprehensive lens for discussing exemplary works on IS and power relations, which makes it suitable for the purposes of this chapter. I use Law's categorization for analytical purposes only after recognizing that some of the studies discussed in the later sections may be classified in more than one type. However, I have classified each study under the category whose influence is predominant. The thrust of this section is to discuss the four types of power according to Law, and examine how they have been approached by IS researchers.

*Power to*

According to Law, 'power to' is power that enables. Barnes (1988), an exponent of this approach, deems that society enables individuals to act. He claims that we are able to do things by virtue of being members of society. Law also places Foucault (1977, 1980, 1982) as a proponent of this type of power. Foucault is classified in this category not only because of his conception of power as embedded in social relations but also because of his concern with discipline. Discipline in this sense concerns strategies, techniques and micro techniques of power that operate through institutions and even bodies, such as, for example, armies. Neither Barnes nor Foucault thinks of power as a zero-sum-game entity. They claim the opposite, that the sum of power parts is greater than the parts. Law characterizes this type of power as productive and enabling, and so he dubs it 'power to'.

The productive and enabling features – that is, the 'power to' – of IS and IT have been the focus of several researchers of IS. Some of them, influenced by Foucault's ideas, have concentrated on the enabling characteristics of an information system when considering it as an electronic panopticon (Zuboff 1988; Sewell and Wilkinson 1992). Another approach to IS is the socio-technical, which views them as a means to conciliate the overall organizational interests of production and profit with those of job satisfaction held by the workforce (Mumford 1972, 1987; Mumford and Henshall 1979). These ideas have been taken further by Hirschheim and Klein (1994), who proposed an IS development methodology for emancipation. Thus, 'power to' has been central in the contributions of the above researchers; some think of IT as enabling production and efficiency and others as an instrument for emancipation. The rest of this subsection discusses these ideas.

*Foucault, the panopticon metaphor and information systems*   The panopticon was envisaged and devised by the British philosopher Jeremy Bentham during the early stages of the industrial revolution. He intended it as an instrument to exercise supervision and surveillance over prisoners: 'The design of the Panopticon consisted of a tower in the centre surrounded by a ring-shaped building composed of cells, each housing a prisoner. The Panopticon allowed for the continuous observation of inmates, while simultaneously requiring few supervisory resources' (McHoul and Grace 1993, p. 67).

Bentham also thought that a panopticon built in a factory could enhance production. Once in place, the panopticon would allow management to instil discipline in their subordinates by letting them know they were under surveillance all the time. Furthermore, the panopticon could give supervisors the opportunity to see their subordinates without the latter being able to see the former. Zuboff (1988) considered IT as the electronic panopticon. She observed that managerial techniques of control and surveillance were supported by IT. The electronic panopticon is represented by IT as it avoids face-to-face contact between managers and employees. The electronic panopticon, Zuboff pointed out, makes work practices visible and emphasizes the division of work. Hence an organization where the electronic panopticon is in place, she claimed, would not tolerate an authoritarian style of management.

The panopticon metaphor is also central to the concept of disciplinary power, which is embedded in routinized social practices. The idea of the panopticon is that power will be internalized, regularized and thereby will secure traditional norms. On those under surveillance, the panopticon produces a state of conscious and permanent visibility that enacts power. It creates the sensation within the individuals that surveillance is permanent, even if it is not; chiefly, because there is no way that individuals might establish whether there are people inside the panopticon. In short, the presence of the panopticon will create disciplinary power:

> Panopticism is the exemplary technique through which disciplinary power is able to function. For it relies on 'surveillance' and the internal training this produces to incite states of docility; it need not rely on displays of physical force or violence. Direct force represents merely frustrated or failed forms of discipline. The subject of surveillance, by contrast, disciplines him- or herself. (McHoul and Grace 1993, p. 67)

An excellent example of how disciplinary power and the panopticon metaphor are related to information systems is in the work of Sewell and Wilkinson (1992), who focus on the just-in-time (JIT) and total quality control (TQC) practices in the manufacturing environment. They argue that these JIT/TQC practices require systems of surveillance better than those offered by traditional bureaucracies; as production became more diverse, supervision has become more important. In this context, the purpose of surveillance systems is to instil discipline and to strengthen central control in order to make production more efficient. Sewell and Wilkinson argue that organizations achieve these goals by introducing two disciplinary forces. The first operates at a horizontal level. It is exerted by the supervision in each manufacturing cell, quality circle or group, by peers. The second is exerted by management information systems that act as surveillance and control systems. This is a vertical process that provides managers with a very close supervision of the shop floor. These two forces are important because JIT/TQC push responsibility downwards to identify responsibility for errors (ibid.).

*Emancipation* To seek emancipation is to aim at freeing individuals and groups from repressive social and ideological conditions that hinder human communication (Honderich 1995). In organizations, individuals will achieve emancipation if they can escape power constraints. However, this can only be achieved in ideal speech situations. Fundamentally these are communication acts that are free from power and authority. According to Habermas (1979), an ideal speech situation will require four main conditions. These refer to the work of Austin (1962) and Searle (1969) on speech acts theory. First, the propositional content of the utterance should be truthful. Second, the illocutionary force should be valid. Third, the utterance should be expressed sincerely by the speaker. Fourth, the speaker and hearer should understand each other in a comprehensive way. This ideal situation will eventually allow participants to acknowledge their real interests (Habermas 1972, 1974; Mumby 1988). Power and authority will interfere with these conditions. In this context, power is perceived as distorting communication and therefore as a factor that hinders emancipation.

In the IS field, the emancipatory approach has been applied mainly to the process of developing information systems. The point is that by incorporating these ideals in the design and development stages, IS can be effective instruments for emancipation. This approach has been analysed in depth mainly by Scandinavian researchers (Bjorn-Andersen et al. 1982; Bjerknes and Bratteteig 1995; Iivari and Lyytinen 1998). In North America, Hirschheim and Klein (1994) have also explored the idea of emancipation linked to IS development. They point out that the Scandinavian experiences of emancipation have consisted principally in transferring control of IS development and design to trade unions. According to Hirschheim and Klein, this transfer of control leads to another type of communication distortion which is introduced by the power structures of trade unions.

Hirschheim and Klein argue that IS developed by a methodology embracing emancipatory principles could generate an ideal speech situation in organizations. To do so, they suggest some modifications to the ETHICS method. The modifications they propose would provide ETHICS with tools to avoid distortions that might come from authority and illegitimate power, peer opinion, time pressure, resource limitations and social differentiation (for example, values, beliefs). Thus, a modified ETHICS would facilitate the debate on organizational problems and concerns by introducing obligatory critical checks.

## Power over

Lukes (1974) criticizes the 'power to' conception because it disregards the relational nature of power that, for him, should involve at least two agencies. The drawback of the 'power to' conception, according to Lukes, is that it ignores conflict. Law classifies Lukes's work as 'power over'. He derives this notion from Lukes's definition of power: 'A exercises *power over* B when A affects B in a manner contrary to B's interests' (Lukes 1974, p. 27; emphasis added). Lukes would call 'power over' power, and instead of using the term 'power' he would use the term 'influence'. Lukes's definition raises the question of how to identify B's real interests. The research problem with this definition is that the realization of interests leads us to moral relativism. Who is going to identify the real interests? Would it be up to an observer or would it be established by interrogating the participants? This difficulty is illustrated in Mintzberg's (1983) remark qualifying politics as illegitimate power and that of Hirschheim and Klein (1994) deeming politics as the dark side of power. Politics is illegitimate for the former because it stands against managerial interests and for the latter because politics reflects personal interests. Both positions, I believe, show the problem of moral relativism in Lukes's 'power over' approach. For Barbalet (1987, p. 8) Lukes's conception of power is sociologically vacuous: 'If to be subject to power is to have one's real interests contravened, and if real interests can be identified only outside of a subordination to power, then it is impossible ever to determine whether one is subjected to power, except when it ceases to matter.'

Lukes's work examines the social science debate between agency and structure. Are our actions determined by our culture, social group, gender or race or do our actions depend on our will? The answers to these questions will divide people into two groups. One includes structuralists and Marxists. In the other group are the voluntarists, and Lukes, and Dahl (1957, 1961) belong to this group. Law argues that 'power to' and 'power over' should go together, one represents capacities and the other relations. How these two relate, he claims, is one of the most important questions in sociology. One attempt to solve this debate in sociology is the work of Giddens (1984). This problem has also been addressed in IS, mainly by those who focus on the relationship between organizations and IT (Orlikowski 1992, 1993, 2000; Walsham 1993, 2002; Walsham and Sahay 1999). The main question asked has been whether IT determines organizational change or is it the other way around. By drawing on Giddens's theory, these authors have answered by indicating that in fact there is a mutual influence. They call this relationship the 'duality of technology'.

*'Power over' in the implementation of information systems* This approach is characterized by the recognition of the technical and political nature of implementing information systems. This political dimension can be understood as a conflict, either overt or covert, by the different interests of users and systems analysts. It also considers the resistance exerted by users against the implementation of an information system (Keen 1981; Wynne

and Otway 1982; Markus 1983; Franz and Robey 1984). The limitation of this type of approach, considering power relations as a conflict of interests, leads us to the moral relativism problem pointed out above. This is clearly illustrated in Keen's (1981) classic paper. Keen understands resistance as a behaviour intended to prevent the implementation or use of a particular system. As a consequence, this resistance prevents the achievement of the system designer's objectives. In this sense, Keen suggests that the only way to differentiate legitimate resistance from genuine sabotage is by reference to the user's conscience: 'Obviously there is a fine line between honest resistance to a project one feels is misguided and selfish sabotages of a necessary innovation. The difference is a matter for conscience and self-scrutiny. In both cases, the response is political, whether "clean" or "dirty" politics' (p. 28).

The problem here is how to distinguish between what is 'clean' from what is 'dirty' without incurring moral relativism.

Both Keen and Markus propose recommendations for systems analysts, including the participation of users in systems analysis, design and implementation (Markus 1983). Keen recommends a tactical response to overcome resistance, called 'countercounterimplementation'. This strategic and tactical position consists in creating alliances, providing incentives, promoting the signing of very specific and detailed contracts, and in defining clearly the scope and objectives of the project. His approach is similar to that of Willcocks and Mason (1987) whose work might suggest managerial interests as paramount. Knights and Murray (1994, pp. 11–12) criticize this type of approach not only for the aforementioned moral relativism but also for ignoring the construction and the base of organizational politics:

> In promoting the sectional interests of IS specialists, they [those researchers] are blind to the contradictions and tensions of organisational life in market contexts and how these make the 'rational' objectives of any one group difficult to achieve. Their research 'cries out' for a broader analysis of markets, socio-economic power and the political nature of managerial labour. Like technological determinism, then, socio-technical approaches avoid the implications of their recognition that politics is a factor in technological and organisational change. Unless politics can be mobilised in favour of managerial goals, it is viewed as disruptive.

Another relevant work regarding power struggles between users and IS professionals is the classic paper by Markus and Bjorn-Andersen (1987). These researchers focus on the power exerted by IS professionals over users. Their conception of power is based on Lukes's (1974) three-dimensional model of power. Hence they suggest that power should be understood from two different perspectives – the users and the system analysts – whom they deem as having contrary interests. They argue that a better understanding of the power exercised by IS professionals over users might have a positive effect on the productivity of both parties. Moreover, understanding users' power and interests is essential to obtain their participation in developing information systems. Consequently, Markus and Bjorn-Andersen reach a pragmatic conclusion: the analysis and awareness of the different types of power exercised by IS professionals over users and vice versa can boost the productivity of both parties.

*IT consultants exercise 'power over'*   In the 1990s, the emergence of IT consultants gave rise to another relevant group of stakeholders whose involvement in power relations attracted the attention of IS researchers. IT consultants exercise power over organizations when they claim to know what is technically possible and what is not. A remarkable example of this situation is the work of Bloomfield and Danieli (1992), who studied the development by IT consultants of an information system in the UK National Health Service (NHS). In their research, Bloomfield and Danieli found that the consultants were acting as IT spokespersons, so they defined what was technical and what was social. The authors show how the IT consultants drew on technical explanations to persuade their counterparts to drop some of their demands about the system. One of the most important resources utilized by IT consultants during these struggles was their alliance with the technical expert in the hospital. This alliance allowed the IT consultants to legitimize their claims about the 'technical' nature of the impediments to incorporate users' demands into the system. In summary this type of research, in addition to studying power relations between IT consultants and their counterparts in organizations, highlights that distinguishing between what is technical and what is not, is in itself an exercise of power.

*Power storage*
Law (1991) suggests that both 'power over' and 'power to' can be stored. In studying power, he points out, researchers need to address the question of whether power can be stored. This question is answered negatively by Foucault (1977), who argues that power is only an end product and therefore it should not be reified. However, useful as this assertion may be – in the sense that we should study power because it prevails wherever and it is only recognized in actions – it does not help with analytical purposes. Our day-to-day experience teaches us, for instance, that some people can be and are effectively more powerful than others, and Foucault's power notion does not account for that. For example, Foucault's conception of power does not explain why army discipline has different manifestations in a soldier and in a general. Law claims that his notion of 'power storage' accounts for that phenomenon. The reason why the military general is more powerful,

that is has more power than the soldier, is the result of the bureaucratic and authority relations (in terms of punishment and rewards) that have been institutionalized in the army. Law (1991, p. 170) makes his claim of the plausibility of 'power storage' very clearly:

[A]s lay people we work routinely on the assumption that both 'power over' and 'power to' can indeed be stored, even if the methods by which they are stored are never entirely secure and we know our store may spring a leak. If this were not the case we would never open bank accounts, we would never accept promises at face value, and neither would we say (surely with some reason, at least most of the time!) that Prime Ministers have 'more power' than back-benchers.

The concern of researchers over 'power storage' can be seen in the applications of resource dependency (Pfeffer and Salancik 1978; Pfeffer 1981) and contingency theories (Hickson et al. 1971; Hinings et al. 1974). Resource dependency theorists see organizational members not as completely autonomous but as interdependent. To act, those members need resources such as money, personnel, technology and information, and to obtain those resources organizational members need to interact and negotiate with those who control them. In this context, the control and possession of resources is a source of power. Contingency theory, on the other hand, addresses organizational phenomena such as power, decision making and change in organizations. This theory explains how it is that particular organizational units can exercise more power than others. For contingency theorists, 'power storage' of organizational units lies in the distinctiveness of their sources of knowledge and skills, their centrality – how the units are related to the rest of the organization – as well as on how easily the units can be replaced. Both theories, resource dependency and contingency, have been applied to the study of power relations between IS units and organizations (Lucas 1984; Saunders and Scamell 1986; Goodhue et al. 1988; Clemons and Row 1992; Gupta et al. 1994; Cavaye and Christiansen 1995, 1996).

The 'power storage' perspective along with resource dependency and contingency theories has led researchers to deem IS units within organizations as powerful. This type of research was more popular in the 1980s than in the 1990s. In the 1980s, IS units were thought to be powerful since they 'possessed' much information and specialized knowledge, and were very difficult to replace (Lucas 1984; Saunders and Scamell 1986). The studies conducted by Lucas and Saunders and Scamell applied the strategic contingency and resource dependency theories to analyse the power relations between IS units and the rest of the organization. Lucas (1984) suggests that IS units might be considered powerful for three reasons: (i) computer-based information systems have created organizational uncertainty that can only be reduced by the information services units; (ii) poor systems documentation also makes it difficult to seek an alternative; and (iii) because of the above, Lucas supposes that information services departments may be highly connected to other departments.

Other researchers have applied contingency theory for understanding the political factors affecting the implementation of information systems (Cavaye and Christiansen 1995, 1996). They argue, by drawing on contingency theory, that IS can change the distribution of power ('power storage') among units within organizations because IS affect access to and control over information. Accordingly, members of those units, perceiving that they would lose power by adopting an information system, would resist its introduction. Cavaye and Christiansen (1996) illustrate their contingency-based framework by applying it to a case study. Although they claim their contribution consists in mapping the power of the organizational units, I believe that their main contribution is in pointing out the limitations of the contingency approach; these will be discussed in the next section.

*Power discretion*
Once power is 'stored', in the sense of enjoying privileged standing conditions, such as that of the general in an army, and if the general or empowered agents have options in their scope of actions, then this will imply discretion. 'Power discretion' concerns the different options that agents have in hand to deploy the power that is stored. Discretion here is understood as the faculty held by an agent either to act or not, or to choose among different ways of action. In other words, power discretion, to paraphrase Law (1991, p. 170), is the capacity of an agent to switch on or off 'power to' or 'power over'. Law gives the example of a bank manager who has different options for investing money. The manager decides either to lend money or not to a particular organization or country; that, Law claims, is 'power discretion'. Sociologists who embrace this approach include Parsons (1937, 1967) and Alexander (1983).

Research on information systems influenced by the 'power discretion' approach has concentrated on the relationship between decision making and power, that is, the political nature of decision making (Pettigrew 1972, 1973; Wynne and Otway 1982; Wilkinson 1983; Davenport et al. 1992; Scarbrough and Corbett 1992; Noble 1995). Knights and Murray (1994, p. 2) classified this type of research as processual, as its focus is localized politics and implies that the exercise of power might be disruptive. The 'power discretion' approach to the study of information systems, particularly that of Pettigrew (1972, 1973), on the one hand, conceives organizations as political arenas where units and members dispute the control of resources. On the other, it assumes that the main motivation of organizational actors is career and self-development.

Pettigrew (1972) shows how particular organizational agents that control the flow of information – the gatekeepers – can influence the outcome of decisions. He illustrates his point by showing in his case study how a gatekeeper influenced the acquisition of specialized IT equipment to boost his power position. Pettigrew's research also points out how information and knowledge can be equated with power, that is, power storage. Furthermore, his work suggests that discretion needs to be disciplined if organizations are going to subordinate individual interests to more general objectives. It is because of these insights that Pettigrew's work remains a classic in the study of politics and information.

In summary, to re-take Law's notion of 'power discretion' in the context of IT, it could be said that the calculations made by agents when they exercise 'power discretion' are highly influenced by career advancement and self-development. This is, as will be discussed in the section below, a view of power similar to the strategic approach proposed by Machiavelli (1958, 1970).

**Discussion about the different views of power**
Law's (1991) study has allowed us to identify four different notions of power: power as a capability ('power to'), power as relational ('power over'), power as standing conditions ('power storage') and power as decisions ('power discretion'). The typology of power formulated by Law has also helped us to classify exemplary literature on power and information systems, and to trace the intellectual origins of the ideas underpinning that research. We have also seen how particular approaches to power and information systems have contributed to our understanding of different aspects of the political dimension of information technology applications in organizations (see Table 3.1). Some studies point out the enabling, constraining, or emancipatory features of information systems while others suggest the conflicting relations and political dimensions of decision making.

*Power to*
The panopticon metaphor shows limitations when responsibility of individuals is involved, as sometimes the disciplinary power comes from the individual and not from surveillance. Individuals' actions, for example, may follow disciplinary codes of ethics internalized as part of their education or by being members of professional groups. The limitation of the panopticon metaphor stems from being developed as the result of studying institutions such as prisons and hospitals where individual responsibility is not a factor (Clegg 1989). Disciplinary power works when individuals know that they are under surveillance; once they know how to break the system, discipline ends.

*Table 3.1 Different views of power and their relation to IS research*

| Type of power | Premises | IS research issue | Unanswered questions |
|---|---|---|---|
| Power to | Power is enabling<br>Power is productive<br>Power can be either hegemonic or emancipatory | IS as electronic panopticon<br>IS for increasing productivity<br>IS can be instruments of emancipation | The panopticon metaphor shows limitations when responsibility of individuals is involved<br>To analyse how IS become stable in organizations we should look at the circuits of power that sustain the systems<br>An emancipatory method for developing IS does not consider how to deal with the 'dark side' of power, i.e., vested interests and hidden agendas |
| Power over | Power is based on agency<br>Power is relational<br>Power is based on interests | IS professionals (system analysts, developers and consultants) exercise power over users | The imputation of interests (i.e. an act of power itself)<br>Exercise of power beyond the agency of consultants and analysts |
| Power storage | Power depends on resources<br>Power depends on regulations, norms and rules | Control over information and IS as a source of power<br>The IS function being powerful in organizations | Evidence did not support the assumption<br>Resource dependency for explaining power can be tautological |
| Power discretion | Power resides in decision making | Those who make decisions regarding IS and the acquisition and deployment of IT are powerful | It does not take into account how discourses both shape the subject-making decisions and limit the available options |

Dhillon (1995), for example, points out that many breaches of information systems in organizations are carried out by insiders.

An in-depth reflection on Foucault's ideas and their relationship with information systems can be found in Introna (1997). Introna conceives IS and their relationship with power not only as electronic panopticons but also as embedded in the micro physics of everyday life, power relations, discourse and knowledge. This is a contribution for those interested on Foucault's ideas and how they are related to the management of information systems. In addition, Introna's work is also relevant for his suggestion that the Foucauldian perspective needs to be complemented if researchers are going to account for how IS become stable, institutionalized or, following Silva and Backhouse (1997), like part of the organization's 'furniture'.

Although the emancipation approach presented by Hirschheim and Klein (1994) might influence organizations in the way they anticipate, I have some reservations, particularly regarding their approach to power; specifically regarding the concept of an ideal speech situation. Hirschheim and Klein themselves recognize some of the limitations of their emancipatory approach since unfortunately, ideal speech situations cannot be achieved in practice (Mumby 1988). Furthermore, emancipation ideals lead to what Benton (1981) calls the 'paradox of emancipation'. According to emancipation principles, the ultimate manifestation of power occurs when power is being exercised and those on the receiving end will not realize it. Thus, how is it possible that users can reach self-awareness of power exerted over them, if IS professionals or managers are exerting that power? Only when power ceases to be exerted can users realize it, but when this is the case, it is of no use to them at all. Therefore, to be emancipated, users need power and knowledge; power and emancipation constitute the two sides of the same coin.

However, the strongest criticism of their ideas might be that they do not consider power relations prevailing within the organizational context. For example, in developing an information system applying their modified version of ETHICS, users still belong to other domains in the organization. Outside the information system within the organization, users still belong to other spheres where authority and domination prevail: managers are managers and employees are employees. Therefore an emancipatory method for developing IS could hardly consider how to deal with the 'dark side' of power, that is, vested interests and hidden agendas. The strategic and tactical nature of power or its dark side, as Hirschheim and Klein call it, is irrefutable and pervasive. Hence the application of ETHICS or any other participatory method will benefit from a political appraisal of the organization that includes both sides of power: either dark or legitimate.

*Power over*

The conception of 'power over' assumes the relational nature of power and its exercise requires agencies exerting power over other agencies against the interests of the latter. As discussed in the previous section, this definition is similar to that of Lukes (1974) and therefore it contains the same problems with his conception of power regarding the assumption of 'real interests'. The identification of real interests will depend on an independent observer who will adopt a relative moral position (Clegg 1989). For example, the socio-technical approach to IS assumes that the real interests of workers are to improve their working conditions and that their interests can be represented by their elected spokespersons (Mumford and Henshall 1979). The identification of real interests will always be an exercise of power itself (Clegg 1989). The second problem with this approach is that technical facts and user values are not so easy to differentiate, not to mention the difficulty of identifying specific users' values; for example, in emphasizing particular requirements, one group of users could argue that their reasons for that emphasis are technical, while concealing (intentionally or unintentionally) other interests.

Research on 'power over' highlights the relationships among different organizational actors involved with IS and IT, namely developers, users, IT consultants and managers. Furthermore, researchers concerned with this type of power have applied sociological theories and interpretive research methodologies to conduct their studies. These works do not provide either an empirical or a theoretical account of how IS become permanent and how these are derived from discourses as well as how techniques of discipline are deployed. However, they show both the viability of sociological approaches to the study of power regarding organizations and IT and that distinguishing the social from the technical aspects of information systems might be itself a matter of power.

*Power storage*

The discussion of the studies under this category showed that IS services were not considered as powerful as might have been expected. Lucas (1984) suggests that this might be because the information services units are not involved in any key decision-making processes. This observation points out that somehow the IS units were unable to store power. This conclusion seems to be a tautology, because if the IS staff were involved in key decisions they might already be regarded as powerful: the cause of power is the effect of power. In this sense, Clegg (1989, p. 190) criticizes theories that consider resources as a source of power because they are in some respects tautological:

How is power to be recognised independently of resource dependency? Resource dependency of X upon Y is the function of Y's power. Equally, Y's independence is the function of X's dependence upon Y, given the previous X–Y relationship. The cause of power is resource dependency. At the same time, the consequence of resource dependency is equivalent to its cause. Hence notions of cause and consequence are meaningless in such formulae. *Part of the problem is the pervasive tendency to think of power as a thing without considering that it must also be a property of relations.* (Emphasis added)

Thus, the limitations of both theories, resource dependence and contingency, suggest that a complete approach to power requires the consideration of the other types of power. The challenges of these approaches stem from their exclusive focus on resources as sources of power without paying attention to how these resources were obtained. Cavaye and Christiansen (1996) point out clearly the limitations of the contingency and resource dependency approaches. On the one hand, they acknowledge that their framework neither contemplates other types of power nor provides an account of the influence of the organizational environment on 'power storage'. On the other, they recognize that contingency theory, by concentrating on organizational units, overlooks the power exercised and held by individual actors.

*Power discretion*
The notion of 'power discretion' is interesting in the sense that emphasizes how authorities, such as managers, can exercise influence over the acquisition of technology or on the processes of design and implementation of information systems. In this sense, Pettigrew (1972) highlighted that political decisions are often led by calculations based on self-advancement. Nevertheless, other works (Wilkinson 1983; Scarbrough and Corbett 1992; Scarbrough 1993) address power relations not only between individual agents but also between groups, namely managers and workers. Wilkinson suggests that IT is mainly adopted by managerial choice influenced and legitimized by the efficiency discourse. Scarbrough and Corbett emphasize that managers make decisions regarding technological innovations based on their knowledge about organizations and technology. They coincide with Wilkinson in highlighting that the predominant discourse in making decisions about technology is Fordist notions of control.

Furthermore, Wilkinson, Scarbrough and Corbett recognize that workers can influence decisions on the acquisition, design and use of IT, but for this to occur it is necessary that workers are conscious of their interests and with a well-established identity. This is shown by Ehn's research and that on the UTOPIA project (Bjerknes et al. 1987; Bodker et al. 1987; Ehn 1991). In order for workers to realize their interests and rights, so that they can be effective decision makers, they would need to work in an institutional environment, such as Scandinavia, in which culture and regulations favour democratic values and workers' right to participate. Thus, one of the challenges of the notion of 'power discretion' is that to be an effective lens for understanding power it needs to account for discourses, particularly on how discourses shape, empower and limit the subject-making decisions.

**Arguing for an integrative framework and a Machiavellian stance**
The foregoing section discussed the particularities, contributions and limitations of the theoretical approaches of exemplary works in the literature of information systems and power. Now I shall reflect on three general issues derived from those works. Let us start by recognizing that there is a common characteristic in most of those studies: they focus on a narrow area of power. As discussed, this restricts the understanding of power relations. Conversely, if a theory of power were to integrate consistently different approaches, it would help researchers to make more sense of power relations. An integral theoretical framework, then, should encompass coherently the contributions to the study of power provided by social and political sciences (Jasperson et al. 2002). It should account not only for how a system becomes stable but also how it is either rejected or abandoned. A framework able to do that could span its scope of application to understand what some scholars regard as failure of information systems, particularly when among the reasons of failure are political and power factors.

*The circuits of power: an integrative framework*
For these purposes I argue that the 'circuits of power' (Clegg 1989) constitutes a powerful analytical tool for the study of power and information systems. The concepts introduced by Clegg derive from relevant advances in the sociology of sciences (Callon 1986, 1987; Law 1986; Latour 1987) and the sociology of organizations (DiMaggio and Powell 1991; Meyer and Rowan 1991). One of the virtues of the circuits framework is that it consolidates power concepts from political sciences and sociology and relates them to organizations. Another of the appealing characteristics of the framework stems from conceiving power as fundamentally strategic. Clegg is interested not only in organizational agents' actions but also in their intentions. Another strength of the framework is that Clegg clearly specifies the different components of his model (Clegg 1989, pp. 187–240).

For Clegg, power is essentially a contested concept, and so he has introduced a theoretical framework of power that incorporates conceptions not only centred on individual and collective agency but also on Foucault's (1977) concept of disciplinary power. As well as those ideas, Clegg also introduces in his framework, from Harre and Madden (1975) and Wrong

(1995), concepts of power as dispositional, considering power as capacities. Another important element in Clegg's argument for his framework is the contradistinction of the 'modern' concept of sovereign power represented by Hobbes's (1962) ideas and Machiavelli's (1958, 1970) notion of power as strategic and contingent. Clegg claims that his analysis of power is more contingent and realistic, closer to a Machiavellian approach and far from sovereign conceptions. However, Clegg's (1989, p. 239) proposal is not radical in the sense of neglecting previous frameworks of power. Hence I argue that Clegg's circuits of power is an integrative framework.

Clegg maintains that most of the organizational studies on power concentrate on 'power over'. He calls this type of power 'episodic' – that is, how A can make B do something B would not do otherwise (Dahl 1957). The study of power, Clegg maintains, should instead be focused more widely than just on Dahl's conception, so as to explain the conditions that allow episodic power to occur. For Clegg, episodic power depends both on rules of meaning and membership and on techniques of discipline and production. In other words, the power exercised by A over B cannot be explained without understanding relational issues that involve norms and regulations concerning the matter of authority, nor without identifying the techniques of discipline and mechanisms of control deployed by A to ensure B's compliance. That is why Clegg complements the circuit of episodic power with the other two circuits of power: social and system integration. The circuit of social integration refers to these rules of meaning and membership, and the circuit of system integration to the techniques of production and discipline. These two circuits stem from Clegg's semiotic view of agency which considers agencies in organizations not only as executors of actions but also as carriers and creators of meanings. This framework has been applied in IS by Introna (1997) and very recently by Silva and Backhouse (2003). The latter presents a detailed account of how the framework can be applied to study the stability of information systems.

### Actor-network theory

The concept of actor-network theory (ANT) was developed by the French sociologists Michel Callon and Bruno Latour (Callon 1986; Callon et al. 1986; Latour 1986, 1987). ANT deems power relationships as strategic: 'Understanding what sociologists generally call power relationships means describing the way in which actors are defined, associated and simultaneously obliged to remain faithful to their alliances' (Callon 1986, p. 224). ANT as a method of social inquiry comprises three methodological principles. The first is about the agnosticism of the observer, which implies that the observer must avoid censoring and making judgements regarding the subjects under study. The second is that of symmetry, which consists in describing scientific, social and technological issues in the same terms.[1] The third is about free association, which implies refusing to accept all a priori differences between social and technological events (Callon 1986).

Walsham (1997) argues about the virtues of applying ANT to the field of IS and he and Sahay have applied the theory for making sense of how information systems become adopted or rejected (Walsham and Sahay 1999). A compelling example of how ANT can illuminate the study of power and IS is presented in the work of Bloomfield and Best (1992). These authors applied the concept of ANT to analyse how organizational problems are defined and how an IT solution is proposed by IT consultants. They focused particularly on how power is exercised throughout this process. Because of the centrality of power in social theory, Bloomfield and Best adopted a sociological inquiry position to approach power exercise regarding organizational IS. The organizational definition, the proposal of the IT solution and its implementation are considered by Bloomfield and Best as a process of sociological translation; hence the appropriateness of approaching their study with ANT.

One of the main problems in studying power is that politics tend to be not only hidden but also regarded as immoral. For example, Mintzberg (1983) calls this dimension of power the 'dark side' of power since organizational members are supposed to comply with regulations and norms; otherwise their behaviour will become illegitimate and unethical. The problem – as can be witnessed by whoever has organizational experience – is that people do not always comply with regulations and norms as they are supposed to. By deeming politics as the dark side of power we are limiting our view of power. Keen (1981, pp. 31–2) in his classic paper expressed the need to study politics for understanding how organizations manage and use IS:

> Unfortunately, 'politics' have been equated with evil, corruption and, worst of all, blasphemy in the presence of the Rational Ideal, but politics are the process of getting commitment, or building support, or creating momentum for change; they are inevitable ... It is absurd to ignore it ... A political perspective on information systems is needed in research. It will of necessity be based on comparative field studies that illustrate theoretical concepts ... It can immensely add to our understanding both of the implications of information technology and the dynamics of effective implementation.

I argue that by virtue of the principle of agnosticism, ANT provides the epistemological tools and the ontological assumptions required to open the 'black box' of politics in the study of information systems. ANT brings the Machiavellian view of power – in the sense that power is strategic – into the principle of agnosticism. This principle indicates that the researcher should abandon any moral or ethical prejudice towards the subject of studies; these prejudices may very well be that the subjects behave according to organizational rules. Of course this principle does not suggest assuming that organizational members will display deviant behaviour. It only suggests that any moral prejudice will hinder the researcher from appreciating the strategic nature of power; that is, the dark side. Thus, ANT offers research a set of research tools to expose power in both its dimensions: legitimate and dark.

In summary, the two frameworks discussed in this section, circuits of power and ANT, can complement each other. On the one hand, the strength of the former is its emphasis on disciplinary techniques and the relevance it gives to meanings as well as recognizing exogenous institutional influences. ANT, on the other hand, is a suitable analytical tool for making sense of the manoeuvres made by powerful actors to create obligatory passage points for weaker actors. ANT emphasizes agency and actions, while the circuits of power centres more on structural aspects such as rules, techniques and norms. Hence in his original formulation of the circuits of power, Clegg (1989) considered the advances made by ANT for studying the episodic circuit of power. Although combining ANT and the circuits of power in studying power will probably end in a long and laborious investigation, the results no doubt will be comprehensive and interesting.

**Conclusion**

This chapter has discussed the different angles that IS researchers have taken in the study of power. Without being exhaustive, I dwelt on exemplary papers for identifying the insights that each approach brings to such a study. By collating their contributions and challenges, the chapter shows how useful an integrative theoretical framework will be to researchers. However, it has not been my intention to demonstrate that both ANT and the circuits of power are the only integrative or strategic tools for the study of power. The objective of the chapter has been to argue that given the complexity of the power phenomenon its study requires a complex and rich theory such as the circuits of power. Moreover, the hidden nature of politics and its negative connotation entail audacious research approaches such as the one offered by ANT. It is my belief that ignoring the politics in and around IS would be as effective as an ostrich burying its head in the sand to avoid danger.

**Note**
1. Callon states that he has chosen the vocabulary of translation terminology (see Callon 1986).

**References**

Alexander, J.C. (1983), *Theoretical Logic in Sociology: The Modern Reconstruction of Classical Thought – Talcott Parsons*, vol. 4, Berkeley, CA: University of California Press.
Alvarez, R. (2002), 'Confessions of an information worker: a critical analysis of information requirements discourse', *Information and Organization*, **12** (2), 85–107.

Austin, J.L. (1962), *How To Do Things With Words*, 2nd edn, Oxford: Oxford University Press.

Barbalet, J.M. (1987), 'Power, structural resources, and agency', *Current Perspectives in Social Theory*, **8**, 1–24.

Barnes, B. (1986), 'On authority and its relationship to power', in J. Law (ed.), *Power, Action and Belief*, Sociological Review Monograph 32, London: Routledge & Kegan Paul, pp. 180–95.

Barnes, B. (1988), *The Nature of Power*, Cambridge: Polity.

Benton, T. (1981), '"Objective" interests and the sociology of power', *Sociology*, **15** (2), 161–84.

Bjerknes, G. and T. Bratteteig (1995), 'User participation and democracy: a discussion of Scandinavian research on system development', *Scandinavian Journal of Information Systems*, **7** (1), 73–98.

Bjerknes, G., P. Ehn and M. Kyng (eds) (1987), *Computers and Democracy: A Scandinavian Challenge*, Aldershot: Avebury.

Bjorn-Andersen, N., M. Earl, O. Holst and E. Mumford (eds) (1982), *Information Society: For Richer, for Poorer*, vol. 2, Amsterdam: North-Holland.

Bloomfield, B.P. and A. Best (1992), 'Management consultants: systems development, power and the translation of problems', *Sociological Review*, **40** (3), 533–60.

Bloomfield, B.P. and R. Coombs (1992), 'Information technology, control and power: the centralization and decentralization debate revisited', *Journal of Management Studies*, **29** (4), 459–84.

Bloomfield, B.P. and A. Danieli (1995), 'The role of management consultants in the development of information technology: the indissoluble nature of socio-political and technical skills', *Journal of Management Studies*, **32** (1), 23–46.

Bodker, S., P. Ehn, M. Kyng, J. Kammersgaard and Y. Sundblad (1987), 'A utopian experience: on design of powerful computer-based tools for skilled graphic workers', in Bjerknes et al. (eds), pp. 251–78.

Callon, M. (1986), 'Some elements of a sociology of translation: domestication of the scallops and the fishermen of St Brieuc Bay', in J. Law (ed.), *Power, Action and Belief*, Sociological Review Monograph 32, London: Routledge & Kegan Paul, pp. 196–233.

Callon, M. (1987), 'Society in the making: the study of technology as a tool for sociological analysis', in W.E. Bijker, T.P. Hughes and T. Pinch (eds), *The Social Construction of Technological Systems: New Directions in the Sociology and History of Technology*, Cambridge, MA: MIT Press, pp. 83–103.

Callon, M. J. Law and A. Rip (eds) (1986), *Mapping the Dynamics of Science and Technology: Sociology of Science in the Real World*, London: Macmillan.

Cavaye, A.L.M. and J.K. Christiansen (1995), 'A framework for estimating power of subunits to explain IS implementation', Paper presented at the 3rd European Conference on Information Systems, Athens, June.

Cavaye, A.L.M. and J.K. Christiansen (1996), 'Understanding IS implementation by estimating power of subunits', *European Journal of Information Systems*, **5** (4), 222–32.

Clegg, S. (1975), *Power, Rule and Domination*, London: Routledge & Kegan Paul.

Clegg, S. (1979), *The Theory of Power and Organization*, London: Routledge & Kegan Paul.

Clegg, S.R. (1989), *Frameworks of Power*, London: Sage.

Clemons, E.K. and M.C. Row (1992), 'Information, power, and control of the distribution channel: preliminary results of a field study in the consumer packaged goods industry', Paper presented at the International Conference on Information Systems, Dallas, TX, December.

Dahl, R. (1957), 'The concept of power', *Behavioural Science*, **2**, 201–5.

Dahl, R.A. (1961), *Who Governs? Democracy and Power in an American City*, New Haven, CT: Yale University Press.

Davenport, T.H., R.G. Eccles and L. Prusak (1992), 'Information politics', *Sloan Management Review* (Fall), 53–65.

Davidson, E.J. (2002), 'Technology frames and framing: a socio-cognitive investigation of requirements determination', *MIS Quarterly*, **26** (4), 329–58.

Debnam, G. (1984), *The Analysis of Power: A Realistic Approach*, London: Macmillan.

Dhillon, G. (1995), 'Interpreting management of information system security', Unpublished PhD, London School of Economics.

DiMaggio, P.J. and W.W. Powell (1991), 'The iron cage revisited: institutional isomorphism and collective rationality in organizational fields', in W.W. Powell and P.J. DiMaggio (eds), *The New Institutionalism in Organizational Analysis*, Chicago: University of Chicago Press, pp. 63–82.

Ehn, P. (1991), 'The art and science of designing computer artifacts', in C. Dunlop and R. Kling (eds), *Computerization and Controversy*, Boston, MA: Academic Press, pp. 288–307.

Foucault, M. (1977), *Discipline and Punish*, New York: Vintage Books.

Foucault, M. (1980), *Power/Knowledge: Selected Interviews and other Writings 1972–77*, Brighton: Harvester.

Foucault, M. (1982), 'Afterword: the subject and power', in H.L. Dreyfus and P. Rainbow (eds), *Michel Foucault: Beyond Structuralism and Hermeneutics*, London: Harvester Wheatsheaf, pp. 208–26.

Franz, C.R., and D. Robey (1984), 'An investigation of user-led system design: rational and political perspectives', *Communications of the ACM*, **27** (12), 1202–9.

Giddens, A. (1984), *The Constitution of Society*, Cambridge: Polity.

Goodhue, D.L., J.A. Quillard and J.F. Rockart (1988), 'Managing the data resource: a contingency perspective', *MIS Quarterly*, September, 373–91.

Griffith, T.L., M.A. Fuller and G.B. Northcraft (1998), 'Facilitator influence in group support systems: intended and unintended effects', *Information Systems Research*, **9** (1), 20–36.

Gupta, P.P., M.W. Dirsmith and T.J. Fogarty (1994), 'Coordination and control in a government agency: contingency and institutional theory perspectives on GAO audits', *Administrative Science Quarterly*, **39** (2), 264–84.

Habermas, J. (1972), *Knowledge and Human Interests*, trans. J. Shapiro, Boston, MA: Beacon.

Habermas, J. (1974), *Theory and Practice*, trans. J. Viertel, Boston, MA: Beacon.

Habermas, J. (1979), *Communication and the Evolution of Society*, trans. T. McCarthy, Boston, MA: Beacon.

Harre, R. and E.H. Madden (1975), *Causal Powers*, Oxford: Blackwell.

Hickson, D.J., C.R. Higgins, C.A. Less, R.E. Schneck and J.M.A. Pennings (1971), 'A strategic contingencies theory of intraorganizational power', *Administration Science Quarterly*, **16** (2), 216–29.

Hinings, C.R., D.J. Hickson, J.M. Pennings and R.E. Schneck (1974), 'Structural conditions of intra-organizational power', *Administrative Science Quarterly*, **9** (1), 22–44.

Hirschheim, R. and H.K. Klein (1994), 'Realizing emancipatory principles in information systems development: the case for ETHICS', *MIS Quarterly*, March, 83–109.

Hobbes, T. (1962), *Leviathan*, ed. M. Oakeshott, with an introduction by R.S. Peters, London: Collier-Macmillan.

Honderich, T. (ed.) (1995), *The Oxford Companion to Philosophy*, Oxford: Oxford University Press.

Howcroft, D. and M. Wilson (2003), 'Paradoxes of participatory practices: the Janus role of the systems developer', *Information and Organization*, **13** (1), 1–23.

Iivari, J. and K. Lyytinen (1998), 'Research on information systems development in Scandinavia: unity and plurality', *Scandinavian Journal of Information Systems*, **10** (1&2), 135–86.

Introna, L.D. (1997), *Management, Information and Power*, London: Macmillan.

Jasperson, J., T.A. Carte, C.S. Saunders, B.S. Butler, H.J.P. Croes and W. Zheng (2002), 'Review: power and information technology research: a metatriangulation review', *MIS Quarterly*, **26** (4), 397–459.

Keen, P.G.W. (1981), 'Information systems and organizational change', *Communications of the ACM*, **24** (1), 24–33.

Kling, R. (1991), 'Cooperation, coordination and control in computer-supported work', *Association for Computing Machinery, Communications of the ACM*, **34** (12), 83–8.

Knights, D. and F. Murray (1994), *Managers Divided: Organisation Politics and Information Technology Management*, Chichester: John Wiley & Sons.

Latour, B. (1986), 'The powers of association', in J. Law (ed.), *Power, Action and Belief: A New Sociology of Knowledge*, Sociological Review Monograph 32, London: Routledge & Kegan Paul, pp. 264–80.

Latour, B. (1987), *Science in Action*, Cambridge, MA: Harvard University Press.

Law, J. (1986), 'On power and its tactics: a view from the sociology of science', *Sociological Review*, **34** (1), 1–37.

Law, J. (1991), 'Power, discretion and strategy', in J. Law (ed.), *A Sociology of Monsters: Essays on Power, Technology and Domination*, vol. 38, London: Routledge, pp. 165–191.

Lucas, H.C. (1984), 'Organizational power and the information services department', *Communications of the ACM*, **27** (1), 1218–26.

Lukes, S. (1974), *Power: A Radical View*, London: Macmillan.

Lukes, S. (ed.) (1986), *Power*, Oxford: Blackwell.

Machiavelli, N. (1958), *The Prince*, London: Everyman.

Machiavelli, N. (1970), *The Discourses*, Harmondsworth: Penguin.

Markus, M.L. (1983), 'Power, politics, and MIS implementation', *Communications of the ACM*, **26** (6), 430–44.

Markus, M.L. and N. Bjorn-Andersen (1987), 'Power over users: its exercise by system professionals', *Communications of the ACM*, **30** (6), 498–504.

McHoul, A. and W. Grace (1993), *A Foucault Primer: Discourse, Power and the Subject*, London: University College London Press.

Meyer, J. and B. Rowan (1991), 'Institutionalized organizations: formal structure as myth and ceremony', in W.W. Powell and P.J. DiMaggio (eds), *The New Institutionalism in Organizational Analysis*, Chicago: Chicago University Press, pp. 41–62.

Mintzberg, H. (1983), *Power in and around Organizations*, Englewood Cliffs, NJ: Prentice-Hall.

Mumby, D.K. (1988), *Communication and Power in Organizations: Discourse, Ideology, and Domination*, Norwood, NJ: Ablex Publishing Corporation.

Mumford, E. (1972), *Job Satisfaction: A Study of Computer Specialists*, London: Longman.

Mumford, E. (1987), 'Sociotechnical systems design: evolving theory and practice', in Bjerknes et al. (eds), pp. 59–76.

Mumford, E. and D. Henshall (1979), *The Participative Design of Computer Systems*, London: Batsford.

Newman, M. and R. Sabherwal (1996), 'Determinants of commitments to information systems development: a longitudinal investigation', *Management Information Systems Quarterly*, **20** (1), 23–54.

Noble, F. (1995), 'Implementation strategies for office systems', *Journal of Strategic Information Systems*, **4** (3), 239–53.

Orlikowski, W.J. (1992), 'The duality of technology: rethinking the concept of technology in organizations', *Organization Science*, **3** (3), 398–427.

Orlikowski, W.J. (1993), 'CASE tools as organizational change: investigating incremental and radical changes in systems development', *Management Information Systems Quarterly*, **17** (3), 309–40.

Orlikowski, W.J. (2000), 'Using technology and constituting structures: a practice lens for studying technology in organizations', *Organization Science*, **11** (4), 404–28.

Parsons, T. (1937), *The Structure of Social Action*, New York: McGraw-Hill.

Parsons, T. (1967), *Sociological Theory and Modern Society*, New York: Free Press.

Pettigrew, A.M. (1972), 'Information control as a power resource', *Sociology*, **6** (2), 187–204.

Pettigrew, A.M. (1973), *The Politics of Organisational Decision Making*, London: Tavistock.

Pfeffer, J. (1981), *Power in Organizations*, Marshfield, MA: Pitman.

Pfeffer, J. and G.R. Salancik (1978), *The External Control of Organizations: A Resource Dependence Perspective*, New York: Harper & Row.

Robey, D. and L.A. Smith (1993), 'Perceptions of conflict and success in information systems development projects', *Journal of Management Information Systems*, **10** (1), 123.

Russell, B. (1938), *Power: A New Social Analysis*, London: Allen & Unwin.

Saravanamuthu, K. (2002), 'The political lacuna in participatory systems design', *Journal of Information Technology*, **17** (4), 185–98.

Saunders, C.S. and R.W. Scamell (1986), 'Organizational power and the information services department: a reexamination', *Communications of the ACM*, **29** (2), 142–7.

Scarbrough, H. (1993), 'Problem-solutions in the management of information systems expertise', *Journal of Management Studies*, **30** (6), 939–55.

Scarbrough, H. and J. Corbett (1992), *Technology and Organization: Power, Meaning and Design*, London: Routledge.

Searle, J. (1969), *Speech Acts: An Essay in the Philosophy of Language*, Evanston, IL: Northwestern University Press.

Sewell, G. and B. Wilkinson (1992), '"Someone to watch over me": surveillance, discipline and the just-in-time labour process', *Sociology*, **26** (2), 271–89.

Sillince, J.A.A., and S. Mouakket (1997), 'Varieties of political process during systems development', *Information Systems Research*, **8** (4), 368–97.

Silva, L. and J. Backhouse (1997), 'Becoming part of the furniture: the institutionalisation of information systems', in A.S. Lee, J. Liebenau and J.I. DeGross (eds), *Information Systems and Qualitative Research*, London: Chapman & Hall, pp. 389–414.

Silva, L. and J. Backhouse (2003), 'The circuits-of-power framework for studying power in institutionalization of information systems', *Journal of the Association for Information Systems*, **4** (6), 294–336.

Walsham, G. (1993), *Interpreting Information Systems in Organizations*, Chichester: John Wiley.

Walsham, G. (1997), 'Actor-network theory and IS research: current status and future prospects', in A.S. Lee, J. Liebenau and J.I. DeGross (eds), *Information Systems and Qualitative Research*, London: Chapman & Hall, pp. 466–80.

Walsham, G. (2002), 'Cross-cultural software production and use: a structurational analysis', *MIS Quarterly*, **26** (4), 359–80.

Walsham, G. and S. Sahay (1999), 'GIS for district-level administration in India: problems and opportunities', *MIS Quarterly*, **23** (1), 39–66.

Wilkinson, B. (1983), *The Shopfloor Politics of New Technology*, London: Heinemann.

Willcocks, L. and D. Mason (1987), *Computerising Work: People, Systems Design and Workplace Relations*, London: Paradigm.

Wrong, D.H. (1995), *Power: Its forms, Bases, and Uses*, London: Transaction.

Wynne, B. and H.J. Otway (1982), 'Information technology, power and managers', in Bjorn-Andersen et al. (eds), pp. 207–17.

Zuboff, S. (1988), *In the Age of the Smart Machine*, New York: Basic Books.

# 4 Are social constructivist approaches critical? The case of IS failure

*Nathalie N. Mitev*

## Introduction

The information systems (IS) literature has recently witnessed an increasing interest in the adoption of a network perspective to studying the information and communication technology (ICT) innovation process. A social constructivist approach, actor-network theory (ANT), has gained popularity in IS research – see, for instance, the recent special issue of *Information Technology and People* on ANT and IS (Hanseth et al. 2004). It is therefore important to examine its application to IS research and its potential for critical IS research, about which there has been some debate already (for example, Walsham 1997). This chapter first reviews the basic premises of social construction and constructivism in general and how science and technology studies (STS) have adopted these theoretical outlooks, long before IS research – indeed, it is mainly through an interest in developments in STS that IS researchers discovered ANT. As a result, some questions are raised concerning the nature of the 'critical', about which there is also some divergence in critical IS research. The notion of IS failure is then used to illustrate the main differences between more mainstream functionalist understandings and interpretivist, constructivist and critical perspectives. The ANT refusal to distinguish between the social and the technical, and its notions of actor networks, symmetry and translation are explored using a few examples of failure case studies in order to assess what elements of criticality can be brought to IS research by social constructivist analyses of technology. Finally, some suggestions are made to ensure that constructivist approaches can be used in a fully critical manner.

## Social constructivism

The notion that reality is socially constructed was proposed by Berger and Luckmann (1966) and derives from Alfred Schutz, who himself drew on Edmund Husserl and Max Weber. It aims at understanding the taken-for-granted and experienced world that each person in a society shares with others. Social constructionism holds that a phenomenon need not have existed, or need not be at all as it is at present, is not determined by the nature of things and is not inevitable. Hacking (1999) identifies some of the main tenets of constructionism as external explanations of stability (non-inherent to the product of science, or to the essence of technology) and contingency (avoiding inevitabilism): 'Process and product are both part of the arguments about construction. The constructionist argues that the product is not inevitable by showing how it came into being (historical process), and noting the purely contingent historical determinants of that process' (p. 38).

This is not to say that everything is a social construct or that nothing can exist unless it is socially constructed (ibid., p. 25). Constructionist statements are usually not meant to imply that there is nothing outside of human experience but that for humans the only things that matter and thus are real are our constructions. This means that we no longer think in terms of objective reality but in terms of meanings, discourses and representations. Hacking (p. 48) offers the following definition: 'Social constructionism means various sociological, historical and philosophical projects that aim at displaying or analysing actual, historically situated, social interactions that led to, or were involved in, the coming into being or establishing of some present entity or fact.'

It can be differentiated from traditional critical forms of 'unmasking', which tend to be functionalist in that they aim to show the functions and interests of dominant ideologies. Constructionism is usually a more local sort of unmasking (ibid., p. 54) although constructionists are also concerned with questions of power and control and showing how categories of knowledge are used in power relationships (p. 58).

Social constructionist approaches have developed in many disciplines over the last 30 years, for example, the social construction of nature, knowledge, gender, emotions, madness, technological systems and so on. There are also different variations – constructionalism, constructivism, constructionism; see also Sismondo (1993), who distinguishes different kinds of social constructivism about science – but the themes and attitudes are not so different as they all believe that things are not what they seem (Hacking 1999, p. 49). These differences will not be discussed in detail here. Instead, the following section concentrates on social constructionism applied to STS, as it is considered of relevance to the design, implementation and use of information systems. We shall first briefly explain what they all share in challenging positivist approaches and then outline the distinctions between the three main approaches present in STS, mild constructionism (social shaping), constructionism (social construction of technology) and strong constructivism (ANT).

The social construction of sciences holds that a successful science did not have to develop in the way it did, but could have had different successes evolving in other ways; and that scientific facts exist only within styles of thinking. For instance, Pickering (1984) holds that the evolution of physics, including the quark idea, is thoroughly contingent and could have evolved in other ways. Constructionists think that stability results from factors external to the overt content of the science and this is illustrated by the Edinburgh school (Barnes et al. 1996). It is taken for granted that science is a historically situated and social activity and that it is to be understood in relation to the contexts in which it occurs (Shapin 1996). The processes of science and the scientific activity are the main objects of study. That is different from doubting the truth or applicability of scientific propositions. Alternative successful science is in general always possible. A fit between apparatus, beliefs about the apparatus, interpretations and analyses of data, and theories is not determined by how the world is, by the technology in existence, the social practices of scientists, the interests or networks – indeed, not determined by anything. Many fits are possible and the actual fit that is arrived at is contingent (Hacking 1999, p. 73). Moving on from science studies, sociologists of technology have developed several approaches with varying levels of rigidity, strong and weak or mild (Brey 1997; see also Howcroft et al. 2004), which discusses the potential of STS for IS research).

The mild constructionist perspective is social shaping of technology (SST) (MacKenzie and Wajcman [1985] 1999) which points to the socially contingent form of technology itself. It seeks to identify factors that influence the form or content of technology and the direction of technological innovation. For instance, it argues that some technologies (for example, typesetting machinery) are a reflection of male dominance in the labour market and society at large. SST explores what shaped the technology; it allows for non-social factors, since there are effects of technology, related to the social context. It believes that there is a division between the social and the technical.

A stronger constructionist brand is the social construction of technology (SCOT) (Collins and Pinch 1982, 1993; Bijker et al. 1987). It has its origins in the sociology of scientific knowledge, which seeks to reveal key points of ambiguity or controversies between competing scientific claims and how one interpretation prevails over others. One of its principles is that all knowledge claims must be treated symmetrically and that the explanation for their creation and acceptance rests on social factors, not on the natural world. This relates to a later point made about treating failures and successes in the same way, symmetrically. In SCOT, technological artefacts are characterized by the meanings that relevant social groups assign to them. There is a division between the social and the technical, but there are no powers or effects of the technology, unlike in SST.

A more extreme approach (Grint and Woolgar 1997), suggests that identifying circumstances such as the interests of particular social groups, which become embodied in technologies, is problematic and is subject to interpretive flexibility. According to actor-network theory proponents (Callon 1986, 1991; Latour 1991) there are no divisions between the social and the technical. Reality is constructed in the interplay of actants (human and non-human) as they come together. The constitutive forces found in the interplay among actors construct reality. ANT introduces a new constructivist way of questioning reality, but based on a realistic ontology. ANT diverges from the previous two approaches. There is contention particularly about the difference between humans and non-humans. ANT researchers believe that both essence and differentiation are the result of attribution work and can be studied empirically. Technology neither dictates nor has any effect independent of human actors involved (Grint and Woolgar 1997, p. 138).

The ANT division between the social and the technical is of particular interest: IS research often designates an entity as either technological or social, and then 'we attribute specific properties to that entity in order to explain its behaviour, thereby adopting an essentialist position' (Tatnall and Gilding 1999, p. 957). Essentialism refers to the view that objects have 'real' essences that causally explain their more readily observable properties, a view which has been much debated more generally in the philosophies of science and of language; for example, about whether the language of our classification of the world should be based on a certain knowledge of the real essences of objects themselves, rather than *our* view of the essential qualities of objects. Anti-essentialist positions about technology believe that 'antecedent circumstances, i.e. design, manufacture and production, are said to be "built into" and/or "embodied" in the final product; the resulting technology is "congealed" social relations' (Willcocks and Grint 1997, p. 103). ANT sees properties as network effects rather than innate or inherent characteristics of an entity.

It is clear that much work in STS has tried to develop alternatives to technology-deterministic explanations, and to the essentialist perspective that sees technical capacity as inherent to the technology. IS research has also recently moved away from deterministic or functionalist (either managerialist or technicist) interpretations that are based on positivist and essentialist epistemologies. IS researchers have explored the use of interpretive sociological approaches such as structuration theory (Walsham 1993), hermeneutics, critical social theory and relativism (Sahay et al. 1994; Wilson 1999), social shaping, social construction and constructivism (Whitley and Bouzari 1999) and actor-network theory (Walsham 1997). As a way of avoiding positivism, the adoption of constructionist principles in IS research is of value and can be quite diverse: as a complementary perspective to the objectivist view of technology (Orlikowski and Barley 2001) or as a fuller exploration of its radical potential.

**Critical perspectives**
Ontologically, interpretive IS research assumes that the social world is not given and that it is produced and reinforced by humans through their action and interaction. It is useful in capturing complex, dynamic, social phenomena that are both context and time dependent. Critical researchers, however, contend that the interpretive research philosophy does not recognize the inherent conflict and contradiction in social relations. Orlikowski and Baroudi (1991, p. 18) identify four deficiencies in interpretive research:

> [it] does not examine the conditions, often external, which give rise to certain meanings and experiences;
> [it] omits to explain the unintended consequences of action ... these unintended consequences of action are often a significant force in shaping social reality;
> [it] does not address structural conflicts within society and organisations, and ignores contradictions that may be endemic to social systems;
> [it] neglects to explain historical change; that is, how a particular social order came to be what it is, and how it is likely to vary over time.

Critical research perspectives offer a different view of the world from those of positivist and interpretive perspectives. Where the latter are content to predict or explain the status quo, the critical perspectives are concerned with critiquing existing social systems and revealing any contradictions and conflicts that may inhere in their structures (ibid., p. 19). System developers, for instance, exist only in the context of a society investing in information technology (IT) as a form of production. Organizations cannot be studied in isolation from the industry, society and nation within which they operate, and which they in part constitute. Critical organizational sociologists (for example, Edwards 1979; Knights and Willmott 1988; Knights and Murray 1994) argue that new technologies are designed and used to serve particular interests and they see organizations as a locus of conflict. Academics in the field of critical management studies (for example, Alvesson and Willmott 1992), maintain that management literature has been dominated by managerialist 'one best way' organizational models of change, which take the form of lists of prescriptions (for example, Burnes 1992); and that the dominant line in management texts presents politics as an aberration from a rational norm. They argue that on the contrary, change is a constant political process requiring the capacity to mobilize power resources. On the other hand, critical research has been challenged in that it may tend to be totalizing or deterministic. Traditional critical research makes the assumption that people are constrained in their actions by various forms of cultural and political domination (Myers 1997). Additionally, Orlikowski and Baroudi (1991, p. 23) claimed that the form of theory and knowledge in the critical tradition is uncertain.

There has been a recent expansion of interest in critical approaches in IS research, exemplified in recent journal special issues – *Journal of Information Technology* (Brooke 2002a), *ACM SIGMIS Database* (Truex and Howcroft 2002), *Information Systems Journal* (Brooke et al. forthcoming) – and it can be said to broadly encompass the following range of tasks, indicating *three different foci on criticality*:

1. the in-depth investigation of the nature of IS phenomena at local levels, particularly through qualitative work;
2. the development of relevant knowledge and practical understanding that enables organizational change and indicates new ways of working; and
3. the critique of taken-for-granted assumptions underpinning organizational, managerial and technological practices.

The first kind is being addressed by straightforward interpretive, hermeneutic and ethnographic approaches introduced a decade ago in IS research (for example, Walsham 1993; Lee 1994; Harvey and Myers 1995; Butler 1998). Another more openly critical strand has used Jürgen Habermas's critical theory with emancipatory aims for IS development (for example, Hirschheim and Klein 1994), and therefore falls into the second category. However, there have been recent calls for pluralism in IS critical research (Adam et al. 2001; Doolin and Lowe 2002) as it is seen as 'over-saturated with Habermasian analyses' (Brooke 2002a, p. 46). Habermasian critical social theory has also been judged unable to theorize the causes and preconditions of power constraints and self-interest in IS research (Brooke 2002b). A more recent development is to add a critical outlook to existing approaches: for instance, critical interpretivism (Doolin 1998), critical hermeneutics (Phillips and Brown 1993; Myers 1994a) and critical ethnography (Myers 1997). These authors attempt to move beyond the immediate narrative of the subjects to the broader historical, social and cultural processes within which narratives are embedded, and thus thrive; this critical outlook belongs to the third category. But there are difficulties.

By focusing on 'hidden agendas' (Ngwenyama et al. 1997), 'underlying sense' (Myers 1994a) or 'deep structures' (Heracleous and Barrett 2001), critical interpretive and hermeneutic traditions entail probing the 'depth model' underneath narratives. However, notions of 'the text and the socially constructed world behind it' and 'the reader bound into the socially constructed world standing behind the text' (Lee 1994, p. 150) show a confusion between interpretivism and social construction. Post-structuralists and constructivists (Dreyfus and Rabinow 1982) deny the existence of an 'underneath'. The assumption of a 'hidden' meaning of discourse and the hermeneutic reclamation of lost, 'real' or even 'true' meaning deny a radical form of social constructivism. The competing approaches of critical hermeneutics and constructivism do not share the same ontological and epistemological perspectives, which has an impact on their criticality.

Critical approaches emphasize the fact that social reality is historically constituted. However, this does not merely mean that the researcher should 'seek to evaluate critically ... the totality of understandings by analysing the participants' understandings historically and in terms of changing social structures' (Myers 1994a, p. 57). Attributing (a) the subjective, the interpretive, the socially constructed and meaning to hermeneutics on the one hand, and (b) the objective, the historical and social reality separately from the critical on the other hand, reflects, respectively, (a) a subjectivist individualist epistemology and (b) an objectivist realist ontology. Constructivism is epistemologically about the social construction of meaning and ontologically about the construction of social reality. It combines a social theory of knowledge with an intersubjective, not an individualist, theory of action. And the analysis of power is central to understanding the reflexive link between these two levels (Guzzini 2000). Meaning attribution and the social world interact; then the political status and the legitimacy of action depend on this interaction, this construction.

A social constructivist stance supports criticality in that the present is not determined by the nature or truth of things; it seeks to 'denaturalize' the apparent natural order of things, thereby questioning the inevitability of the social status quo, and positing as a preliminary the contingency of social orders. Only intersubjective rules, and not some unchangeable truths or realities, give meaning to practices. Social construction is not a kind of idiosyncratic, individual or subjective will to knowledge. Our interpretations are based on a shared system of codes and symbols, of languages, lifeworlds and social practices. Socially constructed knowledge is a 'constitutive factor of social power and the concept of power provides a central link between the construction of knowledge and social order' (ibid., p. 172). So it is not just a matter of IS implementers 'needing to understand the organisational context, the stakeholders and the politics involved' (Myers 1994a, p. 57) which is ontologically realist, but of understanding how a phenomenon is collectively constructed as real, which is ontologically constructivist. It is worth noting that it still becomes real in its social consequences (Hacking 1999).

In the case of existing critical IS research, there are therefore shortcomings in the treatment of technology and its social construction. It is important to adopt a critical and reflective stance in relation to the role that technology plays in maintaining social orders and power relations in organizations (Doolin 1998); hence the use of constructivist insights into the social nature of technology and into the technical orientation towards the world (Feenberg 2000). Interpretivist and constructivist approaches to technology failures are inherently critical of the dominant rationalist functionalist perspective, as found for instance in the well-established factor-based and process approaches to IS implementation research, some of which are mentioned below in relation to IS failure. Rather than assuming that particular IS choices succeed (and others fail) if they solve the objective 'problems' of certain groups, the ways in which 'actors come to build one or other definition of reality, how social definitions may change over the course of events and how the past is reconfigured in the present, become central considerations' (Fincham 2002, p. 6). A critique of IS implementation failure literature is presented below, followed by an exploration of a social constructivist approach to IS failure.

## IS failures

IS failures always attract public attention, and there is a constant flow of cases, for instance in the UK: the failed and tragic introduction of a computer-aided dispatching system at the London Ambulance Service (LAS 1993; Flowers 1996; Robinson 1994; Beynon-Davies 1995); Taurus (Transfer and Automated Registration of Uncertified Stock) at the London Stock Exchange (Drummond 1996); the failed integration of computer systems at Wessex Health Authority (Kelsey and Brown 1993); the controversial cost of energy settlements information systems in the privatized electricity industry (Kelsey 1993); nurses' difficulties with data collection for National Health Service (NHS) information systems (Brindle 1995); the collapse of the Read project intended to facilitate the creation of an individual's medical computer record (Brindle 1996); the Inland Revenue's legal battle with Electronic Data Services (EDS) over the embarrassing failure in the processing of the income tax self-assessments (Farrell 1997); the Passport Office fiasco which delayed and ruined the summer holidays of people applying for passports in 1999 (Hencke 2000); continuing problems with the new computer system at the National Air Traffic Services at Swanwick (Genus et al. 2003); and the difficulties with the London Heathrow Airport swipe card recording system (McMaster and Wastell 2004).

IS failures raise interesting questions. How should one analyse IS case studies? Are there inherent differences between successful and unsuccessful ones? Are there methodological points that should apply when investigating and describing such cases? The usual notion of IS success and failure (for example, Sauer 1993; Flowers 1996; Fortune and Peters 1995) belongs to managerialist and technicist discourses in which management is rational and technology is unproblematic and neutral. Accordingly, reasons for failures are often expressed in statements such as: the company did not know how to manage change; users showed resistance; there was no leadership or vision; the technology and business strategies were not aligned; and so on. These, often retrospective, statements usually draw on the latest management fad, from total quality management, excellence, strategy, change initiatives, re-engineering, to empowerment and the networked enterprise. What these managerialist discourses have in common is a truncated understanding of organizations characterized by: a belief in rational management; a denial of the permanent existence of power relations and conflict; a desire to eliminate organizational politics, for instance by using technology; a tendency to see organizations as individual closed entities, which have to survive in a hostile environment; and a limited focus on the business environment (that is, customers, competitors and suppliers only) which ignores broader social, political, cultural, economic and historical perspectives. This narrow understanding of organizations colours the telling and explaining of failure and success stories. The explanations found in the mainstream IS/ management literature are as simplistic for successes as they are for failures. They often take the form of lists of naive prescriptions in the case of successes (for example, have a champion, manage change, communicate the corporate vision to staff and so on); in the case of failures they retrospectively try to find something/someone to blame, as if using IT was a neutral, objective, rational exercise, which in the 'normal' course of events is successful and unproblematic. Often IS implementation activities are only partial successes/ failures. An important research objective is therefore to move beyond what appears to be common(-sensical) explanations of failure and success, and find more complex and richer ways of describing and understanding the often controversial use of IS in organizations, through the inclusion of broader social, economic, political, cultural and historical perspectives.

Research work on implementation failures has been carried out by academics (for example, Sauer 1993; Flowers 1996; Fortune and Peters 1995; Drummond 1996) in many industrial and commercial sectors, such as the health service (for example, Robinson 1994; Beynon-Davies 1995; Bloomfield 1995), the public sector (Myers 1994b) and the financial services sector (Knights and Murray 1994). This work reflects many different theoretical perspectives: managerialist, positivistic, systemic, interpretive, sociological, ethnographic, critical and constructivist. The evolution of understandings of IS failures will be discussed and presented along the following three dimensions (see Figure 4.1): their epistemologies (functionalism, interpretivism, constructivism and critical theories); their originating disciplines (engineering, information systems, organization theories and sociology of technology); and the focus of failure models/ understandings (technology, individuals, systems, stakeholders, structure, organizations, culture, context, power and politics).

**Disciplines**

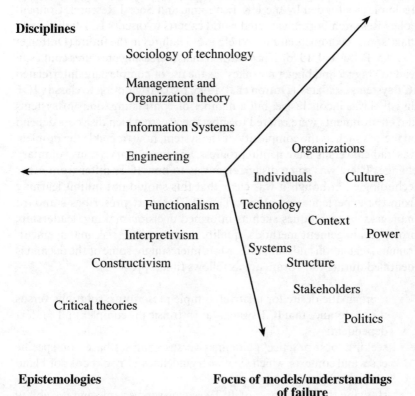

Sociology of technology

Management and
Organization theory

Information Systems

Engineering

Organizations

Individuals          Culture

Functionalism     Technology

Context

Interpretivism                                    Power

Systems

Constructivism                        Structure

Stakeholders

Critical theories

Politics

**Epistemologies**                    **Focus of models/understandings**
                                                       **of failure**

*Figure 4.1   Evolution of understandings of failure*

*Functionalism: technology, individuals, systems, stakeholders, structure*
The disciplines of engineering and information systems and their prevalent functionalist epistemologies have only provided limited explanations of failures in the past. This is related to the theoretical perspective that human action is intentional and rational; and to the quest for universal laws, which disregard historical and contextual conditions as possible triggers of events or influences on human action (Orlikowski and Baroudi 1991, p. 12). Nevertheless, the functionalist approaches have evolved from trying to allocate blame to individuals and perceiving failure situations as systems,

to identifying causes as coming from organizational factors, and considering stakeholders, organizational structure and culture, contingency and context. This represents a shift towards drawing on the disciplines of management and organization theories.

In 1994 a PICT (Programme on Information and Communication Technologies funded by the UK Economic and Social Research Council) Policy Research Forum gathered world experts to discuss ICT failures and make some recommendations to help avoid failures in the future (Dutton et al. 1995; Peltu et al. 1996). They warned that 'increasing pressures could still lead to "bigger and bigger mistakes" as the use of complex and interrelated ICT systems escalates' (Dutton et al. 1995, p. 5). Attempting to classify ICT disasters was inconclusive; but a number of contrasting kinds of systems and environments were offered to show the way in which disasters depend on factors such as the complexity of the system, how tractable the problem was, radical versus incremental progress, and mandatory versus voluntary change. There was some disagreement as to how ICTs differ from other technologies, although it was clear that this should not inhibit learning from the experiences of others. The PICT report prescribes standard management techniques such as informed decision making, leadership, project management methods, quality management, risk management, training, regulation and standards. More interestingly, some of the dilemmas identified during the Forum are as follows (ibid., pp. 48–9):

- a pragmatic desire for relatively simple prescriptive solutions versus the acceptance that ICT systems are intrinsically complex and context dependent;
- seeking 'best practice' guidelines versus analyses based on specific cases and contexts, which view such guidelines as 'cookbooks of bland platitudes'; and
- studying the uniqueness of ICT systems versus exploring the ability to share knowledge from other technologies and disciplines.

The emphasis on people as opposed to the technology itself is present in various forms in the literature. Poor management, ignorance of information technology, human error, poor training and lack of consideration of human factors, are some of the explanations commonly put forward. Jones (1995) found that poor software development management tends to be the primary root cause for many failures. In a similar vein, Neumann (1995, p. 6), studying computer-related risks in a series of sectors, found that problems which occur during system development 'often involve people as an underlying cause'. Requirements are inconsistent, design is misconceived, maintenance is sloppy and outputs are misinterpreted. The blame is commonly put on flawed humans who have to be disciplined to use an intrinsically objective and useful technology. It was noted that people at operational levels, such as systems developers and software engineers, tend to be blamed for failure, for instance in their information gathering. Clarke (1991, p. 62) argues that discourses obscure problems and contradictions that are revealed in practice, 'which might explain how system failure is often explained away as a failure to collect enough data'. More fundamental management and systemic flaws are often the root cause of the many problems caused by increasing use of complex integrated socio-technical systems (Dutton et al. 1995, p. 23).

Perrow (1984, p. 5) encapsulated this systemic understanding of failure by coining the term 'normal accident' which signals that, given the system characteristics, multiple and unexpected interactions of failure are inevitable and that the cause of accidents is to be found in the complexity of systems, not the people. Researching the Three Mile Island nuclear accident, Perrow (p. 7) found that it is the interaction of the multiple failures that explains accidents. His theoretical approach is to see human constructions as systems, not as collections of individuals (p. 351), and the result of unplanned, unwitting, slow evolving human attempts to cope. The value of Perrow's work is in how problems are seen as not coming from *individual* motives or errors, and how he redirects attention towards *systems*, technological and economic.

The PICT experts noted a growing acceptance that technical risk factors 'cannot be extricated from "softer" psychological, social and organisational influences' (Dutton et al., 1995, p. 8), which are less amenable to definitive solutions. It was felt that political, social, economic, technical and organizational factors are so interwoven that they must be considered together at all stages. As a result, the notion of system has been broadened by many researchers to include the behavioural and organizational factors seen as essential ingredients of successful implementation and use – and, by implication, as causes of failure. Of the hundreds of studies that have been conducted on the successful implementation and use of information systems, there are almost as many different measures of success as there are research studies. Pinto (1994) has assembled some of the most commonly identified critical success factors. They include 'behavioural and organizational factors' such as organizational politics, culture, psychological concerns, managerial competence, user participation, training and human resource management. The 'problem' areas within IS implementation have therefore moved from individuals to organizational factors. Some examples of the latter analytical tools are the stakeholders and the configurational fit which are summarized here.

Lyytinen and Hirschheim (1987) offer the concept of 'expectation' failure, a notion that encompasses correspondence (system does not fulfil objectives), process (failure to produce a system) and interaction failure (users do not use the system). Its value is in making explicit the fact that failure is relative to interests which may differ among stakeholder groups, and in that it makes it clear that failure is an evaluation rather than a description. A model suggested by Sauer (1993) is that of a 'natural' system in which IS project organizations pursue their survival through their work on an IS which is intended to serve supporters well enough to yield the support needed for the project to survive. In these formulations of failure, there is an undercurrent which assumes that, if it were not for stakeholders' conflicting interests which lead to lack of support, IS development and use would run smoothly. Sauer's aim (ibid.) is to develop the 'right' management strategies that can enrol the 'right' amount of support from the 'right' stakeholder groups. This is problematic in that support (or lack of it) is not just a matter of how (rightly or wrongly) stakeholders interpret the impact of IS and how they can be persuaded (or not) of its value. Stakeholders are not equal. How are the 'right' stakeholders chosen? What happens to the 'wrong' stakeholders? Perhaps more fundamentally, interpretations and actions cannot be anticipated and therefore 'managed'.

Another organizational view of IS failure derives from the debates about strategy, systems and structure in the organizational theory literature. Sauer et al. (1997, p. 27) propose a configurational theory in which the 'core proposition is that "weak" configurational fit causes failure modes by encouraging behaviours conducive to failure'. Weak fit creates competing motivations for different people in different parts of the organization and there is tension between strategy and structure. It states that 'dysfunctional' behaviour arises from confusion from a configuration in weak fit. Altering structures therefore should guarantee 'good' behaviour. This functionalist way of thinking presumes that conflict-free organizations can be engineered and that, by altering structural conditions, one can prevent conflict, manage behaviour and risk. Instead of structure, Gallivan (1997, p. 246) concentrates on the cultural aspects and on 'the importance of fit between a technology and the adopting organisation by characterising IT systems as "culture bound", indicating that the same system may be subject to different interpretations across different contexts'.

Some IS failure research has demonstrated that change is emergent, unpredictable, contingent and often accompanied by contradictory outcomes in different contexts. Poulymenakou and Holmes (1996) state that we need to understand the relationship of IT with its organizational context, in order to meet effectively the challenges that systems failure presents. Their theoretical approach is that failure should be considered from a contingency viewpoint: 'failure is highly situational ... and dependent upon a number of environmental factors which, although common to the study of failure, manifest themselves very differently in different circumstances' (ibid., p. 37). They classify contextual factors into macro- and micro-contingent variables.

While useful in helping to understand parts of the dynamics, the above concepts necessarily imply a generalization of cause–effect relationships across contexts, which is epistemologically functionalist. The notion of contingent 'variables' implies a deterministic logic and tends to reduce the interrelationship across levels of analysis to simplified top-down cause–effect relationships. The notion of organizational fit is by itself suggestive of a functionalist perception of organization where there is an objectively 'appropriate' relationship along the stated dimensions. It implies not only that there may exist such a state of stable equilibrium conducive to successful implementation of technology, but also that it can be actively managed in order to achieve a desired outcome. The notion of organizational culture fit considers technology explicitly and suggests that there is a relationship between the artefact and users. But there is still a deterministic notion that certain organizational cultures will necessarily be appropriate to technology exhibiting certain features.

The IS failure literature presented so far is predominantly rationalist and subscribes to prescriptive managerialism which claims to offer advice on how to manage IT using a descriptive norm, such as efficiency or fit. The functionalist paradigm is objectivist and regulatory. In this paradigm, organizations are seen primarily as structures for rational economic activity, where managerial interests are paramount. Objective rationality implies that in all like circumstances the correct answer is the same and that there is 'one best way'. However, understandings of efficiency are not rational and scientific but value-laden. Sauer (1999) cites other theories that have been explored more recently to study IS failures in a non-functionalist fashion: interpretivism, critical theory and constructivism, each of which will be reviewed next.

*Interpretivism: organizations, culture, context*
One of the first non-functionalist IS academic traditions to have a recognized presence was the interpretive one (for example, Orlikowski and Baroudi 1991; Walsham 1993, 1995; Orlikowski et al. 1996; Lee et al. 1997; Myers et al. 1998). In contrast to positivist rational–economic interpretations of organizational processes, interpretive research aims at producing an understanding of the context of the information system, and the process whereby the information system influences and is influenced by its context.

Context is concerned with the multi-level identification of the various systems and structures within which the IS is embedded. ... Human actors draw on elements of context, such as resources or perceived authority, to carry out actions, and this activity can reinforce existing systems of resource distribution or power, or can create new systems of authority or meaning. Thus human action draws on context or structure and, in so doing, reinforces existing structures or contexts, or creates new contexts. An investigation of this dynamic process of action/context interweaving is fundamental to an understanding of the process of organizational change within which the IS is one element. (Walsham 1993, p. 5)

Interpretive IS research focuses on the study of the interaction between IS and organizations and many theoretical models have been developed, including before interpretivism became generally recognized. Markus (1983) is one of the first researchers to have questioned commonly used explanations and assumptions about the implementation of information systems in organizations, particularly the notion of user resistance. She developed an 'interaction theory' as opposed to a people-determined, a system-determined or a people-plus-system approach. She states that there are no tactics that are useful in every situation (ibid., p. 441) and she draws on the concepts of power and organizational politics. However, her aim is still to predict resistance and generate strategies that will help to prevent resistance.

Markus and Robey (1988) examine the causal structures found in theories about the relationship between IT and organizational change. Causal agency is classified into the technological imperative, the organizational imperative and the emergent perspective. Markus and Robey (1988) state that the logic of change is based on either variance theories (antecedents are necessary and sufficient conditions for outcomes) or process theories (antecedents are necessary but not sufficient). Levels of analysis can be macro (societies and organizations), micro (individuals and groups) or a mixed macro–micro analysis. Process approaches (for example, Markus and Robey 1988; Davis et al. 1992; Newman and Robey 1992; Sauer 1993) improve upon factor-based research but can tend to try to identify generally applicable causal linkages assumed to exist 'out there'.

In-depth interpretive analyses of technology failure use ethnography to understand the actors' views in order to build a richer understanding. For instance, Vaughan's (1996) study of the *Challenger* disaster (the NASA space shuttle which exploded at launch in January 1986, killing all astronauts on board), is also informed by a consideration of culture; and Drummond's (1996) qualitative study questions the notion of managerial rationality in the decision-making escalation which led to the Taurus fiasco. Vaughan (1996) goes beyond the historically accepted retrospective version of this tragedy and is concerned with understanding the 'native' view of events. She exposes micro–macro links, and reveals a very complex picture that shifts the attention from individual causal explanations to the power of structure and culture. Investigating the meaning that actions and decisions had for participants at the time those actions were taken, enables her to understand many of the actions which were eventually seen as controversial and were not understandable after the accident, since they were judged retrospectively and with hindsight. Her argument illustrates that mistakes and disasters are socially organized and produced by social structures and culture. Her contribution to the analysis of technological failures is particularly interesting in that it shows that actions defined as deviant after the tragedy, can be seen as conforming to rules and culture at the time of the action. She shows how historic changes altered the structure and emphasis of the space agency and created a problematic culture dominated by bureaucratic accountability and political accountability (ibid., p. 198).

Drummond's (1996) analysis is grounded in a substantial exploration of the context and the actors. She found that there was no clear dividing line between the rational and the irrational in decision making, and that information was equivocal and part of the 'ritual' of decision making. Her study highlights 'how decision debacles may be caused not by a breakdown in rationality so much as by *rationality* itself' (ibid., p. 125, original emphasis) and how the process is clothed in a rhetoric of scientific objectivity. She found that escalation is 'simultaneously rational and irrational, bound up with power, politics and opportunity, and influenced by the vagaries of project and organization' (p. 89). This fundamental contradiction explains how everyone acted logically, according to his or her circumstances. A functionalist approach would investigate what variables or factors caused escalation rather than explore discourses about rationality, in this instance.

*Critical perspective: power and politics*
Functionalism is useful in that it brings a focus on processual approaches of IS design, use and implementation, and interpretivism then adds an interest in the organizational context when examining the practical actions of managers, users and designers. Orlikowski and Baroudi (1991, p. 10) observe that in the positivist tradition, when conflict occurs, it is seen as dysfunctional to the social system and is something to be suppressed or overcome. Knights and Murray (1994) argue that a critical perspective is necessary to make reference to the political character of IT developments and their essential contestability. 'Tensions surrounding IT management are systematically related to complex sets of power, managerial and market relations' (Knights and Murray 1997, p. 37). Strategy and technological change are a contested terrain of discourse rather than a description of

a rational process or a prescription for rational action. Organizational change is a political process; change has several objectives, some of them contradictory in their implications, and many giving expression to opportunistic and implicit tactics, agendas or strategies. De facto change emerges from conflicts at tactical level, ad hoc management decisions, and accidents, rather than from a rational planning process: 'Although dominant coalitions will probably be involved, strategy [or change or resistance] can emerge from anywhere in the organisation. Organisational goals are not unitary, may be conflicting, and are frequently left unstated or unclear for political reasons' (Knights et al. 1997b, p. 28). These authors recommend that we should concentrate on the internal political context, as well as on the social and institutional aspects of the external context; and that we should not neglect the way in which organizations both reflect and reproduce the major social inequalities in society, and hence the essentially contestable nature of organizational relations.

Disagreements over technical changes are an inevitable feature of organizational life, and not, as shown for example in the failure of a nursing information system (Wilson and Howcroft 2000), a consequence of resistant users. Gender aspects were seen to be a particular set of interests related to contested identity and power relations. Another example of a critical approach to IS failure is that of Myers's (1994b, p. 198) case study in which he found that 'the new payroll system became a symbol of the government's intention to restructure educational administration', leading to resistance from many teachers to the new information system. However, a constructivist critique of this latter example would say that this should be the starting point rather than the final result of a critical analysis. Myers only identifies these intentions or interests as exogenous and takes them at face value; but, and particularly in relation to technology, we need to examine how the discursive construction of technology is *presented* as a set of external constraints with attendant imperatives. Actors act on the basis of assumptions and in so doing bring about outcomes consistent with that thesis, irrespective of its veracity, and indeed of its perceived veracity. For instance, in this case study, the government's thesis may possibly be that the use of IT streamlines administrative processes, improves customer care, ensures quality control, adds competitive advantage, or increases transparency. For each of these discourses, associated conceptualizations of the relations between technology and, for example, the market, economics, the organization, or management, together with their implications, effects and relationships to other actors' conceptualizations, should be explored further in order to bring criticality to the analysis. If actors believe the discourse to be true (or find it to their advantage to present it as true), they will act in a manner consistent with its predictions, thereby contributing to its perceived truth and naturalness (Hay and Rosamond 2002).

While many IS researchers share the view that an information system is a social system that uses IT, construing these contextual social factors as exogenous separates and isolates/insulates them from the technology and implies the pre-existence of a technological deterministic 'natural trajectory' (MacKenzie 1988) independent of external social 'contexts'. MacKenzie argues that technical trajectories do not exist but are actors' constructs, that technology is never self-directing and that a technological trajectory is a self-fulfilling prophecy. This concept of a natural trajectory is illustrated by Newman and Robey (1992) when they express the hope that IS practitioners can use models to diagnose and predict problems in order to move projects in the 'right' direction. This assumes that there is a normal, successful, natural, right way of using technology and the objective is to trace evidence of failure in terms of discrepancies from this natural and inherent technological development. MacKenzie (1988) suggests that the term 'natural' can be read here as 'asocial'.

## Social constructivism and failure

Social constructivism argues that there is no such thing as a social problem that does not have technological components; nor can there be a technological problem that does not have social components, and that any attempt to make such a division is bound to fail. ANT states that the development of technological devices should be interpreted within an analysis of the struggles and growth of 'systems' or 'networks'. The constructivist approach moves away from making distinctions among technical, social, economic and political aspects of technological development, and uses the 'seamless web', 'system' or 'actor-network' metaphors, which stress the importance of paying attention to the different but interlocking elements of physical artefacts, institutions and their environments, linking the micro and macro levels[1] of analysis. Social constructivist approaches assist in counteracting the weaknesses of determinist analyses; the latter are preoccupied with the 'social impacts' of a predetermined technical 'trajectory' and tend to treat technology as a neutral 'black box'. Failures are of particular interest since the controversy which surrounds them tends to reveal processes that are more easily hidden in the case of 'successful' projects, and more complex relationships between technical choices and social environments can be unravelled. ANT has been used to investigate the success of a number of technological innovations, and to describe a number of failures: for example, Grint and Woolgar (1997) for the Luddite movement; McMaster et al. (1997) for systems analysis by local government; Vidgen and MacMaster (1996) for car parking systems; Latour (1992) for a transport system.

*The technical and the social*

The conventional dichotomy between the social and the technical is problematic as technical and social choices are constantly negotiated and socially constructed (Bloomfield and Vurdubakis 1994), and their construction follows the same logic in successes and failures. For instance, a common debate about IS failures is whether they are management or software failures (Flowers 1996). Technologists blame management and managers get carried away with what they are told the technology can do for them. This reflects a convenient dichotomy between the technical and the social. It is argued here that another way of looking at it is not to see the technical and the social as separate and stable entities. Disentangling the interplay of actors and the construction of technical and social choices can be done by focusing on 'failure' studies: they can show that, at the beginning of and during a project, choices are not obvious or unproblematic, unlike what they appear to be in a successful project. Failure studies also allow for more complex explanations from actors. This leads to richer verbalizations of the complex links between technical choices and the social environment, and more readily so than in the case of 'successes' where choices tend to be seen as obvious.

> Like the sociology of science, the sociology of technology has chosen as its methodological principle to use the same explanatory resources when reporting on successful and unsuccessful innovations. However, to challenge the impression of obviousness which can be given by technical choices that lead to devices which 'perform well', there is no better strategy than concentrating on failure cases to show that it is impossible to distinguish between good and bad decisions. Moreover, in failures and controversial cases, actors facilitate the researcher's work since they express the more complex relationships between technical choice and social environment. (Akrich 1993, pp. 36–7, author's translation)

*Symmetry and failure*

Borrowing from the sociology of scientific knowledge (for example, Pickering 1992; Barnes et al. 1996), sociologists of technology have argued that technology failures are of as much interest as success stories. You cannot, at the start of a project, tell whether it is going to succeed. This implies that the same methods of analysis should be used to describe successful and unsuccessful projects, and hindsight should not be used to describe the problem. The sociology of scientific knowledge recommends that scholars interested in the development of science and technology choose controversy as one important site for research. The controversy is about the truth or falsity of scientific belief, or about the success or failure of a technology, in solving problems. Different groups will define not only the problem differently but also success or failure, and there is not just one possible way, or one best way, of designing an artefact (Bijker et al. 1987, p. 14). The notion of symmetry helps dismantle the 'impression of obviousness' (Akrich 1993, p. 36–7).

Latour's investigation (1992, 1993) into the abandonment of a new revolutionary subway transportation system planned in the South of Paris, *Aramis*, is a good example of how to tackle symmetrically the failure story (*Aramis*) and the success story (*VAL*, a working automatic suburban train in the northern city of Lille). Trying to explain only *Aramis*, since it has been a failure, whereas *VAL* has turned out to be a success, would be 'asymmetric since it would look for social explanations only when something goes wrong – the straight path of happy technical development being, in contrast, self-evident and self-explanatory' (Latour 1993, p. 383). Both projects tie together many interests, and in both cases, these interests do not exist independently of the projects and (potential or eventual) artefacts. In following the design and redesign of *Aramis*, and all the interested groups and actors, and in gathering what they said, did and did not do throughout the project, Latour assembled not only one explanation but at least 20; however, he claims that he does not practise two different interpretations, one about the nature of the artefact and the other about the meaning it has for social groups: 'it is the same task to define the artefact tying together the various groups or the groups tying together one artefact' (ibid., p. 381). Rejecting the division between the social and the technical, social actors are not considered as simply 'pressing their wills on inert passive objects, and artefacts are not pressing their goals onto human actors'. Latour refuses to set the failure in the following dualistic terms: is it because *Aramis* failed that the interpretations diverged so, or because the interpretations are so divergent that the project never became an institution, a stabilized thing?

*Actor networks*
Actor networks are interrelated human and non-human actors who shape the way things are (Callon 1986, 1991; Latour 1989, 1991). This circumvents technological determinism in which technical projects and innovations proceed naturally unless they are actively stopped, and replaces it with the idea that things do not happen unless human and non-human actors make them happen. One of the strengths of the actor-network approach is the systematic avoidance of what can be called methodological dualism: 'Rather than assuming that we are dealing with two separate, but related, ontological domains – technology and organisations – we propose to regard them as but phases of the same essential action' (Latour 1991, p. 129). The separation between technology and organization is a sense-making device, one of the means by which we orient ourselves in the world (Bloomfield and Vurdubakis 1994). For instance, in the case of the use of IS in the NHS studied by

Bloomfield and Vurdubakis (1997, p. 89), the intermediation between the domain of technology and the (social) world of the organization is interlinked with the intermediation between the professional groups of management and clinicians, and their respective rationalities (medical/administrative). Thus in addition to constituting/negotiating the boundary between the 'technical' and the 'social', the IT review at the NHS is an intermediary device which effects translations between the worlds of management and medicine, the commercial ethos of management consultancy and the public service orientation of the NHS (ibid.).

*Translation*
Latour's (1991) alternative to technological determinism, in which things do not happen unless other actors make them happen, implies that each actor who takes the project further may take it in a different direction than that intended by the previous actor. Latour uses the term 'translation' to describe this effect, playing on both of its meanings. The innovation is translated or carried from one position to another in the sense of a mathematical manipulation; the innovation is also interpreted or transposed from one position to another in the linguistic sense of the word 'translation'. Translation operates between actors: an actor gives a definition to another actor, imputes him/her/it/them with interests, projects, desires, strategies, reflexes and afterthoughts (Callon 1991). An actor might be the company that has conceived, produced and distributed a machine, and another actor its users. The translation operation is regulated by conventions that are more or less local, and are always revisable (ibid.). The final shape and position of the innovation is unlikely to be that of the original developers. In each stage of its life, the project is taken and adapted by the actors that become involved in it. Only in the rare case when the future users can be persuaded to follow the initial goals, does the innovation proceed as originally planned. All too often, however, the issue becomes sidetracked and unintended effects occur. Translations take place through '*problematisation*', '*intéressement*' and enrolment of actors (ibid.).

Of particular interest are the related concepts of stability, irreversibility and obligatory passage points. According to Callon (ibid.), convergence and irreversibility of techno-economic networks are both involved in the acts of translation and the networks that they sometimes succeed in forming. Convergence is the degree of accord (alignment and coordination) engendered by a series of translations. Controversies are translation as betrayal. Irreversibility, taken as the predetermination of translations and as the impossibility of a return to competing translations, is synonymous with normalization. A network which is irreversible is a network that has become heavy with immutable, durable devices (frozen elements or 'black boxes') and inscriptions, norms of all sorts, and which as a result slips into a codified information system. Failures can be seen to occur when 'the necessary translation of the system ... is problematic and a stable network of aligned interests is not yet developing' (Aarts et al. 2000, p. 518).

**Contructivism and critical research**
What constructivism, as illustrated above, can bring to the analysis of IS failure will first be summed up. The three different foci on criticality already introduced above will then be used to discuss how constructivism can help IS research to be critical. Finally, the fundamental and related question of whether social constructivist approaches are critical is touched upon, and suggestions are made to complement them further in order to combine the second and third of our three critical foci more effectively, as neither should be the single focus.

*Constructivism can help critical IS research*
As discussed in the previous section, the factor-based approach to IS failure research has not delivered results (Bussen and Myers 1996; Larsen and Myers 1999; Parr et al. 1999), and according to Sauer (1999, p. 290) 'factor research has not satisfactorily isolated causes in a way that allows them to be eliminated in practice'. To summarize, causes and explanations for IS failures have been constructed around: the technology itself; individuals (incompetent software engineers, resistant end-users) (Jones 1995; Neumann 1995); and systems (Perrow 1984). Behavioural and social 'factors' have been seen as responsible, for instance: organizational factors (Ewusi-Mensah and Przasnyski 1994; Peltu et al. 1996); stakeholders (Lyytinen and Hirschheim 1987; Pinto 1994; Seddon et al. 1999); organizational structure (Sauer et al. 1997); and culture (Beynon-Davies 1995; Gallivan 1997). Success 'factors' are said to be (Lyytinen and Robey 1999): top management support, overcoming resistance, having champions, controlling shop floor politics, involving users, managing projects, fitting with organizational culture, managing change and risk, introducing knowledge management, providing organizational learning, empowering staff, providing customer focus and so on. The list of factors is endless, and the components are claimed to be universal, independent of situation and time. This is unsatisfactory; for instance, top management support can easily be seen to be counterproductive in cases of project escalation (Keil 1995; Drummond 1996).

IS failure research is often expected to accumulate knowledge and deliver solutions to prevent failure by eliminating its causes. IS researchers have expressed confidence in the possibility of controlling and mastering the organizational future: 'Future research will ultimately result in the demise of IS failures' (Lyytinen and Hirschheim 1987, p. 301; see also Dalcher and Genus 2003). This basic premise corresponds to assumptions that are socially constructed: they take on a natural 'commonsensical' appearance but in fact are complex and contingent historical constructions. Social constructivism breaks with conventional and commonsensical conceptions of problems by examining them as a 'social process of definition': it is concerned with unravelling how these claims are constructed (Holstein and Miller 1993). One way in which constructivism can help unravel these claims is by bringing an awareness of our tendency to believe in technological trajectories. Many existing approaches to IS failure construe social factors as exogenous from the technology and imply the pre-existence of a 'natural' technological trajectory (MacKenzie 1988) with which social factors 'interfere'. For instance, when Newman and Robey (1992) express the hope that IS practitioners can use models to diagnose and predict IS failures in order to move projects in the 'right' direction, they assume that the technology on its own can be successful through its 'inherent' structure, if its 'normal' development is unhampered by external human or social factors. IS failures are often assumed to be anomalies and diversions from a 'normal', successful course of action. Through notions such as inevitabilism and contingency (Hacking 1999), constructionism helps us to realize that the belief that socio-technical development can be controlled and managed (for example, Flowers 1996; Fortune and Peters 1995) is problematic. ANT and the sociology of translation help us to understand how an innovation is translated or carried, interpreted or transposed, from one position to another, and how translation operates between actors in unexpected ways, leading to the formation of techno-economic networks.

Constructivist concepts can be applied to how researchers understand why attempts to build socio-technical information systems 'deviate' or fail; and to how that cannot be explained solely by recourse to mere technical factors, nor by reference to the supposed effects of some powerful social forces which were always there but somehow mysteriously overlooked (Bloomfield et al. 1997, p. 130). Instead, to explain these deviations in IS development, use and implementation, we can consider several of the processes in the building of heterogeneous actor networks. ANT's inclusion of non-humans, the principle of symmetry, irreversibility and stabilization, and the process of translation have contributed to interpreting IS more radically and pushing beyond previous accounts by providing a conceptual framework for analysing the multiple connections among people, artefacts and institutions in a non-deterministic manner. This has also been illustrated in other IS researchers' attempts at using ANT for the empirical description of actor networks around various ITs, for example, geographic IS (Walsham and Sahay 1999), hospital IS (Bloomfield et al. 1997) and IT infrastructures (Monteiro 2000).

In terms of our three different foci on criticality (that is (i) making local in-depth qualitative investigations, (ii) indicating new ways of organizing and working, and (iii) critiquing taken-for-granted assumptions), constructivist approaches address both the *first* (which interpretivism also does) and *third* foci, the latter being the most valuable contribution to critical IS research.

## Making constructivism more critical

However, extreme social constructivism such as ANT has been accused of disregarding macro social structures and of a weak capacity for explanation, as opposed to description. Walsham (1997) categorizes some of the existing limitations of ANT as follows.

- *Social structures* ANT concentrates on how things get done to the detriment of how broader social structures shape socio-material practices. It gives interesting accounts of local contingencies and material arrangements, without taking into account macro social structures.
- *Humans and non-humans* the symmetry between human and non-human actors has been criticized for having gone too far in erasing all distinctions and reducing people to the status of things. In other words, there are political implications of levelling human and non-human differences.
- *Amoral and apolitical* the disregard for macro structures has led to criticisms of being amoral and apolitical in how it leads to ignoring the political biases that can underlie the spectrum of choices for relevant actors. Star (1991) refers to the 'networks of the powerful' and to how irreversible networks are only stable for some and discriminate against those who do not belong to the community of practice who form, use and maintain the network.
- *Description* ANT is a method for describing, but not for explaining. Callon's answer (1991) is that explanations are only offered by networks which increase their convergence and irreversibility, and that the descriptions delivered by intermediaries turn into explanations. This leaves the question of how to explain the failure to converge in the case of a divergent, reversible and unstable network. If all explanations are the result of a stabilized network already in place, one assumes that one could use explanations of other (previous?) stable overlapping and neighbouring networks, but then the problem is transposed to where does one stop? As Walsham (1997, p. 476) observes, identifying all of the heterogeneous associations within an actor network is difficult enough, let alone those of overlapping networks.

McLean and Hassard (2004) analyse these limitations in a similar manner: inclusion/exclusion; network boundaries; collusion with the powerful actors leading to managerialism; appearing radical but dissolves dichotomies; reliance on spokespersons but delegation of authority is itself a political process. It is clear that constructivism is seen here as not addressing the second of our three critical foci, but a more politically oriented one. Walsham (1997) suggests combining the methodological approach and conceptual ideas of ANT with insights and analyses drawn from other social theories. Some authors are complementing ANT by as varied a range of perspectives as Martin Heidegger (Ciborra and Hanseth 1998), Michel Foucault (Knights et al. 1997a), institutionalization theory (Silva and Backhouse 1997) and circuits of power (Silva et al. 1997; Mitev 2000). To address concerns related to our second critical focus, some argue that what is missing in ANT is the recognition of the role of power and its relationship to networks and knowledge. Knights and Murray (1994, p. xii) argue that 'it is largely through the social interpretation, construction or reconstruction of [broader socio-political, economic and organizational] conditions and what they mean for the organisation that specific political alliances are mobilised and particular information systems are made possible'. Knights et al. (1997a, p. 151) suggest complementing Callon's analysis of the dynamics of network building with a Foucauldian appreciation of how power and knowledge circulate throughout organizations and societies, as a principal medium of network construction and reproduction. They state that 'new "regimes of truth" ... undergo a process of multiple translation and accident as their champions rethink, and are challenged, subverted and blown off course by recalcitrant actors and unexpected intermediations' (Knights et al. 1997a, p. 153). One way of including power is to suggest that translation is a political representation. As illustrated by Bloomfield et al. (1997) in their fieldwork on IT in the NHS, the introduction and application of concepts previously associated with commercial organizations have been the object of ongoing struggles and renegotiations; and 'the internalisation of such constitutive concepts as costs, overheads, assets, customers, quality, etc. and the willingness of an organisation's members to construct their world and their work in terms of these concepts, is an instance of the exercise of disciplinary power' (ibid., p. 115).

A similar critical exploration of constructivism is to be found in the STS literature, with a view to making its approach to studying the innovation process more explicit (Klein and Kleinman 2002). Questions raised relate to: the theoretical attack on macro-contextual issues, seen as having political implications; how the 'descriptive turn' and its attendant 'value-free relativism' has been a turn towards or away from the political agenda of STS; how taking into account specific concerns of commercially-driven innovation networks is lacking; how actors are representatives of organizational agendas and shift in and out of the network; how the capture of innovation as networks and knowledge-generating activities can be (post-structurally) politicized; and how to reawaken a critical sociological position in order to contextualize innovation and infuse social analysis into social constructivism.

Clearly, research concentrating on our third critical focus only is unsatisfactory. However, in response to these criticisms, ANT proponents make it clear that they are not indifferent to the possibility of judgement, but only refuse to accept judgements that transcend situations: 'both constructivism and deconstruction rightly insist on the power of intermediaries that make impossible any direct access to objectivity, truth and morality' (Latour 2002, p. 6).

### The necessity of both politics and deconstruction

Deconstruction and constructivism do point to the many dangers (for example, totalizing and transcendental discourses; see also Wilson 1999) associated with carrying out research on our second critical focus on its own. McLean and Hassard (2004), for instance, despite their criticisms mentioned above, still find it valuable to draw upon actor-network analyses of the social achievement of technological innovations through the construction of webs or networks of actors. They value actor-network insistence that technologies are constructed through social processes comprising accident, fortuitous circumstance and political action. Constructivism emphasizes the network of events and agents that lies behind an item of knowledge and that is intended as an unmasking of established order, since the notion of contingency undermines authority. At the core, though, there is a tension between (a) the desire of liberation from domination which implies some transcendental value judgement (our second critical focus), and (b) the recognition of the social construction of these values and the appeal of the force of some of the critique (our third critical focus); and it can be difficult, if not impossible, to reconcile these two positions (Hacking 1999, p. 96).

To combine both the second and third foci of criticality, McLean and Hassard (2004) suggest concentrating not on what actors do but on what provides actors with their actions: subjectivity, intentionality and morality. They draw on Star (1991) who pointed out the problem of hierarchies of distribution being ignored in the ordering of actor-network accounts; on Bowker and Star's (1991) understanding of how narratives (that seem universal) may have been constructed, of how to recover their multivocality, but how far from unproblematic it is to do as it requires some form of ordering and classification, which explains the constitution of truth. 'Problems relating to the issue of orderings and the distributions of power should be acknowledged to a greater extent within the methods employed in the selection and representation of actors and how we inscribe our accounts' (McLean and Hassard 2004, p. 510). They also suggest using the concept of governmentality after Rose (1989, 1999) and Rose and Miller (1992) as complementary to ANT rather than as an alternative, to provide an opening through which to adopt critique as an intellectual and political activity, based on notions of politics, ethics, distributions and the making of judgements in accounts. These suggestions would help address the issues of overlapping networks and boundaries, differences between small and large actors, directional flows of translation, and power logics of return in ANT. It may help elaborate a more critical social constructivist IS agenda which incorporates a richly informed, historically contextualized understanding of the social ordering of epistemological categories leading to patterns of inequity and hidden assumptions embedded in IS knowledge and practice.

An important aim still remains, to investigate in what manner social order itself arises (our third critical focus), which has not attracted much attention in IS research, including critical IS research. This seems particularly crucial as some IS researchers tend to 'apply' the ANT network idea to their systems and forget that they are 'effects or outcomes', in other words not given in the order of things (Latour 2004). Both political and deconstruction agendas should be crucial in IS research, as much IS design, implementation and use is historically situated, socially constructed and corresponds to time-dependent managerial ideas and trends used in specific contexts for complex reasons. Specifically, managerialism and the growing use of management as a value and its elevation to a more significant and visible position since the 1980s is related to 'its enmeshment with highly contested changes [such as] public sector restructuring, downsizing and cultural re-engineering' (Fournier and Grey 2000, p. 11; see also Clarke and Newman 1993) and the associated constant flow of 'new' managerial solutions which need to be deconstructed, particularly in their relations with ICTs.

**Note**
1. Although ANT proponents would deny the distinction between the micro and macro levels.

**References**
Aarts, J., E. Goorman, H. Heathfield and B. Kaplan (2000), 'Successful development, implementation and evaluation of information systems: does healthcare serve as a model for networked organisations?', in R. Baskerville, J. Stage and J.I. DeGross (eds), *Organizational and Social Perspectives on Information Technology*, Proceedings of the International Federation for Information Processing (IFIP) TC8 WG8.2 International Working Conference, Aalborg, Denmark, 9–11 June 2000, Boston, MA: Kluwer Academic, pp. 518–20.

Adam, A., D.A. Howcroft and H. Richardson (2001), 'Absent friends? The gender dimension in IS research', in N.L. Russo, B. Fitzgerald and J.I. DeGross (eds), *Realigning Research and Practice in Information Systems Development: The Social and Organizational Perspective*, Proceedings of the International Federation for Information Processing (IFIP) Working Group 8.2 Conference, Boise, ID, 27–29 July 2001, Boston, MA: Kluwer Academic, pp. 333–52.

Akrich, M. (1993), 'Les objets techniques et leurs utilisateurs' (Technical objects and their users), in *Les Objets dans l'action, raisons pratiques* (Objects in Action, Practical Reasons), vol. 4, Paris: Éditions de l'École des Hautes Études et Sciences Sociales, pp. 35–57.

Alvesson, M. and H. Willmott (eds) (1992), *Critical Management Studies*, London: Sage.

Barnes, B., D. Bloor and J. Henry (1996), *Scientific Knowledge: A Sociological Analysis*, London: Athlone.

Berger, P.L. and T. Luckmann (1966), *The Social Construction of Reality: A Treatise in the Sociology of Knowledge*, Garden City, NY: Doubleday.

Beynon-Davies, P. (1995), 'Information systems "failure": the case of the London Ambulance Services' computer aided despatch system', *European Journal of Information Systems*, **4**, 171–84.

Bijker, W.E., T.P. Hughes and T. Pinch (eds) (1987), *The Social Construction of Technological Systems: New Directions in the Sociology and History of Technology*, Cambridge, MA: MIT Press.

Bloomfield, B.P. (1995), 'Power, machines and social relations: delegating to information technology in the National Health Service', *Organization*, **2**(3/4), August/November, 489–518.

Bloomfield, B.P., R. Coombs, J. Owen and P. Taylor (1997), 'Doctors as managers: constructing systems and users in the National Health Service', in B.P. Bloomfield, R. Coombs, D. Knights and D. Littler (eds), *Information Technology and Organizations: Strategies, Networks and Integration*, Oxford: Oxford University Press, pp. 112–34.

Bloomfield, B.P. and T. Vurdubakis (1994), 'Boundary disputes: negotiating the boundary between the technical and the social in the development of IT systems', *Information Technology and People*, **7**(1), 9–24.

Bloomfield, B.P. and T. Vurdubakis (1997), 'Paper traces: inscribing organisations and information technology', in B.P. Bloomfield, R. Coombs, D. Knights and D. Littler (eds), *Information Technology and Organizations: Strategies, Networks and Integration*, Oxford: Oxford University Press, pp. 85–111.

Bowker, G. and L.S. Star (1999), *Sorting Things Out: Classification and Its Consequences*, Cambridge, MA: MIT Press.

Brey, P. (1997), 'Philosophy of technology meets social constructivism', *Techne: Journal of the Society for Philosophy and Technology*, **2**(3–4), Spring-Summer, www.scholar.lib.vt.edu/ejournals/SPT/v2 n3n4html/brey.html, accessed 15 June 2004.

Brindle, D. (1995), 'Paperwork key to nurses' strike action. Failure to collect data can hit employers but not patients', *The Guardian*, 17 May.

Brindle, D. (1996), 'Crucial NHS project "faces collapse"', *The Guardian*, 18 April.

Brooke, C. (guest editor) (2002a), Special issue on Critical Research in Information Systems, *Journal of Information Technology*, **17**(2), June.

Brooke, C. (2002b), 'What does it mean to be "critical" in IS research?', *Journal of Information Technology*, Special issue on Critical Research in Information Systems, **17**(2), June, 49–57.

Brooke, C., D. Cecez-Kecmanovic and H.K. Klein (guest editors) (forthcoming), Special issue on Exploring the Critical Agenda in IS Research, *Information Systems Journal*.

Burnes, B. (1992), *Managing Change: A Strategic Approach to Organisational Development and Renewal*, London: Pitman.

Bussen, W. and M. Myers (1996), 'Executive information systems failure: a New Zealand case study', *Journal of Information Technology*, **12**(2), 145–53.

Butler, T. (1998), 'Towards a hermeneutic method for interpretive research in information systems', *Journal of Information Technology*, **13**, 285–300.

Callon, M. (1986), 'Some elements of a sociology of translation: domestication of the scallops and the fishermen of St Brieuc Bay', in J. Law (ed.), *Power, Action and Belief*, London: Routledge & Kegan Paul, pp. 196–233.

Callon, M. (1991), 'Techno-economic networks and irreversibility', in J. Law (ed.), *A Sociology of Monsters: Essays on Power, Technology and Domination*, London: Routledge, pp. 132–64.

Ciborra, C. and O. Hanseth (1998), 'From tool to Gestell: agendas for managing the information infrastructure', *Information Technology and People*, 11(4), 305–27.

Clarke, J. and J. Newman (1993), 'The right to manage: a second managerial revolution', *Cultural Studies*, 7, 427–41.

Clarke, R.J. (1991), 'Discourses in systems development failure', in S. Aungles (ed.), *Information Technology in Australia: Transforming Organisational Structure and Culture*, Sydney: New South Wales University Press, pp. 45–62.

Collins, H. and T. Pinch (1982), *Frames of Meaning: The Social Construction of Extraordinary Science*, London: Routledge & Kegan Paul.

Collins, H. and T. Pinch (1993), *The Golem: What Everyone should Know about Science*, Cambridge: Cambridge University Press.

Dalcher, D. and A. Genus (guest editors) (2003), Special issue on Avoiding IS/IT Implementation Failure, *Technology Analysis and Strategic Management*, 15(4), December.

Davis, G., A.S. Lee, K.R. Nickles, S. Chatterjee, R. Hartung and Y. Wu (1992), 'Diagnosis of an information system failure: a framework and interpretive process', *Information and Management*, 23, 293–318.

Doolin, B. (1998), 'Information technology as disciplinary technology: being critical in interpretive research on information systems', *Journal of Information Technology*, 13, 301–11.

Doolin, B. and A. Lowe (2002), 'To reveal is to critique: actor-network theory and critical information systems research', *Journal of Information Technology*, Special issue on Critical Research in Information Systems, 17(2), June, 69–78.

Dreyfus, H. and P. Rabinow (1982), *Michel Foucault: Beyond Structuralism and Hermeneutics*, Brighton: Harvester.

Drummond, H. (1996), *Escalation in Decision-making: The Tragedy of Taurus*, Oxford: Oxford University Press.

Dutton, W.H., D. MacKenzie, S. Shapiro and M. Peltu (1995), 'Computer power and human limits: learning from IT and telecommunications disasters', Policy Research Paper No. 33, Uxbridge: Programme on Information and Communication Technologies, Economic and Social Research Council. (Discussion based on a PICT Research Forum Policy Studies Institute, London, 20 October 1994.)

Edwards, R. (1979), *Contested Terrain: The Transformation of the Workplace in the Twentieth Century*, London: Heinemann.

Ewusi-Mensah, K. and Z.H. Przasnyski (1994), 'Factors contributing to the abandonment of information systems development projects', *Journal of Information Technology*, 9, 185–201.

Farrell, N. (1997), 'Outsourcing: learning from past mistakes', *Information Week*, 16, 18–22.

Feenberg, A. (2000), 'Constructivism and technology critique: replies to critics', *Inquiry*, 43, 225–38.

Fincham, R. (2002), 'Narratives of success and failure in systems development', *British Journal of Management*, 13, 1–14.

Flowers, S. (1996), *Software Failures – Management Failures: Amazing Stories and Cautionary Tales*, Chichester: Wiley & Sons.

Fortune, J. and G. Peters (1995), *Learning from Failure: The Systems Approach*, Chichester: Wiley & Sons.

Fournier, V. and C. Grey (2000), 'At the critical moment: conditions and prospects for critical management studies', *Human Relations*, 53(1), 7–32.

Gallivan, M.J. (1997), 'The importance of organizational culture fit: a technology implementation success story', *International Journal of Failure and Lessons Learned in Information Technology Management*, 1(4), 243–57.

Genus, A., A. Rigakis and K. Dickson (2003), 'Managing large-scale IT projects: the case of the National Air Traffic Services' new en route centre at Swanwick', *Technology Analysis and Strategic Management*, Special issue on Avoiding IS/IT Implementation Failure, **15**(4), December, 491–504.

Grint K. and S. Woolgar (1997), *The Machine at Work: Technology, Work and Organization*, Cambridge: Polity and Oxford: Blackwell.

Guzzini, S. (2000), 'A reconstruction of constructivism in international relations', *European Journal of International Relations*, **6**(2), 147–82.

Hacking, I. (1999), *The Social Construction of What?*, Cambridge, MA: Harvard University Press.

Hanseth, O., M. Aanestad and M. Berg (guest editors) (2004), Special issue on Actor-network Theory and Information Systems, *Information Technology and People*, **17**(2), 116–239.

Harvey, L.J. and M.D. Myers (1995), 'Scholarship and practice: the contribution of ethnographic research methods to bridging the gap', *Information Technology and People*, **8**(3), 13–27.

Hay, C. and B. Rosamond (2002), 'Globalization, European integration and the discursive construction of economic imperatives', *Journal of European Public Policy*, **9**(2), April, 147–67.

Hencke, D. (2000), 'Passport officials savaged by MPs', *The Guardian*, 1 February.

Heracleous, L. and M. Barrett (2001), 'Organizational change as discourse: communicative actions and deep structures in the context of information technology implementation', *Academy of Management Journal*, **44**(4), 755–78.

Hirschheim, R. and H.K. Klein (1994), 'Realizing emancipatory principles in information systems development: the case of ETHICS', *MIS Quarterly*, **18**(1), 83–109.

Holstein, J.A. and G. Miller (1993), *Reconsidering Social Constructionism: Debates in Social Problems Theory*, New York: Aldine de Gruyter.

Howcroft, D.A., N.N. Mitev and M. Wilson (2004), 'What we may learn from the social shaping of technology approach', in L. Willcocks and J. Mingers (eds), *Social Theory and Philosophy of Information Systems*, Information Systems Series, Chichester: John Wiley, pp. 329–71.

Jones, C. (1995), *Patterns of Software System Failure and Success*, London: International Thomson Computer Press.

Keil, M. (1995), 'Pulling the plug: software project management and the problem of escalation', *MIS Quarterly*, **19**(4), December, 420–47.

Kelsey, T. (1993), 'Electricity consumers left with needless £15m bill. Power companies were forced into costly computer contract during privatisation', *The Independent*, 7 June.

Kelsey, T. and C. Brown (1993), 'Government accused of misleading parliament over Wessex health authority's computer contracts: former Tory ministers linked to wasted £63m', *The Independent*, 15 March.

Klein, H.K. and D.L. Kleinman (2002), 'The social construction of technology: structural considerations', *Science, Technology and Human Values*, **27**(1), Winter, 28–52.

Knights, D. and F. Murray (1994), *Managers Divided: Organisation Politics and Information Technology Management*, Chichester: Wiley & Sons.

Knights, D. and F. Murray (1997), 'Markets, managers and messages: managing information systems in financial services', in B.P. Bloomfield, R. Coombs, D. Knights and D. Littler (eds), *Information Technology and Organizations: Strategies, Networks and Integration*, Oxford: Oxford University Press, pp. 36–56.

Knights, D., F. Murray and H. Willmott (1997a), 'Networking as knowledge work: a study of strategic inter-organizational development in the financial services industry', in B.P. Bloomfield, R. Coombs, D. Knights and D. Littler (eds), *Information Technology and Organizations: Strategies, Networks and Integration*, Oxford: Oxford University Press, pp. 137–80.

Knights, D., F. Noble and H.W. Willmott (1997b), 'We should be total slaves to the business: aligning information technology and strategy – issues and evidence', in B. Bloomfield, R. Coombs, D. Knights and D. Littler (eds), *Information Technology and Organizations: Strategies, Networks and Integration*, Oxford: Oxford University Press, pp. 13–35.

Knights, D. and H. Willmott (1988), *New Technology and the Labour Process*, London: Macmillan.

Larsen, M.A. and M.D. Myers (1999), 'When success turns into failure: a package-driven business process reengineering project in the financial services industry', *Journal of Strategic Information Systems*, **8**, 395–417.

Latour, B. (1989), *La science en action: Introduction à la sociologie des sciences*, Paris: Gallimard, Folio Essais. (In English: *Science in Action: How to Follow Scientists and Engineers through Society*, Cambridge, MA: Harvard University Press, 1987.)

Latour, B. (1991), 'Technology is society made durable', in J. Law (ed.), *A Sociology of Monsters: Essays on Power, Technology and Domination*, London: Routledge, pp. 103–31.

Latour, B. (1992), *Aramis ou l'amour des techniques*, Paris: Éditions La Découverte. (In English: *Aramis, or the Love of Technology*, trans. C. Porter, Cambridge, MA: Harvard University Press, 1996.)

Latour, B. (1993), 'Ethnography of a "high-tech" case. About Aramis', in P. Lemonnier (ed.), *Technological Choices: Transformations in Material Culture since the Neolithic*, London: Routledge & Kegan Paul, pp. 372–98.

Latour, B. (2002), 'The promises of constructivism', in D. Idhe (ed.), *Chasing Technoscience: Matrix or Materiality*, Indiana Series for the Philosophy of Technology, Bloomington, IN: Indiana University Press, www.ensmp.fr/~latour/articles/article/087.html, accessed 28 November 2003.

Latour, B. (2004), 'On using ANT for studying information systems: a (somewhat) Socratic dialog', in C. Avgerou, C. Ciborra and F. Land (eds), *The Social Study of Information and Communication Technology*, Oxford: Oxford University Press, pp. 62–76.

Lee, A.S. (1994), 'Electronic mail as a medium for rich communication: an empirical investigation using hermeneutic interpretation', *MIS Quarterly*, **18**(2), June, 143–57.

Lee, A.S., J. Liebenau and J.I. DeGross (eds) (1997), *Information Systems and Qualitative Research*, Proceedings of the International Federation for Information Processing (IFIP) WG8.2 International Conference on Information Systems and Qualitative Research, Philadelphia, PA, 31 May–3 June, London: Chapman & Hall.

London Ambulance Service (LAS) (1993), *Report of the Inquiry into the London Ambulance Service*, London: LAS, South West Thames Regional Health Authority, February.

Lyytinen, K. and R. Hirschheim (1987), 'Information systems failures: a survey and classification of the empirical literature', *Oxford Surveys in Information Technology*, **4**, 257–309.

Lyytinen, K. and D. Robey (1999), 'Learning failure in information systems development', *Information Systems Journal*, **9**, 85–101.

MacKenzie, D. (1988), '"Micro" versus "macro" sociologies of science and technology', PICT (ESRC Programme on Information and Communication Technologies) Working Paper No. 2, Research Centre for Social Sciences, Edinburgh University.

MacKenzie, D. and J. Wajcman (eds) ([1985] 1999), *The Social Shaping of Technology: How the Refrigerator Got Its Hum*, 1st edn, Milton Keynes; Open University Press, 1985, 2nd edn, Buckingham: Open University Press, 1999.

Markus, M.L. (1983), 'Power, politics and MIS implementation', *Communications of the ACM*, **26**(6), June, 430–44.

Markus, M.L. and D. Robey (1988), 'Information technology and organizational change: causal structure in theory and research', *Management Science*, **34**(5), May, 583–97.

McLean, C. and J. Hassard (2004), 'Symmetrical absence/symmetrical absurdity: critical notes on the production of actor-network accounts', *Journal of Management Studies*, **41**(3), May, 493–519.

McMaster, T., R.T. Vidgen and D.G. Wastell (1997), 'Towards an understanding of technology in transition: two conflicting theories', in K. Braa and E. Monteiro (eds), *Proceedings of the 20th Information Systems Research in Scandinavia*, Conference (IRIS20), University of Oslo, Hanko, Norway, 9–12 August, www2.cs.utu.fi/IRIS/iri.hrm, accessed 24 February 2005.

McMaster, T. and D. Wastell (2004), 'Success and failure revisited in the implementation of new technology: some reflections on the Capella project', in K. Kloutz, B. Fitzgerald and E. Wynn (eds), *Proceedings of the International Federation for Information Processing (IFIP)*

*Working Group 8.6 Conference of IT Innovation for Adaptability and Competitiveness*, Leixlip, Co. Kildare, Ireland, 30 May–2 June, http://ifip8point6.com, accessed 24 February 2005.

Mitev, N.N. (2000), 'Towards social constructivist understandings of IS success and failure: the introduction of a computerised reservation system', Paper presented at 21st International Conference on Information Systems, Brisbane, Australia, December.

Monteiro, E. (2000), 'Actor-network theory and information infrastructures', in C. Ciborra (ed.), *From Control to Drift: The Dynamics of Corporate Information Infrastructures*, Oxford: Oxford University Press, pp. 71–83.

Myers, M.D. (1994a), 'Dialectical hermeneutics: a theoretical framework for the implementation of information systems', *Information Systems Journal*, **5**, 51–70.

Myers, M.D. (1994b), 'A disaster for everyone to see: an interpretive analysis of a failed IS project', *Accounting, Management and Information Technologies*, **4**(4), 185–201.

Myers, M.D. (1997), 'Critical ethnography in information systems', in Lee et al. (eds), pp. 276–300.

Myers, M.D., A.S. Lee and M.L. Markus (1998), 'Qualitative research in information systems', ISWorld_Net, www.isworld.org/ isworld/ isworldtext.html, accessed 4 May 1998.

Neumann, P.G. (1995), *Computer-related Risks*, New York: ACM Press and Addison-Wesley.

Newman, M. and D. Robey (1992), 'A social process model of user–analyst relationships', *MIS Quarterly*, June, 249–66.

Ngwenyama, O.K., L. Harvey, M.D. Myers and E. Wynn (1997), 'Ethnographic research in information systems: an exploration of three alternative approaches to ethnography', Paper presented at 18th International Conference on Information Systems, Atlanta, GA: Association of Information Systems, pp. 533–4, Panel 17, 14–17 December.

Orlikowski, W.J. and J.J. Baroudi (1991), 'Studying information technology in organizations: research approaches and assumptions', *Information Systems Research*, **2**(1), March, 1–28.

Orlikowski, W.J. and S.R. Barley (2001), 'Technology and institutions: what can research on information technology and research on organizations learn from each other?', *MIS Quarterly*, **25**(2), 145–65.

Orlikowski, W.J., G. Walsham, M.R. Jones and J.I. DeGross (eds) (1996), *Information Technology and Changes in Organizational Work*, Proceedings of the International Federation for Information Processing (IFIP) WG8.2 Working Conference, Cambridge University, 7–9 December 1995, London: Chapman & Hall.

Parr, A.N., G. Shanks and P. Darke (1999), 'Identification of necessary factors for successful implementation of ERP systems', in O.K. Ngwenyama, L.D. Introna, M.D. Myers and J.I. DeGross (eds), *Information Technologies in Organizational Processes: Field Studies and Theoretical Reflections on the Future of Work*, Proceedings of the International Federation for Information Processing (IFIP) Working Group 8.2 Conference, St Louis, MO, 31 May–3 June 1999, Boston, MA: Kluwer Academic.

Peltu, M., D. MacKenzie, S. Shapiro and W.H. Dutton (1996), 'Computer power and human limits', in W.H. Dutton (ed. with M. Peltu), *Information and Communication Technologies: Visions and Realities*, Oxford: Oxford University Press, pp. 177–95.

Perrow, C. (1984), *Normal Accidents: Living with High-risk Technologies*, New York: Basic Books.

Phillips, N. and J.L. Brown (1993), 'Analyzing communication in and around organizations: a critical hermeneutics approach', *Academy of Management Journal*, **36**(6), December, 1547–76.

Pickering, A. (1984), *Constructing Quarks: A Sociological History of Particle Physics*, Edinburgh: Edinburgh University Press.

Pickering, A. (ed.) (1992), *Science as Practice and Culture*, Chicago: University of Chicago Press.

Pinto, J.K. (1994), *Successful Information System Implementation: The Human Side*, Lansing, MI: Project Management Institute.

Poulymenakou, A. and A. Holmes (1996), 'A contingency framework for the investigation of information systems failure', *European Journal of Information Systems*, **5**, 34–46.

Robinson, B.A. (1994), 'And treat those imposters just the same: analysing systems failure as a social process', Paper presented at PICT (Programme on Information and Communications Technologies) Doctoral Conference, Edinburgh University, August.

Rose, N. (1989), *Governing the Soul: The Shaping of the Private Self*, London: Routledge.

Rose, N. (1999), *Powers of Freedom: Reframing Political Thought*, Cambridge: Cambridge University Press.

Rose, N. and P. Miller (1992), 'Political power beyond the state: problematics of government', *British Journal of Sociology*, **43**(2), 172–205.

Sahay, S., M. Palit and D. Robey (1994), 'A relativist approach to studying the social construction of information technology', *European Journal of Information Systems*, **3**(4), 248–58.

Sauer, C. (1993), *Why Information Systems Fail: A Case Study Approach*, Henley-on-Thames: Alfred Waller.

Sauer, C. (1999), 'Deciding the future for IS failures. Not the choice you might think', in R.G. Galliers amd W. Currie (eds), *Rethinking Management Information Systems: An Interdisciplinary Perspective*, Oxford: Oxford University Press, pp. 277–309.

Sauer, C., G. Southon and C.N.G. Dampney (1997), 'Fit, failure and the house of horrors: toward a configurational theory of IS project failure', Paper presented at 18th International Conference on Information Systems, Atlanta, GA: Association for Information Systems, 14–17 December.

Seddon, P.B., S. Staples, R. Patnayakuni and M. Bowtell (1999), 'Dimensions of information systems success', *Communications of the Association for Information Systems*, **2**, 20.

Shapin, S. (1996), *A Social History of Truth*, Chicago: University of Chicago Press.

Silva, L. and J. Backhouse (1997), 'Becoming part of the furniture: the institutionalisation of information systems', in Lee et al. (eds), pp. 389–416.

Silva, L., G. Dhillon and J. Backhouse (1997), 'Developing a networked authority: nature and significance of power relationships', in R. Galliers, S. Carlsson, C. Loebbecke, C. Murphy, H.R. Hansen and R. O'Callaghan (eds), *Proceedings of the 5th European Conference on Information Systems*, Department of Accounting, finance and information Systems, University Cork College, Ireland, 19–21 June, pp. 511–25.

Sismondo, S. (1993), 'Some social constructions', *Social Studies of Science*, **23**, 515–53.

Star, S.L. (1991), 'Power, technologies and the phenomenology of conventions: of being allergic to onions', in J. Law (ed.), *A Sociology of Monsters: Essays on Power, Technology and Domination*, London: Routledge, pp. 26–56.

Tatnall, A. and A. Gilding (1999), 'Actor-network theory and information systems research', *Proceedings of the 10th Australasian Conference on Information Systems*, School of Communications and Information Management, Victoria University of Wellington, New Zealand, 1–3 December, pp. 955–66.

Truex, D. and D.A. Howcroft (guest editors) (2002), Special issue on Critical Analyses of Enterprise Resource Planning (ERP) Systems, *ACM SIGMIS Database*, **33**(2), Winter.

Vaughan, D. (1996), *The Challenger Launch Decision: Risky Technology, Culture and Deviance at NASA*, Chicago: University of Chicago Press.

Vidgen, R.T. and T. McMaster (1996), 'Black boxes, non-human stakeholders and the translation of IT through mediation', in Orlikowski et al. (eds), pp. 250–71.

Walsham, G. (1993), *Interpreting Information Systems in Organisations*, Chichester: Wiley & Sons.

Walsham, G. (1995), 'The emergence of interpretivism in IS research', *Information Systems Research*, **6**(4), December, 376–94.

Walsham, G. (1997), 'Actor-network theory and IS research: current status and future prospects', in Lee et al. (eds), pp. 466–80.

Walsham G. and S. Sahay (1999), 'GIS for district-level administration in India: problems and opportunities', *Management Information Systems Quarterly*, Special issue on Intensive Research in Information Systems, **23**(1), March, 39–65.

Whitley, E.A. and S. Bouzari (1999), 'An anti-essentialist reading of intranet development: what is the role of technology?', in L. Brooks and C. Kimble (eds), *Information Systems: The Next Generation*, Proceedings of the 4th UKAIS (UK Academy of Information Systems) Conference, 7–9 April, University of York, Maidenhead: McGraw-Hill, pp. 97–104.

Willcocks, L. and K. Grint (1997), 'Re-inventing the organization? Towards a critique of business process re-engineering', in I. McLoughlin and M. Harris (eds), *Innovation, Organizational Change and Technology*, London: International Thomson Business Press, pp. 87–110.
Wilson, F. (1999), 'Flogging a dead horse: the implications of epistemological relativism within information systems methodological practice', *European Journal of Information Systems*, **8**, 161–9.
Wilson, M. and D. Howcroft (2000), 'The role of gender in user resistance and information systems failure', in R. Baskerville, J. Stage and J.I. DeGross (eds), *Organizational and Social Perspectives on Information Technology*, Proceedings of the International Federation for Information Processing (IFIP) TC8 WG8.2 International Working Conference, 9–11 June, Aalborg, Denmark, Boston, MA: Kluwer Academic, pp. 453–71.

# 5 Taking a critical linguistic turn: using critical discourse analysis for the study of information systems

*Rosio Alvarez*

## Introduction

Nearly two decades ago Enid Mumford wrote: 'we have been looking critically at the kinds of research associated up to now with information science, and discussing the need for new approaches' (Mumford et al. 1985: foreword). At the time, there was growing concern by information systems (IS) researchers that traditional methods could not adequately investigate social needs and problems of IS design, implementation and use. Researchers critiqued the dominant 'scientific method' that most studies employed, and while not rooted in a single theoretical perspective, these studies were overwhelmingly based on positivist assumptions (Orlikowski and Baroudi 1991). Now, almost 20 years later, a cursory sampling indicates a changing research landscape with approaches such as actor-network theory (Bloomfield et al. 1992; Latour 1996; Wilson 2002), critical social theory (Hirschheim and Klein 1989, 1994; Ngwenyama 1991; Lyytinen 1992; Päivärinta 2001) structuration theory (Orlikowski and Robey 1991; Orlikowski 1992; Yates and Orlikowski 1992) and action research (Avison et al. 2001; Kock and Lau 2001), all of which critically view IS development as a socio-organizational and, simultaneously, technological phenomenon. This chapter continues in this tradition by presenting critical discourse analysis as an approach for understanding IS as a discursively constructed phenomenon embedded within social structures.

Critical discourse analysis fundamentally concerns itself with critically analysing language or semiotics in the context of social interactions. But why should IS researchers concern themselves with language? This chapter will explore this question and present an argument for understanding IS design and use as the production and exchange of semiotic products. I argue that as researchers of IS, we are already examining the production and exchange of semiotic products in the form of, for example, requirements analysis and technical support calls. Moreover, language is to be thought of as social action which has a performative aspect. That is, language accomplishes 'things' in its use, such as establishing one's identity. And finally, the 'critical' component of critical discourse analysis permits us to look at how these accomplishments create and reproduce relationships of dominance, power, inequality and control as they are expressed, constituted and legitimized in language use. While critical discourse analysis is an approach rather than a methodology, facework, narrative analysis and tropes are presented as methods for analysis that have been previously used by the author. The chapter concludes with a summary of other linguistic work by IS researchers to highlight the importance of the semiotic and information systems.

**Semiotic products and IS research**
The fundamental substance of much IS work depends on interactional talk. Think, for instance, of requirements analysis. In its simplest form, requirements analysis entails encoding into the system design the requirements that clients verbalize. The analyst works with end users to establish an understanding of organizational information processing needs, designs system alternatives, and, finally, communicates the results to users and other members of the organization. While a number of tools and techniques are used to elicit information from users, the interview continues to be a dominant elicitation technique (Agarwal and Tanniru 1990). The interview relies on the exchange of talk: questions are asked about business information needs by analysts and answers are given by users. As another example, consider the typical technical support call. During this exchange, users call in and attempt to describe the nature of their problem. The technician asks a variety of questions in an attempt to identify the problem and provide a solution. This is perhaps the quintessential semiotic product that information system organizations provide.

The information exchange in the above practices can be viewed in a number of ways depending on one's epistemological stance. A positivist stance would suggest that these social interactions are aimed at extracting pre-existing pieces of information that reside inside user's minds. They are nuggets of information and the analyst simply needs the right tools to mine them. An interpretive position – such as the one taken in this chapter – assumes that the 'truth' does not simply exist as a matter of course outside the social actors or interaction, but rather it is produced in the context (Putnam 1983). Independent of one's epistemological frame, these interactions depend on language use, and produce new 'data' or 'solutions' through language. In a sense, these exchanges produce semiotic products which are an outcome of interactions between technical analyst and clients during IS design and use. If we understand the information associated with IS as a semiotic product, then the design, implementation and use of these systems fundamentally depends on the exchange of semiotic products.

The importance of examining the semiotic products that IS so deeply depend upon has not been lost on IS researchers. A quick glimpse of the field shows a growing 'turn' towards linguistic analysis. For instance, one stream of literature focuses on organizational semiotics based on the 'speech act' approach of John Searle and J.L. Austin (Lehitinen and Lyytinen 1994; Clark 2001). This approach is described as an attempt to fully grasp the meanings conveyed through everyday conversation (Iivari et al. 1998). The argument suggests that IS are not about the design of physical things, but about the design of practices and possibilities realized through linguistic communication systems (Flores et al. 1988). For the most part, this perspective focuses on the illocutionary point and propositional content of speech acts. These speech acts form larger parts of networks of conversations and discourses (Winograd and Flores 1986; Klein and Truex 1996).

Another stream of related research is that of genre analysis. In this research, genre is considered to be a socially recognized type of communicative action, such as a memo, meeting, résumé or workshop, which is habitually enacted by members of a community to effect particular social purposes (Yates and Orlikowski 1992). What appears to be of importance to this line of work is not so much the individual 'motive' for communicating but the socially constructed meaning that is attached to the genre. As such, these researchers focus on the social context in which the genre is constructed, recognized and used, particularly when examining electronic communications (Yates et al. 1999).

Other researchers focus more directly on discourse analysis. Several of them have adopted a critical hermeneutic view that uses discourse analysis to examine technology implementation and use (Myers and Young 1997). For instance, Wynn and Novick (1996) examine the issue of 'turns' during cross-functional meetings. They find that what is considered a 'valid' contribution is based on discourse style. In particular, they found that listeners receive the story, as opposed to the professional style of discourse, differently. Other scholars such as Sayer and Harvey (1997) study implementation discourses. They examine how the use of an electronic mail system is used as a technology of power to manipulate discourses during a business process reengineering (BPR) project. Suchman and Bishop (2000) examine discourses of 'innovation' that function to conserve rather than change existing institutional orders.

More recently, a collection of writings examined organizational discourse about information technology (IT) (Wynn et al. 2002). While the contributions to the collection take a variety of approaches to discourse, some of the pieces that are more relevant to the way in which discourse has been discussed in this chapter include the work of Wilson (2002), who examines resistance by users in the context of a hospital. Wilson uses the social shaping of technology approach to examine discrepancies between 'legitimate' rhetoric and the actual use of the system. Kvasny and Trauth (2002) conducted a critical analysis of the responses from underrepresented groups to the dominant discourses about power and found that these groups had different responses for coping with the notion of IT as a vehicle of power. These researchers show a growing interest in the notion of critique via the examination of discursive exchanges. The following section outlines one approach for doing critical linguistic work in IS.

**Basic concepts for studying discourse**
Critical discourse analysis does not represent a unified theoretical frame, but rather it consists of several approaches based on the work of theorists such as Norman Fairclough, Ruth Wodak, Teun van Dijk, Malcolm Coulthard, Jonathan Potter, Linda Wood and Rolf Kroger. A comprehensive treatment of these authors' contributions to critical discourse analysis can be found in other reviews (see Fairclough 1992a; Wodak 1996). The following discusses some of the more important and commonly shared foundational concepts about language and how it is studied using critical discourse analysis. Specifically, this section argues for a shift in thinking about talk as action rather than as distinctly separate, and examines the function of talk and its role in producing identities and finally examines the content and form of talk.

Before enumerating and expanding on these concepts, it is important to define what is meant by the term 'discourse'. It has been used in various disciplines and has a variety of meanings within and between these fields. To examine the multiple definitions of discourse across these disciplines would take us too far afield. Instead, in this chapter, the definition of discourse is given as a specific form of language use (spoken or written) and a specific form of social interaction, both understood as a complete communicative event in a social situation (van Dijk 1990). As Potter (1997) suggests, discourse is text and talk in social practices. Therefore, the focus of analysis is not on language as an abstract entity such as a set of grammatical rules (as in linguistics) or a system of differences (as in structuralism) or a set of rules for transforming statements (as in Foucauldian genealogies) but on the actual medium of interaction, on what people do with language. Through talk, people create their social worlds. Therefore, talk is constitutive of social life; it does not reflect a pre-existing discourse or independent reality, but rather continuously creates the social world in which we live and work.

The first fundamental concept of discourse concerns how we think of talk. If we understand talk and utterances as not just being about things (that is, having meaning) but also as doing things, then, we can think of talk *as* action (Wood and Kroger 2000) carrying with it a performative quality. This is perhaps a very difficult move, given the privileged status afforded to action over talk. Familiar expressions such as 'talk is cheap' or 'actions speak louder than words' are part of our everyday discourse that perpetuates the distinction between talk and action while privileging the latter. The prevalence of these expressions requires a re-programming of researchers working with discourse to no longer think of talk as simply words but rather as something people do with words.

Another central concept of critical discourse analysis is examining the function of talk. Conceptualizing talk as going beyond meaning to include its function or 'force' has its foundations in speech act theory (Austin 1962). In this way, talk or utterances not only have meaning but they also have force, or accomplish things. Specifically, utterances are considered in terms of: (i) what they are about (locutionary); (ii) what the person speaking does with them (illocutionary); and (iii) the effect they have on the hearer (perlocutionary). In other words, to analyse discourse involves analysing the function that discourse serves and not just its content. Take, for example, the statement 'You hit your wife'. In this utterance, the speaker is describing an event (locutionary) but also accusing the listener (illocutionary) and angering or embarrassing the listener (perlocutionary). One could also say that through this discourse the identity of the listener is constructed as a violent or sexist man and the speaker as a person concerned about domestic violence and perhaps even a feminist. The performative quality of talk allows for identity, in this case a gendered identity, to emerge from discourse (Bucholtz 1999).

The emergence and performance of identity is especially true of the interview, a data-gathering tool used very frequently during IS development and also by IS researchers. Unlike sermons, political speeches or educational discussions, the interview as a discourse genre is one where the subject is expected to 'confess'. Confession is used here in the Foucauldian (1980, 1981, 1991) sense where the confessional is a power relationship which operates through avowal; the individual verbalizes intentions, troubles, desires and whatever transgressions that are otherwise difficult to tell. It is through this ritual that self-reflection, self-knowledge and self-examination about the speaking subject are obtained (Foucault 1991). Here the confessional act serves to construct the confessor's identity as a kind of speaking subject (that is, a 'criminal', 'deviant' or 'sinner'). Whether a gendered, transgressive, professional or some other type of identity is produced, all of these discursive constructions point to the performative function of talk. While not all interviews might require confession, the information requirements interview seems to demand this of interviewees. The confessional act during the interview does not take place alone; it does so in the presence of an 'authority who requires the confession, prescribes and appreciates it, and intervenes in order to judge' (Foucault 1981: 61). Clients confess their actions and possible transgressions with information (mis)use to the systems expert or a highly paid consultant. The information worker discloses information, thereby making finer and more intimate regions of worklife available for surveillance, judgement, evaluation and classification by these experts.

Content is another issue that critical discourse analysis addresses. While examining content is not central to critical discourse analysis, it is by no means ignored. Referential content tends to be the focus of the more conventional conversation analysis. To the extent that content focuses on the words and their referential aspects, critical discourse analysis examines how things get accomplished with those words (often referred to as 'style' or 'form') and not on the actual objects, events or persons that the words are referring to. It can be the case that a word may be semantically empty in that is has no referential meaning, but can function at another level. Take, for example, the utterance 'What are you good at?'. This utterance may have no relation to obtaining the qualities in which the listener excels, but rather might be a reprimand or threat to face or even an invitation to social interaction. Analysing the linguistic form of the utterance as a question versus a statement also has implications for content. The example above uttered as a statement might serve as a challenge to the recipient. Other verbal features such as the use of formal versus informal language accomplish very different functions in social interactions. In sum, the content of discourse should be examined at many different levels: lexical, pragmatic and social. And more importantly, content and form or style should be analysed together (Fairclough 1992b).

Finally, critical discourse analysis requires shifting our understanding of how we use talk. For researchers trained in the positivist tradition, the goal of most exploration and research is to obtain the 'truth' or what 'really' happened. Talk, in this instance, would then be viewed as the 'route' (Wood and Kroger 2000) to what really happened. Critical discourse analysis requires shifting the focus of interest so that we no longer view talk as a tool to explain behaviour but rather focus on talk as behaviour. This erases the distinction between thought and talk; they are one and the same and both are constituted discursively. This will pose a particularly difficult challenge to IS researchers who will have to divorce themselves from being concerned with what clients or interviewees 'really' think or mean or want. We no longer examine words in order to get at those nuggets inside heads; instead we are more interested in the phenomena that are constructed discursively by those words in their context (for example, discrimination, anger, abuse or control).

Using critical discourse analysis to study IS development and use can provide researchers with additional tools that assist them in producing better information systems. But additionally, and perhaps more importantly, given the nature of this volume, critical discourse analysis can be an opportunity for IS researchers to examine power relations by deconstructing language used, and how power is mobilized through language, thereby giving way to emancipatory possibilities. This is discussed further in the next section, which addresses critique and its role in studying discourse.

**The 'critique' in critical discourse analysis**
Thus far, I have laid out the concepts and guidelines for conducting discourse analysis as informed by the interpretive philosophical approach. That is, unlike positivist approaches which regard the social context as 'noise' and therefore a variable that must be controlled or somehow factored out (Harvey and Myers 1995), interpretive approaches focus on the social context and attempt to understand its discursive construction and the meanings assigned to it by people. But unlike the interpretive approach, critical discourse analysis carries with it an inherent 'critique' component. To be critical implies taking distance from the data (language), embedding the data in its context, taking an explicitly political stance and an attempt at self-reflection (Wodak and Meyer 2001). Volumes have been written on the history of 'critical' thought and theories and current debates within that field. The intent of this section is not to summarize these but rather identify the issues most relevant to critical discourse analysis that differentiate it from interpretivism and more specifically to identify issues relevant to IS researchers.

The notion of critically viewing language has its roots in the work of Karl Marx, post-structuralism and the Frankfurt school. For instance, under the framework of Marxist theory, Althusser (1971) and Gramsci (1971) have focused on the importance of ideology while Pecheux (1982) has identified discourse as the core linguistic form of ideology. In other realms, Foucault (1979) has highlighted the importance of technologies of power and their intertwined relationship with discourse. Habermas (1970, 1984) has focused on the notions of communicative action and the subordination of the 'lifeworld' by the purposive-rational action of the economy and state. He sees a privileging of 'strategic' language (that used to succeed and get people to do things) over 'communicative' language (that used for achieving understanding). The issues that surface from the work of these theorists and that have become a constant for those influenced by critical social theory and critical discourse analysis are those of ideology, power and emancipation.

The concept of ideology has been studied in a number of fields by many theorists (Althusser 1971; Williams 1977; Hall 1996). To elaborate the nuances of their agreements and contradictions in detail would go beyond the purpose of this chapter. The following presents a rudimentary sketch of ideology that is informed to some degree by the Frankfurt school and subsequent challenges to this school of thought. This summary will aid the reader in understanding the role of ideology when studying language.

Thompson (1990) suggests that ideology refers to social forms and processes within which, and by means of which, symbolic forms circulate in the social world. If one is to study ideology it would involve examining the ways in which meaning is constructed and conveyed by all types of symbolic forms, including spoken words, visual images and/or written texts. Ideology is seen as a means through which unequal power relations are established and maintained. The investigator's role is to determine whether the production and deployment of symbolic forms establish and/or sustain relations of domination. For the critical discourse analyst, certain uses of language and other symbolic forms are ideological, namely those that serve to establish or sustain relations of domination. Think of a simple example: the use of the word 'girl'. We do not usually hear people refer to male adults, say, in their mid- to late twenties, as 'boys'. But it is not uncommon to hear people refer to female adults in the same age bracket as 'girls'. There is a certain ideology of sexism embedded in this discursive practice that has become naturalized or what Gramsci would refer to as 'common sense'. This is when ideology is most effective, functioning to deceive and obscure people's interests and needs without their knowledge. The role of critical discourse analysis is to 'enlighten' and expose these delusions.

However, Volosinov (1973: 13) takes a stand that distances itself from seeing ideology as a fact of consciousness but instead sees words or utterances as 'the ideological phenomena par excellence'. Manifestations of ideology cannot be divorced from speech. To study ideology one must trace out the social life of the sign, which is produced through social interaction and class struggle. In other words, according to Volosinov, the word is 'mutable' or what is more commonly referred to as 'polysemic', implying that its meaning is not given in advance but is produced through concrete social practice and class struggle.

To be critical is to show connections and causes which are hidden, but also to provide the resources for intervention (Fairclough 1992a) and hence the groundwork for emancipation. The role of the critical researcher is to expose these hidden contradictions that are obscured through ideology, and therefore attempt to reframe and potentially enact a different kind of social order.

A number of theories have been proposed for achieving emancipation but perhaps the best known is Habermas's (1984) theory of communicative action. Habermas proposed the concept of a 'lifeworld' as a transcendental site where speaker and listener meet in mutual understanding. In this space, any semantic differences are negotiated and consensus is reached. In communicative actions, participants pursue their goals cooperatively on the basis of a shared definition of the world. In contrast, purposive-rational action is strategic. It is oriented towards rational opponents and follows decision rules to maximize individual interests. This action is means–ends oriented. A number of IS studies use a Habermasian framework (compare the above citations on critical social theory and the *Journal of Information Technology*, special issues 2002, Vol. 17, Nos 1 and 2). None, however, explicitly examines the discursive environment using critical discourse analysis.

Finally, power is a key component of the critical agenda and Foucault is perhaps the most influential in defining and understanding power. In a chapter of this length it is not possible to do justice to the richness of Foucault's thesis on power. The purpose here is to highlight some of the more important characteristics of his analysis of power. Foucault's notion of power is quite different from prevailing notions of oppressive power. Although he recognizes that power often works as a negative and oppressive force, his concern is with how it produces the knowable – objects, subjects, practices and, in general, daily social life. Power, according to Foucault, 'is exercised by virtue of things being known and people being seen' (1980: 154). He shows us that power and knowledge are different sides of the same 'social relations' coin. For example, if we think of how we are able to act upon or control any object, such as a car, we must first know its properties, characteristics and mechanics before we can act on it (that is, if we know, we can to some degree control). In other words, we must render its unknown parts knowable so that we can have power over it as an object. Knowledge of the object or subject invests us with a certain amount of information that structures our interactions with the object or subject of interest, and allows for our intervention (that is, management, government). As such, power is a relational activity; it is not a property external to someone or something, but rather a relationship or network of relationships that structures our interactions with the others. Thus, to understand how power works we must understand the techniques, practices and procedures that render people and objects knowable. Extending Foucault's notion of power, this chapter argues that linguistic forms can be seen as a technique that renders objects knowable and structures our unequal interactions with those objects. It is not that language contains power, or that power is derived from language, but rather language indexes power relations, expresses power relations, and can therefore be used to challenge, subvert or alter power relations.

**Towards a methodology for critical discourse analysis**
As I have already suggested, there is no single theory that informs critical discourse analysis. Likewise, there is no one method prescribed by critical discourse analysis for collecting and analysing data. Critical discourse analysis is in fact an 'approach' for understanding social phenomena and not a method or a series of rules that determine how one is to collect data. However, critical discourse analysis data collection is influenced by the hermeneutic tradition where lines between data collection and analysis are blurred. Similar to grounded theory, data collection is iterative, requiring analysis after every data collection exercise. One collects data, analyses, revises questions, expands or omits concepts, then collects more data and may begin the cycle again. However, the approach is 'modified' from standard grounded theory (Glaser and Strauss 1967; Turner 1981) in the sense that the research does bring certain theoretical orientations and perspectives to the data. One expects, for example, that power relations are negotiated and that certain forms of domination exist in particular social contexts that must be uncovered by the researcher.

While data collection and analysis may blur, critical discourse analysis relies on linguistic material and categories for analysis. A definitive list of linguistic devices relevant for critical discourse analysis cannot be given, partly because the nature of the research problem will determine the linguistic features that are of interest. Meyer (2001) presents a good summary of several preferred methods of theorists. The linguistic features most relevant for the author are based on those proposed by van Dijk (2001). These include stress and intonation, word order, lexical style, coherence, local semantic moves, topic choice, rhetorical figures, syntactic structures, false starts, turn taking, hesitations and repairs.

Interpretation and analytic strategies are again not prescribed in a unified sense for critical discourse analysis. There are recommendations for analysis mentioned by both van Dijk and Meyer, depending on the nature of the research question. In previous research, the author has used three analytical strategies: 'footings, facework and frames' (Alvarez 2001, 2002), 'narrative analysis' (Alvarez and Urla 2002) and 'tropes' (Alvarez 2004). These strategies for analysis are described below along with examples from research that has used these approaches for interpretation and analysis.

*Footings, facework and frames*
As speakers communicate verbally, they choose from a wide range of social attributes and roles that are made available to them and which they perceive as best fit to the situation. Erving Goffman (1981) uses the term 'footing' to refer to these social roles which define the relationship between speakers. At one moment the speaker may be a 'friend' concerned about the health

and well-being of an employee; at another the same speaker may be a 'peer' competing for control of resources. As we speak, we shift footing and move in and out of social roles, all of which assist us in establishing a relationship with others such that the meaning of the utterance is understood.

In addition to footings, the concept of 'face' and associated facework is a useful heuristic for understanding linguistic interactions. Goffman describes face as 'an image of self delineated in terms of approved social attributes – albeit an image that others may share' (1967: 5). The showing of face involves the person taking on verbal and non-verbal acts by which views about the situation and evaluation of others are expressed. Facework is necessary, because 'face is something that is emotionally invested, and that can be lost, maintained or enhanced and must be constantly attended to in interaction' (Brown and Levinson 1978: 61). Facework involves a complex array of resources, actions and strategies that are adopted to protect one's self-presentation. The management of face may take the form of verbal statements about roles and responsibilities, or be managed through prosodic and linguistic markers such as change in tone or hesitation.

And finally, 'framing' is defined as the speaker's instructions to the listener about what has been said and how to understand the utterance (Bateson 1972; Goffman 1974; Tannen and Wallat 1987). It provides a metamessage about the context (Tannen 1986). Through subtle signals like pitch, voice, intonation and facial expression, the contextual information is jointly created. Gumperz (1982) refers to these signals as 'contexualization cues' which may be prosodic, paralinguistic and non-verbal. These messages function to call up shared experiences. They are a powerful means of negotiating social identity and legitimating preferred styles of communicating in the predominantly asymmetrical interactions of workplace settings (Sarangi and Roberts 1999). The person proposing the frame during an interaction establishes how talk is to be understood in that context (Tannen 1986). Out-of-frame behaviour is usually resisted because it threatens the context and derails the main line of proposed activity.

How, then, might these concepts be used in IT research? Facework, framing and footing can be used to critically examine the discursive context of a requirements analysis process (Alvarez 2002). The research shows that a 'technologist' frame is dominant during the requirements analysis interviews. The technologist frame is one that provides the analyst with control and authority. This frame establishes and maintains asymmetrical power relations. Clients occasionally resist the technologist frame by proposing a 'personal' or lifeworld frame. While in the personal frame, the client regains control of the interview and creates a more socially relevant context.

In other research (Alvarez 2001), the decommissioning of a legacy system and the implementation of a new system are critically examined.

The findings show that removing a technology raises the possibility that something is 'wrong' and therefore participants try to manage this by valorizing the past, when the legacy system was at its prime, through deft facework and reframing. Clients discursively construct the legacy system as an effective technology, at least for its time, and concurrently construct their identity as seasoned and knowledgeable workers. Participants also confess to complex transgressive acts that subvert the legacy system but at the same time function to save face of speakers and get work done.

## Narrative analysis

Conversational narratives are 'stories' that are dynamically and often mutually produced. A story is an embedded and fragmented process in which gaps are filled in by the teller and the listener through cues offered. Cues are responded to by the speaker, thereby directly shaping the telling and meaning of the story. Recipients are able to immediately show how they have assessed the speaker's meaning but in so doing, also contribute to its shared creation and interpretation.

Theorists concerned with narratives have developed various definitions for describing their structure and function. Labov and associates (Labov 1972, 1982; Labov and Waletsky 1967) suggest that narratives are stories about specific past events. These stories follow a chronological sequence where the order of events moves in a linear way through time. From this perspective, a narrative is always responding to the question 'and then what happened?'. Reissman (1993) extends this definition by arguing that stories, with beginnings, protagonists and culminating events, are but one narrative form. Other genres include habitual narrative (repetitive event with no peak in action) and hypothetical narrative (events that did not happen).

Narratives are both a form of representing experience as well as a tool of persuasion. Commenting on their persuasive nature, Mumby (1987: 114) describes the narrative as a 'politically motivated production of a certain way of perceiving the world which privileges certain interests over others'. They are used to create believable explanations for the teller's actions. In an effort to convince the audience (of what? His or her point of view? Something else?), the teller may mix and juxtapose narrative genres (Reissman 1993). For instance, the story may be juxtaposed with a hypothetical narrative to distinguish 'what is' from 'what could have been'. In general, different genres, with distinctive styles, are modes of representation that are selected and invoked by tellers for different reasons and therefore vary in their power to persuade. According to Reissman, stories 'make us care about a situation to varying degrees as they pull us into the teller's point of view' (ibid.: 18).

In previous research that has used narrative analysis to critically examine requirements analysis process during an enterprise resource planning (ERP) implementation (Alvarez and Urla 2002), findings show that narratives provide knowledge about users' ways of working with information: how they collect what they need; how they categorize and process it; and how they deliver it to others. The plot structures identified in the study are those of 'deviant customers' with whom staff worked and a tendency to deflect blame towards the system for inefficient manual processes that were in place. Both the narrative of deviant subjects and deflecting blame are seen as indices of workers' attempts to negotiate the boundaries of their work responsibilities so as not to be perceived as blamable for inadequacies of their job performance. The teller of the stories attempts to persuade the listener as to the rationality of her/his actions under work conditions that are less than optimal. These stories serve as diagnostics of unequal power relations and how workers deal with such inequality.

### Tropes

Philosophers of language have long examined the role of tropes in vocabulary (Henle 1962; Alston 1964). According to these scholars, no vocabulary is without interstices or 'holes', and tropes, especially metaphors, function to seal these 'holes'. In this way, tropes function to counter what has been termed the 'designative inadequacy' (Weinreich 1964) of lexical systems. Tropes mitigate these lexical gaps because they introduce new meanings and thereby extend the semantic range of language as well as increase the speaker's expressive potential.

The concern with the relation among metaphor, metonymy, synecdoche and irony has given rise to the notion of the 'play of tropes' (Fernandez 1986) in anthropological studies. This notion implies a focus on the entirety of the tropes in dynamic relation as they interact with and are interpreted by social actors. Of the various tropes, those most often examined are metaphor, metonymy and synecdoche. However, metaphor has occupied a privileged position in the minds and writings of scholars. Independent of which trope is used, the purpose of examining these linguistic techniques is to understand what tropes 'do' in social interactions and not necessarily what they are in a formal analytic sense. In other words, through the examination of tropes we are able to explore human interaction.

Metaphor states an equivalence between terms taken from separate semantic domains (Sapir 1977). It consists of the employment of an attribute of a given semantic domain as a representation of an attribute of a different domain, on the basis of a perceived similarity between the two attributes (Turner 1992). Metaphor presents us with an A is B relation where A is the 'tenor' and B the 'vehicle'. The meaning that is generated by the interaction of the two is considered the 'ground'. For instance, in this metaphorical expression 'justice is blind', justice is the tenor, the thing that we want to know more about, and blind is the vehicle, the part that explains justice to us in terms of concrete and more familiar notions. The ground is the meaning produced by the combination of the two terms. In this interactional model, the ground produced by the two members of the metaphoric equation necessarily entails the creation of a new meaning, not simply the recognition of a pre-existing one (Richards 1950; Black 1962). In the metaphor 'justice is blind', we imbue both justice and blindness with a new meaning not reducible to that which each has in its original semantic domain.

Metaphor can be illustrated as shown in Figure 5.1, where T1 is the first term (the tenor), in this case, justice, C represents the common features and common ground and T2 the second term (the vehicle), in this case blind. We start with T1 and then move to T2 by way of a group of shared features.

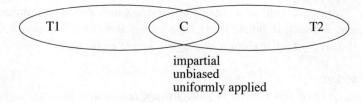

impartial
unbiased
uniformly applied

*Figure 5.1    Metaphor illustrated*

Metonymy is the use of an entity to refer to another that is related to it. It can be illustrated as shown in Figure 5.2. Metonymy replaces or juxtaposes contiguous terms that occupy a separate place within what is considered a common semantic domain. For instance, an adolescent may say 'I like Michael' (= she likes the music of Michael Jackson). In this case Michael (T1), the person, is juxtaposed to signify Michael Jackson's music (T2); T1 and T2 share a common domain but do not share common features.

And finally, similar to metonymy, synecdoche draws both its terms from a common domain but one term is included as a 'part for the whole'. For instance, in the synecdoche 'all hands on deck', hands (part) signifies the entire body or person (whole). Synecdoche can be illustrated as shown in Figure 5.3. Here, hands (T1) are indexical of the whole person (T2) but both are part of a common domain.

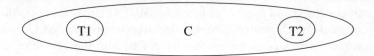

*Figure 5.2    Metonymy illustrated*

*Figure 5.3    Synecdoche illustrated*

In general, the use of tropes is not simply a game of substitution but rather a creative exercise where the interplay of two disparate terms provides insights that may reveal important and deep understandings not otherwise available. The use of these devices in discourse serves to organize interactions and construct the social world. Current research by the author (Alvarez 2004), for example, examines the play of tropes during technical support calls. Tropes are used as a lens to understand how the 'communication problem' between technical support specialist and client is manifest, and how lexical gaps are overcome during discursive exchanges.

**Conclusion**

The purpose of this chapter is to encourage researchers to continue in an emerging linguistic vein by offering critical discourse analysis as a framework for studying information systems. Specifically, this chapter offers the tools for examining the semiotic products that are exchanged during IS design, implementation and use. The framework offered here assumes that IS are not mere tools and technique, but rather they are social artefacts that are in part constructed and shaped by language. Critical discourse analysis provides one avenue for making transparent the political and contested nature of IS development and use by critically examining language.

But how might critical language analysis bring with it a change in unequal power relations? In other words, will changing language change detrimental working conditions for workers? The social forms that contribute to unequal and exploitative conditions are produced by people and can be changed by people rather than being seen as though they are part of nature. Critical theorization about language can illuminate these conditions and 'denaturalize' them, thereby opening them up for change, but also show what unrealized alternative directions exist – how certain aspects can enhance the human condition and others can be detrimental. Often, these normalized ways of speaking achieve a certain naturalness that is not contested. Unveiling how certain discourse achieves this hegemony and thereby achieves a misperception of arbitrariness can show how it comes to be seen as reflecting certain (economic) realities rather than constructing them.

Exposing these misperceptions may not have a direct impact on the individual who sits at the computer carrying out daily tasks. The relationship is slightly more distant and complex. The critical analysis of discourse can bring into democratic control aspects of the social use of language that are currently outside the democratic control of people. Critical discourse analysis advocates a critical awareness of the centrality of language in creating a democratic society, because language is so central to the negotiations and struggles over power and material resources. One cannot fully grasp one's social circumstances without a critical awareness of how language figures within them. Critical discourse analysis is a tool to assist both the researcher in the academic institution as well as the worker in the organization in achieving this end.

## References

Agarwal, R. and Tanniru, M.R. (1990), 'Knowledge acquisition using structured interviewing: an empirical investigation', *Journal of Management Information Systems*, **7** (1), 123–40.

Alston, W.P. (1964), *Philosophy of Language*, Englewood Cliffs, NJ: Prentice-Hall.

Althusser, L. (1971), 'Ideology and ideological state apparatuses', in L. Althusser (ed.), *Lenin and Philosophy and Other Essays*, London: New Left Books, 127–86.

Alvarez, R. (2001), '"It was a great system": face-work and the discursive construction of technology during information systems development', *Information, Technology and People*, **14** (4), 385–405.

Alvarez, R. (2002), 'Confessions of an information worker: a critical analysis of information requirements' discourse', *Information and Organization*, **12**, 85–107.

Alvarez, R. (2004), 'The play of tropes in the discourse of knowledge workers: examining technical support services', *Proceedings of the American Conference on Information Systems*, New York: Association for Information Systems, August, pp. 67–79.

Alvarez, R. and Urla, J. (2002), 'Tell me a good story: using narrative analysis to examine information requirements, interviews during an ERP implementation', *Database*, **33** (1), 38–51.

Austin, J. (1962), *How to Do Things with Words*, Oxford: Clarendon.

Avison, D., Baskerville, R. and Myers, M. (2001), 'Controlling action research projects. Information', *Technology and People*, **14** (1), 28–45.

Bateson, G. (1972), *Steps to an Ecology of the Mind*, New York: Ballantine.

Black, M. (1962), *Models and Metaphors*, Ithaca, NY: Cornell University Press.

Bloomfield, B.P., Coombs, R., Cooper, D.J. and Rea, D. (1992), 'Machines and manoeuvres: responsibility accounting and the construction of hospital information systems', *Accounting, Management and Information Technologies*, **2** (4), 197–219.

Brown, P. and Levinson, S.C. (1978), *Politeness: Some Universals in Language Usage*, Cambridge: Cambridge University Press.

Bucholtz, M. (1999), 'Transgression and progress in language and gender studies', in M. Bucholtz, A.C. Liang and L.A. Sutton *Reinventing Identities: The Gendered Self in Discourse*, New York: Oxford University Press, pp. 3–26.

Clarke, R.J. (2001), 'Organizational semiosis: integration and separation between system features and workpractices', *Australian Journal of Information Systems*, **8** (2) 103–14.

Fairclough, N. (1992a), *Discourse and Social Change*, Cambridge: Polity.

Fairclough, N. (1992b), 'Discourse and text: linguistic and intertextual analysis within discourse analysis', *Discourse and Society*, **3**, 193–217.

Fernandez, J.W. (1986), *Persuasion and Performances: The Play of Tropes in Culture*, Bloomington, IN: Indiana University Press.

Flores, F., Graves, M., Hartfield, B. and Winograd, T. (1988), 'Computer systems and the design of organizational interaction', Association for Computing Machinery (ACM), *Transactions on Office Information Systems*, **6** (2), 153–72.

Foucault, M. (1979), *Discipline and Punish: The Birth of the Prison*, Harmondsworth: Penguin.

Foucault, M. (1980), *Power/Knowledge: Selected Interviews and Other Writings 1972–1977*, ed. C. Gordon, New York: Pantheon.

Foucault, M. (1981), *The History of Sexuality*, vol. 1, London: Penguin.

Foucault, M. (1991), 'Politics and the study of discourse: questions of method and governmentality', in G. Burchell, C. Gordon and P. Miller (eds), *The Foucault Effect: Studies in Governmentality*, Chicago: University of Chicago Press, pp. 53–72.

Glaser, B.G. and Strauss, A. (1967), *The Discovery of Grounded Theory: Strategies for Qualitative Research*, New York: Aldine.

Goffman, E. (1967), *Interaction Ritual: Essays on Face-to-face Behavior*, Garden City, NY: Doubleday Anchor.

Goffman, E. (1974), *Frame Analysis*, New York: Harper & Row.

Goffman, E. (1981), *Forms of Talk*, Philadelphia, PA: University of Pennsylvania Press.

Gramsci, A. (1971), *Selections from the Prison Notebooks*, ed. and trans. Q. Horar and G. Nowell Smith, London: Lawrence & Wishart.

Gumperz, J.J. (1982), *Discourse Strategies*, Cambridge: Cambridge University Press.

Habermas, J. (1970), *Toward a Rational Society*, Boston, MA: Beacon.

Habermas, J. (1984), *The Theory of Communicative Action*, vols 1 & 2, Boston, MA: Beacon.

Hall, S. (1996), 'The problem of ideology: Marxism without guarantees', in D. Morley and H. Chen (eds), *Stuart Hall: Critical Dialogues in Cultural Studies*, London: Routledge, pp. 25–46.

Harvey L. and Myers, M.D. (1995), 'Scholarship and practice: the contribution of ethnographic research methods to bridging the gap', *Information, Technology and People*, **8** (3), 18–27.

Henle, P. (ed.) (1962), *Language, Thought and Culture*, Ann Arbor, MI: University of Michigan Press.

Hirschheim, R. and Klein, H.K. (1989), 'Four paradigms of information systems development', *Communications of the ACM*, **32** (10), 1199–216.

Hirschheim, R. and Klein, H.K. (1994), 'Realizing emancipatory principles in information systems development: the case for ETHICS', *MIS Quarterly*, **18** (1), 83–109.

Iivari, J., Hirschheim, R. and Klein, H.K. (1998), 'A paradigmatic analysis contrasting information systems development approaches and methodologies', *Information Systems Research*, **9** (2), 164–93.

Klein, H.K. and Truex, D. (1996), 'Discourse analysis: a semiotic approach to the investigation of organizational emergence', in P.B. Andersen, B. Holmquist and H. Klein (eds), *Signs of Work: Semiosis and Information Processing in Organisations*, Berlin: Walter De Gruyter, pp. 227–68.

Kock, N. and Lau, F. (2001), 'Information systems action research: serving two demanding masters', *Information, Technology and People*, **14** (1), 1–11.

Kvasny, L. and Trauth, E.M. (2002), 'The digital divide and work and home: the discourse about power and underrepresented groups in the information society', in Wynn et al. (eds), pp. 249–72.

Labov, W. (1972), *Language in the Inner City: Studies in the Black English Vernacular*, Philadelphia, PA: University of Pennsylvania Press.

Labov, W. (1982), 'Speech actions and reactions in personal narrative', in D. Tannen (ed.), *Analyzing Discourse: Text and Talk*, Washington, DC: Georgetown University Press, pp. 217–47.

Labov, W. and Waletzy, J. (1967), 'Narrative analysis: oral version of personal experience', in J. Helm (ed.), *Essays and the Visual Arts*, Seattle, WA: University of Washington Press, pp. 12–44.

Latour, B. (1996), 'Social theory and the study of computerized work sites', in W.J. Orlikowski, G. Walsham, M.R. Jones and J.I. DeGross (eds), *Information Technology and Changes in Organizational Work*, London: Chapman & Hall, pp. 295–307.

Lehitinen, E. and Lyytinen, K. (1994), 'Action based model of information system', *Information Systems*, **11** (4), 299–317.

Lyytinen, K. (1992), 'Information systems and critical theory', in M. Alvessson and H. Willmott (eds), *Critical Management Studies*, London: Sage, pp. 159–80.

Meyer, M. (2001), 'Between theory, method and politics: positioning the approaches to CDA', in Wodak and Meyer, pp. 14–31.

Mumby, D.K. (1987), 'The political functions of narrative in organizations', *Communication Monographs*, **54**, 113–27.

Mumford, E., Hirschheim, R., Fitzgerald, G. and Wood-Harper, T. (1985), *Research Methods in Information Systems*, Amsterdam: North-Holland.

Myers, M.D. and Young, L.W. (1997), 'Hidden agendas, power and managerial assumptions in information systems development', *Information Technology and People*, **10** (3), 224–40.

Ngwenyama, O.K. (1991), 'The critical social theory approach to information systems: problems and challenges', in H.E. Nissen, H.K. Klein and R. Hirschheim (eds), *Information Systems Research: Contemporary Approaches and Emergent Traditions*, Amsterdam: North-Holland, pp. 267–80.

Orlikowski, W. (1992), 'The duality of technology: rethinking the concept of technology in organizations', *Organization Science*, **3** (3), 398–427.

Orlikowski, W.J. and Baroudi, J.J. (1991), 'Studying information technology in organizations: research approaches and assumptions', *Information Systems Research*, **2** (1), March, 1–28.

Orlikowski, W. and Robey, D. (1991), 'Information technology and the structuring of organizations', *Information Systems Research*, **2** (2), 143–69.

Päivärinta, T. (2001), 'The concept of genre within the critical approach to information systems development', *Information and Organization*, **11**, 207–34.

Pecheux, M. (1982), *Language, Semantics and Ideology*, London: Macmillan.

Potter, J. (1997), 'Discourse analysis as a way of analyzing naturally occurring talk', in D. Silverman (ed.), *Qualitative Research: Theory, Method and Practice*, London: Sage, pp. 144–60.

Putnam, L.L. (1983), 'The interpretive perspective: an alternative to functionalism', in L.L. Putnam and M.E. Pacanowsky (eds), *Communication in Organizations: An Interpretive Approach*, Beverly Hills, CA: Sage, pp. 31–54.

Reissman, C.K. (1993), *Narrative Analysis*, Newbury Park, CA: Sage.

Richards, I.A. (1950), *The Philosophy of Rhetoric*, New York: Oxford University Press.

Sapir, J.D. (1977), 'The anatomy of metaphor', in J.D. Sapir and J.C. Crocker (eds), *The Social Use of Metaphor: Essays on the Anthropology of Rhetoric*, Philadelphia, PA: University of Pennsylvania Press, pp. 3–32.

Sarangi, S. and Roberts, C. (1999), 'The dynamics of interactional and institutional orders in work-related settings', in Sarangi and Roberts, *Talk, Work and Institutional Order: Discourse in Medical, Mediation and Management Settings*, Berlin: Mouton de Gruyter, pp. 1–60.

Sayer, K. and Harvey, L. (1997), 'Empowerment in business process reengineering: an ethnographic study of implementation discourses', in K. Kumar and J. DeGross (eds), *Proceedings of the Eighteenth International Conference on Information Systems (ICIS)*, Atlanta, GA: Association for Information Systems, pp. 427–40.

Suchman, L. and Bishop, L. (2000), 'Problematizing "innovation" as a critical project', *Technology Analysis and Strategic Management*, **12** (3), 327–33.

Tannen, D. (1986), *That's Not What I Meant!*, New York: William Morrow.

Tannen, D. and Wallat, C. (1987), 'Interactive frames and knowledge schemas in interaction: examples from a medical examination/review', *Social Psychological Quarterly*, **50** (2) 205–16.

Thompson, J.B. (1990), *Ideology and Modern Culture*, Cambridge: Polity.

Turner, B. (1981), 'Some practical aspects of qualitative data analysis: one way of organizing the cognitive processes with the generation of grounded theory', *Quality and Quantity*, **15**, 225–47.

Turner, T. (1992), '"We are parrots", "twins are birds": play of tropes as operational structure', in J.W. Fernandez (ed.), *Beyond Metaphor: The Theory of Tropes on Anthropology*, Stanford, CA: Stanford University Press, pp. 121–58.

Van Dijk, T.A. (1990), 'Social cognition and discourse', in H. Giles and W.P. Robinson (eds), *Handbook of Language and Social Psychology*, New York: John Wiley & Sons, pp. 163–86.

Van Dijk, T.A. (2001), 'Multidisciplinary CDA: a plea for diversity', in Wodak and Meyer (eds), pp. 95–120.

Volosinov, V.N. (1973), *Marxism and the Philosophy of Language* (trans. L. Matejka and I.R. Titunik), Cambridge, MA and London: Harvard University Press.

Weinreich, U. (1964), *Languages in Contact: Findings and Problems*, The Hague: Mouton.

Williams, R. (1977), 'Ideology', in *Marxism and Literature*, Oxford: Oxford University Press, pp. 55–71.

Wilson M. (2002), 'Rhetoric of enrollment and acts of resistance: information technology as text', in Wynn et al. (eds), pp. 225–48.

Winograd, T. and Flores, F. (1986), *Understanding Computers and Cognition: A New Foundation for Design*, Norwood, NJ: Albex.

Wodak, R. (1996), *Disorders of Discourse*, London: Longman.

Wodak, R. and Meyer, M. (2001), *Methods of Critical Discourse Analysis*, London: Sage.

Wood, L.A. and Kroger, R.O. (2000), *Doing Discourse Analysis*, Thousand Oaks, CA: Sage.

Wynn, E.H., Whitley, E.A., Myers, M.D. and DeGross, J.I. (2002), *Global and Organizational Discourse about Information Technology*, Boston, MA: Kluwer Academic.

Wynn, E. and Novick, D. (1996), 'Relevance conventions and problem boundaries in a work redesign team', *Information Technology and People*, **9** (2), 61–80.

Yates, J. and Orlikowski, W. (1992), 'Genres of organizational communication: a structuration approach to studying communication and media', *Academy of Management Review*, **17** (2), 299–326.

Yates, J., Orlikowski, W. and Okamura, K. (1999), 'Explicit and implicit structuring of genres in electronic communication: reinforcement and change of social interaction', *Organization Science*, **10** (1), 83–103.

# 6 Against rules: the ethical turn in information systems

*Alison Adam*

## Introduction

This chapter offers a discussion of an important issue relating to the separation of information systems (IS) and information or computer ethics, namely the implications for the development of the nascent discipline of critical IS and the question of whether it is possible to develop a critical IS ethics to bridge the gap between IS and computer ethics. In this discussion, the argument against rule-focused ethics, and their encapsulation in professional codes of ethics, is paramount in developing a more situated, phenomenological approach towards ethics for critical IS.

Both information systems and computer ethics are young disciplines which address the social and ethical contexts of IS, information and communication technologies. Given such a large overlap of interest it is perhaps surprising that the two disciplines have grown up quite so separately. Walsham (1996) notes that while papers in IS journals often mention ethical issues, they rarely focus on such topics in terms of explicit ethical concepts and systems of ethics, nor do they tend to cite computer ethics research overtly, although there are some attempts to integrate ethical reasoning into systems methodologies. Similarly, computer ethics research does not often cite mainstream IS research. Some of the reasons for this split may reside in the way that computer ethics arose separately from IS, where the former has more links to philosophy, the latter to management and organizational studies.

Whatever the reasons, a number of implications follow from this apparent separation. Importantly, it is difficult to see how ethical practice can be fruitfully integrated into IS development, either in education or in the workplace unless the two disciplines can be woven together more effectively. The need for integration of the two disciplines manifests itself in different ways. For instance, witness how problematic IS failure is regarded when such a high proportion of IS projects fail (Sauer 1993). IS failure is almost never seen as an ethical problem. Instead, the focus often rests on human failing, reluctance of users and so on.

Were we to consider ethical aspects of IS failure we could then bring to the fore issues, for instance, such as the ways that users may be pushed into using systems and why they resist (Howcroft and Wilson 2002). Other places where IS and computer ethics might fruitfully come together, although rarely recognized to date, include research on the ways in which vendors of software packages may sell customers functionality they do not require (Light and Adam 2004) and the difficulties of teaching ethics to IS students in ways which they can then apply in professional practice (Bell and Adam 2004).

However, the focus of the current chapter is on the related issue of how ethics may be more effectively integrated into the critical wing of IS. There are a number of implications of this split which have yet to be addressed, in detail, in critical IS. In its attempt to offer a more rational discourse, and the alleviation of technocratic oppression through the possibility of emancipation, critical IS clearly covers a number of interests which have also been studied within the discipline of computer ethics. Nevertheless, such discussions have not significantly overlapped, to date.

On the surface, critical IS would seem to have much better ethical credentials than mainstream IS, given its connection to the work of Jürgen Habermas and his communicative ethics. Indeed, it is possible that the development of critical IS could help bridge the gap between IS and ethics, yet its trajectory has also remained largely separate from that of computer ethics. The question is, then, whether it is feasible to develop a new strand of computer ethics from the critical wing of IS and, although not explored in this chapter, whether such a 'critical IS ethics' would offer new opportunities for the perennial difficulty of integrating ethical practice into IS practice. Critical IS carries its ethical credentials implicitly. It emphasizes theory and critique, rather than practice, but so far there are no critical IS methodologies, if indeed that is what we want. This suggests that there is considerable scope for research in this area.

**The rise of computer ethics: codes of conduct as social contract**
The rise of computer ethics, as a discipline, involves the intersection of several vectors – philosophy, social studies of technology, information systems, organizational studies and, more particularly, professional codes of conduct. Importantly, the emphasis on professional codes can be seen as part of the professionalization strategy of the emerging computing/ information technology (IT) profession (Adam 2001). The notion of a 'social contract' is important here. As citizens, we subscribe to a social contract, an agreement to act in particular ways towards each other and with regard to the instruments and institutions of the state. This takes place at a tacit level, where we behave in ways that keep the wheels of society in motion, but also at a more formal level, where we act according to the rules of society, and more expressly, forms of legislation, or expect to face

the consequences. The problem with most social contract theories is that they imply an original 'state of nature', where no social contract exists and possibly no morality, such that rational beings would naturally want to enter into a social contract to provide justice and morality. Rawls (1971) extended such ideas to argue that justice will not spontaneously emerge from a social contract, as individuals are naturally self-interested and so will want rules that favour themselves. Therefore we have to stand back from what individuals might argue for; we cannot expect them to be other than biased and we must propose some general principles of justice, which will ensure fairness to all. One problem with such a view is that, in most forms, it implies a raw, savage nature as a natural state, where there are no social laws, and also seems to suggest that individuals will act selfishly even when laws are made. Justice and rights then have to be imposed on society. Such views, if extended to professional life, imply that we cannot expect professionals to behave in an altruistic way towards others. Therefore they must be regulated, not only to ensure that everyone is treated justly, but also to ensure that everyone's rights are respected.

Following this, it can be argued that the social contract takes on additional burdens when applied to professions, beyond those expected of the individual members of society. A profession has particular duties towards its users and a wider public, not only to do them no harm but also, more positively, to act in their interests according to the dictates of the profession. For instance, the medical profession subscribes to a rigorous code of ethics, and thereby enters into a social contract with its public that it will act in a proper manner towards its patients in return for recognition of the right to practise medicine. The computing industry, in subscribing to codes of ethics, attempts to enter into a similar social contract. However the journey of the emerging IT/IS profession towards professional status is just as rocky as that of the medical profession in the eighteenth and nineteenth centuries. Indeed, it can be argued, that the IT/IS profession hardly matches any of the traditional indicators of professional status, for example, standard education, professional autonomy or regulatory body.

Computing codes of conduct and practice, as an explicit representation of the justice and rights encapsulated in the social contract, have several goals: to capture the essence of the profession's commitments and responsibilities, as a basis for ethical decision making; and to convince the public that the profession is capable of self-regulation (Laudon 1995; Walsham 1996). This can be characterized as a contract between a profession and society: accountability of the profession and its members is given in return for the trust, confidence and respect of the public (and the accompanying increased social and economic rewards) (Mason et al. 1995). Early versions of the codes of bodies, such as the Association for Computing Machinery

(ACM), tended to be regulatory, but in the 1990s these codes become more normative in nature, possibly indicative of a profession growing in maturity. Gotterbarn (1997) sees normative codes as reflecting some sort of consensus of the traditions of a particular profession. It is possible to read the change in emphasis of these codes in Rawlsian terms where the earlier version reflected more of a 'state of nature' within the IS profession where rules had to be regulatory, explicitly spelling out which actions were or were not permitted to members of the profession. In a more mature society, or here a more mature professional context, justice and rights have become accepted into the profession's ethos, reflected in more normative codes.

To some extent, the ethical code formalizes the social contract between profession and public, yet much of the social contract is tacit, not written down and not strictly enforceable. This is especially the case in the computing/IT/IS profession where most practitioners practise perfectly well without reference to professional membership and one need not be licensed in order to practise. This reinforces Gotterbarn's point. It is not so much that the code of ethics strictly lays down rules for the profession to follow, rather that they reflect the maturity of the social contract into which the profession has developed.

This serves to emphasize that although codes can help rule out unacceptable decisions, they are not prescriptions for action, and they do not explicitly spell out a set of rights. Much of the reason for this is because, especially in later form, ethical codes tend to display the 'open texturedness' we expect from a good rule, where all the states to which the rule applies are not written down in advance (they cannot be); rather the rule is subject to interpretation in each new case. In effect, the meaning of the rule is made, through interpretation, in subsequent cases. Open texturedness is accepted by the legal profession as not only inevitable but also desirable (Twining and Miers 1991). However, other than in Gotterbarn's (1997) analysis, the notion that open texturedeness might be desirable in ethical codes is largely absent from attempts to formalize ethical decision making in IS.

For instance, the above discussion casts doubts on the practical usefulness of the relatively few ethical methodologies which have been suggested for IS practice, for instance, Mason et al.'s (1995) 'supersession', where the highest-order ethical rule takes precedence in ethical decision making. This methodology rests on both the power of the code of ethics to help achieve a decision and also a view that rationalist goal-centred approaches are the essence of ethical decision making. Additionally, there is the whole question of the ineffectiveness of professional codes in an industry which is largely unregulated. Rationalistic ethical methodologies place too much reliance on formal processes of rational decision making, which ignores the question of how far moral activity is directed into activities other than decisions; in other words, into the more tacit, less explicit areas of the social contract, the things we do to keep the wheels of society turning.

**Adding 'critical' to critical information systems ethics**
In the discussion above, a number of concerns over the implications which derive from the separation of IS and information ethics, have been expressed. There are a number of problems with approaches which attempt to integrate ethical analysis more explicitly into systems methodologies as, inevitably, given that ethics is attached to well-established system development methodologies, the ethical considerations can look as if they are 'bolted on'.

The seeming intransigence of this problem is at least part of the reason for turning to critical IS to consider how far the apparently more ethically inspired critical wing of IS may provide a model for an ethically integrated IS which could also provide pointers towards an alternative model for integrating ethics into IS education and practice.

There are (at least) two, clearly related, ways that critical IS ethics can be conceived. On the one hand we may start with the notion of critical ethics and think of how this may be applied to critical IS. On the other hand we may start with critical IS and expand its ethical dimension. Starting with critical ethics is problematic in itself since there are at least two meanings to the term. 'Critical ethics' is used in mainstream philosophy as an alternative term for meta ethics – in other words the way that one may justify having ethical beliefs, what ethics means and so on; in other words, reasoning about ethics rather than doing ethics. This can be juxtaposed with normative ethics which has as its subject matter the business of how we ought to behave in given circumstances. Interesting and important though it may be to reflect upon the whole business of doing ethics, this is not the job we particularly require of a critical IS ethics. Nevertheless, as described below, it is possible to retain this meaning while accommodating a deeper meaning of the term 'critical'.

More pertinently, the term 'critical ethics' has also been used by theorists addressing the 'turn to ethics' in the humanities and social sciences, particularly in the wake of postmodernism, with some, but not all of the interest, generated via critical theory (Rainsford and Woods 1999). Part of this project sets up critical ethics as a critique of the traditional ethics of deontology, consequentialism and so on; in other words, a critique of the legitimacy of the project of ethical theory itself (Critchley 1999).

This last point is one of the most useful aspects of critical ethics which could potentially inform critical IS ethics. How may we criticize the project of ethics, yet retain it and integrate it more effectively into IS? Robinson (1999) has developed the concept of critical ethics in ways which reflect the latter meaning, that is, the critique of traditional ethics, to the critical theory of Habermas. Although Robinson's project is the relationship of international relations to the feminist ethics of care, there may well be important lessons for the integration of ethics into critical IS:

> A critical ethics of care does not seek to arrive at an account of moral philosophy which presents a justification for action dependent on the application of principles and rules, rather it is ... a phenomenology which starts from the ways in which we experience our ethical lives: as 'human beings connected in various ways ... responding to each other by engaging together in a search for shareable interpretations of their responsibilities'. (Robinson 1999: 39–40, quoting Walker 1998: 114)

In constructing a critical ethics, Robinson is explicitly arguing against principles and rules and arguing for a phenomenology of morality where moral behaviour is embedded in everyday life. This suggests that looking towards the application of rules as the focus of moral life, for example, as in codes of ethics, does not capture the important activities to be encapsulated in a critical IS ethics.

According to Robinson, a critical ethics of care must not preserve existing power relations but must critically examine how existing structures of social and personal relations lead to marginalization or break down to cause suffering: 'This kind of moral thinking encourages us to see such problems not only as moral but also as social and political' (Robinson 1999: 40). Thus the exposure of the structures of oppression are crucial to Robinson's politicized critical ethics of care. When it comes to the issue of voices being heard, we would need to attend to the structures which permit or deny others the ability to be heard. These issues clearly relate to Habermas's communicative ethics, and Benhabib (1992) has explicitly sought to connect Habermas's theory with a critical ethics of care. Although she believes that Habermas provides us with ways of getting to universal norms, she contends that his theories are too abstract and formalized, and too much inspired by Immanuel Kant with concomitant emphasis on rights, individual moral agents and universalizable moral laws.

If we look to critical IS itself, to think about ways in which its ethical dimensions may be better characterized and to make a preliminary exploration of how this may or may not inform IS practice, we may see how some of the arguments above can apply. To date, the major influence on critical IS has been the work of Habermas and the communicative ethics of his critical social theory (Hirschheim and Klein 1995). Given its strong ethical foundations, it is surprising that critical IS does not seem to make much of its ethical credentials. Nevertheless, the focus on emancipation can clearly be cast as an ethical issue.

Commentators (Waring 2000) have noted that Habermas's theories are notoriously difficult to apply in the world of IS. Some of this may mirror Benhabib's (1992) point that Habermas is too abstract to be immediately applicable. But there is also the question of exposing and dealing with power structures. The concept of communicative rationality, where all have a right to speak, ignores the structures of power and oppression, where individuals may or may not be able to speak, as both Benhabib and Robinson (1999) note. The political nature of organizations within which information systems must be implemented is well recognized by contemporary IS researchers, but it is as if critical IS needs to take this on board more substantially. In doing this, a critical IS ethics would extend the communicative ethics of Habermas, along the lines suggested by Benhabib, to include a critical ethics of care which acknowledges the powerful and the powerless.

How might such issues be helpful in weaving ethics into IS practice? The vector of much teaching on information or computer ethics is Kantian in inspiration. Similarly, despite its critical credentials, critical IS appears to be broadly Kantian in nature. For all its emphasis on rights, deontological theory is individualistic in approach and takes little account of the wider culture in which ethical behaviour takes place. A potential way forward lies in further concentration on empirical rather than theoretical studies of critical IS, such as that of Waring (2000), and, crucially, more empirical IS studies which specifically attend to ethical issues set in a wider culture. These would provide a bank of case studies with which to teach critical IS with a more explicit ethical dimension. Given that critical IS is much more concerned, from the outset, with communication and emancipation, this would seem to be a much more appropriate place to look for means to integrate computer ethics with IS teaching than normative approaches towards systems design, even those, such as Rogerson et al. (2000) or Wood-Harper et al. (1996), which combine elements of ethical analysis into traditional systems methodologies.

**Conclusion**

This chapter engages with a number of issues relating to the connection, or lack of connection between IS and computer or information ethics. Integration of ethics into IS education and practice remains problematic, partly because ethics is usually taught as a separate subject, partly because computer ethics follows traditional Kantian ethics in emphasizing the ethical decision making of supposedly individual moral agents. The relatively few attempts to integrate ethical analysis into systems development methodologies appear to be at an early stage of development and have not spawned a research tradition. Given the emphasis on emancipation and communicative rationality within critical IS, further empirical work in this field would provide more appropriate case studies of integration of ethics into IS, especially critical IS, particularly where these can be integrated into political and social contexts as suggested by Benhabib (1992). This would serve to feed back into work on computer ethics, ideally to de-emphasize rule-based decision making in ethics and to further stress the phenomenological, embedded nature of moral behaviour in IS.

## References

Adam, A. (2001), 'Computer ethics in a different voice', *Information and Organization*, **11**, 235–61.

Bell, F. and Adam, A. (2004), 'Whatever happened to information systems ethics? Caught between the devil and the deep blue sea', in B. Kaplan, D.P. Truex, D. Wastell and A.T. Wood-Harper (eds), *Information Systems Research: Relevant Theory and Informed Practice*, Boston, MA: Kluwer, pp. 159–74.

Benhabib, S. (1992), *Situating the Self: Gender, Community and Postmodernism in Contemporary Ethics*, Cambridge: Polity.

Critchley, S. (1999), 'The original traumatism: Levinas and psychoanalysis', in Rainsford and Woods (eds), pp. 88–104.

Gotterbarn, D. (1997), 'Software engineering: a new professionalism', in C. Myers, T. Hall and D. Pitt (eds), *The Responsible Software Engineer: Selected Readings in IT Professionalism*, London: Springer-Verlag, pp. 21–31.

Hirschheim, R. and Klein, H.K. (1995), *Information System Development and Data Modelling: Conceptual and Philosophical Foundations*, Cambridge: Cambridge University Press.

Howcroft, D. and Wilson, M. (2002), 'Re-conceptualising failure: social shaping meets IS research', *European Journal of Information Systems*, **11**, 236–50.

Laudon, K.C. (1995), 'Ethical concepts and information technology', *Communications of the ACM*, **38**, 33–9.

Light, B. and Adam, A. (2004), 'Selling packaged software: an ethical analysis', Paper presented at European Conference on Information Systems, Turku, Finland, June.

Mason, R.O., Mason, F.M. and Culnan, M.J. (1995), *Ethics of Information Management*, Newbury Park, CA: Sage.

Rainsford, D. and Woods, T. (eds) (1999), *Critical Ethics: Text, Theory and Responsibility*, Basingstoke: Macmillan.

Rawls, J.A. (1971), *A Theory of Justice*, Cambridge, MA: Harvard University Press.

Robinson, F. (1999), *Globalizing Care: Ethics, Feminist Theory, and International Relations*, Boulder, CO: Westview Press.

Rogerson, S., Weckert, J. and Simpson, C. (2000), 'An ethical review of information systems development', *Information Technology and People*, **13**, 121–36.

Sauer, C. (1993), *Why Information Systems Fail: A Case Study Approach*, Henley-on-Thames: Alfred Waller.

Twining, W. and Miers, D. (1991), *How to Do Things with Rules: A Primer of Interpretation*, 3rd edn, London: Butterworth.

Walker, M.U. (1998), *Moral Understandings: A Feminist Study in Ethics*, New York and London: Routledge.

Walsham, G. (1996), 'Ethical theory, codes of ethics and IS practice', *Information Systems Journal*, **6**, 69–81.

Waring, T.S. (2000), 'The systems analyst and emancipatory practice: an exploratory study in three NHS hospitals', Unpublished PhD thesis, University of Northumbria at Newcastle.

Wood-Harper, A.T., Corder, S., Wood, J.R.G. and Watson, H. (1996), 'How we profess: the ethical systems analyst', *Communications of the ACM*, **39**, 69.

# 7    Management fashions and information systems

*Chris Westrup*

## Introduction

Management fashion appears to be the antithesis of rational management and far removed from the straw man of management engaged in an unrelenting pursuit of extracting surplus value from labour. This is both a strength and a weakness. Perhaps an exploration of management fashion can open up understandings of management as varied, uncertain and aping rationality, and management knowledge as contestable and provisional? On the other hand, a focus on fashion can overemphasize an aesthetic notion of management and downplay continuities in processes of change. It is the contention of this chapter that a critical engagement with the notion of management fashion can shed light on the development and use of information systems (IS) and reflexively say something about the field of IS research. To explore this, I shall mainly consider the example of enterprise resource planning (ERP) systems with some discussion on business process re-engineering, e-business and customer relationship management (CRM). By even mentioning these examples, it is clear that fashion is a strong contender in any explanation of these phenomena. Willmott (1995) even considers that we could be engaged in a 'turkey shoot' with easy targets for academics to aim at, but perhaps more is at stake here. For example, managerial fashion is often linked with management best sellers and management gurus. Michael Hammer's article in the *Harvard Business Review*, 'Don't automate, obliterate' (1990) and the subsequent books on business re-engineering are a classic instance of the rise of a management guru and a management fashion which have been very influential (see Jackson 2001). For academics and universities, management fashions and gurus are a threat to ambitions to be the authoritative source of managerial knowledge.

The chapter begins by discussing what a management fashion is and how management fashion has been theorized, before moving on to look at possible management fashions in IS. The next step is to consider whether technologies can be treated in the same way as management fashions and then to explore some critical issues that emerge from regarding IS as fashions.

**Management fashion**

What is a management fashion?[1] Abrahamson (1996: 257) in an influential article defines management fashion as 'a relatively transitory collective belief, disseminated by management fashion setters, that a management technique leads to rational management progress'. In this definition we have an interesting association of different issues. 'Transitory' indicates the temporal nature of fashion; 'collective belief' shows a sharing of an emotional commitment; 'management fashion setters' suggests an active process by someone or a group to spread these ideas; 'management technique' illustrates that a fashion must be linked to specific management techniques; while the notion of 'rational management progress' sits rather uneasily with the invoking of belief and of transience. Indeed, one of the important tensions in identifying management fashions is that between rational progress on the one hand and the continual turning over of management fashions on the other.

Many management fashions have been identified. Abrahamson (1996) uses the technique of quality circles as an exemplar of a management fashion (see Figure 7.1). He shows a typical bell-shaped curve based on a measure of the number of articles in the ABI Inform management database. Quality circles become evident in 1977, peak in 1982 and fall back to a low level by 1986. All in all, this phenomenon occurs over ten years. Succeeding fashions can also be identified. Abrahamson and Fairchild (1999) see a series of management fashions from quality circles, to total quality management to business process re-engineering. Gibson and Tesone (2001: 124) identify five fads: management by objectives, representative of the 1950s; sensitivity training, representative of the 1960s; quality circles, representative of the 1970s; total quality management, representative of the 1980s; and self-managed teams, representative of the 1990s. Some authors have argued for numerous fashions. Grint (1997), for example, identifies eight fashions between 1986 and 1995 as culture; leadership; business process re-engineering; outsourcing; downsizing; empowerment; total quality management; and competencies. Other authors have identified many more (see, for example, Pascale 1990). Kieser (1997) suggests that management fashions are becoming more common and their duration is becoming shorter.

*Explaining management fashions*

In the last dozen years, an interesting literature has developed on management fashions and fads (see Abrahamson 1991, 1996; Kieser 1997; Abrahamson and Fairchild 1999; Gibson and Tesone 2001; Jackson 2001; Newell et al. 2001; Scarbrough and Swan 2001; Spell 2001). The discussion is centred on the importance and frequency of change in the techniques and discourses

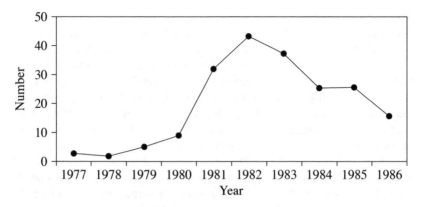

*Source*:   After Abrahamson (1996).

*Figure 7.1   Number of articles using the term 'quality circle'*

of management. As I have discussed earlier, this is not necessarily seen as pathological, as the terms 'fashions' or 'fads' imply. Abrahamson has been influential in developing this debate, and I shall explore some of his definitions and ideas before looking at alternative conceptualizations.

Abrahamson (1996: 255) argues that management fashions are not just aesthetic fashion, but are 'deadly serious matters' for business schools and scholars. If business schools and their academics are seen to be lagging in management progress then they may be seen as undeserving of societal support. Second, he argues that the demand for management fashions is shaped by socio-physiological forces, and by 'a desire to learn about management techniques that would help them [managers] respond to organizational performance gaps opened up by real technical and economic environmental changes' (ibid.). He argues that the choice of management technique is guided by twin norms: that management knowledge will progress over time (progressive and normative) and that management techniques will be rational; they are efficient means to attain important goals. Abrahamson and Fairchild (1999), using again the example of quality circles, show that they began in Japan in the early 1960s; became widely adopted in Japan; were introduced into the United States in the mid-1970s; by 1982, 90 per cent of the top Fortune 500 companies had adopted quality circles; and by 1988, some 80 per cent of those top Fortune 500 companies had abandoned them. They provide evidence to show that fashions both follow each other and are interdependent. For example, job enrichment was replaced by quality circles; quality circles were replaced by total quality management; and total quality management by business process re-engineering. Further, they suggest that demand for each new fashion arose from the collapse of demand for the previous fashion.

Abrahamson's argument is based on institutional theory and the idea that organizations seek to attain isomorphism with similar organizations. This draws on the ideas of Meyer and Rowan (1977), that organizations seek to mimic other organizations without necessarily following them in practice. Partaking of fashions furthers isomorphism. This is linked with the notion of progress which, as others have remarked, sits uneasily with that of institutional theory (Kieser 1997: 53). Kieser makes two other points: first he suggests that Abrahamson seeks to differentiate between management techniques and rhetoric: a distinction he argues cannot be maintained; second, he takes issue with Abrahamson's contention that it is socio-physiological forces that shape demand whereas Kieser argues that rhetoric is the most important feature and that management fashions are analogous to fashion in aesthetic forms.

Kieser suggests that while rhetoric is the 'main input currency', it takes place in an arena of management fashion where different groups are in contention: consultants, professors, publishers, the trade press and so on: 'The participants can achieve their individual goals of highest possible profit … by widening the arena through luring further participants into it' (ibid.: 57). Kieser goes on to argue that the management best seller is a key ingredient in the popularization of management fashions. These are often associated with the creation of management myths based on examples of extraordinary change credited to companies that have used the new fashion. In short, a management fashion holds the promise of bringing order to a disorganized world. Managers are the most important players in the arena. It is they who must pick up fashions – to enhance their power relations; to avoid missing the boat – and it is they who are the consumers of fashions.

Kieser's argument is more persuasive than Abrahamson's as it focuses more satisfactorily on the role of rhetoric in management fashion. It shows a relational arena where different actors attempt to extend networks of influence through rhetorical means. Let us see how they each consider the dynamics of management fashion, beginning with the rise of a management fashion.

Abrahamson argues that rhetoric is important, but this argument is tempered by propositions such as 'if there exists *unmet demand* for a certain type of management technique, then one or more techniques belonging to this type will become fashionable, if they are created, selected, processed, and disseminated by the management-fashion-setting community' (Abrahamson 1996: 257, emphasis added). This notion of unmet demand needs further exploration. In terms of rhetoric, we should expect that a discourse relating to ERP systems should also shape the objects that it refers to. Therefore, we can suppose that unmet demand is as much a manifestation of the discourse as a force external to rhetoric as Abrahamson proposes. He argues that the forces influencing demand centre around six forces: psychological desires of managers to appear individualistic and progressive; management action in the face of disappointment of managerial expectations; as a response by high reputation organizations to the adoption of a fashion by lower reputation organizations; macroeconomic fluctuations; labour strife; and finally as a response to technical contradictions within organizations (ibid.: 258–60). If we consider fashion as rhetoric then, following Foucault and those who have interpreted his ideas in organizational studies (for example, Knights and Willmott 1989), a focus on discourse would suggest, contra Abrahamson, that most of the forces can be explained differently. Individuals and subjectivity are shaped by discourse and practices rather than relying on psychology (Foucault 1980); shortfalls in managerial expectation are created through discourses; responses to macroeconomic indicators are, in turn, mediated by discourses; both labour strife and managerial response are also mediated through discourse (Knights and Collinson 1987); and finally, technical contradictions are as much manifestations of discourse as they are self-evident facts (Bloomfield and Vurdubakis 1994).

Turning to the decline of a management fashion, Abrahamson has two lines of explanation. The first is a usage of forces such as macroeconomic conditions, labour strife and technical contradictions. Similar arguments to those advanced above can be used to question this explanation. A second line of argument is proffered in Abrahamson and Fairchild (1999: 713), who argue that there are a variety of possible exogenous forces but the 'exogenous forces that do trigger management fashions are the few, among the many, that management discourse both pushes to the top of many fashion consumers' agendas and relates to organisational performance gaps that management techniques could eliminate'. This appears to be a more congenial argument in relation to rhetoric, but it still ignores the probability that performance gaps are themselves identified, measured and articulated as part of discourses that are linked to the promotion of a new managerial fashion. In other words, rather than as Abrahamson and Fairchild propose (that one management fashion collapses before another takes hold), a focus on discourse suggests that the decline of one management fashion is intimately linked with the rise of another as it seeks to explain the shortcomings of a previous fashion in terms of the novel fashion's benefits.

Kieser's (1997: 68–9) argument on the demise of management fashions is more appealing. He argues that the success of a management fashion leads first to it becoming diverse and even meaningless as it is reinterpreted in a multitude of ways and second, to other fashion designers denouncing existing fashions and replacing them with their own – 'murder' as he calls it. He also suggests that sometimes a fashion produces dysfunctional effects that lead to a counter fashion.

So far, I have focused on two authors who analyse management fashion as primarily rhetorical/institutional accomplishments which seek to explain some of the processes by which management fashions rise and fall. Grint (1997) provides a convenient classification of different approaches to the explanation of management fashions and the related phenomenon of the management guru. His framework produces four quadrants depending on whether a management fashion is taken as logical or emotive on the one hand, and whether it is explained rather by individuals (internalist) or by external forces (externalist) (see Table 7.1). In addition a fifth category – an institutional perspective – is placed in the centre of the four quadrants.[2]

*Table 7.1  Grint's classification of approaches to management fashion*

|  | Externalist | Internalist |
|---|---|---|
| Emotion | Distancing | Charismatic |
|  | Institutional |  |
| Logic | Structural | Rational |

*Source*:   After Grint (1997).

Abrahamson's and Kieser's explanations are placed in the distancing/ institutional categories. Rational arguments in the internalist/logical quadrant propose that fashions are tried by management in organizations and depending on the outcomes, they are accepted or rejected. Once a fashion is adopted, it tends to lose its identity and becomes part of general business practice. Because of this increasing management base of experience, subsequent fashions have to be 'at equal or higher levels than preceding processes' (Gibson and Tesone 2001: 122). In other words, management fashions are examples of a market mechanism/selection process at work with acceptance or rejection depending on whether they work or not. Charismatic accounts bring us to the management guru: 'the management fashion setters' of Abrahamson's definition at the beginning of the chapter. For some management fashions, the management guru and the fashion are very closely intertwined. The celebrated case of Tom Peters, his promotion of excellence and the accompanying book *In Search of Excellence* (Peters and Waterman 1982) are exemplars of the management guru and an accompanying management fashion. These examples can be multiplied easily, with Michael Hammer and the rise of business process re-engineering being a pertinent example in the IS area. Structural explanations form the final quadrant. For example, Barley and Kunda (1992), using evidence over the last hundred years, argue that managerial thought swings between two poles, broadly depending on economic circumstances. In times of increasing economic activity, managerial approaches based on employee participation and solidarity predominate, while in times of recession, approaches based on formalization and rationalization are evident. These they term 'normative' and 'rational' rhetorics, respectively. Having identified ways in which management fashions have been theorized, we can move on to consider them in relation to information systems.

**Information systems fashions**
The area of IS is no more immune from management fashion than others. Of the fashions listed earlier, outsourcing, downsizing and business process re-engineering have had important relationships with information technologies (ITs). In each of these fashions, the role of IS was often seen as pivotal. Equally, each of them could be introduced with IS having a minor or even a non-existent role. For example, Baxi, an English manufacturer of heating appliances, was put forward as an exemplar of business process re-engineering. However, their use of the technique did not involve IS at all (see Kennedy 1994). From about 1997, there has been a change in the way fashions and IS combined. Prior to that date, although IS were often promoted as important in specific fashions – business process re-engineering is a classic example – the technique could be implemented with sometimes quite limited use of IS. Subsequent fashions in such systems – enterprise systems, e-business and customer relation management systems, for instance – are all centred on interventions using specific technologies.

Two things have happened here. First, the nature of IS technologies changed. The move was from customized systems built either by in-house expertise or by contractors, to IS that are commodity products built by large vendors, which are purchased or licensed and installed in companies. This happened for all sizes of systems, but for large organizations, the advent of ERP systems was an example of commodity IS products becoming available for their type of company. Second, having IS as commodity products made it easier to have fashions based on them because they had become a tangible entity that now could be replicated and sold to numerous companies. Let us look at the case of ERP systems as an example of an IS-predicated management fashion which, arguably, was the first of this type.

I shall not begin by defining what ERP systems are. Indeed, a contention of this chapter is that ERP systems are to be found in the circumstances of their engagement in the world rather than elsewhere.[3] ERP systems are seen by some as 'the answer to the Information Age's wildest dreams' (Davenport 2000: 6). More prosaically, to others, they are 'comprehensive packaged software solutions that integrate organizational processes through shared information and data flows' (Shanks and Seddon 2000: 243).

The measurement of a management fashion is an interesting issue, but identifying changing management practice is very difficult. Instead, most authors try to measure either academic analysis or articles in the popular management press (see Thomas 1999). Both Abrahamson and Kieser use the number of publications as a measure of the popularity of a specific management fashion (see Abrahamson 1996: 258; Kieser 1997: 51).[4] Similar processes were used to seek to measure the popularity of ERP systems using three sets of data. First, the contents of a popular internet-based IT journal *InformationWeek* were surveyed. Second, the titles of papers submitted to three well-known IS conferences were analysed. Finally, the contents of the ABI Inform management database (only refereed articles) were measured. The results of these three sources are shown, respectively as Figure 7.2, Table 7.2, and Figure 7.3. These measures were seeking to identify frequency in the popular IT press (Figure 7.2) and usage in academic conferences (Table 7.2) which should be quicker to publish than in academic journal articles (Figure 7.3). Broadly, the figures bear out what we might expect of a management fashion. Figure 7.2 shows that the term ERP appeared in 1996, reached a peak in1999 and has fallen back almost as swiftly to a relatively low level in 2002. In other words, the frequency of usage of ERP in the popular press has peaked and shows a bell-shaped curve. In the conference literature, ERP as a term appears in 1997 and reaches a plateau in the years 1999, 2000 and 2001. In 2002, the number of conference papers decline significantly except in the European-based ECIS. Academics' interest in ERP systems reached a plateau which coincided with (or slightly lagged behind) the peak of interest found in the popular press. In the academic published literature, ERP grows, albeit unevenly, up to the latest available data in 2002 (see Figure 7.3). It appears that published articles may have just reached a peak and lag behind the decline of interest exemplified in the popular IT press by some two to three years.

These figures show, using measures of a management fashion, that ERP systems have a typical bell-shaped curve of a specific fashion (see Figure 7.1) in terms of interest in the popular management/IS literature. Published academic interest lags behind. Two other terms, e-business and CRM, were also analysed in the business and academic published literatures. In *InformationWeek*, e-business as a term has a more marked bell-shaped curve than ERP and peaks in 2000 about 18 months after ERP. In published academic literatures, a steep rise in the use of the term starts to decline slightly after 2001. In Figure 7.2, CRM has a much lower peak of use

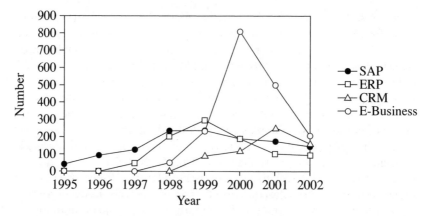

*Note*:   SAP = SAP is the leading vendor of ERP systems; ERP = enterprise resource planning;
CRM = customer relationship management.

*Source*:   *InformationWeek* (various years).

*Figure 7.2    Number of articles using specific words in* InformationWeek

*Table 7.2    Conference papers using ERP in title in three major IS conferences*

| Conference | 1997 | 1998 | 1999 | 2000 | 2001 | 2002 |
|---|---|---|---|---|---|---|
| ICIS[1] | 1 | 3 | 5 | 6 | 4 | 3 |
| AMCIS[2] | 1 | 1 | 29 | 24 | 29 | 4 |
| ECIS[3] | 0 | 2 | 1 | 3 | 2 | 6 |
| Total | 2 | 6 | 38 | 33 | 35 | 13 |

*Notes*:
1. International Conference on Information Systems.
2. Americas Conference on Information Systems.
3. European Conference on Information Systems.

*Sources*:   Klaus et al. (2000); conference websites.

in 2001 and starts to decline in 2002, whereas in the published academic
literatures the use of CRM has continued to rise up to 2002. What can we
make of these figures?

Arguably, we have three terms, ERP, e-business and CRM all acting as
we might expect an archetypical management fashion to behave. Evidence
is seen first in the popular press which peaks and then declines. Interest in
academic literatures lags behind: a peak of interest in the academic conference
literature peaks about a year later[5] while attention in the published academic

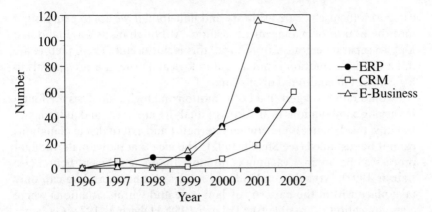

*Source*: Proquest ABI Inform databases.

*Figure 7.3    Number of articles using specific words in ABI Inform refereed publications*

literature peaks about a year after that. Each of these three fashions appears to last about six or so years in the popular management literature and each has succeeded the previous one at yearly intervals: ERP appears in 1997; e-business in 1998; and CRM in 1999.

## Management fashions and information systems

So far, I have sought to establish what a management fashion is, and that trends in IS are similar to management fashions identified elsewhere, and introduced some of the theorization of management fashion. We are now in a position to assess the notion of management fashions from a critical perspective in relation to IS. I shall approach this in three moves: first, by considering what the notion of management fashions tells us of IS as an arena of management and an area of academic scrutiny; second, to delineate issues in the consumption of management fashions; and finally, to consider more overtly what a critical stance brings to an exploration of this area and what are the ramifications of such a position.

### The notion of management fashion

As Grint's analytic categories show, explanations of management fashions can range from appeals to logic or emotion on the one hand, to individuals or society on the other. As all positions in his quadrant are occupied, arguments exist for all of these positions. In one sense this is self-defeating as we could be left scrabbling around for reasons external to this framework to justify choices of a relevant explanation.[6] Instead, I shall argue that the categories themselves are arbitrary and unhelpful if we are to gain insight into the notion of management fashion. Although many have laboured long to separate emotion from logic, this is not useful. These factors are not a dualism: emotion is not absent in logical debate; nor are appeals to logic absent in emotional discussion.

I would rather suggest that both emotion and logical analysis are found in varying combinations in all forms of analysis, argument and judgement.[7] Equally, the demarcation between internalist and externalist explanations cannot be sustained (see Shapin 1992). The idea that individuals' thought processes operate in a vacuum is no more than a convenient fiction (see Latour 1993). Arguably, individuals' modes of understanding can only take place within the patterns of language and within situations where communication is possible (see Polanyi 1958; Habermas 1972; Gadamer 1975). External forces need articulation to become noticed and, arguably, cannot be simply seen as extra linguistic categories separate from individual (and group) processes of understanding and explanation. In short, we must look elsewhere for explanations, and a good starting point is the issue of relatedness.

Westrup et al. (2003) have used the creation of networks and the translation of concepts and techniques to explain the movement of (yet) another management fashion (world class management: WCM) from consultants in the United States to small companies in north-west England. That study shows that concepts and techniques travel and are appropriated by different groups to advance their own agendas, and when the utility of that label is exhausted for specific groups they pragmatically ditch the name even if some of the practices still remain in some form. In that case, Schonberger's packaging of Japanese management experience in the 1980s led him to coin the term 'WCM' (Schonberger 1982). In the UK, other consultants adopted a similar name while changing some of the practices, and used this packaging to sell training courses to newly created regional development agencies. The agencies enthusiastically adopted these training packages as it consolidated a practical role for them in providing support to companies. Businesses that were trained in the scheme claimed to be using WCM, but, on closer inspection, had a very selective uptake of practices. In one or two cases, companies adopted accounting practices that were diametrically opposed to WCM, found them useful, and considered that these were the benefits of WCM. This example boils down to the argument that management fashions conceal diversity within movements of the same name and that a variety of actors such as consultants, companies, development agencies and management appropriate management fashions to redefine themselves and further their interests in usually unpredictable ways. What can this suggest for information systems?

A major implication and self-evident point, shared by many other authors in this volume, is that IS are not a self-contained area. We have to move away from any residual understanding of IS as simply technical to realizing that the technical is shot through by the social (see Latour 1987; Bloomfield 1992). When it comes to management fashions, we can see that wide-ranging sets of relations are set in train. For example, enterprise systems such as ERP are licensed from vendors – SAP, a German-based multinational, being the market leader. The implementation and development of these systems in organizations are normally the business of SAP partners who are consultancy companies (see SAP 2004). Why ERP systems are to be used at all depends on what we can call 'visions' of what ERP systems might be (ibid.), how they can benefit businesses and, in pre-millennial times, how they would be able to banish the spectre of legacy systems crashing in the year 2000 (Vurdubakis 2001). Within a company, ERP systems become an underlying organizational motif showing how different aspects of the business can be and are in fact linked through the sharing of common ERP-encoded information (Westrup and Newman 2003). In other words, these IS link together and redefine a variety of areas and actors both within and outside companies. A corollary of the multifaceted relations of ERP systems is that academic understanding and analysis must be equally multifaceted. Academic demarcations particularly in the area of management are becoming less useful as approaches such as ERP become widely used in organizations.

Spell (2001) has shown for several management fashions that they first appear in the business press, before academic publications. This result is supported in the evidence given earlier in this chapter. Spell charitably suggests that one explanation is the longer lead times for publication in academic journals. A more disquieting possibility for some academics, who still consider that academic research leads businesses, is that they are simply commenting on trends in management rather than actively advancing management knowledge which is to be applied in businesses. In part, an eclipse of the academy as the prime producer of knowledge gives credence to Gibbons et al.'s (1994) argument that knowledge production has moved from one mode to another. Mode 1 was argued to have been disciplinary-led research arising in universities, whereas mode 2 is more diverse, interdisciplinary and developing in the sites of production. A reason for this shift is the ubiquity of IT, which enables communication and the development of markets for knowledge. To this could be added the importance of an educated management cadre that can be involved in the production of new techniques/new knowledges and in the consumption of these self-same management techniques. In other words, management fashions point towards the decline of universities as a major source of management knowledge and towards the importance of other modes of knowledge production that are often interdisciplinary in outlook.[8]

*Delineating issues in the consumption of management fashions*
Turning to the second point, discussions of management fashions are useful in moving our attention from the understanding that the implementation of IS is not simply a matter of technical utility. We are instead faced with issues of the production and consumption of IS as commodities. This is traditionally seen as the sphere of economic activity and explanation *par excellence*. Clearly, vendors of IT products must be profitable and are faced with demands to create ever-increasing profits. SAP is a good example. In the early 1990s it outperformed the stock market, but by the late 1990s, exponential growth began to fall away.[9] In part, this was because the market for ERP systems in large companies within developed countries was becoming saturated. SAP, and others, changed their products to continue to expand sales. For example, they changed ERP systems to produce more industry-specific variations of ERP so as to increase the number of possible sites where they could be used. By 2001, SAP were seen as very successful in reorganizing their products even though their sales were not increasing at the rates of the 1990s (Aberdeen Group 2001). As has been argued elsewhere, in the recent new world of IS as commodity products, vendors have an interest in continuing to develop their products to create new revenue streams and to make previous products obsolete (Westrup and Knight 2000). Thus, an economic explanation is useful to clarify why there is instability in the emerging market for IS. But, we cannot leave this activity to economic explanations alone because, as Granovetter (1985) shows, we are left with an under-socialized account of what is occurring. Management fashion draws us to considering the consumption as more than simply economic activity.

Once an item has been sold to the recipient then it moves from the market to a private area of consumption. This is usually allied with the notion that the consumer has sovereign choice and that consumption is voluntary (Douglas and Isherwood 1996: 36). However, another position is that the material possessions carry social meanings and that assessing the technologies and techniques is not always a question of efficiency and efficacy, but can draw on how they make and maintain social relationships (ibid.). I have already alluded to the idea that management fashions can be useful to managers by providing them with new techniques which can show their awareness of latest thinking to their peers and subordinates. As Gibson and Tesone (2001: 131) argue, 'understanding management fads and translating them into practice within the organisation is the mark of the manager who stays current to both theory and practice'.

New technologies such as an ERP system can show a company to be a user of the latest technologies. This can be useful for external audiences such as customers (with calls for improving customer service), shareholders (by improving efficiency) and for audiences within the organization to demonstrate that the organization can be joined up through shared information mediated through an ERP system. As institutional theory argues, the consumption of ERP systems is also a mimetic act: if other companies use these systems then we are doing likewise. For ERP systems, this activity is taken one step further. Not only are the users of such a system on a par with other organizations, but they are also gaining access to best business practice that is encoded in the processes of the system. The prize here is something better than what any one specific company does. CRM systems are associated with similar promises. The users of these systems will be able to manage a relationship with a customer(s) that derives from the ability to collect and analyse diverse information and organize tailored marketing for that (those) specific customer(s). For both ERP and CRM, these expectations are often seen as failing in practice, leading to the elaboration of these systems or their replacement by others (Westrup and Newman 2003).

Consumption is not straightforward for many management fashions. How are the insights of a specific management fashion to be applied in a specific organization? Arguably, consultants are a key actor in these processes. Take, for example, a large multinational manufacturing company in the northwest of England using SAP.[10] When they first installed SAP in 1997, they had a large number of consultants who spent over a year on installation. Now they rarely use these consultants except when they put in a new part of the SAP system such as CRM in 2003, though they still retain a consulting contract to give expert help on specific issues that arise from time to time. Senior IS management consider that they are better than consultants in most areas. As one manager said, 'if we have done it before [with consultants], we will do it again [without consultants]'. Although reliant on consultants at first, management are confident in most areas about how to use the ERP system to best advantage in their company. In short, considerable management and workforce learning is needed to configure systems such as SAP to make them work in any particular setting. Consumption of these systems appears to be a process whereby consultants, managers, the workforce and the technology are all engaged in realigning themselves. All these issues remain largely unresearched at the moment.

### A critical stance
This section considers what is critical about an analysis of management fashions and information systems. Critical theory recognizes both the dark

side of appeals to rationality and the instable and relentless pressures of capitalism (Horkheimer and Adorno 1972; Braverman 1974). Management fashions can be seen as mirroring them both. Management, continually looking for new ways to extract surplus from labour and other resources, is active in its consumption of the latest management fashion. Each fashion is cloaked in appeals to its rationality as a better way to manage organizations in turbulent times. Yet beneath this rationality is often the destruction of employment and social forms of life. Business process re-engineering is one example of a rationality that seeks to institute a year zero approach to organizing and, with technologies, to engineer a new future that will be more productive than before (Grint and Willcocks 1995). ERP systems can be seen as the commodity IS package that seeks to provide predictability to the re-engineering of the organization based on the 'best business practices' encoded in the system (Westrup and Knight 2000). Do we end up with the iron cage of Max Weber: 'mechanised petrifaction embellished with a convulsive self importance ... [with] specialists without spirit, sensualists without heart' (Weber 1958, pp. 181–2)? IS fashions when based on technologies appear to be more resilient than techniques based on management fashions such as quality circles (Westrup 2003). Although evidence in the printed/electronic media of IS technologies such as ERP reduces as we expect for a management fashion, they appear to remain in place for a long time afterwards. ERP systems, for instance, are often called 'digital concrete', but more appropriately they are examples of the congealing of social relations in and around technologies. In turn, management gain specific roles in the use of these technologies. With ERPs they can become the process owners, guardians of the purity and efficacy of certain global business processes which only 'work' because they are mediated by ERP technologies.[11] It appears that managers gain new aspects of identity in relation to technologies such as ERP systems. Workers are subjected to similar processes. ERP systems, when implemented in organizations, are used to try to fix roles for both management and workforce alike. Each has roles that link up to their login accounts on the system. Whether this is a process of deskilling is not straightforward or clear at present. What I would like to emphasize is that the users of these systems and the system itself are not stable. Workers (or management) appear not to be passive dupes of the system, but exercise agency in the use of them. The attempt to create a rational system based on IS technologies is no more than partly successful. There is always room for interpretation and reinterpretation of the processes of work as the discussion on consumption shows. As Barley and Kunda (1992) argue, such moves seem to be no more than one pole in an oscillation that then moves towards normative/group processes of working. Whether there is any real difference is highly questionable (Willmott 1993).

Looking at the processes in the rise and decline of management fashions foregrounds managers, but there are many who benefit from the cycling of different management fashions. I have already discussed the role of the management guru and the vendors of technologies. The academic, though perhaps more peripheral than in the past,[12] also has an important role, as textbooks, degree programmes and executive courses attest. Recently a well-known IS academic expressed his concern to me about what he was going to teach executives in the future, as there seemed to be a dearth of new ideas and those that were around were already widely known. However, some of the most interesting parties that come into view when looking at processes, are management consultants and consulting companies. It is they who package and repackage management knowledge and techniques and, in a marketplace that is itself constructed, they gain by having new ideas and solutions and sidelining the past (see Clark and Fincham 2002; Jones 2003).

### Conclusion

This chapter began by setting out how management fashions are represented and it has sought to show that recent trends in IS can be seen as waves of management fashion. A key difference, however, is that IS fashions tend to be linked to more durable technologies rather than techniques which can be relatively ephemeral. A teleology of process in management understanding based on a series of passing fashions is not convincing. When it comes to IS technologies, there is evidence of increasing proficiency with enterprise systems even though the more extravagant claims placed on these technologies have not (and are unlikely to) come to pass. Clearly, further work needs to be done looking at specific instances of the coming and going of management fashions and their legacy in organizing specific companies. Various explanations of management fashions were discussed before looking more specifically at management fashion and IS. I have argued that being aware of management fashions in IS shows how it is increasingly difficult to defend IS as an isolated area of study either in practice or in management education. Although it is certainly acceptable to foreground IS as an area of interest, they are not simply artefacts or systems. Instead, through a focus on management fashions, we find them in IS highlighting circuits between vendors, consultants, the business press, companies, managers and workforces. These circuits are economic but they are much more than that as they are also resources for the definition and redefinition of actors. Through the use of ERP systems, companies become leading-edge companies applying cutting-edge technologies. Managers become knowledgeable in the latest techniques and so on. For academics, the prognosis is less appealing. Some management gurus are academics who have shed their skins to emerge as global players. However, most management fashions appear not to arise in universities, and scholarly analysis seems to be more of a critical commentary of unfolding events. As Bauman (1987) suggests, academics are less akin to legislators and find themselves interpreting events. For many, this is no bad thing.

The consumption/implementation of management fashions is more than either a simple following of a unidirectional management imperative to increase profitability or the exercise of sovereign choice by management as economic theory assumes. Instead, the chapter draws on the idea that consumption is as much about the construction and maintenance of social relationships and meaning. This idea suggests that the rhetorics that are placed on IS are of prime importance in giving different groupings, such as management, ways to realign themselves. Consultants are arguably an important conduit in this process as they seek to speak for new technologies and, in turn, provide new roles for management, workforce and technology. As the term 'management fashions' suggests, these processes seem to be continually unstable even though technologies do perhaps give more permanence to social processes than other management fashions. This, too, remains an area for further research.

Finally, identifying the succession of management fashions throws into relief the tensions in seeking an increasing control of organizations. Techniques and, at a slower rate, technologies, are applied, found wanting, and replaced by the next technique and/or technology. Whether management knowledge advances is very unclear: organizations haltingly appear to be more productive by some measures, but the cost in disruptions for both management and workforce is rarely discussed. In that sense we are all fashion victims.

**Acknowledgements**
I would like to thank Hannah Knox, Damian O'Doherty and Theo Vurdubakis, my co-workers on the Economic and Social Research Council (ESRC) project 'The role of ICT-based applications in business knowledge processes'. I would like to acknowledge the support of the ESRC in assisting with fieldwork reported in this chapter.

**Notes**
1. I shall use the terms 'fashion' rather than 'fad'. Note that the two labels present differing associations: 'fashion' has associations with fashion in consumption such as clothing; home décor; the design of cars; and so on. 'Fad' has an even more pejorative association equivalent to the stampede for certain children's toys – Buzz Lightyear or the Brat dolls – at Christmas. In the literature, the terms tend to be interchangeable.
2. Jackson (2001: 22), when using the framework, places the institutional approach with the distancing one as he suggests that it is difficult to separate out work that uses these approaches. I shall follow his approach.

3. This draws on a statement by Ingold (1996: 152): 'Thus, the meaning of speech, like that of song, lies in the circumstances of the speaker's *engagement* with the world: it is not something that precedes that engagement, and which it serves to deliver' (original emphasis).

4. Abrahamson uses the ABI Inform database and also measures the thickness in inches of an annual proceedings of a conference in the area; Kieser uses the WISO journal database.

5. Evidence only given for ERP systems.

6. The perils of reflexivity in this situation are well put by Jackson (2001: 36–7).

7. If we need an appeal to authority rather than our own experience in these matters, I would choose a non-Western (and therefore non-Freudian) system of psychological thought that is broadly Buddhist in origin. In the Abhidhamma, all thought processes have feeling (*qua* emotion) as part of their constituents (see Watts 1975; Gethin 1998).

8. Academics have other roles such as consultancy and, of course, teaching MBAs.

9. This comes as no surprise. For example, sustained large growth rates require larger and larger increases in sales as a company's turnover increases.

10. The name of the company has to remain confidential. The fieldwork is part of an ongoing study on the role of ICT-based applications in business knowledge processes, an ESRC-funded project (RES-334–25–0012). Some 20 interviews have been conducted to date at this site.

11. This is what we found in the northwest UK company discussed above. The work of the organization has been re-engineered into global business processes and each business process has a business process owner. No change can take place unless the business process owner considers it to be of global significance to the company and approves it.

12. In itself an interesting research issue.

## References

Aberdeen Group (2001), 'SAP: the once and future king', Aberdeen Group Insight Report, June, www.aberdeen.com, July.

Abrahamson, E. (1991), 'Management fads and fashion: the diffusion and rejection of innovations', *Academy of Management Review*, **16**: 586–612.

Abrahamson, E. (1996), 'Management fashion', *Academy of Management Review*, **21**(1): 254–85.

Abrahamson, E. and Fairchild, G. (1999), 'Management fashion: lifecycles, triggers, and collective learning processes', *Administrative Science Quarterly*, **44**: 708–40.

Barley, S. and Kunda, G. (1992), 'Design and devotion: surges of rational and normative ideologies of control in managerial discourse', *Administrative Science Quarterly*, **37**: 363–99.

Bauman, Z. (1987), *Legislators and Interpreters on Modernity, Post-Modernity, and Intellectuals*, Ithaca, NY: Cornell University Press.

Bloomfield, B. (1992), 'Understanding the social practices of systems developers', *Journal of Information Systems*, **2**: 189–206.

Bloomfield, B. and Vurdubakis, T. (1994), 'Re-presenting technology: IT consultancy reports as textual reality constructions', *Sociology*, **28**(2): 123.

Braverman, H. (1974), *Labor and Monopoly Capital*, New York: Monthly Review Press.

Clark, T. and Fincham, R. (eds) (2002), *Critical Consulting: Perspectives on the Management Advice Industry*, Oxford: Blackwell.

Davenport, T. (2000), *Mission Critical: Realizing the Problems of Enterprise Systems*, Harvard, MA: Harvard Business School Press.

Douglas, M. and Isherwood, B. (1996), *The World of Goods: Towards an Anthropology of Consumption*, London: Routledge.

Foucault, M. (1980), *Power/Knowledge: Selected Interviews and other Writings 1972–77*, ed. C. Gordon, Brighton: Harvester.

Gethin, R. (1998), *The Foundations of Buddhism*, Oxford: Opus.

Gadamer, H.-G. (1975), *Truth and Method*, New York: Seabury.

Gibbons, M., Limoges, C., Nowotny, H., Schwartzman, S., Scott, P. and Trow, M. (1994), *The New Production of Knowledge: The Dynamics of Science and Research in Contemporary Societies*, London: Sage.

Gibson, J. and Tesone, D. (2001), 'Management fads: emergence, evolution, and implications for managers', *Academy of Management Executive*, **15**(4): 122–33.

Granovetter, M. (1985). 'Economic action and social structure: the problem of embeddedness', *American Journal of Sociology*, **91**: 481–510.

Grint, K. (1997), *Fuzzy Management: Contemporary Ideas and Practices at Work*, London: Oxford University Press.

Grint, K. and Willcocks, L. (1995), 'Business process re-engineering in theory and practice: business paradise regained?', *New Technology, Work and Employment*, **2**: 99–109.

Habermas, J. (1972), *Knowledge and Human Interests*, Boston, MA: Beacon.

Hammer, M. (1990) 'Re-engineering work: don't automate, obliterate', *Harvard Business Review*, **67**(4): 104–12.

Horkheimer, M. and Adorno, T. (1972), *Dialectic of Enlightenment*, New York: Continuum.

Ingold, T. (1996), 'Introduction to a debate "Language is the essence of culture"', in T. Ingold (ed.), *Key Debates in Anthropology*, London: Routledge, pp. 149–53.

Jackson, B. (2001), *Management Gurus and Management Fashions: A Dramatistic Inquiry*, London: Routledge.

Jones, M. (2003), 'The expert system: constructing expertise in an IT/management consultancy', *Information and Organization*, **13**(4): 257–84.

Kennedy, C. (1994), 'Re-engineering: the human costs and benefits', *Long Range Planning*, **27**(5): 64–72.

Kieser, A. (1997), 'Rhetoric and myth in management fashion', *Organisation*, **4**(1): 49–74.

Klaus, H., Rosemann, M. and Gable, G. (2000), 'What is ERP?', *Information Systems Frontiers*, **2**(2): 141–62.

Knights, D. and Collinson, D. (1987), 'Disciplining the shop floor: a comparison of the disciplinary effects of managerial psychology and financial accounting', *Accounting Organisations and Society*, **12**(5): 457–77.

Knights, D. and Willmott, H. (1989), 'Power and subjectivity at work: from degradation to subjugation', *Sociology*, **23**(4), 535–58.

Latour, B. (1987), *Science in Action*, Milton Keynes: Open University Press.

Latour, B. (1993), *We Have Never Been Modern*, Cambridge, MA and London: Harvard University Press.

Meyer, J. and Rowan, B. (1977), 'Institutionalized organizations: formal structure as myth and ceremony', *American Journal of Sociology*, **83**: 340–63.

Newell, S., Robertson, M. and Swan, J. (eds) (2001), 'Management Fads and Fashions', *Organisation* (Special Issue), **8**(1): 5–15.

Pascale, R. (1990), *Managing on the Edge*, New York: Touchstone.

Peters, T. and Waterman, R. (1982), *In Search of Excellence: Lessons from America's Best Run Companies*, New York: Harper & Row.

Polanyi, M. (1958), *Personal Knowledge: Towards a Post Critical Epistemology*, New York: Harper & Row.

SAP (2004), www.sap.com/company, accessed January 2004.

Scarbrough, H. and Swan, J. (2001), 'Explaining the diffusion of knowledge management: the role of fashion', *British Journal of Management*, **12**: 3–12.

Schnonberger, R. (1982), *Japanese Manufacturing Technology: Nine Hidden Lessons in Simplicity*, New York: Free Press.

Shanks, G. and Seddon, P. (eds) (2000), 'Editorial', Special issue on ERP systems, *Journal of Information Technology*, **15**: 243–44.

Shapin, S. (1992), 'Discipline and bounding: the history and sociology of science as seen through the externalism-internalism debate', *History of Science*, **30**: 333–69.

Spell, C. (2001), 'Management fashions: where do they come from, and are they old wine in new bottles?', *Journal of Management Inquiry*, **10**(4): 358–73.

Thomas, P. (1999), *Fashions in Management Research: An Empirical Analysis*, Aldershot: Ashgate.

Vurdubakis, T., (2001) 'The machine stops: time and technology in the great millennial bug hunt', Paper presented at the International Conference on Spacing and Timing, Palermo, November.

Watts, A. (1975), *Psychotherapy East and West*, New York: Vintage.

Weber, M. (1958), *The Protestant Ethic and the Spirit of Capitalism*, New York: Scribner's.

Westrup, C. (2003), 'Discourse, management fashions, and ERP systems', in E. Wynn, E. Whitley, M. Myers, J. DeGross (eds), *Global and Organisational Discourse about Information Technology*, Dordrecht: Kluwer, pp. 401–18.

Westrup, C., Hopper, T. and Jazayeri, M. (2003), 'Free beer tomorrow! World class manufacturing, idealised accountability and how companies and the state aspire to become competitive', Working Paper, School of Accounting and Finance, University of Manchester.

Westrup, C. and Knight, F. (2000), 'Consultants and enterprise resource planning (ERP) systems', Paper presented at European Conference on Information Systems, Vienna, July.

Westrup, C. and Newman, M. (2003), 'Creating new areas of expertise: management accountants and the advent of ERP systems', Working Paper, School of Accounting and Finance, University of Manchester.

Willmott, H. (1993), 'Strength is ignorance; slavery is freedom: managing culture in modern organizations', *Journal of Management Studies*, **30**(4): 515–52.

Willmott, H. (1995), 'Managing the academics: commodification and control in the development of university education in the UK', *Human Relations*, **48**(9): 993–1028.

# 8 Flexibility, freedom and women's emancipation: a Marxist critique of at-home telework[1]

*Anita Greenhill and Melanie Wilson*

## Introduction: Marxism and the critical IS agenda

The main aim of this chapter is to describe how Marxist theory can assist in furthering the critical and gender studies projects in information systems (IS) research. This is to be achieved by applying established theoretical developments in Marxist approaches concerning technology and the labour process, on the one hand, and women's oppression, on the other. A useful illustration – because of its contemporary and contextual applicability to the analysis – is at-home telework. Our critical intention is to challenge assumptions associated with technological innovations such as telework. The critique is intended for use by agencies responsible for workers' welfare (such as trades unions), to contribute to preventing deterioration in working conditions, and/or hopefully to ameliorate them.[2] However, as the reader will discover, our agenda for emancipation in IS research is set against a broader landscape of radical change on a societal level. Drawing on earlier Marxist writings, we take the opportunity to outline what we believe extensive emancipation entails.

An emancipatory project in IS is nothing new (Orlikowski and Baroudi 1991). It has been a common theme among critical writers who have maintained a focus on issues of equality and inequality for some time (Hirschheim and Klein 1989; Ngwenyama 1991; Mingers 2000; Cecez-Kecmanovic 2001; Maru and Woodford 2001).[3] In generating a critical agenda it is essential to be clear about disputed areas, at least to enable us to draw up common areas of agreement (and struggle). Gender is a significant parameter for application of a critical approach since issues of inequality abound – nowhere more so than in the IS profession (Rasmussen and Hapnes 1991; Van Zoonen 1992; MacKinnon et al. 1993; Klawe and Leveson 1995; Webster 1996; Turner and Hovendon 1997; Trauth 2002) and in relation to IS (Kwan et al. 1985; Frenkel 1990; Green et al. 1993; Adam et al. 1994; Grundy 1996; Wilson and Howcroft 2000; Adam et al. 2002; Wilson 2002, 2004). An increasing number of these writings have brought in feminist research from other quarters (organizational behaviour, science and technology studies, sociology) and applied these to the IS arena and issues. However, despite the fact that Marxism and feminism share the common goal of opposing women's oppression, there are few examples of research where the former has been systematically applied to the field of IS and gender. This is our main contribution to the handbook.

Marxists begin with the position that every form of class society creates its own form of archetypal family, and has maintained the oppression of women at its centre (Vogel 1983). In 'traditional' family forms, women serve to care for the next and current generation of workers at minimal cost to society and the state. Further to this, although alternative family forms are on the increase,[4] nevertheless, the heterosexual couple with '2.2' children archetype is held up as the ideal model to which we all should aspire, with other relationships and households relegated in relevance and validity. Since Marxists believe that the imposition of this model as the 'true' or proper family unit has implications for the formation and socialization of all women's identity, the privatized capitalist family is the focus of the critique in this chapter. In so doing we hope to undermine the conservative agenda that seeks to relegate other family forms.

Central to a thorough liberation for women would be the creation of new family arrangements enabled by the provision of an alternative to the services provided within the privatized family: places where food is prepared, children cared for, washing done. Responsibility for children, the old and the sick, and ensuring adequate care outside the family for those who need it, would be taken by the whole community, not by individual women (and men) within the home (German 2003). Starting with this radical alternative serves to put in context the misguided, even regressive nature of much of the rhetoric surrounding teleworking at home. This socio-technical innovation, associated with talk of the 'Third Wave' and the 'Electronic Cottage' (Toffler 1987) has been mooted as enabling better management of the home–work balance. However, little is written about the societal costs of teleworking.

We argue that at-home telework is a regressive step. When scrutinized from a critical standpoint, the proposition to resituate women in the home distances them from the very point where they are potentially strongest and able to radically change society, namely: at work. Uncritical acceptance associated with the benefits of telework for workers assists the domination of housework, home responsibilities, isolation and powerlessness over paid work in the socialized public arena where collective resistance is possible.

In order to construct the case for a Marxist-inspired critical approach to IS, the chapter is organized as follows. The next section introduces the selected IS topic of at-home telework which will be subjected to a Marxist assessment of emancipation. This is followed by an explanation of the employee-centred Marxist approach to gender and IS by reference to the labour process literature, as well as cultural perspectives on the gender–technology relationship. As the family is central to Marxist analysis of women's oppression, this argumentation is carried over to the following section, which delineates the difference between Marxist and feminist approaches to women's twin roles as paid employees outside the home and as unpaid domestic workers in the home. The penultimate section draws the points made in the chapter into a sustained Marxist critique of at-home telework. The contribution to the handbook is summarized in the last section.

**Telework: a socio-technical ensemble**
In this section we describe the chosen IS phenomenon for our critical approach, providing background information on telework and outlining the promises made on its behalf for women workers. The example of home working, as a form of telework, magnifies the conflict of roles that women experience in attempting to equalize the work–life balance. The critical approach to IS adopted in this chapter will contest claims made for teleworking's inevitably emancipatory potential for women by examining the implications of at-home teleworking for women's lives – specifically asking if and how such new work practices can result in amelioration of working conditions and even 'freedom'. The tradition initiated by Braverman (1974) inaugurated a radical critique of the use of technology in organizations because of the potential of increased exploitation of the workers. For the IS researcher this implies an examination of the construction and use of IS to further increase the process of exploitation on the part of management and at the expense of employees (lengthening of the working day, reduction in working conditions, increased productivity and so on). In this regard we would be hesitant to accept on face value promises of flexibility, choice and emancipation for employees without scrutiny of its potentially detrimental effects. Furthermore, our critique has a gender dimension since many of the benefits will be particularly directed towards women workers and their family responsibilities.

*Background on telework*
'Telework', is defined as work that is carried out at a distance from the core organization through the medium of information and communication technologies (Sullivan 2003). As Gray et al. (1993, p. 6) state, teleworking entails: 'working remotely from an employer, or from a traditional place of work, for a significant proportion of work time. Teleworking may be on either a full-time or part-time basis. The work often involves electronic processing of information, and always involves using telecommunications'. Telework is generally agreed as encompassing three broad classifications

of work forms: home-based teleworking, teleworking from remote offices (call centres) and mobile teleworking (Gray et al. 1993). While there has been a wealth of studies concerning call-centre workers in recent years, there is significantly less research concentrating on the other types of teleworking practices. This may well reflect aspects of the phenomena, for the actual numbers of teleworkers employed full-time to work at home is overall very small – about 2 per cent of the UK labour force (TUC 2003) or just under 400,000 people (IES 2003). Qvortrup (1998, p. 8) delineates three categories of home workers, with full-time home workers belonging to the first: (a) 'substitutors', those who substitute work done at home for work done in a traditional setting; (b) 'self-employed', working online from their homes; and (c) 'supplementers', who bring home work from their traditional offices. Despite the fact that the trend for telehome workers is set to increase (TUC 2003), few studies have focused primarily on the employee's perspective, or gender and the impact of such work practices on the home–work, family boundary.

Aside from substantial data collated by employee welfare agencies (such as the Trades Union Congress in the UK[5]), in academia, balancing the work–life or family–work interface has been studied from different perspectives by various writers, including: its effects on family relations (Baines and Gelder 2003); supervisory/human resource practices (Felstead et al. 2002; Batt and Valcour 2003; Dimitrova 2003); job characteristics and work environment (Berg et al. 2003); work organization and intensity, employee involvement and job satisfaction (Felstead et al. 2002); interpersonal relationships at work (Dimitrova 2003); and psychological impacts of teleworking including stress, emotions and health (Mann and Holdsworth 2003). Industries where telework already exists are: manufacturing, electricity, gas and water, wholesale and retail, transport and storage, financial services, other business services, public administration, education, health and social work (Hogarth et al. 2000). IS work is almost exclusively non-manual labour (Felstead et al. 2002) and the occupations of potential interest include: managers and administrators, professionals, associate professionals and technical, clerical and secretarial positions. Marxists will be interested in how men and women experience the home–work balance differently as well as how individual socio-economic groups manage to overcome the renegotiation of boundaries.

*Telework as beneficial and emancipatory for women*
According to the literature, from the individual's perspective, employees can expect reduced commuting time and costs (Di Martino and Wirth 1990; Ward and Shabha 2001) leading to reduced stress and a better quality of

life (Huws 1993). Additionally, there is an appeal of a greater sense of freedom in avoiding an area of life that connotes the end of leisure time, as well as more contact with children and sustained membership in non-work communities. On the other hand, this absence from the host organization brings a cost of 'invisibility'. The improved working conditions of employees is said to bring benefits to the organization: managers see workers as more productive than on-site staff due to fewer interruptions and motivation problems, reduced travel time and greater job satisfaction (ibid.); and a reduction in turnover and absenteeism rate (Frolick et al. 1993; Bricknell 1996). Hitherto excluded groups, such as disabled people and women tied to the home through family responsibilities are offered 'inclusion' (Daniels et al. 2001). Daniels et al. summarize these issues using a table of hypothesized costs and benefits (see Table 8.1).

*Table 8.1   Hypothesized costs and benefits of teleworking*

| Hypothesized individual benefits | Hypothesized individual costs |
| --- | --- |
| Chance to remain in work despite moving home, becoming ill or taking on family care roles | Fewer chances for development or promotion, and the perception that teleworkers are not valued by their managers |
| More time for home and family | Increased conflict between work and home |
| Reduced commuting | Limited face-to-face contact with colleagues and social isolation |
| Greater job autonomy | Routinization of tasks |
| Less disturbance while working | More time spent working |
| More flexible hours | Lower job security |
| | Weakened collective representation |

*Source*:   Daniels et al. (2001, p. 1152).

Later in the chapter we shall subject these hypothesized benefits and costs to a Marxist critique. In relation to IS and organizations, a critical approach implicitly challenges views of organizations which do not seek to explore the contradictions emanating from their conflictual nature (Spencer 2000). Hence we shall offer an explanation of the Marxist position on both women's oppression and the labour process and in so doing make reference to the claims made on behalf of teleworking.

**Marxism, gender and the IS labour process**
In this section we shall build on existing IS research into gender and technology which examines the disadvantaged relationship of women and IS from an anti-determinist standpoint, making the case for a cultural perspective to overcome the problems associated with essentialism and determinism (Wilson and Howcroft 2000; Wilson 2002, 2004). In keeping with a radical critical philosophy and adhering to an emancipatory project, this social constructivist approach does not eschew a historical materialist grounding. We shall highlight the distinct contribution of Marxism to the topic which leads to novel approaches and insights.

*Marxism and a cultural perspective of gender and IS*
There is evidence of an increasing range of studies on both the gender differences in relation to computerized IS (Kwan et al. 1985; Frenkel 1990; Grundy 1996) as well as the underrepresentation of women in the computing and IS profession (Rasmussen and Hapnes 1991; Van Zoonen 1992; Klawe and Leveson 1995; Turner and Hovendon 1997). However, the undertheorization of the role of gender and IS (Adam et al. 2002) has only recently been addressed in IS research. The legacy of the liberal feminist 'add-more-women' approach (Grundy 1996) still lingers. The latter is problematic: not least because it assumes that 'success' is constituted by the victory of computer systems projects and thus entails a managerialist slant; but also because it is technologically determinist, with technology itself never being questioned (Van Zoonen 1992, p. 14) and computers being seen perforce to be a good thing. It is also a sign of a limited emancipatory agenda.

Those who have attempted a theorization of women's situation in relation to IS (for examples, MacKinnon et al. 1993; Wilson and Howcroft 2000; Adam and Green 2001; Adam et al. 2002; Wilson 2002, 2004) share an understanding that technology is made more explicable by analysing it as a culture, and therefore historically and materially contingent. Explanations of women's participation in IS which reject sexist, essentialist and deterministic arguments and explanations are based on the role of socialization in creating gender difference. Girls are socialized into having an orientation towards activities related to home creation, child rearing and care of others as part of their preparation for womanhood. Socialization is all-encompassing in two respects. First, it affects both men and women, differently but symmetrically (Davies 1995). Second, women internalize the views of society and (resistance aside) are shaped by it. Notions about the natural place of women in society are not only held by men.

While both Marxism and feminism will broadly agree on the socially constructed nature of gender characteristics (masculinity and femininity), they dispute the causes of this division. This affects both the choice of topic for study as well as the lens applied to the area. So, for example, drawing on technology studies, feminists have focused on issues of domestic ideology and gender and (de-)skilling, including the practices of male trade unionists to exclude women (for example, Cockburn 1988). There is much in Cockburn's work that is useful. However, approaches such as this have been challenged by those informed by Harry Braverman's seminal Marxist work *Labor and Monopoly Capital* (1974) which offers a means to examine the role of technology in exploitation under Taylorist capitalism. Such an approach seeks to challenge views of an unambiguous struggle of male unionists and employers to promote the interests of men over women, showing how the single theme of male dominance neglects other factors (Wightman 1999).

From a Marxist perspective, liberal feminists have recourse to the term 'patriarchy' which tends to imply a universality that obscures the contingent and localized character of gender roles. Patriarchy is used to describe the 'masculinist project of the domination and control of women and nature' (Wajcman 1991, p. 17). However, the imposition of a 'strong notion of a universal "patriarchy" or "gender patterns" is problematic' (Alvesson and Billing 1997, p. 4). Further, patriarchy can be viewed as a sort of conspiracy theory, perceiving as it does the intentional oppression of all women by a unity among all men (German 1986). Currently and historically, this ignores the diversity of interests (especially of class) among men, as well as the moments of solidarity between male and female workers in improving women workers' conditions (ibid.). The reliance on patriarchy theory entails a vision of women's oppression as an eternal feature of society and falling prey to biological determinism and essentialism which universalizes the experience of women. In contrast, a social constructivist approach to gender states that the term 'human nature' is in fact a generalization from observations of human behaviour, since there is always a tendency to read off from one's immediate reality, the natural state of the world.

*Agency and self-emancipation: IS and women users*
Despite the differences described above, in looking at the technology relationship, a Marxist approach need not eschew the work of feminists in technology studies, where the paradigm of social construction has been developed for the study of the gender–technology relationship (Wajcman 1991). This provides a platform on which to build our critical approach to IS which also incorporates the materialist, radical writing on organizations and technology, in the vein of Braverman's critique of technology and the labour process. In studying organizations, the emancipatory desire contained in Braverman's approach for structures that are wanted, needed and egalitarian

sets it automatically in an antithetical relation to the two dominant and fatalistic notions of managerialism and technological determinism.

To combat this fatalism, we must avoid concentrating on women only as victims of patriarchy, thereby treating them as mere objects of history. Instead, Marxists focus on where women are strongest: in the unions, at the height of struggles. This broad and rich history of working-class women's struggles has many peaks from which we can gain a clearer view of emancipation (Cliff 1984; Louie 2001; Naples 2002; Ehrenreich and Russel Hochschild 2003). The examples of women agitating collectively to change society – and in so doing managing to change themselves – serve to emphasize the fact that isolation in the home constitutes a step away from freedom for women and represents a retreat into the home both physically and ideologically. The question of agency and self-emancipation is key to a Marxist approach and a critical analysis should assume an active agency on the part of employee/users in relation to the development and use of IS. As socio-technical ensembles, IS always necessitate innovations in organizational behaviour required to complement the system (including changes in work practices).

Marxists and feminists agree that family responsibilities play a crucial role in shaping women's employment. Women form part of the workforce on an unprecedented scale but they come to the labour market still carrying the burden of women's oppression: lower earnings than men over a lifetime and constituting the bulk of part-time workers (Sutcliffe 2001). In addition, the lack of availability and high cost of childcare means that the majority of working-class women with young children are forced to 'choose' between living at home on benefits while caring for their children, and working inconvenient shifts which fit in with their partner's work. Evidently, some women have better conditions than this. However, for every career woman on a high salary, with car, house and nanny or au pair, there are many more in low-paid work with few of the material advantages which can help lessen the burden of women's oppression (Ehrenreich and Russel Hochschild 2003). For those without access to this type of 'alternative' to the double burden of the family, at-home teleworking is held out as a potential solution. For those with more means at their disposal, it seems to offer the allure of autonomy and control. Ironically, such technical fixes to the social problem of incompatible responsibilities, with the allure of 'flexibility', 'choice' and 'autonomy', may ultimately serve to take women back into more traditional and oppressive roles.

By espousing only the beneficial aspects for society, organizations and individuals of at-home telework, its advocates neglect the negative effects of a return to the home for working women. For example, Robey and Jin (2004, p. 151) claim that 'work is increasingly mediated by technologies that potentially liberate workers from specific places and times'. Teleworking, it is argued, will bring benefits to those (predominantly women) workers who struggle with the double burden of responsibilities of paid work and family care. The benefits are realized by the offer of 'flexibility' (Huws 1993; Sturgeon 1996; Daniels et al. 2000) which will remove those barriers deemed to stand in the way of easier management of this burden. Conversely, others have been sceptical towards the potential for (women's) emancipation through teleworking precisely because of traditional home responsibilities (Adam and Green 1998). This critical response to the legacy of traditional roles in the family is fully investigated in the next section.

**Marxism and the centrality of the family**
In this section we shall describe in more detail the Marxist position on women's oppression to show the materialist explanation for the current state of affairs in terms of women's oppression, as well as offering ideas for liberation. Feminism is far too broad a category to attempt to describe even the main trends here.[6] For now we shall use broad brushstrokes to draw generally recognized differences between the common elements of feminism and Marxism. The fundamental differences – especially between Marxism and the liberal feminist project – are highlighted when applicable. The intention is to clarify debates rather than score sectarian points. Despite areas of communality between feminist and Marxist approaches to women's relationship to IS, the differences shape both the paradigms employed to carry out research and the goal of study in terms of what it is we intend to prove. The significance for IS is outlined later by drawing out implications for at-home telework.

*Function and origins of the privatized family*
The heart of our critique of at-home telework as a response to women's double burden of work and family responsibilities is constituted by the Marxist view of the family as central to women's oppression. The privatized heterosexual family in capitalist society is underpinned by the need to ensure that workers meet the physical and mental requirements of paid labour, and to bring up the next generation of workers (German 2003). Socialized reproduction was not a possibility in the early stages of capitalism, and it is unlikely that global capitalism would invest in it now: the full socialization of childcare would require a level of investment unacceptable to the ruling class; the ideology of the family continues to be very important for the stability of the system (Davies 1982); the current period of economic crises has recourse to the backward 'defense of the family' to manipulate problems in the labour supply (Harman 1984, p. 11). Within the nuclear family it was expected that the man would work full-time outside the home and the

woman would take charge of refreshing man's labour power, as well as giving birth to and rearing children. Today, women increasingly work outside the home, yet continue with their role as wife and mother.

However, evidence continues to confirm that males' at-home obligations remain traditionally defined. No matter what discrepancies exist in age or educational level, fathers, husbands, partners all take on far fewer obligations than women to use their time for caretaking and domestic tasks; women with children are likely to work half as much again at home as at their workplace (Perin 1998). For Marxists, the prime beneficiaries are companies, given the priority of profit (Acker 1994).[7] The lack of ambition conventionally ascribed to women and their expectations of finding fulfilment in the family sphere facilitates adaptation to the modestly skilled jobs available in contemporary working life. So, the role of wife and mother shapes women's attitudes to work outside the home (Colgan and Ledwith 1996). The value of this ideological byproduct of the family for the capitalist class should not be underestimated (Davies 1982). Ideologically, it also created a split in the working class, encouraging men to identify with certain values of the exploiters (German 1986). Still more importantly for the current research on at-home teleworking is the condemnation by Marxists of any retreat of women into the family: 'the isolation of women in the home could cut them off from wider social movements. Their oppression reduced their ability to struggle against the system much of the time, and so opened them up to conservative views of society' (Harman 1984, p. 6).

A materialist explanation that locates women's position in society as ultimately determined by their role in the family is useful in a number of respects. First it reverses the pessimism of an acceptance of eternal patriarchy, as well as the essentialist overtones in describing males as 'naturally' oppressive. Second, it overcomes the rather untenable 'conspiracy theory' that men from all walks of life and different backgrounds with differing economic interests colluded in the subjugation of women. Third, it at least offers a coherent and consistent explanation which gives voice to the fact of the existence of women's oppression while not succumbing to the negative acceptance that things are as they are. Lastly, it is a historical theory which relies on reference to alternative views of human behaviour (and thus nature) to show that it is at least possible for men and women to live as equals. Further to these, it should be clear that this perspective automatically forces questions about promises for women's emancipation within the home.

Since it is culturally accepted that women will still take the major responsibility for childcare, their working lives have become structured by that responsibility. Indeed, the duties of childcare (rather than servicing male needs in the home) is by far the most influential factor shaping women's working lives (German 1986). Once again, this has implications for our view of teleworking.

In sum, for feminists the fundamental antagonism in society is between men and women: for Marxists it is between the classes not the sexes. Marxists conceive of an inescapable interrelationship among exploitation, oppression and liberation.

*Marxism and agency: going out to work as a precondition for liberation*
The theory of self-emancipation central to Marxism means that going out to work offers the only opportunity for women to radically change themselves in the process of changing their conditions. Working outside the home increases egalitarian attitudes among those women and their male partners (Cliff 1984). Increased participation in the workplace offers an alternative to the ideology of oppression and identifies the point at which women have strength. Yet the Marxist focus on the workplace can be at odds with a feminist approach. It is the case that liberal feminists since the 1960s onwards have tended to consistently focus on areas where men and women are in highest conflict: rape, battered women and wages for housework (McGregor 1989). At the same time, important struggles where women are more likely to win the support of men, such as strikes, the resistance to cuts in welfare, the fight for equal pay, abortion rights and unionization have been largely neglected (German 1988).

Karl Marx and Friedrich Engels argued that women's incorporation into social production was a precondition for their liberation. The involvement of women in work outside the home has constituted a crucial factor in women's struggles (Cliff 1984). The strength and confidence come from the gains of workplace participation: economic independence, a possibility of social worth, and collective action. This should make us wary of any technology-enabled 'solutions' to women's situation, such as at-home telework, which represent a return to women's isolation ideologically and physically in the home. Isolation leads to a sense of powerlessness. If women only worked at home as housewives, the picture would be grim. In relation to teleworking, if women's place in the home is privileged over other roles, there is a danger that this will lead them away from the potential to improve their lot, individually or collectively – but especially the latter – as described below.

*Unpaid work in the family: the home as haven and prison*
Marx and Engels had a dialectical approach to the family (Engels [1884] 1978), describing it as a haven in a heartless world, yet a place where people were socialized into continuing with their roles. Building on their work, Cliff (1984) outlines the contradictory nature of the working-class family

as haven and prison. First, the family is oppressive for (working-class) women, as women's own conception of themselves contradicts the actual situation where they are both earners and housewives. Instead of an escape to freedom from the control of the parental home and from boring and dreary jobs, marriage and home turn into a prison. Second, the family is oppressive not just for women, but for men too where a man's worth and self-esteem are adjudged on the basis of his ability to 'bring home the bacon'. Third, the family is more oppressive for working-class people than for other classes, since for them work and home are worlds apart. Evidently, women from different classes experience the home–work divide and family constraints and burdens differently.[8] Professional middle-class people, by contrast, lead far more active social lives than working-class people due to increased access to funds and common cultural activities. Fourth, the institution of the family imposes the harshest oppression on those who contravene its rules or just do not fit: lesbians and gays (Cliff 1984). We are all thus enslaved by the sex-role stereotypes connected with the family. Lastly, despite all these facts, in the face of no viable alternatives, the family is embraced as it does provide a sort of haven in a capitalist world: 'Out of loneliness the nuclear family gains strength. The institution of the family oppresses the woman. She, on her part, participates in creating the chains that bind her, decking them with flowers of love' (ibid., p. 221). While the home offers men an escape from the alienation of paid labour, the home is the very site of housewives' alienated situation.

The dual aspect of the family and home as refuge and site of unpaid labour is extremely significant for at-home telework prospects. When history has offered an opportunity, Marxists, in condemning the drudgery of 'domestic slavery' (Stites 1978), have attempted to socialize domestic labour and childcare (through maternity homes, nurseries, kindergartens, schools, communal dining rooms, communal laundries and mending centres) as the only way for women to be truly liberated. Under capitalism there is not even a discussion of such transformations of the nature of domestic labour because 'the capitalist economy is structurally hostile to the industrialization of housework' (Davies 1982, p. 223). In sum, Marxists are against moves to enable housework and the unpaid labour carried out in the home to continue – it is altogether a move in the wrong direction. In addition, moving paid work into the home is likely to have negative consequences for the home as a haven from alienation – a double disadvantage.

**Teleworking: a Marxist critique**
In this next section, we apply a Marxist critique to the claims made on behalf of technology, making a comparison with the Marxist agenda for women's liberation in order to contextualize the claims of amelioration for (women)

employees' working lives. The benefits teleworking provides to individuals as identified by Daniels et al. (2001) largely concern promises of flexible working hours, the option to work from home, and the opportunity to raise a family while pursuing a career (Sturgeon 1996). Indeed, this is summed up by one of the most-cited writers on the subject (Huws 1993, p. 45): 'the ability to combine work harmoniously with the demands of raising a family is often the main advantage of teleworking'.

By contrast, application of the Marxist analysis of the family combined with the Braverman critique of the labour process applied to IS leads to the following critique of hypothesized benefits for women to be delivered by telework.

*Anti-technological and biological determinism: cultural perspective of gender and IS*

In critical IS research, it can be expected that we would criticize notions associated with: managerialism for promoting fundamentally capitalist values such as increasing productivity and curtailing worker resistance; and technological determinism, which also excludes human choice, intervention and responsibility. A focus on the worker's employment experience in the teleworking phenomenon challenges the dominant ideology that technology always constitutes the best answer to social problems. In line with existing writing on gender and IS that deals with the disadvantaged relationship of women and IS from an anti-determinist standpoint, we have furthered the case for a cultural perspective to overcome the problems associated with essentialism and determinism. An analysis of this relationship as a cultural one, means also considering its historical and material contingency. For Marxists, the exploitation of some people by others, the existence of an oppressive state and the subordination of women to men in the nuclear family are products of human history and therefore open to change.

This means we should bear in mind that the socio-technical ensemble of at-home telework, like other IS, is a product of a capitalist system and society. It is subject to the critique of Braverman as a tool of increased exploitation over human emancipation within organizations, underpinned by fundamentally contradictory and conflictual interests. Increased profits can come only at the expense of increased exploitation and alienation. In analysing women's oppression and disadvantaged position at work, the Marxist focus is on the use made by capitalists of low-paid workers. At-home telework has many overlapping themes as part-time work (IES 2003). The need for women to accept low-paid part-time work is due to a lack of choice about at-home responsibilities. The capitalists have benefited twofold in that the burden of ensuring the refreshment and replenishment of the next generation of workers is provided for free in the privatized home. At the same time this can be used to drive down wages through part-time work – the ideological battering ram of the domination of housework and home responsibilities over a social role in the workplace.

### Increased alienation versus 'flexibility', 'choice' and 'autonomy'

By looking to writings and records of demands made by women and men for the amelioration of women's situation from the highpoint of struggle, Marxists have a benchmark against which to compare other claims – such as emancipation, or, in the case of telework: flexibility, choice and autonomy. These three terms imply that there are a set of alternatives on offer for work and home responsibilities. Evidently, with no real alternatives for the acceptable arrangement of childcare or other family duties, there is little real choice on offer. Home working may be the only option for managing childcare and work. Likewise, flexibility is seen as a benefit since it enables women to deal with their double burden and can be alternatively interpreted as reinforcing a view of women as 'always available for others' – even when struck by illness. Furthermore, Jenkins (2004) has shown how, in the case of part-time female workers, flexibility is restricting and offers little opportunity for career development. The extent to which employees can exercise autonomy will vary but will not necessarily decrease the routinization of tasks. Indeed, Dimitrova (2003) states that some managers use extensive supervisory procedures to counteract the inability to observe workers directly.

### Commuting and more time for family

The criteria on which to assess telework as an advance/progress will be according to rates of exploitation, which can be measured in terms of length of working day in relation to rewards and rate of profit created. Although this is quantitative in nature, it will be a social measure of technical capacity, and does not preclude subjective assessments of the worker's experience of this process. While the prospect of less commuting by working remotely may be appealing, this 'technical fix' obscures the complexity of the problem. Further, managers are likely to attempt to exploit the hours retrieved and there are restrictions about when activities have to take place. The ability to control hours of work must come at the expense of a working day without boundaries. The issue of flexibility arises again, with employees potentially expected to be always available to the organization.

The claim that the chance to remain at home to work for an organization will lead to workers having more time for family relations ignores the fact that these activities may be mutually exclusive, leading to increased conflict between work and home. If childcare is going on simultaneously with other work, then there may be increased/different disturbance (from family and community members) while working, which would negate those claims of teleworking as a solution to the distraction of the office. One cannot promote increased contact with family and community without equally allowing for unsolicited contact. If the family represents a refuge from loneliness and some limited respite from the alienation of capitalism, then it follows that bringing the lower levels of IS work into the home will signify the potential loss of one of the positive aspects of the home/family.

There is clear evidence here of the traditional view of family roles critiqued in the chapter: the care of children is unquestioningly the prerogative of women in the home within a structure of the capitalist, privatized family. This assumption precludes suggestions for broader alternative societal arrangements (Segal 1994). The critical researcher would maintain a sceptical distance from such technologically enabled utopias, since there are many reasons for concern that past exclusion patterns may be reproduced in the future (Wood 1999). Traditional home responsibilities severely reduce the potential for emancipation through occupations such as teleworking (Adam and Green 1998).

*Nature of work and (in)visibility*
The rhetoric of 'inclusion' is especially hollow for two reasons: absence from the host organization brings a cost of 'invisibility' from the reward system operated by management; and isolation in the home guards against traditional ways of collectively organizing in the workplace for resistance. Isolation leads to a sense of powerlessness. The managerialist view of work underpinning the promises is evident: work is largely portrayed as an individual rather than a collective act, since interaction with other tasks and workers is overlooked. In addition, the meaning of work for employees is limited to the perfunctory execution of tasks for the organization; other activities, such as socializing, satisfaction and sense of worth are thereby relegated in significance or even deemed dysfunctional. There is an implicit work ethic underlying the benefits for individuals: work must occur no matter what else happens in the individual's life (including sickness).

As for opportunities for women to overcome their situation, the view of work as an individual, functional act underestimates the social purpose of work in the workplace. From the aspect of managements' response to employees, the significance of presence and visibility of employees for recognition of their efforts is ignored, although 'invisibility' has historically played a negative role in women's career prospects, as the example of part-time (especially) women workers has consistently shown. This invisibility also impinges on employees' subjectivity and sense of belonging (and security).

*Agency and opportunities for collective action*

The Marxist focus on active employees/users, instead of a fixation on the manager as actor, embraces innovations to resist and subvert the process of exploitation (misbehaviour). Work has a social attraction (Hochschild 1997) partly constituted by the potential for collective activity. However, this opportunity is undermined by at-home telework, making it increasingly difficult for agencies to organize to protect employees' welfare (Bibby 2003), and for people to organize themselves. The additional difficulties in organizing workers who are disparate and whose sense of collective identity is likely to be weaker than in older forms of work has been noted (Danford et al. 2003).

Even if the withdrawal from socialized labour within an organization does not affect the economic independence of women, home work will certainly curtail the potential for collective action. Hence it would constitute a step away from women's struggles. In respect of strategies for effecting real change for women, as we have seen, the gains made in women's situation in the second half of the twentieth century have largely been a result of the increasing presence of women in the labour force. By contrast, the suggested solution of at-home telework as an aid for women to manage their work and family duties in a modern society may serve to promote other problems.

Critical IS research should be directed towards assisting those agencies responsible for workers' welfare (such as trades unions), at the very least to contribute to the prevention of the deterioration in working conditions, but hopefully more concretely to ameliorate them. Emancipation is not just limited when discussing the potential benefits of telework; more than this, telework is a regressive step ideologically. Talk of improved working conditions of telework when observed from a Marxist perspective is turned on its head, for at-home telework is likely to contribute to the distancing of women from the very point where they are potentially strongest (economic independence, a possibility of social worth and collective action) and able to radically change society, in the collective at work.

*Socio-economic groups: class differences*

Women from different classes experience the home–work divide and family constraints and burdens differently. In Marxist terms, we would be especially interested in socio-economic (class) groups. Given the discrepancy in work situations and family life between professional and working-class women, areas of investigation for the critical researcher include access to at-home telework, how the problems and solutions in relation to telework are variously perceived and varying impacts. The prior arrangements of housework and childcare due to disposable income disparity would also be of interest.

Further, we shall increasingly find at-home teleworkers carrying out clerical work, often involving the transaction-processing functions at the bottom end of an organization's work ranking. Webster (1996) reports that, despite the changes in skill requirements due to developments of office technology, there have not been equal improvements in career opportunities, influence or clerical salaries for women. It is unlikely that telework will remedy differences in access and conditions, as suggested by Felstead et al. (2002). Teleworking may appear as an option to feminists, viewed as a reform to accommodate the double burden of the family. It is especially an option for middle-class professionals, yet the double burden is usually managed by paying for the labour of others in the home (usually working-class women). However, we believe that there are few feminists who would see things this way. Teleworking is more about an adjustment within capitalism – a new form of work – to continue with exploitation and to employ the rhetoric of freedom.

On a societal level, from the Marxist perspective, society may pay a high price for the retreat of women back into the home. Given the situating of women's oppression in the family and successful struggle in collectivized and social workplace situation, the critical researcher would be very sceptical as to promises of freedom offered on behalf of at-home telework. Hence, uncritical acceptance associated with the benefits of telework for workers constitutes a means of assisting the domination of housework, home responsibilities, isolation and powerlessness over paid work in the socialized public arena where collective resistance is possible.

**Contribution of chapter for critical IS research**

In contrast to liberal feminists who look to confine the agenda to reforms under existing capitalism, Marxists maintain that there can be no women's (and with it sexual) liberation without a fundamental change to the means of production and social reproduction (that is, the end of the capitalist systems and the initiation of socialism); and vice versa – there cannot be a socialist society in which women are oppressed.[9] We believe that by making apparent how the reproduction of social structures and relations stand in the way of emancipation, then we are potentially in a position to consider alternative structures and solutions. In fulfilling this aim we have contributed to the handbook in the following ways:

1. In relation to the IS topic chosen for our critical approach, telework is seen as a socio-technical ensemble. We have provided a succinct overview of the teleworking literature, a background and definitions to the phenomena.

2. While interested in societal and organizational explanations for outcomes, we have taken the perspective of individual employees and their interaction with broader structures. The aim was to look at technology in diffusion and to 'put the labour back in', assuming the centrality of studying users' agency in shaping the development and outcome of systems, as well as a view of women as subjects of history and their self-emancipation.

3. Concerned with emancipation, our focus has been on the implications of home teleworking for women, specifically asking if and how such new work practices can result in amelioration of working conditions – even 'freedom'. We have thus contributed significantly to the discussion of emancipation, which is key to the critical agenda. By reviewing the visions of Marxists from the peaks of struggles, we have set a benchmark of aspirations against which others can draw their own boundaries.

4. The radical nature of the critique means that the main target has been the 'black-boxing' of the double burden of the home. Underpinning the claims to choice and flexibility is a rather traditional view of family roles: not just that it is women – rather than men – who often take on the care responsibilities, but that this is within a privatized family, where societal responsibility for childcare is minimal. Locating women's oppression within their role in the privatized family unit means taking a critical stance against 'solutions' that take women back into the home and out of the public sphere.

As a consistent practical conclusion of the type of critical approach adopted here, we suggest that future research should retain a commitment to work in conjunction with unions and other agencies which have as their goal the amelioration of workers' conditions. Finally, in terms of the subject for research, although the critique here is aimed at telework, the exposition of that which constitutes and shapes women's oppression and disadvantaged situation at work can be applied to other IS innovations and associated new work practices.

**Notes**

1. Elements of the research presented here in relation to at-home telework have been presented in Wilson and Greenhill (2004a, 2004b, 2004c).
2. Organizing teleworkers is doubly difficult: high-tech workers have been awkward to unionize (Van Jaarsveld 2004), and the disparate physical location of teleworkers adds another order of difficulty to the task (Bibby 2003).
3. In this regard, Bhaskar's (1998: 676) dialectic of equality can be a useful definition: 'the principle of sufficient practical reason states that there must be ground for difference. If there is no such ground then we are rationally impelled to remove them'.
4. For example, in the UK single parenthood continues to rise and cohabitation of both gay and straight couples has significantly increased; by 1997 heterosexual marriage rates had

halved since 1970; divorce rates are higher than other EU countries; teenage pregnancy rates have increased (German 2003).
5. See www.tuc.org.uk/changingtimes/worktrends.htm.
6. Given the overarching topic of technology we direct readers who wish to pursue an analysis of the feminist trends to Judy Wajcman's excellent work, *Feminism Confronts Technology* (1991).
7. Cited in Alvesson and Billing (1997).
8. See, for example, Angela Davies's (1982) eloquent application of Engels's writings on the family to black and white women in the United States.
9. This incidentally provides a criteria or benchmark for assessing those systems that do claim or have claimed to be socialist.

## References
Acker, J. (1994), 'The gender regime of Swedish banks', *Scandinavian Journal of Management*, **10**, 117–30.
Adam, A., Emms, J., Green, E. and Owen, J. (eds) (1994), *Women, Work and Computerization: Breaking Old Boundaries: Building New Forms*, Amsterdam: North-Holland.
Adam, A. and Green, E. (1998), 'Gender, agency, location and the new information society', in B.D. Loader (ed.), *Cyberspace Divide: Equality, Agency and Policy in the Information Society*, London: Routledge, pp. 83–97.
Adam, A. and Green, E. (2001), *Virtual Gender: Technology, Consumption and Identity*, New York: Routledge.
Adam, A., Howcroft, D. and Richardson, H. (2002), 'Guest editorial', *Information Technology and People*, **15** (2), 94–97.
Alvesson, M. and Billing, Y.D. (1997), *Understanding Gender and Organizations*, London: Sage.
Baines, S. and Gelder, U. (2003), 'What is family friendly about the workplace in the home? The case of self-employed parents and their children', *New Technology, Work and Employment*, **18** (30), 223–34.
Batt, R. and Valcour, P.M. (2003), 'Human resource practices as predictors of work–family outcomes and employee turnover', *Industrial Relations*, **42** (2), 189–220.
Berg, P., Kalleberg, A.L. and Appelbaum, E. (2003), 'Balancing work and family: the role of high-commitment environments', *Industrial Relations*, **42** (2), 168–88.
Bhaskar, R. (1998), 'Dialectical critical realism and ethics', in M. Archer, R. Bhaskar, A. Collier, T. Lawson and A. Norrie (eds), *Critical Realism: Essential Readings*, London: Routledge, pp. 641–87.
Bibby, A. (2003), 'Trade unions and telework', www.andrewbibby.com, accessed 5 October 2003.
Braverman, H. (1974), *Labor and Monopoly Capital: The Degradation of Work in the Twentieth Century*, New York: Monthly Review Press.
Bricknell, G. (1996), 'Time you did your homework', *Facilities*, **14** (12/13), 42–4.
Cecez-Kecmanovic, D. (2001), 'Doing critical IS research: the question of methodology', in E.M. Trauth (ed.), *Qualitative Research in IS: Issues and Trends*, Hershey, PA: Idea Group Publishing, pp. 141–62.
Cliff, T. (1984), *Class Struggle and Women's Liberation: 1840 to Today*, London: Bookmarks.
Cockburn, C. (1988), 'The gendering of jobs: workplace relations and the reproduction of sex segregation', in S. Walby (ed.), *Gender Segregation at Work*, Milton Keynes: Open University Press, pp. 91–107.
Colgan, F. and Ledwith, S. (1996), *Women, Work and Organizations*, Basingstoke: Macmillan.
Danford, A., Richardson, M., Upchurch, M., Cooper, S. and Danforth, A. (2003), *New Unions, New Workplaces: Strategies for Union Revival*, Routledge Research in Employment Relations, London: Routledge.

Daniels, K., Lamond, D. and Standen, P. (2001), 'Teleworking: frameworks for organizational research', *Journal of Management Studies*, **38** (8), 1151–85.

Davies, A. (1982), *Women, Race and Class*, London: Women's Press.

Davies, C. (1995), *Gender and the Professional Predicament in Nursing*, Buckingham: Open University Press.

Di Martino, V. and Wirth, L. (1990), 'Telework: a new way of working and living', *International Labour Review*, **129** (5), 529–54.

Dimitrova, D. (2003), 'Controlling teleworkers: supervision and flexibility revisited', *New Technology, Work and Employment*, **18** (3), 181–91.

Ehrenreich, B. and Russel Hochschild, A. (2003), *Global Woman: Nannies, Maids, and Sex Workers in the New Economy*, New York: Metropolitan Books.

Engels, F. (1978), *The Origin of the Family, Private Property and the State*, Peking: Foreign Languages Press (originally published 1884, Zurich).

Felstead, A., Jewson, N., Phizacklea, A. and Walters, S. (2002), 'The option to work at home: another privilege for the favoured few?', *New Technology, Work and Employment*, **17** (3), 204–23.

Frenkel, K.A. (1990), 'Women and computing', *Communications of the ACM*, **33** (11), 33–46.

Frolick, M., Wilkes, R. and Urwiler, R. (1993), 'Telecommuting as a workplace alternative: an identification of significant factors in American firms' determination of work-at-home policies', *Journal of Strategic Information Systems*, **2** (3), 206–22.

German, L. (1986), 'Frederick Engels: life of a revolutionary', *International Socialism Journal*, Special Issue on The Revolutionary Ideas of Frederick Engels, **25**, Winter, 3–46.

German, L. (1988), 'Rise and fall of the Women's Movement', *International Socialism Journal*, **2** (37), Winter, 3–49.

German, L. (2003), 'Women's liberation today', *International Socialism Journal*, **101**, Winter, 3–34.

Gray, M., Hodson, N. and Gordon, G. (1993), *Teleworking Explained*, Chichester: Wiley.

Green, E., Owen, J. and Pain, D. (eds) (1993), *Gendered by Design: Information Technology and Office Systems*, London: Taylor & Francis.

Grundy, F. (1996), *Women and Computers*, Exeter: Intellect.

Harman, C. (1984), 'Women's liberation and revolutionary socialism', *International Socialism Journal*, **2** (23), Spring, 3–42.

Hirschheim, R. and Klein, H.K. (1989), 'Four paradigms of information systems development', *Communications of the ACM*, **32** (10), 1199–216.

Hochschild, A.R. (1997), *The Time Bind: When Work Becomes Home and Home Becomes Work*, New York: Henry Holt and Company.

Hogarth, T., Hasluck, C., Pierre, G., Winterbottom, M. and Vivian, D. (2000), *Work–life Balance 2000: Baseline Study of Work–Life Balance Practices in Great Britain – Summary Report*, London: Department of Education and Employment.

Huws, U. (1993), *Teleworking in Britain: A Report to the Employment Department*, London: Employment Department.

Institute for Employment Studies (IES) (2003), 'Further analysis of labour force survey on telework', www.employment-studies.co.uk, 7 October.

Jackson, P.J. and Van der Wielen, J.M. (eds) (1998), *Teleworking: International Perspectives. From Teleworking to the Virtual Organization*, London: Routledge.

Jenkins, S. (2004), 'Restructuring flexibility: case studies of part-time female workers in six workplaces', *Gender, Work and Organization*, **11** (3), 306–33.

Klawe, M. and Leveson, N. (1995), 'Women in computing: where are we now?', *Communications of the ACM*, **38** (1), 29–35.

Kwan, S.K., Trauth, E.M. and Driehaus, K.C. (1985), 'Gender differences and computing: students' assessment of societal influences', *Education and Computing*, **1** (3), 187–94.

Louie, M.C.Y. (2001), *Sweatshop Warriors: Immigrant Workers Take on the Global Factory*, Cambridge, MA: South End Press.

MacKinnon, A., Blomqvist, M. and Vehvilainen, M. (1993), 'Gendering computer work: an international perspective', *AI and Society*, **8**, 280–94.

Mann, S. and Holdsworth, L. (2003), 'The psychological impact of teleworking: stress, emotions and health', *Technology, Work and Employment*, **18** (3), 196–211.

Maru, Y.T. and Woodford, K. (2001), 'Enhancing emancipatory systems methodologies for sustainable development', *Systemic Practice and Action Research*, **14** (1), 61–77.

McGregor, S. (1989), 'Rape, pornography and capitalism', *International Socialism Journal*, **2** (45), Winter, 3–34.

Mingers, J. (2000), 'An idea ahead of its time: the history and development of soft systems methodology', *Systemic Practice and Action Research*, **13** (6), 733–55.

Naples, N. (2002), *Women's Activism and Globalization: Linking Local Struggles and Transnational Politics*, London: Routledge.

Ngwenyama, O.K. (1991), 'The critical social theory approach to information systems: problems and challenges', in H.E. Nissen, H.K. Klein and R. Hirschheim (eds), *Information Systems Research: Contemporary Approaches and Emergent Traditions*, Amsterdam: North-Holland and London: Elsevier Science.

Orlikowski, W.J. and Baroudi, J.J. (1991), 'Studying IT in organizations: research approaches and assumptions', *Information Systems Research*, **2** (1), 1–28.

Perin, C. (1998), 'Work space and time on the threshold of a new century', in P. Jackson and J.M. Van der Wielin (eds), *Teleworking: International Perspectives from Teleworking to the Virtual Organization*, London: Routledge.

Qvortrup, L. (1998), 'From teleworking to networking: definitions and trends', in Jackson and Van der Wielen (eds), pp. 21–39.

Rasmussen, B. and Hapnes, T. (1991), 'Excluding women from the technologies of the future?', *Futures*, December, 1107–13.

Robey, D. and Jin, L. (2004), 'Studying virtual work in teams, organizations and communities', in M.E. Whitman and A.B. Woszczynski (eds), *The Handbook of Information Systems Research*, London: Idea Group Publishing, pp. 150–65.

Segal, L. (1994), *Is the Future Female? Troubled Thoughts on Contemporary Feminism*, 2nd edn, London: Virago.

Spencer, D.A. (2000), 'Braverman and the contribution of labour process analysis to the critique of capitalist production – twenty-five years on', *Work, Employment and Society*, **14** (2), 223–43.

Stites, R. (1978), *The Women's Liberation Movement in Russia: Feminism, Nihilism and Bolshevism 1860–1930*, Princeton, NJ: Princeton University Press.

Sturgeon, A. (1996), 'Telework: threats, risk and solutions', *Information Management and Computer Security*, **4** (2), 7–38.

Sullivan, C. (2003), 'What's in a name? Definitions and conceptualizations of teleworking and homeworking', *New Technology, Work and Employment*, **18** (3), 158–65.

Sutcliffe, B. (2001), *One Hundred Ways of Seeing an Unequal World*, London: Zed Books.

Toffler, A. (1987), *The Third Wave*, New York: Random House Value Publishing.

Trades Union Congress (TUC) (2003), 'The future of work: looking ahead – the next ten years', http://tuc.org.uk/em_research/, 7 October.

Trauth, E. (2002), 'Odd girl out: an individual differences perspective on women in the IT profession', *Information Technology and People*, **15** (2), 98–118.

Turner, E. and Hovendon, F. (1997), 'How are we seen? Images of women in computing advertisements', in R. Lander and A. Adam (eds), *Women in Computing*, Exeter: Intellect Books, 60–71.

Van Jaarsveld, D.D. (2004), 'Collective representation among high-tech workers at Microsoft and beyond: lessons from WashTech/CWA', *Industrial Relations*, **43** (2), 364–85.

Van Zoonen, L. (1992), 'Feminist theory and information technology', *Media, Culture and Society*, **14**, 9–29.

Vogel, L. (1983), *Marxism and the Oppression of Women: Toward a Unitary Theory*, London: Pluto.

Wajcman, J. (1991), *Feminism Confronts Technology*, Cambridge: Polity.

Ward, N. and Shabha, G. (2001), 'Teleworking: an assessment of socio-psychological factors', *Facilities*, **2** (1–2), 61–71.

Webster, J. (1996), *Shaping Women's Work: Gender Employment and Information Technology*, London: Longman.

Wightman, C. (1999), *More Than Munitions*, Harlow: Addison Wesley Longman.

Wilson, M. (2002), 'Making nursing visible? Gender, technology and the care plan as script', *Information Technology and People*, **15** (2), 139–58.

Wilson, M. (2004), 'A conceptual framework for studying gender in information systems research', *Journal of Information Technology*, **19** (1), 81–92.

Wilson, M. and Greenhill, A. (2004a), 'Gender and teleworking identities in the risk society: a research agenda', *New Technology, Work and Employment*, **19** (3), 207–21.

Wilson, M. and Greenhill, A. (2004b), 'A critical deconstruction of promises made for women on behalf of telework', Paper presented at the Second International CRIS Workshop, on Critical Reflections on Critical Research in IS, Salford, July.

Wilson, M. and Greenhill, A. (2004c) 'Gender and teleworking identities: re-constructing the research agenda', Paper presented at the 12th European Conference on Information Systems, Turku, June.

Wilson, M. and Howcroft, D. (2000), 'The role of gender in user resistance and IS failure', in R. Baskerville, J. Stage and J. DeGross (eds), *The Social and Organisational Perspective on Research and Practice in Information Technology*, Berlin: Kluwer Academic, pp. 453–71.

Wood, T.A. (1999), 'Gender and educational equity: the emergence of the Internet', CITE Report, No. 247, Milton Keynes: The Open University.

# 9 Critical management studies: towards a more mature politics
*Christopher Grey*

## Introduction

Critical management studies (CMS) has become the term of choice for a wide and growing array of academics working not just in management but in various cognate fields including accounting and information systems. Many date the use of the term from Alvesson and Willmott's (1992) eponymous edited collection although, as I shall indicate, it has many antecedents. If we *do* date it from 1992 then we can make, with almost equal validity, the remark that CMS has achieved an enormous amount and that it has achieved almost nothing. An enormous amount precisely because it has become a term which is so widely used and because it has generated so much in the way of conferences, meetings, journal papers, debate and discussion. Yet almost nothing because, outside of itself, it is hardly known about and has hardly touched the way in which management operates and is invoked in wider society. Indeed, even within the limited terrain of the business and management schools where it has been most influential, its impact upon the 'mainstream' of those institutions has been minimal. We might at least expect that those versions of management studies which are under critique would have mounted a defence of themselves, even if they hadn't been persuaded to reform. But almost nothing like this has happened. What has happened, however, is a series of vituperative debates *inside* CMS so that the proverbial Martian might reasonably conclude that the only people interested in CMS are its adherents and that even they don't like it very much. In the heyday of punk there was a song title which became a popular graffito: 'pop will eat itself', and if CMS is the rock 'n' roll of business schools then it could well suffer a similar fate.

Now of course I want to resile from what I have just said before the ink has even dried. I do not think that CMS has no achievements to its name, nor do I subscribe to the self-flagellation, common among academics, about their own irrelevance. Ideas are worth expressing even if few listen; internal debate has some merits over slavish conformity and influence is a slow and indirect business. But – and it is a big but – precisely because influence is a slow and indirect business, intellectual movements need to nurture

*174*

themselves as they grow, rather than kick themselves down before they have started to walk. In this chapter, I shall argue that CMS has begun to have a small influence but that this will not be advanced if it collapses into internal feuding when it has hardly begun to have the influence it warrants.

I see developments in the critical analysis of information systems (IS) as being part and parcel of this wider development: CMS. And I assume that the politics of critical IS are very similar to those in the management field more generally. More than that, I assume that the growing interest in critical approaches to IS, of which this handbook is one example, are indicative of the influence which CMS is having upon intellectual developments in a range of fields.

However, in this chapter I want to stress not so much CMS as an intellectual development but the (clearly) related theme of CMS as a political movement. Perhaps movement is too loaded and too grandiose a term. Yet it is unavoidable to read CMS in political terms. Much of its impetus comes from some version of leftist politics. It arises predominantly within university business schools,[1] the development of which has its own political story, some of which I shall tell. One consequence of that story is that the mainstream orthodoxy of business schools, to which CMS is in large part a reaction, can in a general (and often a particular) way be associated with some version of rightist politics. So CMS is a broadly left-wing movement nested inside a broadly right-wing institution. This presents an interesting political situation, containing both important possibilities but also obvious difficulties. It is aspects of this situation that I wish to explore in this chapter. More specifically, I shall articulate what I am calling a 'mature' politics for CMS, by which I mean a politics which is inclusive, outward facing and which utilizes the strategic possibilities of its business school location.

I shall begin by outlining some contextual features of CMS, focusing principally upon the business schools within which it has primarily arisen. In the next section I shall give a brief explanation of what is distinctive about CMS and the ways in which it has developed so far. I shall then explore at greater length the internal debates and controversies associated with CMS before developing in depth the main new argument I am making in this chapter: that CMS needs a more mature politics in the sense that I have just defined.

## The context of CMS

The term 'critical management studies' contains within it two related but slightly different propositions. One is a critique of management. The other is a critique of the study of management. Certainly these are linked, for if the critique of the study of management is successful then a new form of studying management emerges – one which engages in the critique of management. However, these two meanings carry with them different implications for the politics of CMS.

The critique of management operates on a large scale of analysis because management itself is insinuated not just into the organization of business corporations but also into political administration and, even, into the fundament of 'modern' world views in which nature and the social order are seen as amenable to, and in need of, management. This clearly positions CMS as connecting to some very large issues within politics and philosophy. It also links CMS to a much longer history of thought and action than might be implied by those who date it from 1992. The management of corporations, the state, nature and the social order have been the subject of critique whenever it has been practised or proposed. If this is what we mean by CMS then it would be wholly naive to think either that it could proceed in isolation from a huge variety of intellectual histories and political movements which are concerned with some kind of critique of management. But it would also be naive to castigate CMS – a movement of, at most a few hundred people in, predominantly, business schools in, predominantly, Northern Europe, Australia, New Zealand and the United States – for having failed to make a huge amount of progress in the transformation of debate about management, let alone its practice.

Understood as a critique of management *studies*, CMS looks rather different. If management studies means the academic discipline located within universities then it has a much shorter history and denotes a much more limited terrain. Relatively speaking, it also makes CMS a much more original set of ideas, to the extent that most of management studies in this meaning has been 'uncritical'. Management studies has a history of perhaps no more than 120 years and, as a research-based discipline operating on any great scale, perhaps less than 60 years. Even against that background, it is important to recognize that the size and longevity of CMS is relatively small but it does suggest that here is a domain which might be more amenable to influence than that of management *per se*. But by the same token, we might judge CMS all the more harshly if it fails to have that influence.

The conjoining of these two things – a longstanding set of traditions and debates within a relatively new kind of institution – is what makes CMS of some potential importance. Business schools have become a significant nodal point within contemporary society, connecting intellectuals with businesses and government. In many ways, business schools have a similar character and function to that of the medieval universities which connected intellectuals with church and court. Business schools may be 'servants of power' (Baritz 1960), but it is precisely this that makes them an important place for the instantiation of all of those debates and critiques which have always attended management. Adherents of CMS may not be saying anything that sociologists and social activists are not saying, but they are doing it in places within shouting distance of where power, if it lies anywhere, lies. That does not mean that CMS can or will be more influential than those other voices – and the likelihood of its co-option is much greater – but it does impose a particular set of possibilities and impossibilities, of tactics and dilemmas, which are peculiar to itself. It is this institutional positioning which must set the context for anything which, politically, CMS can expect, or be expected, to achieve.

Given these possibilities, it might be a surprise that CMS has been so slow to get going. It is certainly true that there are plenty of examples of CMS *avant la lettre*. In the UK there was a radical movement in organization studies, in particular, from the 1970s (for example, Clegg and Dunkerley 1977) and also in accounting (for example, Hopwood 1974). Peter Anthony (1986) prefigured many of the CMS themes about, specifically, management. In the United States, writers such as Walter Nord and John Jermier (for example, Jermier 1981) were, from the 1970s onwards, making similar observations. And undoubtedly one could find, without too much effort, a recognizably critical analysis from one business school academic or another at any time during the last century. However, the more obvious thing about business schools is the extent to which they developed, throughout the twentieth century, and especially in the latter half of that century, a quite stifling orthodoxy in which positivism, economism and managerialism ruled the roost. To a very large extent they still do.[2]

One reason for that was that in the United States, where management studies developed earliest and most extensively, business schools were deliberately re-invented in the post-war era around the 'new paradigm' (Locke 1989). In this new paradigm, management studies were, under the influence of the Gordon and Howell Report and the Pierson Report, both published in 1959, to be placed on a proper 'scientific' footing. Research would provide a knowledge base for reliable predictions and interventions. Teaching would equip fledgling managers with the results thus garnered. This model was both enthusiastically embraced, in the United States, and successfully exported, most especially although variably, to Europe (Engwall and Zamagni 1998). This may be read in many ways. In part it was certainly (as with business schools since their inception in the nineteenth century) to do with attempts to boost the status of 'business' to match that of professions such as law and medicine. In part, it was to do with another kind of status-building project, that by management academics themselves to be taken as seriously as their colleagues in, if not the sciences then at least the social sciences. As Jim March wittily observed (March 2000), if economists have long suffered physics-envy then management scientists have suffered economics-envy.

These are some small-p political issues around management studies and they are worth mentioning both as an explanation of the context of CMS and as a reminder that CMS is not new or unique in pursuing political agendas in business schools. But the spread of what I suppose[3] can be called the 'mainstream' version of management studies can also be read in big-P politics terms. The export of US management studies on a large scale was inextricably bound up with the cold war in two slightly different, although plainly related, ways. One was that an economistic and managerialist version of the business school was part and parcel of the general espousal of capitalist ideologies: the market economy and hierarchy being two obvious generic examples. But in a more precise way, as historian Robert Locke (1996) explains, it was widely believed that US management technique was the best in the world and that this had been demonstrated by the logistical basis of the US war effort. This, and the long post-war boom, was the basis of what he calls the 'American management mystique'.[4] If Western Europe was to resist the seductions of Communism then it was necessary to ensure that its industry was not just effective but superior to that of the Soviet bloc – and management, along with management education, was one answer. The enmeshment of business schools with the political imperatives of Western capitalism continues to be one of their most obvious defining features. They simultaneously provide the personnel for the investment banks and consulting practices along with one source of the ideological resources of such undertakings (Frank 2001; Grey 2002; Parker 2002).

And this is why it is important to understand the political context within which business schools emerged and still operate. North American schools, in particular, but also European institutions like INSEAD (the European Institute of Business Administration), the London Business School and others bear the imprint of this history and also transmit it to the extent that they define what a 'proper' business school is. At the same time, it would be wrong to see Europe as the passive recipient of a North American orthodoxy. For a start, over time, that orthodoxy has become progressively more heterogeneous and, in particular, the collapse of the 'American management mystique' opened up even the heartlands to other influences, most notably some version of Asian management practice. But in any case, as many of the contributions to Engwall and Zamagni (1998) show, the US model was always modified or even rejected on the basis of local and culturally specific factors. Thus, for example, it has not, until very recently, had much purchase in Germany; Scandinavia was as much influenced (for better or worse) by the German tradition of business economics and France has retained the *Grandes Écoles* as a route to the staffing of elites even though it has incorporated some US-style business schools. CMS can in part be read as one of the various reactions to the influence of the orthodox North American model of business schools and management studies.

Most interesting of all in this regard is the UK case, and I say this not, I hope, through any kind of parochialism but because it is in the UK that CMS seems to have been most popular. The first thing to note is that business schools do not exemplify anything like the more general story which could be told of many institutions of a transition from British to American global reach (or, as some unreconstructed folk might say, imperialism). That is: there was relatively little UK business school tradition in place prior to the large-scale development of US provision and so there is little in the way of an imperial legacy in UK management studies. Certainly there had been a largely non-university-based history of 'commercial education' (Pollard 1965) – bookkeeping, navigation, commercial law and so on. There had also been some university-led provision of administrative studies, for example at Manchester, the London School of Economics and Political Science (LSE) and – hooked into the British and Imperial Civil Service – Henley. But the development of business schools – and I suppose I mean MBA providers which also conduct research – did not occur until the mid-1960s. Their subsequent take-up has been more enthusiastic and certainly more extensive in the UK than anywhere else in Europe, if not the world. The UK produces more MBA graduates a year (about 12,000) than the rest of Europe put together; about 13 per cent of UK undergraduates major in management and, in total, almost a third take management as part or all of their degree.

This has developed very rapidly, so that within the last 20 years the number of business schools has grown from about 35 to perhaps 118 (there is an imprecision about what constitutes a business school, but the overall picture is clear enough). 'The last 20 years' is very significant, for several reasons. One is that it suggests – and there can be no doubt that there is a causality – that the rise of UK business schools is related to the rise of the New Right, of a hegemony around market ideologies and of a utilitarian approach to education in general and higher education in particular. Second, it means that these schools have developed since the collapse of the 'American management mystique', and so in a context where alternative management models were becoming legitimate. Third, this was a period during which cold war politics was diminishing in intensity, or had ceased altogether, but in which the new politics of global turbo-capitalism[5] was in the ascendant. Fourth, it means that the emergence of UK business schools post-dates the 'linguistic turn'[6] and the widespread questioning, or even discrediting, of the positivism upon which both 'new paradigm' business schools and the social sciences which underlie management studies had been predicated.

So then there is a fifth consequence, which binds together – or comes out of – much of what I have just said and which is crucial to the development of CMS. As UK business schools grew they needed, for reasons of legitimacy, faculty who were academically trained and, for labour market reasons, largely home grown. This was probably the only area of universities which experienced significant and sustained growth in faculty numbers over the period in question. These faculty came in large part from the junior ranks of the social sciences, where academic jobs had, under the impact of the New Right, largely dried up. This brought a collection of people, trained to be hostile to positivism, trained in critical traditions in social science, and often radicalized by the class, feminist and ecological politics of the 1980s into the growing business schools. That was often aided by existing faculty who had been informed by the 'antecedents' of CMS but was in any case dictated by, perversely, the market-led growth of management studies in higher education. This new cohort unsurprisingly brought their attention to bear upon the corporate excesses of an increasingly deregulated capital and the managerialist and technocratic politics which proceeded from the 'post-history', 'post-ideology' landscape of the aftermath of the cold war. Or, in another variant, a cohort attuned to the identity politics of consumer society and the anti-brand analysis of what in due course became the anti-globalization movement brought its attention to bear upon marketing, retailing and consumption.

I said that I do not want to be parochial and certainly I do not want to discount or ignore that a move to CMS came in other places and for other reasons, or for local variants of similar reasons.[7] But, for all that there is not a singular story to be told, it is clear to me that the story I have just told accounts for a major impetus for CMS. However, whether or not this is true, the more important issue is to recognize that CMS has a context, political and institutional, which needs to be understood as a prelude to saying more about what it stands for and what it might achieve.

**The nature of CMS**
I have suggested that CMS is a broadly leftist approach to management and management studies, and have already implied something of what it stands for. Now I shall delineate it somewhat more precisely. Along with Valerie Fournier, I argued that CMS organizes itself around some core propositions: de-naturalization, anti-performativity and reflexivity (Fournier and Grey 2000).

The first refers to what I think is crucial to any oppositional politics. The existing order, whatever it may be, always justifies itself by reference to nature and necessity. *Of course* men dominate women, whites dominate blacks, capital dominates labour. It's natural: whether based on evolution or social function the answer is the same. Things *have* to be the way they are because otherwise they would *not* be that way – the false syllogism of every piece of cod Darwinism and elitist self-congratulation since time immemorial. In management, the proposition is that someone has to be in charge, that of course they know more, or else they would not be in charge, so of course they deserve more money. Hierarchy is taken as natural; the idea that coordination implies superiority is taken as natural; the idea that hierarchical coordination licenses higher rewards than production is taken as natural; markets are natural and so on. CMS disputes all of these assertions.

The second feature of CMS is perhaps a special case of the first. Anti-performativity denies that social relations should be (naturally) thought of instrumentally: in terms of maximizing output from a given input. And it is striking how many of those who have discussed this aspect of our description of CMS have struggled with it. Critics and supporters have asserted that since we wish to see a different kind of world then we too are performative; we too want to make 'something happen'. Well, the latter is true, but the former is not. The term 'performative' emphatically does not mean *any* kind of action or simply (and perhaps this is where the confusion lies) performing. It means that particular version of action or performing in which there is a means–ends calculus with economic efficiency as the guiding theme, and ethics and values are ignored, truncated or subsumed within efficiency. In Weberian terms, performativity is the elevation of an exclusively instrumental rationality to the detriment of value rationality. Thus performativity does not by any means exhaust all the possibilities of action or 'performance'. The fact that some commentators think that it does only goes to show how far instrumental apprehensions of action and preformative apprehensions of performance have been naturalized.

The third feature of CMS, according to the Fournier and Grey article, is reflexivity. This refers to the capacity to recognize that accounts of organization and management are mediated by those, typically researchers, who give that account. Reflexivity consists, in part, of a recognition of the role of researchers in this respect. But I think more importantly that it consists of a recognition of the cultural conditions of production of research. In this way, CMS evinces a methodological and epistemological rejection of the objectivism and scientism inherent within mainstream positivist research. Under the guise of the production of value-free facts, such research is inattentive to (or unreflexive about) the assumptions which guide both its choice of what to research and the manner in which that research is conducted (see Tinker et al. 1982).

These three features, taken together, stake out a ground for CMS which is compatible with quite a large variety of different theoretical and political positions – a point I shall return to – and yet marks some boundaries which separate CMS from mainstream, orthodox and managerialist positions both as regards management and the conduct of management research. For this reason, CMS has been able to exert an attraction to a relatively large group of academics within business schools and has in recent years come to a growing prominence. This is indexed in part by the growing volume of work which self-positions itself, either explicitly or through citation, as being informed by CMS. Such work is increasingly found within 'top' international journals and can be seen to inform handbooks, such as this one, positioning themselves as in some ways alternative to orthodoxy. Although this has been most obvious in the area of organization studies, the critical approach has also been strongly articulated in most parts of the management studies field, especially accounting (Chua 1986) and information systems (Orlikowski and Baroudi 1991).

There have also been a number of analytical treatments of CMS, some of which are referred to elsewhere in the chapter and which include a special issue of *Organization* arranged around a series of responses to Zald (2002). And CMS is not just discussed in the literature, but has begun to institutionalize itself through conferences, especially the CMS conference which has run three times since 1999, with a growing number of delegates. In the United States, a CMS workshop has grown into a special interest group of the American Academy of Management and a recent commentary suggests that the prospects for CMS to gain a hearing in the US, and to influence the practice of management education, are promising (Walsh and Weber 2002).

All of this, while scarcely earth-shattering, tends to suggest an expansion of interest in and legitimacy for CMS. It also indicates a growing number of people who self-identify with CMS and who can be expected to support and nurture research groups and networks with a critical orientation. So this might be seen as good news for those who share this orientation. However, as CMS has grown it has attracted a considerable amount of criticism and, as I stated earlier, not so much from those it is critical of as from those who might be expected to be sympathetic to its general position.

### Debates within CMS
The development of CMS was, as I suggested earlier, by no means a bolt from the blue. It had been prefigured by a series of analyses of organizations, accounting and management, and owed a considerable debt to some pre-existing traditions. In particular, the existence of Marxist and neo-Marxist studies of organizational and industrial sociology was especially important. Some versions of CMS, most notably those inspired by Jürgen Habermas and earlier Frankfurt school luminaries, are effectively versions of Marxism and,

even where the debt is not explicit, analyses both of capital accumulation and of the seductions of consumer society lurk as recognizable if sometimes unannounced guests at the CMS party. Other versions of CMS invoke post-structuralist and postmodern analysis, all too often treated within CMS as if they were the same thing, with Michel Foucault, Jacques Derrida and Jean-François Lyotard being primary sources. Still other versions draw upon feminist analysis, itself often reliant upon readings of neo-this and post-that. And one could find many other strands to CMS, some weird, some wonderful and some, but very occasionally, both.

All of which has posed some interesting challenges to those who had been advancing recognizably similar arguments to CMS before it became labelled as such, and to the various research groups inspired by them. In just the same way that management studies in general, in its mainstream development, has a micro politics, so too has CMS, and it is worth dwelling upon these a little for the simple reason that the outcome of the small-p politics will go some way to influencing the big-P prospects of CMS.

Many of those advancing CMS-type arguments before it emerged as a 'named' approach seem to have been sanguine about its development. For example, Stewart Clegg, who had prefigured many, if not most, CMS arguments in the organization field has continued to work with his own developing intellectual agenda and has not engaged in polemics against the new grouping. Along with one of the main precursors of CMS in the United States, Walter Nord, he has collaborated to produce an influential handbook (Clegg et al. 1996) which brings to bear many strands of CMS analysis and advances them. In an earlier work (Clegg 1990), he set out a transition between Marxist and post-structuralist theorizations of power. In this way, Clegg has remained for three decades one of the most influential voices in critical management studies (uncapitalized). Paul Adler has more enthusiastically embraced the CMS label and has been instrumental in institutionalizing CMS in the United States as well as contributing to its internal debates (Adler 2002) and making extensive attempts to connect CMS to political activism. David Boje, too, has, perhaps more than anyone else, made links to activists while supporting the elaboration of CMS, and one could give many other examples.

In the UK, where, as I have suggested, much of the intellectual impetus for CMS has arisen, there has been a somewhat more sour reaction, however. For many years, a major 'home' for the critical analysis or organizations and management was the Labour Process Conference (LPC), established by David Knights and Hugh Willmott in the 1980s, which drew upon the labour process analysis inspired by Karl Marx and Harry Braverman as well as upon British traditions in industrial sociology, among other things. Willmott went on to become one of the progenitors of CMS by that name, while Knights, more than anyone else in the field, was responsible for the introduction of post-structuralist (more specifically: Foucauldian) analysis into organization and management theory.

These developments, which had an international influence, grew out of the LPC that they had founded, but posed a profound challenge to it. So too did an emerging group of CMS academics in the UK who, directly and indirectly, developed out of the Knights–Willmott 'axis' and which came to be called the 'Manchester school' of organizational analysis (Thompson and Ackroyd 1995; Wray-Bliss 2002). It would hardly be in the spirit of the reflexivity which I claimed for CMS if I failed to mention that I am sometimes named as a member of this school.[8]

The LPC responded to all this in at least two ways. One, which is difficult to take too seriously, was on the conference floor itself. Here, in a series of plenaries but also in standard sessions, there were savage attacks upon the supposed renegades of post-structuralism, complete with flourishings of Braverman's book and even, on one slightly desperate occasion, volume 3 of Marx's *Capital*. Whether volume 3 had a particular significance, it is difficult to say. The second was certainly more serious, and should not be dismissed. In 1995, Paul Thompson and Stephen Ackroyd published a lament for the way that industrial sociology had been side-tracked by post-structuralism,[9] an argument consistent with the more general critique of the influence of postmodernism on organizational analysis made by Thompson (1993). Attempts to address these conflicting views, even when expressed in the most respectful and tolerant terms (for example, Parker 1999) attract spectacular vitriol (Thompson et al. 2000). And at the 2001 LPC, Thompson delivered a full-blown attack upon, specifically, CMS. Ironically the hostility and immoderation of these various attacks has had the effect that many of those formerly sympathetic to LPC have ceased to attend it, while CMS conferences attract ever-growing numbers. And this underlines the point that I shall make later: a political position cannot be built if any departure from a narrowly defined orthodoxy is not only not tolerated but reviled. The result can only be that an ever smaller number of people meet in complete agreement but also complete irrelevance. This I would define as 'immature politics'.

Although written at different times and with slightly different targets in mind, these and other LPC-inspired writings exhibit a shared analysis of CMS. At the heart of this analysis is that CMS is another term for post-structuralism and that post-structuralism is disabled by relativism and an overfocus upon identity. This makes CMS both intellectually suspect, because it is inattentive to real structures of domination in organizations and society, and, at best, ambivalent about resistance; and politically suspect, because its relativism makes it incapable of sustaining an oppositional politics.

For these reasons, which I have glossed but not, I hope, misrepresented in their essence, CMS should be abjured by those of a neo-Marxist and/ or critical realist persuasion. In Thompson's 2001 paper, moreover, CMS, specifically, is attacked for being a careerist bandwagon and (worst of all, perhaps) a 'brand'. Now, I shall resist the temptation to reply point-by-point to the arguments in these contributions – not least because the last of them took some of my work (Fournier and Grey 2000) as its main whipping boy (or girl, if one prefers to equalize such things). I am not interested in trying to settle personal scores here; but I *am* interested in trying to advance to political projects of CMS. So I shall make two brief comments which are relevant to the particular points I want to make in this chapter. One is that the argument involved a curious sleight of hand. The defining features of CMS (as repeated earlier in this chapter) were dismissed as being no more than standard attributes of critical social science and therefore could not be used to define CMS – because CMS is 'really' post-structuralist. So precisely those things which were used to *include* a variety of theoretical positions were ruled out on the a priori ground that CMS could not contain variety. It is difficult to see how a debate can be conducted in these terms: if every proposal to define CMS more widely than post-structuralism is dismissed for its width, and CMS itself is dismissed for its post-structural narrowness!

My second, and main, comment is that to read Fournier and Grey (2000) as defining CMS as post-structuralism involves ignoring the explicit claims that were made there, and certainly to misrepresent my own view. Fournier and Grey (ibid.: 16) argue that CMS is defined by: 'a broad range of positions including neo-Marxism (labour process theory, Frankfurt School of Critical Theory, Gramscian 'hegemony theory'), post-structuralism, deconstructionism, literary criticism, feminism, psychoanalysis, cultural studies, environmentalism'. They went on to say that: 'if CMS is to have any future as a "movement" – if such it be – then it would seem more important to create alliances between Marxists and post-structuralists ... than to degenerate into recondite squabbles about differences' (ibid.: 26).

At the risk of being self-aggrandizing, this is also the same point that I tried to make in an earlier debate (Neimark 1990; Grey 1994) between neo-Marxism and post-structuralism in critical accounting: 'My own hope would be that [critical accounting] would not divert its attention too much from the critique of mainstream accounting theory and practice. In the relatively small field of critical accounting there is a legitimate place for analyses which derive inspiration from Foucault, Marx (or Derrida, Latour etc)' (Grey 1994: 7).

In fact, there are several common threads which run between the early 1990s debate about critical accounting and that more recently conducted about CMS. Many of the same protagonists are present and, certainly, many of the arguments resurface. In accounting, one of the most distinguished and insightful neo-Marxist analysts has been Tony Tinker (for example, Tinker 1985) who took a similar role in the accounting debates to that taken by Thompson in the CMS debates, and who has himself castigated CMS, both in some forceful conference interventions and in print (Tinker 2002), for the fact that, in his view, departures from the orthodoxy of Marx and the Frankfurt school represents a political cul-de-sac.

But CMS has been attacked on another flank, too. Just as the neo-Marxists feel that their status as the sole voice of authentic critique has been undermined by the supposed 'postmodernism' of CMS, so too do some postmodernists object to CMS. Edward Wray-Bliss (2002), in particular, criticizes the self-same 'Manchester school' to which Thompson and Ackroyd (1995) object for a lack of reflexivity and embodied ethics in their research practice, a charge vigorously rebutted by Collinson (2002) on (ironically, in view of the Thompson critique) largely realist grounds (including the rather legitimate point that Wray-Bliss knew nothing about the unpublished relations between the authors he criticized and their research subjects). From a different position altogether, Peter Anthony, who might almost be seen as a high priest of CMS, has abjured what is done in its name, and stakes a claim to a privileged knowledge of reality when he accused CMS of failing to address it (Anthony 1998).

Beyond published criticisms of CMS, its conferences, which aim towards pluralism, have been attacked as masculinist conspiracies to silence women. There has also been a sense, again not articulated in print, but certainly in formal and informal conference discussions, that the growth of CMS means a dilution of its intellectual purity – a view more common among the 'postmodernists' than anywhere else. Sometimes expressed in crassly anti-American terms, sometimes in the pure accent of intellectual snobbery (and often both together) the complaint is, in effect, that these dreadful people obviously do not understand the nuances of whichever newly discovered continental thinker is under discussion. CMS, on this view, should be the exclusive preserve of a few favoured keepers of the true flame.

**Towards a mature politics for CMS**
All this is, for those amused by it, very amusing and, for those engaged in it, very engaging. However, and this is the central point which I want to make in this chapter, it shows a quite remarkable irresponsibility on the part of those involved. CMS represents the possibility of drawing together those elements within business schools (and cognate areas) that share some oppositional tendencies. That is: oppositional to established power and ideology; to managerial privilege; to hierarchy and its abuse; to, to put it at its most generic, not only the established order but the proposition

that the established order is immutable. *Of course* we can debate endlessly what any of these terms mean, which of them we might wish to delete, what terms we might wish to add. But to do so is to fail, in the most self-indulgent and irresponsible way, to understand either the possibilities or the frailties of CMS.

CMS has developed an umbrella – not especially original, certainly not beyond critique – under which disparate kinds of opposition to orthodoxy can gather. That can be dismissed as a 'brand', but to do so fails to understand that some kind of term with which to identify is a prerequisite of any political endeavour. It can be dismissed as an institutionalization, but to do so is to imagine that influence can be achieved by the individual production of sophisticated analyses (or not to care about having influence at all). Both the criticism of branding and that of institutionalization fail to recognize that these are important ways in which those who may be very isolated within their own institution can claim an identity and a legitimacy which enables them to justify their work. And if, in the process, individuals build careers, then so what? Should CMS writers abstain from applying for promotion? On the contrary, aren't critical ideas about management more likely to get a hearing if they are espoused by senior as well as junior faculty? No sensible person would imagine that embracing CMS rather than orthodoxy would be a good careerist strategy, since by definition the opposite is true.

Leaving aside these rather snide criticisms, the more important point is this. CMS has a small chance of influencing the business schools it largely inhabits and, if it does so, an even smaller chance of leveraging the position of business schools within the wider social order so as to make an impact upon *that*. So there is a choice to be made: either to develop a common front against managerialism and all the assumptions to which it is related – hierarchy, globalization, masculinism, the primacy of markets, anti-unionism and so on – or to engage in an endless debate about how this confrontation is to be effected, what are the right theoretical resources, which terms are most important and what their correct interpretation is.

I suppose that my own view is already clear, but let me spell it out. I still think, as I did in relation to the accounting debates in the 1990s, that the differences between the various critical positions are far, far less significant than those between critical and managerial positions. Neo-Marxists can accuse post-structuralists of an ambivalence which might give succour to neo-conservatives. Post-structuralists can accuse neo-Marxists of a realism which might give succour to positivists. But they must surely know that these possibilities can be weighed against the certainty that the alliance of managerialists and the neo-liberal and neo-conservative Right proposes something with which no strand of critical thought could be content.

And, in this respect, I think the situation has changed, for the worse, in recent years. We now have a world in which the United States, the most powerful economic, cultural and military force in the world is in the grip of a most extraordinary fundamentalism. A fundamentalism in which the rights of workers and the rights of women are being steadily eroded. A fundamentalism which proposes itself as a Christian crusade. A fundamentalism in which an actual imperialism of imposed rule goes alongside a metaphorical imperialism of culture and consumption. We have a world in which globalization is being enforced in a way which is destroying local cultures, destroying public provision of goods and services, destroying ecologies but validating a growing racism around the globalization of labour. We have a world in which an ever-more inequitable distribution of wealth and healthcare is making concentration camps of the South and pockets of the North. And where any departure from the orthodoxy of these monstrous developments is met with vicious economic and physical brutality.

Management is by no means the only, and not even the most important, aspect of this world. But it is certainly intimately linked to every single one of these issues. Organizations, accounting, finance, marketing, economics, information systems – all the familiar segments of the MBA curriculum – are implicated. So too are the managers produced each year in their thousands by business schools; the managers who staff the global corporations and consultancies – and, increasingly, the polities, charities and non-governmental organizations – of the world I have just described.

All of this poses a significant challenge for what I (still) think can be called the Left, and, specifically, for the Left within business schools. The history of the Left has been an interesting and in some ways depressing one, and perhaps especially so when compared to the Right. The Right has always had internal schisms. One of the most obvious, especially in recent years, has been between neo-liberals and conservatives. The former believe in the primacy of markets, the latter in the primacy of traditional morality. It is obvious that these are in contradiction, for the market inevitably undermines traditionalism. Unlike conservatism, neo-liberalism has no good reason to oppose drugs, abortion or the decline of religion. It might support the right of managers to manage, but opposes the elitism of managerial (as against shareholder) interests. Conservatism has no good reason to support globalization, and might well support managerial elitism. But the Right rarely allows these differences to get in the way of getting on with things. It is the Left which treats issues of doctrinal purity, orthodoxy and heresy, as being of prime importance, and while it debates these issues, the world is re-made by the Right.

This has been the story of the Left, whether we take the example of the 1872 split at the Basel conference between Marx and Mikhail Bakunin, Marxism and Anarchism, Scientific and Utopian Socialism; or the fragmentation of the 1968 student and industrial protests into '*les groupuscules*', each defending as absolute quite miniscule differences in tactics or ideology. And its attempts to overcome disunity have been scarcely more, and perhaps rather less, endearing. The rigid party discipline of Bolshevism was certainly effective in securing power, as, in a more benign way, have been the 'Third Way' coalitions of recent electoral politics. But since the one led to totalitarianism and the other to an almost wholesale acceptance of the neo-liberal settlement, neither offers promising templates. The first was too intolerant, the second far too tolerant. Yet there is an alternative – a Left movement which is tolerant of internal difference yet uncompromising with its opponents. And there is a model for such a movement – the Popular Front against Fascism. The Popular Front was a response to the rise of Fascism in Europe in the 1930s which asked all those who opposed Fascism, whether from the perspective of Communism, Liberal Democracy, Anarchism or anything else, to sink their differences in the realization that they had more in common as anti-fascists than divided them.[10] Ultimately, the Popular Front strategy, although motivated by quite complex diplomatic, military and political manoeuvrings, can be seen as the key to the alliance between the United States, the Soviet Union and the UK that defeated the Fascist Axis.

Now I am not suggesting for one minute that CMS should be thought of in anything like the grandiose terms which might be inferred from these examples. It has nothing like that level of significance. Nevertheless, it is a political grouping and one which connects with wider political concerns. Just as the development of business schools is inseparable from the politics of corporate power and cold war international relations, so too is CMS plugged into issues that are not (or need not be) parochial to business schools. And CMS, both in terms of the ideas upon which it draws, and the people involved, is not isolated from wider politics. One of the axioms of Popular Front politics was that even small things made a difference – nothing was outside the overall struggle. Business schools may not be the most important or glamorous of sites for political engagement, but nor are they entirely negligible. Those who prefer to squabble about this or that nuance may be saying, in effect, that business schools do not matter that much. If so, they mistake the way in which such schools are significant nodes in contemporary Western capitalism. As Thomas Frank (2001: 177–8) explains, business schools are 'processing plants for the faking of intellectual authority', an authority which gives succour to the institutions of global capitalism. They make a difference, not overwhelming but none the less real: so, then, can CMS.

Much of what I have written is, implicitly and occasionally explicitly, targeted at the more traditional Left of CMS – the neo-Marxists. But they may well be aware, as I am, that what I have said will call forth raised eyebrows and, even, contemptuous dismissal from some of the more post-structuralist and postmodern within the CMS camp who will shudder at the crude 'with us or against us' politics I have articulated. For example, some feminists may think that I have not just downplayed their work but reinscribed a confrontational duality that bespeaks of pure masculinism. Some post-colonialists may think that not only have I downplayed their favourite issues but that I have provided highly eurocentric examples. And all of these things may very well be true. But to readers who have this reaction I would say just the same thing as I have said to the neo-Marxists. There is a choice to be made, and it is one imposed not by theoretical priorities but by the brute fact, and brutal practice, of a political Right in the ascendant. The nuances of which theoretical position is favoured over others may seem important to many of us. But they are as nothing compared with what a rejuvenated and unopposed Right will, and does, champion, and as nothing compared with the unthinking and indifferent subscription of the managerialists in business schools to the values of this Right. We all – we who oppose the managerialist hegemony – have to get a sense of our priorities; or else we can indulge ourselves while that hegemony remains unchallenged in business schools and challenged by others outside business schools.

I do not mean by this that CMS should not continue to develop new insights from a whole variety of perspectives, nor that it should abjure intellectual sophistication. But the purpose of these insights and this sophistication should not be that of winning contestations within CMS. It should rather be part of an attempt to use CMS to shift understandings within the orthodox and managerialist majority in business schools, and more extensively. What that implies is that we 'critics' need to engage with our less critical colleagues as a political project of influence. We can do this not just through our writings but also, and perhaps more importantly, through the myriad of 'administrative' transactions we have with our colleagues about course content or journal status. If we can create a bridgehead in which critical teaching is seen as legitimate and journals that carry critical material are seen as respectable, then this helps to legitimize the critical project. These are small pickings, and initially less satisfying than satisfying the impulse to mount root-and-branch objections to orthodox thinking, including that which permeates our employing institutions. And I am sure that I have, on occasion, done all of the things I am counselling against.

But I am increasingly convinced that to do so is not helpful to securing a wider hearing for CMS.

I want to make a final point. The politics of CMS can be thought of in terms of the large scale of politics of the Left, and I have invoked this in my attempt – call it a plea – for an end to infighting within our journals, conferences and elsewhere. But CMS's main political possibilities lie in much more modest endeavours. Although we sometimes write papers which imply that the whole world is hanging on our words, this is rarely – no, let's not be silly – it is *never* the case. But that does not mean that we have no influence at all. On the contrary, CMS can have a considerable influence. The most important way may be through teaching. We have in our institutions managers and future managers, even future business leaders. This is important, and it means that CMS, as a body of scholarship, may be less important than the critical management education which it informs (Grey 2002, 2004). In addition, working in business schools gives a legitimacy to the voices of those of us within them. On professional bodies, government committees and in the media we can use the institutions we work for – even if we have reservations about them, even if we sometimes wish we did not work for them – to give legitimacy to critical ideas. Precisely because business schools are hooked into global capitalism and the reproduction of global managerial elites, they offer those of a critical persuasion a platform which, if skilfully used, can give influence. Sure, such influence is going to involve compromise. Sure, it is not going to transform the world. There is probably no form of radical politics for which this is not true, and if there is then it certainly is not CMS.

**Conclusion**

I have sought to depict CMS as essentially a political movement, as much as, or more than, a scholastic one. Certainly it is nested within a set of institutions, primarily university business schools, which are themselves contextualized by, and associated with, the politics of Western capitalism. In one way this means that CMS is of only modest importance; business schools are but one, relatively minor, institution within a massive ideological–institutional bloc. In another way it means that CMS is of some significance; business schools are, perhaps more than most parts of intellectual life, hooked in to political and corporate power. Moreover, of the various institutions of global capitalism, business schools are relatively unusual in having a sizeable minority of left-leaning members. All of this presents a political opportunity, not for societal transformation, but, more modestly, for a degree of influence.

That influence needs to take two forms, matching the two propositions I identified earlier as those made by CMS: influence over management studies and business schools, and influence over management itself, both in terms of management practice and in terms of the value placed upon it within politics and society. The first part of that project is easier than the second, but in itself will be remarkably difficult. The aim cannot be simply to destroy business schools. For, as Martin Parker has said, in an insightful discussion of CMS:

> When the B-schools become empty, when the corridors contain dead leaves and the roofs leak, then they will be converted to sociology departments or housing for the elderly and CMS will have done its job [but] if the limit of your ambition is to put yourself out of a job, the prospects ... do not seem to be bright. (Parker 2002: 132)

That is not my ambition for business schools, for CMS or, for that matter, for myself. For business schools to be a viable vehicle for CMS to exert influence they have to continue to exist in something like their present form, so that they can be used strategically as a platform for the critique of management in wider society.

Even to achieve these modest goals will require a great deal more political maturity than has been shown by many sections (or potential sections) of CMS so far. I have indicated that those people committed to critical ideas, whether in organizations studies, accounting, information systems or some other field, need to refrain from self-indulgent squabbling and a self-righteous search for theoretical purity. Perhaps I have done so in rather harsh terms. However, these seem to me to be justified by the seriousness of the present political conjuncture, which does not allow too many niceties, and my appraisal of the possibilities and limits of CMS for influence within that conjuncture. As always in social relations and political action there is a choice, albeit not made 'under conditions of our own choosing'. One such choice facing CMS is whether to be adolescent, or whether to be adult.

### Notes
1. I shall use the term 'business schools' to denote not just institutions with this name, but also management and administrative studies schools and similar entities. Departments of accounting or of information systems may not quite fall within this term, although they often contribute teaching to management and business courses, and sometimes fall administratively into business schools; so I do not draw a hard and fast line between these departments and business schools. To say that CMS is mainly associated with business schools is to suggest that it has been less associated with discipline-based social science departments in universities, rather than to draw distinctions between different areas of management and business studies.
2. I sometimes have the impression that those CMS academics whose main contacts are with each other fail to appreciate quite how marginal they are within the wider context of business schools. If so, this perhaps encourages them to think that internal debate rather than external critique should be the main purpose of CMS.
3. It is not straightforward, because another part of the mainstream has always been humanistic and psychologistic, and the relation of such approaches to what I am calling the mainstream and to CMS itself, is interesting.

4. It was a mystique not least because the undoubted logistical sophistication of the Normandy landings was not the primary reason for the Allied defeat of Nazi Germany in Western Europe. Arguably more important was the fact that, with massive loss of life, the Soviet Red Army had wiped out the cream of the German army in 1943. But this fact was not something which the United States was able to recognize in the context of the cold war.

5. By this I mean the 'footloose' capitalism which switches production at ever faster rates between cheaper labour zones but also (and no doubt associatedly) configures constant, radical change as the defining feature of organizations (Grey 2003). This is not a 'purely economic' phenomenon: rather it has been bolstered by political decisions to de-regulate and liberalize trade.

6. Briefly, the view that language constitutes, rather than reflects, the reality it appears to describe.

7. Australia and New Zealand, for example, shared a colonial legacy that made them in some ways similar to the UK and experienced, earlier and in some respects more drastically, the impact of New Right politics. In Scandinavia, however, where CMS has also been influential, a mainly social democratic polity has prevailed and CMS can be seen as allowed by, rather than forced by, politics. Scandinavian academics often work in English, which may also be significant, for it is notable that CMS has not had so much purchase in more sealed language communities such as France and Germany. But there are undoubtedly many complexities in different countries that would require detailed analysis.

8. So too, if the accounts I have referred to are to be believed are: Jo Brewis, David Collinson, Deborah Kerfoot, Glenn Morgan, Martin Parker (although he, alone among those named, never worked or studied in Manchester), Andy Sturdy, John Roberts and Theo Vurdubakis. Apologies if I have excluded any who would wish to be included or included any who would prefer not to be.

9. What is perhaps even more remarkable is the way that sociology has almost entirely ceased to say anything much, post-structuralist or otherwise, about work organizations.

10. Sometimes the term 'popular front' is used more specifically to denote the governments in France (1936–38) and Spain (1936–39) which sought to incorporate this principle.

## References

Adler, P. (2002), 'Critical in the name of whom and what?', *Organization*, **9** (3), 11–32.

Alvesson, M. and H. Willmott (eds) (1992), *Critical Management Studies*, London: Sage.

Anthony, P. (1986), *The Foundations of Management*, London: Tavistock.

Anthony, P. (1998), 'Management education: ethics versus morality', in M. Parker (ed.), *Ethics and Organization*, London: Sage, pp. 269–81.

Baritz, L. (1960), *Servants of Power*, Middletown, PA: Wesleyan University Press.

Chua, W.-F. (1986), 'Radical developments in accounting thought', *Accounting Review*, **61** (4), 601–32.

Clegg, S. (1990), *Frameworks of Power*, London: Sage.

Clegg, S. and D. Dunkerley (eds) (1977), *Critical Issues in Organizations*, London: Routledge and Kegan Paul.

Clegg, S., C. Hardy and W. Nord (eds) (1996), *Handbook of Organization Studies*, London: Sage.

Collinson, D. (2002), 'A response to Wray-Bliss: revisiting the shopfloor', *Organization*, **9** (1), 41–50.

Engwall, L. and V. Zamagni (eds) (1998), *Management Education in Historical Perspective*, Manchester: Manchester University Press.

Fournier, V. and C. Grey (2000), 'At the critical moment: conditions and prospects for critical management studies', *Human Relations*, **53** (1), 7–32.

Frank, T. (2001), *One Market Under God*, London: Weidenfield & Nicholson.

Grey, C. (1994), 'Debating Foucault: a critical reply to Neimark', *Critical Perspectives on Accounting*, **5** (1), 5–24.

Grey, C. (2002), 'What are business schools for? On silence and voice in management education', *Journal of Management Education*, **26** (1), 496–511.

Grey, C. (2003), 'The fetish of change', *Journal of Critical Postmodern Organizational Science*, **2** (2), 1–19.

Grey, C. (2004), 'Re-inventing business schools: the contribution of critical management education', *Academy of Management Learning and Education*, **3** (2), 178–86.

Hopwood, A. (1974), *Accounting and Human Behavior*, London: Prentice-Hall.

Jermier, J. (1981), 'Infusion of critical social theory into organizational analysis', in D. Dunkerley and G. Salaman (eds), *The International Yearbook of Organization Studies*, London: Routledge and Kegan Paul, pp. 195–211.

Locke, R. (1989), *Management and Higher Education since 1940*, Cambridge: Cambridge University Press.

Locke, R. (1996), *The Collapse of the American Management Mystique*, Oxford: Oxford University Press.

March, J. (2000), 'Plenary address', 16th EGOS Colloquium, Helsinki University, Finland, July.

Neimark, M. (1990), 'The king is dead, long live the king', *Critical Perspectives on Accounting*, **1** (1), 103–14.

Orlikowski, W. and J. Baroudi (1991), 'Studying information technology in organizations: research approaches and assumptions', *Information Systems Research*, **2** (1), 1–28.

Parker, M. (1999), 'Capitalism, subjectivity and ethics: debating labour process analysis', *Organization Studies*, **16** (4), 553–64.

Parker, M. (2002), *Against Management*, Cambridge: Polity.

Pollard, S. (1965), *The Genesis of Modern Management*, London: Penguin.

Thompson, P. (1993), 'Fatal distraction: postmodernism and organization theory', in J. Hassard and M. Parker (eds), *Postmodernism and Organizations*, London: Sage, pp. 41–62.

Thompson, P. (2001), 'Progress, practice and profits: how critical is critical management studies?', Paper presented at Labour Process Conference, Royal Holloway College, University of London, March.

Thompson, P. and S. Ackroyd (1995), 'All quiet on the workplace front: a critique of recent trends in British industrial sociology', *Sociology*, **29**, 615–33.

Thompson, P., C. Smith and S. Ackroyd (2000), 'If ethics is the answer, you've been asking the wrong questions: a reply to Martin Parker', *Organization Studies*, **21** (6), 1149–58.

Tinker, A. (1985), *Paper Prophets*, New York: Praeger.

Tinker, A. (2002), 'Disciplinary spin', *Organization*, **9** (3), 419–27.

Tinker, A., B. Moreno and M. Neimark (1982), 'The normative origins of positive theories', *Accounting Organizations and Society*, **7** (2), 167–200.

Walsh, J. and K. Weber (2002), 'The prospects for critical management studies in the American Academy of Management', *Organization*, **9** (3), 402–10.

Wray-Bliss, E. (2002), 'Abstract ethics, embodied ethics: the strange marriage of Foucault and positivism in labour process theory', *Organization*, **9** (1), 5–39.

Zald, M. (2002), 'Spinning disciplines: critical management studies in the context of the transformation of management education', *Organization*, **9** (3), 365–85.

# 10 The wrong trousers? Beyond the design fallacy: social learning and the user

*James Stewart and Robin Williams*

**Introduction**

This chapter reflects critically upon how a substantial body of writings in technology studies and user-oriented computing have sought to conceptualize design – and their tacit and explicit presumptions about what is wrong with technology design/development processes as currently practised.[1] Many of these analyses share a paradoxical view of design: presenting on the one hand a rather heroic view of design as successfully embedding a range of explicit purposes and implicit values (a view we refer to as the 'design fallacy'), while on the other hand demonizing design practices and outcomes. The chapter argues that this account is inadequate and derives from a flawed 'design-centred' perspective – that focuses narrowly on particular design episodes and conceives these as leading to finished solutions to social/ organizational needs.

The chapter presents an alternative view of the role of design in the development of new technologies, particularly in relation to new information and communication technologies (ICTs), that has emerged in the course of the European Union Social Learning in Multimedia (SLIM) research project.[2] A social learning perspective is outlined that sees design outcomes/supplier offerings as inevitably unfinished in relation to complex heterogeneous and evolving user requirements. Further innovation takes place as artefacts are implemented and used. To be used and useful, ICT artefacts must be 'domesticated' and become embedded in broader systems of culture and information practices. In this process, artefacts are often reinvented and further elaborated ('innofusion').

The social learning perspective (Rip et al. 1995) analyses particular design episodes as located within longer-term processes of innovation across multiple cycles of technology design and implementation. It offers an evolutionary model of how societal requirements and technological capabilities may be coupled together. Although concepts of evolution and of learning may convey a sense of smooth and seamless interaction, our analysis points to the complex and often difficult interaction between them, offering an analytical framework that is more open (i) to the necessarily incomplete nature of the design process; (ii) to the unpredictability of outcomes; and (iii) to the multiplicity of actors and sites of innovation.

## The design-centred perspective in technology studies

*A problematic intellectual inheritance from early technology studies*

The issue of design was central to the emergence of technology studies as an area of debate and field of study. Starting from an assessment of newly emerging technologies that focused upon their undesirable social and environmental implications, critical socio-economic analysis moved on to ask 'what was giving rise to technologies that were having these effects?'; critiques were advanced of the dominant form of technologies developed (MacKenzie and Wajcman 1985). For example, the 'social shaping of technology' perspective sought to investigate the choices inherent in technological design and development and how these were influenced by the various values and interests involved. The archetypal 'social shaping' study by Noble (1979) pointed to the explicit intentions of the developers (of automated machine tools), and the suppression of one technology (record playback) in favour of another (numerical control). A similar conception of the significance of design underpinned the espousal by socially concerned engineers of alternative approaches to technological design (for example, in ideas of human-centred technologies and participatory design; see Ehn 1988). In much of these early writings we find an 'essentialist' account (Wajcman 1991) of the relationship between technology and social values, in which the design of the artefact is a more or less simple reflection of the values and priorities of designers and developers – values which are assumed to be reproduced (or at least favoured; see Winner 1980) when these artefacts are deployed and used. In this view, consumers are seen as passive recipients of the technology and its embedded values (Sørensen 1994). Although critical of the substance of design, this view sees technology design/development as a straightforward vehicle for social values and intentions.

The subsequent development of empirical research and analysis has called this view into question. Recognition of frequent failures in technological development, of unintended technical and social outcomes, and of the complexity of social interactions around the development and use of technology (and in particular of the influence upon innovation processes of intermediate and final 'users' of an artefact) has called for the revision of various elements of this simplistic model (Sørensen and Williams 2002). However, we suggest that prevalent social shaping and constructivist analyses of design still bear the imprint of their past intellectual inheritance. We point to the continuation of a view of design that tacitly retains some modernist presumptions, in terms of an essentialist and somewhat mechanistic view of how values and preferences may become embedded in design and may be reproduced when those artefacts are subsequently consumed/used. Such a view would appear to be informed by a 'linear' rather than 'interactive' model of innovation, and conveys more than a hint of technological determinism. In particular, we argue that much of this analysis shares what we have described as a 'heroic view' of design, which at the same time demonizes engineers. It is heroic in the sense that designs are portrayed as finished products inscribing particular views of the user, user activities and priorities into the artefact. The 'design problem' is then conceived in terms of the failings of design practitioners – through ignorance of users (their purposes and contexts) or their commitment to different priorities – embedding the wrong values/specification of user requirements in design, with imputed serious negative consequence for the usability and use of those artefacts for particular purposes and by particular groups. We shall return to this argument about the socio-economic analysis of design. But first, we shall examine, under the rubric of 'the design fallacy' the implications for design practice.

## The design fallacy

An important line of critique of design practice has centred around the perceived failure of ICT offerings to match the culture and requirements of users and in particular of the 'final users' who must operate the system. Failings of newly developed systems were attributed to the shortcomings of dominant 'technocratic' design approaches, and the difficulties experienced by computer scientists and engineers in capturing user requirements; to their narrow, functionalist understandings of the tasks being automated and their lack of understanding of the intricate culture and specific practices of the various users of information systems; and to the consequent gulf between designed systems and the circumstances and practices of the various groups of potential and actual users. Traditional requirements capture techniques, which emerged from the successful automation of routine record-processing tasks in early commercial computing, could not readily be applied to more complex activities involving the exercise of judgement and in novel applications where user requirements were not readily specified. Requirements capture is a potentially difficult problem because the needs of various current and potential users, and the means by which they may be fulfilled, are not fixed entities, but evolve, partly in the face of new technical capabilities and practices. In the face of these perceived problems, a range of user-centred design initiatives was launched which sought to develop richer understandings of the context and purposes of the user and build them into technology design. New design methodologies and models were proposed. Often user-centred design involved the deployment of social scientists alongside technology developers to study user contexts or to bring user representatives into the design process directly. Some interesting work has been done (see, for example, Ehn 1988; Bødker and Greenbaum 1992; Green et al. 1993).

However with hindsight, these kinds of project seem to have had only modest influence over system design overall, and some serious questions can be raised about their effectiveness – most immediately in relation to the uptake and wider applicability of models that emerged from user-centred design initiatives. More fundamentally, it can be noted that such initiatives failed to generate distinctively different models of artefact from those emerging from conventional design settings.[3]

While the shift towards user-centred design represents a significant and positive development, we need to avoid the pitfalls of what we have termed the 'design fallacy': the presumption that the primary solution to meeting user needs is to build ever more extensive knowledge about the specific context and purposes of various users into technology design. In large degree, the shortcomings of this view arise because the emphasis on the complexity, diversity and thus specificity of 'user requirements and contexts' (and the consequent importance of local knowledge about the user) is taken up within an essentially linear, design-centred model of innovation to emphasize the need for artefacts to be designed around the largely unique culture and practices of particular users. By seeing computer artefacts, once designed, as largely fixed in their properties, and thus privileging prior design (Procter and Williams 1996), the key question becomes one of building ever more extensive amounts of knowledge about the context, culture and purposes of users into the designed system.

Following on from this, socio-economic research, and in particular ethnographic studies of users, were proposed to identify the *right* values and overcome the design problem, by capturing the increasing amounts of knowledge about specific groups of users and their purposes, practices and thus requirements that could be incorporated into the design of the artefact. Ethnographic and in particular ethnomethodological approaches were advanced as being uniquely suited to addressing the intricacy of specific contexts and practices – identifying the crucial differences and distinctions that conventional requirements capture techniques would all too easily overlook (Anderson 1997). Although this point goes somewhat beyond the scope of the current chapter, it can be observed that there are obvious limitations to the role of ethnography as a method for requirements capture.[4] However ethnographic approaches could be used in addition to or as an alternative to 'user participation' in design – in which representatives of various current and potential users could express their requirements for the new system and contribute directly to requirements specification and to design and development decisions.

*Rethinking design – beyond the design fallacy*
The design-centred model, with its exclusive preoccupation with prior technological design ('the design fallacy'), can be criticized on a number of grounds:

- it is unrealistic and simplistic;
- it may not be effective in enhancing design/use; and
- it overlooks important opportunities for intervention that are revealed, for example, if a design-implementation life-cycle model is adopted.

In particular we argue against the model of design as an inductive process of accumulating ever more information about current user requirements. Recognition of the complexity and diversity of user settings does not necessarily imply that technological design will or should be entirely shaped around the detailed needs of particular users.

## The constructivist theorization of design: its conceptualization of the user and use

A central concern for social shaping and constructivist analyses of design has been to assess critically the way in which certain priorities and outcomes may be built in to technology development and therefore may be advantaged when those technologies are used (Winner 1980). In relation to new applications of technology, analysis has revolved around the way in which the future user and use of an artefact has been conceived. Indeed, in designing and developing an artefact, some model is needed of the anticipated user, the ways in which the artefact will be used and of the social and technical context in which use will take place. Designers do not simply develop an artefact – they must inevitably also develop some concept of the use context and lifestyle (van Lieshout et al. 2001). These *representations* (Vedel 1994) of the user/use may be more or less specific.

But how are these representations developed and implemented in designed artefacts? If design is shaped by the values and context in which technologies are developed, how are these values embedded, and how can they be identified?

We argue that social shaping and constructivist analyses have tended to veer, implicitly and perhaps unconsciously, towards a rather 'politicized' view of technological design as being *richly informed* by a set of specific values and presumptions from the development context, and in particular by specific and questionable conceptions of the user and use.

Noble's (1979) machine tool case refers to a highly polarized and visible context: the explicit intentions of the developers of automated machine tools around the choice of an operating interface that offered clear (apparently self-evident) implications for the outcomes – reducing the role of craft machinists. More sophisticated methodologies and explanatory concepts may be needed to grasp design choices in other contexts.

Important insights have emerged from analysts with roots in semiotic analysis and discourse theory. Thus Akrich (1992a) and Akrich and Latour (1992) claim that we may interpret the endeavours of designers as efforts to inscribe certain preferred programmes of action by users (which Akrich describes as 'scripts' or 'scenarios') in the design of a given artefact or technological system. Designers visualize a script of preferred reactions to the artefact, and they try to shape the technology in order to make these reactions as mandatory as possible (Sørensen 1996). In a similar vein, Woolgar (1991) describes designers as seeking to 'configure the user' – in terms of defining the characteristics of the user and how they may respond. By 'setting parameters for the user's actions' (ibid.: 61), the behaviour of the user is configured by the designer and the user is disciplined by the technology.[5] In this sense, the technology (and the designer) constructs 'the user'. This concept of configuring the user has been widely taken up.

A body of work has emerged from this perspective (for example, Woolgar 1991; Akrich 1992a, 1992b). Much of this conveys a view that design incorporates a comprehensive *representation* of the intended users, their purposes and the context of use. The user may be represented, for example, in terms of presumptions in relation to their skills, their identities (for example, in terms of gender, see Cockburn and Furst-Dilic 1994, or other social categories such as race and class) and the activities that may be seen as appropriate and inappropriate.

We argue that this kind of critical analysis has paradoxically often produced a rather simplified, 'stylized' and overpoliticized account of how the social context shapes the content of design (for example, regarding which social values and relationships become embedded in design and how) – which can thus readily be 'read off' by the analyst. We identify a tendency, which we describe as 'narrative bias', towards a particular kind of story about technology.[6] The first move in such an analysis is, typically, to identify the representation of the user underpinning a particular design/development. The second move is then to examine whether these may be 'the wrong values', based on an inadequate or misleading view of users and their requirements. Thus researchers have tended to look for the problems that may arise where that representation is restrictive or out of line with the actual users that arise or can be anticipated to arise. One common example highlights the problems arising where engineers have relied on their personal experiences and presumptions to articulate a rather unrepresentative model of the user (Akrich 1995; Nicoll 2000) – a strategy which Oudshoorn and Pinch (2003) have described, following Akrich (1995) as the 'I-methodology'.

It can be noted that these studies of 'designers configuring the user' do not in general address both the design and the implementation of particular artefacts. There are many reasons for this – not least that product development cycles tend to be longer than the lifetime of most social science research projects.[7] The impact of design choices on the user is thus largely imputed.

We would suggest that, when detailed empirical analysis of design/ development settings is actually undertaken, it turns out to be rather hard to discern the sets of objectives and presumptions underpinning design. Design/development choices are dominated by the 'taken for granted' aspects of the innovation – and by a series of design choices that will tend to be justified in technical or pragmatic terms. Indeed, design is rarely conducted by a single actor, but emerges through a multiplicity of actors in interaction with various concerns and agendas in relation to a host of factors (price, technical constraints, interoperability standards and concepts of the user market). Design is often done by committee (or through more complex arenas), working to tight deadlines under conditions of conflict and accommodation, yielding compromises that may satisfy no-one. What can be 'read' about the user and the setting of use is typically underspecified, fragmentary and inconsistent. And when the designed artefacts are subsequently implemented and used, the design presumptions are by no means expressed in a straightforward way.

The implication in the idea of 'configuring the user' that users are recipients, of course, stands in contrast with another, increasingly influential, stream of analysis which emphasizes the 'interpretive flexibility' and choice that users and others are able to exert regarding the meanings and use of a technology (Pinch and Bijker 1984). Indeed, Latour, Akrich and other writers, from a discourse theoretic background, see technology as a 'text' that is capable of different readings (even though their writings also convey a strong sense that the technology inscribes a preferred reading). A growing body of recent accounts, influenced by developments in cultural and consumption studies, portray consumption as an active and creative process (Sørensen 1994). These emphasize that, although the designer may seek to prefigure the user – and thus implicitly to constrain the ways in which the product is used – ultimately users still retain flexibility regarding the meanings they attribute to technologies, and over choices about how the artefact will be appropriated. We capture these processes – and specifically, the key processes of domestication and innovation – within the more general heading of social learning. Recognition of social learning offers a very different view of the character and significance of design activities.

**The social learning framework**
The social learning framework is proposed as an extension to the social shaping of technology perspective that focuses in particular upon opportunities for reflexive practice in the development of technologies.[8] It draws upon concepts from the developing evolutionary tradition in economics and economic history which have long recognized 'learning curves': the gradual improvements that often arise in the performance of a technology over time. Arrow (1962) described as 'learning by doing' the idea that workers, individually as well as collectively, develop more efficient ways of employing machinery through their experience from usage. Similarly, Rosenberg (1982) characterizes as 'learning by using' the process through which a user gains familiarity with a given piece of technology and develops skills in making use of it. These concepts point to the fact that the properties of a technology (its affordances and limitations) may not be immediately apparent, but are discovered, learned and enhanced through experience, often in relation to particular productive processes and activities. As Sørensen (1996) puts it:

> Social learning can be characterised as a combined act of discovery and analysis, of understanding and giving meaning, and of tinkering and the development of routines. In order to make an artefact work, it has to be placed, spatially, temporally, and conceptually. It has to be fitted into the existing, heterogeneous networks of machines, systems, routines, and culture.

However, social learning is not limited to the site of technology application (what Fleck 1988a describes as the 'implementation arena'), important though this is. Such learning by doing provides a potentially very important source of information on the effective use of a technology. By giving suppliers access to what users have learned about their products and what deficiencies and potentialities they have discovered, it could provide invaluable information for subsequent product innovation. It has been further noted that this information is often not systematically collected and used – perhaps because of the strength of the rhetorics of technology supply (on the grounds that, if a new product already fulfils user requirements as claimed, what need is there to examine the problems that may arise in its implementation and use). This underlines the importance of the *linkages* between users and producers that can act as a vehicle for this kind of knowledge exchange. To innovate successfully, producers may depend critically on information from users, and vice versa. This is the basis of the idea of the learning economy (Andersen and Lundvall 1988). The social learning framework draws attention to the way in which these knowledge flows are achieved (often through the efforts of key intermediaries) through processes that Sørensen (1996) describes as 'learning by interaction'.

When using the term 'social learning' we are not referring narrowly to individual cognitive processes but are crucially addressing collective learning processes – conceived in the broadest sense to include not only knowledge flows but also interactions between actors and processes of negotiation and struggle. It thus includes processes of 'learning by regulation' (ibid.) in which the circumstances for the 'proper' operation of a technology are achieved.

We can further distinguish two related social learning processes by which users contribute to technology development and use: innofusion and domestication.

*Innofusion*
This view of innovation draws on Fleck's (1988a) concept of 'innofusion' (= innovation + diffusion) to demonstrate that the innovation of an artefact (robotics and industrial automation in his original exegesis) was not limited to the research and development laboratory, but continued as the artefact was diffused in its implementation and use. Innofusion refers to the 'processes of technological design, trial and exploration, in which user needs and requirements are discovered and incorporated in the course of the struggle to get the technology to work in useful ways, at the point of application' (ibid.: 3).

*Domestication (or appropriation)*
Silverstone's studies of the consumption of household technologies highlighted the choices available to family members in terms of where the product is located and how it is incorporated within family routines (Morley and Silverstone 1990; Silverstone et al. 1992). However, a broader usage of the concept of 'domesticating' technology has emerged, in the sense of *taming* the technology. This often involves innovation by the consumer: using artefacts in ways not anticipated by the designer (Berg 1994). Domestication (Silverstone et al. 1992; Sørensen 1994; Lie and Sørensen 1996) and the related concept of appropriation (Pacey 1983; du Gay et al. 1997) are used to highlight the efforts of users to integrate ICT applications within their particular contexts and purposes. In the case of information systems at work, domestication may include, for example, the development and redevelopment of: working and information practices; work-arounds to overcome faults/limitations in the designed system; and systems of meaning (for example, the classification of cases; see Star and Bowker 1999).

These two facets of social learning over technology – innofusion and domestication – are not separate. However, these concepts were coined separately and for differing purposes. They draw attention to differing aspects of the innovation process, respectively, the evolution and biography of artefacts (Pollock et al. 2003) and the evolution and biography of user (and user organization) practices/culture. The social learning framework combines these to achieve an integrated perspective – and one that addresses innovation over different phases of the cycle of product development and use and in different sites.

**A social learning perspective on design**
The social learning perspective on design thus locates design within a broader context. Episodes of design are not viewed as snapshots in isolation – temporally from what precedes and follows it, or socially from its broader context – but are seen as moments of innovation across multiple cycles of design, implementation, consumption and further enhancement that are dispersed across a wide range of players, sites or phases.

We have elaborated and tested this framework through a series of case studies of digital experiments and trials, conducted under the SLIM project – an eight-country study funded by the European Commission. The SLIM case studies unusually sought to encompass the design, implementation and consumption of new multimedia systems across a range of contexts – commercial, education, public administration, community information and everyday life. This work has highlighted the pertinence of the social learning framework to understanding technology design.

A schema has been developed for understanding innovation in ICT applications. As this portrays a rather different view from received models, it is helpful to briefly outline some of the salient points. However, it is first important to address important changes that have taken place in both the form of ICT applications and its attendant design/development processes captured by the analysis of ICT as 'configurational technology'.

*ICT applications as configurational technology*
Social shaping of technology research has produced a number of important insights into the form of technology (particularly in respect of ICT applications), the process of innovation and the opportunities for influence by various players. It reveals that today, ICT development virtually never takes the form of *ab initio* design of complete systems (as is tacitly presumed by the design-centred account). Instead, ICTs are typically 'configurational technologies' (Fleck 1988b), created from selections of existing (often standard, commodified) component technologies and tools and some customized elements configured together.[9]

The configuration and customization of cheap, generic component technologies has proved a remarkably effective way of acquiring ICTs (and one that has had far more impact than user-centred design). The trade-offs between price and scope and so on yield a range of technology supply/ acquisition strategies between, for example, customizing a large generic application (involving a small number of 'large grain' components) for a particular context and the knitting together of a 'fine-grained' array of simpler flexible components (for example, standardized components and tools) selected and configured around the requirements of a particular user (Fincham et al. 1994).

*Opportunities for user influence vary with the form of technology: user-led innovation in configurational technologies*
These differing circumstances offer varying opportunities for user influence (which Koch 1997 has characterized as 'bricks and clay' in the hands of the local user). In the latter case we find that the organizational user is able to exercise considerable choice over the final configuration/solution. Indeed, it could be argued that this configuration activity opens up opportunities for a kind of user-led design, despite the user's virtually total exclusion from the prior design of the component technologies.[10]

Recognition that ICT applications take the form of configurational technologies also changes our view of the character and sites of design activity. Design of configurational technologies is most immediately about the appropriate selection and artful combination of the array of standard components as well as the creation of customized components. The user can exert considerable choice over the final configuration. What is critical in terms of this current discussion is that the development of configurational technology is a model in which *technology design and implementation are closely coupled.*

*Supplier ICT offerings inevitably fail to provide finished solutions*
One of the reasons for innofusion/domestication and the emergence of user-led creation of configurational technologies is the implausibility of the expectation that design outputs/supplier offerings could immediately and completely match user needs (not least since user needs are inchoate, varied, complex and evolving). This is particularly marked when we are dealing with ICT applications in complex organizational and cultural contexts. In other words, supplier offerings are inevitably unfinished; work must be done to adapt them to the technical and social contexts of use. This is a process of mutual shaping in which, on the one hand, the artefact may be reworked to meet specific user exigencies, while on the other, the artefact, in being incorporated within local systems of practice and meaning, may open up new ways of doing things. The social learning perspective seeks to capture these intertwining innofusion and domestication processes in

the implementation and use of technologies as well as the possibility of drawing lessons for future technological supply.

### Design as specific or generic

For example, we need to bear in mind that artefactual design is inevitably generic to some degree in relation to specific users. Since not all users can be directly involved in design, selected users must inevitably to some extent stand proxy for their peers and for future potential users. Indeed, successful system design depends on an ability not just to capture the specificities of the user context, but also to translate these into a form in which they can be more widely used. While the design fallacy conceives the improvement of design in terms of building in ever more knowledge about users into the artefact, there are also risks in trying to prefigure too closely the users and their purposes; in seeking to foreclose user choice around the expressed preferences of particular sets of users. There are issues around the building of representations of the user. Moreover, design is subject to a number of contradictory paradoxes – between making a solution specific and generic; between aligning with and moving beyond current practices and models.

These factors may mandate in favour of adopting more generic design approaches. We thus see strategies to build upon successful specific applications, but to design out from the artefact reference to its specific contexts of origination and use which might limit its future use and market – or more precisely to 'redesign' and re-present the artefact to make it more generic and open it up to broader markets. Designers may need to balance between building solutions that are very tightly configured around particular local requirements – which may, for example, act as a barrier to utility and use in other contexts – and keeping the system more flexible. Schumm and Kocyba (1997) have described the related processes as involving on the one hand 'decontextualization' of this knowledge (its separation from particular contexts, its codification to make it more widely applicable) and of 'recontextualization' (to implement this generic knowledge within particular artefacts). This involves a shift in perspectives from particular users to a generic representation – of 'the user' or a set of classes of user. Despite the rhetorics of the accountability of design to the user, designers and developers may have only a limited understanding of, or concern about actual users. 'The user' is thus a construct – a projection of potential users – built around various kinds of partial knowledge of actual users together with other agendas (for example, supplier capabilities and commercial strategies).[11] For example, in the creation of a packaged ICT application for an organization, we may find a shift from a niche solution designed around specific organizational users to a generic solution built around suppliers' decisions about their intended market and its common features. In the case of novel mass-market products, there may be no existing users to refer to. While the preferences of users may be assessed through panels and trials with selected proxy users, the product will be developed and promoted around rather diverse sets of categories and knowledge from, for example, market research (for example, demographic information, established languages and statistics for characterizing lifestyle groups and market segments).

There are important trade-offs between making artefacts unique and making them standardized. For example, the cost and other benefits of re-using software 'code' generates a trade-off in software acquisition strategies between the *increased utility* to the particular user and *higher cost* of solutions custom built around their particular requirements and cheaper generic solutions which may match their requirements less exactly (Brady et al. 1992; Fincham et al. 1994). We see increasing resort to commercial off-the-shelf (COTS) software solutions (Pollock et al. 2003). Suppliers may seek to adapt applications developed in one context to sell them on as niche or generic solutions, securing additional returns on their development effort. Users may choose to adapt to the constraints of cheaper packaged software for a variety of reasons.[12] Thus the rapid spread of packaged software and tools reminds us that the possible price (per unit functionality) advantages of mass-produced standard solutions may outweigh the costs to particular users of adapting systems or adapting their activities to system constraints and affordances. The attractiveness of standardized offerings is further increased by the possibility of combining them with customized elements into configurational technology solutions. This is further assisted by conscious attempts to design such component technologies to be readily linked together and customized.

### Design as a hypothesis about the user

This perspective involves a shift away from the idea of the supplied artefact as a finished solution for particular users. Instead, we took the broad view that artefactual design embodies something of a *hypothesis about the user* (Lobet-Maris and van Bastelaer 1999). In this sense, digital experiments and trials can be seen as providing an opportunity to *test* these hypotheses. However, the SLIM investigations have shown, across a range of case studies, that in the design and development process for multimedia products and services, these hypotheses about the user and use often remain implicit and underspecified. The presumptions made about the user typically remain largely unstated and are often poorly elaborated. These presumptions are then tested – for example, under simulated or actual conditions of use. We return to this in the following section when discussing how an effective representation of the user is achieved.

**Representation of the user – revisited**
Our critique of the main tradition of analysis of design highlighted the difficulties in generating an adequate model, or 'representation' (Vedel 1994), of the user and user requirements. Despite this, it remains the case that development/design needs to prefigure a number of elements about the context, purposes and activities of the user. However a richer understanding of the representation process is perhaps called for.

Representation relates to a number of different elements. For example, Nicoll's (2000) 'contextual usability' model conceives the usability of technology as a complex of interdependent elements within a particular context, including *usefulness*, (the development of) *usage* patterns, and the particular social and cognitive exigencies of situated *use*. Following on from this we suggest that representation encompasses: the technical configuration of the system, content, usage, uses and 'rules' (formal and informal) about proper usage/users.

In principle, the hypotheses embodied in the design/representation are attempts to prefigure these very dimensions of the eventual use of the artefact. However, it is difficult, indeed impossible to prefigure these reliably – hence the importance of social learning, both in testing and refining the design hypotheses whether through 'synthetic' social learning processes in the course of development, or by securing feedback from actual social learning processes in the appropriation of artefacts in real-life contexts to future technology design/representation (Akrich 1995).

There are, then, a number of ways by which designers may seek to 'configure the user' (in the Woolgarian sense – comprising attempts both to prefigure/incorporate the user in the design of the artefacts and to align actual users to that view). Vedel (1994) identifies a range of mechanisms through which developers seek to configure the user – including, for example, advertisements, directions for use and technical guides – as well as technical design. Van Lieshout (1999) takes this further to include representations of the context for operating the technology. Developing these ideas, Lobet-Maris and van Bastelaer (1999) identify the different elements of the artefacts through which the user may be configured (in the design of 'Digital Cities'):

1. the interface, and in particular, the way information is presented in the interface (for example, the metaphors that are used will 'configure' the user and induce a specific usage);
2. the language and terminology used in the interface;
3. services offered – the types of information;
4. rules allowing or forbidding particular behaviours;

5. access possibilities – for example, where equipment is accessible, opening hours and so on imply different types of user; and
6. training.

However, design is not a one-off act, but is part of an iterative series of activities, informed by earlier design practice and feedback from the appropriation and use of other systems (earlier technologies in this application domain; similar technologies in related domains). Figure 10.1 shows schematically the various moments involved in a particular cycle of development, and the relationships between them. It shows the iteration between the articulation of *representations* of user/use at the outset of, their materialization in particular *designs/configurations* and finally testing the implemented design hypotheses through processes of innofusion and domestication in particular contexts of use followed potentially by feedback to future technology supply/design.

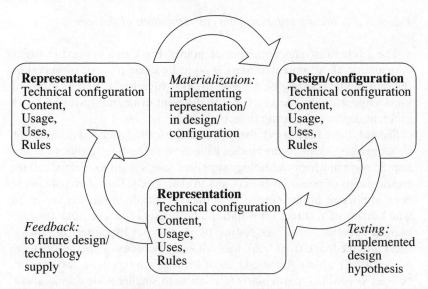

*Source*:   Williams et al. (2005).

*Figure 10.1    Schematic diagram of user representation and appropriation*

Following on from this we ask what intellectual resources do designers and developers have for building a representation of the potential user? Figure 10.2 shows some of the sources of ideas and information that designers/developers may deploy.

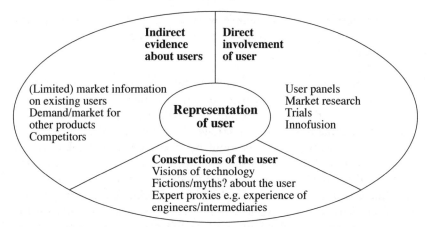

*Source*:   Williams et al. (2005).

*Figure 10.2    Resources for building representations of the user*

The figure illustrates a number of points. First, in a context in which information about potential users is typically incomplete or of uncertain reliability, players may be obliged to 'knit together' different kinds of knowledge from diverse sources with different evidential status and with different degrees of gearing to 'actual' users.

Second, there may be relatively little empirically grounded information about existing users. Many studies have drawn attention to the crude and limited ways in which technology suppliers have sought to understand the requirements of potential users (Cawson et al. 1995). There have, of course, been important improvements over the last decade in the techniques by which firms gain direct information about users (for example, through market surveys, consumer testing of prototypes by panels of 'proxy' users and feedback from 'real' users of early versions of the product; see Akrich 1995), although these kinds of exercise are expensive and may not be seen as justified, particularly in relation to smaller-scale development. In the absence of direct knowledge of users, there may be resort to more or less well-justified indirect constructions of the user – for example, by extrapolating from similar technology applications. Constructions of the user, created by 'experts' (for example, engineers or intermediaries) may, for example, be derived from their own personal experience and culture (Nicoll 2000) or may be more firmly rooted in experiences in this or other product markets. Expert constructions may be informed not only by rigorous evidence and pertinent experience but also by visions of technology and narratives (myths?), including anecdotes or stereotypes about the user which may turn out to be more or less close to actual users and their behaviours. Developers do not work in a vacuum – but may be influenced here by popular opinion, media views and in particular by the behaviour of peers and competitors – which may be reflected in clustering of supplier offerings or the mutual reinforcement of supplier visions and presumptions. These kinds of alignment of expert views, and consequent mission-blindness, have been identified as the root of a number of high-profile and expensive failures of ICT systems (Collingridge 1992).

The potential weaknesses of the latter forms of evidence are clear – informed as they are by 'implicit' presumptions and knowledge of uncertain evidential status rather than the systematic application of explicit verifiable techniques (Akrich 1995). However, it would be misleading to see the application of formal techniques as obviating the uncertainties surrounding users and their requirements. We would like to carry this argument further. Our third point is that all the forms of information about future users carry their own uncertainties and difficulties. For example, the most systematic empirical information available about user choices and preferences (as revealed, for example, in aggregate form through market behaviour) is likely to exist only in relation to established products (even then, user preferences may change over time as some elements come to be seen as essential features in a particular product market – for example, in the way that every mobile phone sold today includes the relatively recent SMS (Short Messaging Service) innovation. In contrast, where products are changing, expert views are liable to be rooted in prior experiences in other related markets. The question arises as to how far one can extrapolate from such information. The problem perceived in relation to 'radical innovations' is that knowledge about the users and uses of existing applications may not provide a reliable guide to the novel application. There is inevitably a metaphorical leap.

Empirically grounded information about users of a new product may be sought through a variety of methods: the direct involvement of proxy users in panels; market research surveys; and trials (ibid.). However, various difficulties arise regarding the interpretation of such direct information about potential (and ultimate actual) users. For example, user panels need to be introduced to new technologies and given some training in their use – however, their selection and training mean that they are in some ways no longer independent and representative of wider publics. Sørensen (1996, section 2.3) describes this as 'simulated social learning', involving as it does 'people that are supposed to act as if they were users, but under artificial, laboratory-like circumstances'. Initiatives for 'user involvement' in the design/use of prototypes raise similar problems about representativeness. Since, in most organizational settings, not all current users can be involved, user involvement (directly in design or in panels and trials) is inevitably based on an incomplete sample of existing users (let alone future, as yet unknown, users), which throws up a set of further uncertainties and choices. How should appropriate 'proxy users' be selected? Is their behaviour in the laboratory a good basis for understanding behaviour in everyday life? Would their responses provide a secure foundation for anticipating the larger cohort of 'real' users that the supplier wanted to attract? For example, we know that many initial users of a technology may be 'enthusiasts' who, in their skills and interest in a technical field, may differ substantially from later adopters in terms of their expectations and requirements (Rogers 1983; Norman 1988). This may be one of the reasons leading to the development of baroque technologies (for example, the video machine or microwave oven) with features that most users cannot fully utilize.

Many of these considerations tend to mandate in favour of live digital experiments and trials – which would allow experimentation around the acceptance and utility of a product in relatively naturalistic settings (Nicoll 2000).

The proliferation of digital experiments and trials over the last decade underpin the potential importance of social learning in the innofusion and domestication of ICT applications – in that it can provide rich sources of more direct and reliable information about 'actual' user responses to supplier offerings (though issues arise about how such appropriation experiences can be fed back to generate more robust user representations for future design).

It remains the case that it is not possible to produce through experiments and trials a fully comprehensive and wholly representative account of the user's reactions (just as we observed in relation to requirements capture). The knowledge base is, of necessity, incomplete and potentially open to challenge. It is, in consequence, necessary to exercise judgement in a context of uncertainty.

### Reconceptualizing the design process

The goal of this chapter is a more adequate and intricate understanding of design, its various 'audiences' and how they are incorporated in the design process and its outcomes. The analysis we have presented calls for some rethinking of certain common presumptions about design. For a start, we argue for a broad understanding of design, as involving a range of decisions about system design, development and deployment. In parallel with this we move away from a conception of design as an individual cognitive process, embodied in a particular designer, to seeing it as a negotiation process; a collective endeavour involving many players, including, for example, project managers as well as just design specialists. Design is, to use John Law's (1988) term, 'heterogeneous'. Third we stress that design has a number of audiences as well as the projected final users and the organizational user who may have commissioned the design. This may include, for example, developers/designers of complementary products as well as managers linked to the particular development project, standard setters and others who may act as gatekeepers or proxies for ultimate potential users. MacKay et al. (2000) make a similar point when arguing that the designer is 'configured' by the context of design.

*Design as a configuration process*
We would also make a slightly different point, deriving from our analysis of configurational technology (see above), that design is a constrained configuration process. This contrasts with the heroic account of design by seeing the process of design not as an open search,[13] but as constrained, enabled and channelled by its insertion in a broader setting and history of prior design choices. An important feature of many system design processes is thus the creative selection and configuration together of a selection of already existing bundles of knowledge, practices, artefacts, as well as novel elements. Design in this context is revealed as a process of *configuration*: in the sense of an artful selection and combination of diverse fixed and malleable elements but operating largely within existing repertoires (which Whipp 1985 described as structural repertoires of established problem diagnoses and designed solutions).

Our use of the term 'configuration' draws attention to the application of relatively restricted sets of rules for reconfiguring (that is, selecting, reworking, adapting and combining) existing knowledge and practices.[14] Design may 'configure' the user (Woolgar 1991) but it is also conditioned by its context and history.

*'Design as accountability'*
The design fallacy and ideas of participatory and ethnographically informed design can be seen as linked to the more general idea, which we can find across a range of socially oriented computer contributions, that 'good' computer system design would be a design process that is subject to the requirements of these diverse user groups. Indeed a rather similar conception underpins more formalized structured systems design methodologies. We have described this as a model of 'design as accountability', in which the requirements of all stakeholders are to be represented and seen to be represented in the eventual design. The designer's role is thus to receive this specification and to embed it authentically and reliably in the eventual designed system. However, this represents a rather restricted, bureaucratic and uncreative view of the role of the designer and the character of design work.

*'Design as creativity'*

Although designers may see advantage in presenting their role in this neutral technical manner, design is, of necessity, more than simply induction from articulated user requirements. For example, designers inevitably play an active role in establishing which requirements are prioritized in a context of potentially conflicting requirements or competing demands on limited resources. Our critique of the conceptualization of computer-systems design in terms of the *accountability* model suggests an alternative model of design as a *creative* process, and one that valorizes *authorship*. In this mode the designer is given leave to construct new concepts of use – to reconstruct the user and transform existing genres of use (albeit within the bounds of what particular users can be convinced is acceptable/attractive, based on whatever evidence may be deployed regarding user preferences). This is particularly evident when we consider the design of novel applications (especially for mass-market products) where there are no existing users.

When actual design settings are studied (for example, in the SLIM case studies), the primary design goals and purposes of a project were not typically induced from user responses, but were instead invoked in the original conception of the project. The cases varied in the emphasis given to user objectives and uses; in some, there were relatively clear sets of parameters emerging from consideration of user requirements, while in others, the technical potential (and its imputed self-evident advantages) were more central.

We can explore this by examining the analyses that have been advanced of the development of a class of community information systems known as Digital Cities. Amsterdam Digital City (DDS), the forerunner of many European initiatives, was studied both by Lobet-Maris and van Bastelaer (1999), for the SLIM study and subsequently by Oudshoorn et al. (2004) for another European Commission project – SIGIS.[15] Lobet-Maris and van Bastelaer argue that failure in some Digital City projects to focus upon specific user groups resulted in technical criteria prevailing over design decisions.[16] Rommes (2002) and Oudshoorn et al. (2004) take this point further, arguing that in DDS where interfaces are designed for 'everybody', instead of with a specific user group in mind, the tacit default user will continue to be the 'typical Internet-user' (the highly educated, white young male with extensive computer experience).

In contrast, it seems that those design cases in which a clear and determined attempt was made to transform existing gendered presumptions, designers found it helpful to conjure up stereotypical representations of users – not with any implication that these were actual representations of particular groups of actors, but as self-consciously stylized archetypes – as tools for rethinking design presumptions.

**Conclusion**

This brief review has sought to lay out a more comprehensive and more realistic[17] view of the process of design, building on insights from research into the social shaping of technology (particularly in relation to ICTs) and the emerging social learning perspective.

We have criticized the 'design fallacy' and the common presumptions of user-centred design and major currents within social shaping and constructivist analyses of current design, which see a solution to shortcomings in current design practices in terms of 'building in' to artefactual design an increasing body of knowledge about the requirements of diverse specific users.

The design-centred model is criticized on the grounds of theory and practice: on the one hand it provides a simplistic and unrealistic stereotypical account of the design process; on the other, it overlooks important opportunities for intervention and improvement in design processes if a design-implementation life-cycle model is adopted. In particular, we argue against the model of design as an inductive process of accumulating ever more information about current user requirements. Recognition of the complexity and diversity of user settings does not necessarily imply that technological design will or should be entirely shaped around the accumulated detailed needs of particular users. When design is viewed in its broader context of multiple overlapping cycles of design–implementation–use, we see many routes for matching evolving technical affordances against emerging usages/user requirements in addition to merely contributing to prior technological design. The way in which technological development may cater for different social purposes and players is equally complex. Thus, in addition to designing specific requirements into artefacts, there may be a need to 'design out' references to specific users/contexts of use in the creation of generic solutions. This process of making a product generic may well be at the expense of meeting the specific requirements and relevances of particular users – indeed, the creation of standardized mass-market solutions may exclude many in favour of the majority (Pollock et al. 2003). In some circumstances this may not be problematic. We must bear in mind that many of the most successful ICT applications in recent years have been media and communications technologies (e-mail, mobile telephony, SMS, the internet and the world-wide-web) which make few presumptions about the kinds of activity being supported. This is one of a number of paradoxes surrounding design that need to be resolved in particular design episodes – between making designs specific or generic; standardizing and providing unique solutions; prefiguring user requirements and keeping artefact design and usage open; between matching current practices and considering future extensions.

Increasingly sophisticated methods are being adopted to obtain more robust evidence about users' requirements – through direct knowledge of specific proxy 'users'; and through forms of social learning in more or less natural contexts of use. The importance of these more naturalistic sites of social learning is demonstrated by the explosion in social experiments and technical trials in new ICT applications. However, design must confront the inevitable metaphorical leap in creating a representation of 'the user' in a context of incomplete information about current users and their requirements (let alone future users who do not yet exist).

The social learning perspective being developed opens up our understanding of the innovation process. It offers some cautious grounds for optimism, in place of the pessimism of the design-centred account, for a range of avenues for improvement in practice rather than merely one rather prescriptive route. It draws attention to the multiplicity of sites and spaces for intervention:

- involving different avenues and kinds of activity;
- involving (directly and indirectly) a wider and more diverse range of actors including non-specialists;
- affording varying opportunities for influence, depending on the context and form of technology; and
- requiring various kinds of tools and support.

This exploration has offered some important insights. However, the challenge may be for a more systematic study of technology design and development (in its broad setting, encompassing multiple cycles of design and implementation), which has potentially important lessons for design and development.

## Notes

1. This chapter is based upon a talk initially presented at the European Association for the Study of Science and Technology (EASST) 2002 (York, 1 August 2002). An earlier version appears in Harald Rohracher (ed.) (2005), *User Involvement in Innovation Processes: Strategies and Limitations from a Socio-technical Perspective*, Munich: Profil-Verlag.
2. The SLIM project was funded under the Targeted Socio-Economic Research programme of the European Commission Fourth Framework Programme (Contract 4141 PL 951003). Some findings appeared earlier, notably in van Lieshout et al. (2001). The main findings are published in Williams et al. (2005). We are grateful to our European collaborators for their contribution to the ideas and material on which this analysis is based.
3. This was true also of some of the multimedia social experiments explored in the SLIM study, reported here, which had broader ambitions to be exemplars and fulfil certain social ambitions.
4. There are obvious limitations to the role of ethnography as a method for requirements capture; it is an expensive and slow method for data capture. Effective requirements capture and design is much more than the accumulation of knowledge of diverse user requirements; you could never carry out enough ethnography to create an all-inclusive

account of, for example, a large organization; nor could you simply induce a design solution from such a knowledge base. Effective design also requires generalization, based on some kind of accommodation, satisficing and prioritization between the specific requirements and preferences of multiple individuals and groups. The undoubted strength of ethnographic methods is in picking up and providing insights into the intricacy of work contexts and practices at a level of detail which does speak to design. However, in most circumstances its role can only be as a resource to deepen other methods of requirements analysis rather than as a primary requirements capture methodology.

5. Mackay et al (2000: 737–57, note 18) draw attention to the diverse formulations that Woolgar has deployed for configuring which include defining the identity of future users and setting constraints upon their likely future actions (Woolgar 1991: 59 note 17).

6. We use the concept of 'narrative bias' to refer to the shortcomings that have characterized much writing in this domain in which certain elements and issues are pulled into the foreground, and others downplayed, to produce a stylized and simplified story which seems to hold a certain narrative compulsion to that group. Particular (sub)disciplines seem to favour particular types of narrative (for example, the demonization of designers). Often this serves to augment the perceived social significance and centrality of the locales and actors under study.

7. In mass consumer products, consumption is far removed in time and space from development. The small number of case studies where design and implementation are both addressed are almost always those of the development of specific organizational IT applications – in which designer and organizational users are part of a linked institutional nexus (as well as our own work, Williams et al. 2000, 2005, see, for example, McLaughlin et al. 1999; Mackay et al. 2000). Following on from this, many studies of design have been snapshots, focusing upon the activities of designers and underplaying the extent to which design operates as part of a broader process involving commercialization, implementation and application and feedback into future design/development.

8. We are influenced here by work from organizational studies (for example, on 'organizational learning', Schon 1983) and elsewhere which has emphasized the adaptive and reflexive capabilities of actors.

9. Indeed, the development of configurational technologies is now so pronounced that it is difficult to find examples that correspond to Fleck's (1988b) counter example of *system technologies.*

10. This is, of course, a very different model of user input to design and development than the conventional concept of users contributing to the specification and design choices around specific technologies (component or whole applications). It is, however, a model in which the user is able to exercise considerable influence over the final designed system.

11. While designers think of the user through the 'lens' of a technical artefact, others may have different understandings of these people – as customers, clients, patients, citizens, ratepayers – not revolving around technology systems.

12. Users may find additional benefits from adapting to standard offerings – notably various network externality benefits from the interoperability of standardized technologies – including, for example, the greater availability of skills to maintain and use a package.

13. As might be inferred by Latour's (1988) portrayal of technical specialists as *Modern Princes* ('Sartrean engineers') acting with a high degree of autonomy.

14. Dan Shapiro and co-workers have deployed Levi Strauss's concept of *bricolage* to describe this process (Büscher et al. 2001).

15. The latter study was undertaken for another EC project on Strategies for Inclusion, Gender and the Information Society (IST 2000 26329 funded under the Information Society Technologies Programme). SIGIS seeks to understand how design and development choices may exclude certain actors (focusing in particular on the gender dimension) and in particular what strategies might promote social inclusion.

16. This does not mean, of course, that there was no scope for social learning and experimentation in the more technically focused projects. For example, the SLIM portfolio of cases included a number of projects that were primarily concerned to develop and test a new technical infrastructure. However, there is a sense that technological objectives have taken first

place, and only after they have been realized has space emerged for experimentation about usages (for example, in the above cases, about educational objectives). The presumption that the technology would provide a solution *per se*, meant that users have had to grapple with the constraints and affordances of new technologies under circumstances of use and according to the parameters configured in design. However, this testing has required the implementation of particular applications to run on the infrastructure and presumptions. Some form of user experimentation has needed to take place even though this had, to some extent, to be 'smuggled in' (Jaeger et al. 2000).
17. We seek a realistic understanding in the sense of a more intricate account and one that presents a more adequate account of design/development practice that might, for example, be recognized by practitioners. We have sought to avoid the pitfalls of 'narrative bias' described earlier.

### References
Akrich, M. (1992a), 'The description of technological objects', in W. Bijker and J. Law (eds), *Shaping Technology/Building Society*, Cambridge, MA: MIT Press, pp. 205–24.
Akrich, Madeleine (1992b), 'Beyond social construction of technology: the shaping of people and things in the innovation process', Chapter 9 in M. Dierkes and U. Hoffmann (eds), *New Technology and the Outset: Social Forces in the Shaping of Technological Innovations*, Frankfurt and New York: Campus/Westview, pp. 173–90.
Akrich, Madeleine (1995), 'User representations: practices, methods and sociology', in Rip et al. (eds), pp. 167–84.
Akrich, M. and B. Latour (1992), 'A summary of a convenient vocabulary for the semiotics of human and nonhuman assemblies', Chapter 9 in W. Bijker and J. Law (eds), *Shaping Technology/Building Society*, Cambridge, MA: MIT Press, pp. 259–64.
Andersen, E.S. and B.-Å. Lundvall (1988), 'Small national systems of innovation facing technological revolutions: an analytical framework', in C. Freeman and B.-Å. Lundvall (eds), *Small Countries Facing the Technological Revolution*, London: Pinter, pp. 9–36.
Anderson, Bob (1997) 'Work, ethnography and system design', Technical Report EPC-1996-103, in A. Kent and J.G. Williams (eds), *The Encyclopedia of Microcomputers*, vol. 20, New York: Marcel Dekker, pp. 159–83.
Arrow, K (1962), 'The economic implications of learning by doing', *Review of Economic Studies*, **29**, 155–73.
Berg, Anne-Jorunn (1994), 'Technological flexibility: bringing gender into technology (or is it the other way around)?', Chapter 5 in Cockburn and Furst-Dilic (eds), pp. 94–110.
Bødker, Susanne and Joan M. Greenbaum (1992), 'Design of information systems: things versus people', Computer Science Department, Aarhus University, Aarhus.
Brady, Tim, Margaret Tierney and Robin Williams (1992), 'The commodification of industry applications software', *Industrial and Corporate Change*, **1** (3), 489–514.
Büscher, Monika, Satinder Gill, Preben Mogensen and Dan Shapiro (2001), 'Landscapes of practice: bricolage as a method for situated design', *Computer Supported Cooperative Work*, **10** (1), 1–28.
Cawson, Alan, Leslie Haddon and Ian Miles (1995), *The Shape of Things to Consume: Delivering IT into the Home*, Aldershot: Avebury.
Cockburn, Cynthia and Ruza Furst-Dilic (eds) (1994), *Bringing Technology Home: Gender and Technology in a Changing Europe*, Milton Keynes: Open University Press.
Collingridge, David (1992) *The Management of Scale: Big Organizations, Big Decisions, Big Mistakes*, London and New York: Routledge.
du Gay, Paul, Stuart Hall, Linda Janes, Hugh Mackay and Keith Negus (1997), *Doing Cultural Studies: The Story of the Sony Walkman*, London and New Delhi: Sage.
Ehn, P. (1988), *Work-Oriented Design of Computer Artifacts*, Stockholm: Arbetslivcentrum.
Fincham, Robin, James Fleck, Robert Procter, Harry Scarbrough, Margaret Tierney and Robin Williams (1994), *Expertise and Innovation: Information Strategies in the Financial Services Sector*, Oxford: Oxford University Press/Clarendon.

Fleck, James (1988a), 'Innofusion or diffusation? The nature of technological development in robotics', Edinburgh *Programme on Information and Communication Technologies* (PICT) Working Paper No. 7, Edinburgh University.

Fleck, James (1988b), 'The development of information integration: beyond CIM?', Edinburgh PICT Working Paper No. 9, Edinburgh University. A digest of this paper, prepared for the Department of Trade and Industry, is available as 'Information-integration and industry', PICT Policy Research Paper No. 16, Economic and Social Research Council, Oxford, 1991.

Green, Eileen, Jenny Owen and Den Pain (eds) (1993), *Gendered by Design? Information Technology and Office Systems*, London and Washington, DC: Taylor & Francis.

Jaeger, Birgit, Roger Slack and Robin Williams (2000), 'Europe experiments with multimedia: an overview of social experiments and trials', *The Information Society*, **16** (4), 277–302.

Koch, Christian (1997), 'Production management systems: bricks or clay in the hands of the social actors?', in C. Clausen and R. Williams (eds), *The Social Shaping of Computer-Aided Production Management and Computer Integrated Manufacture*, vol. 5, COST A4, Social Sciences, European Commission DGXIII, Luxembourg: Office for Official Publications of the European Communities, pp. 131–52.

Latour, Bruno (1988) 'How to write "The Prince" for machines as well as machinations', in Brian Elliot (ed.), *Technology and Social Process*, Edinburgh: Edinburgh University Press, pp. 20–43.

Law, John (1988), 'The anatomy of a socio-technical struggle: the design of the TSR 2', in Brian Elliot (ed.), *Technology and Social Process*, Edinburgh: Edinburgh University Press, pp. 44–69.

Lie, M. and K.H. Sørensen (eds) (1996), *Making Technology Our Own? Domesticating Technology into Everyday Life*, Oslo: Scandinavian University Press.

Lobet-Maris, Claire and Beatrice van Bastelaer (eds) (1999), 'Digital Cities Final Report', mimeo, CITA, University of Notre Dame de la Paix, Namur, www.info.fundp.ac.be/~cita/publications/SLIM/, accessed February 2005.

Mackay, H., C. Carne, P. Beynon-Davies and D. Tudhope (2000), 'Reconfiguring the user: using rapid application development', *Social Studies of Science*, **30** (5), 737–57.

MacKenzie, Donald and Judy Wajcman (eds) (1985), *The Social Shaping of Technology: How the Refrigerator Got Its Hum*, Milton Keynes: Open University Press.

McLaughlin, J., P. Rosen, D. Skinner and A. Webster (1999), *Valuing Technology: Organisations, Culture and Change*, London: Routledge.

Morley, D. and R. Silverstone (1990), 'Domestic communications: technologies and meanings', *Media, Culture and Society*, **12** (1), 31–55.

Nicoll, D.W. (2000), 'Users as currency: technology and marketing trials as naturalistic environments', *The Information Society*, **16** (4), 303–10.

Noble, David (1979), 'Social choice in machine design: the case of automatically controlled machine tools', in A. Zimbalist (ed.), *Case Studies on the Labour Process*, New York: Monthly Review Press, pp. 18–50.

Norman, D. (1988), *The Psychology of Everyday Things*, New York: Basic Books.

Oudshoorn, Nelly and Trevor Pinch (2003), *How Users Matter: The Co-Construction of Users and Technologies*, Cambridge, MA: MIT Press.

Oudshoorn, Nelly, Els Rommes and Marcelle Stienstra (2004), 'Configuring the user as everybody: gender and design cultures in information and communication technologies', *Science, Technology and Human Values*, **29** (1), 30–63.

Pacey, Arnold (1983), *The Culture of Technology*, Oxford: Blackwell.

Pinch, Trevor and Wieber Bijker (1984), 'The social construction of facts and artefacts: or how the sociology of science and the sociology of technology might benefit each other', *Social Studies of Science*, **14** (3), 399–441.

Pollock, N., R. Williams and R. Procter (2003), 'Fitting standard software packages to non-standard organisations: the "biography" of an enterprise-wide system', *Technology Analysis and Strategic Management*, **15** (3), 317–32.

Procter, Robert N. and R. Williams (1996), 'Beyond design: social learning and computer-supported cooperative work: some lessons from innovation studies', Chapter 26, in Dan Shapiro, Michael Tauber and Roland Traunmueller (eds), *The Design of Computer-Supported Cooperative Work and Groupware Systems*, Amsterdam: North-Holland, pp. 445–64.

Rip, Arie, Thomas J. Misa and Johan Schot (eds) (1995) *Managing Technology in Society: The Approach of Constructive Technology Assessment*, London and New York: Pinter.

Rogers, E.M. (1983), *Diffusion of Innovations*, New York: Free Press.

Rommes, Els (2002), 'Worlds apart: exclusion-processes in DDS', in M. Tanabe, P. van den Besselaar and T. Ishida (eds), *Digital Cities II: Second Kyoto Workshop on Digital Cities*, Kyoto, Japan, 18–20 October 2001, Lecture Notes in Computer Science, vol. 2362, Heidelberg: Springer-Verlag, pp. 219–32.

Rosenberg, N. (1982), *Inside the Black Box: Technology and Economics*, Cambridge: Cambridge University Press.

Schon, Donald A. (1983), *The Reflective Practitioner: How Professionals Think in Action*, London: Temple Smith.

Schumm, W. and H. Kocyba (1997), 'Recontextualisation and opportunities for participation: the social shaping of implementation', in C. Clausen and R. Williams (eds), *The Social Shaping of Computer-Aided Production Management and Computer-Integrated Manufacture*, vol. 5, COST A4, Social Sciences, European Commission DGXIII, Luxembourg: Office for Official Publications of the European Communities, pp. 49–62.

Silverstone, R., E. Hirsch and D. Morley (1992), 'Information and communication technologies and the moral economy of the household', in R. Silverstone and E. Hirsch (eds), *Consuming Technologies: Media and Information in Domestic Spaces*, London: Routledge, ch. 1, pp. 15–31.

Sørensen, Knut H. (1994), 'Adieu Adorno: the moral emancipation of consumers', in A.-J. Berg and M. Aune (eds), *Domestic Technology and Everyday Life: Mutual Shaping Processes*, vol. 1, COST, Social Sciences, Science Research and Development, European Commission DGXIII, Luxembourg: Office for Official Publications of the European Communities, pp. 157–69.

Sørensen, Knut H. (1996), 'Learning technology, constructing culture: socio-technical change as social learning', STS Working Paper no. 18/96, Centre for Technology and Society, University of Trondheim.

Sørensen, Knut H. and Robin Williams (eds) (2002), *Shaping Technology, Guiding Policy: Concepts, Spaces and Tools*, Cheltenham, UK and Northampton, MA, USA: Edward Elgar.

Star, S.L. and G.C. Bowker (1999), *Sorting Things Out: Classification and Its Consequences*, Cambridge, MA: MIT Press.

van Lieshout, M., T. Egyedi and W.E. Bijker (eds) (2001), *Social Learning Technologies: The Introduction of Multimedia in Education*, Aldershot: Ashgate.

van Lieshout, M. (1999), 'The digital city of Amsterdam: between public initiative and private enterprise', in Claire Lobet-Maris and Beatrice van Bastelaer (eds), *1999 Digital Cities Final Report*, mimeo – Faculté Université de Notre Dame de la Paix, Namur: CITA, ch. 7, pp. 61–110.

Vedel, Thierry (1994), 'Introduction à une socio-politique des usages', in André Vitalis (ed.), *Médias et nouvelles technologies: pour une socio-politique des usages*, Rennes: Éditions Apogée, pp. 13–34.

Wajcman, Judy (1991), *Feminism Confronts Technology*, Cambridge: Polity.

Whipp, Richard (1985), *Innovation and the Auto Industry: Product, Process and Work Organization*, London: Pinter.

Williams, Robin, with Roger Slack and James Stewart (2000), *Social Learning in Multimedia: Final Report to European Commission*, DGXII, Edinburgh, Research Centre for Social Sciences: Edinburgh University.

Williams, Robin, James Stewart and Roger Slack (2005), *Social Learning and Technological Innovation: Experimenting with Information and Communication Technologies*, Cheltenham, UK and Northampton, MA, USA: Edward Elgar.

Winner, Langdon (1980), 'Do artifacts have politics?', *Daedalus*, **109** (1), Winter, 121–36. Reprinted in Donald MacKenzie and Judy Wajcman (eds) (1985), *The Social Shaping of Technology*, London: Open University Press, pp. 26–38.

Woolgar, S. (1991), 'Configuring the user: the case of usability trials', in J. Law (ed.), *A Sociology of Monsters. Essays on Power, Technology and Domination*, London: Routledge, pp. 57–102.

# PART II

# THEORY AND APPLICATION

# 11 Critical engagement: why, what and how?
## Geoff Walsham

### Why critical engagement?

In seeking a definition for critical research in the information systems (IS) field, the early article by Orlikowski and Baroudi (1991) remains helpful. They describe the critical researcher's beliefs about reality, knowledge and the role of research as follows:

> [S]ocial reality is historically constituted ... everything possesses an unfulfilled potentiality, and people, by recognizing these possibilities, can act to change their material and social circumstances ... knowledge is grounded in social and historical practices ... the role of the researcher is to bring to consciousness the restrictive conditions of the status quo, thereby initiating change in the social relations and practices, and helping to eliminate the bases of alienation and domination. (pp. 19–21)

Bearing in mind the clear anti-establishment agenda of the above mission statement for the critical IS researcher, it is no great surprise that Orlikowski and Baroudi recorded that critical studies in four 'major information systems outlets' were non-existent. These outlets were *Communications of the ACM, ICIS Proceedings, Management Science* and *MIS Quarterly.* Over a decade later, the position would be not dissimilar in the conservative mainstream. Although the 'major outlets' would now probably include *Information Systems Research*, and exclude one or two of the original set, the proportion of 'critical' articles in these outlets remains very low.

However, the overall position of the IS field has changed somewhat. There is increasing interest in critical studies, as reflected in this book, for example. It is also reflected in a significant number of the articles published in 'alternative' outlets such as *Information and Organization* and *Information Technology and People.* This increased interest in critical work is also manifested in the broader domain of management studies research, as demonstrated by a series of conferences on critical management studies and special issues of journals. It may be that critical studies will follow interpretivism in moving from a marginalized position in the IS field to a more central role (Walsham 1995). This has already happened to some extent with respect to critical management studies, particularly in Europe: 'Although this should not be overstated, critical management studies is less marginally positioned in Europe than in the USA' (Grey and Willmott 2002, p. 412).

But why are these movements with respect to critical IS and management studies research occurring? This is a complex question to answer, and largely beyond the scope of this short chapter. However, I would like to argue that it is not surprising that some researchers at least, in both IS and management studies more generally, are adopting critical approaches. Enormous asymmetries of wealth and power exist in the world, and the 'restrictive conditions of the status quo' and 'bases of alienation and domination' noted in Orlikowski and Baroudi's definition of critical research remain highly relevant to the contemporary world.

Let me give a few examples. Globalization is hard to define, but Beck (2000, p. 9) argues that its complexity is often reduced to the ideology of 'globalism': 'By globalism I mean the view that the world market eliminates or supplants political action – that is, the ideology of the rule of the world market, the ideology of neoliberalism'. Beck argues strongly against this ideology, citing many different reasons. For example, he notes that globalism 'sings the praises' of worldwide 'free trade', but that we live in a world far removed from any fair model of free trade due to enormously skewed initial conditions. The failure of the 2003 World Trade Organization summit to reach agreement provides an ironic example of the rich countries' support for free trade when it is to their own advantage, but not otherwise. For example, the massive agricultural subsidies provided to US and European farmers are in clear breach of anything resembling a level playing field.

The plight of poor people in the world remains a major illustration of the inadequacies of the current world order. Their poverty is not simply material, but also in the capabilities (Sen 1999) which they have to make choices and take action with respect to their lives. Poor people do not necessarily come from poor countries, and Castells (1998) defines the Fourth World as the underprivileged anywhere, including the urban poor in the rich Western countries, for example. The position of women in the world may have improved somewhat in some contexts over the last century, but women are often disadvantaged in a male-dominated world, for example in the privileging of male workers and their competencies (Woodfield 2002).

Information and communication technologies (ICTs), the primary focus of the IS field, are deeply implicated in all of the above issues. ICTs are involved in the way that we as individuals carry out our work and leisure activities, in the way that we organize ourselves in groups, in the forms that our organizations take, and in the type of societies that we create. I argued in a recent book (Walsham 2001) that we should be trying to make a 'better' world with ICTs, not merely in economic terms, but also related to a wider global agenda of social and spiritual welfare. This implies the need for IS researchers to adopt a critical approach to the existing status quo, in order to explore current material and social circumstances in their historical and cultural context, and thus to try to initiate positive change.

In addition to 'critical', the title of this chapter also includes the word 'engagement' as a way of thinking about the role of the critical IS researcher. One meaning of the word is that of an undertaking or prolonged course of action, and I shall argue that critical IS research needs this type of long-term approach, since the issues to be addressed are complex and deep-seated in nature. A second meaning of the term is as a metaphor from the area of military activities where an engagement is conceived of as a battle against an enemy. Critical research implies challenging the status quo and in some cases therefore, opposing existing vested interests. This can sometimes be a painful and even on occasions a dangerous process. Finally, I wish to suggest engagement as a descriptive term in its sense of a duty or moral commitment. Researchers are often in a privileged position themselves; for example, I am able to write this chapter without any censorship, except no doubt for a review by a sympathetic colleague. This freedom should carry with it a sense of responsibility, since many working people, for example managers in business organizations, do not have this freedom to write what they wish, and may suffer severe sanctions if they challenge powerful vested interests.

So, I have said something in this introduction about the 'why' of critical engagement and I have made a brief mention of the 'what', namely some broad topics for study. I shall address later in the chapter the 'how' of critical engagement through different modes and styles of work. Before that, in the next three sections, I wish to provide some specific examples of the 'why' and 'what' of critical IS research. These are largely drawn from the published work of other researchers, although in all three cases I have had some personal involvement with the research work myself. All of the examples are taken from work in so-called developing countries. This should not be taken to imply that work in such contexts is more important than critical research in the richer countries of the world. However, many of the chapters in this book deal with these latter contexts, and I hope that the illustrations in this chapter will provide a valuable complement.

**Health information systems in South Africa**
This case study concerns work carried out in South Africa over the last ten years under the label of HISP (Health Information Systems Program). A summary and analysis of the work from 1994 to 2001 is given in Braa and Hedberg (2002). The basic objective of the work has been to develop locally relevant health information systems and associated data collection procedures, linked to a national strategic approach to improving health

standards across the country as a whole. The HISP approach is in the process of being extended to other African countries such as Mozambique and developing countries in other regions such as India, but the focus of this section will be the South African work only.

The work needs to be viewed within the political context of post-apartheid South Africa. Following an armed struggle and international pressure, the notorious apartheid system was ended in South Africa in the early 1990s. A democratically elected government of national unity was formed in 1994 under the leadership of Nelson Mandela. The government brought with it a new policy agenda, and health was regarded as a key area. Government health policy stated that the health system would be decentralized to focus on districts, subdivisions of the country containing between 50 000 and 500 000 people. Part of the plan was the development of a new national health information system to support the changed focus, and work on HISP formed part of this.

*The HISP approach and achievements*
In its first phase up to 1998, HISP aimed at supporting the emerging decentralized structures in three pilot districts in Cape Town, the main town in the province of the Western Cape. A key goal of the approach was the empowerment of local health workers. In terms of data collection and related computer-based IS, this translates into the need to create, analyse and use data at the same level at which it is collected. This contrasts with the 'typical' approach in many developing countries, and certainly in apartheid South Africa, where the health data collected by local-level workers are passed up the hierarchy, and data collection is perceived as a burden by local workers, irrelevant to their work with sick people. As an illustration of work under HISP to address such issues, Thompson (2002) describes changed data collection approaches in some large Cape Town clinics in the poorest areas of the city. These were based on the use of simple tools such as hand-held counters (for example, for patients arriving at the clinic) and simplified and more transparent procedures and forms for data collection.

One metaphor used by the researchers to describe their approach to the development of locally relevant information systems is that of 'cultivation'. The argument is that particular information systems (hardware/software/standards) may be planted in specific locations, so that the seeds are similar, but local growing conditions are infinitely variable. Thus the developing plant needs to be tended and nurtured through people at the lower level who have ownership and commitment towards it. Braa (1997) argued that a participatory design process is crucial in helping to create such ownership, and thus a bottom-up approach to IS development is essential.

However, although local empowerment and commitment is crucial, there is a need at the higher policy levels, both in districts and nationally, to create standardized data. A key rationale for this is to identify and target areas of need as described by Braa and Hedberg (2002, p. 114): 'striving for equity between geographical areas and racial groups will require a system of national standards to measure and monitor the extent to which this policy is being achieved and to pinpoint areas where more resources and efforts are needed'.

Braa and Hedberg discuss a tension between this need for standardization and the flexibility needed for effective localization. They describe their approach to resolving this tension through a hierarchy of standards, where each level in the health system has freedom to define its own standards as long as they align with the standards of the level above.

With respect to the progress of HISP following the Cape Town pilot projects, the South African Department of Health adopted the strategies, processes and software developed in the pilot districts as a national standard. Braa and Hedberg report that 'these are currently being rolled out to all districts (in South Africa)' (ibid., p. 113). As noted earlier, other countries are experimenting with the HISP approach, and it is also worth noting that the HISP software has been deliberately designed as open source, based on the political view that such systems should be freely available to other developing countries.

### Critical engagement of the researchers

The action research on HISP has been a collaborative endeavour, initially involving the University of Oslo in Norway, the University of the Western Cape in South Africa and the Department of Health in South Africa. More recently, a range of other individuals and institutions have been included. However, a core team has worked on the project since its inception. This core team offers a classic example of critical engagement, and I shall justify this assertion below by relating their actions and motivations to the characteristics of critical engagement described earlier.

Orlikowski and Baroudi's definition of critical research emphasized the importance of recognizing *unfulfilled potential* and therefore the possibility of people acting *to change their material and social circumstances*. The unfulfilled potential in South Africa can be related directly to the oppression of non-white people during the apartheid years and, in the specific context of the health system, change includes the need to provide improved health services through decentralization and locally relevant information systems. This was a key motivation for the core team, as described by Braa and Hedberg (2002, p. 113):

As a legacy of apartheid, the new South Africa (post-1994) inherited one of the least equitable health care systems in the world ... the new government launched the Reconstruction and Development Program ... with a title that clearly expressed its intent: the reconstitution and development of communities that suffered under apartheid. The restructuring of the health sector ... is based on a decentralized system of health districts. Development of new national health information systems to support the restructuring of the health sector is part of this plan.

A second feature of Orlikowski and Baroudi's definition of critical research is the recognition that *knowledge is grounded in social and historical practices.* The South African health system provides an excellent example of this, where the data collected during the apartheid years, and thus the 'knowledge' concerning the health of the overall population, was subordinated to the need to discriminate between the various races. Again, this is well recognized and articulated by Braa and Hedberg (2002, p. 113): 'The politics of apartheid – segmentation, centralism and exclusion of "black" South Africans – have all been deeply inscribed into all the bits and pieces of the information systems in which standards for data collection are basic elements'.

Finally, Orlikowski and Baroudi's definition suggests the role of the critical researcher as bringing to consciousness the restrictive conditions of the status quo, initiating changes in social relations and practices and thus *helping to eliminate the bases of alienation and domination.* The whole work through HISP has been geared to achieving such ends by means such as the development of decentralized systems through local prototyping, the empowerment of local-level health workers, and the improved ability to target poor areas and disadvantaged parts of the population by comparing standards across districts and the country as a whole.

I argued earlier for the use of the term 'engagement' as a valuable characteristic of critical IS researchers, and its meanings as an *undertaking,* a *battle* and a *duty* or *commitment.* With respect to the first of these meanings, an undertaking implies a long-term approach in order to address complex and deep-seated problems and inequities. HISP has been operating for ten years already and its scope is widening rather than narrowing. The researchers have engaged with the complexity of the area across a wide range of activities as noted by Braa and Hedberg (2002, p. 116): 'The authors have been deeply and directly involved in strategic planning, daily implementation, political brokering, software prototyping, institutional development, and training at all levels.'

Turning to the metaphor of engagement as a battle, it is notable that Braa and Hedberg entitle their paper: 'The struggle for district-based health information systems in South Africa'. They articulate their political motives for engaging in this struggle as follows:

> It is important to note that the original key members of the HISP team have background as social/political activists in the antiapartheid struggle and other social movements, and that we have always explicitly and implicitly seen ourselves as political actors in a larger development process. (Ibid., p. 114)

Engagement as a 'duty or commitment' is also captured in the above quotation from the long-term members of the core HISP team.

I would like to end this subsection on a note of caution. I am not saying that all the actions of the HISP team were always well-conceived, or that their goals were always attained. The struggle continues. Nevertheless, I believe that much has been achieved over the ten years of HISP and, in the context of this chapter, that the HISP project provides a good example of all of the features of critical engagement on the part of IS researchers.

**GIS for land management in India**

This case study describes research carried out on attempts in India to use geographical information systems (GIS) for district-level administration and planning, with a particular focus on land management. GIS appear to have considerable potential at this level where many issues are spatial in nature: for example, the planning and upgrading of roads, the location of health facilities, the choice of areas for particular agricultural development, or the management of natural and planted forests. India has a population of more than one billion people, the considerable majority of whom live 'off the land' and have very low incomes. Better land management in India offers, therefore, the prospect of improving the material circumstances of large numbers of poor people.

The research carried out in this area was in two phases. The first phase took place over the period from 1993 to 1996 and involved all district-level GIS initiatives in India at that time, although a key focus was ten projects carried out under the direction of the Ministry of Environment and Forests (MOEF) of the government of India. Detailed descriptions of the research in this phase can be found in Sahay and Walsham (1997) and Walsham and Sahay (1999). The second phase of the research was carried out in 2002–03 and investigated eight different sites, with rather more emphasis on what was happening at the village level in addition to the actions of GIS scientists and government administrators. Descriptions of this phase can be found in Puri (2003) and Puri and Sahay (2003).

*Outline of the GIS experiences*

One of the research questions motivating the first phase was whether the use of GIS in this context had been successful. The researchers give a clear and negative answer: 'we must give the broad answer "no" to the issue of whether GIS has been used successfully to date, defining success in this case as substantive use' (Walsham and Sahay 1999, p. 55).

What were the reasons given by the researchers for this state of affairs? Basically, that the systems were developed in a top-down manner by GIS scientists with a technological agenda, and that little effort or thought was directed to involving local-level administrators in the design and implementation of the systems. In addition, it was argued that India is not a map-based culture, in the sense that most Indians do not use maps to conceptualize spatial issues. Thus, the incorporation of 'alien' GIS systems into local-level use by administrators, or even more so villagers, would require much more than the development of technical systems supplemented by some rudimentary 'training'.

The field research in the second phase found similar experiences in some of the field sites, but in one site in particular, the district of Anantpur in the state of Andhra Pradesh, a more optimistic picture was emerging:

> Field work in several districts reflected the persistence of the cultural divide between scientist, line department officials and communities (e.g. villages). On the other hand, the exposure gained in Anantpur was in sharp contrast as decentralization of development, empowerment of people, implicating local knowledge in GIS design and use were in evidence. (Puri 2003, p. 91)

The second-phase researchers argue from their evidence that two complementary elements are needed to move beyond the unsuccessful top-down model of GIS development, and that both of these elements were present in Anantpur district. First, that it is important to recognize the value of the 'indigenous knowledge' of local people such as farmers and other villagers of their own location, what is feasible there and how best to implement new land management practices. They distinguish this from the 'technical knowledge' of GIS developers and general 'scientific knowledge' of land, soil or water, for example. The argument is not that these last two forms of knowledge are irrelevant, but that all three types of knowledge must be harnessed for effective use of GIS to support improved land management practices at the district and village level. This was achieved in Anantpur district by participatory design approaches. Puri and Sahay (2003, p. 189) report the words of a local government official as follows:

> A striking feature of the development methodology adopted in Anantpur is that all such programs (for improved land management) are determined, finalized and implemented by the villagers as per their felt needs, with power to incur expenditure within allocated budget. The government only plays the role of a motivator and adviser, and also oversees the progress of implementation and financial expenditure.

This leads to the second element of the relative success in Anantpur, namely the role played by government institutions. The researchers emphasize that participation in itself is not enough, but that efficacious outcomes depend also on the creation of favourable institutional conditions. They identify four such conditions in Anantpur: a local watershed-based approach to development; devolution of budgets down to this watershed level; the setting up of a local (as distinct from distant) GIS unit; and changing the GIS scientists' responsibilities to include a local implementation focus. They also note that the setting up of these institutional conditions was greatly helped by the enthusiastic support of the district collector (the most senior administrator in the district), in the context of the state of Andhra Pradesh whose chief minister at that time, Chandrababu Naidu, was well-known for his advocacy of the potentially beneficial role of ICT in development.

*Critical engagement of the researchers*
The first phase of the research was carried out by two academic researchers, Sundeep Sahay and Geoff Walsham, and the second phase by Sahay and a PhD student, Satish Puri. However, it is important to note that Puri was, in the first phase, the MOEF official in India in charge of GIS projects. Thus, Puri moved from the role of a key participant in the first phase to an academic researcher in the second phase. This background is relevant to the following discussion of critical engagement.

The recognition of unfulfilled potential and the need to change the material and social circumstances of the rural people of India was a key motivation of all the researchers during both phases. The recognition that knowledge is grounded in social and historical practices grew more gradually. In the early stages of the first phase of the research, the importance of local knowledge was certainly not emphasized either by the researchers or by the GIS teams. Themes such as village-level participation and the need to change institutional conditions at the village level were certainly not present in the first phase. Puri (2003, p. 72) gives an honest account of influences on his own thinking in these areas being partly derived from his later experiences as a PhD student in Scandinavia:

> Gaining some insight into the value systems of democratization of workplace and empowerment of workers that motivated much of this participatory research (in Scandinavia) has been a moving experience, which has shaped my thinking about the potential liberating role of IS in particular and ICTs in general in societal contexts.

This quotation also relates to a further element of the goal of a critical researcher, namely *helping to eliminate the bases of alienation and domination*. It has to be said that, in the context of India, the use of GIS in the Anantpur case is rather a 'drop in the ocean', and that capabilities (Sen 1999) for people to make choices and take action in their lives are still very limited in most of rural India. Favourable institutional conditions and participatory approaches are the exception rather than the rule. Nevertheless, the Anantpur case is encouraging, and a stimulus to further action to cultivate such approaches more widely.

What of the engagement of the researchers in this case? The long-term nature of the research, over ten years now since the early work, justifies using the term 'an undertaking', carried out to address complex and deep-seated problems and inequities. Although one of the researchers in the second phase was also a practitioner in the first phase, the engagement has not, however, been as strong and comprehensive as that reported in the South African case earlier. The first-phase researchers moved only gradually from a more detached position to the position of action researchers:

> We see a continuum of research positions here from the role of 'independent observer' with a mainly descriptive objective through the strongly prescriptive stance of an 'action researcher' with active involvement in the change process. In our research project, we started in the former position, but we gradually became more involved as time went on. (Walsham and Sahay 1999, p. 45)

Although this process has continued in the second phase, with involvement at the local village level for example, the research still stops short of the *battle* metaphor in many respects. The researchers have had only peripheral involvement in the deeply political processes governing the nature of institutional conditions, and have not set up or facilitated the participatory approaches carried out in Anantpur district, for example.

The view of the research as a *duty or commitment* has, however, been present throughout. In the first phase, the researchers noted that they felt 'a particular moral imperative to get involved in advising on possible courses of action ... in Indian districts, whose economic prosperity is amongst the lowest in the world' (ibid., p. 45). Puri (2003, p. 123) closes his thesis with an appeal for more research on whether ICTs are contributing to create a better world in which we live: 'This thesis is closed with a re-emphasis on [this] question, and the need to foreground it more emphatically in IS research, more so when these systems implicate and impact the poor and already marginalized communities'.

### Digital inclusion projects in Brazil
The phrase 'digital divide' is used widely, not just in academic circles but also in the media, for example. However, it is important to note that the provision of access to the internet, or to ICT more generally, is not a sufficient response, since people need to be enabled also to use the technology effectively. This is

the focus of so-called 'digital inclusion' projects, and this section will outline some digital inclusion projects in the context of Brazil. Many different actors and institutions are involved in such projects, including central, state and city governments, non-governmental organizations (NGOs), international agencies such as the World Bank, and private sector companies.

The material below will briefly outline some of the digital inclusion projects in the city of São Paulo, a mega-city of 17 million people. In particular, the projects have involved the setting up of 'telecentres' in poor areas, with hardware and software, internet access and support staff. Typical numbers of computers in such centres are in the range of 10–20 machines. Research on the design, implementation and use of these telecentres is being carried out at the University of São Paulo by a PhD student, Marie Ann Macadar, and her supervisor, Nicolau Reinhard. I am involved as Macadar's co-supervisor, and I had the opportunity to visit ten São Paulo telecentres over a three-day period in September 2003. Macadar and Reinhard's (2002) paper (in Portuguese) describes early experiences in São Paulo, and also in the city of Porto Alegre.

*Telecentres in the city of São Paulo*
The first telecentre in the city was established in 2001, but the number of such centres is now into the hundreds. The government of the city of São Paulo is a major player, with about 100 centres in 2004. They have chosen the location of their telecentres based on an adapted version of a human development index, selecting poorer areas for the establishment of new centres. Their digital inclusion policy is stated as follows:

> Eliminating Digital Exclusion can only be possible if such mission is faced as a duty of the State and turned into a public policy. Education, for instance, has only become universal when the government finally decided to take full responsibility on it.
> We should ban technological inequalities and digital illiteracy, granting people with the right to access knowledge via net. The São Paulo City Hall with its Digital Inclusion Plan, has been working on the idea of bringing the right to connection and information accessible to all. The City Hall is setting up and supporting Telecenters on the most socially excluded areas, around the entire town. (www.telecentros.sp.gov.br/English)

Funding for the centres is provided by the city government, and facilities are free to users. However, there is a strong emphasis on the use of open-source software to keep down costs. The centres provide a certain number of machines for free internet access at the users' own choice (except pornography sites), and typical uses are to find job adverts, to create CVs, to play games and to engage in e-mail and other forms of digital social interaction. The centres also provide specific training courses for groups of people on topics such as the use of e-mail and various software packages, and internet access, searching and website creation.

My overall impression of telecentres in the city of São Paulo, supported by the Brazilian researchers' more extensive fieldwork, is that some good things are happening from a combination of the various initiatives. Both 'open access' and 'training course' approaches are being widely utilized, although primarily by the younger end of the population, and the fact that the provision of facilities is free is crucial in encouraging use in poor areas. An interesting impression, from a field researcher used to working in places like India, is that the gap between the rhetoric of 'what is happening' according to senior officials in government offices, and what is visible 'on the ground' at the field sites, is relatively small.

However, I do have some reservations about the current status and usefulness of the telecentres. It is not obvious that the centres are helping community activities in a proactive enough way. A good example is community enterprise or entrepreneurial activity taking place in poor communities. The effective use of ICT, including the internet, to support such activities would require, at least, a dedicated team of small enterprise specialists, working with computer specialists. One cannot expect small-scale entrepreneurs to have the know-how to use ICTs in their businesses without specialist help, and computer specialists are necessary but not sufficient.

More generally, there are many positive uses of the technology in the existing telecentres, but one senses that the 'match' between the communities' needs and the computer technology requires a more vigorous and diverse effort than was present in 2004. The head of an NGO with a long-term commitment to telecentres supported this view when he said that: 'We need to go back to the communities … to find out what they really want … some good things are happening *but* … I am the one saying but'.

A further qualification concerning the success of the telecentre initiatives is to ask whether the approach is hitting the really poor, or even the children of the really poor. I suspect that the answer is no, but perhaps this is an impossible goal at the present time, where such people need more basic provision of housing, of education and so on. I would not wish to end this subsection on a negative note. The 'digital inclusion' projects in São Paulo are many in number, substantive and worthwhile. The challenge for the future is to extend their scale and scope, and to ensure that they serve communities' needs more fully than they do at present.

*Critical engagement of the researchers*
The recognition of *unfulfilled potential* and the need to *change the material and social circumstances* of the more disadvantaged communities in São

Paulo, and more generally in Brazil, is a key motivation of the digital inclusion projects themselves and of the researchers working on them. Macadar and Reinhard (2002) describe the *'exclusão digital'* as a *'trágica situação'*. They argue the need for research to look at the experiences of the digital inclusion projects taking place in order to 'analyse the difficulties encountered and the solutions attempted', and thus to learn how to make the projects more effective.

With respect to the recognition that *knowledge is grounded in social and historical processes*, it could be argued that, as in the later stages of the GIS projects in India, more attention should be paid to the importance of indigenous knowledge. In other words, that the telecentres have something of the air of 'technology push' about them, and that this needs to be balanced by a fuller exploration of the knowledge held by the communities themselves, and how the ICT-based initiatives can complement this. The brief discussion above of the need to go 'back to the communities', as described by the NGO leader, reflects such an understanding.

*Eliminating the bases of alienation and domination*, for the poor of São Paulo as elsewhere, is of course a Herculean task. One example of this is provided by one of the Brazilian researchers: 'most of the Brazilian population is not used to participative tools in their lives; some of the tools used by the (digital inclusion) projects are extremely democratic in character (e.g. a management council) ... they are quite new for this reality' (Macadar, private communication).

What can be said concerning the engagement of the researchers in this case? The research work on the digital inclusion projects is relatively recent and thus the long-term *undertaking* aspect is less visible than in the South African or Indian cases. Nevertheless, the work forms part of a longer-term concern on the use of ICTs for development at the University of São Paulo, and there is commitment to continue the work on digital inclusion into the future. As with the Indian case, and different from the South African case, some aspects of the research do not fit well to the *battle* metaphor in the sense that the researchers have not been deeply involved in managing the digital inclusion projects themselves, or confronting any vested interests which may be harmful to the projects. Nevertheless, there is clear political involvement by the research team in the way in which they interact with senior political figures in the area, such as those in the digital inclusion programmes of the federal government in Brasilia.

The *duty or commitment* view of engagement on the part of the Brazilian researchers can be clearly seen from their negative descriptions of the digital divide, and related global inequities, and the strong imperative to do something about it. With respect to my own position, being involved with these projects is one approach to a concern as to whether our technologies and systems are perpetuating, and indeed reinforcing, existing inequity (see Walsham 2001 for a fuller exposition). The digital inclusion projects in São Paulo may be limited in scope and scale, but I believe that they are a step in the right direction.

**Modes of engagement**
The chapter so far has outlined three critical IS research projects, and has discussed related action taken in the specific context. However, critical engagement should not be viewed as only involving local research and action. Publications and teaching are ways to reach wider audiences. With respect to the IS field as a whole, valuable actions include attempts to shift the field towards carrying out more critical research, or to a more sympathetic attitude towards it. This section will discuss these alternative modes of engagement, but first I shall make some further brief comments on critical research projects.

*Research*
All three research projects described above could be classed as involving critical research, although with some differences in the style and degree of engagement. Although the close engagement of researchers in the HISP project in South Africa is to be commended, such depth and continuity of involvement is not always possible. Both the GIS research in India and the digital inclusion research in Brazil have involved some engagement in local action, not least in influencing the ideas of practitioners in the field sites, but the researchers have not been as involved in directing and undertaking local action as in South Africa. However, this statement should not be seen as a judgement of the relative merits of the work in the three cases. The long-term effects of research projects are complex and subtle, and we should be careful in judging outcomes solely on the metric of degree of local engagement.

Can we learn anything from the three research projects as to how to get the funding and other resources needed in order to conduct critical IS research in developing country contexts? One should be wary of generalizing from this small sample, but it is noticeable that all the projects involved collaboration between indigenous and foreign researchers, used PhD students as resources, and had the support of local government administrators and officials. These cases suggest that it is necessary to build long-term networks of support to enable critical research engagement to be carried out.

*Publications*
It is obvious that all academics need to publish their work, in outlets such as conference papers, articles and books, in order to reach a wider audience

than their local field sites. However, bearing in mind the scarcity of critical IS research publications, there is a particular need for more written output of this type. It is easy to see how critical IS researchers, particularly those deeply engaged in their local domain, could prioritize local action over global dissemination, but both types of engagement should be valued highly. With respect to the three cases reported in this chapter, the cited publications are useful, but I would argue that more written dissemination is needed in all three cases.

With respect to the type of publications, academic- and practitioner-oriented outlets both serve valuable if different functions. I would like to see more academic papers describing critical IS research in 'mainstream' academic publications. This would be one way of influencing the IS field as a whole towards a recognition of the value of such research, or at least of its existence. Practitioner-oriented publications need to be different in style, and some would argue more 'conservative', but it is possible to introduce some 'critical' issues into more traditional written pieces. One of my papers (Walsham and Sahay 1999), published in the mainstream outlet *MIS Quarterly*, had a deliberate agenda of widening the geographical scope of the journal away from its excessively Western-centric focus.

### Teaching

I am sure that it will not have escaped the notice of many 'critical' readers of this chapter that I am talking above about the need for a 'struggle' against the existing power structures in academia, represented, for example, by journal editors and reviewers. This struggle for a critical voice to be heard also applies in the domain of teaching, perhaps particularly in business schools. Zeld (2002, p. 379) articulates the problem in the context of trying to introduce critical management studies teaching into business schools:

> However, it is certain that both the students who come to business schools to get training to participate and climb in management, and the elites who support the business schools, are deeply identified with the exact values and commitments that much of Critical Management Studies critiques.

Nevertheless, although difficult to do, surely there is a moral imperative for critical researchers not to completely abandon their critical stance when confronted by a class of MBA students, for example. The majority of the class may be indifferent or even hostile to the introduction of some critical spice into the curriculum, but students are not customers in my view. Academics have the right and duty to set the curriculum in the best interests of the students as they see it, not to follow exactly what the students feel that they want. More engagement and effort is needed in the introduction of a critical agenda into the teaching area, as captured in this appeal from Fulop (2002, p. 434): 'I only wish that as a community of CMS (critical management studies) scholars we could develop a rich array of strategies to teach CMS rather than push this issue to the back of papers or conference programmes.'

### Structuring the IS field

I have already commented on some ways of influencing the IS field towards including more critical voices, for example, by critical researchers publishing their papers in mainstream journals. However, this is only feasible if such journals have at least some editors and reviewers who are sympathetic to critical research. Therefore, a further engagement role for critical researchers is to get themselves on to editorial boards and conference committees to provide a possible route for critical papers. It is worth noting that this does not imply my support for a lowering of editorial or reviewing standards, but for critical papers not to be rejected 'out of hand', just because they are critical. An analogy can be made with the state of interpretive IS research in the late 1980s, where the explicit policy of *MIS Quarterly*, for example, was to exclude such papers (Walsham 1995). This is no longer the case, and interpretive researchers are now adequately represented on the editorial board for this journal.

There is a paradox, to some extent, in what I have said above. If mainstream journals, which generally support the status quo, introduce critical papers which oppose precisely this, then do such mainstream journals become self-contradictory in content? And does this mean that other journals will then become the new mainstream, perhaps even more opposed to critical voices? I have no simple answer to this latter question, but I would like to think that some intermediate position may be possible where 'conventional' and 'critical' papers can sit side by side in a mainstream journal, with a creative if contested debate between them. At the very least, I would like to see some debate, at conferences for example, about mainstream journal content in the IS field, and its lack of criticality.

### On being engaging

There is a danger in adopting a critical research stance of being seen as negative, unconstructive and miserable. This is captured, amusingly, in the conductor Sir Thomas Beecham's description of critics in the theatrical world: 'drooling, drivelling, doleful, depressing, dropsical drips' (quoted in Metcalf 1986, p. 65).

In contrast, it is important for the critical researcher to be engaging, used in the sense of attractive and interesting. The emphasis of the work is of course on questioning the status quo, but this can be done in a way which is constructive and optimistic, geared to building a better world.

A related point concerns the need to come across as not adopting a 'holier than thou' position. One should avoid demonizing others, such as managers in conventional organizations or non-critical researchers. With respect to the first of these groups, many managers are trying to do a good job within the constraints within which they operate, and even in some cases trying to shift those constraints. It is much harder to be critical of the status quo when one is operating inside rather than outside a conventional organization. With respect to non-critical researchers, there is a need for work that addresses the question as to how to be more efficient and effective within existing groups, organizations or societies.

Grey and Willmott (2002), both critical researchers themselves, note that the very existence of critical research in business schools depends on the more conventional side of the work carried out there: 'CMS (critical management studies) is in this sense parasitical, or at least dependent on, business schools being essentially institutions whose function is to provide knowledge *for* management rather than knowledge *of* management' (p. 416). They argue that CMS should, therefore, see itself as part of the overall field of management studies, but not the only important part, and not existing in isolation from the other parts: 'In short, CMS should not be overvalued in the general scheme of things, and its proponents should be alert to dangers of becoming too introspective and self-regarding' (p. 412).

Their message applies to the IS field also, in my view. Those of us who identify ourselves as 'critical' IS researchers should not try to operate independently of more mainstream, conventional work, but rather should try to complement and sometimes critique that work. There is a certain irony in me writing this, since my own work is often labelled as 'interpretive' (Walsham 1993), rather than critical. I have, however, always thought of my research as having critical elements to it. For example, my engagement with the inequities in so-called developing countries goes back nearly 40 years.

In summarizing my own research 'journey' over the last decade or so, I would say that I have moved from a position where my critical agendas were largely implicit/covert to the current time when I am attempting to be more open about these agendas. A second component in this shift relates to theory. In my earlier work, critical elements were not normally theorized, whereas currently, in this chapter, for example, I am attempting to introduce more critically oriented concepts and theories. The boundaries between interpretive and critical research are fuzzy in my view, but the distinction remains an important one to discuss.

## Conclusions

I have defined critical research in this chapter based on the definition of Orlikowski and Baroudi (1991), but I have added the concept of engagement. I have viewed this as involving long-term commitment, a struggle against elements of the existing status quo, and a moral duty or commitment to engage. I have argued that the 'why' of critical engagement essentially derives from the enormously asymmetric world in which we currently live, for example, in terms of wealth, power to act, and access to resources. This presents a challenge for us all, namely to analyse and critique existing conditions, and to engage with others in trying to change things for the better, particularly for the currently disadvantaged.

In terms of the 'what' of critical IS research, I have outlined three cases taken from so-called developing countries in each of Africa, Asia and South America. In each case, the work was concerned with trying to use ICT to benefit relatively poor communities: to support improved healthcare in South Africa; better land management in India; and digital inclusion in Brazil. As I noted earlier in the chapter, I am not, however, privileging developing countries as being the sole preserve of critical research, since there are a wide range of areas for work in the rich countries. I would add that we have only scratched the surface so far. There are many other topics and issues in all geographical areas which would benefit from critical research.

With respect to 'how' to be critically engaged in the IS area, I have argued that there are different modes of engagement, including field research, publications, teaching, and contribution to structuring the IS field through being involved with institutions such as conferences and journals. I have also argued the need to be engaging, and not to demonize others who do not adopt critical positions as their main research activity. I would like to add a final word. Although I have taken a relatively conciliatory position with respect to existing research in IS, and more generally in related fields such as management studies, I do think that it is unfortunate that there is so little work which adopts an explicitly critical stance. The world is staggeringly inequitable in many respects. We need more research which addresses the question as to why this is the case, what we should do about it, and how to make things better.

## References

Beck, U. (2000), *What is Globalization?*, Cambridge: Polity.
Braa, J. (1997) 'Use and design of information technology in third world contexts with a focus on the health sector: case studies from Mongolia and South Africa', PhD thesis, Department of Informatics, University of Oslo, Oslo.
Braa, J. and Hedberg, C. (2002) 'The struggle for district-based health information systems in South Africa', *The Information Society*, **18** (2), 113–27.

Castells, M. (1998), *End of Millennium*, Oxford: Blackwell.

Fulop, L. (2002), 'Practising what you preach: critical management studies and its teaching', *Organization*, **9** (3), 428–36.

Grey, C. and Willmott, H. (2002), 'Contexts of critical management studies', *Organization*, **9** (3), 411–18.

Macadar, M.A. and Reinhard, N. (2002), 'Telecentros Comunitários Possibilitando a Inclusão Digital: um Estudo de Caso Comparativo de Iniciativas Brasileiras' (Community telecentres creating possibilities for digital inclusion: a comparative case study of Brazilian initiatives), Proceedings of the 26th ANPAD Meeting (Associação Nacional dos Programas de Pós-Graduação em Administração), Information Systems Track (ADI), Salvador-BA-Brasil, 22–25 September.

Metcalf, F. (ed.) (1986), *The Penguin Dictionary of Modern Humorous Quotations*, London: Penguin.

Orlikowski, W.J. and Baroudi, J.J. (1991), 'Studying information technology in organizations: research approaches and assumptions', *Information Systems Research*, **2** (1), 1–28.

Puri, S. (2003), 'The challenges of participation and knowledge in GIS implementation for land management: case studies from India', PhD thesis, Department of Informatics, University of Oslo, Oslo.

Puri, S. and Sahay, S. (2003), 'Participation through communicative action: a case study of GIS for addressing land/water development in India', *Journal of Information Technology for Development*, **10** (3), 179–99.

Sahay, S. and Walsham, G. (1997), 'Social structure and managerial agency in India', *Organization Studies*, **18** (3), 415–44.

Sen, A. (1999), *Development as Freedom*, Oxford: Oxford University Press.

Thompson, M.P.A. (2002), 'Cultivating meaning: interpretive fine-tuning of a South African health information system', *Information and Organization*, **12** (3), 183–211.

Walsham, G. (1993), *Interpreting Information Systems in Organizations*, Chichester: Wiley.

Walsham, G. (1995) 'The emergence of interpretivism in IS research', *Information Systems Research*, **6** (4), 376–94.

Walsham, G. (2001), *Making a World of Difference: IT in a Global Context*, Chichester: Wiley.

Walsham, G. and Sahay, S. (1999), 'GIS for district-level administration in India: problems and opportunities', *MIS Quarterly*, **23** (1), 39–66.

Woodfield, R. (2002), 'Women and information systems development: not just a pretty (inter)face?', *Information Technology and People*, **15** (2), 119–38.

Zeld, M.N. (2002), 'Spinning disciplines: critical management studies in the context of the transformation of management education', *Organization*, **9** (3), 365–85.

# 12 Towards critical interpretivism in IS research

*Bill Doolin and Laurie McLeod*

## Introduction

This chapter proposes and outlines a critical approach to interpretive research on information systems (IS). The chapter first establishes the need for such a critical research project by rehearsing the existing critique of interpretive research. It then proposes a solution in the form of 'critical interpretivism'. Critical interpretivism is grounded in three principles: (i) the construction of detailed, local and situated empirical interpretation; (ii) a reflective approach that reveals and disrupts the assumptions and certainties that reinforce the status quo in organizations; and (iii) the connection of interpretation to broader considerations of power and control.

The chapter illustrates the application of critical interpretivism to IS research through three case studies. Each case study draws on a particular theoretical perspective to inform the critical interpretation and analysis of the development or implementation of different information systems. The different theoretical perspectives emphasize the plurality of critical approaches possible within critical interpretivism (see Thomas 1993). The first case study mobilizes a Foucauldian conception of power to understand the implementation of and resistance to a medical management information system; the second utilizes actor-network theory (Law and Hassard 1999) to explain the development and abandonment of an executive information system; and the third draws on a structurational model of information technology (IT) to conceptualize the development and use of a company intranet.

Central to the argument in this chapter, is that interpretive IS researchers need to consciously adopt a critical and reflective stance in relation to the role that the ITs which they describe play in maintaining social orders and power relations in organizations. By utilizing perspectives such as those discussed in this chapter, interpretive IS researchers can marry the thick description of interpretive research with the broader sweep of critical social theory (see Hull 1997).

## Being critical about interpretive IS research

Interpretivism is the result of a long history of critique of positivism as the sole basis for understanding human activity. It asserts that reality and our knowledge of it are social products that cannot be understood independently of the social actors who construct and make sense of that reality. A shared social reality is produced and reproduced through ongoing social interaction and can only be interpreted, rather than 'discovered' (Orlikowski and Baroudi 1991). Actions cannot be understood without reference to their meaning.

Interpretive research involves the study of social practices in the context in which they occur. This close involvement with the subject of research means that ethnographic techniques and participant observation are favoured as sources of qualitative research evidence. As Law (1994, p. 2) says: 'I listened to participants, I watched them and I asked them questions.' The presentation of the evidence typically involves detailed 'thick descriptions' of organizational contexts and practices, emphasizing the perceptions and explanations of human actors in the context studied.

The primary purpose is to offer an account or interpretation of and for human conduct. The researcher moves beyond the descriptive properties of the studied scene and informant interpretations of those properties by attempting to provide a contextualized understanding. Interpretive research does not seek to generalize in the positivist sense. Instead, a theoretical understanding of the phenomenon is sought, which can then be used to inform other settings (Orlikowski and Baroudi 1991; Knights 1995). From an interpretive position, the validity of doing so relies on the plausibility of the reasoning used in describing the results and in drawing conclusions from them (Walsham, 1993). As Geertz (1973, p. 25) observes of ethnography: 'What generality it contrives to achieve grows out of the delicacy of its distinctions, not the sweep of its abstractions.'

The use of interpretivism as a legitimate approach for understanding human interaction with and around IT is now relatively established in the IS field (for example, Walsham 1993, 1995; Lee et al. 1997; Myers 1997). We might characterize interpretive IS research by an intention to understand 'the context of the information system, and the process whereby the information system influences and is influenced by its context' (Walsham, 1993, pp. 4–5). It is based on the belief that: 'The same physical artifact, the same institution, or the same human action, can have different meanings for different human subjects, as well as for the observing social scientist' (Lee 1991, p. 347).

Although IS have a physical component that permits their technical operation, they are designed and used by people operating in a complex social context. Thus, an information system is understood (constructed) differently by different individuals, and is given meaning by the shared understanding of such phenomena that arises out of social interaction. This is a dynamic process since the information system itself is not static, either in terms of its physical components and data or in the changing human perceptions of the information system and its output (Walsham 1993). Viewed thus, IS form part of an environment, within which managers, developers and users interact in order to develop shared meanings and interpretations of an ambiguous social reality. These shared meanings form a basis from which action is constructed (Boland 1979).

IS research that has its primary motivation in interpretation attempts to describe, interpret and understand IS phenomena, often utilizing an alternative perspective to the technical view of the mainstream, positivist tradition. For example, Hirschheim and Newman (1991) challenge the orthodox view that IS development is a normative process reflecting conventional economic reality. As an alternative basis for understanding the actual practice of IS development, they used the concept of symbolism to interpret the social actions and behaviour of developers and users in the development process. Wastell and Newman (1993) examined the behavioural dynamics of IS development, utilizing a stress perspective, and concluded that:

> The rational-technical view of systems development presented in most textbooks is a caricature. Information system development is a complex, protean, social phenomenon; conflict is endemic ... Simple prescriptions such as 'get top management support' or the pious call for user involvement grotesquely oversimplify the exacting realities of actual systems work. (pp. 142–3)

In their discussion of a broad critical research project for management studies, Alvesson and Deetz (2000) essentially argue for an 'empirical turn' in critical management research. They suggest that much of the critical scholarship in management is characterized by a conceptual emphasis and a lack of grounding in empirical work. We agree with Alvesson and Deetz (ibid., p. 17), that one of the tasks of critical research is to generate 'insight' or 'local understandings' of the phenomena under study. It is through the development of rich empirical material, based on organization-specific and micro-level aspects of local forms of phenomena that meaningful and insightful interpretations are constructed (Alvesson and Skoldberg 2000).

By emphasizing empirical research, we are not advocating naive empiricism, in which data can somehow be separated from interpretation, or where empirical material can act as an objective judge of or mirror on reality (Alvesson and Deetz 2000). Rather, empirical data are the results of interpretation (Alvesson and Skoldberg 2000), and the generation of empirically grounded, local understandings is an essential component for critical research. As Alvesson and Skoldberg (ibid., p. 257) put it, this form of empirical research is 'data-driven' as opposed to 'data-centred'.

We believe that the growing tradition of interpretive IS research, with its detailed empirical knowledge of organizational activity that is local and contextualized, can contribute much to such an expanded conception of the critical management research agenda.[1] However, Putnam (1983) points out a tendency for much research on human activity in organizations to utilize a managerial perspective that perpetuates managerial-based definitions of organizational reality and the status quo. While positivist research, which has an orientation towards technical control, is particularly prone to this, any research is capable of being unreflective and uncritical. Indeed, much interpretive IS research has been criticized for its failure to explain the unintended consequences of action, which cannot be explained by reference to the participants and which are often a significant force in shaping social reality. Such research has also been criticized for its frequent neglect of historical change, and a failure to recognize the inherent conflict and contradiction in social relations (Jönsson 1991; Orlikowski and Baroudi 1991).

Tinker (1998) criticizes interpretive IS research for what he perceives as its uncritical appreciation of the social and historical context of technological developments. He suggests that this unreflective accommodation with IT reflects an equivocation that inadvertently helps legitimate (and accelerate) technological changes that degrade the quality and quantity of work. By disregarding the historical and social contexts in which IT in organizations is designed and used, representations of IS phenomena are grounded in the status quo (Orlikowski and Baroudi 1991).

Many interpretive IS researchers would disagree with this criticism, suggesting that indeed it is hard to avoid being critical when conducting interpretive research. Nevertheless, there is a danger that interpretive researchers may become preoccupied with exhaustive and comprehensive description in attempts to provide authoritative and definitive accounts of empirical reality (Knights 1995). While interpretive IS research is grounded in a desire to describe and understand organizational reality, it need not do so without questioning the power structures that maintain the status quo. We need to consider the implications of unreflective accounts of IT in perpetuating the status quo in organizations.

Knights (ibid.) advocates dispelling the illusion of neutrality that many academics seek to cultivate around their research. He argues that a more reflexive approach to both self and other is necessary. Knights suggests that the contribution of interpretive research lies not only in adding depth to more conventional approaches, but also in that the in-depth analysis facilitates the disruption of existing assumptions and certainties. He notes, however, that the disruption of one set of representations involves the elevation of another that, in its turn, remains to be disrupted. Thus, interpretive research sets in motion continual possibilities of the production, transformation and reproduction of representation.

We see this as being reflective in the conduct of research, where reflection is 'the interpretation of interpretation' (Alvesson and Skoldberg 2000, p. 6). By reflection, we mean not only a form of reflexivity in which the researcher critically reflects on his or her own interpretations and the conditions within which they are constructed, but also the reflective and critical consideration of taken-for-granted assumptions and ideas, alternative interpretations, and an appreciation of how things could be otherwise.

We can avoid the danger of unreflective accounts of IT not only by questioning and deconstructing the taken-for-granted assumptions inherent in the status quo (Hull 1997), but also by connecting local understandings or interpretations of IS to broader considerations of social power and control (Thomas 1993; Alvesson and Deetz 2000) and by asking how these have come to be shaped or organized in a certain way, and for whose benefit they operate (Downing et al. 1995). Partly this involves adopting a more politically informed position regarding the agency of IT in social and technological change (Tinker 1998). Technology is both a condition and a consequence of power relations in organizations and society (Knights 1995). Without a critical consideration of IT, such research not only maintains taken-for-granted assumptions about the technology, it also deflects criticism away from IS and encourages their reification (Joerges and Czarniawska 1998).

Based on the above discussion, we suggest that critical interpretivism in IS research can be achieved through adherence to three fundamental principles:

1. The construction of detailed, local and situated empirical interpretation (Alvesson and Deetz 2000; Alvesson and Skoldberg 2000).
2. A reflective approach that reveals (and disrupts) the assumptions and certainties that reinforce the status quo in organizations (Knights 1995; Alvesson and Skoldberg 2000).
3. The connection of interpretation to the wider historical and societal context, and considerations of power and control (Thomas 1993; Alvesson and Deetz 2000).

In particular, to be critical, interpretive IS research must extend beyond the development of IT into the larger historical, economic, ideological, political and cultural context within which such developments occur (Alvesson and Deetz 2000). This wider context of particular technological outcomes involves preconceptions of power that impact on present and future events – events that must be interpreted in the light of these power relationships (Putnam 1983).

To do so, we need to inform our interpretations with appropriate social theories that help us theorize the empirically grounded understandings we derive from our research. As Alvesson and Skoldberg (2000) suggest, interpretive research is an intellectual project rather than a technical one. Critical social theories can act as sensitizing devices to provide a more reflective character to empirically-based interpretive research. Such theories challenge the legitimacy of established or hegemonic interpretations, and provide the basis for alternative representations (ibid.). Similarly, Walsham (1997) argues that in order to examine ethical and moral implications related to IS, we need to incorporate political, ethical and moral theories in our research.

There exists a continuum of possible critical approaches (Thomas 1993), and IS researchers can be critical while utilizing a range of theoretical perspectives. In this chapter, we present three theoretical perspectives that we believe are especially relevant to the critical analysis of IS in organizations. We do not attempt to privilege these over any other. They simply reflect approaches that we have found useful in our research on IS.

The first perspective uses the relational notion of power developed by Michel Foucault (1977, 1980) to conceptualize IT as a disciplinary technology. That is, how IS are implicated in mobilizing particular representations of organizational reality and in the governance of the conduct and subjectivity of organizational participants (Knights 1995; Hull 1997). The second perspective draws on a stream of work within the sociology of science and technology that has come to be known as 'actor-network theory'. In this perspective, IS are treated as heterogeneous and relational networks of actors, both human and non-human (Law 1992). The third perspective is based on the structuration theory of Anthony Giddens (1979, 1984), which provides a way of examining the mutually interactive relationship between structure and agency in organizational activities. In particular, Orlikowski (1992, 2000) has integrated an explicit consideration of IT into structuration theory.

**Foucault and power**

The Foucauldian perspective offers a useful approach to studying information systems in organizations from a critical perspective (Doolin 1998). According to Foucault (1977, 1980), power is not possessed but is exercised. It is a capacity for action that resides in social relations. In their daily lives, individuals are faced with a field of possible responses and reactions. Power operates by structuring this field of possible actions (Foucault 1982). It is manifested in the numerous knowledges, practices and technologies that are brought to bear on the actions of others (Hindess 1996). In particular, power operates by enhancing the calculability of individuals.

Various technologies of evaluation and calculation make visible the activities of individuals and calculate the extent to which they depart from a norm of performance (Johnson 1993; Miller 1994). Contemporary examples include the comparative application of performance information, or other forms of surveillance (such as supervision, routinization, rationalization, formalization and mechanization) which seek to increase control of organizational members' behaviour (Clegg 1989).

Increasingly, IT mediates this process. Representational, inscriptional and computational techniques associated with IS render individuals calculable, and thus knowable and governable. Some activities are given an existence and attention, while others remain unrecognized, enabling managerial knowledge to make stronger truth claims (Boland and Schultze 1996) and engendering compliance in those subject to such scrutiny: 'Calculative technologies make it possible to render visible both the near and the distant activities of individuals, to calculate the extent to which they depart from a norm of performance, and to accumulate such calculations in computers and files and compare them' (Miller 1994, p. 246).

The majority of attempts to apply a Foucauldian perspective to IS have been concerned with the capacity of such systems to make visible aspects of organizational activity. For example, Zuboff (1988), in highlighting the 'informating' capacity of IT applied to work processes, acknowledges the potential for new forms of surveillance through IS. Zuboff's work, together with subsequent studies (for example, Sewell and Wilkinson 1992; Ball and Wilson 2000) invoke the notion of an informational or electronic 'panopticon', in which organizational participants are subject to a disciplinary gaze through computerized monitoring and surveillance.

Linked to a centre of calculation, individuals are made not only calculable but also more calculating with respect to their own actions. Individuals learn to survey and discipline themselves through forms of self-monitoring and self-control (Clegg 1989). Foucault (1977) uses Jeremy Bentham's central, elevated watch-tower, the panopticon, as a metaphor for the exercise of this disciplinary power. The impossibility of avoiding the supervisory gaze of the all-seeing (but unseen) observer in the tower engenders a realization in the occupants of the surrounding cells that they are always subject to surveillance. The occupant becomes his or her own guardian, even in the absence of the supervisor. This constitutes a new, internalized, discipline of norms that influence individuals' judgements about what is legitimate and non-legitimate behaviour (Clegg 1989; Bloomfield and Coombs 1992).

In the arena of organizations, individuals participate in a range of discourses and practices that constitute the truth of what is normal in social and organizational relations (Knights and Murray 1994). In doing so, individuals are transformed into subjects who derive their sense of meaning and identity through their internalization of the social and institutional norms that make up this shared understanding of organisational reality. IS play an important role in mobilizing particular representations of organizational reality. In the fabrication of IS, the constitutive concepts of the dominant discourses and knowledges instituted in organizational practices have to be defined, and organizational phenomena reconciled with them (Bloomfield and Coombs 1992).

IS thus mediate and reinforce certain views and meanings. In doing so, they underpin the framework of meaning within which organizational participants regulate their own behaviour in accordance with the norms and values associated with societal and organizational knowledges and discourses (Orlikowski 1991; Bloomfield and Coombs 1992). As Bloomfield (1995, p. 511) comments: 'Staff ... become increasingly locked into a whole new ensemble of routinized everyday practices whose regularity is mediated and reinforced through the actions delegated to information systems.'

For example, in her study of how IT mediated work processes in a multinational software consulting firm, Orlikowski (1991) shows how IT can reinforce established forms of organizing and intensify existing mechanisms of control, rather than undermining it.

*Power and resistance in the implementation of a casemix information system*

In order to illustrate the utility of a Foucauldian perspective in constructing a critical analysis of the implementation and use of IS, we shall briefly discuss the implementation of a 'casemix' information system in a New Zealand hospital. A casemix system is an information system that links detailed information on individual patient clinical activity with the associated costs, for use by managers and service providers as a basis for contracting and for revealing the relative efficiency of clinical resource usage. The information provided by casemix IS mobilizes new categories for construing medical activity (Bloomfield 1991).

The casemix information system studied was developed and implemented in a context of New Zealand public health sector reform in the late 1980s and early 1990s (see Doolin 1999a, 2004 for more detail). The introduction of such IS into public hospitals was ostensibly concerned with improving operational efficiency and the allocation of limited economic resources. The problem of funding healthcare was translated into one of a lack of the appropriate information required to control costs. This translation was accompanied by an implicit delegation to IT that involved keeping track of resource usage (see Bloomfield 1995).

The detailed information provided by the casemix information system offered hospital management the possibility to increase control over doctors' use of clinical resources by monitoring and making visible the financial implications of clinical decisions. The information from the casemix system provided a view on clinical practice that highlighted variances between the performance of individual clinicians or clinical specialities. Using this information, managers could make stronger truth claims in their attempts to influence decisions on admissions, treatment, length of stay and discharge. Management's view was also that peer pressure and the visibility accorded to comparative information on resource usage would engender a sense of resource efficiency in doctors as less-expensive treatment protocols were pursued and doctors conformed to 'normal' work practices (see Chua and Degeling 1993).

In this we can see the potential for doctors to be made both more calculable in terms of the comparative performance information produced by the casemix system and more calculating with respect to the financial implications of their clinical practice. However, the use of IS to monitor and control organizational activity does not constitute organizational participants as passive victims of computerized surveillance. Those over whom power is exercised are recognized and maintained as people who act and could do otherwise, implying the necessary existence of resistance in power relations (Foucault 1982; Knights and Morgan 1991). Those subject to power and control are able to resist by means of challenging or diverting the systems and rules imposed on them (Clegg, 1989; Covaleski et al. 1993). Further, comparative surveillance IS are not exclusively constraining. Such systems are 'double-edged', in that they also empower by providing a legitimate discursive space for action (Bloomfield and Coombs 1992).

Various strategies were utilized by doctors in the hospital studied to resist the monitoring and scrutiny afforded to management through the casemix information system. Doctors challenged the accuracy of the casemix information and the validity of the procedures used to construct it. They produced alternative explanations for clinical outliers or variances between individual clinicians' practices. Other doctors argued that the diagnostic categories used in the casemix system were not sufficiently detailed for clinical management purposes. Differences between clinical specialities also had implications for the ability of management to impose control through the casemix system. In surgical specialities, types of treatment and patient episodes were often well defined and standardized, whereas in some of the medical specialities doctors often worked in teams and patients moved through several specialities during their treatment. Some clinicians were even able to subvert the casemix information towards their own ends, principally in arguing for more resources in an environment of constrained financial resources.

During the height of the reform period, it seemed as if the information produced from the casemix system would become the prevalent framework within which discussions on resource allocation in the hospital were structured. Casemix information became implicated in the daily work of many hospital staff, providing a particular discourse representation of organizational reality, which helped give meaning to the various transactions and organizational practices in which it was utilized. These included the management and operation of clinical units in the hospital and the basis for contracting with funding authorities. In the words of Morgan and Willmott (1993, p. 12), it was forming the 'currency of debate, the principal media through which claims to legitimacy and control are processed'.

However, despite considerable efforts to interest doctors in accepting and using casemix information to evaluate and manage their clinical practice, resistance to casemix management continued within the medical staff. A reluctance of senior management to challenge the long tradition of medical privilege and autonomy (see Chua and Degeling, 1993) in enforcing the use of casemix information meant that full implementation of the system and widespread use of its information throughout the hospital did not occur. The casemix information system became relegated to a relatively minor role as a tool for measuring performance against contracts rather than a tool for the comparative evaluation and control of clinical performance (see Bloomfield et al. 1997). Without the routine use of casemix information and the discursive practices associated with it by hospital doctors in their everyday work and talk, the potential for their self-regulation as subjects of the casemix discourse did not eventuate.

The Foucauldian perspective described above provides a detailed analysis of the implications of IS as a means of surveillance and control. It highlights the way in which such comparative systems can render organizational participants more calculable, and thus susceptible to management control, while acknowledging countervailing practices of resistance. It also highlights the potential for certain IS to facilitate self-disciplinary behaviour in those who use them, through the particular representations of organizational reality that these systems embody.

Although the Foucauldian perspective offers a useful critical approach to studying IS in organizations, Joerges and Czarniawska (1998) suggest that Foucauldian studies have often gone too far in their use of technical metaphors for organizational discipline, power and control, to overwrite the social with the technical. Technology proper becomes once again largely taken for granted, its significance residing in its involvement as the material component of human practices (Hull 1997; Joerges and Czarniawska 1998). An alternative perspective that retains a view of reality in which the social and the technical mutually define one another is actor-network theory (Law and Hassard 1999).

**Actor-network theory**

Actor-network theory (ANT) has its origins in the work of sociologists of science and technology such as Michel Callon (1986a, 1986b), Bruno Latour (1987) and John Law (1987). Since then its popularity has grown, and this has seen its application to a range of research fields including organization studies (Hassard et al. 1999) and IS (Walsham 1997). These translations have, to an extent, resulted in its 'black-boxing', and it is important to remember that ANT is less a fixed theoretical position than a 'heterogeneous work in progress' (Law 1999, p. 9). Nevertheless, we shall attempt to provide a brief outline of concepts commonly associated with ANT (see also Law 1992).

ANT perceives contemporary society as constituted by heterogeneous collectivities of people, technology, machines and objects. These collectivities are theorized as networks of actors (human and non-human), each of which is itself the effect of a network of heterogeneous elements – hence 'actor-network' theory, for each actor is also a network. ANT has gained some notoriety from the agnosticism it holds towards the nature of the actors involved in an actor-network, and hence the generalized symmetry with which it analyses human and non-human actors (Callon and Latour 1992; Michael 1996).

A fundamental aspect of actor-networks is their relationality. Actors, both individual and collective, are defined and interactively constituted in their relationships with other actors in the actor-network. Such actors are constituted as objects only to the extent that the actor-network stays in place (Law, 1992). The relative durability of actor-networks is a consequence of their heterogeneity. That is, actor-networks come in a variety of material forms, such as people, texts, machines and architectures. Actor-networks are made relatively cohesive and stable by the way they are intimately bound up with the material and the technical (Latour 1991).

In building an actor-network, an agent defines, mobilizes and juxtaposes a set of materially heterogeneous actors, obliging them to enact particular roles and defining the relations between them. The agent becomes the spokesperson of the actors constituted in this 'translation'. Translation involves the production of 'intermediaries' – texts, artefacts or people, which circulate between actors and, in doing so, define the relationship between them. The 'enrolment' of allies in a network involves persuading other actors that they share a common interest or problem. The agent seeks to enrol other actors by a process of 'problematization', presenting a problem of the latter in terms of a solution belonging to the former. By this, the enrolling agent attempts to become an 'obligatory passage point' in the network of relationships being established, through which the others must pass in the attainment of their interests (and in doing so, help further the interests of the agent). However, resistance is possible, and translation is only achieved when actors accept the roles defined and attributed to them ('simplification'). If an actor resists enrolment and defines itself differently, it becomes complex, possibly leading to the modification or disintegration of the actor-network (Callon 1986a, 1986b; Latour 1987, 1996; Law 1992; Lea et al. 1995).

ANT emphasizes the local and the contingent, and how these contribute to the production of social order. Critics of ANT argue that this emphasis neglects the reverse role that institutionalized social structures play in influencing the local process of social interaction (Walsham 1997). Traditional critical theory tends to assume the inevitable presence of conflict brought about through predetermined and pre-existing social structures. Yet, in ANT, social structures are themselves the relational achievements. As Latour (1991, p. 118) puts it: 'the macro-structure of society is made of the same stuff as the micro-structure'.

This emphasis on 'relational materiality' (Law 1999) reflects an unwillingness to accept a priori the pre-existence of social structures and differences as somehow inherently given in the order of things. ANT avoids the tendency to reify social relations as given entities, 'constructed as macro-actors and shut away into black boxes', focusing instead on how they are actively enrolled as resources in sustaining an actor-network (Ormrod 1995, p. 44). The aim is to open up these 'black boxes', these simplifications that we take for granted, and expose the way that translations occur and associations are generated (Somerville 1999). And in doing so, explore how social relations are ordered so as to 'generate effects like organizations, inequality, and power' (Law, 1992 p. 381).

ANT often attracts charges of apoliticism or moral relativism. This derives from the position that the various perspectives, interpretations and identities of actors implicated in the actor-network should not be presumed or fixed by an observer when they are subject to negotiation (Callon 1986b). However, Latour (1991) argues that ANT is not indifferent to the possibility of moral judgement, but rather rejects judgements that transcend the network, somehow originating from outside the empirical events and relationships that the theory describes. In this sense, ANT is similar to Foucault's rejection of the possibility of normative justification, in that the imposition of moral consequences from beyond the actor-network is itself an operation of power (see Ormrod 1995) in which we exchange one form of domination for another.

This agnosticism means that ANT is able to 'record the discriminations that are performed and the boundaries that are constructed in the activities it studies' (Lee and Hassard 1999, p. 392). There are differences between 'the powerful and the wretched', but these are 'differences in the methods and materials that they deploy to generate themselves' (Law 1992, p. 390;

emphasis removed). As Michael (1996) observes, it is through exposing this contingency that critique derives. In doing so, ANT reveals how things could have been otherwise (Law 1992; Michael 1996).

Recalling the appeal of Alvesson and Deetz (2000) for a broader critical project based on detailed empiricism, the reflective and empirical inquiry that ANT offers make it effective as a critical research perspective (Doolin and Lowe 2002). ANT is concerned with unravelling the heterogeneous materials and processes in which networks and actors are shaped and stabilized. In doing so, it reveals the assumed, the mundane and the status quo. ANT is a good way of defamiliarizing the taken-for-granted (Calas and Smircich 1999), and of exploring how distinctions are produced, status is constructed and social relations are stabilized. As Ormrod (1995, p. 45) suggests: 'If we are to successfully challenge the relations ... we think are worse, unfair, wrong, then we need to be able to discuss them in all their specificity and difference.'

For example, Walsham and Sahay (1999) provide some critical insights in an actor-network analysis of geographic information systems (GIS) in India. Their initial choice of exploring IT use in a developing country suggests some empathy with a critical agenda, and in tracing the networks implicated in their case studies they question the desirability of global pressures and influences in these contexts. In particular, by providing an analysis situated in the social, political and cultural context of India, they are able to demonstrate how the inscription of Western values in the GIS technology reflected assumptions about rational decision making, spatial thinking and coordinated action – assumptions that to some extent conflicted with Indian values in the implementation of the GIS there.

*The executive information system that never was*
We shall illustrate the utility of ANT in critical analyses of IS development by briefly discussing the proposed development and implementation of an executive information system (EIS) in a New Zealand hospital (see Doolin 1999b, for more detail). In order to build a coherent and stable actor-network, the diverse interests of heterogeneous actors had to be accommodated within the EIS. Ultimately, the failure to unify the multiplicity of interpretations surrounding the proposed system meant that the project ceased to exist. In this particular story of IS development, no object, no tangible information system actually resulted. No hardware or software was purchased, installed or used. This failure of the information system to materialize makes it difficult to explain in conventional terms of technical or social appropriateness. ANT offers a way to understand the organizational activity surrounding this particular event, which Latour (1996) might describe as a fiction attempting to become true.

The attempted development of the EIS involves the efforts of various actors, both individual and collective, to order the organization and work of other actors, both human and non-human. It occurred in a wider environment of public sector reform in New Zealand. During the 1980s and 1990s, a trend towards international acceptance of economic rationalism encouraged the development of a new discourse in healthcare in many countries, including New Zealand. This discourse was characterized by the importation of values, techniques and skills from the private sector in the pursuit of efficiency, value for money and greater accountability. In New Zealand, the ideology of market competition and the profit-seeking enterprise was applied to hospital management. Framed in this discourse, healthcare services were portrayed as undermanaged, and clinicians and their managers as ill-informed. This allowed a solution to be presented in terms of better management and more information (see Chua and Degeling 1993). IT was seen as the obvious antidote to this lack of information (Bloomfield 1995).

However, rather than diffusing unchanged through society, the new discourse in healthcare was translated differently as it was reproduced in different locations (Bloomfield, 1991). Organizational participants negotiated the discourse in terms of their pre-existing interpretive schemes, their actions reflecting a modified form of the hegemonic projects occurring at the broader political level (Maile 1995). The localized nature of this translation meant that different organizational arrangements developed, as participants in various hospitals attempted to react to the demands placed on them by central government.

One of the more influential actors in the hospital studied was the General Manager (GM) Information Systems, who had been a deliberate appointment to strengthen information management and strategy within the hospital. Given the importance placed on IT as an essential element in modern managing, being the official spokesperson for IT conferred considerable status and authority on this general manager. Consistent with the new discourse, he problematized hospital management as running a business and appealed to the efficacy of performance information for managing the hospital. Better management required information with which to manage, and a technology with which to access this information. The GM Information Systems could provide the 'solution', in the form of an EIS – a computerized information system that would allow senior management to access data collected from the hospital's IS and thus intervene more effectively in the running of the hospital. Conceived as such, the EIS represented a valuable aid in addressing the 'problem' of information management in the hospital.

The GM Information Systems and the project team he assembled used a number of tactics in an attempt to enrol allies. Essentially, they tried to attribute identities, interests, roles and courses of action to various actors. The project team talked about 'setting expectations' in relation to the EIS, defining what the system as an actor would be, and how the other actors would relate to it and with it. They defined the users of the EIS as senior management, as they perceived the impact of an EIS to be at higher organizational levels. The project team talked of the need to get all the hospital general managers to 'buy into' the EIS, defining a role for the general managers in which their use of the EIS was central. However, many of the general managers did not anticipate using the EIS personally. They resisted their definition as personal computer users or envisaged making use of intermediaries. In effect, they were redefining the EIS as an information access tool for all staff rather than as an executive management tool.

The project team discussed the 'political' aspects of the proposed system development and decided to 'sell the idea' by piloting the system in one of the hospital's divisions, hoping to enrol further general managers through the obvious appeal of a successful demonstration. The project team considered each division's suitability as a demonstration site, including its status in the hospital, the availability of computerized data, and the existence of a supportive general manager as a sponsor.

Attention focused on the human resources division. Piloting the EIS there would align the known interest of a number of the general managers in human resource information with the goals of the project team. In discussing the EIS with the human resources division, the project team appealed to their common interests, pointing out that situating the pilot there would support the division proposal for a human resource information system with an EIS-type interface. They also attempted to assert themselves as an obligatory passage point, stating that if they identified a suitable EIS solution, human resources should not purchase its own.

However, network building is a process of mutual shaping and the EIS was just one possible problematization of healthcare management within the hospital. The GM Finance offered an alternative problematization. While he conceptualized the healthcare 'problem' in much the same way as the GM Information Systems did (that is, in terms of 'information to manage' and information 'necessary to run businesses'), in his view the information and existing report tools associated with the hospital's financial information system were an appropriate solution.

The GM Finance utilized a counter-enrolment based on the relative priority for IS development. He subordinated the role of the EIS to that of other IS, which he argued were more important to the survival of the hospital in the new healthcare environment in New Zealand. The effectiveness of his enrolment strategy lay in the way in which he translated the interests of other general managers, some of whom had an interest in other IS related to their divisions, so that they were congruent with perceived interests of the hospital.

Ultimately though, it was an inability to enrol the non-human actors that undermined the attempt to build the EIS actor-network. In IS development it is necessary to expand the actor-network to include the artefacts as well as the human actors involved (Hanseth and Monteiro 1997). An actor-network's durability is limited by the durability of the weakest links within it. If one of the non-human actors does not play its part, the network breaks down in much the same way as if a human actor had rejected a new technology (Latour 1987; Bloomfield 1995).

The weak link in the EIS actor-network was the credibility of the information that the EIS would draw upon and summarize. There was widespread concern among the general managers that the feeder IS for the EIS contained inaccurate or inconsistent information. This concern fed directly into the GM Finance's counter-enrolment. He argued that without 'clean' and standardized information there was little point in computerizing information that managers had no confidence in. The role of the EIS articulated by the GM Information Systems, in summarizing and representing a concrete organizational reality and in providing access to the detailed data that supposedly objectively constituted that reality, was undermined and the incipient actor-network began to unravel.

An IS project becomes real by assembling sufficient elements so that it ends up existing independently of our opinion of it. If it interests very few actors, it remains an idea, a concept, an argument. It does not become realized. An information system as actor-network must unify a multiplicity of interpretations, so that the enrolled actors can agree on a common object. If the range of interests gathered around it cannot be accommodated within it, then that object does not come into existence (Latour 1993, 1996). In the case of the EIS, it survives only as another story about IS development, and to reinforce the need to study ITs while they are still projects (Latour 1993).

The strength of using ANT to inform the analysis presented above is that it focuses attention on the IT itself. However, rather than simply treating the technology as an artefact, it elevates it to the same status as a human actor. This provides an alternative perspective on IS as the precarious stabilization of heterogeneous elements in a network of relationships that constantly threatens to unravel. In this perspective, IS are not taken-for-granted entities, but are the effect or accomplishment of ongoing sociotechnical processes of organizing and ordering (Law 1992, 1994).

As noted above, one of the criticisms of analyses based on ANT is that they provide an inadequate consideration of social structures and the influence of these on actors' behaviour (Walsham 1997). While advocates of

ANT counter that social structures are themselves relational effects, a social theory that deals more explicitly with the relationship between structure and agency is the structuration theory of Anthony Giddens.

## Giddens and structuration

Giddens's (1979, 1984) structuration theory is an attempt to overcome a perceived dualism in the social sciences between objective social structures and subjective human agency. Giddens proposes that structure and agency are a mutually interacting duality. While social structures enable or constrain human action, recurrent human interaction produces and reproduces social structures. While a detailed explanation of structuration theory is beyond the scope of this chapter, we shall briefly outline some key elements of the theory (see also Jones 1999).

For Giddens, structure is the set of enacted rules and resources that mediate social action through three modalities – interpretive schemes, facilities and norms. These modalities link agency and structure in the recursive 'process of structuration' (Giddens 1979). Interpretive schemes are the shared knowledge that humans draw on to make sense of behaviour and events in social interaction and communication. In doing so, they enact structures of meaning, which Giddens calls 'structures of signification'. Facilities or resources are the capabilities available to human agents to act intentionally and exercise power over people (authoritative resources) or material objects (allocative resources). Asymmetries of resources become institutionalized as 'structures of domination'. Norms are rules and conventions governing legitimate human conduct. Human agents draw on these to sanction their actions and, in doing so, reproduce 'structures of legitimation' (Orlikowski and Robey 1991; Walsham and Han 1991).

The separation of structure and agency into three dimensions is purely analytical since in practice they are inextricably interlinked. For example, although language is integral to communication within structures of signification, it may express elements of power (structures of domination) or moral sanction (structures of legitimation). It is also important to note that, for Giddens, structures are not external material constraints but 'traces in the mind' that are enacted when drawn on in human action and interaction. Humans are considered to be knowledgeable agents capable of reflexive monitoring of the consequences of their actions. This, together with the unintended consequences of intentional action, opens up the possibility of change. In this way, structures are not only reproduced through human interaction but may also be transformed (Walsham and Han 1991; Jones 1999).

For Giddens, conflict between agents or groups is the expression of structural contradictions in societal systems. Giddens suggests that contradictions involve divisions of interest, divergent modes of life and distributions of life chances. Conflict is likely to occur if agents perceive that these differences adversely affect their interests, and they are able and motivated to take action of some sort (Giddens 1984; Walsham 2002).

While Giddens did not appear to explicitly consider IT in the development of his structuration theory, his ideas have been an important influence in a growing body of IS research (Orlikowski and Robey 1991; Walsham and Han 1991). Examples include studies of computer-supported cooperative work (Lyytinen and Ngwenyama 1992), IS strategy formation (Walsham and Han 1993), executive IS (Jones and Nandhakumar 1993), computer conferencing systems (Orlikowski et al. 1995), IT implementation (Karsten 1995; Montealegre 1997), intranets (Scheepers and Damsgaard 1997), e-commerce IS (Chiasson 2002), and cross-cultural software production (Walsham 2002).

One of the more influential interpretations of Giddens's work in the IS field is that of Orlikowski (Orlikowski and Robey 1991; Orlikowski 1992, 2000). Orlikowski integrates an explicit consideration of technology into structuration theory, in an attempt to explain how the use of IT is implicated in the production and reproduction of social structures. In her structurational model of technology, she conceptualizes IT as both the product of human action and structuring human action through its routine use in organizations. How an IT is designed and appropriated in a given context is influenced by structural properties that, in turn, are reaffirmed or transformed through human use of the technology.

In her 2000 paper, Orlikowski corrects the misconception present in some structurational analyses of IT, which treat use of technology as the appropriation of embedded social structures that are built into it by human agents during design and development (see also Jones 1999). Bearing in mind Giddens's notion of structures as 'traces in the mind', she reminds us that structures are emergent and enacted in recurrent social practices:

> While a technology can be seen to have been constructed with particular materials and inscribed with developers' assumptions and knowledge about the world at a point in time … it is only when this technology is used in recurrent social practices that it can be said to structure users' action. That is, it is only when repeatedly drawn on in use that technological properties become constituted by users as particular rules and resources that shape their action. (Orlikowski 2000, p. 408)

Orlikowski (2000) terms this set of enacted rules and resources 'technology-in-practice' – a specific structure that is enacted in the situated use of a technology. The relationship is recursive, in that, through routine practices associated with a technology, users shape the technology structure that shapes their use of that technology. Technologies-in-practice are neither invariant nor final. They may be undermined or modified through the actions of knowledgeable agents, whether deliberately, inadvertently, or by improvisation in response to unexpected events.

Enactment of technology-in-practice is situated within other nested and overlapping social systems. Interaction with a technology may enact and reproduce other social structures, such as those that reflect the system of authority in an organization or a normative professional culture, in addition to a technology-in-practice. Orlikowski's model focuses specifically on technologies-in-practice as being particularly relevant to technology use in organizations. As Giddens (1979, p. 411) notes, 'in any structurational analysis, one must foreground some structures and background others'.

*Social structures and situated action in the use of an intranet*
In order to demonstrate how a structurational analysis can provide a critical consideration of the use of IS, we shall briefly discuss the implementation of an intranet in a New Zealand company. The description of the case is drawn from the work of Alleyne (2002), who was supervised by one of the authors. The structurational analysis presented here is new.

The case organization is a large, well-established New Zealand company processing commodity products from a primary industry. The company is considered to be a leader in the application of IT in process control. It operates in a highly competitive global market. The company employs some 3000 people, geographically dispersed over all parts of New Zealand. It has a decentralized organizational structure, and information flows between its various business units are considered to be critical to its success.

The intranet studied evolved from an initial need of the company's IT department to implement and deploy a set of new corporate applications to the dispersed user community in the company. In organizational terms, the intranet was a minor project, with little top management support. The initial development in 1997 was conducted by two in-house staff, who used resources left over from an earlier project. For the next four years, ad hoc development of the intranet proceeded slowly under the aegis of the IT department, who perceived the intranet as 'just a repository'. Their 'low maintenance' approach to the intranet was partly shaped by their interpretive understanding of the user community as lacking in the necessary technical skills to make more than limited use of the intranet.

Around 2001, there was a rapid growth in interest in the intranet from the company's business units, who demanded a presence on the intranet. This placed the IT department under pressure in terms of time and staff resources. Initially, they drew on their allocative facility over the technical resources (human and infrastructural) necessary to develop Web pages and intranet applications to limit action arising from the business units' requests. In exercising power in this way, the IT department sanctioned their behaviour by drawing on an existing structure of legitimation that reflected organizational norms as to who should conduct IS development.

Part of this 'conflict' between the IT department and the business units was the result of the lack of a mutual structure of signification with regard to the intranet. For the IT department, the intranet was understood as a tool for deploying corporate applications and information. The business units did not interpret the intranet in the same way, perceiving the intranet as a valuable way to promote their units' activities within the organization. In doing so, they drew on structures of signification and legitimation that conceptualized IT as a legitimate strategic resource for operating in the company's competitive environment. Eventually, the increasing interest from the business units forced the IT department to delegate some responsibility and activity for the intranet to the business units. This reflected an organizational structure of legitimation, in which the IT department had a role of providing a service function to the decentralized business units.

This delegation defined specific members of each business unit who would be responsible for the management and content of their unit's Web pages on the intranet. Within the units, existing procedures were modified or new ones created to deal with the generation, collection and authorization of content. Thus, new organizational procedures involving action around the intranet were introduced and, with time, became institutionalized as a new structure of legitimation governing Web page content management. The IT department attempted to impose guidelines and standards for Web page layout in the form of a style guide and a Web page template. However, the use of these was not policed, and user departments developed their own formats and styles. It appears that the IT department lacked authoritative facility over the business units in this regard.

These developments do not necessarily reflect the attainment of a mutual or shared structure of signification for the intranet between the IT department and the business units. Instead, we suggest that the solution negotiated between the two groups enabled the coexistence of their respective structures of signification. The business units continued to view the intranet as a promotional tool, and the IT department were able to retain their interpretation of the intranet as a deployment tool since they distributed responsibility and tools for content management across it. The structural contradiction between the two groups still existed, but the agents involved no longer perceived the contradiction as negatively affecting their interests.

Other, established, organizational practices were reproduced in the way the intranet was used. For example, reporting unit performance against targets on the basis of key performance indicators was a company-wide process that was placed on the intranet. The processing and authorization of accounts was also transferred to the intranet. Routine use of the intranet in such ways reproduced structures of domination within the organization, in that it incorporated existing reporting relationships and hierarchical authority structures.

Following Orlikowski (2000), we can distinguish two different technologies-in-practice that were enacted by the two main groups described in this case study. The IT department enacted what we might call a 'deployment' technology-in-practice. In their recurrent practices based around the intranet, staff in the department drew upon a range of interpretive schemes, facilities and norms. For example, they drew on their knowledge of intranets as technical projects and as a solution to implementing corporate applications across a decentralized organizational structure. Their prior experience of the user community within the company influenced their perceptions of the users' abilities to manage and use an intranet. In exercising allocative facilities over their technical expertise and equipment, they drew on norms that reserved IS development and management to professional IT staff. Some of these elements were constitutive of structures that related to the division of labour within the organization and the company's decentralized organizational structure. The enactment of the 'deployment' technology-in-practice reproduced and reinforced (at least initially) these existing structures.

The business units enacted what we might call a 'promotion' technology-in-practice. In doing so, they drew upon their interpretations of the competitive environment in which they operated and the role of IT as a strategic resource. Their actions were influenced by organizational norms that legitimated their relative autonomy and emphasized the service role of the IT department within the decentralized organizational structure.

What is interesting is how the enactment of these two technologies-in-practice transformed the division of labour structure in the organization. The responsibility for managing IT that had previously been the domain of the IT department under this structure was modified to pass responsibility for the content and management of their part of the intranet to the individual business units. This change reflected changes in the interpretation of the technical capabilities of users and in organizational norms related to who should manage IT in the company.

The structurational analysis of the intranet begins to explore the processes by which various social structures influence the actions of organizational participants in their use of IT. At the same time, it highlights how these structures were constituted and even transformed through ongoing sociotechnical interactions within the organization. In particular, Orlikowski's (2000) concept of technologies-in-practice provides a useful vehicle for examining how such structures are enacted in the appropriation and use of an information system.

## Discussion and concluding remarks

From an interpretive perspective, the requirements for researching IT in organizations include focusing on action and interaction in organizational settings, analysing specific situations in which individuals experience phenomena, and recognizing the symbolic uses of technology while transcending the actors' purely subjective interpretation (Boland and Pondy 1983). We have argued in this chapter that the emphasis it places on detailed, local and contextualized empirical knowledge means that interpretive IS research is ideally suited to participate in a critical research project of the type outlined by Alvesson and Deetz (2000).

However, such research must involve a critical appreciation of the way in which IT is implicated in organizational activity. To do so requires a reflective approach that challenges taken-for-granted assumptions and questions how the status quo is constructed and maintained in organizations. IT needs to be analysed as a condition and a consequence of a broader set of social, political, economic and ideological issues. In other words, the 'black box' of IT needs to be opened up to reveal the power relations inscribed within it that may repress or constrain (Thomas 1993; Knights and Murray 1994).

We suggest that the above can be encapsulated in three fundamental principles of a critical interpretivism in IS research: (i) the construction of detailed, local and situated empirical interpretation; (ii) a reflective approach that challenges the assumptions and certainties that underlie the organizational status quo; and (iii) connecting the interpretation and representation of IS phenomena to a broader consideration of power and control. Following Walsham (1997) and Alvesson and Skoldberg (2000), we advocate informing interpretive IS research with appropriate critical social theories. Three such theoretical lenses were discussed in the chapter, each of which provides a relevant perspective for developing a critical appreciation of the way IT is implicated in processes of organization and technological change.

Using the relational notion of power developed by Foucault (1977, 1980), the concept of IT as a disciplinary technology was outlined. The case study of the implementation of a casemix information system intended to monitor the activity and performance of hospital doctors provided a 'fine-grained' analysis (see Ball and Wilson 2000) of the implications of computer-based surveillance systems as a means of management control. Such systems enhance the calculability of individuals through the comparative application of measures that reference the norm. However, doctors at the hospital studied were able to both challenge and circumvent the casemix system in order to escape the 'disciplinary gaze'.

In most critical social theories, the focus tends to be on questions of human agency (Whitley 1999). Technology is often ignored or relegated to a role as a tool of oppression, domination and control. However, actor-network theory restores the role of what Latour (1992) calls the 'missing masses' in stabilizing the heterogeneous actor-networks that make up organizations and society. As Walsham (1997) notes, challenging the rigid separation of human and non-human seems valuable – particularly where the boundaries between the social and the technical are continually negotiated and defined, such as in IS (Bloomfield and Vurdubakis 1994). The second case study in this chapter relates an attempt to construct an actor-network around an executive information system in a hospital. The actor-network approach allows us to understand how various actors went about translating an organizational situation in terms of particular 'solutions', and perhaps why the EIS was not implemented, but remained merely an assembly of quarrelling human actors and a stack of documents (Latour 1993).

The third case study focused on the links between social structure and human agency in the development and use of an intranet. Giddens's (1979, 1984) structuration theory was used to explore the structural contradictions between two groups within the company, and the way that issues arose from their respective interpretations of the purpose and meaning of the intranet. The recursive relationship between structure and agency can be seen in the way the intranet was structured and organized. That is, the IT department provided infrastructure and development tools, while content management was performed by individual business units. This pattern of interaction around the intranet both reflected and reinforced the decentralized organizational structures of the company and its concomitant structures of signification, domination and legitimation.

Although constraints on space preclude greater presentation of empirical data, each of the three case studies is based on detailed empirical interpretations generated from in-depth fieldwork. In constructing our accounts of IS development and use, we have tried to be reflective in our interpretations. For example, we explicitly considered the exercise of power in the deployment of IS, the relational character of IS development (and how things could be otherwise), and the enactment of organizational structures that shape (and are shaped by) people's use of IT.

In doing so, we have attempted to avoid privileging dominant – such as managerialist – perspectives on IS in organizations that would simply reinforce the received view of such phenomena. Our reflective approach was informed by ideas drawn from the social theories of Foucault, Latour and others, and Giddens. This critical theorization enabled us to connect the empirically-based interpretive research presented in the case studies with the broader socio-political conditions of possibility within which IS development and use occurs.

To conclude, we have argued that interpretive IS research needs a critical edge if it is to avoid an unreflective accommodation with how IT is implicated in organizations and society. To achieve this, such research needs to complement its empirical richness with a reflective approach that reveals how the status quo has come to be and who benefits from existing arrangements of IT and organization. Further, the interpretation needs to be connected to broader considerations of power and control.

## Note

1. We have chosen to locate our discussion of critical interpretivism within critical management studies because of our interest in the organizational implications of IS. Equally, other traditions (such as science and technology studies) could provide a suitable platform from which to build a case for critical interpretive research on IT.

## References

Alleyne, G. (2002), 'How does intranet technology affect organizational structure?', unpublished dissertation, University of Waikato, Hamilton, New Zealand.

Alvesson, M. and Deetz, S. (2000), *Doing Critical Management Research*, London: Sage.

Alvesson, M. and Skoldberg, K. (2000), *Reflexive Methodology: New Vistas for Qualitative Research*, London: Sage.

Ball, K. and Wilson, D.C. (2000), 'Power, control and computer-based performance monitoring: repertoires, resistance and subjectivities', *Organization Studies*, 21(3): 539–65.

Bloomfield, B.P. (1991), 'The role of information systems in the UK National Health Service: action at a distance and the fetish of calculation', *Social Studies of Science*, 21(4): 701–34.

Bloomfield, B.P. (1995), 'Power, machines and social relations: delegating to information technology in the National Health Service', *Organization*, 2(3/4): 489–518.

Bloomfield, B.P. and Coombs, R. (1992), 'Information technology, control and power: the centralization and decentralization debate revisited', *Journal of Management Studies*, 29(4): 459–84.

Bloomfield, B.P., Coombs, R., Owen, J. and Taylor, P. (1997), 'Doctors as managers: constructing systems and users in the National Health Service', in Bloomfield, B.P., Coombs, R., Knights, D. and Littler, D. (eds), *Information Technology and Organizations: Strategies, Networks and Integration*, Oxford: Oxford University Press, pp. 112–34.

Bloomfield B.P. and Vurdubakis, T. (1994), 'Boundary disputes: negotiating the boundary between the technical and the social in the development of IT systems', *Information Technology and People*, 7(1): 9–24.

Boland, R.J., Jr. (1979), 'Control, causality and information system requirements', *Accounting, Organizations and Society*, 4(4): 259–72.

Boland, R.J., Jr. and Pondy, L.R. (1983), 'Accounting in organizations: a union of natural and rational perspectives', *Accounting, Organizations and Society*, 8(2/3): 223–34.

Boland, R.J., Jr. and Schultze, U. (1996), 'From work to activity: technology and the narrative of progress', in Orlikowski, W.J., Walsham, G., Jones, M.R. and DeGross, J.I. (eds), *Information Technology and Changes in Organizational Work*, London: Chapman & Hall, pp. 308–24.

Calas, M.B. and Smircich, L. (1999), 'Past postmodernism? Reflections and tentative directions', *Academy of Management Review*, 24(4): 649–71.

Callon, M. (1986a), 'The sociology of an actor-network: the case of the electric vehicle', in Callon, M., Law, J. and Rip, A. (eds), *Mapping the Dynamics of Science and Technology: Sociology of Science in the Real World*, London: Macmillan, pp. 19–34.

Callon, M. (1986b), 'Some elements of a sociology of translation: domestication of the scallops and the fishermen of St Brieuc Bay', in Law, J. (ed.), *Power, Action and Belief: A New Sociology of Knowledge?*, London: Routledge & Kegan Paul, pp. 196–233.

Callon, M. and Latour, B. (1992), 'Don't throw the baby out with the bath school! A reply to Collins and Yearley', in Pickering, A. (ed.), *Science as Practice and Culture*, Chicago: University of Chicago Press, pp. 343–68.

Chiasson, M.W. (2002), 'The tail and the dog: agency and structure influences on the development of an e-commerce information system in a new venture startup', *Database for Advances in Information Systems*, **33**(4): 24–37.

Chua, W.F. and Degeling, P. (1993), 'Interrogating an accounting-based intervention on three axes: instrumental, moral and aesthetic', *Accounting, Organizations and Society*, **18**(4): 291–318.

Clegg, S.R. (1989), *Frameworks of Power*, London: Sage.

Covaleski, M.A., Dirsmith, M.W. and Michelman, J.E. (1993), 'An institutional theory perspective on the DRG framework, case-mix accounting systems and health-care organizations', *Accounting, Organizations and Society*, **18**(1): 65–80.

Doolin, B. (1998), 'Information technology as disciplinary technology: being critical in interpretive research on information systems', *Journal of Information Technology*, **13**(4): 301–11.

Doolin, B. (1999a), 'Casemix management in a New Zealand hospital: rationalisation and resistance', *Financial Accountability and Management*, **15**(3&4): 397–417.

Doolin, B. (1999b), 'Sociotechnical networks and information management in health care', *Accounting, Management and Information Technologies*, **9**(2): 95–114.

Doolin, B. (2004), 'Power and resistance in the implementation of a medical management information system', *Information Systems Journal*, **14**(4), 343–62.

Doolin, B. and Lowe, A. (2002), 'To reveal is to critique: actor-network theory and critical information systems research', *Journal of Information Technology*, **17**(2): 69–78.

Downing, J., Mohammadi, A. and Sreberny-Mohammadi, A. (eds) (1995), *Questioning the Media: A Critical Introduction*, Thousand Oaks, CA: Sage.

Foucault, M. (1977), *Discipline and Punish: The Birth of the Prison*, London: Penguin.

Foucault, M. (1980), *Power/Knowledge: Selected Interviews and Other Writings 1972–1977*, New York: Pantheon.

Foucault, M. (1982), 'The subject and power', in Dreyfus, H.L. and Rabinow, P. (eds), *Michel Foucault: Beyond Structuralism and Hermeneutics*, New York: Harvester Wheatsheaf, pp. 208–26.

Geertz, C. (1973), *The Interpretation of Cultures*, New York: Basic Books.

Giddens, A. (1979), *Central Problems in Social Theory*, Basingstoke: Macmillan.

Giddens, A. (1984), *The Constitution of Society*, Cambridge: Polity.

Hanseth, O. and Monteiro, E. (1997), 'Inscribing behavior in information infrastructure standards', *Accounting, Management and Information Technologies*, **7**(4): 183–211.

Hassard, J., Law, J. and Lee, N. (1999), 'Preface to themed section on actor-network theory and managerialism', *Organization*, **6**(3): 387–90.

Hindess, B. (1996), *Discourses of Power: From Hobbes to Foucault*, Oxford: Blackwell.

Hirschheim, R. and Newman, M. (1991), 'Symbolism and information systems development: myth, metaphor and magic', *Information Systems Research*, **2**(1): 29–62.

Hull, R. (1997), 'Governing the conduct of computing: computer science, the social sciences and frameworks of computing', *Accounting, Management and Information Technologies*, **7**(4): 213–40.

Joerges, B. and Czarniawska, B. (1998), 'The question of technology, or how organizations inscribe the world', *Organization Studies*, **19**(3): 363–85.

Johnson, T. (1993), 'Expertise and the state', in Gane, M. and Johnson, T. (eds), *Foucault's New Domains*, London: Routledge, pp. 139–52.

Jones, M. (1999), 'Structuration theory', in Currie, W.L. and Galliers, R.D. (eds), *Rethinking Management Information Systems: An Interdisciplinary Perspective*, Oxford: Oxford University Press, pp. 103–35.

Jones, M.R. and Nandhakumar, J. (1993), 'Structured development? A structurational analysis of the development of an executive information system', in Avison, D., Kendall, J.E. and DeGross, J.I. (eds), *Human, Organizational and Social Dimensions of Information Systems Development*, Amsterdam: North-Holland, pp. 475–96.

Jönsson, S. (1991), 'Action research', in Nissen, H.-E., Klein, H.K. and Hirschheim, R. (eds), *Information Systems Research: Contemporary Approaches and Emergent Traditions*, Amsterdam: North-Holland, pp. 371–96.

Karsten, K. (1995), 'Converging paths to Notes: in search of computer-based information systems in a networked company', *Information Technology and People*, **8**(1): 7–34.

Knights, D. (1995), 'Refocusing the case study: the politics of research and researching politics in IT management', *Technology Studies*, **2**(2): 230–54.

Knights, D. and Morgan, G. (1991), 'Corporate strategy, organizations and subjectivity: a critique', *Organization Studies*, **12**(2): 251–73.

Knights, D. and Murray, F. (1994), *Managers Divided: Organisation Politics and Information Technology Management*, Chichester: Wiley.

Latour, B. (1987), *Science in Action: How to Follow Scientists and Engineers Through Society*, Cambridge, MA: Harvard University Press.

Latour, B. (1991), 'Technology is society made durable', in Law, J. (ed.), *A Sociology of Monsters: Essays on Power, Technology and Domination*, London: Routledge, pp. 103–31.

Latour, B. (1992), 'Where are the missing masses? The sociology of a few mundane artifacts', in Bijker, W.E. and Law, J. (eds), *Shaping Technology/Building Society: Studies in Sociotechnical Change*, Cambridge, MA: MIT Press, pp. 225–58.

Latour, B. (1993), 'Ethnology of a "high-tech" case: about Aramis', in Lemonnier, P. (ed.), *Technological Choices: Transformation in Material Cultures since the Neolithic*, London and New York: Routledge, pp. 372–98.

Latour, B. (1996), *Aramis or the Love of Technology*, Cambridge, MA: Harvard University Press.

Law, J. (1987), 'Technology and heterogeneous engineering: the case of Portuguese expansion', in Bijker, W.E., Hughes, T.P. and Pinch, T.J. (eds), *The Social Construction of Technological Systems: New Directions in the Sociology and History of Technology*, Cambridge, MA: MIT Press, pp. 111–34.

Law, J. (1992), 'Notes on the theory of the actor-network: ordering, strategy, and heterogeneity', *Systems Practice*, **5**(4): 379–93.

Law, J. (1994), *Organizing Modernity*, Oxford: Blackwell.

Law, J. (1999), 'After ANT: complexity, naming and topology', in Law and Hassard (eds), pp. 1–14.

Law, J. and Hassard, J. (eds) (1999), *Actor Network Theory and After*, Oxford: Blackwell.

Lea, M., O'Shea, T. and Fung, P. (1995), 'Constructing the networked organization: content and context in the development of electronic communications', *Organization Science*, **6**(4): 462–78.

Lee, A.S. (1991), 'Integrating positivist and interpretive approaches to organizational research', *Organization Science*, **2**(4): 342–65.

Lee, A.S., Liebenau, J. and DeGross, J.I. (eds) (1997), *Information Systems and Qualitative Research*, London: Chapman & Hall.

Lee, N. and Hassard, J. (1999), 'Organization unbound: actor-network theory, research strategy and institutional flexibility', *Organization*, **6**(3): 391–404.

Lyytinen, K.J. and Ngwenyama, O.K. (1992), 'What does computer support for co-operative work mean? A structurational analysis of computer supported co-operative work', *Accounting, Management and Information Technology*, **2**(1): 19–37.

Maile, S. (1995), 'Managerial discourse and the restructuring of a district authority', *Sociological Review*, **43**(4): 720–42.

Michael, M. (1996), *Constructing Identities: The Social, the Nonhuman and Change*, London: Sage.

Miller, P. (1994), 'Accounting and objectivity: the invention of calculating selves and calculable spaces', in Megill, A. (ed.), *Rethinking Objectivity*, Durham, NC: Duke University Press, pp. 239–64.

Montealegre, R. (1997), 'The interplay of information technology and the social milieu', *Information Technology and People*, **10**(2): 106–31.

Morgan, G. and Willmott, H. (1993), 'The "new" accounting research: on making accounting more visible', *Accounting, Auditing and Accountability Journal*, **6**(4): 3–36.

Myers, M.D. (1997), 'Qualitative research in information systems', *Management Information Systems Quarterly*, *Discovery*, archival version, www.misq.org/discovery/MISQD_isworld/index.html, accessed 2 March 2005.

Orlikowski, W.J. (1991), 'Integrated information environment or matrix of control? The contradictory implications of information technology', *Accounting, Management and Information Technologies*, **1**(1): 9–42.

Orlikowski, W.J. (1992), 'The duality of technology: rethinking the concept of technology in organizations', *Organization Science*, **3**(3): 398–427.

Orlikowski, W.J. (2000), 'Using technology and constituting structures: a practice lens for studying technology in organizations', *Organization Science*, **11**(4): 404–28.

Orlikowski, W.J. and Baroudi, J.J. (1991), 'Studying information technology in organizations: research approaches and assumptions', *Information Systems Research*, **2**(1): 1–28.

Orlikowski, W.J. and Robey, D. (1991), 'Information technology and the structuring of organizations', *Information Systems Research*, **2**(2): 143–69.

Orlikowski, W.J., Yates, J., Okamura, K. and Fujimoto, M. (1995), 'Shaping electronic communication: the metastructuring of technology in the context of use', *Organization Science*, **6**(4): 423–44.

Ormrod, S. (1995), 'Feminist sociology and methodology: leaky black boxes in gender/technology relations', in Grint, K. and Gill, R. (eds), *The Gender-Technology Relation: Contemporary Theory and Research*, London: Taylor & Francis, pp. 31–47.

Putnam, L.L. (1983), 'The interpretive perspective: an alternative to functionalism', in Putnam, L.L. and Pacanowsky, M.E. (eds), *Communication and Organizations: An Interpretive Approach*, Beverly Hills, CA: Sage, pp. 31–54.

Scheepers, R. and Damsgaard, J. (1997), 'Using internet technology within the organization: a structurational analysis of intranets', in S.C. Hayne, W. Prinz, M. Pendergast and K. Schmidt (eds), *Proceedings of the International ACM SIGGROUP Conference on Supporting Group Work: The Integration Challenge*, Phoenix, AZ, 16–19 November, New York: ACM Press, pp. 9–18.

Sewell, G. and Wilkinson, B. (1992), '"Someone to watch over me": surveillance, discipline and the just-in-time labour process', *Sociology*, **26**(2): 271–89.

Somerville, I. (1999), 'Agency versus identity: actor-network theory meets public relations', *Corporate Communications*, **4**(1): 6–13.

Thomas, J. (1993), *Doing Critical Ethnography*, Newbury Park, CA: Sage.

Tinker, T. (1998), 'Hamlet without the prince: the ethnographic turn in information systems research', *Accounting, Auditing, and Accountability Journal*, **11**(1): 13–33.

Walsham, G. (1993), *Interpreting Information Systems in Organizations*, Chichester: Wiley.

Walsham, G. (1995), 'The emergence of interpretivism in IS research', *Information Systems Research*, **6**(4): 376–94.

Walsham, G. (1997), 'Actor-network theory and IS research: current status and future prospects', in Lee, A.S., Liebenau, J. and DeGross, J.I. (eds), *Information Systems and Qualitative Research*, London: Chapman & Hall, pp. 466–80.

Walsham, G. (2002), 'Cross-cultural software production and use: a structurational analysis', *MIS Quarterly*, **26**(4): 359–80.

Walsham, G. and Han, C.-K. (1991), 'Structuration theory and information systems research', *Journal of Applied Sciences Analysis*, **17**: 77–85.

Walsham, G. and Han, C.-K. (1993), 'Information systems strategy formation and implementation: the case of a central government agency', *Accounting, Management and Information Technologies*, **3**(3): 191–209.

Walsham, G. and Sahay, S. (1999), 'GIS for district-level administration in India: problems and opportunities', *MIS Quarterly*, **23**(1): 39–66.

Wastell, D. and Newman, M. (1993), 'The behavioral dynamics of information system development: a stress perspective', *Accounting, Management and Information Technologies*, **3**(2): 121–48.

Whitley, E.A. (1999), 'Habermas and the non-humans: towards a critical theory for the new collective', Centre for Social Theory and Technology, Keele University, Keele, www.keele.ac.uk/depts/stt/cstt2/papers/whitley.htm, accessed 2 March 2005.

Zuboff, S. (1988), *In the Age of the Smart Machine: The Future of Work and Power*, New York: Basic Books.

# 13 Consuming passions in the 'global knowledge economy'

*Helen Richardson*

## Introduction

What a whirlwind the past couple of decades have been – blink and you may have missed it. Open your eyes now and wonder on the revolutionary transformation. Everything is new and different. We are in a new digital age, in new relationships and communities – virtual and in cyberspace. There's a new economy – it's global and knowledge-based. We have new ways of working in transformed organizations – management has been flattened and work is team-based. We've gone e-mad in a fantasy digital global dream world. We're on-line everywhere and anywhere signifying new ways of living, loving, being governed and educated. The family, the High Street, the workplace, the School and particularly the individual and self and identities have been turned on their heads. Moreover we must consume with a passion and in new and different ways. We must immerse ourselves in Information and Communication Technologies (ICTs) and engage in the on-line feeding frenzy with a hunger that can never be sated. If you're not in – you're out. Miss it and miss out whether deprived of access or a digital 'refusenik'.

This is one side of the hyperbole – that everything is new and changing and in a revolutionary way. Equally mystifying is the other side that says nothing has changed, globalization does not exist and the ubiquitous 'e' has had little or no impact, nor will it. In this chapter, I consider this 'revolution' and in particular focus on cultures of consumption in relation to ICT use in our everyday lives. Castells (1996) describes a 'brave new world' where industrial society has apparently been left behind; knowledge has eclipsed manufacturing and where the human mind is a productive force. On the face of it, it is a consumer-led society where collective identities have ceased to exist (Campbell 1995). Instead, it is said that individual patterns of consumption appear to be important and individual expressions – like that of shopping behaviour, sexuality and many other manifestations of class, gender, ethnicity and culture – seem to shape our atomized, particularized experience. I define my field of study as looking at 'cultures of consumption' and the political, historical, social, cultural and economic context that is implied. I shall provide a brief critique of notions of a 'global knowledge economy' and postmodern ideas of culture and consumption divorced from the material. In this chapter I intend to reclaim the social and international from ideologies of individualism and globalization that dominate the argument of cultures of consumption in the so-called 'global knowledge economy'.

Critical research has often been criticized for being too theoretical and esoteric (Boudreau 1997). Moreover, critical social theory has had limited exposure in information systems (IS) research and therefore there is a lack of field experience. This is what this handbook is seeking to redress and the contribution from this chapter is to consider the critical research approach taken during two pieces of research. I include two illustrative cases – of home e-shopping and work on the 'front line' in telephone call centres. These individual testimonies from households and workplaces can shed light on what Bourdieu has called the 'collective malaise' in his manifesto to resist the 'new myths of our time' (Bourdieu 1998). Using the tools of analysis from critical social theory, I suggest a different perspective and understanding of society and individuals in it. I attempt to demonstrate that critical research in IS – following the traditions of critical research in other disciplines – challenges orthodoxy, questions what is often ignored or taken for granted and recognizes the influence of history, culture and social positions on beliefs and actions (Alvesson and Deetz 2000). A feature of critical research is to set the political agenda of research at the start, and in this account the political agenda is to challenge dominating institutions and interests and tell stories that are often left untold.

The chapter will proceed by discussing what is old and new in the so-called 'global knowledge economy', followed by an overview of differing viewpoints of 'cultures of consumption'. After explaining my understanding of critical IS research, I shall then present my two illustrative case studies. In conclusion I review my contribution to the theory and practice of critical research and finally suggest alternative futures focusing on liberation and emancipation, and stressing solidarity rather than segregation and disintegration.

**What is new and old in the so-called 'global knowledge economy'?**
The first task is to introduce the historical, political, social and economic context of the case research. In doing so, I am endeavouring to relate technology to culture – regarded as an 'admirable if elusive pursuit' (Slack and Wise 2002: 486). Indeed, at times this research has seemed daunting and challenging, stumbling as it does through a myriad of interdisciplinary debates – on modernism and postmodernism, on the idea of culture, on mass consumption in a globalized world, on what a knowledge economy means, on the nature and use of ICTs in organizational change and on technological determinism and domestication of technology. Few would argue that

cultures of consumption and analysing the global knowledge economy are not multidisciplinary projects. Yet what does multidisciplinary research really mean when each discipline has its own spheres of reporting in terms of its own journals and terminology? What this chapter will be arguing is that critical research in IS can provide a distinctive multidisciplinary bridge or at least has a modest aim to construct this.

So what is a global knowledge economy – does it exist and if so, what is old and new about it, has history been forgotten and in trying to understand the modern world are we engaged in 'the politics of amnesia' (Eagleton 2003: 18)? This is a critique of the ideas of a global knowledge economy but only the most blinkered observer could deny that technologies feature in most of the lives of the UK population in the twenty-first century. We have shops and homes full of digital gadgets, for example, and those with access to e-mail can communicate with friends and colleagues around the world, almost instantaneously. Students can find thousands of pieces of text in just one keyword search of the internet. Rarely can a journey be taken without the phenomena of human beings clasping bits of plastic to their ears and speaking in loud voices, or bashing keys in a frenzy of communication through 'texts'. Moreover the reality of global capitalism is domination by large transnational corporations (TNCs) like General Motors, Siemens and Shell (Webster 2004) and the global marketplace is revealed to us through consumer goods provided by distant countries or customer services outsourced offshore.

How is the global knowledge economy defined? In fact a single definition is problematic, with many expressions applied – often interchangeably – even though they are not synonymous. This entire chapter could be about what terms are used, when and why. When describing economic features generally, 'global knowledge economy', 'new economy' or 'digital economy' are employed. Societal commentators adopt phrases like 'post-industrial society', 'information society' and 'knowledge society'. Then there are the epochal observers heralding the 'digital age' or 'information age'. When discussing the UK as a global economic player in 2004, then the model of a so-called 'global knowledge economy' and 'information society' most closely represent the dominant arguments. It is debatable whether we can use an all-encompassing term. However, although definitions are problematic, what follows is a brief discussion of some important features of a global knowledge economy that have been identified. I have selected some of the most prominent authors and make use of the terms as they employ them.

Touraine (1974) speaks of a 'post industrial society' where cultural services have replaced material goods at the core of production. In the 'post industrial society', Daniel Bell (1973) suggests that there has been a sea-change from a manufactured goods-producing economy to a service sector. Moreover, this is apparently a society based on services where 'what counts is not raw muscle power or energy but information' (ibid.: 20). Masuda (2004), an advocate of the idea of an 'information society', develops this theme, writing about, in his view, how it is the production of information values and not material values that are the driving force behind the formation and development of society. It is Castells's work that perhaps most comprehensively sets out the characteristics of this 'information age'. A useful summary of the Castellian thesis can be found in Webster (2004) and I present a brief and partial summary of this as the 'case for' the predominant view of this 'new' economic and social era before presenting 'the case against'. Castells (2004) first describes an informational economy where sources of productivity and competitiveness depend on knowledge, information and the 'technology of processing'. Second it is a global economy – not the world economy that has been developing since the sixteenth century, but where 'the core strategically dominant activities have the potential of working as a unit in real time on a planetary scale' (ibid.: 140). Then it is a 'network enterprise' – the heart of the global economy being connectivity with new forms of organization that can be ad hoc and ephemeral units. Fourth, there is a transformation of work and employment and the United States and the UK in particular have 'de-industrialized' with the 'organization man' out and the 'flexible woman' in. Lastly, a characteristic is social polarization and social exclusion. The nation-state declines in importance and there is a demise of social identity like 'citizen' and 'family', for example. Castells concludes that although the information age does not have to be the age of stepped-up inequality, polarization and social exclusion – for the moment, it is.

As with any futuristic account, I have the benefit of hindsight, statistical accounts and time to deconstruct the 'revolutionary' thesis. So, are we living in a 'global knowledge economy' – a 'post-industrial society'? There has indeed been a decline in the numbers employed in manufacturing in the UK – but only a decline. Between 1983 and 2003, for example, the total number of manufacturing jobs declined by a third, but productivity increased by about a quarter (*UK 2004 Yearbook*) and in 2001, 3.9 million still worked in manufacturing in the UK. The worldwide decline is also not apparent, for example, industrial production and the state of the manufacturing sector has remained stable in countries like Germany and there has been vast expansion, for example, in China, Southeast Asia and Mexico (Reich 2004).

To speak of a 'global knowledge economy' also suggests that Castells's characteristics are available on a planetary basis. Clearly this is not the case. Personal computers (PCs) producing the 'information age' are certainly not accessible to the global workforces manufacturing them (Campbell 1995). In terms of access to information technology (IT), 91 per cent of the world's users of the internet are drawn from only 19 per cent of the world's population with a concentration of hosts in the United States and northern Europe (Ramonet 2004). Most people in the world lack access to a telephone let alone the internet or indeed clean water (Curtis 2003). The old fault line is the North/South divide, with the North accommodating about 15 per cent of the world's population and absorbing 80 per cent of its economic output and the South about 85 per cent of its population and consuming 20 per cent of its output (Hirst and Thompson 1998; Ramonet 2004).

To write the obituary of the nation-state is also premature. Kraak (2001) has pointed out how nation-states still wield huge economic and decision-making power. This can be seen during major world negotiations like the G8 summits and world trade talks. Nation-states also set out a social and technical infrastructure – a prerequisite for development to take place (ibid.). Nation-states forge links with other states and groupings, starkly illustrated through the 'special relationship' of US President George W. Bush and UK Prime Minister Tony Blair during the 2003 war on Iraq. Genuine TNCs are also rare – most are locally based but trade multinationally. TNCs and financial markets certainly operate worldwide but most things – like the production and consumption of most goods and services – still occur at a national level (Hirst and Thompson 1998). Trade, investment and financial flows are in fact concentrated in the Triad of Europe, Japan and North America. Further, global markets are by no means beyond regulation and control – the above Triad do much of it.

It is important to locate the roots of the globalization 'myth', which arose after a variety of events following the period of economic growth after the Second World War and almost full employment in advanced capitalist countries. Then came the OPEC (Organization of Petroleum-Exporting Countries) oil crises in the 1970s and 1980s and a series of domestic policy failures in the UK (Hirst and Thompson 1998; Curtis 2003). These included, for example, the 1976 crisis of the financial markets where the value of the UK currency started to collapse against other currencies in the world, particularly the US dollar. The then-prime minister, Jim Callaghan, called in the International Monetary Fund and this began an era of harsh monetarist-based so-called 'economic reforms'. In the 1980s, the UK also faced sharp recession and economic downturn, including facing the aftermath of a massive stock market collapse in 1987. To compensate, financial institutions and manufacturers sought wider outlets for investment and markets. In addition, post-Second World War US foreign policy strove to create an 'open-door' access to other countries' markets and resources. Today the World Trade Organization has become the organizing body for the global economy to 'liberalize trade' (Curtis 2003). Such 'liberalization' is clearly a one-way street and globalization can be seen as a powerful force, described by Bourdieu as a myth in the strong sense of the word and representing not homogenization but an extension of the hold of a small number of dominant nations (Bourdieu 1998).

So what of the 'knowledge' part of the 'global knowledge economy'? The distinctive issue confronting contemporary business we are told is not the centrality of knowledge but rather the opportunities there are to intensify its production and utilization (Castells 1996). Yet there are many contradictions with IT-driven knowledge management. Some stress the need to see production of knowledge in the context of its use (Gibbons et al. 1994). Others view knowledge management as a whole as 'hype' and to suppose that the 'use of computers can suddenly provide us with the ability to manage something we don't understand is humbug' (Bentley 1999: 13). What is also often overlooked is that power structures play a large part in the making and accepting of knowledge (Adam and Richardson 2001) and how technologists so often lack understanding of the situated work practices of the system's user communities (Kvasny and Truex 2000). Yet global knowledge economic rhetoric has certainly shaped commercial and government policy in the UK. Government rhetoric on the global knowledge economy would seem to stress a belief that digital technologies and the utilization of people as a resource are the key enablers in the knowledge-driven economy and, accordingly, government policy must reflect this. ICTs and in particular the internet are said to bring to the 'digital economy', what is defined by the UK government as a 'transformational impact' on the business environment (Mandelson 2001). In the race for competitive advantage, to be without access to ICTs and the internet is seen as a risk to economic prosperity (Keeble and Loader 2001).

Much government discourse about the inevitability of globalization also invokes new IT as an autonomous and largely unassailable influence. Johnson (2000) notes how technocratic discourse, globalization and free market economics coalesce into an extremely powerful ideological force. Wajcman (2002) observes that governments everywhere legitimate much of their policy in terms of a technological imperative and that we should not underestimate the increasing role that technological determinist understandings of the economy play in political discourse. Castells speaks of social polarization and social exclusion but suggests that the rise of the network enterprise means the end of struggle between capital and labour. Other 'upbeat' analyses suggest an individualization of society, capitalism without social classes – instead of social inequality based on risk and choice (Giddens 1984; Beck 1992). In my view, the 'death of class conflict', heralded almost desperately from time to time, is a premature announcement. Bourdieu (1998) suggests that these analyses are a submission to the values of the economy where a return to individualism means not only blaming victims for their own misfortune but also an attempt to destroy any notion of collective responsibility lest this may interfere with commercial interests. In this chapter, I conclude with a determination to reclaim collective identity from the individualistic 'human as sovereign consumer' that pervades the dominant ideology of global knowledge economic rhetoric.

Reflecting on the debates over what a global knowledge economy may be, we can observe two conflicting perspectives. On the one hand, the global knowledge economy means a prosperous global community living peacefully together as an 'interconnected human family'. On the other hand, ICTs serve as a means to maintain or worsen the gap between the haves and the have-nots by traditional socio-economic factors and the 'digital divide' (Nordenstreng 2004). Kvasny (2004) suggests that a clearer term is 'digital inequality', and that digital divides cannot be discussed solely on the terrain of IT where oversimplified constructions of IT and its values leads to social justice being reduced to bottom-line calculus and only tolerated when costless. She continues graphically to describe how some sections of society as a result are 'catching hell', in other words are at the sharp end of social suffering and hardship. As far as the global knowledge economy is concerned, Eagleton (2003) has noted that the great mass of men and women are really neither here nor there in the Castellian vision, and it is the rich that are global and the poor that are local. At the same time, however, 'in principle capitalism is an impeccably inclusive creed: it really doesn't care who it exploits' (ibid.: 19). Jonathan Rowe (2000) in the *New Internationalist* magazine also questions whether this is a 'new economy' or the old economy on 'economic steroids'. In these terms there is not much that is new to report.

This section has largely given a critique of the notion of a revolutionary and global knowledge economy. This is in the spirit of understanding the danger of separating theorizing of technology from history, culture, society, economics and politics in that it is easy to be swayed by the rhetoric of revolution and what Winner (1985) describes as 'mythinformation'. Other elements of this 'brave new world' now have to be defined and discussed, namely concepts of culture and consumption, and the culture of consumption.

**Cultures of consumption: definitions and debates**
If the history of political economy shaped the ideas about a disputed philosophy of globalization, so cultures of consumption are influenced heavily by the postmodern ideas of the 1980s. The so-called 'cultural logic of late capitalism' (Campbell 1995) is one where apparently consumption replaces production as the core element in the economy. Changes to contemporary culture were said to be wide-ranging, involving 'new modes of theorization' in the artistic, intellectual and academic fields. Changes in

the broader cultural sphere include a shift in interdependencies between groups – again the end of class society heralded by apparent changes in everyday practices of different groups developing new ways of orientation and identity (Featherstone 1991).

In this section, I argue against a postmodernist and individualistic and consumption-led discourse. I view human consciousness and the production and reproduction of our social life as rooted in materialism. In these terms I concur with the view of Alvesson and Skoldberg (1999), who describe the postmodernist discourse as a perfect ideology for an era where the market ruled. The 'roaring 80s' of the 'Reaganomic' derivatives market described as 'a free play in a vacuum liberated from all reference to mundane occurrences' was 'a whirlwind of signs without regard to boring realities' (ibid.:159). In the UK, this free market ideology is perhaps best illustrated with reference to a government advertising campaign called 'Ask Sid', involving the utilities shares sell-off to the general public. 'Sid' was portrayed as a canny 'man-in-the-street' who bought individual shares when previously nationalized companies were touted on the stock exchange. 'Sid' could then allegedly rake in the dividends as a private shareholder if the stock remained buoyant or sell the stock to gain an investment bonus and 'feel' individually superior from those who had not availed themselves of this opportunity. This was the era of UK Prime Minister Thatcher's[1] so-called 'no such thing as society' and UK Prime Minister Major's[2] 'classless society' where individual stock shareholding was further encouraged through private purchase of 'social housing' previously available only in the rented sector. Such ideologies were exposed as 'wishful thinking', however, with the persistence of collective resistance – illustrations are numerous, such as the 1984 miners' strike and the 1990 'poll tax' demonstrations. Bourdieu (1998) conceptualizes such individualistic ideologies as being material, symbolic and everyday acts of violence by the state. He notes, for example, how privatization leads to a loss of collective gains – such as affordable good quality social housing – and this loss is rarely accounted for in profit and loss calculations. He also notes how this is often accompanied by the preaching of the 'gospel of self-help' – all of this justified by the endlessly repeated need to reduce costs for companies (ibid.: 3).

After the 1980s, the 'free market forces' hit a brick wall and it must have seemed as though all wishes had come true again with the dotcom free market anarchy. Everyone started busily redefining the economy and the High Street; ways of organizing business and so on were to be transformed. Individualism apparently reigned again – it was to be each individual's choice whether to be a dotcom millionaire or not; only imagination was a barrier. The view of social divisions being an irrelevancy (Featherstone 1991) or a matter of individual risk and choice (Beck 1992) of course is essential in perpetuating these myths (Howcroft 2001). At this stage it was ironic to see that e-commerce was equated with SMEs (small and medium-sized enterprises); indeed, it seemed in the UK that stories of the same small businesses – sausage production in East Yorkshire, Angora rabbit farms in Devon and so on – appeared at every e-commerce promotion.[3] Of course, we can now see that the 'old economy' flourished and global e-commerce is dominated by TNCs not SMEs. Fortunately the dotcom collapse has tempered the excesses of postmodern pontificating, but what the modernism–postmodernism debate unleashed was a dramatic upsurge of interest in the issue of culture, although Featherstone (1991) has noted that explicit cultural studies and treatments of technology are rare. Yet to understand the consuming passion ideology in the UK today, such an analysis needs to be done.

The 'idea of culture' (Eagleton 2000) is one that fills many an academic tome. From 'culture as worship' originating with William Caxton in the fifteenth century (Williams 1976, 1980), culture is equated with a 'whole way of life' of people, not what we live by but what we live for (Eagleton 2000) and both a way of life and a whole range of cultural practices such as artistic appreciation and practice, consumption of mass-produced commodities and so on. Although culture appears to be politically neutral, Eagleton has observed that it is 'precisely in this formal commitment to many sidedness that it is most clamorously partisan' (ibid.: 17). The word 'culture' indeed 'encodes a number of philosophical issues' and Eagleton spells these out in terms of freedom and determinism, agency and endurance, change and identity, the given and the created, the dialectic between the artificial and the natural and what we do to the world and what the world does to us.

When we are being urged to consume with a passion, the notion of consumption requires discussion, too. Consumption is regarded as involving both material goods and symbolic meaning (Featherstone 1991). In the debating chamber, those in the Baudrillard and Lyotard corner are concerned with the making of identities (Poster 1988) and consumption as a symbol rather than instrumental activity. In the opposing corner, which I subscribe to, are those who stress how identities and who we are cannot be abstracted from the material. Bourdieu (1979) shows how class distinctions, for example, circulate round the cultural and symbolic as well as the material and economic axes.

Karl Marx's analysis of alienation is a good starting point to understand the implications of ideas of culture and consumption. Lee (1993: 7) suggests, for example, that the 'ontological rupture between labour and need appears objectified as the petrified or dehumanized product of estranged labour' and that this 'overriding sense of rupture' is seen as 'the undeniable hallmark of capitalist societies'. Consumption of mass-produced commodities constitutes a 'vital dimension of the modern capitalist economy' (Campbell 1995: 111) despite being a neglected area of study (Miller 1987). Warde (2003) furthermore, suggests that consumer culture – a culture where what we consume and the way in which we consume goods and services provided in economic markets – has come to represent our identities, mediate our interactions with others and even shape our politics. In these terms, Featherstone (1991) stresses how important it is to focus on 'cultures of consumption' rather than seeing consumption as arising in an unproblematic way from production. It can be seen that the ideology of consuming with passion rests on dreams – keeping people going on dreams of consumer goods and consumer experiences in 'dream worlds' as Benjamin (2002) has called arenas of consumption like shopping malls, for example (Campbell 1995). Bocock (1993: 50) commented:

> Consumerism, that is, the active ideology that the meaning of life is to be found in buying things and pre-packaged experiences, pervades modern capitalism. The ideology of consumerism serves both to legitimate capitalism and motivate people to become consumers in fantasy as well as in reality.

Here there are contradictions and conflicts – between those describing the emotional pleasure of consumption and 'celebration of desire' (Featherstone 1991) in modern consumption and the 'fault finding cultural critic' as Jürgen Habermas described the Frankfurt school (Alvesson and Skoldberg 1999). The perspective of consumer culture is often that of 'seductive containment' of the population (Featherstone 1991) and the way that support of mass media and effective marketing achieves an objectifying, controlling and streamlining of human needs and desires (Campbell 1995). Aldred (2004: 121), however, points out that 'people are not just prisoners of received ideas however strong they seem when the world is quiet: when we try and change the world we often start to see it differently'. She goes on to suggest that seduction by neo-liberalism's false promise of omnipotence – in the guise of the 'sovereign consumer' comes about through a sense of a fundamental *lack* of agency. Indeed, Harvey (1989; cited in Aldred 2004: 121) notes that: 'The capitalist market produces the giddy fantasy of consumer power *and* the nightmare of complete *powerlessness* under the unchallengeable "invisible hand" which deems that wages and benefits are always too high.' So as Sørensen and Williams (2002) succinctly point out, culture is not uniform or fixed – it is a complex social construction implicated both in creativity and the generation of opportunities and in restricting openness and variety.

So far I have set the historical, political, social and economic context of my case research. Now I shall take a critical research approach and briefly present some illustrative cases.

**Critical research in IS – illustrative cases**

In presenting my illustrative research cases, I address the three tasks set by Alvesson and Deetz (2000) in taking a critical approach: providing insight, critique and transformative redefinition. Insight, it could be argued, is something that most interpretive studies do to a greater or lesser extent. Critique involves challenging taken-for-granted assumptions, beliefs, ideologies and discourses. Again, this can sometimes lead to research being a mere polemic, always being 'anti' something and never providing alternatives. A critique can also mean little more than a brief but gratifying rant against the worst forms of management aggression or workplace injustice – not entirely unrewarding but perhaps limited in its scope. It is the third task – that of transformative redefinition – that provides perhaps the greatest challenge. This is developing critical and relevant knowledge to understand and facilitate change (Howcroft and Trauth 2004). Here, theory is crucially linked to practice and the notion of emancipation and liberation introduced, needing explanation and application to practice. A fundamental objective, therefore, in taking a critical approach to IS research – to paraphrase Marx – is to understand the world and so to change it. Whether research is about IT and organizational change or home e-shopping, an analysis of cultures of consumption in the global knowledge economy unearths contradictions. Have organizations been flattened and workers empowered or is there more intense control and deepened oppression through peer pressure and teamwork? Are we active and self-engaged consumers or passive and manipulated? Is society and everyday life centred on individual risk and choice or on community and therefore there is potentially collective resistance?

The critique and insight gained through taking a critical research approach contributes to the development of theory that is linked to emancipatory practice. Transformative redefinition manifests itself through this dynamic relationship. Where does an analysis of cultures of consumption in a global knowledge economy fit in here then? Eagleton (2000: 131) has said that culture is not only what we live by. It is also, in great measure, what we live for, and here he recounts some of those things – affection, relationship, memory, kinship, place, community, emotional fulfilment, intellectual enjoyment and a sense of ultimate meaning. This is a far cry from disintegration and individualism espoused by the 'new economy' advocates.

So what is emancipation and how is it to be achieved? The ideology of a global knowledge economy means a corporate and governmental stranglehold on what is the future, yet there can be a number of visions of a 'new society'. Perhaps 'it is not hard to imagine affluent communities of the future protected by watchtowers, searchlights and machine-guns, while the poor scavenge for food in the waste lands beyond'. On a more optimistic note 'in the meantime, rather more encouragingly, the anti-capitalist movement is seeking to sketch out new relations between globality and locality, diversity and solidarity' (Eagleton 2003: 22). In redefining the global knowledge economy, the World Social Forum (WSF)[4] are making an important active and theoretical contribution. A major maxim adopted by the WSF to be found on their posters and banners is that 'Another World is Possible'. This counters the morale-sapping notion of the inevitability of the global knowledge economic condition assumed by the dominant discourse.

What does taking a critical approach mean – in terms of method and practice – Alvesson and Skoldberg (1999) emphasize that a theoretical frame of reference is crucial to counterbalance any tendency on the part of the researcher to get trapped by empirical data. Deep meanings, making critical interpretations and reflection, override emphasis on collecting and processing empirical material. However, Sørensen and Williams (2002) suggest that even small studies or individual case analysis can provide rich insights for intervention and the ability to explain what choices were made. Bourdieu (1998) would agree, explaining his encounter with many everyday people caught in the contradictions of the social world and how these contradictions are experienced through 'personal dramas'. These can then contribute to a critique and a disrupting of actual social realities in a critical research approach that combines interpretive understanding with an emancipatory interest in knowledge (Alvesson and Skoldberg 1999). Linking critical social theory to research practice is therefore crucial, and this is what I have attempted to do in the following illustrative cases. In the first case – that of customer relationship management (CRM) systems use in telephone call centres – critical theory helped in understanding and analysing case data and the 'logic of practice' (Bourdieu 1990), providing insightful tools in the consideration of IT and organizational change. In the second case – that of home e-shopping and the domestication of ICTs – the emphasis is more on how the empirical evidence and underpinning theory are inextricably linked and enable an understanding of both. The main themes of this chapter inform both illustrative cases – to critique individualism and consumption-led ideologies of culture and identity; to exemplify the tensions between global knowledge economic rhetoric and the realities of our everyday lives; to question what it means to be an individual in the global knowledge economy; to contribute to fieldwork that takes a critical research approach and in particular which tries to provide a multidisciplinary bridge in relation to the seemingly disparate strands.

*The case of CRM systems in telephone call centres*
This subsection is about individuals and their experiences as employees of call centres in the northwest of the UK, and specifically draws on the

conceptual tools provided by Pierre Bourdieu. In terms of understanding consuming passions in the global knowledge economy, more than any other writer, Bourdieu has been able to extend Marx's original logic of capital into the cultural domain (Lee 1993). Bourdieu was a 'resister' appearing on various anti-globalization platforms before his death in 2002. He also challenged the orthodoxy and what is legitimate or not in terms of research and research findings. In *Weight of the World*, for example, Bourdieu (1999) seeks to give a voice to those not usually heard to bring to light the 'requirements of domination' (Skeggs 2002).

Bourdieu tries to convey that the social space and individuals that occupy it are as a result of historical struggles, and individuals produce the social space they live in and are produced by it. Therefore they both incorporate and objectify social structures that they inhabit (Wolfreys 2000). The relationship between the individual and society, or structures and agencies, is expressed in an analogy: compare social activity to an individual sense of play – people are free to act but they can only do so within the constraints of the game that they are playing. The game or social activity allows for improvisation and manipulation of rules, and coming to terms with the game is called the logic of practice. This is not just coming to terms with the rules, nor is it a wholly unconscious experience, nor is it purely as a result of rational calculation. It is that people develop strategies of behaviour but these are shaped by their objective situation (ibid.). The feel for the social game becomes an instinctive part of the make-up of individuals via the habitus that becomes a way of behaving based on a sense of what might be achieved (ibid.), so people have internalized the objective chances they face (Skeggs 2002).

In what Bourdieu describes as the dominant circular path – a causal loop of generation and reproduction – actors internalize the structure of the field as 'habitus'. Habitus in turn generates practice and practices serve to reproduce the structure of the field. Habitus – as a product of history – is an open system of dispositions that is constantly subjected to experiences, and affected by them in ways that either reinforce or modify its structures. It is important to note here that, though durable, these are not eternal (Lawler 2002).

Practices are generated by dynamically combining past experience, present situation and implicit anticipation of the future consequences of these very actions. Also, there is the question of how power relations exist and are maintained alongside habitus. Domination is maintained in society by means other than direct repression. Society, as stated, is made up of different fields, for example, fields of education, politics, economics and so on. Within each field, people compete for 'capital'. This could, for example, be cultural or monetary capital – any capital that is at stake within that particular field. Different forms of capital can be converted to other forms. Once the credentials of this capital become generally acknowledged and legitimized, then power relations no longer exist between individuals but become 'objective mechanisms and social institutions that reproduce relations of domination without the need of direct intervention by the dominant group in society' (Wolfreys 2000). The term symbolic violence is coined – acknowledgement and legitimization of the form of capital at stake in a particular field resulting in reproduced relations of domination. It is 'gentle and invisible' violence and internalized relations of power (Bourdieu and Wacquant 1992), being a legitimate call for deference to authority.

In terms of conducting critical research, the concept of habitus, arising out of, shaped by and reflecting the fields in which its operates, allows Bourdieu to 'forsake the false problems of personal spontaneity and social constraint, freedom and necessity, choice and obligation' (Bourdieu and Wacquant: 20) and side-steps the micro-macro debate that 'forces a polarized, dualistic social ontology' (ibid.: 168). Bourdieu discusses on the one hand, the unity and regularity of systems and their practical coherence, and on the other, their 'fuzziness' and irregularities which are both being equally necessary and inscribed into the logic of practice (Bourdieu 1990).

In their framework for field analysis, Bourdieu and Wacquant (1992) suggest analysing the position of the field *vis-à-vis* the field of power. Then there is a need to map out the objective structure of the relation between positions occupied by agents or institutions and finally to analyse the habitus of agents – those systems of dispositions they have acquired by internalizing a determinate type of social and economic condition, and which find a definite trajectory within the field under consideration.

With this framework in mind, I shall discuss an interpretive field study of telephone call centres in the northwest of England (Richardson and Richardson 2002). Ironically these are often housed in the old mills and engineering shops once at the forefront of the industrial revolution but long since idle – that is, until the 'virtual' age. It is interesting to consider whether this is indeed the new economic era, or history repeating itself. The area of study has the largest number of call-centre jobs in the UK (TUC 2001). There are many types of call centres but rather than taking an organizational or case-study model representing examples from each call-centre type, this research instead aimed to follow the fortunes of call-centre workers in what is described as a mobile field study (Richardson 2003). In these terms, four call-centre workers were involved with the researchers in a two-year study. As the four changed workplaces for a variety of reasons, so this enabled aspects of CRM system use in nine different call centres to be analysed. The researchers were mobile, moving as 'shadows' rather than fixing themselves in the organizations and taking snap-shot views. In practice, they all met up regularly, sometimes engaged in group discussions, sometimes in one-to-one interviews. Consent was sought for the content and direction of the research as an ongoing concern. Participants supported the research and wanted their voice to be heard and stories told. The powerful tales are of stress, burn-out, sacking,[5] job changes and frustration, but also of community, solidarity and collective action. Interviews were transcribed and reflexive stories written down, but shown to and discussed with the individuals concerned.

This illustrative case focuses on the use of CRM systems that operate to handle the 'front-line' communication with customers, control and to various degrees automate the gatekeeping roles, capture and standardize sales knowledge and oversee customer service. This front-line work is vital and significant to an organization. It is often strategically important work. CRM system use is aimed at streamlining and shortening the key business processes that define a global organization's relationship to the markets and customers – it is a strategic business issue that requires technology support (Ciborra 2000). CRM systems mean codifying intellectual capital (Light 2001), with software providing 'scripts' enabling monitoring and call analysis. This metaphorically, if not physically, welds the worker and machine into a streamlined and controlled knowledge system. This account in contrast aims to throw the spotlight on the individuals' working on the call centre 'front line' and tell the stories often left untold in studies of IS and change (Alvesson and Deetz 2000).

In the workplaces studied, labour turnover was high. In one centre, labour turnover was expected to be 100 per cent in their first year. Scripts and monitoring aspects of CRM software were utilized. Practices like 'hot-desking'[6] were imposed with a goal of de-personalizing work stations with the view to concentrating minds on productivity. Workers were generally organized in teams, with a team supervisor receiving very little enhanced pay but there to disseminate orders from the top down. Management tried various techniques to try to establish control of teams, enhance productivity and instil peer pressure on 'the weakest link'.[7] These included incentives such as awarding of food vouchers for improved sales figures, to the use of punitive actions such as imposing star charts to encourage behaviour modification.

The monitoring aspects of CRM system use means that no aspect of the call-centre workers' day was unaccounted for. They were profiled, listened in to, their opening remarks analysed and wrap-up time and phrases used. The sales content of their conversations, achievement of call numbers and sales targets were scrutinized. Call times were strictly monitored with pressure on for quick 'closure'. Their off-line frequency and intimate toilet habits were considered and discussed at teamwork supervision sessions, as were perceived attitudes displayed during conversations with customers.

The use of scripts, rules and codes with CRM systems even result in codifying responses to stress and also involve the way team working is used to self-regulate. CRM requires that exact phraseology is imposed for monitoring and analysis purposes. One worker explained that calls were dissected into four parts: (i) a welcome and introduction; (ii) offering products and services; (iii) recap call; and (iv) positive close. She faced difficulties with management for failing to use the exact words 'and to recap'. Supervisors made her put labels on her monitor with the words on and she had to tick a 'star chart' when she used the words. Her calls were monitored closely and listened in to. Saturdays were colloquially called the 'sacking day'. It was easier and less obvious for management to dismiss someone on a Saturday. One Saturday, she was sacked for again using words similar to, but not actually 'and to recap'.

Call-centre work can be very stressful and alienating. Despite facing frequent and sustained verbal abuse from customers, call-centre staff had to control their responses. This has been described as an aspect of 'emotional labour' where employees have to publicly display an emotion not necessarily felt (Hochschild 1983). However, the call-centre workers did enjoy the opportunities for rich communication and dealing with complex issues presented by the customers. At this point, scripts were often bypassed and ignored. Often advice about debt and so on was given beyond that stipulated by the script. Call-centre work is also a story of solidarity and community. Management methods often intimidated, yet solidarity helped in many cases. During the study there was a major official strike against bullying in one of the call-centre organizations. This precipitated the Trades Union Congress and call-centre organizations to consider good practice (TUC 2001).

Reflecting on Bourdieu and Wacquant's framework, the field of CRM use in telephone call centres in the northwest of England is one of startling contrast. For the consultants and employers, CRM use in call centres means knowledge-intensive, strategic use of technology, flexible working and utility of all those new ways of working, such as 'flattened' organizations, teamwork and empowerment. For others, they are the 'sweatshops of the 21st century' (Belt et al. 2000: 368). Working in call centres also means coming to terms with uncertain and casual employment. Bourdieu (1999) has commented that a feature of work today is generalized and permanent conditions of insecurity. He discusses how a constant threat of unemployment, for example, shapes a new type of domination aimed at compelling workers to submit to and accept exploitation. This is experienced in the call-centre teams we looked into. He further emphasizes that insecurity is the product, not of an economic inevitability but of a political will (Bourdieu 1998: 84). Concepts of 'empowerment' and freedom of individual decision making may be seen to rest on an increasing manipulation of the individual by centralized forms of managerial surveillance and cultural control (Wilson 1995). Yet as I have shown, resistance is always possible, particularly as contradictions are exposed in practice.

In terms of fulfilling the tasks of insight, critique and transformative redefinition, this study attempts to go beyond a more traditional view of stakeholder analysis to give a wider political picture and to question the assumptions that perhaps just focus on the efficaciousness of software or the constraints or otherwise of IS. To analyse the habitus of agents means stretching the scope of the research beyond the organization and the study. In this case, for example, an important fact is that call-centre staff in the northwest of England are recruited heavily from the gay and lesbian community, from the vast student population and from women seeking part-time employment. This results in a casual and transient workforce with a distinct profile and contributes to the 'personal dramas' (Bourdieu 1998). Holistic reflection therefore needs consideration of these agents' habitus – as far as a researcher can uncover internalized dispositions. Even so, the quest and endeavour to do so can result in a richer and political consideration of the research study.

Bourdieu helps us understand the complex historical and cultural factors involved in the social relations of IS use. This comes specifically through analysis of the competing fields, understanding of the role of habitus, contradictions apparent through the application of symbolic violence as a mode of domination, and how the relationships between structures and agencies involved manifest themselves in the logic of practice.

Critical research and Bourdieu's analysis in particular shows us that there are wider institutional and ideological issues to be discussed when studying IS and organizational change (Bourdieu 1990; Alvesson and Deetz 2000). A clear motivation for this research has been to highlight the contradictions between CRM rhetoric and the reality for call-centre workers on the 'front line'. It aims to let their stories be heard. Alvesson and Skoldberg (1999) show how critical approaches stimulate reflection and encourage multiplicity, and that this in turn gives the 'marginalized quieter voices' a greater chance of being heard as well as enhancing the political relevance of the research.

This research has now reached what Eisenhardt (1989) calls 'closure'. The four call-centre employees have dispersed – to travel, to other jobs, to 'pastures new'. The next illustrative case is part of an ongoing and larger study at its 'in-the-field' stage. What follows is mainly an approach where the literature is examined with a critical lens helping to shape the research, although some preliminary analysis is presented where appropriate. The fieldwork includes a longitudinal study of households and their e-shopping experiences and use of ICTs in the home. Interviews held in and outside of the households enabling observations and in-depth discussions, contribute to the empirical material. I also developed an on-line questionnaire that is 'live' at the time of writing.[8]

### The case of home e-shopping: opening up the 'black box' of home consumption and the domestication of ICTs

My investigation into home e-shopping and consumption is in the context of family and households in everyday life. I began this ongoing research in 1998 at the height of the dotcom boom. At the time, the literature was divided. In the utopian hyped fantasy world, the High Street by now would have ceased to exist (De Kare-Silver 1998). It was predicted that we would all be engaged in shopping through various media, and shopping would have been transformed beyond recognition. On the other side of the spectrum, commentators suggested that e-shopping would have 'no impact' (Markham 1998) and be an irrelevance.

Of course the dotcom collapse in 1999 dented the e-shopping hype, nevertheless the dotcom myths (Howcroft 2001) still reappear and reinvent themselves when the next 'revolutionary' media appears on the scene. For example, 3G mobile phones, which can send images or 'smart' phones that can alert you to a retail 'bargain' nearby, are hyped as the next revolutionary change to the shopping experience. The UK Christmas 2003 'must have'– the iPod – is said to render the making and purchase of music albums immanently obsolete.

Home e-shopping, though, enables consideration of engagement with ICTs in the very personal and private sphere and how technologies become embedded into everyday life. This research considers domestication of ICTs into the household – a political and contested social space (Silverstone and Hirsch 1992) where scarce resources have to be competed for (Green and Adam 1998). One way we are being urged to consume with a passion is to engage with ICTs in the home. We are encouraged to use PCs in the home as an aid to study, for leisure and for electronic governance and to e-shop, using a variety of home-based media.

Part of the aim of my research is to consider home e-shopping in relation to gender and household relationships and gendered technology. It is to see how gender is shaping use of domestic technologies, particularly ICTs – not only what is done, when and by whom, but also the household spaces the technology occupies. So what is the state of gender and home e-shopping and what can we learn about its relation to global knowledge economic rhetoric and the ideology of individualism?

On-line home shopping today has its origins in the traditional mail-order business. In the 1850s, 'Shilling' or 'Turn Clubs' brought credit to customers otherwise denied it. After the Second World War, these 'clubs' became a major way to purchase. In effect they offered interest-free loans. A significant feature of this traditional mode of home shopping is provision of credit, with women being community providers of credit as catalogue agents, and also consumers of credit as major catalogue users. Mail-order catalogue home shopping is a localized market, centred on household-related goods. Its customers are mainly poorer women who are economically vulnerable. Women, as catalogue agents and therefore community credit providers, work part-time at this task and generally this fits in with their social and economic circumstances. There are social aspects involving meeting with relatives and neighbours while collecting weekly payments, and hence it is a club and community endeavour. This regulated form of credit and also unregulated forms like using so-called 'loan sharks'[9] or informal loans to friends and family, are crucial to low-income households as a mechanism to manage poverty.

For many people, 'doing the shopping' conjures up a picture of weekly purgatory – a stress-filled domestic chore to be endured. Yet 'going shopping', particularly for women, is a pleasurable leisure pursuit involving browsing, meeting with friends and the anticipation of returning home clutching bulging carrier bags. It is not surprising therefore that shopping for pleasure is the most popular out-of-home leisure pursuit for women (Mintel 1996). On-line shopping is far from achieving that status.

Clearly, women are not a homogeneous group when it comes to predictions of on-line shopping behaviour. It has been identified that a woman's socio-economic group affects access to disposable income, and e-shopping demands internet access and credit power. However, women in the UK are underwhelmed by the on-line shopping experience, and on-line shoppers are at present, technically aware, fairly affluent and predominantly young men (Richardson 2000).

With such consuming passions, the household becomes the focus of enhanced consumption and so the lens shifts to the family. Many policy makers and commentators decry the 'new' family in the 'new economy'. There has been a dramatic increase in lone-parent-headed households in the past two decades (German 2003). Viewpoints sway from 'women should be in the workforce' to 'women should be at home caring for children' on an almost daily basis – depending on whose 'think-tank' is reporting. Throughout history there has always been a contradiction between ideology of 'the family' and realities of everyday family life. In the early days of factory labour in the eighteenth century, men, women and children worked but had a very low life expectancy and were not being reproduced in the quantity and quality required by capitalist development (Richardson 1984). The 'family' had to be 'reinvented' after this unintended consequence of industrialization and urbanization, aided by protective legislation, including restricting the working hours of women and children. In the twentieth century, for example, Thatcher showed a startling volte-face from the post-war boom era when she proclaimed in 1952 that 'I should like to see married women carrying on with their jobs', and then during an economic recession in 1980 'I feel very very strongly that women should not leave their children to come home to an empty house' (Marshall 1982: 8). Just as in an analysis of the current 'global knowledge economy', such statements have to be scrutinized with an understanding of historical, political and economic context.

In these terms, Giddens (1984) drawing on Beck's 'individual and risk society' thesis, suggests that the changing situation of men and women in the family and at work must be seen as individual choice. This is put forward in terms of choices in relation to freedom and liberation and in the context of analyses that patterns of work will inevitably change – the women working flexible hours in casual jobs, replacing men working in one occupation for life. Such a dramatic change in the UK labour market and employment patterns – like so much of the 'new economy' writing – is premature in predicting the disappearance of the full-time permanent male employee. However, critical inquiry into such futuristic predictions helps us understand our social world. Bourdieu's 'new mode of domination' is one example where there is insecurity through casualization of work and 'flexploitation', to use his term (Bourdieu 1998: 85). However, as German (2003) explains, the family is both broken down by the effects of capitalism but also maintained and reinforced by capital as the cheapest, most convenient and most socially stable way of caring for the existing generation of workers and reproducing the next generation. The family fulfils too precious a role to be left to 'free market' individualism. In reality, three-quarters of households are still headed by two-parent families and men and women are moving closer together in terms of work and domestic life, but not in circumstances of their choosing. They do so 'against a backdrop of continuing women's oppression and intensified exploitation for both men and women' (ibid.: 31). Fitting into these roles is hard work – for women it means working for less than equal wages and for men increased unpaid childcare in the home. In these terms individual men and women are 'sold an image of themselves which goes well beyond the old roles of breadwinner and homemaker' (ibid.: 32).

For the purposes of passionate enhancement of cultures of consumption, clearly an issue is how new technologies have impacted not only on home e-shopping but in the household generally. Green and Adam (1998) have noted how little is considered about the way in which ICTs impact on everyday life in the home, and in particular they observe the gendered social relation of domesticity which surrounds the use of ICTs. As Silverstone and Hirsch (1992) have pointed out, the household is a complex social, economic and political space that powerfully affects both the way technologies are used and their significance. We know little about the economic or social context of the use of technologies in the home and how ICTs are appropriated and consumed in households, including the gender dimensions of this and the negotiation involved.

My fieldwork so far concurs with Green (Green et al. 1990; Green 2001), whose studies of women's leisure continue to show time synchronization and time fragmentation dominating most women's lives, leading them to find 'snatched' spaces for leisure and enjoyment rather than planned activities. A striking feature of everyday lives from my analysis to date is how little leisure time people have or perceive themselves to have. Leisure time is also often taken in snatched and fragmented moments and at times that precludes pre-planning. Leisure researchers also suggest that there is an objective decline in leisure time, often referred to as 'time squeeze'. This is as a result of multiple role conflict and role overload (Peters and Raaijmakers 1999). The competing demands of labour market and domestic work are associated with a perception of a loss of control over time, often called 'time crunch', and research suggests that women with children feel more time crunched than men (ibid.).

In my study so far I have also found that the 'time poor' seize moments for essential household maintenance. A quick grocery shop, for example, is fitted in on the way home or before work. In these terms, e-shopping is anticipated as a way to help make everyday tasks quicker and easier and reduce the demands of everyday living. However, in reality, stress is often increased when the e-shopping experience fails to meet expectations and problems have to be dealt with like incorrect items delivered or inconvenient delivery times. E-shopping has not yet dealt with 'old-fashioned' logistical problems like loading lorries with the right goods and transferring them successfully from A to B.

Whatever the case, it is clear that the household is a central arena where consumption is located (Silva 2002) and again Bourdieu's conceptual tool of habitus is useful here in analysing the significance of the everyday, including domestic routines and responsibilities embedded in family life (ibid.). In consideration of the domestication of ICTs, understanding the objects that people need and use cannot ignore household practices and relationships within the household (Morrison 1998). A clear theme emerging from my study is that household maintenance tasks are not shared equally and so there is unequal access to 'spare time'. The households in my study are home to a plethora of technological gadgets associated with leisure and communication. What is absent is the leisure time to use them. However, the PC has particular significance, often housed in communal spaces and taking up more physical space. In addition, the PC has a symbolic link embedding a subtext of personal improvement through its reported educative role. Home PC ownership also has a strong association with the daily bombardment of digital divide rhetoric, demanding an individual commitment and responsibility to 'self-help'. In other words the message is, embrace the ICT 'revolution' or be a victim of digital 'have-not-ness' brought about, it is implied, by personal inadequacy and culpable neglect. Many people in my study are 'catching hell' (Kvasny 2004), living busy lives with an overload of domestic and work commitments in the everyday struggle to 'make ends meet'. Use of ICTs in the home in this context is just another thing to be dealt with.

By way of Bourdieu and Wacquant's (1992) analytical framework, the habitus of the agents involved in UK domestic households cannot be considered apart from consideration of gender and the role of the family in capitalism today. Bourdieu describes ways of being and doing where individuals acquire the 'practical sense'[10] and this includes gendered ways of knowing and being which become an 'inextricable part of the intimate details of everyday life' (Silva 2002: 175).

**Reflecting on alternative consuming passions: a critical theory of practice**
In claiming to have taken a critical research approach to the two illustrative cases, what does this mean in relation to interpreting the research and enabling an alternative understanding of consuming passions in the global knowledge economy? Alvesson and Skoldberg (1999) suggest that an important principle is to think in a dialectic way. It is the state of tension between different realized ideas and practices on the one hand and alternatives to these on the other, that helps to avoid getting caught by established ideas and institutions. They stress how the natural tendency is to interpret existing social reality from a taken-for-granted cultural stance and that this must be counteracted.

Throughout the chapter I have addressed the tasks of insight, critique and transformative redefinition while seeking to provide an alternative analysis of cultures of consumption in a global knowledge economy. The task has also been to critically interpret unconscious processes, ideologies, power relations and other expressions of dominance to prevent the privileging of certain interests over others, whereby the form of understanding appears to be spontaneously generated (ibid.). In this context I have therefore flagrantly favoured literature taking a critical view of the dominant ideologies to question what it means to be an individual within the tensions and contradictions of our social world. I have also tried to provide alternative voices seldom heard. In these terms there are versions of the future and the future can be described as a 'contested entity'. Moore (2003) describes the corporate versions that seek to produce corporate identities presenting a future that is ultimately knowable through expertise resting on the valued endpoint of competitive advantage. She continues to highlight the inexorable logic of future-oriented technological determinism. Research about CRM use in call centres and domestication of ICTs in this context, highlights a dominant viewpoint of the essentialist assumptions held about technologies and those who consume them. However, the future and what technologies we have and how they are used is not inevitable, and critical interpretation means a shift in focus from what appears to be self-evident, natural and unproblematic on the one hand and what can be interpreted as the freezing of social life, irrational and changeable on the other (Alvesson and Skoldberg 1999). In this context, this account aimed to build a distinct multidisciplinary bridge to move in favour of emancipatory change.

In fulfilling the third task set – that of transformative redefinition – I am contesting that there is a critical theory of practice and in doing so I concede that it is crucial to link critical social theory to research practice. In the cases presented here, I have used the analytical tools and framework provided by Pierre Bourdieu. A poignant illustration perhaps of how theory is linked to practice is given by Eagleton (1996: 5):

> One of the most moving narratives of modern history is the story of how men and women languishing under various forms of oppression came to acquire, often at great personal cost, the sort of technical knowledge necessary for them to understand their own condition more deeply, and so to acquire some of the theoretical armoury essential to change it.

Kvasny (2004) suggests that instead of seeing the wisdom of everyday people, the more common response is to produce discourses that discount their values and that it is becoming extremely difficult for non-market values to gain a foothold. Justice, care and kindness, for example, are all non-market values that provide sanctuary from the brutal realities of everyday life in global capitalism. Bourdieu (1998) would agree, urging us to radically question that which individualizes everything. He suggests an alternative 'economics of happiness' with all violence paid for.

So how can we understand a critical theory of practice? Kvasny (2004) advocates the need for a questioning spirit to constitute new understandings that can serve as springboards for the future. Bourdieu (1998) supports blocking the forced feeding of globalization by criticizing the words themselves and equipping people with weapons of resistance.

My contribution with this chapter is to reclaim the social and collective through my interpretation of resistance and solidarity of call-centre workers, despite the compulsion to fulfil individual performance targets and be controlled by team and peer pressure. By critically analysing the family and households today, I am reclaiming the social and collective from the force and dominance of the ideology of individualism. I also reclaim the international from prevailing arguments of the inevitability and omnipotence of global economic forces by critically disrupting the dominant arguments about what it means to live in a global knowledge economy. In questioning what emancipation and freedom really are in the global knowledge economy, is another world possible? Indeed it is.

## Notes

1. Margaret Thatcher, UK Prime Minister 1979–90.
2. John Major, UK Prime Minister 1990–97.
3. Pointed out by Dr Sarah Green from the Department of Social Anthropology at the University of Manchester, UK and researcher in the ESRC project 'Social contexts of Greater Manchester'.
4. This is an ad hoc grouping of various anti-globalization, trade union and other activists who share a commitment to emancipatory change.
5. 'Sacking' is a term used when an employer terminates employment as a result of a breach of contract or other misdemeanour by the employee.
6. This is the practice whereby workers are not allocated their own work station or work space but sit at the nearest available desk. Individualization of work space is not permitted.
7. During team meetings, supervisors encourage analysis of the team performance and identification of individuals who appear to be the weakest link in terms of productivity and so on. Teams were encouraged to assert peer pressure on the individuals identified in order to improve team performance.
8. See www.hr.arcbits.co.uk/Shopping.php (August 2004).
9. Loan sharks are people who loan money to be repaid at extremely high rates of interest.
10. Bourdieu's work has been translated from the French as *The Logic of Practice* (Bourdieu 1990). However, the original work is called *Le Sens pratique* (Bourdieu 1980) and perhaps 'the practical sense' as described here gives a clearer understanding. Thanks to Frantz Rowe for pointing this out.

## References

Adam, A. and Richardson, H. (2001), 'Feminist philosophy and IS', *Information Systems Frontiers*, **3** (2), 143–54.

Aldred, R. (2004), 'In perspective: Judith Butler', *International Socialism*, **103**, Summer, 115–35.

Alvesson, M. and Deetz, S. (2000), *Doing Critical Management Research*, London: Sage.

Alvesson, M and Skoldberg, K. (1999), *Reflexive Methodology*, London: Sage.

Beck, U. (1992), *Risk Society: Towards a New Modernity*, London: Sage.

Bell, D. (1973), *The Coming of the Post-Industrial Society*, Harmondsworth: Penguin.

Belt, V., Richardson, R. and Webster, J. (2000) 'Women's work in the information economy: the case of telephone call centres', *Information Communication and Society*, **3** (3), 366–85.

Benjamin, W. (2002), *The Arcades Project*, Cambridge, MA: Harvard University Press London.

Bentley, T. (1999), 'Knowledge management? Humbug!', *Management Accounting*, April, 13–15.

Bocock, R. (1993), *Consumption*, London: Routledge.

Boudreau, M.-C. (1997), 'Report on the panel discussion assessing critical social theory research in IS', International Federation of Information Processing Working Group 8.2 Working Conference in Philadelphia, PA, 31 May to 3 June.

Bourdieu, P. (1979), *Distinction: A Social Critique of the Judgement of Taste*, London: Routledge.

Bourdieu, P. (1980), *Le Sens pratique*, Paris: Éditions Minuit.

Bourdieu, P. (1990), *The Logic of Practice*, Cambridge: Polity.
Bourdieu, P. (1998), *Acts of Resistance. Against the New Myths of Our Time*, Cambridge: Polity.
Bourdieu, P. (1999), *The Weight of the World*, Cambridge: Polity.
Bourdieu, P. and Wacquant, L.J.D. (1992), *An Invitation to Reflexive Sociology*, Cambridge: Polity.
Campbell, C. (1995), 'The sociology of consumption', in Miller, D. (ed.) *Acknowledging Consumption*, London: Routledge, p. 111.
Castells, M. (1996), *The Rise of the Network Society*, Oxford: Blackwell.
Castells, M. (2004), 'An introduction to the information age', in Webster (ed.), pp. 138–50.
Ciborra, C.U. (ed.) (2000), *From Control to Drift: The Dynamics of Corporate Information Infrastructures*, Oxford: Oxford University Press.
Curtis, M. (2003), *Web of Deceit: Britain's Real Role in the World*, New York: Vintage.
De Kare-Silver, M. (1998), *E-shock: The Electronic Shopping Revolution. Strategies for Manufacturers and Retailers*, London: Macmillan.
Eagleton, T. (1996), *The Illusions of Postmodernism*, Oxford: Blackwell.
Eagleton, T. (2000), *The Idea of Culture*, Oxford: Blackwell.
Eagleton, T. (2003), *After Theory*, Harmondsworth, Penguin.
Eisenhardt, K.M. (1989), 'Building theories from case study research', *Academy of Management Review*, **14** (4), October, 532–50.
Featherstone, M. (1991), *Consumer Culture and Postmodernism*, London: Sage.
German, L. (2003), 'Women's liberation today', *International Socialism*, **101**, December, 3–45.
Gibbons, M., Limoges, C., Nowotny, H., Schwartzman, S., Scott, P. and Trow, M. (1994), *The New Production of Knowledge: The Dynamics of Science and Research in Contemporary Societies*, London: Sage.
Giddens, A. (1984), *The Constitution of Society*, Cambridge: Polity.
Green, E (2001), 'Technology, leisure and everyday practices', in Green, E. and Adam, A. (eds), *Virtual Gender: Technology, Consumption and Identity Matters*, London: Routledge, pp. 173–89.
Green, E. and Adam, A. (1998), 'On-line leisure: gender and ICTs in the home', *Information, Communication and Society*, **1** (3), 291–312.
Green, E., Hebron, S. and Woodward, D. (1990), *Women's Leisure, What Leisure?*, Basingstoke: Macmillan.
Harvey, D. (1989), *The Condition of Postmodernity*, Oxford: Blackwells.
Hochschild, A. (1983), *The Managed Heart: Commercialization of Human Feeling*, Berkeley, CA: University of California Press.
Howcroft, D. (2001), 'After the goldrush: deconstructing the dotcom market', *Journal of Information Technology*, **16**, 195–204.
Howcroft, D. and Trauth, E. (2004), 'The choice of critical information systems research', in Kaplan, B., Truex, D., Wastell, D., Wood-Harper, T. and DeGross, J. (eds), *Information Systems Research: Relevant Theory and Informed Practice*, Boston, MA: Kluwer Academic, pp. 195–211.
Hirst, P. and Thompson, D. (1998), *Globalisation in Question*, Oxford: Blackwell.
Johnson, C. (2000), *Governing Change: from Keating to Howard*, Brisbane: University of Queensland Press.
Keeble, L. and Loader, B. (eds) (2001), *Community Informatics: Shaping Computer-Mediated Social Relations*, London: Routledge.
Kraak, A. (2001), 'Debating Castells and Carnoy on the network society: the Gauteng seminars', *Umrabulo*, no. 9, November, www.ancdocs/pubs/umrabulo/umrabulo9.html, accessed 22 February 2005.
Kvasny, L. (2004), 'The existential problem of evil and IT in the hotel civilization', www.isi. salford.ac.uk/cris, 14 July.
Kvasny, L. and Truex, D. (2000) 'Information technology and the cultural reproduction of social order: a research paradigm', in Baskerville, R., Stage, J. and DeGross, J. (eds), *Organisational and Social Perspectives on IS*, Boston, MA: Kluwer Academic, pp. 277–93.

Lawler, S. (2002) 'Rules of engagement: habitus, power and resistance', Workshop on After Bourdieu: Feminists Evaluate Bourdieu, University of Manchester, UK, 11 October, http://les.man.ac.uk/sociology/Seminar/afterbourdieu.shtm, accessed 30 November 2003.

Lee, M.J. (1993), *Consumer Culture*, London: Routledge.

Light, B. (2001), 'A review of the issues associated with customer relationship management systems', Paper presented at the 9th European Conference on Global Co-operation in the New Millennium, Bled, Slovenia, 27–29 June.

Mandelson, P. (2001), 'Foreword', in *Competitive Advantage in the Digital Economy*, London: Department of Trade and Industry, www.dti.gov.uk/comp/competitive/pdfs/ec_pdf1.pdf, 15 July 2002.

Markham, J.E. (1998), *The Future of Shopping: Traditional Patterns @nd Net Effects*, Basingstoke: Macmillan.

Marshall, K. (1982), *Real Freedom: Women's Liberation and Socialism*, London: Junius.

Masuda, Y. (2004), 'Image of the future information society', in Webster (ed.), pp. 15–21.

Miller, D. (1987), *Material Culture and Mass Consumption*, Oxford: Blackwell.

Mintel (1996), *Leisure Trends*, London, Chicago, Belfast, Sydney: Mintel Leisure Intelligence.

Moore, K. (2003), 'Versions of the future in relation to mobile communication technologies', PhD thesis, University of Surrey, Guildford, UK, September.

Morrison, D. (1998), 'A virtual ethnography of the dynamics of social change in relation to new technology', http://virtualsociety.sbs.ox.ac.uk/projects/morrison.htm, accessed 5 December 2003.

Nordenstreng, K. (2004) 'Divisons', in Webster (ed.), pp. 255–60.

Peters, P. and Raaijmakers, S. (1999), 'Time crunch and the perception of control over time from a gendered perspective: the Dutch case', *Society and Leisure*, **21** (2), Autumn, 417–33.

Poster, M. (ed.) (1988), *Jean Baudrillard: Selected Writings*, Cambridge: Polity.

Ramonet, I. (2004), 'Gaps in the net', http://mondeediplo.com/2004/01/01Ramonet, accessed 20 January 2004.

Reich, R. (2004), 'The three jobs of the future', in Webster (ed.), pp. 204–12.

Richardson, H.J. (1984), 'Job evaluation and equal pay for women workers in the British labour market', unpublished MA thesis, University of Kent at Canterbury, UK, April.

Richardson, H. (2000), 'It's shopping but not as we know it – women and home e-shopping in the UK', presented at the Gemisis Conference on Innovative Solutions for the Digital Age, University of Salford, UK, 16–18 May.

Richardson, H. (2003), 'CRM in call centres – the logic of practice', in Korpela, M., Monteleagre, R. and Poulymenakou, A. (eds), *Organizational Information Systems in the Context of Globalization*, Boston, MA: Kluwer Academic, pp. 69–81.

Richardson, H. and Richardson, K. (2002), 'Customer relationship management systems and information ethics in call centres – you are the weakest link, goodbye!', *Australian Journal of Information Systems*, May, 485–501.

Rowe, J. (2000) 'Eat, sleep, buy, die', *New Internationalist*, NI329, November, www.newint.org, accessed 22 February 2005.

Silva, E.B. (2002), 'Time and emotion in studies of household technologies', *Work, Employment and Society*, **16** (2), 329–40.

Silverstone, R. and Hirsch, E. (1992), *Consuming Technologies: Media and Information in Domestic Spaces*, London: Routledge.

Skeggs, B. (2002), 'Exchange value and affect: against polite society', Workshop on After Bourdieu: Feminists Evaluate Bourdieu Workshop, University of Manchester, UK, 11 October, http://les.man.ac.uk/sociology/Seminar/afterbourdieu.shtm, accessed 30 November 2003.

Slack, J.D. and Wise, J.M. (2002), 'Cultural studies and technology', in Lievrouw, L. and Livingstone, S. (eds), *The Handbook of New Media*, London: Sage, pp. 485–501.

Sörensen, K.H. and Williams, R. (eds) (2002), *Shaping Technology Guiding Policy. Concepts, Spaces and Tools*, Cheltenham, UK and Northampton, MA, USA: Edward Elgar.

Touraine, A. (1974), *The Post-Industrial Society: Tomorrow's Social History: Classes, Conflicts and Culture in the Programmed Society*, London: Wildwood House.

Trades Union Congress (TUC) (2001), 'It's your call: TUC call centre workers campaign', Trades Union Congress, February.

*UK 2004 Yearbook*, www.statistics.gov.uk, 12 January.

Wajcman, J. (2002), 'Addressing technological change: the challenge to social theory', *Current Sociology*, **50** (3), 347–63.

Warde, A. (2003), 'ESRC cultures of consumption programme', Centre for Research in Innovation and Competition, University of Manchester and UMIST, http://les1.man. ac.uk/cric/Alan_Warde/currres.htm, accessed 22 February 2005.

Webster, F. (ed.) (2004), *The Information Society Reader*, London: Routledge.

Williams, R. (1976), *Keywords: A Vocabulary of Culture and Society*, London: Fontana/Croom Helm.

Williams, R. (1980), *Problems in Materialism and Culture: Selected Essays*, London: Verso and New Left Books.

Wilson, F. (1995), 'Managerial control strategies within the networked organisation', *Information Technology and People*, **18** (3), 57–72.

Winner, L. (1985), 'Do artefacts have politics?', in MacKenzie, D. and Wajcman, J. (eds), *The Social Shaping of Technology*, Milton Keynes: Open University Press, pp. 28–41.

Wolfreys, J. (2000), 'The radicalism of Pierre Bourdieu', SWRecordings 235 Bookmarks, audiotape, London: Bookmarks Publications.

# 14 Rationalities and emotions in IS innovation

*Chrisanthi Avgerou and Kathy McGrath*

## Introduction

The information systems (IS) field is saturated with technical/rational thinking on the development and role of information and communication technology (ICT) amidst the dynamics of contemporary organizations. The take-up of ICT in organizations is studied as a process of technical reasoning and acting governed by a mix of concerns about the engineering of software and other ICT artefacts, administrative control and economic gain. The knowledge developed to address each of these concerns has the form of a closed system of reasoning geared to specific ends. Assuming the desirability of technology innovation, survival and growth of self-governed organizational units of work, and economic maximization in free market conditions, the engineering, the administrative and the economic rationalities determine consistent plans of action for their optimal achievement. Nevertheless, as the technology construction, administrative integrity and economic gain are invariably intertwined in ICT innovation, the currently prevalent instrumental knowledge on IS tends to combine these three rationalities in complex techno-economic reasoning. The literature on systems development, IS planning and outsourcing is concerned with strategies and tactics of a combined effort towards a desirable technological, managerial and economic effect.

Of course the IS field is well aware of the shortcomings of its core of instrumental knowledge. A constant theme in IS research on pragmatic obstacles that erode the integrity of professionals' rational interventions has made widely noticeable a persistent malaise with symptoms such as 'user resistance' and multiple forms of system 'failures' (Keen 1981; Sauer 1999). A stream of studies have pointed out that the technical/rational models misrepresent the real processes of IS innovation. They juxtaposed other types of behaviour – spontaneous action, tacit knowledge, political action – not as problematic attitudes that subvert the technically reasoned professional activities, but as constructive behaviour observed in cases of successful innovation (Suchman 1987; Knights et al. 1997; Ciborra et al. 2000). Such critiques of the type of IS knowledge and practice within the field itself echoes more general positions in social theory, which, from a broader perspective, have questioned the significance of instrumental knowledge in modernity. Notable is the influence of recent analyses in the field of science and technology studies, such as Latour (1993).

Furthermore, since the early 1990s, a substantial literature of non-instrumental analyses of ICT in organizations has been developed, quite distinct from the technical/rational tradition – what we can call the 'social study' of ICT (Avgerou et al. 2004). Drawing from contemporary social theory, such as structuration theory and the various strands of the sociology and history of technology, a body of IS knowledge came to address ICT and organizations in terms of individual actors' behaviour embedded in social context, that is, human interactions supported or inhibited by institutionalized modes of practice (Barley 1986; Orlikowski 2000). Such studies bring to the fore aspects of the ICT innovation process which are not dictated by imperatives of systems of consistent reasoning, but associated with human agency in its complexity as constituted by life experience in relation to the technical, natural and social world.

No assumptions of rationality, of consistent reasoning to meet universally desirable ends, are evoked in such studies. Nevertheless, the legacy of rationality continues to be present in most social studies of ICT in two basic ways.

First, social studies of ICT tend not to problematize what drives the techniques, the political behaviour, or the attitudes towards technology innovation. For example, Orlikowski's stucturational studies on the way ICT is implicated in incremental and improvisational organizational change assumes that actors are committed to pursuing the overall organizational goal of competitive advantage. This position takes for granted the assumptions inherited from the technical/rational legacy, namely actors striving for their benefit in the context of organizations competing in a market economy (Orlikowski 1996, 2000; Orlikowski et al. 1996). Their tactics may differ, for example, forming adversarial or collaborative work practice, but we are expected to understand their behaviour as single-mindedly serving the economic success of the firm.

Second, most studies focus on cognitive aspects of human action and intentional behaviour, even though this behaviour is seen not to be limited to technical reasoning but to involve political alignments and improvisational elements. Less attention is given to the diffused processes of technology domestication, the lived experiences with technologies shapeable through everyday use, without design, policy and political strategies (Monteiro 2004). Only marginally the emotional and almost never the aesthetic dimensions of human existence are acknowledged.

From a critical perspective, the lurking assumption of a rationality oriented towards universally desirable ends as a driving force in the way human agency is implicated in ICT and organizational change bears significant limitations. Failing to address the contingent nature of underpinning desirable ends of rational action, social studies of ICT run the risk of a-contextual and a-historical generalizations. Such generalizations may be particularly detrimental to the transfer of knowledge from one research domain to another, for example, from a business domain to government or from the socio-cultural setting of the Western societies to developing countries that have not followed socio-economic trajectories similar to the Western modernization. Also, by narrowing human agency to its cognitive dimensions, IS studies retain an impoverished conception of the relationship of ICT innovation to the human condition, unable to consider the totality of human capacities that are either positively or negatively engaged with innovation processes.

In other words, maintaining covert assumptions about the desirable ends towards which the cognitive/calculative action of ICT innovation may be directed, and eliminating from analytical attention the emotional dimensions of human agency, sustains a very limited view of what ICT innovation involves. First, because it misses important aspects of the dynamics through which ICT innovations result in winners and losers, and second, because it leaves unacknowledged areas of the dynamics through which human actors are engaged with, and cope with the consequences of, ICT innovation and organizational change.

In this chapter we set out to explore the possibilities for an analytical perspective that allows us to account for the rational and the emotional as two constituent dimensions of human agency in ICT innovation. Our exploration has gained valuable insights from examining the distinct literatures on rationality and emotions, which we present in the following section. We then outline some conceptual premises for addressing in common rationality and emotions as inseparable aspects of human experience by drawing from Foucault's analytical perspective. The penultimate section demonstrates these ideas by reinterpreting a case study of a failed attempt to introduce an IT-based system in the London Ambulance Service (Page et al. 1993; Beynon-Davies 1995; Hougham 1996). Finally, in the conclusions, we highlight the critical nature of the Foucauldian analysis of this case.

**The literatures on rationality and emotions**

*Rationality*
A relativistic view of rationality is not a new proposition in social theory. At the beginning of the twentieth century, when the course of modernity

was already quite advanced, Max Weber elaborated on the 'rational' consistency of fundamental institutions of modernity, namely the order that sustains organizations and the functioning of the free market economy (Weber 1947). In analysing the formal rational type of the modern economy, Weber acknowledged that the outcome of economic action is judged differently in relation to different underlying ends – what he calls 'substantive rationality'.

In the substantive sense, the modern Western economic rationality, in which people orient their decisions towards maximizing efficiency and weighing costs and benefits, conveys one particular set of values that historically came to dominate over others. These values involve the ethical sanction of acquisitive activity and a propensity to seek new solutions to problems rather than adhere to traditions. But other societies subscribe to different values, hence strive to attain different ends. Such ends may include ethical, political or utilitarian considerations, such as social equity, social justice, or the furtherance of power of a political unit. Indeed, in terms of substantive rationality, economic activity itself may be of secondary importance, or in conflict with the attainment of particular social values of a society. Thus, the notion of the substantive rationality provides a wider perspective to view the modern economic system. Several authors have highlighted the need to understand better how different kinds of rationalities prevail and perpetuate, and the consequences of sustaining or subverting particular biases to certain values over others (Parsons and Smelser 1956; Smelser 1978; Strange 1988).

Similar arguments have been made in organizational studies, with many authors highlighting examples of organizations in which individual and collective action does not comply with principles of rational organizational behaviour on the basis of which organizations in Western market societies are assumed to function. The organizational behaviour patterns in East Asian countries – mainly Japan, South Korea and Taiwan – have been repeatedly discussed as examples of alternative underlying substantive rationalities (Hamilton and Biggart 1988; Orrù et al. 1991), or what Clegg calls 'modes of rationality' (Clegg 1990).

In acknowledging differences in substantive rationality, research on organizational behaviour associates modes of rationality with the historically developed social relations of a locality, whether a country or an otherwise defined region; it directs attention to local meanings and legitimate action. For example, differences in the degree to which rational action in organizations is driven by trust and cooperation – or competition and antagonism – are traced in broader, historically formed, structures of social relations. It remains, nevertheless, a crude thesis, mainly because focusing on the differences among underlying substantive rationalities across local communities makes assumptions on homogeneous beliefs and behaviours within them, overlooking the coexistence of multiple beliefs within a community as well as an organization.

This pitfall is avoided in a stream of science and technology studies that have recently been subjected to scrutiny and critique the assumption of rationality in the way science and technology advance and come to bear on modern society (Hughes 1983; Law 1991; Bijker and Law 1992). Studies on the social construction of technology not only challenge the formal rational perspective that views technology engineering as a closed system obeying its own rules of technical rationality, but they also avoid drawing sweeping relationships between trajectories of technology innovations and social structures. In effect, they recognize that multiple rationalities are implicated in the shaping of technology innovation, but they do not attempt to predetermine what these rationalities are by reference to established social features, to social institutions. Rather, emphasis shifts to the particular actors, historical circumstances and events; to how the technologies we live with are the product of those actors who took advantage of, and struggled against, an apparently random range of opportunities, obstacles and alternative options that defy the neatness of structuralist social theory.[1]

Many see such relativism as lacking critical might because it does not expose the social conditions that enable certain actors to mobilize human allies and techno-scientific resources (non-human actors/intermediaries) in order to achieve results of their interest while others fail to do so. In effect, social studies of technology point to dynamics of power relations among multiple actors, but they generally do not enter into an analysis of what these dynamics are. However, by refusing to offer generalized or 'ideal' models of human behaviour that identify the 'rational' means of serving a particular end, these studies challenge the long-established divisions between rational and irrational behaviour. Thus the main contribution of most contemporary social constructivist perspectives on technology innovation is the elimination of the distinction between the rational character of processes techno-scientific and the idiosyncratic, irrational character of processes seen as political.

Summarizing so far, the recognition of multiple, historically developed, substantive rationalities and congruent modes of organizing overcomes the problem of a universalistic conception of rationality that determines strategies and rules of rational behaviour without reference to social context. However, the notion of substantive rationality provides limited scope for understanding how actors with diverse interests can be mobilized to convert an idea into reality. Social constructivist perspectives on technology innovation address such mobilizations, challenging the long-established divisions between rational and political behaviour (Latour 1999) without the need of structuralist social theory that predetermines where political power and rational capacity lie in society. Nevertheless, they remain vague on two major aspects: about the way power dynamics relate to what is considered rational, or taken to be true knowledge, and about the way the agency of the 'actor' – so important in the dynamics of translation – is constituted as the bearer of the observed rational/political competence. The analytical perspective we develop later on addresses these issues, as well as those arising from the following review of the literature on emotions.

*Emotions*
The study of emotions has received less attention within the IS field than in other disciplines concerned with issues of work and organization, notably management and organization studies, sociology and psychology. Indeed, despite being influenced by the writings of a broad range of social and organizational theorists, IS researchers have consistently ducked the issue when it comes to engaging in a substantive way with the affective domain. Moreover, IS professional practice sees emotions largely as an attribute – usually, an undesirable one – of the users of its innovations (Wastell and Newman 1996; Wastell 1999). While a detailed review of the diverse literatures on emotions and their relationship with work and organization is beyond the scope of this chapter, we highlight some key readings that indicate the nature of the work done to date and the substantive issues arising.

Within organization studies, Fineman has been a significant contributor (Fineman [1993] 2000, 1996). In the second edition of *Emotion in Organizations*, Fineman (2000) identifies two broad schools of research in this area – informed on the one hand by psychodynamic theory and a psychoanalytical perspective, and on the other by the concepts and ideas of social constructionism. In the first case, researchers are concerned with the unconscious processes of the human mind – the hidden or repressed thoughts and desires, and the social defences adopted by individuals or organizations to a range of emotions, generally anxiety related. From a psychoanalytical perspective, such defence mechanisms are seen as dysfunctional or irrational, and, as in the clinical application of such research, they need a treatment. For example, Brown and Starkey (2000) focus on five ego defences adopted by organizations to maintain collective self-esteem and continuity of their existing identity. Such defences, they argue, block organizational change, hence there is a need for organizational learning to promote critical reflection on identity to militate against such dysfunctional behaviour.

Social constructionist research addresses the intersubjective nature of emotions; the way that systems of meaning shape emotional behaviour and how emotional codes of conduct are socially and culturally constituted.

While some social constructionist studies focus on the 'rules' of emotional expression that operate within specific work organizations (Hochschild 1983; Van Maanen 1991), others focus on the emotions of broader societal groups. Departing, in the latter case, from the focus on particular groupings of adults, Bendelow and Mayall (2000) study the emotions of children, arguing that they should not be rendered invisible within the social order of primary schools.

Fineman (2000) argues for breaking down the distinctions outlined above – for theory that draws insights from both schools of thought, and for building explanations interrelationally by collapsing from the outset individual, organizational and societal levels of analysis. From his perspective, rationality and emotionality are also inseparable, and he argues that the work of Giddens and Foucault might be exploited with these considerations in mind.

In a more critical commentary on the current state of emotion research, Meyerson (2000) finds that a managerialist agenda predominates – the major focus is emotional labour, or the management of emotions, and not the nature of them. In effect, Hochschild's research on emotional labour – addressing efforts to make front-line service agents (such as flight attendants) conform to managerially prescribed rules of emotional expression towards customers (Hochschild 1979, 1983) – is too easily abused. Even though Hochschild argues that the labour involved to display the prescribed emotional appearance can cause psychological damage to front-line workers, inevitably her work has caused others to exploit the potential for emotion engineering (engendering the 'right' way to feel). Meyerson (2000) is critical of both enterprises, seeing the latter as serving single-mindedly the end of improving performance, while the former can do no more than suggest treatments for 'sick' – meaning flawed or incompetent – workers who fail to serve this end. She asks what work and research would be like if emotions were honoured: if burnout was not sick but 'OK' – something that could be talked about and cared for as part of the job; if such caring was valued and rewarded; and if social scientists abandoned their illusory ethics that human experience can be understood from a position of emotional detachment.

Within social theory, Giddens (1990, 1991) uses the concept of existential anxiety to refer to how individuals experience a crisis of identity about who they are and what their role is in the context of the transformations taking place in the modern era. Nevertheless, he argues that feelings of anxiety are with us from the early days of life. And just as an infant's caretaking agent (usually the mother) seeks to establish habits and routines, which provide the child with a defence against anxiety and a way of encountering an unfamiliar world, so too do we develop such practices throughout our lives. These routines form the basis of a framework of ontological security, a collection of emotional and behavioural 'formulae' that are a part of our everyday practice and help us to cope with potential dangers. In Giddens's argument, anxiety is free-floating, in the sense that it lacks a specific object. However, it may intensify if people are unable, or prevented from, carrying out the routines of their everyday practice, and it may become fixed on a specific object or situation in response to a perceived threat. The transformations occurring in the modern era, in which information technology (IT) is deeply implicated, may give to such an uprush in anxiety as well as providing a target for it. Most writers agree that fear is the way to characterize the step change in anxiety that occurs when a specific object or situation appears threatening.

Some IS researchers, sensitized by their reference theories have paid attention to aspects of emotionality. For example, Wastell (Wastell 1996) draws from psychodynamic theory to demonstrate how a structured systems development methodology was used as a social defence to contain anxiety during IS development. In a later paper (Wastell 1999), he argues that transitional objects (entities that provide temporary emotional support) should be used to break down these defensive processes. Consistent with a psychoanalytic perspective, Wastell sees anxiety and the social defences to it as dysfunctional, and seeks to eliminate them.

Barrett and Walsham (1999) draw from Giddens's writings on modernity and its consequences (Giddens 1990, 1991) to explore the concept of existential anxiety. They show how IT adoption in the London insurance market was implicated in such anxiety among brokers and underwriters, who began to feel significantly troubled about what the new information system and the forms of knowledge it inscribed would mean for them. This move marks a departure from cognitive–rational structurationist studies of IT adoption (for example, Orlikowski 2000) which avoid engaging with the affective domain. Nevertheless, Barrett and Walsham tend to bracket emotion, in the sense that it seems important to discuss market participants' anxiety largely in the context of introducing new information technology. The question of what emotion they felt before introduction of the new system, or whether they were anxious about the process of assessing risk – however achieved – in an increasingly complex and risky society (Beck 1992, 1994) is not significantly addressed. In short, we might easily conclude that the brokers' and underwriters' actions always implicated a type of rationality, but only at certain times implicated a type of emotion.

Ciborra, drawing on Heidegger (1962), is explicit that we always act within an emotional medium. We have, he argues, a fundamental attunement with a situation – a way of encountering the world – through a mood;[2] and even though moods can change, we are never without one (Ciborra 2002, p. 161). In this view, purely rational action is not possible. Moreover, some moods are intense, such as panic and profound boredom (when we are empty, and want nothing from a particular situation); in this form of attunement, alternative courses of action are closed off, and any type of effective action becomes problematic. Conversely, when moods are not intense we engage in everyday practices, which may be seen as an effort to drive a mood away (ibid.). This position echoes arguments expressed elsewhere, for example, the view that in order to deal with anxiety – the less intense form of fear or panic – we enact everyday practices established within our framework of ontological security (Giddens 1991).

Overall, IS research has shown less interest than other disciplines in exploring the view that emotions are fundamental to our lived experiences. Although a small number of researchers of ICT innovation have done occasional work addressing the emotional dimensions of human action, in general, affectedness in all of its forms – emotions, moods, dispositions – is not even acknowledged, far less explored, within social studies of ICT. This is all the more surprising when one examines a body of work where the authors make use of the concept of situatedness, yet fail to explore its meaning in the original phenomenological sense of Heidegger and Husserl (Ciborra, 2004). Citing a number of such studies – in particular, Suchman (1987) and Orlikowski (1996, 2000) – Ciborra (2004) explains that, in the phenomenological tradition, 'situated' referred not just to the emerging circumstances of the surrounding world, but also to the inner situation (the affectedness) of the actor. In short, studies presenting a situated account of ICT innovation, and more generally, studies adopting other types of contextualist perspective to examine the innovation process, are failing to explore a key aspect of the situation/context: the moods, dispositions and affections of the actors – in other words, the actors' emotions.

*Concluding remarks*

In summary, the critical perspective we develop and use in the remainder of this chapter is influenced by the following key insights gained from our review of the literatures on both rationality and emotions. First, we must not only look for and engage with alternative substantive rationalities (Avgerou 2002), but also recognize, express and honour feelings (Meyerson 2000), rather than labelling so many behaviours as dysfunctional responses to an assumed universal model of instrumental reasoning. Second, emotions colour every encounter we have with the world (Ciborra 2002), and anxiety is a particularly pervasive emotion with which we cope by developing everyday routines and practices that are key to maintaining a feeling of normality (Giddens 1991). Third, we need theory that will allow us to build explanations interrelationally, rather than adhering to our preferences for studying phenomena from individual, organizational or societal levels of analysis, or making distinctions between rationality and emotionality (Fineman 2000).

**Rationality and emotions: a common perspective**
The work of Michel Foucault provides a critical perspective of rationality and emotions as historically constituted aspects of human agency. In his studies of the way Western societies developed human sciences (Foucault 1970, 1972) and the way they came to identify and deal with madness, illness, criminality and sexuality (Foucault 1971, 1973, 1977, 1978, 1985, 1986), Foucault hardly found it necessary to explain that human agency involves reason and emotions. He took for granted that these are constituent aspects of an individual as a practising subject in the societies of any historical era. The histories of events he traced uncover actors' rationality in their working out of strategies for desirable ends and the deployment of techniques and tactics for their efficient achievement. Similarly, although he did not explain that madness, illness, criminality and the ways societies have dealt with them implicate emotions, it does not surprise the reader that his history of human conduct regarding such an area as sexuality is replete with instances of desire, pleasure and anxiety about the care of self.

In Foucault's perspective, the rational and emotional conduct of an individual is formed within a society's systems of power, knowledge and morality. His studies of specific areas of social practice – regarding insanity, illness, criminality and sexuality – reveal a plurality of rational actions and emotions, which are not to be understood in terms of universal truths about human nature or society, but in terms of the knowledge that came to be believed to be true and the striving for moral conduct under dynamics of power in particular historical conditions.

Foucault's emphasis on the relationship among knowledge, power and morality changed through time, and it was only in the last few years of his life that the dimension of morality became prominent. His early work is best known for associating reason with power, but this association is also essential for understanding his particular notion of ethics.

*Rationalities in power/knowledge relationships*
Foucault's analyses of human sciences as discursive systems are concerned with showing the historical conditions of their existence, rather than their value in pursuing truths. Also, his study of psychiatry, medicine and later of penal systems, treated these areas as fields of knowledge and practice which are linked with institutions, economic requirements and political issues and which are enmeshed in political dynamics of multiple actors. In such studies he distinguished a number of manifestations of power. In its most widely recognizable form, power is exercised by a juridical mechanism

that forces particular truths, that inhibits certain behaviours while allowing others. Power is exercised blatantly by institutions such as the courts of law, the police and the army with the use of physical force, but in Western societies increasing significance came to be acquired by power exercised through discipline and control of individuals' behaviour by institutions such as state administration and education. Such disciplinary power relies less on physical force and more on knowledge of the population and rational/ scientific techniques for classification and categorization of what is normal and what is deviant.

Fundamental in this approach is a conceptualization of power as something which cannot be a priori judged as negative, as interference with rational actions that restricts the discovery of truth. Power mechanisms may be seen as resulting in useful order and compliance with common patterns of socially acceptable behaviour, thus making warlike tactics unnecessary. Also, power is not seen only in dyadic domination relationships of oppressors and oppressed, such as the authority of the state controlling its population, or the church repressing its believers. Power dynamics are pervasive in the micro practices of specific social domains, sometimes exercising a forced domination of one way of thinking and behaving over others, sometimes maintaining normalized thinking and behaving, and sometimes triggering alternative logics of thinking and counteractions. General conditions of domination may be created by such multiform, localized, power-laden relations integrated into overall strategies. But, relations of power are often accompanied by resistances, which are also multiple in form and can be integrated to form larger strategies for the overthrow of dominant orders.

Foucault uses the term 'regime of truth' to capture this notion of socially constructed, power-constituted determination of what is rational – in other words, of what is a valid way to distinguish between true and false. Regimes of truth are the rules according to which truth is determined and specific effects of power are attached to the true. His historical analyses of rationality uncover also the 'knowledges' that were disqualified as inadequate and naive in the struggles and conflicts of the formation of particular social institutions, what he calls the 'subjugated knowledges'.

*Incorporating emotions through an ethical dimension*
In the late 1970s and until his death in 1984, Foucault sought to account for the 'constitution of the subject' in a more general way as shaped by the way people live their lives. In effect, he broadened the power/knowledge perspective by shifting attention to the ethical dimension of human behaviour. Thus, sexuality, a highly emotional domain of individuals' conduct, is seen to be determined in terms of the morality underpinnings of their society. Morality, too, is seen to be a domain of multiple games of

power and truth. Nevertheless, power/knowledge here is clearly not a purely cognitive relationship. In the societies studied – classical Greek, Hellenistic and Roman – sexual ethics is seen neither to obey universal ideals nor to be a cognitive matter of identifying individuals' true sexual nature. The games of power and truth are seen as an exercise of freedom by subjects concerned with a more general problematization of getting their lives right, which Foucault attempts to capture with the term 'aesthetics' of their existence.

Thus, notwithstanding the view that Foucault had an ongoing concern with the power/knowledge relationship, his focus on the subject and on affections, and hence on ideas of personal and voluntary rules of conduct that are morally laden, opens a route for addressing emotions.[3] Indeed, reflecting on his work in progress shortly before his death, he argued: 'you can say, in general, that in our society the main field of morality, the part of ourselves which is most relevant for morality, is our feelings' (Foucault 1984, p. 352). This work was not completed, but Foucault's notion of ethics, which concerns the kind of relationship one ought to have with oneself, provides an analytical direction for understanding emotions in human conduct.

The relationship to oneself has four interrelated aspects concerned with how individuals constitute themselves as moral agents (Foucault 1985). First, the 'ethical substance' refers to the part of oneself that is to be made the focus of moral conduct. This may take the form of a desire or an act, or it may reside in our feelings about the quality of our relationships with others. Foucault (1984) emphasizes the third form in modern society. Second, the 'mode of subjection' refers to the way that individuals are induced to recognize their moral obligations, which may be because they belong to a group that accepts the moral code, they see the obligations as quasi-juridical, or their perception of self requires compliance, say, as someone who must give an example. Third, the 'techniques of the self' are the means by which individuals try to change themselves in order to behave ethically, which may include moderating one's behaviours, renouncing certain acts, or continually monitoring and questioning how one behaves and why. Finally, the *telos* of the ethical subject is the mode of being to which individuals aspire when they behave in an ethical way – the moral goal.

The grid of analysis that emerges from the two last volumes of *The History of Sexuality* (Foucault 1985, 1986) thus involves acts, a moral code, and the relationship to oneself. The acts are the real behaviours of individuals in relation to a moral code that is recommended to or imposed on them, while the relationship to oneself refers to the manner in which one ought to conduct oneself if acting in line with the prescriptions of the code.

A more in-depth discussion of Foucault's views on individuals' care for their lives is beyond the scope of this chapter. It suffices to point out that, from this perspective, individuals' rational acting stems from the beliefs on right or wrong sustained by their social context. They are reflective actors whose beliefs and feelings are constantly tested in the domain of their professional and personal lives. The kind of cognitive and moral challenges that justify alternative tactics as rational courses of action and trigger emotionally charged behaviour are demonstrated in the case presented in the following section.

## An empirical example

The British National Health Service (NHS) is engaged in a process of modernization that has been ongoing for more than 20 years. Ever since the Griffiths report (DHSS 1983) called for more professional management of the NHS, there has been a series of administrative and economic reforms of the health service that embody the efficiency logic of a managerialist rationality. In the early 1990s, this effort involved introducing a limited market economics, in which district health authorities purchased the services they required from hospitals, ambulance services and other health service providers on a contractual basis that supported competitive tendering (DOH 1989). The 'internal market' logic was superseded in 1997 by a system of clinical governance 'called "integrated care"', [which is] based on partnership and driven by performance' (DOH 1997, ch. 1, pp. 1–2). While aiming to encourage more collaboration among healthcare actors, this system extended the drive to improve performance, by creating national centres charged with safeguarding clinical quality and cost effectiveness, and merging health authorities into larger units with increased powers to negotiate contractual obligations with service providers.

British governments, past and present, have been prime movers in these efforts to transform a centralized, publicly funded NHS into an efficient, 'consumer-led' model of healthcare provision that meets public expectations of a modern health service. Joint needs to change the culture of the NHS and to mobilize the potential of information technology are cited repeatedly in managerial and ministerial discourses about this modernization initiative. In this context, few examples are more familiar in the IS literature than the case of the London Ambulance Service (LAS). This case has been presented as a managerial and technical failure (Page et al. 1993; Beynon-Davies 1995; Hougham 1996), as a politically motivated attempt to automate the human role and increase managerial control (Wastell and Newman 1996) and as the unintended and unpredictable outcome of the interplay of power relations (Introna 1997).

All of these accounts deal with what happened at the LAS in 1992, when an attempt was made to introduce information technology as a response to the government's internal market initiative. Each one presents a story of a staff-management conflict, in which managers tried to implement a modernization regime based on an assumed universal rational model of best practice, while staff – still smarting from the effects of a bitter national pay dispute – mounted a challenge to their efforts to increase efficiency. The authors give little or no sense of finding an alternative *regime of truth* with its own substantive rationality and morality – rather than just resistance to change – in the actions of ambulance workers. Although Wastell and Newman highlight stress as a key dimension for analysis in their comparative study of London and Manchester ambulance services, they give little analytical attention to emotions in the LAS case. So the dominant explanation of what happened at the LAS in 1992 is a cognitive–rational one, guided mostly by an instrumental rationality perspective – in short, that ambulance workers successfully resisted the introduction of a new system that incompetent or irrational managers sought to impose upon them.

Here, we suggest not just one rationality system with competent or incompetent proponents and opponents, but different regimes of truth, each constituting a community of rational and moral agents whose behaviours make perfect sense when viewed from the vantage point of their particular value system. In our analysis, we focus less on what happened and more on examining the social conditions that made certain courses of action possible while constraining or ruling out others, seeking to expose those rationalities and emotions whether apparently dominant or subjugated within the power dynamics of instrumental reasoning. We draw from McGrath's longitudinal study of the LAS case to present our arguments. Full details of the study, including a description of the research methodology, are contained in McGrath (2003).

*The traditional command and control regime*
Throughout the 1980s, the LAS made several attempts to introduce information technology into its established, manual modes of working. A management information unit was set up, and although some progress was made in developing spreadsheet applications to analyse a small percentage of the monthly performance statistics, the core operational areas remained largely untouched by technology. Specifically, the emergency staff, which constitutes the vast majority of employees of the service, continued to work with pen and paper, supported by telephones and a radio system for maintaining contact between the control centre and ambulances attending emergency incidents.

At that time, the dominant *regime of truth* operating within the LAS was a 'command and control' regime, organized along militaristic lines of discipline and reflecting the historic connection between the ambulance and the armed services, in which most ambulance officers were ex-military personnel (Preston and Hutchison 2001). All operational staff wore uniforms, and protocols and procedures structured the way that work was carried out, nevertheless human judgement was seen as the final arbiter in responding to patients – a judgement that was acquired only by repeated exposure to emergency situations.

Both officers and staff had an operational focus, so considerations of working within budget and achieving performance targets set by government were not high-profile issues. The authority vested in officers was a mark of their seniority – a sign that they had already gained the operational experience necessary to command. Over 90 per cent of the operational workforce belonged to a trades union, and union officials were active and influential figures within the LAS. In this regime, information technology that tried to enforce compliance with a managerial efficiency logic was not seen as serving the accepted rational and ethical behaviours.

*An emerging professional management regime*
Following publication of the government's plans to introduce an internal market (DOH 1989) a major reorganization took place at the LAS. An 'arm's-length' board was created to be responsible for the day-to-day management of the service, while the regional health authority retained the statutory obligation of accountability (Page et al. 1993). The new appointments to the roles of chair, chief executive, and directors of operations, human resources and finance marked a move to introduce professional managers into the LAS. Twenty per cent of the officer posts were disbanded, while those that remained were redesignated as management roles, for which incumbent staff had to reapply. The new senior management team undertook a radical programme of organizational reform and technological rationalization in just two years, in which the LASCAD (London Ambulance Service Computer Aided Dispatch) system was a crucial element.

The aim was to introduce a highly innovative system that fully automated the command and control functions of the LAS – from receipt of an emergency call at the control centre, through decisions on which ambulance to allocate to the call, to mobilization of the appropriate resources to the incident. Call details would be captured online, tracking devices would be fitted to ambulances so that their locations could be monitored continually, and mobilization instructions would be passed via an electronic link from the control centre to either mobile data terminals in the vehicles or printers on ambulance stations. Managers pressed ahead with this innovative project, despite the more measured approach taken by other ambulance services, the concerns raised by computer professionals who tendered for LASCAD, and the issues highlighted by reviewers of the project.

*Reinterpreting the dominant explanation of LASCAD*

On the surface, LASCAD was an attempt to enact a techno-managerial rationality, in other words, to link a management-driven efficiency rationality with information technology as the way to improve the performance of the LAS to standards set by government. Key among these standards were those derived by ORCON (Operational Research Consultancy) – the response time targets of 8 and 14 minutes, respectively, for responding to 50 and 95 per cent of emergency calls. In the LASCAD effort, the instrumental model of human behaviour implicated in the techno-managerial rationality of the emerging professional management regime ran counter to the substantive *sui generis* model enacted by members of the command and control regime. The dominant explanation suggests that the ensuing conflict between staff and management ultimately led to the demise of the system.

We suggest that adopting a broader Foucauldian perspective of rationalities and emotions reveals that such an explanation has distinct limitations. First, whether by implication or absence, it assumes that the managers at the LAS were ideologically aligned with senior politicians and ministers in the Conservative governments of Margaret Thatcher and John Major. It fails to explore the conflict between these groups which, although more covert, was also more insidious in the way it came to bear on the LASCAD project than the staff–management conflict that has received so much attention. Second, in neglecting to examine how actors were constituted rationally and emotionally, it finds in effect only one value system, in which actors who fail to achieve techno-managerial objectives are seen to be incompetent, while actors who resist such goals are, by implication, behaving irrationally. Such attributions miss important aspects of the dynamics involved in IS innovation (Avgerou and Madon 2004). In the remainder of this section, we endeavour to reveal them in this case.

*On the rationality and emotions of LAS managers*

As mentioned above, presenting the LASCAD affair as a local staff–management conflict either overlooks the key role of the Conservative government of the day in what occurred or assumes that the rationality of that government was harmoniously combined within the professional management regime emerging at the LAS. In the early 1990s the Conservative government had a very low ranking in the opinion polls, to the extent that there was a growing belief that it would lose the next general election, which under parliamentary law had to take place by summer 1992. In a period of economic recession and high unemployment, a success story in the health sector – an area historically constituted as a prime concern of British electors – might have done much to boost confidence in the government.

The implementation of LASCAD, originally scheduled for 8 January 1992, would have been both fitting and timely.

Public inquiries highlight the concerted political pressure exerted on LAS managers to meet timescale and cost (Page et al. 1993), chronic, long-term government underfunding of the LAS (HOCSCOH 1995), and the vested interests of senior health officials and government ministers who nevertheless sought to avoid responsibility for their actions (ibid.). Explaining what happened largely in terms of the faulty execution of a computer contract, and hence as the failure of management at a local level to adhere to best practice in ICT innovation, neglects these wider concerns and the way they constrained professional action by LAS managers. Some understanding of the conflict arising is possible by exposing the contradictions that existed between the ideology of the Conservative government of the day and the way that the actors within a professional management regime are constituted as the bearers of their particular competences.

Within a professional management regime, standards of best practice and human actors are linked together in a control regime intended to achieve efficiency and effectiveness of operations, in which 'value for money' is a central concern. Professional standards of best practice are evident in the fields of accountancy, law, human resource management and information technology, among others – a list that includes specialisms practised by members of the LAS board. Practitioners in these fields often show more allegiance to the professional practices of their own discipline than to operational considerations within a given market sector, not least because such practices are relatively enduring, embody transferable knowledge and skills, and constitute the discipline as one that can be regulated largely by its members.

On the other hand, the socio-political and economic rationality that framed government policy making and enactment in the early 1990s was espoused in the concepts of a free market ideology, and the reform of collectives – notably the trades unions – that would see things otherwise. Participants to this discourse included a coalition of government ministers and senior health service officials that sought not just operational efficiency, but a complete re-establishment of the basis of health sector operations within a market-driven NHS and associated reform of established negotiating bodies.

The government's agenda to introduce market-driven practices into the NHS shared the 'value for money', administrative efficiency concerns of a professional management regime. However, the free market ideology at the heart of this agenda reflected a more fickle, consumer-driven, economic rationality when compared with the relatively stable, self-regulated, commercial interests of the disciplines described by a professional management regime. Moreover, professional practice is not premised on trades union disempowerment. Rather than arguing that best practice concerns received only lip service by members of the LAS board, we suggest that the discourses they attempted to enact were those of two distinct regimes that had not harmoniously been combined. In effect, the notions of commercial best practice enshrined in particular professional disciplines were colonized by the tenets of a more totalizing, consumer-oriented, public relations discipline propagated by the political 'spin-doctors'.

On a narrow lens, the LASCAD project was an attempt to enact a techno-managerial rationality; adopting a broader perspective, its rationality was framed by, in conflict with, and often subjugated to a socio-political and economic rationality of the free market, an acquisitive individualism, and an associated programme of trades union reform. Even while the project was being conceived and the tendering process was taking place – in other words, while members of the operational staff were onlookers to what happened – the discourse was already imbued with contradiction and conflict.

A question that arises is how the professional managers at the LAS were constituted as moral agents within this discourse. A key aspect of the management philosophy espoused by the chief executive, John Wilby, was that managers should gain respect from others by the way they do their jobs and not by virtue of their rank – in effect, they should recognize their moral obligation to be an example to others. He combined this *mode of subjection* to a professional management philosophy with an aggressive 'can do' approach, employing *techniques of the self* which meant mastering any emotions – such as anxiety – that might give a negative message.

In this light, the circumstances surrounding his report to senior health officials, and ultimately government ministers, that 'there is no evidence to suggest that the full system software, when commissioned, will not prove reliable' (Page et al. 1993, p. 35) bear further examination. That such a person should give only negative assurance about a critical system suggests that on 1 April 1992 even John Wilby was wavering in his modernization mission. But his political masters ignored his message, leaving him to carry on with the implementation and account for what happened – an outcome that within 36 hours of the system going live had cost him his job.

Those who chose to remain on the sidelines following John Wilby's report – and other warnings (*Financial Times* 1992; *The Guardian* 1992) – were criticized later on (HOCSCOH 1995), with commentators suggesting that their ethical conduct was in question because they did not intervene to correct the incompetent and irrational behaviours. However, John Wilby's report was dated days before the general election of 1992. At that time, the overwhelming opinion of the electorate and the media was that the Labour party would form the next government, to the extent that a few days later news programmes showed Neil Kinnock celebrating victory at a Labour party rally – even before the votes had been cast. The broadcasters' message was clear – opinion polls demonstrated that the mood of the country was such that these celebrations were well founded: after nearly 13 years in office, the Conservative government was staring defeat in the face.

Ministers and senior health officials now had cause to reflect upon their rational and emotional attachments to the LASCAD project and associated wider reform programmes, in light of the imminent role for the incumbent government as the party of opposition. That things turned out otherwise was an election outcome that took everyone by surprise, and only fuelled the spin-doctors' message that the Conservative party – now celebrating a record fourth consecutive term in office – would continue to dominate British politics because there was no longer a credible alternative.

*On the rationality and emotions of LAS staff*
Clearly, presenting the LASCAD case without either alternative rationality or emotional dimensions misses important aspects of how human actors approached, engaged with, and gained or lost in the process of ICT innovation. This position can be exemplified further by examining what happened when members of the operational staff became involved in the LASCAD discourse – specifically, by analysing the role played by the simple technology of the allocator's activation tray in constituting members of the operational staff as rational and moral agents.

In the command and control regime, staff recognized their obligations to patients through an articulated and accepted rule of their community, which required them to use their knowledge and skills to respond to a call for help, and to develop empathy with the patient using their experience of similar situations. In this way, each individual's *mode of subjection* to their moral obligations was in large part a personal one, a self-styled mode of caring for themselves and others, rather than a quasi-juridical disciplinary mode mandated by ORCON standards. In this regime, staff subscribed to a substantive rational and ethical position, historically and culturally constituted by their prior lived experiences, and central to enacting this position was the allocator's activation tray.

In the manual system that operated prior to LASCAD, each of the three allocators in the control centre had an activation tray. Using an intricate system of slotted holes, coloured tags, and differently coloured forms that might face backwards or forwards, each allocator was able to maintain in his or her tray a profile of resource usage in the sector of London for which s/he was responsible. Call takers entered details of the incidents on the coloured forms, and then passed them to the allocation point; allocators updated the forms with details of the resources allocated; guided by the allocators, dispatchers used the forms to issue instructions to ambulance crews; crews radioed in their availability so that the forms could be turned backwards and then signed off at the end of each call; any of these staff might notify the allocators of exceptional circumstances (for example, police called to an incident) so that the forms could be updated. At the start of each shift, ambulance stations notified the allocators of the crews on duty in their sector so that the coloured tags could be updated. Throughout the shift, allocators listened for calls from each other for spare resources, and if a crew was temporarily reassigned, again the contents of the activation tray were updated.

Each form (or set of related forms) was intended to tell the story of an incident, and the trays were filled with and emptied of them as the incidents unfolded. Each member of the operational staff had a part to play in keeping these forms as complete and current as possible. If the network broke down, patients' lives might be at risk, but so also might the safety of the crews. The combination of attending to patient care and crew safety formed the *telos* of the operators' ethical subject, the ultimate goal of their job – to foster the health of the nation. This was not a straightforward goal because it involved conflicting concerns – as when a patient needs urgent assistance and the scene is dangerous, say, because an assailant is still present. Getting all of the relevant information from the caller, making sure it was passed through to the crew as soon as it became available, and notifying changes as they happened were vital tasks. Anxiety was always free-floating in this job, but the activation trays and the well-established routines that had developed around them acted against the fixing of it; they were key to maintaining a feeling of normality.

Nevertheless, this system had significant drawbacks. Allocators could not view details of the calls as they were being taken, so vital minutes were lost before crews could be assigned; dispatching by telephone and radio was slow because a member of the crew had to transcribe and then confirm key details relating to a call; and the exact location of crews was only known when they made contact with the control centre. On the last point, when crews were available but mobile (for example, returning to their stations to await further work), an allocator needing to assign resources to a new call had to estimate the crews' approximate locations to decide which one was nearest to the incident. These decisions were often contested between control centre staff and vehicle crews. Features of the LASCAD system, specifically online call taking, printers on ambulance stations, mobile data terminals, and aerials on vehicles aimed to address all of the above concerns.

Throughout parallel running of the LASCAD system, reliance on the activation trays endured. If anything, continuing problems with the new system, changes made to it 'on the fly', and an increased workload for staff increased attachments to the paper system. Far from resolving disputes about allocation decisions, new and more serious conflicts arose with LASCAD. In particular, the well-established system in which allocators had learnt spatially to match and collate forms when multiple calls were received for the same incident – as may happen when a road traffic accident occurs – proved more difficult to enact using the windows of a graphical user interface. As a result, there were many instances where several crews were sent to the same call, and several instances where no crew was sent. As parallel running continued, tensions heightened between control staff and vehicle crews, but while voice communications continued they vented on each other, while striving in public to adhere to their *techniques of self* in which patients' anger, stress or frustration did not prompt a response in kind.

In this situation, anxiety was no longer free-floating because members of staff were starting to find that they could no longer execute the behaviours that kept it that way. Their emotion was now focused, the perceived threat was the LASCAD system, and if those feelings intensified, fear would be the outcome. That step change occurred on 26 October. The activation trays were removed, the control room layout was reconfigured, the familiar team structures were disbanded as the system went live pan-London – a move from the parallel running mode in three sectors – and voice communications were replaced by electronic data transfer. What happened next has been documented in previous accounts (*The Guardian* 1992; *Independent* 1992; Page et al. 1993; Beynon-Davies 1995) – the breakdown of the system, the delays to patients, the allegations of at least 20 deaths, the resignation of the chief executive, and the subsequent public inquiry.

Although these accounts have little or nothing to say about emotion, they generally mention that sabotage occurred. From a critical perspective, mentioning one without the other, or even mentioning both without an attempt to constitute the emotions and rationalities involved in a substantive way of the subjects' knowledge and morality, seems at best incurious. Moreover, even bearing in mind the allegation of John Wilby – who lost his job over the incident – that 39 cases of sabotage occurred (HOCSCOH 1995), this begs the question as to how the other 2000 operational staff involved were responding.

In this situation, as in others where a group has experienced fear (for example, Weick 1993), there were a range of responses. The participants in our study stated that some cases of sabotage did occur, in which staff struck back at the threatening object – the technology – but most described the varying degrees of crippling effects and sense of helplessness they had experienced. Deprived of voice communications in an operation that historically had addressed every task with talk, these feelings were acute in some cases. Unsurprisingly, in the control room, which was both the heart of the operation and a confined space in which many were enclosed, panic spread quickly. Ironically, because managers had been so successful in blocking the ways of reverting to the paper system, staff could find no way of coping.

**Conclusions**
In summary, in this chapter we suggested that the following conceptual perspective on rationality and emotions can be drawn from Foucault's work. First, Foucault's approach does not distinguish between reason and emotions as separate capacities laden with different significance in human conduct: rationality being the superior characteristic of human existence of Cartesian philosophy, and feelings being irrational tendencies that true knowledge comes to tame. Second, in the study of knowledge and morality no reference is made to an essential human nature or psychology, no universal categories are required for such analysis, no distinction is offered between scientific true knowledge and false perceptions or ideologies; no theory of nature or society is evoked. Third, both rational and moral conduct are considered in relation to systems of power that shape perceptions of what is at issue, determine what true knowledge is, and regulate practice. Fourth, individuals are considered as subjects forming their own knowledge and ethical conduct. In other words, power is not a crude force of domination which imposes the truth of the powerful on the weak of a society or represses and manipulates instincts and emotions. Instead, the individual is constituted as a knowing, feeling and acting subject amidst the micro-power relations across the multiple domains of his or her life – as sanity, health and moral integrity.

Foucault's basic question throughout his work was to address how, why and in what forms a particular area of human practice was constituted as an object of inquiry, in relation to which the question of truth could be posed. His analyses have been concerned with the problematizations through which particular ways of being are constituted as 'problem' domains in which intervention is necessary, and with the practices – within a system of power relations – that shape the problematizations and are modified by them. He was interested in exposing the power/knowledge relationship, in which the objects of knowledge involve both rationality and emotions, and the power regimes are not only juridical, but may be disciplinary or involve personal choice.

In this chapter we suggested that this perspective provides a pertinent critical view of IS knowledge and practice, and in conclusion we can draw some critical remarks from the LASCAD case. Without denying the significance of the technical rationalities deployed for the construction of ICT artefacts and the management of organizations towards administrative and economic targets, the Foucauldian perspective leads us to look at such rationalization techniques as instruments employed in a regime of truth. The focus on the techno-managerial strategies and tactics that was taken in the discourse within the IS field that sought to explain the LASCAD failure privileged a particular rationality and ignored other logics, socio-political goals, and tactical action that on closer inspection can be seen as legitimate in the context of the events that comprise this case.

In Foucault's spirit we argue that if the social sciences (in which we include information systems) claim to study human activities, then they must take account of context in all of its aspects – historically and culturally, and in terms of rationalities and emotions. From our critical perspective, social science, as it is currently practised, is not adequately accomplishing its objective (Meyerson 2000). In general, researchers are not engaging with emotions, but nor are they curious enough to look for explanations of the failure of instrumental rationality, other than in terms of resistance to change.

As far as professional practices are concerned, we argue that there is a need to reconsider what counts as 'work'. In the ambulance services, response time targets are at the heart of determining quality of service, but constituting 'caring work' in such narrow terms has a general dehumanizing effect. How patients experience the service they receive can have as much to do with the empathy established between them and the members of the service with whom they interact, as it has to do with the number of minutes it takes the ambulance to arrive. Rewarding those who meet their response times, while ignoring or taking for granted the emotional competencies involved in caring work, impoverishes the human condition and condemns aspects of the authentic nature of human being as illegitimate.

Overall, research and practice in the IS field tends to comply with a regime of truth in which normalized professional and academic knowledge holds particular assumptions on what purposes IS innovation serves, through what strategies and tactics they are achieved, and, conversely, where we should look to account for mistakes and misconduct if the assumed rational targets are not realized. The techno-managerial regime of truth is blatantly inadequate to cope with the complexity of cases of IS projects such as LASCAD at the current time of an ongoing search for reform of the NHS, that is, while established principles of governance are questioned and no effective new ones have been adequately institutionalized. Yet, the acceptance of getting the technical and administrative efficiency as the unquestioned rational aim of an IS project is so dominant that it obscures alternative logics, and disqualifies from analytical attention the emotionally charged experiences of participants. The Foucauldian perspective reinstates not only the rationality of action that complies with subjugated knowledges and concerns, but also the emotionally charged behaviour, as constituents of subjectivity through which the course of IS innovation is realized.

## Notes

1. This kind of analysis is best presented by proponents of actor-network theory (ANT). See, for example, Callon and Law 1989; Latour 1988, 1991).
2. Writers suggest that affective phenomena include emotions, moods and dispositions (Oatley and Jenkins 1996). While some authors define these phenomena in terms of their duration or stability, intensity and target, others are less prescriptive.
3. Foucault (1984) claims that his work has been to create a history of the different modes by which human beings are transformed into subjects. He identifies three such modes: 'in relation to truth through which we constitute ourselves as subjects of knowledge [studied in *The Birth of the Clinic* and *The Order of Things*] ... in relation to a field of power through which we constitute ourselves as subjects acting on others [studied in *Discipline and Punish*] ... in relation to ethics through which we constitute ourselves as moral agents [studied in *The History of Sexuality*]' (p. 351). Our common perspective for rationality and emotions takes account of all three modes, an approach Foucault argues was present in a confused fashion in *Madness and Civilization*.

## References

Avgerou, C. (2002), *Information Systems and Global Diversity*, Oxford: Oxford University Press.

Avgerou, C., Ciborra, C. and Land, F. (eds) (2004), *Social Study of Information and Communication Technology*, Oxford: Oxford University Press.

Avgerou, C. and Madon, S. (2004) 'Framing IS studies: understanding the social context of IS innovation', in Avgerou et al. (eds), pp. 162–82.

Barley, S.R. (1986) 'Technology as an occasion for structuring: evidence from observations of CT scanners and the social order of radiology departments', *Administrative Science Quarterly*, **31** (1), 78–108.

Barrett, M. and Walsham, G. (1999), 'Electronic trading and work transformation in the London insurance market', *Information Systems Research*, **10** (1), 1–22.

Beck, U. (1992), *Risk Society: Towards a New Modernity*, London: Sage.

Beck, U. (1994), 'The reinvention of politics', in Beck, U., Giddens, A. and Lash, S. (eds), *Reflexive Modernization*, Cambridge: Polity, pp. 1–55.

Bendelow, G. and Mayall, B. (2000), 'How children manage emotion in schools', in Fineman (ed.), 2nd edn, pp. 241–54.

Beynon-Davies, P. (1995), 'Information systems "failure": the case of the London Ambulance Service's computer aided despatch project', *European Journal of Information Systems*, **4**, 171–84.

Bijker, W.E. and Law, J. (eds) (1992), *Shaping Technology/Building Society*, Cambridge, MA: MIT Press.

Brown, A. and Starkey, K. (2000), 'Organizational identity and learning: a psychodynamic perspective', *Academy of Management Review*, **25** (1), 102–20.

Callon, M. and Law, J. (1989), 'On the construction of sociotechnical networks: content and context revisited', *Knowledge and Society*, **9**, 57–83.

Ciborra, C.U. (2002), *The Labyrinths of Information: Challenging the Wisdom of Systems*, Oxford: Oxford University Press.

Ciborra, C.U. (2004), 'The mind or the heart? It depends on the (definition of) situation', New ESRC Transdisciplinary Research Seminar Series, London: London School of Economics, 2 June.

Ciborra, C.U., Braa, K., Cordella, A., Dahlbom, B., Failla, A., Hanseth, O., Hepso, V., Ljundberg, J., Monteiro, E., and Simon, K. (eds) (2000), *From Control to Drift*, Oxford: Oxford University Press.

Clegg, S.R. (1990), *Modern Organizations: Organization Studies in the Postmodern World*, London: Sage.

Department of Health (DOH) (1989), *Working for Patients*, London: HMSO.

Department of Health (DOH) (1997), *The New NHS: Modern, Dependable*, London: HMSO.

Department of Health and Social Security (DHSS) (1983), *Report of the NHS Management Inquiry*, London: HMSO.

*Financial Times* (1992), 'Bottomley was warned on ambulance software', 30 October, 22.

Fineman, S. (ed.) ([1993] 2000), *Emotion in Organizations*, London: Sage, 2nd edn 2000.

Fineman, S. (1996), 'Emotion in organizing', in Clegg, S., Hardy, C. and Nord, W. (eds), *The Handbook of Organization Studies*, Thousand Oaks, CA: Sage, pp. 543–64.

Foucault, M. (1970), *The Order of Things*, London: Routledge.

Foucault, M. (1971), *Madness and Civilization*, London: Routledge.

Foucault, M. (1972), *The Archaeology of Knowledge*, London: Routledge.

Foucault, M. (1973), *Birth of the Clinic*, London: Tavistock.

Foucault, M. (1977), *Discipline and Punish: The Birth of the Prison*, London: Penguin.

Foucault, M. (1978), *The Will to Knowledge: The History of Sexuality*, vol. 1, London: Penguin.

Foucault, M. (1984), 'On the genealogy of ethics: an overview of work in progress', in Rabinow, P. (ed.), *The Foucault Reader*, London: Penguin, pp. 340–72.

Foucault, M. (1985), *The Use of Pleasure: The History of Sexuality*, vol. 2, London: Penguin.

Foucault, M. (1986), *The Care of the Self: The History of Sexuality*, vol. 3, London: Penguin.

Giddens, A. (1990), *The Consequences of Modernity*, Cambridge: Polity.

Giddens, A. (1991), *Modernity and Self-Identity*, Cambridge: Polity.

*Guardian, The* (1992), 'Ambulance chief resigns', 29 October, 1.

Hamilton, G.G. and Biggart, N.W. (1988), 'Market, culture, and authority: a comparative analysis of management and organization in the Far East', *American Journal of Sociology*, **94**, S52–S94.

Heidegger, M. (1962), *Being and Time*, New York: Harper & Row.

Hochschild, A. (1979), 'Emotion work, feeling rules, and social structure', *American Journal of Sociology*, **85** (3), 551–75.

Hochschild, A. (1983) *The Managed Heart: Commercialization of Human Feeling*, Berkeley, CA: University of California Press.

Hougham, M. (1996), 'London Ambulance Service computer-aided despatch system', *International Journal of Project Management*, **14** (2), 103–10.

House of Commons Select Committee on Health (HOCSCOH) (1995), *Second Report on London's Ambulance Service*, London: HMSO.

Hughes, T.P. (1983), *Networks of Power: Electrification in Western Society, 1880–1930*, Baltimore, MD: Johns Hopkins University Press.

*Independent* (1992), 'Software failure may be behind ambulance crisis', 30 October, 2.

Introna, L.D. (1997), *Management, Information and Power: A Narrative of the Involved Manager*, Basingstoke: Macmillan.

Keen, P.G.W. (1981), 'Information systems and organisational change', *Communications of the ACM*, **24** (1), 24–33.

Knights, D., Noble, F. and Willmott, H. (1997), '"We should be total slaves to the business": aligning information technology and strategy – issues and evidence', in Bloomfield, B.P., Coombs, R., Knights, D. and Littler, D. (eds), *Information Technology and Organizations*, Oxford: Oxford University Press, pp. 13–35.

Latour, B. (1988), 'Mixing humans and nonhumans together: the sociology of a door-closer', *Social Problems*, **35** (3), 298–310.

Latour, B. (1991), 'Technology is society made durable', in Law (ed.), pp. 103–31.

Latour, B. (1993), *We Have Never Been Modern*, New York: Harvester Wheatsheaf.

Latour, B. (1999), *Pandora's Hope: Essays on the Reality of Science Studies*, Cambridge, MA: Harvard University Press.

Law, J. (ed.) (1991), *A Sociology of Monsters: Essays on Power, Technology and Domination*, London: Routledge.

McGrath, K. (2003), 'Organisational culture and information systems implementation: a critical perspective', PhD dissertation, London School of Economics, London, http://is.lse.ac.uk/research/theses/mcgrath.pdf.

Meyerson, D. (2000), 'If emotions were honoured: a cultural analysis', in Fineman (ed.), 2nd edn, pp. 167–83.

Monteiro, E. (2004), 'Actor network theory and cultural aspects of interpretative studies', in Avgerou et al. (eds), pp. 129–39.

Oatley, K. and Jenkins, J. (1996), *Understanding Emotions*, Cambridge, MA: Blackwell.

Orlikowski, W.J. (1996), 'Improvising organizational transformation over time: a situated change perspective', *Information Systems Research*, **7** (1), 63–92.

Orlikowski, W.J. (2000), 'Using technology and constituting structures: a practice lens for studying technology in organizations', *Organization Science*, **11** (4), 404–28.

Orlikowski, W.J., Walsham, G., Jones, M.R. and DeGross, J.I. (eds) (1996), *Information Technology and Changes in Organizational Work*, London: Chapman & Hall.

Orrù, M., Biggart, N.W. and Hamilton, G.G. (1991), 'Organizational isomorphism in East Asia', in Powell, W.W. and DiMaggio, P.J. (eds), *The New Institutionalism in Organizational Analysis*, Chicago: Chicago University Press, pp. 361–89.

Page, D., Williams, P. and Boyd, D. (1993), *Report of the Inquiry into the London Ambulance Service*, London: South West Thames Regional Health Authority.

Parsons, T. and Smelser, N.J. (1956), *Economy and Society*, New York: Free Press.

Preston, H. and Hutchison, J. (2001), 'Science or art: performance turnaround in emergency service system status planning', in Roberts, M., Moulton, M., Hand, S. and Adams, C. (eds), *Proceedings of the 6th UKAIS (United Kingdom Academy for Information Systems) Conference*, Manchester: Zeus Press, pp. 300–309.

Sauer, C. (1999), 'Deciding the future for IS failures: not the choice you might think', in Galliers, B. and Currie, W.L. (eds), *Rethinking Management Information Systems*, Oxford: Oxford University Press, pp. 279–309.

Smelser, N.J. (1978), 'Reexamining the parameters of economic activity', in Epstein, E.M. and Votaw, D. (eds), *Rationality, Legitimacy, Responsibility: Search for New Directions in Business and Society*, Santa Monica, CA: Goodyear, pp. 19–51.

Strange, S. (1988), *States and Markets*, London: Pinter.

Suchman, L. (1987), *Plans and Situated Action*, Cambridge: Cambridge University Press.

Van Maanen, J. (1991), 'The smile factory: work at Disneyland', in Frost, P., Moore, L., Louis, M., Lundberg, C. and Martin, J. (eds), *Reframing Organizational Culture*, Newbury Park, CA: Sage, pp. 58–76.

Wastell, D. (1996), 'The fetish of technique: methodology as a social defence', *Information Systems Journal*, **6**, 25–40.

Wastell, D. (1999), 'Learning dysfunctions in information systems development: overcoming the social defences with transitional objects', *MIS Quarterly*, **23** (4), 581–600.

Wastell, D. and Newman, M. (1996), 'Information systems design, stress and organisational change in the ambulance services: a tale of two cities', *Accounting, Management and Information Technologies*, **6** (4), 283–300.

Weber, M. (1947), 'Sociological categories of economic action', in Parsons, T. (ed.), *Max Weber: The Theory of Social and Economic Organization*, New York: Free Press, pp. 158–323.

Weick, K. (1993) 'The collapse of sensemaking in organizations: the Mann Gulch disaster', *Administrative Science Quarterly*, **38** (4), 628–52.

# 15 Evaluating e-governance projects in India: a focus on micro-level implementation

*Shirin Madon*

## Introduction

The reform of government administration and the provision of improved services to citizens has long been acknowledged as a major criterion for development and today's drive towards e-governance can be considered part of this wider developmental goal. The term 'e-governance' is taken to refer to a wide spectrum of applications of information technology (IT) in government described by some writers in terms of a continuum with a particular logic according to which information and communication technology (ICT) is first used for e-administration and e-services tasks and finally for e-democracy (Ranerup 1999; Heeks 2001a). This logic appears to have become something of a blueprint among international policy makers as revealed in their increased focus on e-governance activity in developing countries (DfID 2000).

The Indian experience in e-government can broadly speaking be divided into two main phases. The first from the late 1960s/early 1970s to the late 1990s, and the second from the late 1990s onwards. In the first phase, efforts to develop e-government were concentrated on the use of IT for in-house government applications with a principal focus on central government requirements such as defence, research, economic monitoring and planning, and certain data-intensive functions related to elections, conducting of national censuses, and tax administration (GOI 1985). During this first phase, the introduction of IT in the public sector did not result in the automation of many key departmental activities. In the second phase, the implementation of the national IT task force and state government IT policies symbolized a paradigm shift in e-governance policies towards using IT for a wider range of sectoral applications, reaching out to a large number of people in rural as well as urban areas with greater input of non-governmental and private sector organizations in providing services to the public (GOI 2000).

Today in India, many different types of e-governance projects are being implemented in parallel, as displayed on the website of the World Bank funded E-governance Centre located at the Indian Institute of Management, Ahmedabad in Gujarat state (Centre for Electronic Governance 2001). Some projects described on the website aim to introduce IT automation in individual government departments. Some aim to improve transparency and accountability within government by introducing electronic file handling and public grievance systems. Others specifically aim to enhance the delivery of government services through IT for a range of high-volume routine transactions such as the payment of bills and tax dues to government. E-governance initiatives are also being introduced under the label 'telecentres' which are normally owned by local entrepreneurs and offer a range of government services and serve as a hub for local entrepreneurial activity.

Approaches and frameworks used to evaluate e-governance projects have, in general, been supply focused in terms of measuring the deployment of infrastructure, the number of applications and the commitment of resources. For example, both the Accenture eGovernment and the eEurope eGovernment benchmarking approaches place greater attention on the supply of e-government applications in terms of the percentage of basic public services available online (Accenture 2002). Moreover, these frameworks focus exclusively on evaluating front-end e-services applications, neglecting back-end administrative reform, changes in the nature of governance, and real benefits in terms of improvements in the social well-being of citizens. Janssen (2003) and other writers argue that a benchmarking of process as learning exercises might be more valuable than benchmarking of results.

In the context of developing countries, e-governance evaluation has tended to emulate this focus on supply-side benefits of ICT infrastructure based on the assumption that enormous benefits will flow from these activities (Heeks 2001a; Unnithan 2002). For example, Heeks (2001a,b) draws on 'network readiness' criteria originally formulated at the Harvard Centre for International Development to serve as a framework for the assessment of a country's stage of development (Kirkman et al. 2002). Heeks bases his framework for assessing the value of e-governance projects in developing countries in terms of rankings of their access and usage in different sectors.

The government of India's composite index for evaluating e-governance activities in different states of the country (GOI 2003), which is based on the Harvard e-Readiness criteria, contains the following indicators:

- special efforts made to promote e-governance in particular sectors;
- online facilities made available to the public;
- government network coverage;
- computerization of records;

- development of skills among government employees;
- re-engineering of government processes.

A small group of telecentre evaluation studies from the International Development Research Centre (IDRC) have considered the extent to which projects actually benefit the community (Harris 1999; Hudson 1999). But the vast majority of evaluation frameworks continue to be based on supply-side criteria and fail to understand how end-users and beneficiaries place value on the e-governance project and how this value changes over time. A more focused evaluation approach is therefore suggested to ensure that these investments result in improvements in administrative effectiveness and in service delivery to citizens. Many government services need to be re-engineered to benefit from IT-enabled services. There is also an inherent distrust among citizens of the service delivery mechanisms which needs to be improved with confidence-building measures (Rama Rao 2003).

In this chapter, we argue that consideration of supply-side needs should be complemented with other kinds of analyses related to understanding the process and value of e-governance projects. The main argument put forward is that value in terms of development priorities can only be assessed through an in-depth understanding of the process of information systems (IS) implementation. In the next two sections, we review critical research issues related to the evaluation exercise and which underlie the concepts of governance and development. Following the presentation of our conceptual framework and methodology, we then present our case study of e-governance activity in the south Indian state of Kerala. Finally, we draw on our conceptual framework to evaluate Kerala's e-governance activity and propose some theoretical implications.

**Drawing insights from evaluation literature**

*Evaluation research*
The development and expansion of evaluation theory and practice is at the core of several different disciplines, and this body of knowledge has evolved a number of forms. While earlier evaluation studies, mainly in education, focused on the measurement of students' abilities with little questioning of the objectives of school curricula, Ralph Tyler in the 1950s insisted that an important component of evaluation should be the stated objectives of change programmes which should serve as criteria for the evaluation exercise. Consequently, a variety of new evaluation models were proposed, taking predefined objectives as the main evaluator (Tyler 1950). Subsequently, the work of Scrivens represented a radical departure in evaluation research by introducing the concept of 'goal-free' evaluation.

According to Scrivens (1973, 1974), the focus of evaluation should be on the effects or outcome of the programme rather than whether these were intended. However, the model failed to come to grips with the question of what effects to look at, and what should be assessed. This eventually led Scrivens to admit that goal-free evaluation was best used as a supplement to goal-based evaluation.

Guba and Lincoln's (1989) 'responsive evaluation' was developed as an emergent form of evaluation that built on many of these ideas. Rather than a distant activity that was conducted without addressing the concerns and issues of different stakeholder audiences, these writers and other evaluation scholars argued that the criteria for evaluation could be found only through an ongoing process of discussions with local stakeholders affected by the initiative (Stake 1975; Guba and Lincoln 1981; Legge 1984). The work of evaluation scholars referred to above was important in an era marked by public sector interventions, particularly in education in Europe and North America. The main message from this body of work was that evaluation criteria should come 'from the field', meaning that it should reflect felt needs and priorities of users of the project rather than predefined objective criteria. The 1980s saw the adoption of modern management techniques, including information systems to support 'best practices' in organizations in both the public and private sectors and IS evaluation was increasingly perceived as a crucial activity for measuring organizational performance.

*Information systems evaluation*
Much research has been conducted in the IT/IS evaluation area over the years. Smithson and Hirschheim (1998) provide a useful review of IS evaluation literature in which they identify a continuum from highly rational/objective to subjective/political. They found that in the majority of cases, IS evaluation tends to be typically perceived as a rational process that performs an objective assessment. A growing number of scholars have been arguing for greater attention to be placed on the evaluation of social costs and benefits of IT investment. For example, Land (2000) argues for the need to overcome weaknesses of traditional evaluation methods by valuing social changes such as organizational learning, user satisfaction and improvements in the quality of working life. Other writers have recognized that evaluation of IT investment is a complex and subjective activity and have presented useful frameworks that combine contextual and processual elements (Farbey et al., 1993; Smithson and Hirschheim 1998).

Approaches which focus on value as the prime driver of an IS evaluation exercise are increasingly found in the literature. According to these approaches, value can only be ascertained through an in-depth understanding of the process of information system implementation. One such approach is the 'value scorecard' evaluation technique developed by Remenyi (2002). These writers argue that any evaluation exercise must necessarily reach a common understanding between stakeholders of what changes are needed to meet overall objectives. The value of the system is then assessed, based on the degree to which these changes have taken place. The concept of IS actability developed by Agerfalk et al. (2002) encourages a more situational evaluation whereby an attempt is made to ascertain the value of an information system in its real use context. This approach takes as its point of departure the social actions performed by the use of information systems. The idea, similar to that developed by evaluation researchers, was that the criteria for evaluation would emerge from the field except now the focus is on system usage.

During the 1970s, the development in many social sciences of perspectives such as phenomenology, hermeneutics and interpretive approaches has influenced the growing body of constructivist IS evaluation research. The focus came to be on social processes and the idea that all IS initiatives were constituted in a complex process of understanding and interaction. Wilson and Howcroft (2000) argue that IS evaluation has many political and social aspects, and advocate a social shaping approach according to which great importance is placed on the identification of relevant social groups which may differ in their social and political interests and their motivation for wanting or not wanting to use the information system. These groups shape the success/failure process through their engagement in the evaluation process. The issue of power in IS evaluation is also dealt with more directly by other writers (Introna and Whittaker 2002; Cordoba and Robson, 2003), who argue that the task of evaluation is as much a political as an understanding process. According to Introna and Whittaker, evaluation does not presume prior thought in the way that motion presumes the existence of some prior force. Instead, they perceive evaluation as an ongoing conversation without a specific start and end, reflecting a unity of cognition and action. This conversation is immersed in the organization which exists in the world and which is constituted and reconstituted through the power asymmetries upon which it depends for its functioning.

An alternative to traditional IS evaluation approaches has recently been discussed by some writers, based on the philosophy of critical realism which has become an important perspective in modern philosophy and social science (for example, Bhaskar 1978, 1989, 1998). Already influencing a number of social sciences fields such as organizational studies and evaluation research, critical realist writers have begun to identify its value in IS research and evaluation (Mutch 2002; Carlsson 2003). These writers argue that a major problem with IS evaluation approaches is their inability to grasp underlying structural and institutional mechanisms of society, including sets of ideas, which are in some respects independent of the reasoning and desires of stakeholders, but which none the less affect the IS initiative and the negotiation process.

In this section, we have reviewed criteria that have been identified as important in the literature on evaluation research and IS evaluation. These criteria relate to process and value in the following way. First, the decision regarding what to evaluate should primarily draw on the formal objectives of the project. Second, project evaluation should be perceived as a process which is inextricably linked with organizational/institutional reform. This has been described in the literature as a subtle, incremental process of organizational learning rather than through legislation. Third, while the formal objectives of a project need to be understood as a starting point for evaluation, the relevance of these objectives need to be 'validated' through a careful study of the felt needs of direct and indirect end users who are actually engaged in the implementation of the project. Here, project evaluation should aim to uncover the underlying mechanisms and structures within society that direct project outcome. Finally, evaluation should include an assessment of the effects or outcomes of the project on the end-users and beneficiary community. Table 15.1 summarizes relevant criteria for a project evaluation from the literature reviewed above, indicating the origin of each component and the reference.

*Table 15.1   Performance criteria suggested in evaluation literature*

| Origin of each component | Reference |
| --- | --- |
| Formal objectives of project | Tyler (1950) |
| Organizational/institutional reform | Smithson and Hirschheim (1998); Land (2000) |
| Felt needs and priorities of users of the project 'from the field' | Stake (1975); Bhaskar (1978, 1989, 1998); Guba and Lincoln (1981, 1989); Legge (1984); Land (2000); Remenyi (2002) |
| Effects or outcome of project | Scrivens (1974); Land (2000); Remenyi (2002) |

In the next section we try to understand critical issues which underlie the concepts of governance and development. To be able to evaluate an e-governance project in terms of the extent to which institutional change has occurred, we need to understand the nature of governance activity and its constituent elements. To be able to evaluate an e-governance project in terms of its impact on development, we need to be specific about how we perceive development and improvements in social well-being.

## Governance and development

### *Understanding governance activity*

Reforming public services is a central task for all governments and the concept of 'public value' offers a useful way of setting out the ultimate goals of public service reform (Jackson 2001). Public value provides a broader measure than is conventionally used within the new public management literature, which often emphasized narrow concepts of cost efficiency and administrative efficiency over other considerations which are difficult to measure such as equity, trust and accountability. Public value refers to the value created by government, and in a democracy this value is assumed to be ultimately defined by the public themselves. As a general rule, the key things that citizens value tend to fall under the three categories of services, outcomes and trust (Jackson 2001; Kooiman 2003; Kjaer 2004). First, citizens derive benefits from the personal use of public services that are very similar to the benefits derived from consuming services purchased from the private sector. User satisfaction is considered critical for measuring services, and from past experience it is likely to be shaped by how people are treated by staff, and by the amount of information that is available about the service (Kooiman 2003). Second, the public has always seen outcomes as a core part of the contract with government. Outcomes often overlap with services since, for example, the service provided by a health centre is linked to the outcome of a healthier population. However, outcomes and services are clearly distinct and need to be managed differently as there is a value in a healthy population beyond the performance of health centres. Yet most governments have increasingly sought to focus attention on outcomes in the form of targets. The third main source of public value relates to issues of trust, legitimacy and confidence. Trust is at the heart of the relationship between citizens and government and even if formal service and outcome targets are met, a failure of trust will destroy public value. Each of the three elements described above of service quality, outcomes and trust are interrelated sources which contribute to overall public value. For example, success in the delivery of an outcome could increase trust in government and satisfaction with services.

Kelly and Muers (2003) argue that while many elements of public value are addressed in government performance evaluation exercises such as service outputs and financial costs to citizens and government, many other significant components such as public involvement, satisfaction and trust in government are often absent from formal appraisal processes yet have a significant bearing on eventual outcome. This leads us to support the notion that e-governance activity and evaluation could usefully be thought of as a continuum ranging from applications related to back-end administrative processes to applications aimed at improvements in government/citizen interaction (Ranerup 1999; Heeks 2001a). In this chapter, we suggest that adopting a public value perspective offers a broader yardstick against which to gauge the performance of government interventions such as e-governance projects.

Table 15.2 draws on the literature on governance activity reviewed above to expand on institutional reform in terms of administrative reform and governance reform.

*Table 15.2    Performance criteria suggested in evaluation and governance literature*

| Origin of each component | Reference |
|---|---|
| Formal objectives of project | Tyler (1950) |
| *Administrative reform*: efficiency, coordination, management | Ranerup (1999); Heeks (2001a, 2001b); Kooiman (2003) |
| *Governance reform*: public value | Jackson (2001); Kooiman (2003); Kelly and Muers (2003); Kjaer (2004) |
| Felt needs and priorities of users of the project 'from the field' | Stake (1975); Bhaskar (1978, 1989, 1998); Guba and Lincoln (1981); Legge (1984); Land (2000); Remenyi (2002) |
| Effects or outcome of project | Scrivens (1973); Land (2000); Remenyi (2002) |

*Understanding development*
Social assessment methods using public participation have recently found their way into World Bank procedures, and a significant body of literature has arisen in development studies which addresses the problem of how best to evaluate development interventions by listening to the voice of the people. The difficulty is that participatory techniques that have been used have focused on a limited range of interpretations of social well-being (Chambers 1995). But apart from this, a more serious issue is that there is no systematic methodology for obtaining information on indirect effects of projects and externalities which may influence any positive effects of the intervention.

Sen's notion of capabilities tries to resolve this by moving away from evaluation in terms of resources and utilities to what he calls 'the space of capabilities'. Sen argued that what we should evaluate is not only primary goods, nor mental states such as happiness or trust and confidence in government, but also what he calls 'functionings' – the various things a person may value doing or being. The functionings relevant for well-being vary from elementary ones such as escaping morbidity, being adequately nourished, being mobile, to complicated ones such as achieving self-respect or taking part in the life of the community. Sen argues that any evaluation of impact has to assess the 'capabilities' or extent to which these desired states of being or doing (functionings) are achievable which in turn depends on the institutions within which individuals operate. Capabilities, then, become important criteria for evaluation, as they reflect the real opportunities which exist to achieve desired functionings (Sen 1999; Chopra and Duraiappah 2001). Much of what Sen says may appear very theoretical and abstract, but it is important to stress that ultimately he is concerned with pragmatic questions of policy assessment which he tries to achieve by deciding on the 'value space' within which our assessments are to be made (Alkire 2002).

The conceptual basis for assessing impacts using the capabilities approach is an objective, normative one, influenced by the work of critical realist writers. Sen argues that the values which matter are not infinitely diverse but can be reduced across cultures into a most basic set of ideas or rationales, and used in assessing the value of a development intervention such as e-governance. The goal is for participants to identify all valued benefits/disbenefits by engaging with the chains of practical reasoning that they already use – that is, their own reasons for doing things (ibid.). Participants would then attempt to rank the wide set of impacts from strongest to weakest. This identification of a basic set of values has been followed by other development theorists, notably Nussbaum (1992) and Max-Neef (1993). The argument made by these writers is that in any given society, at a given period, it is possible to arrive at an objective assessment of needs.

The discussion of whether Sen's approach constitutes an all-encompassing theory of human choice and freedom, and whether it is ever possible to identify a universal set of basic functionings is indeed part of a lively current debate in development studies (Apthorne 1997; Gasper 2001; Corbridge 2002). But for our purposes, we find that the notion of capabilities is useful for evaluating of the eventual developmental outcome of e-governance activity since it enables us to focus on the real availability of opportunity and the real achievement of functionings rather than needs. Indeed, the impetus to work with selected elements of Sen's work has been spurred by recent writers who have tried to apply the capabilities approach for the study of ICT access in society, raising the important question of whether new options, such as being able to hold government accountable, should be added to the capability set of individuals, communities, organizations and states (Garnham 2000; Mansell 2001). We therefore use the concept of 'capabilities' to understand the effects or outcome of e-governance projects.

**Research methodology**
A longitudinal research design was selected in order to trace the micro-level dynamics of e-governance activity in the south Indian state of Kerala. Our interest in Kerala derives from its unique social indices and history of political mobilization. Since 2001, the author has been involved in studying how ICT is being used to improve the delivery of services to citizens in urban areas and to promote socio-economic development within one pilot district in northern Kerala, called Mallepuram (Madon and Kiran 2002; Madon 2003).

Fieldwork has been organized at roughly six-month intervals over the past 15 months. During the course of the research, a total of 75 interviews were conducted with government officials, politicians, non-government organizations, private sector employees and various citizens. A number of these were repeat interviews – that is, the same person was met more than once at different points in time. For the interviews, we did not have a fixed schedule of questions, but a set of issues that we felt were important, drawn from our literature review on evaluation research, governance and development. We encouraged the respondents to comment on these issues as they related to their experiences, to identify new issues, and to describe how they were dealing with them. Over time, as we met people for the second and third time, there already existed a shared understanding between us and we could start the conversation where we had left off at the previous meeting. All the interviews were conducted in face-to-face settings in the location of the interviewees' workplace. The duration of the interviews ranged from a few minutes to an hour, and we were invariably interrupted by phone calls and by the entry and exit of various other people coming into the office to meet the same person that we were interviewing. None of the interviews was tape-recorded. Although data collection was done mainly through semi-structured interviewing, additional data was obtained through participant observation, attendance at public meetings, study of press reports, study of websites and various other sources.

The starting point of our analysis was to understand at the micro level the implementation of various e-governance initiatives in Kerala by obtaining information about elements related to process and value. While acknowledging the formal objectives of the project, our analysis concentrates on three main performance criteria which have hitherto been neglected in the evaluation studies of e-governance projects in developing countries. First, we focus on processes of administrative reform and the degree to which e-governance implementation has been able to trigger more substantial back-end reform in terms of efficiency, coordination and management. Second, we consider an important criteria for evaluation to be the processes of governance reform describing the interaction between the implementation of e-governance initiatives and the building of trust relations amongst government employees and between government and citizens. Third, we place importance in the evaluation exercise on the effects or outcomes of the project. Here, following Sen's ideas, we value the project in terms of improvements in 'instrumental' as well as 'substantive' gains in social well-being. Following Sen's capabilities approach, this necessitates an understanding of the felt needs and priorities of users.

Our analysis proceeded using an interpretive approach (Walsham 1995; Yin 2002) starting from field notes being created by the researcher of the interviews and the identification of key themes drawn from the conceptual framework. Table 15.3 presents this framework, which will guide the analysis of our empirical data.

*Table 15.3   Framework for evaluation*

| Origin of each component | Reference |
| --- | --- |
| *Administrative reform*: efficiency, coordination, management | Ranerup (1999); Heeks (2001a, 2001b); Kooiman (2003) |
| *Governance reform*: public value | Jackson (2001); Kelly and Muers (2003); Kooiman (2003); Kjaer (2004) |
| *Effects or outcome of project*: capabilities | Sen (1999); Alkire (2002) |

**E-governance activity in Kerala: a focus on micro-level implementation**

Kerala is a socially advanced state in India, and some important studies have highlighted certain key development achievements of this state since the 1970s, especially in health and education (Ramachandran 2000). Of interest to scholars of development was the paradox that a third-world region such as Kerala could achieve high indices for human development of its people in spite of sharing almost all the other signs of underdevelopment, particularly in terms of low rates of industrial development and employment. But by the mid-1970s, there were already signs of vulnerability in the state, with stagnation of agriculture and industrial sectors of the economy slowing down the rate of growth in employment and income generation in the state.

All this has threatened the sustenance of achievements made in human development indices.

There has been increased expectation in Kerala that ICT could act as an enabler of the region's economic development and as a growth engine to provide solutions to some of its most important problems such as high unemployment and low income-generating capacity (Subrahmanian and Abdul 2000). Kerala has already developed a sound telecommunications infrastructure in terms of fully digital telephone exchanges and high telephone density, and this strategy has permitted high-speed international communication between non-resident Keralites and their relatives within the state, although the penetration of ICT within Kerala in the absence of state intervention has remained confined to a few selected sections of the society (KSITM 2002). Kerala has also placed greater emphasis on its comparative advantage in terms of human resources, especially on developing knowledge-based and service industries in order to accelerate the growth of income and employment.

The state is showing interest in becoming a major player in the use of ICT in various sectors of the economy. In 1999, the state government set up the Information Technology Mission Group to selectively induct IT in sectors of the economy and departments where there could be immediate and tangible benefits to the citizen. In order to achieve results, it was recognized that substantial changes were required in administrative processes and procedures. Following the devolution of powers to local government initiated in the late 1990s, the Kerala government became committed to the task of procedural simplification and administrative reform, with backing from the Asian Development Bank under its modernizing government programme (ADB 2001). Thirty-four departments were identified in which substantial administrative reforms would have to be introduced first, as a precursor to IT implementation. For instance, the Administrative Reforms Committee of the government found that a single file would have to be handled by as many as 60 people before a decision was taken on it. Simple automation of existing processes was therefore not deemed to be an effective solution and it was recognized that what was needed was a complete overhaul of administrative procedures and information flows. The state government therefore decided to adopt a two-pronged strategy – a long-term strategy to reform the administration and a medium-term strategy involving high visibility people-oriented projects.

*Long-term strategy: Information Kerala Mission (IKM)*
The long-term strategy has been attempted through the IKM project, launched in 1999 and introduced alongside the devolution of local government under the Panchayati Raj legislation. The IKM aimed to

introduce modern management practices and an improved information system in the 100 gram panchayats (village councils) in the state. The systems which prevailed in these local bodies had not been updated since 1967 and the IKM project took approximately one year to produce a comprehensive seven-volume critical evaluation of how systems could be improved in terms of the information flows, work processes and financial transactions of gram panchayats. The document was accepted by the government and formed the basis for the development of an information system for the handling of public services in the gram panchayats. A training programme was introduced for various categories of panchayat officers, from political leaders to bureaucrats, covering various topics such as the digital divide, public service delivery, and contextual issues regarding IS implementation. The IKM pilot system is currently running in Vellanad district before being rolled out to other districts.

*Medium-term strategy: FRIENDS*

The medium-term strategy of the Kerala state government focused on introducing high-visibility 'people-oriented' projects such as FRIENDS – an acronym for fast, reliable, instant, effective network for disbursement of services – which was launched in June 2000 on a pilot basis by the state IT department, and rolled out to all 14 districts by 2001. The basic idea of FRIENDS was taken from the popular e-Seva project in Andhra Pradesh which provides a single-window, IT-enabled counter to citizens for the payment of bills, rather than having to personally visit individual department payment counters located in different parts of the city. FRIENDS centres are open from 9am to 7pm seven days a week, and offer a modern, clean environment facilitated by a computerized queue management system for citizens in their interaction with government. Capital expenditure for equipment for each centre is incurred by the government, and the salaries for the personnel required for operating the counters (service officers) are provided by the eight currently participating government departments. Each centre incurs recurring expenses such as maintenance charges for ICT equipment, and bills for rent, electricity, stationery and salaries to Kudumbasree employees (below-poverty-line women employed as casual labourers in the FRIENDS centres). At present, the average monthly expenditure per centre comes to about Rs. 65000 (approx. £870) while the only revenue is from the collection of telephone bills amounting to a monthly average of only Rs. 12000 (approx. £185). While more income could be generated through advertising, the strategy of the state government so far has been to let the FRIENDS system become fully accepted by citizens before using the centres as point of purchase advertisement spots.

At present, about 1000 different types of bills are paid by citizens on production of a demand notice from the utility company, and many new services are being planned such as the issuing of licences for electrical installations, passenger reservations for railways, long-distance road transport tickets and other services (Madon 2003). Bills can be settled by cash or draft and service officers issue a receipt to each customer as legitimate evidence of payment. Queries generated by citizens are being dealt with by service officers from the department concerned liaising by phone with the department office. The current mechanism for updating departmental registers is via floppy disk being sent by the Kudumbasree women employees to each of the seven departments, printed out and then pasted onto departmental registers. Some departments are now introducing plans to automate their records and many departments are beginning to experiment with online data transfer from FRIENDS to the department. Remittance of money from citizen payments to individual departments is normally swiftly executed, via the district treasuries, although at times the state government has issued a 'treasury ban', causing a delay in transferring money from the treasury to individual departments.

The active participation and enthusiasm of service officers in the FRIENDS project has been critical for the success of the project. Initially, ten junior-level officers from each of the participating departments were recruited and given the common designation of service officer irrespective of their position in their parent department (from which they continued to draw their salary). The selected personnel, all of whom had no previous exposure to computers, underwent a one-week training on computer awareness and usage to deal with the transactions of all departments, and on personality development and public relations. It is interesting to note that the majority of service officers joined FRIENDS voluntarily, attracted by the enhanced office environment, although some officers have recently asked for extra remuneration for providing a daily payment facility to citizens. Many centres have started opening side activities such as running a canteen, thereby generating extra revenue for the Kudumbasree employees. The majority of these female casual employees reported an overall improvement in their working environment at FRIENDS compared with individual government departments.

Despite the alleged success of the FRIENDS initiative, the fact remains that the overall penetration of ICTs within the state is highly limited. Madon and Kiran's study (2002) revealed that public support for the FRIENDS centres has been overwhelming only among Kerala's middle-class population (the highest-income bracket did not pay bills themselves while the lowest-income bracket had too few payments to warrant making a trip to the district FRIENDS centre). In total, about one-third of targeted customers made use of the FRIENDS service and just under a half of them had not even heard about the facility (ibid.). In order to bridge this digital divide, the state government introduced an e-governance initiative called Akshaya in October 2002.

### Medium-term strategy: Akshaya

Akshaya has established multipurpose community technology centres in rural Kerala using a business model involving investment of approximately 1.5 lakhs Rs. (approx. £2300) from local entrepreneurs in any particular village. At the start of 2005, about 555 centres have been set up in the pilot district of Malappuram in north Kerala, chosen precisely because it is the most socially backward district in the state. Each centre is now equipped with between five and ten machines, which were purchased by entrepreneurs in negotiation with local vendors. In December 2002, of some 1000 entrepreneurs who showed interest in the programme, 555 were selected in consultation with gram panchayats to start centres. Panchayat coordinators were identified by the gram panchayat to mediate between each entrepreneur and the panchayat. The fixing of locations for the 555 centres was based on coverage of households, with each centre serving about 1000 households. An Akshaya centre was within easy access (2 km. distance) of every household, following the earlier Kerala model of development for locating hospitals, schools and public distribution outlets. Following some initial bank delays, the entrepreneurs were able to acquire loans to start their centres.

The first phase of Akshaya aimed to impart basic functional ICT literacy to 1000 families over three months. About 2500 trainers were trained by the government for this purpose and so far about 80 per cent of the population of Malappuram, mainly within the 15–65 year age group, has been covered. In lieu of this, entrepreneurs received Rs. 140 (approx. £2) for each person trained from the government, resulting in entrepreneurs recovering 30 per cent of their initial investment within three months of the start of the initiative. The second phase of Akshaya is now under way, with connectivity established in all centres. In this phase, the emphasis is on providing more training, content and utilities. Further training has been requested by the public on spoken English, accounting, and secretarial work, and will be offered on a payment basis of Rs. 20 (approx. 30p) per session.

Despite its initial thrust on training, Akshaya is not perceived by the government as an ICT-literacy programme. Rather, ICT is considered to be only the premise for promoting socio-economic development in the state. The centres are gradually being perceived as hubs for ICT-enabled agricultural, health and education literacy, offering help to citizens in filling out forms and making applications to government for assistance under social welfare schemes. Technical committees have been established in key sector areas in order to generate ideas for relevant content, and about 128 proposals have been received from local content providers with ideas for developing relevant content. Initially, the state government will pay 50 per cent of the cost of content creation in three to four key sectors. Thereafter, content development will become commercially owned by the providers, who will ask for subscriptions from each Akshaya centre. In this second phase of Akshaya, the telecentres are gradually becoming connected to the FRIENDS centre at district level. With access to the FRIENDS database at district level, each Akshaya entrepreneur will offer a service to local citizens of collecting payments for bills up to a certain amount of credit agreed with the local bank, and then depositing that amount into the bank.

**Evaluating Kerala's e-governance activity**
In this section, we evaluate Kerala's e-governance activity, drawing on our three analytical elements of administrative reform, governance reform and effects or outcome of the project on end-users.

*Administrative reform*
Our starting point for the evaluation of e-governance activity in Kerala is to consider the reform of government administration as essential for the promotion of socio-economic development within the country. In the case study we have presented, it is clear that the interaction between the long- and medium-term strategies of government can only be studied at the micro level through the implementation of the FRIENDS, IKM and Akshaya projects over time. Despite the alleged success of FRIENDS in terms of its popularity among citizens, without comprehensive back-end computerization, FRIENDS cannot really become a fully-fledged IT delivery mechanism. At the same time, it shows that a critical mass of front-end e-governance applications could be viewed as a first step to more substantial administrative reform. For example, since the FRIENDS centres have been in operation, many government departments have begun to computerize their records, and two departments are offering online file transfer facilities to the centre. The strategy adopted in Kerala can be contrasted with that in Andhra Pradesh, where significant back-end institutional changes were brought about in terms of networking the administration and file transfer to the district level, but this has not been accompanied by a critical mass of front-end applications as with FRIENDS.

Apart from back-end computerization, a second key point relating to administrative reform processes relates to fundamental changes in devolution of power brought about in parallel with the onset of e-governance activity in the state. IKM was introduced at the same time as the restructuring of the Panchayati Raj system of democratic political decentralization in Kerala. While legislative measures for decentralization were taken in other states of the country, only the gram panchayats in Kerala were entrusted with financial resources. The IKM system, launched under the aegis of the Panchayat Raj department, was introduced to collect data on financial transactions of the local village bodies, and came to be perceived as a natural progression of earlier restructuring rather than as an e-governance intervention that aimed to delegate power to local administrative bodies.

A third key point related to administrative reform in Kerala concerns the management of e-governance activity, in particular the will to integrate the functioning of individual departments. Initially, many departments had wanted to start computerized counters of their own rather than subscribe to FRIENDS. While this would have promoted increased efficiency and computerization within individual departments, such systems would not have provided citizens with an integrated service for the payment of bills. While the management of many IT-enabled payment and utilities centres in India and elsewhere is outsourced to private companies, FRIENDS continues to be managed by the government. Each FRIENDS centre is managed by a project officer and a team of service officers, belonging to different parent government departments but none the less providing a seamless government interface to citizens. This strategy was influenced by the thrust towards integration and improved management practices within government by the chief minister of the state. IT has undoubtedly been a major catalyst in improved coordination between departments, and the FRIENDS centres have promoted the desire for organizational learning within government departments. For example, a log has been created of frequently asked questions from citizens about different department schemes and benefits and responses from service officers. From early 2005, apart from payment centres, the FRIENDS centres will begin to function as call centres for dealing with telephone inquiries about any issues dealt with by government departments.

Evaluation of FRIENDS from an administrative reform point of view also needs to take into consideration the handling of human resources. FRIENDS has resulted in a major cultural change within government, with the breaking down of hierarchy within administration. The selection of officers for the FRIENDS project was made specifically from a younger generation of employees to facilitate the combining of varying designations of officers from their parent department to one uniform ranking of service officer. This was a major experiment in government and one of the main elements for the smooth functioning of the centres. But the handling of human resources in the future will be critical, with one key question now being how to maintain employee levels of commitment to the service they are offering citizens.

A final issue relating to administrative reform concerns the need to identify an appropriate organizational form for Akshaya as it evolves from a pilot project in one district to a state-wide implementation. The project has been managed so far by the IT Mission taking the lead by holding intensive workshops for entrepreneurs and panchayat officers, monitoring the 555 centres and trouble-shooting in the villages. As the project is rolled out to other districts in the state, there is need for a professional group to manage the centres.

*Governance reform*

A starting point for evaluating e-governance projects should be the issue of governance itself. If we understand governance as a process by which institutions, organizations and citizens 'guide' themselves (UNDEPA 2002), we need to identify critical elements which have influenced this process though our micro-level study of e-governance in Kerala.

One overriding factor relating to governance has been the element of trust among different actors involved in e-governance activities within the state of Kerala – namely, government, citizens, participating departments, Kudumbasree employees, entrepreneurs, banks and local politicians. The FRIENDS project has been able to demonstrate to the common citizen that with appropriate training and skill enhancement, the very same government officers who once may have been considered arrogant and customer unfriendly, could be turned to play the exact opposite role. The role of the government in Akshaya has been instrumental in providing legitimacy to the project. For example, historically there has been a great distrust of the private sector and capitalist exploitation in the state. But with Akshaya, the perception of entrepreneurs has been that their investment is 'safe' and that any risk they undertake is underwritten by government. The perception of citizens in the first phase of Akshaya has been that the centres offer a safe environment for training since they are 'government endorsed'. The majority of trainees have been women for whom these centres have offered the possibility of leaving the house and engaging in a learning activity for the first time. In general, Keralites are suspicious of the private sector in Kerala, and even though the Akshaya centres are owned and managed by private entrepreneurs, the government banner has been important in instilling trust and legitimacy into the project.

The continued role of the state in e-governance projects in Kerala will be crucial, although the nature and extent of involvement may change. In the future, the FRIENDS and Akshaya centres may well generate their own revenue, with several models currently being discussed. For example, sustainability of the FRIENDS centres depends on the possibilities of self-support. The authorities are now thinking of adding more services, including those from the private sector, with a view to generating a healthy revenue stream for each centre. Here the question of whether the public should be asked for the first time in history to pay for government information is currently being discussed, and will become even more relevant when the Akshaya centres begin to offer content and services. Once again, while the role of government may lessen in terms of providing financial resources, the government's brand name will continue to remain important in sustaining citizen trust in the venture.

The issue of trust is not only important between citizens, entrepreneurs and the government – it is equally crucial with panchayat members. An example is the kind of damage that can be caused due to lack of communication between different actors in the smooth running of a project such as Akshaya. There was an initial delay of a few months when the IT Mission team tried to obtain bank loans for local entrepreneurs. However, the reasons for the delay were not communicated back to local panchayat members, resulting in a serious breakdown of relations and trust between the panchayat members and the IT Mission team, which eventually had to be restored by the Malappuram District Collector.

Related to the issue of trust among actors is the confidence that has been engendered among citizens regarding IT applications and their benefits. The FRIENDS case reveals that public opinion is a matter of great importance for e-governance projects. Success of the projects depends to a great extent on the opinion and perception of the people who are the beneficiaries of such projects. Over 80 per cent of customers in the FRIENDS study feel that IT could act as an efficient tool for providing better citizen services. Such a perception is having a major impact on the future of e-governance in the state with Akshaya. This confidence is not unique to citizens. The fact that participating departments see FRIENDS as positive despite a lessening of their authority, signals that employees are confident that the single-window concept of FRIENDS is better equipped than their own offices to provide improved services to citizens.

*Effects or outcome of the project*
An important but neglected aspect of e-governance evaluation is the way in which the project has improved the well-being of citizens. Typically, this criterion has been difficult to study because of the ambiguous meaning behind 'well-being'. We evaluate well-being in terms of Sen's capability concept – that is, the extent to which people have real opportunities to benefit from the project. FRIENDS has been successful in providing citizens in Kerala with a real opportunity or 'capability' to pay their bills in a clean,

safe and efficient manner compared to earlier systems of bill payments. FRIENDS has also been successful in creating employment opportunities for below-poverty-line women's groups. An important positive implication of this has been the real opportunity provided to these women to associate with government systems and develop a high degree of networking with employees in government.

With telecentre projects like Akshaya, it is important not to get carried away by images of elderly fishermen or members of the tribal community using computers. Our interest lies in the difference these centres have made to their well-being. For many citizens, the training sessions have given them a new lease of life and diversion from normal routine. For example, as many as 40 per cent of trainees requested that Akshaya hosts further training in IT and non-IT subjects such as computing, spoken English, basic accounting, garment-making and other topics. Nearly all of the trainees interviewed were sorry to have reached the last module of their course. In particular, a major outcome of the Akshaya project has been the confidence and self-esteem that many women have felt for having ventured out from their homes to complete a computer training course.

The role of relevant content in the next phase of Akshaya will be important for influencing the capability set of individuals and groups by disseminating information on various dimensions of socio-economic development such as health, education, agriculture, and small industrial activities. But at the same time, the provision of content is influenced by the vagaries of demand and supply. In Kerala, the high population density ensures a regular stream of activity. In other telecentre project locations, this may not be the case. A typical rural setting would result in local content providers finding little demand for their products and as a result not finding it worthwhile to create content for a handful of users. In such a case, local users would not come to the telecentre if there was no content that was perceived to be relevant. Therefore a critical mass of both users and telecentres is vital for local content to improve the well-being of people.

While the realization of many important activities has been achieved through Akshaya, an important question that remains is the extent to which this 'development' can be sustained using the existing social structures. The gram panchayats are the bastions of social structure in the state and have been consulted every step of the way during the implementation of Akshaya. It is imperative that strong relations of trust are maintained between the panchayats, the entrepreneurs and the citizens.

**Some reflections on evaluation as an ongoing activity**
The aim of this chapter is to go beyond existing frameworks for evaluation of e-governance initiatives in developing countries. These frameworks had

assumed that the evaluation activity was an end in itself quite distinct from implementation. Evaluation criteria were typically based on formal targets of achievement in terms of the extent of infrastructure coverage, the number of applications implemented within government and the number of services offered to citizens. While acknowledging that costs and infrastructure are important factors to take into account when evaluating a project, it has been argued in this chapter that this type of evaluation exercise reveals little about the extent to which e-governance projects have resulted in the achievement of improved administrative procedures, governance structures and social well-being.

The main argument in this chapter has been to regard the evaluation exercise as a continuous process to be carried out during the implementation of e-governance activity. Viewed in this way, a processual perspective has enabled us to highlight many aspects that would have been overlooked using a conventional evaluation approach. First, the process of administrative reform does not occur through legislation but through a subtle and incremental organizational learning process. Through our research, we have been able to study over time some of the interactions that have taken place between government strategies, for example, the influence of front-end applications on triggering back-end reforms. Second, a focus on process has enabled us to study the extent to which the formal objectives of governance reform in Kerala manifested through decentralization and improved coordination strategies have been supported by e-governance initiatives launched in the state. The study has described a subtle process of cultural change that is occurring within government as a result of the common designation of service officers in the FRIENDS project. Third, we have been able to report on improved trust between providers and recipients of e-governance applications. For example, improved citizen trust in government services in both the FRIENDS and the Akshaya projects, and improved trust relations between the local panchayat and the IT Mission team. These aspects, which have been the focus of the current research, are often glossed over by politicians in the rush to implement and evaluate e-governance projects. An important element of any e-governance evaluation exercise must therefore be to understand the process by which citizens and other agents develop trust relations.

Our focus on value of e-governance projects resonates well with Sen's capabilities approach according to which development is considered for its instrumental value as well as its substantive value. For example, we regard the opportunity for citizens to pay bills efficiently, to generate income and to gain self-esteem as important criteria for development regardless of ultimate outcome. At the same time, difficulties lie in identifying and attaching a weight to different capabilities. Each of these different capabilities may be more or less relevant to different socio-economic groupings within a locality. For example, freedom to pay bills may be more relevant for middle-income groups in Kerala than for the low-income fishing community in Kerala. Conversely, freedom to generate income from local economic activities might be more important for tribal youth than for elderly people living in the area.

We have taken a holistic approach to evaluating e-governance activity in Kerala, taking into consideration three major initiatives which are ongoing within the state. One of the main findings from our methodology of evaluation has been that the three activities taken together form a potentially powerful network to guide and support socio-economic development, and provide fertile ground for a micro-level evaluation exercise focusing on processes of reform and social well-being. A major finding from our study is that e-governance evaluation cannot be based on return-on-investment models for individual projects because what is crucial for these projects is not significant profit margins, but a critical mass of continued and sustained stream of activities and linkages between back- and front-end applications.

There are serious policy implications emanating from our evaluation of e-governance activity in Kerala which provide key lessons for policy makers in other developing countries as well. By focusing on processes and value, the whole evaluation exercise becomes more focused on the achievement of governance and development priorities, with consequent implications for policy makers. If key functionings such as paying bills or acquiring functional literacy depend on relational capabilities such as the opportunity to live without being hassled by bribery or the ability to generate income, then policy must not only be directed towards the provision of e-governance infrastructure, but must also address itself to building such capability among individual and organizational end-users of the applications.

### Conclusion

India is one of many developing countries currently launching major e-governance projects aiming to improve government processes, connect government to citizens and promote socio-economic development. However, from the existing literature it remains uncertain as to what contribution, if any, many of these projects are making to overall development priorities. This is because the criteria for evaluation of e-governance projects have typically been based on measures of infrastructure and service provision rather than on substantive issues of governance and development.

The principal objective of our chapter has been to propose an alternative evaluative space for assessing the impact of e-government projects, drawing on elements from relevant strands of literature on evaluation, public sector reform, governance and human development. We have considered e-governance evaluation as an ongoing activity which cannot be separated from the implementation of projects on the ground. Our main argument has been that this framework provides a more meaningful measure of the effectiveness of e-governance activity than earlier models.

## References

Accenture (2002), 'eGovernment leadership – realizing the vision', Third Annual eGovernment Benchmarking report, London.

Agerfalk, P., Sjostrom, J., Cronholm, S. and Goldkuhl, G. (2002), 'Setting the scene for actability evaluation – understanding information systems in context', in Brown, A. and Remenyi, D. (eds), *Proceedings of the 9th Conference on Information Technology Evaluation*, Université Paris-Dauphine, Paris, July, Reading: MCIL, pp. 1–11.

Alkire, S. (2002), *Valuing Freedoms: Sen's Capability Approach and Poverty Reduction*, Oxford: Oxford University Press.

Apthorne, R. (1997), 'Human development reporting and social anthropology', *Social Anthropology*, **5** (1), 21–34.

Asian Development Bank (ADB) (2001), 'Asian municipalities project: enhancing municipal service delivery capability', Project Report, Asian Development Bank, Manilla, Philippines, www.adb.org/projects/benchmarking/implementation.asp, accessed 23 February 2005.

Bhaskar, R. (1978), *A Realist Theory of Science*, Brighton: Harvester Press.

Bhaskar, R. (1989), *Reclaiming Reality*, London: Verso.

Bhaskar, R. (1998), *The Possibility of Naturalism*, London: Routledge.

Carlsson, S. (2003), 'Realistic information systems evaluation research', in Berghout, E. and Remenyi, D. (eds), *Proceedings of the 10th European Conference on Information Technology Evaluation*, Madrid, 25–26 September, Reading: MCIL.

Centre for Electronic Governance (2001), www.developmentgateway.org/topic/index?page_id+3647.

Chambers, R. (1995), 'Poverty and livelihoods: whose reality counts?', IDS Discussion Paper, 347, Institute of Development Studies, Sussex University, Brighton.

Chopra, K. and Duraiappah, A. (2001), 'Operationalising capabilities and freedom in a segmented society: the role of institutions', Paper presented at conference on 'Examining Sen's capability approach', Von Hugel Institute, Cambridge University, Cambridge, June.

Corbridge, S. (2002), 'Development as freedom: the spaces of Amartya Sen', *Progress in Development Studies*, **2**, (3), 183–217.

Cordoba, J. and Robson, W. (2003), 'Finding the value of power-ethics strategies in the evaluation of information systems', in Berghout, E. and Remenyi, D. (eds), *Proceedings of the 10th European Conference on Information Technology Evaluation*, Madrid, 25–26 September, Reading: MCIL.

Department for International Development (DfID) (2000), 'Making e-government work for poor people: governments and electronic information and communication technologies (eICTs) in development', DfID Target Strategy Paper Executive Summary Report, London.

Farbey, B., Land, F. and Targett, D. (1993), *How to Assess Your IT Investments: A Study of Methods and Practice*, Oxford: Butterworth-Heinemann.

Garnham, N. (2000), 'Amartya Sen's "capabilities" approach to the evaluation of welfare and its application to communications', in Cammaerts, B. and Burgelmans, J.C. (eds), *Beyond Competition: Broadening the Scope of Telecommunications Policy*, Brussels: VUB University Press, pp. 25–37.

Gasper, D. (2001), 'Is the capability approach an adequate basis for considering human development?', Paper presented at conference on 'Examining Sen's capability approach', Von Hugel Institute, Cambridge University, Cambridge, June.

Government of India (GOI) (1985), 'Seventh Five Year Plan 1985–1990', Government of India, New Delhi.

Government of India (GOI) (2000), 'Electronic governance: a concept paper', Ministry of Information Technology, Government of India, New Delhi.

Government of India (GOI) (2003), 'E-readiness assessment of states in India', Report prepared by the National Council of Applied Economic Research, New Delhi.

Guba, E.G. and Lincoln, Y.S. (1981), *Effective Evaluation*, San Francisco: Jossey-Bass.

Guba, E.G. and Lincoln, Y.S. (1989), *Fourth Generation Evaluation*, Newbury Park, CA: Sage Publications.

Harris, R. (1999), 'Evaluating telecentres within national policies for ICTs in developing countries', in Gomez, R. and Hunt, P. (eds), *Telecentre Evaluation: A Global Perspective (Report of an International Meeting on Telecentre Evaluation)*, Far Hills Inn, Quebec, 28–30 September, IDRC, www.idrc.ca/telecentre/evaluation/nn/01 TOC.html, accessed 25 February 2005.

Heeks, R. (2001a), 'Understanding e-governance for development', iGovernment Working Paper Series, No. 11, Institute of Development Policy and Management, University of Manchester, www.man.ac.uk/idpm/idpm_dp.htm#ig, accessed 25 February 2005.

Heeks, R. (2001b), 'Building e-governance for development', iGovernment Working Paper Series, No. 11, Institute of Development Policy and Management, University of Manchester, www.man.ac.uk/idpm/idpm_dp.htm#ig, accessed 25 February 2005.

Hudson, H. (1999), 'Designing research for telecentre evaluation', in Gomez, R. and Hunt, P. (eds), *Telecentre Evaluation: A Global Perspective (Report of an International Meeting on Telecentre Evaluation)*, Far Hills Inn, Quebec, 28–30 September, IDRC, www.idrc.ca/telecentre/evaluation/nn/01 TOC.html, accessed 25 February 2005.

Introna, L. and Whittaker, L. (2002), 'The phenomenology of information systems evaluation: overcoming the subject/object dualism', in Wynn, E.H., Whitley, E.A., Myers, M.D. and DeGross, J.I. (eds), *Global Organisational Discourse about Information Technology*, Dordrecht: Kluwer Academic Publishers, pp. 155–75. Barcelona, December.

Jackson, P. (2001), 'Public sector added value: can bureaucracy deliver?', *Public Administration*, **79** (1), 5–28.

Janssen, D. (2003), 'Mine's bigger than yours: assessing international e-government benchmarking', in Bannister, F. and Remenyi, D. (eds), *Proceedings of 3rd European Conference on e-Government*, Trinity College, Dublin, 3–4 July, Reading: MCIL, pp. 209–16.

Kelly, G. and Muers, S. (2003), *Creating Public Value: An Analytical Framework for Public Service Reform*, London: Strategy Unit, Cabinet Office.

Kerala State Information Technology Mission (KSITM) (2002), 'Project Akshaya', document released by the KSITM on the occasion of the inauguration of the project by the President of India, 18 November 2002.

Kirkman, G., Sachs, J., Schwab, K. and Cornelius, P. (eds.) (2002), *The Global Information Technology Report 2001–2002: Readiness for the Networked World*, Centre for International Development at Harvard University and World Economic Forum, New York: Oxford University Press.

Kjaer, A.M. (2004), *Governance*, Cambridge: Polity.

Kooiman, J. (2003), *Governing as Governance*, London: Sage.

Land, F. (2000), 'Evaluation in a socio-technical context', in Baskerville, R., Stage, J. and DeGross, J.I. (eds), *Organisational and Social Perspectives on Information Technology*, MA: Kluwer Academic, pp. 115–26.

Legge, K. (1984), *Evaluating Planned Organizational Change*, London: Academic Press.

Madon, S. (2003), 'IT diffusion for public service delivery: looking for plausible theoretical approaches', in Avgerou, C. and la Rovere, R. (eds), *Information Systems and the Economics of Innovation*, Cheltenham, UK and Northampton, MA, USA: Edward Elgar, pp. 71–89.

Madon, S. and Kiran, G.R. (2002), 'Information technology for citizen–government interface: a study of FRIENDS project in Kerala', World Bank Global Knowledge Sharing Program (GKSP), World Bank, Washington, DC, www1.worldbank.org/publicsector/bnpp/egovupdate.htm, accessed 25 February 2005.

Mansell, R. (2001), 'New media and the power of networks', first Dixons Public Lecture, London School of Economics and Political Science, London, 23 October.

Max-Neef, M. (1993), *Human Scale Development: Conception, Application, and Further Reflections*, London: Apex.

Mutch, A. (2002), 'Actors and networks or agents and structures: towards a realist view of information systems', *Organization*, **9** (3), 477–96.

Nussbaum, M. (1992), 'Human functioning and social justice: in defence of Aristotelian essentialism', *Political Theory*, **20** (2), 202–46.

Rama Rao, T.P. (2003), 'Electronic governance: lessons from experience', *International Federation of Information Processing (IFIP) WG9.4 Newsletter*, **13** (1).

Ramachandran, V. (2000), 'Kerala's development achievements and their replicability', in Parayil, G. (ed.), *Kerala: The Development Experience*, London: Zed Books, pp. 86–116.

Ranerup, A. (1999), 'Internet-enabled applications for local government democratisation', in Heeks, R. (ed.), *Reinventing Government in the Information Age*, London: Routledge, pp. 117–94.

Remenyi, D. (2002), 'The value scorecard: beyond the business case', in Brown, A. and Remenyi, D. (eds), *Proceedings of the 9th Conference on Information Technology Evaluation*, Université Paris-Dauphine, Paris, July, Reading, UK: MCIL, pp. 209–16.

Scrivens, M. (1973), 'Goal-free evaluation', in House, E.R. (ed.), *School Evaluation: The Politics and Process*, Berkeley, CA: McCutchan, pp. 1–4.

Scrivens, M. (1974), 'The pros and cons about goal-free evaluation', *Evaluation Comment*, **3**, 1–4.

Sen, A. (1999), *Development as Freedom*, Oxford: Oxford University Press.

Smithson, S. and Hirschheim, R. (1998), 'Analysing IS evaluation: another look at an old problem', *European Journal of Information Systems*, **7**, 158–75.

Stake, R.E. (1975), *Evaluating the Arts in Education: A Responsive Approach*, Columbus, OH: Merrill.

Subrahmanian, K.K. and Abdul, E. (2000) 'Industrial growth in Kerala: trends and explanations', Working Paper no. 310, Centre for Development Studies, Trivandrum.

Tyler, R.W. (1950), *Basic Principles of Curriculum and Instruction*, Chicago: University of Chicago Press.

UNDEPA (2002), 'Benchmarking e-government: a global perspective', New York, www.unpan.org/egovernment2.asp, accessed 23 February 2005.

Unnithan, C. (2002), 'e-Governance in India – initiatives and drivers: a preliminary investigation', Paper presented at the 2nd European Conference on e-Government, Oxford, October.

Walsham, G. (1995), 'Interpretive case studies in IS research: nature and method', *European Journal of Information Systems*, **4**, 74–81.

Wilson, M. and Howcroft, D. (2000), 'The politics of IS evaluation: a social shaping perspective', in Orlowski, Wanda J., Ang, Soon, Weill, Peter, Kramer, Helmut and DeGross, J.I. (eds), *Proceedings of 21st International Conference on Information Systems*, Atlanta, GA: ICIS, pp. 94–103.

Yin, R.K. (2002), *Case Study Research, Design and Methods*, 3rd edn, Newbury Park, CA: Sage.

# 16 Rethinking urban poverty: forms of capital, information technology and enterprise development

*Lynette Kvasny and Lakshman Yapa*

## Introduction

In this chapter, we introduce a social theory that incorporates IT-based projects aimed at empowering inner-city communities. This social theory, called 'rethinking urban poverty', challenges the economic determinism that informs much of the prevailing discourse surrounding urban poverty in the United States. We posit that poverty is not entirely an economic condition, and thus has no purely economic solution. Instead, we offer a social theory that provides insights into using social and cultural capital to address issues of poverty. While so-called 'poor neighbourhoods' have relatively few economic resources, they possess other material and symbolic resources such as indigenous knowledge, public spaces, local products, community organizations, and social networks. A more hopeful and pragmatic discourse enables us to discover and harness the untapped resources that exist within inner-cities to improve the quality of life of their inhabitants. Instead of passively waiting for the infusion of jobs and funds from external entities, residents can proactively engage in highly tangible projects that leverage their skills and knowledge.

The 'rethinking urban poverty' framework emerged from a sustained programme of research and outreach that brings together Penn State University faculty and students, and local business owners, non-profit organizations and residents to address community concerns. This research and outreach programme has developed over a seven-year period through sustained relationships and partnerships with the people and organizations in the Belmont neighbourhood in West Philadelphia. The project was initiated by Lakshman Yapa in 1998 under the title, 'Rethinking Urban Poverty: Philadelphia Field Project'.[1]

In what follows, we describe the demographic and physical conditions of Belmont to portray both the despair and the hope that coexist in this neighbourhood. We also present the prevailing discourse on poverty and community development to give a sense of how people in positions of power talk about places such as Belmont. Next, we present the rethinking urban poverty theory, and relate this to Pierre Bourdieu's theory of capital. We conclude the chapter by demonstrating how we use this theory to inform enterprise development projects that utilize IT to enhance social and cultural capital among small businesses.

## Neighbourhood profile of Belmont

Poverty in the United States has traditionally been defined as an economic condition that occurs when a family's income falls below the official government threshold. In one of the richest countries in the world, a large and growing number of people are living in official poverty. In 2002 the poverty rate was 12.1 per cent (34.6 million people), up from 11.7 per cent (32.9 million) in 2001 (Proctor and Dalaker 2003). The number of families in 'severe poverty', defined as those with family incomes below one-half of their poverty threshold, represented 40.7 per cent of the poverty population or 4.9 per cent of the total US population. Moreover, 'a disproportionate share of people in poverty live inside central cities: 39.9%', as compared to suburban and rural areas (ibid., p. 14). The poverty rate for people living inside central cities has held constant at 26.7 per cent even as the population in central cities continues to fall. Thus, central cities experience the effects of poverty more intensively than any other region of the United States. Many low-income families are socially isolated in central cities and have no other recourse but to remain in these neighbourhoods. Scarce opportunities exist to overcome the vicious cycle of poverty, illiteracy, sporadic work, racial and ethnic discrimination and criminal activity (Wilson 1987, 1996).

A person working full-time at minimum wages for 40 hours a week, 52 weeks per year still earns a near poverty level income, hence the large number of people counted among the working poor (Bureau of Labor Statistics 2002). There are limits to how much the minimum wage can be increased when American workers have to compete in a global labour market where multinational firms pay workers from poor countries far less than the minimum wage paid in the United States. The failure of the conventional model of economic growth to eradicate poverty is particularly evident in our study area. West Philadelphia is home to the University of Pennsylvania, the largest job provider in the city. There are three other major universities in the area: Drexel University, the University of the Sciences and St Joseph's University. The University City area of West Philadelphia has been a major recipient of federal funds for development since the 1960s, and today it is a very prosperous area of new office and classroom buildings, affluent shops and restaurants, and residential neighbourhoods with quiet tree-lined streets and historic mansions. The popular Philadelphia Zoo and the Fairmont Park are both located in West Philadelphia. Nevertheless, in the year 2000 over 40 per cent of the residents in the Belmont neighbourhood, in the heart of West Philadelphia, lived below the poverty level. Considerations such as these led us to our scepticism with the search for economic solutions to the poverty problem.

West Philadelphia, like the rest of the city, is a mosaic of distinct neighbourhoods. The Philadelphia City Planning Commission defines the neighbourhood of Belmont as comprising census tracts 106 and 107. In the United States, a census tract is a small geographic area into which a large city is divided for statistical purposes. It is usually homogeneous in demographic and economic characteristics, and contains somewhere between 2500 and 8000 individuals. The total population in the two tracts in 2000 was about 5236, living in about 1889 households. The US Census defines a poverty area as one with a poverty rate exceeding 20 per cent. In 2000, with a poverty rate of 42 per cent, Belmont was declared an 'official' poverty area twice over. Once an area of thriving businesses, today Lancaster Avenue between 40th and 44th Streets is in a state of visible decline. With dilapidated buildings housing an array of small businesses and fading commercial signs, the avenue has the appearance of a permanent flea market selling cheap second-hand goods. There are no commercial banks in the entire corridor, although there are a large number of pawnshops and cheque-cashing establishments that also sell items such as cigarettes and alcohol. There are approximately 70 businesses in the Belmont section of Lancaster Avenue, seven of which are restaurants and the others are engaged in personal services and the sale of apparel, jewellery, furniture, hardware, groceries and electronics. None of the businesses represents national franchises or outlets of national chains.

The streetscape in Belmont along Lancaster Avenue is unattractive to potential shoppers. Rubbish is strewn about the sidewalks, and many of the businesses are housed in dilapidated buildings interspersed with vacant and abandoned structures. The economic base of surrounding households is far too small to support a diversified commercial strip. According to the 2000 census, the median household income in Belmont was $16000. To provide a comparative reference, the poverty threshold for a two-parent, two-children household was $17463 in 2000. In addition to the small local economic base, while the avenue is widely used by suburban commuters travelling to workplaces in downtown Philadelphia, very few of them stop here to shop. The University of Pennsylvania and Drexel University are adjacent to Belmont; however, students from these universities are specifically advised to avoid the neighbourhood, as the area is considered unsafe. Perhaps most importantly, merchants on Lancaster Avenue do not seem to be aware of the city, state and federal programmes available for small business development. For example, the merchant leaders were only vaguely familiar with the business services offered by the Small Business Development Center (SBDC) programme housed in the Wharton School of the University of Pennsylvania. The SBDC programme and the US

Small Business Administration in Philadelphia maintain excellent web pages detailing their services. However, the Belmont merchants in general do not access these web pages as there is no online culture.

Away from the Lancaster Avenue business corridor, Belmont is an area of residential streets. Homeownership rates in Belmont, a good index of neighbourhood stability, have fallen from 55.6 per cent in 1990 to 48.8 per cent in 2000 as compared to West Philadelphia (51.85 to 49.8 per cent) and Philadelphia (62 to 59.3 per cent). According to the 2000 US Census, the vacancy rates of housing in Belmont stood at 22 per cent, double the rate of the City of Philadelphia. The landscape of the residential streets presents stark contrasts. Well-maintained houses with neatly trimmed hedges and porches with potted plants stand next to vacant lots and burnt-out structures that are literally falling apart. There are many rubble-strewn empty lots, but not all are that way. Some residents have fought back to reclaim these spaces with gardens growing vegetables and flowers. In fact, the group of neighbourhoods north of Market Street and East of 52nd Street, which includes Belmont, contain more private and community gardens than any comparable area of the entire county of Philadelphia (Hu 2003).

The contrasts in the physical landscape mirror what exists in the social world of Belmont: hope, love, kindness and faith reside side by side with despair, cynicism, simmering anger and crime. Civic society in Belmont is at best quite weak. During the seven years that Penn State has worked in the Belmont neighbourhood, we found only three functioning community organizations, each with a small membership. In fact, one of the three, the Belmont Improvement Association, closed its doors in early 2003 under allegations of financial misappropriation. The association was functioning again in the summer of 2004 under the patronage of a local family with access to political power in the City Council. The other two organizations, the Lancaster Avenue Business Association and the Holly Street Garden Literacy Association, are small and do not have a community-wide reach. Stronger organizations like the People's Emergency Center are well-funded service providers, not grassroots community organizations. Creating cultural and social capital in Belmont requires the prior development of social networks for informal learning and knowledge sharing. This means strengthening groups such as the Lancaster Avenue Business Association. As we shall discuss in the following section, social and cultural capital are two integral factors in the economic development of communities, and IT can play a role in facilitating the creation of social and cultural capital.

**Rethinking urban poverty through forms of capital**
The US Census defines Belmont as a 'poverty area' and, as we have demonstrated, residents of this neighbourhood face very serious problems

of material deprivation. The principal academic answer to the problem proposes increased investment, job creation, education, workforce training and rebuilding the physical infrastructure. Even within Belmont, community leaders privilege this economic discourse by talking about 'good jobs' as the golden key to solving problems of the community. *The Plan for West Philadelphia*,[2] a Philadelphia City Planning Commission report, addressed the economic problems of West Philadelphia and proposed a detailed strategy for enhancing the physical environment. The document was published in 1994 after a five-year process of community-based planning, and specifically mentioned the commercial area of Belmont as in need of revitalization. The authors made a tacit assumption that once the planning projects were specified, funds would become available through the city, the state, and the federal government, but they did not. Conventional wisdom views the infusion of economic capital as the principal answer to the problems of neighbourhoods such as Belmont. However, insisting on economic capital is problematic because that is precisely what is in short supply and most likely will remain that way for the foreseeable future.

The approach that we advocate goes beyond economics, physical planning, jobs and incomes. We do not believe that poverty in Belmont can be corrected only through more jobs and higher incomes. Belmont competes in a global labour market where American companies can get skilled and unskilled labour for a fraction of what they pay in the United States. It is difficult to see why large companies would want to move into this area and create jobs that pay living wages. Hence, the challenge to academics is to produce a social theory that will inform interventions that improve quality of life in places such as Belmont in ways that go beyond the futile logic of waiting for economic capital and jobs programmes.

Instead of asking why households do not make more income, suppose we ask the substantive question of why poor households have problems with adequate nutrition, housing, transport, healthcare and other life chances. The answers we get to these questions are different from those that use the conventional approach. Consider commuting costs as an example: such costs depend upon the geographical distribution of residences and jobs, available modes of transport and insurance rates. Finding ways to reduce transport costs of poor people, of course, is another way of increasing their effective income. We can do this by studying transport patterns in the space economy, and helping to initiate action programmes that promote car-pooling, public transport, relocating work and telecommuting. For another example, consider health. Good health is not necessarily about purchasing expensive high-tech healthcare. In West Philadelphia, the principal health problems include high blood pressure, obesity, diabetes, heart failure, back pain and allergies excluding asthma.[3] Many of these ailments have their origin in poor diet and lack of exercise. Therefore, the lack of money, as serious as it is, may not pose insurmountable obstacles to improving health. Thinking along these lines, we hope to find how people can meet their basic needs through less expensive, technically more benign and ecologically less destructive ways. We have to develop a new discourse of cultural and social capital that could revalorize the inner city by focusing on locally relevant issues such as urban gardening and architecture, rebuilding homes with local effort, alternative modes of transport, telecommuting instead of physical commuting, and creative ways of making safe neighbourhoods.

The lack of economic capital should not be a deterrent to improving the quality of life in places such as Belmont. Bourdieu (1985) has argued that there are other forms of capital besides economic, such as cultural and social, and that these forms are readily convertible from one to another. Indeed, according to Bourdieu, cultural and social capital are economic capital in disguise:

> So it has to be posited simultaneously that economic capital is at the root of all the other types of capital and that these transformed, disguised forms of economic capital, never entirely reducible to that definition, produce their most specific effects only to the extent that they conceal (not least from their possessors) the fact that economic capital is at their root, in other words – but only in the last analysis – at the root of their effects. (Ibid., p. 252)

Although Bourdieu's principal intent was to produce a general theory of exchange and social practice, his notion of three types of capital and their convertibility has a special significance for addressing poverty problems in community settings such as Belmont. The vigorous growth of small Asian businesses in urban America is perhaps illustrative of the connection between economic capital and social capital, rooted in networks of kinship and community.

'Cultural capital' refers to the collective value of knowledge, skills, competencies, family background, social class and investments in education. Cultural capital helps us to understand differences in taste, cultural distinctions and value judgements. People from different backgrounds will appreciate, appropriate and consume art, food, music, sports or other cultural goods in distinct ways. These distinctions serve as markers that can be used to differentiate social dimensions of class, race, gender and geographic location (Bourdieu 1984).

For Bourdieu, people can neither consume nor produce a cultural good unless they possess the requisite cultural capital. This holds for music, art, scientific formulae, literature and IT. For instance, ownership of and familiarity with IT such as personal computers and the internet is a type of cultural capital. It is simply expected that one is confident with technology in business, school, home and civic settings. It is a mark of the professional and erudite (Kvasny and Truex 2000).

Bourdieu (1985) has identified three forms of cultural capital: *embodied* cultural capital is incorporated within the body of the individual, and represents an individual's knowledge and capacity. Embodied cultural capital can be increased through self-improvement and education, but it cannot be accumulated beyond the appropriating capacity of a given individual. The individual's physical and mental abilities, as well as personal sacrifices of time and money help to define the appropriating capacity. In fact, economic capital enables the personal investment of time and money for higher education. In this way, external wealth (that is, economic capital) facilitates the accumulation of bodily wealth (that is, embodied cultural capital) which in turn increases one's earning capacity. Moreover, embodied cultural capital derives its scarcity value because the economic and cultural means to acquire it are unequally distributed among individuals.

The *objectified* form of cultural capital consists of cultural goods such as artefacts, books, paintings, music and technologies. Cultural goods can be materially acquired with economic capital, but the use and enjoyment of such a good requires embodied cultural capital. For example, to appropriate a personal computer, an individual must possess embodied cultural capital such as file-management, word-processing and information-seeking skills.

Cultural capital in its *institutionalized* form refers to formal credentials and certificates for academic qualifications. Bourdieu has argued that objectifying a cultural good in the form of an academic certificate is one way of neutralizing some of the biological limits of embodied capital which can be used only by its bearer. In addition, unlike embodied cultural capital which can be called into question, institutionalized cultural capital certifies competence and legally guarantees qualifications.

'Social capital' consists of all actual or potential resources linked to possession of a durable network of more or less institutionalized relationships of mutual acquaintance or recognition (Bourdieu 1985). An important aspect of these relationships is the benefits that one can potentially receive from participating in communities and networks (Bourdieu and Passeron 1979; Bourdieu 1990). These benefits come in the form of information, support, guidance or additional social contacts. Since colleagues, friends and relatives provide many informational resources, social capital is an important variable affecting access to and use of IT (Warschauer 2002). For instance, in a longitudinal study of people making use of community technology centres in the United States, researchers (Chow et al. 2000) found that gaining access to new social resources is as critical as gaining access to hardware in assisting people to become computer literate. The study also indicates how the users of community technology centres extend their own relationship to technology by later assisting their own friends, relatives and associates. One way to promote effective use of information and communication technology in communities is to first examine the social networks that already exist, and then to use the technology to help amplify and extend those social networks (Chapman and Rhodes 1997).

For Bourdieu, social capital is an asset that provides tangible advantages to those individuals, families or groups that are better connected. The central premise of social capital is that social networks have value (Wellman 2001). Social capital is an important sociological category for understanding poverty and other forms of social inequality because marginalized members of society typically have less social capital to draw upon (Bourdieu 1990). Social capital works through multiple channels that include information flows, mutual aid, collective action and the formation of collective identity. In the context of central cities, examples of social capital include informal neighbourhood crime-watch programmes, neighbours engaged in childcare and caring for the old and sick, and youths engaged in organized sports.

## A framework for projects

This section outlines how we are applying our social theory of rethinking urban poverty in the Belmont neighbourhood in West Philadelphia. Earlier we argued that we can go beyond economics by employing cultural and social capital to focus on substantive themes such as nutrition, housing, health, transport and safety. However, within these themes, how do we assess and prioritize the needs of an area such as Belmont when in fact the list of needs is infinitely long? Belmont has problems with adequate housing, home maintenance, safe neighbourhoods, quality schools and playgrounds, childcare, health, diet, nutrition, exercise, jobs, income, retirement benefits, use of open spaces, horticulture, gardening, jobs and so on. Which of these are more important and where should community development begin? The truth is that there is no known social theory that helps us to rank these topics in some order of relative importance (Yapa 1996, pp. 717–20). No one can say that a campaign for AIDS prevention is more or less important than drug rehabilitation, or that either of these topics is more or less important than nutrition, exercise or job creation. So-called 'root causes' such as drug abuse, lack of education, or unemployment are constituted from still other causes that are present in never-ending cycles of causation.

Despite our inability to prioritize one set of needs over another, the Belmont community–university partnership has undertaken a large number of projects in the area in the past seven years. What we have actually done in Belmont by way of projects are the products of a negotiated statement between the university and community leaders. The projects that we are currently engaged in, and those that we propose are the result of three considerations: (i) input from community residents and businesspeople; (ii) emphasis on cultural and social capital instead of economic capital; and (iii) the existing stock of particular skills and competencies (cultural capital) of Penn State faculty and students, and community participants who have come together to work in Belmont. So far, we have undertaken a large number of projects such as enterprise development, urban gardening, food security, consumer choices and cartographic mapping.[4]

**Information technology for enterprise development**
Consistent with our framework for projects, the larger Belmont community–university partnership has several points of entry, but what we describe here are projects related to IT and economic development. Many scholars have noticed that IT has the potential to exacerbate social divisions, and to reproduce power relations (Moolenkropf and Castells 1991; Schiller 1996; DiMaggio et al. 2001; Kvasny and Kiel 2002; Strover et al. 2003). However, this is only one possible outcome. When designed from a socially conscious and culturally sensitive standpoint, IT-enabled solutions also have the potential for empowering historically excluded and marginalized groups (Portney and Berry 1997; Castells 2001; Schement 2001; Payton 2003; Kvasny forthcoming).

From a theoretical perspective, we believe that IT can positively contribute to the creation of social and cultural capital. However, we do not believe that the community can be organized around the abstract concepts of social and cultural capital. The building of these capital resources requires the implementation of a series of limited, concrete, visible, collaborative projects that will not only deliver tangible outputs but will also lead to the long-term building of capacity in the community.

We selected economic development as the project domain for two pragmatic reasons – community needs and researcher expertise. Poor enterprise development negatively affects the quality of life in Belmont because it provides few jobs, offers very poor consumer choices to the residents, and brings in very little external money. In addition to these economic concerns, poor enterprise development negatively affects socio-cultural outcomes such as limited collective action among merchants, restricted access to valuable resources external to the neighbourhood, and scant knowledge of how IT can be used to augment and support business processes. The economic and socio-cultural concerns are related. For instance, the local Girl Scout troop recently solicited funds from merchants for the purchase of new uniforms. The majority of merchants did not contribute funds. And while the residents believe that the merchants do not give back to the community, the merchants counter that they are struggling financially and cannot afford to subsidize community programmes. This contributes to the tension that already exists between residents and merchants, and as a result, there is a mounting effort by residents to boycott local businesses. Even with the looming threat of a boycott, merchants continue to assert that they will not contribute funds.

One way to improve economic and socio-cultural climate along the business corridor is to improve the economic viability of the local stores. We do so by focusing on low-cost IT solutions that facilitate enterprise development. In particular, internet commerce provides opportunities for extending the customer base and bringing much-needed funds into the community. However, before we can engage in internet commerce projects, we have to develop basic IT literacy skills within the community. Such an approach is well suited to the needs of local merchants, and matches very well with the type of resources and the competencies that we have as researchers.

The Lancaster Avenue Business Association (LABA) has been our primary community partner in the IT and enterprise development projects. Yapa has worked with the LABA for the last six years, and over the last two years Yapa and Kvasny have met with members of the LABA executive committee about once a month. Our partnership with the LABA is maintained on two levels. First, we fund a Volunteers In Service to America (VISTA) IT coordinator to help with research, education and information dissemination. VISTA is a US government programme in which citizens volunteer one year of service to non-profit organizations working to alleviate poverty in America. Second, we have a series of concrete project activities that are coordinated through LABA, thus adding to its technical capacity. The projects provide opportunities for theorizing and implementing effective uses of IT. Effective uses of IT occur when individuals have a targeted purpose for using the technology apart from mere curiosity (Gurstein 2003). In what follows, we shall present two examples of effective use of IT. First, we shall discuss how members of the local business association and youths develop and apply computing literacy and skills (embodied cultural capital). Next, we shall describe how IT is used to convert objectified cultural capital such as paintings, jewellery, dolls and recipes into saleable goods (economic capital). As we present details of the projects, we shall point out how they illustrate our concern with cultural and social capital, and convertibility among the forms of capital.

*Computer literacy for merchants*
In the summer of 2003, we initiated a programme of computer literacy among the members of the LABA. The International Computer Driving License (ICDL), programme[5] is recognized in more than 100 countries as the standard for basic computer skill certification. It provides the tools to produce skilled, accredited workers and entrepreneurs. Thus, the

ICDL programme provides institutionalized cultural capital by validating participants' proficiency in areas such as file management, the internet, e-mail, spreadsheets, presentations and databases. Philadelphia is the first major US city to launch this computer certification programme on a broad basis.

This project is designed to build the technical capacity of the LABA by developing and expanding the professional services that it offers to the business community. ICDL instruction is provided by Penn State students and the VISTA IT coordinator. Thus, embodied cultural capital is cultivated through the transfer of IT skills and training to ICDL participants. University funds subsidize the enrolment fees for a small group of merchants from Lancaster Avenue. The ICDL training will be provided to one or more people in each of the 70 enterprises on Lancaster over a three-year period. Also, refurbished computers will be provided to merchants upon completion of the ICDL training. In this way, each member of the business association will have both the objectified cultural capital – a PC – and embodied cultural capital – IT skills – that enable them to effectively use the computing resources. In addition, the participants receive institutionalized cultural capital in the form of an ICDL certificate.

Ongoing computer support services for Lancaster Avenue merchants will be provided through the Penn State Education Partnership Program (PEPP). This is an after-school outreach programme directed by Elmore Hunter, Director of Penn State Cooperative Extension and Outreach in Philadelphia. Over 100 high-school students have already received training in computer programming and in the maintenance of computer hardware. Youth involvement is important because they, more so than the adults of working age, have the time to devote to acquiring and teaching IT skills. Graduates of the PEPP programme will act as paid interns to provide continued computer support for Lancaster Avenue merchants. This will not only involve high-school students in their own community development (that is, social capital), earning their own wages (that is, economic capital) but will also provide a low-cost method to sustain all of our IT projects. In addition, social capital increases as students and merchants work together, which may bridge the longstanding misunderstandings and increase trust between the merchants and the community youths.

By bringing IT skills into the business corridor and using these skills to strengthen the technical capacity of organizations and individuals, small businesses may be better able to run their businesses more efficiently and to increase their effective income. To determine the impact of this training, we shall periodically conduct in-depth inquiries with each business to understand how they are using IT to support their business, the perceived benefits and limitations of computer literacy on everyday life and business operations, and the sustainability of their IT use. We shall also assess the economic impact of IT use on profit margins and inventory control, as well as the general level of computer integration in the day-to-day conduct of business. In sum, we seek to understand how and to what extent social and cultural capital enabled by the computer literacy training are converted into positive economic outcomes.

*Internet commerce for inner-city products*
Since the surrounding households do not have sufficient income, and more affluent residents of the nearby University City district avoid the Lancaster Avenue business corridor west of 40th Street, we posed the question: are there cultural products that Belmont could produce and sell to the outside world without customers having to physically visit the neighbourhood? One solution was to identify a range of products that could be produced locally that would be appropriate for online marketing and selling. In consultation with the community, we began to draw on the stock of embodied cultural capital represented in the competencies of university faculty and students, and the skills and knowledge possessed by local merchants. Faculty and students have embodied and institutionalized skills including web development, advertising, digital photography, implementing eBay auctions, online payments, and packaging and delivery of goods. Community members possess embodied and objectified forms of cultural capital such as knowledge of horticulture, doll making and artisanship. Of the 70 businesses in the neighbourhood, about seven of them have potential online markets. These include a craftsperson who makes very high-quality African-American dolls; a cabinet-maker; a maker of beautiful floral arrangements; a travel agency; a shop specializing in African art objects; and two jewellery stores. Moreover, some members of the business association now have a variety of embodied cultural capital in the form of computing skills and objectified cultural capital in the form of computing machinery that they acquired through the computer literacy project. We also plan to encourage a few businesses to move into new product lines that have online marketing potential. For example, a few restaurants specialize in southern-style African-American cuisine and Black Muslim cooking, for which they can be encouraged to produce cookbooks and market ingredients. Thus, local skills and talents in the form of embodied cultural capital are employed to create a variety of products (that is, objectified cultural capital) which are then sold and converted into economic capital.

Since Lancaster Avenue itself cannot provide a physical site to market these products, the internet may provide an amenable site for obtaining additional sales and new markets. Since individuals, government entities, schools and firms have all found success using eBay, we decided to use this as a first foray into internet commerce. A pilot project, begun in the summer of 2004, is being conducted in which we sell dolls depicting the variety of clothing styles adopted by Muslim women throughout the world. Penn State students work with the LABA to develop the eBay advertisement and associated web pages. The process will be documented in a detailed fashion so that the LABA can instruct other organizations seeking to sell items online. Eventually, the LABA will be able to market 'the eBay setup' as a service to its members, and begin to create institutional cultural capital through eBay ratings that would certify the LABA as a competent and trustworthy seller.

The benefits from this project also flow from the community to the university. We argued earlier that economic academic discourses have contributed to exacerbating problems of poverty. This project allows us to develop and test an alternative social theory of poverty, IT and community development. Such knowledge leads to the publication of research articles, student theses, an alternative pedagogy on poverty, and the creation of a new class of scholars who are producing powerful public scholarship and civic engagement.

Social capital will begin to flow from the activities associated with these projects. Currently, LABA has not attained its potential as a strong community organization, and only a small fraction of the merchants on the Avenue are members of this organization. Our discussion with merchants revealed that some of them were not certain as to the value of the services offered by LABA. By making the LABA a centre for knowledge of internet marketing and sales[6] merchants may find membership in the organization more attractive. Thus, turning LABA into a valued and sought-after community organization requires that we first increase its technical capacity to be of service to merchants.

LABA's charter refers to the value of cultural diversity in the community. Members of the executive committee of LABA have always reached out to Muslim, Christian and Korean merchants on the Avenue. Bringing these groups together is an important function that LABA can serve. In the summer of 2004, for instance, there was some tension between the Korean merchants and African-American residents of Belmont. Some residents were of the opinion that the Korean merchants were not contributing enough to the community. If LABA were a stronger organization, it could serve as an important intermediary in defusing such tension.

**Conclusion**
In this chapter, we have presented a social theory for rethinking urban poverty. This social theory is critical in that it brings to light the restrictive and alienating economic discourses that typify urban poverty (Klein and

Myers 1999). Our approach is also emancipatory in that we use Bourdieu's notions of cultural, social and economic capital to inform interventions that leverage existing community resources to improve the quality of life. Specifically, we theorize the forms of capital and the conversions among the forms of capital through two economic development projects – IT literacy for merchants and internet commerce for inner-city products – conducted in the West Philadelphia neighbourhood of Belmont. These projects are not just about the transfer of skills. For instance, in the internet commerce project, we consciously considered appropriate cultural products and community partners, and the IT training and resources were geared towards this particular end. Through these projects, we present a more optimistic discourse on urban poverty that counters the traditional approach of waiting passively for well-intended but often ill-designed economic programmes from government and corporate entities. We also demonstrate how inner-city communities can assume a more active role in their economic development by cultivating cultural and social capital through tangible projects that leverage IT. While we believe that people can consciously act to change their social and economic conditions, as critical theorists, we also recognize that human agency is constrained by various forms of social, cultural and political domination as well as natural laws and resource limitations (Kincheloe and McLaren 1998). Therefore, we adopt a praxis orientation that connects theory to tangible projects in an attempt to understand and confront the injustices experienced by inner-city residents. Finally, the university–community partnership illustrates how in the absence of economic capital the transfer of cultural capital from the university is helping to create social capital in the community. The transfer is a two-way process as the university is gaining a new class of scholars versed in a new social theory of poverty.

## Notes

1. See www.geog.psu.edu/phila.
2. See www.penn-partners.org/wp/plan/.
3. See the West Philly Data InfoR at http://westphillydata.library.upenn.edu/infoR_WestPhiladelphia.htm#healthtable.
4. A list of past student projects is available at www.geog.psu.edu/phila.
5. See www.icdlus.com.
6. They already have a LABA web page – www.thelaba-cdc.org – created with the help of Penn State resources.

## References

Bourdieu, P. (1984), *Distinction: A Social Critique of the Judgement of Taste*, Cambridge, MA: Harvard University Press.

Bourdieu, P. (1985), 'The forms of capital', in J. Richardson (ed.), *Handbook of Theory and Research for the Sociology of Education*, New York: Greenwood Press.

Bourdieu, P. (1990), *Reproduction in Education, Society and Culture*, Thousand Oaks, CA: Sage.

Bourdieu, P. and Passeron, J.-C. (1979), *The Inheritors*, Chicago: University of Chicago Press.

Bureau of Labor Statistics (2002), 'A profile of the working poor, 2000', US Department of Labor: Report 957, www.bls.gov/cps/cpswp2000.htm, accessed June 2004.

Castells, M. (2001), *Internet Galaxy: Reflections on the Internet, Business and Society*, New York: Oxford University Press.

Chapman, G. and Rhodes, L. (1997), 'Nurturing neighborhood nets', *Technology Review*, October, 48–54.

Chow, C., Ellis, J., Walker, G. and Wise, B. (2000), 'Who goes there? Longitudinal case studies of twelve users of community technology centers', CTCNet, Cambridge, MA, www.ctcnet. org/resources/longrep3.doc, accessed June 2004.

DiMaggio, P., Hargittai, E., Neuman, R. and Robinson, J. (2001), 'Social implications of the internet', *Annual Review of Sociology*, **27**, 307–36.

Gurstein, M. (2003), 'Effective use, local innovation and participatory design', *First Monday*, www.firstmonday.org/issues/issue8_12/gurstein/index.html, accessed 9 July 2004.

Hu, E. (2003), 'Using computer mapping for community development in Belmont-Mantua', Honors thesis, Pennsylvania State University, University Park, PA.

Kincheloe, J. and McLaren, P. (1998), 'Rethinking critical qualitative research', in N. Denzin and Y. Lincoln (eds), *Handbook of Research on Qualitative Research*, Thousand Oaks, CA: Sage, pp. 260–99.

Klein, H. and Myers, M. (1999), 'A set of principles for conducting and evaluating interpretive field studies in information systems', *MIS Quarterly*, **23** (1), 67–97.

Kvasny, L. and Keil, M. (2002), 'The challenges in redressing the digital divide: a tale of two cities', in L. Applegate, R. Galliers and J.I. DeGross (eds), *Proceedings of the International Conference on Information Systems (ICIS)*, Barcelona, Spain, 15–18 December, pp. 812–28.

Kvasny, L. (forthcoming), 'Let the sisters speak: understanding the digital divide from the standpoint of the "other"', in *The Data Base for Advances in Information Systems*.

Kvasny, L. and Truex, D. (2000), 'Information technology and the cultural reproduction of social order', in R. Baskerville, J. Stage, and J. DeGross (eds) *Organizational and Social Perspectives on Information Technology*, New York: Kluwer Academic, pp. 277–94.

Moolenkropf, J. and Castells, M. (1991), *Dual City*, Thousand Oaks, CA: Sage.

Payton, F.C. (2003), 'Rethinking the digital divide', *Communications of the ACM*, **46** (6), 89–91.

Portney, K. and Berry, J. (1997), 'Mobilizing minority communities: social capital and participation in urban neighborhoods', *American Behavioral Scientist*, **40** (5), 632–44.

Proctor, B. and Dalaker, J. (2003), 'Poverty in the United States: 2002', US Census Bureau, US Department of Commerce, Current Population Reports, Washington, DC.

Schement, J. (2001), 'Of gaps by which democracy we measure', in B. Compaine (ed.) *The Digital Divide: Facing a Crisis or Creating a Myth?*, Cambridge, MA: MIT Press, pp. 303–7.

Schiller, H. (1996), *Information Inequality: The Deepening Social Crisis in America*, New York: Routledge.

Strover, S., Chapman, G. and Waters, J. (2003), 'Beyond community networking and CTCs: access, development and public policy', in *Proceedings of the Telecommunications Policy Research Conference*, Arlington, VA, http://tprc.org/papers/2003/230TIF_evaluation.pdf, accessed February 2005.

Warschauer, M. (2002), 'Reconceptualizing the digital divide', *First Monday*, **7** (7), www. firstmonday.dk/issues/issue7_7/warschauer/, accessed February 2005.

Wellman, B. (2001), 'Physical place and cyberplace: the rise of networked individualism', in L. Keeble and B. Loader (eds), *Community Informatics: Shaping Computer-Mediated Social Relations*, New York: Routledge, pp. 17–42.

Wilson, W.J. (1987), *The Truly Disadvantaged*, Chicago: University of Chicago Press.

Wilson, W.J. (1996), *When Work Disappears*, New York: Vintage Books.

Yapa, L. (1996), 'What causes poverty? A postmodern view', *Annals of the Association of American Geographers*, **86**, 707–28.

# 17 'Global but local': mediated work in global business organizations

*Dagfinn Hertzberg and Eric Monteiro*

## Introduction

Globally operating business organizations are caught in a deep dilemma. On the one hand, there is a strong emphasis on being 'close' to their customers. This stems, in part, from the critiques of Fordist modes of production such as flexible specialization or lean production which underscore the growing differentiation in consumption and demand (Piore and Sabel 1984; Womack 1990; Nohria and Ghoshal 1997; Ger 1999). As Keat (1990: 3) notes, 'meeting the demands of the 'sovereign' consumer becomes the new and overriding international imperative'. There are reasons to doubt the extent to which we have actually entered the age of post-Fordist production (Dicken et al. 1994), yet crucial for interpretive studies of organizational dynamics 'there is no doubt that managerial representations of the customer as a means of restructuring organizations, and of influencing employees' behaviour and attitudes, are of real importance' (du Gay and Salaman 1992: 619). On the other hand, global business organizations want to retain the traditional economy of scale based on extensive routinization and standardization. They also need to present a reasonably coherent and uniform front stage to ensure that they are perceived as the 'same', preserving an identity or a brand (Leidner 1993; Ger 1999). The dilemma of globally operating production and service organizations is, so to speak, to combine the better of two worlds (Jones et al. 1998: 1048). We analyse this dilemma, focusing on the strategies, challenges and experiences around acquiring 'closeness' despite mediated, distanced relationships and patterns of communication.

Our interpretive study is empirically based on Rolls-Royce Marine (RRM). A 5000 employee division of Rolls-Royce, RRM is a highly competitive producer of ship and off-shore equipment for commercial marine enterprises worldwide. Traditionally a high-quality producer of equipment, RRM is in the midst of a transformation into a more service-oriented, customer-focused enterprise. Organizationally, these repair, maintenance and spare parts delivery services are predominantly delivered through a globally dispersed, 500-employee branch of RRM (the Global Support Network,

GSN). The espoused operational strategy of RRM is 'global but local', thus combining the traditional (and fairly centralized) production with a stronger local presence and closeness with customers. On the programmatic level, this global but local strategy is not unlike many other strategies. Our study aims to analyse the dynamics, contingencies and controversies embedded in this transformation. Empirically we focus on local sites in the GSN, supplemented with perceptions at the production sites (the 'principals') and the headquarters to analyse how the closeness with customers is realized. More specifically, we study the 'disembedded' (Giddens 1990) nature of the relationship between the globally dispersed GSN sites and the Scandinavian-based production sites and headquarters. The direction of our analysis is aimed at the following set of questions. How is the espoused ambition of the global but local strategy played out within the organization? Bowing to the pressure to streamline and make more uniform the work routines, procedures, roles and formats of reporting, what are the conditions for locally grounded cultivation of customer relationships? How is the quality of products and services affected by the contradictory demands from local interaction and global uniformity? How is the balance between local autonomy and centralized control negotiated and perceived? How is trust dynamically and provisionally constructed in the relationship between the local sites and headquarters?

In the next section we describe the background for and discourse around the problem of mediated social relationships. We elaborate a perspective on abstract (or institutional, non-personal) trust, a prerequisite for disembedded communication to function (ibid.), as provisional, fragile and emotional. We then present some context for our study as well as a description of our research method. The subsequent section analyses the dynamics of the ongoing reorganization efforts, pursuing three threads: the implications in terms of practices and competences of being 'close' to the customers; the tension between globally applicable routines and locally embedded strategies; and the dynamics and characteristics of how trust is established and cultivated. The final section contains concluding remarks.

**Conceptualizing mediated communication in global business organizations**
Global business organizations are of course not new. In a useful classification, Ghoshal and Barlett (1989) outline three ideal types of organizational configurations: multinational, international and hybrid. The multinational, exploited by the expanding European firms, where the local (national) businesses enjoy extensive autonomy, thus producing a loosely coordinated portfolio of largely independent businesses. The international model, promoted by US-based firms after the Second World War, where the local businesses are more tightly coordinated and are more dependent on

the centre for competence and skill. The strong aspect of the international model, according to Ghoshal and Barlett (ibid: 58–9) is its ability to: 'leverage the knowledge and capabilities of the parent company. But its resource configuration and operating systems make it less efficient than the global company, and less responsive than the multinational company'.

Hence, there is a need to work out new hybrid models of global organizations as existing models fail to combine the benefits of centralization (international model) and decentralization (multinational model). Exactly how such businesses are to be configured remains the topic of an unresolved debate.

The increasing pressure for responsiveness to local customers' demands, getting close to the customers, is particularly intense for interactive service work (Leidner 1993; Jones et al. 1998) – or, as is the case for RRM, the increasing level of interactive service work also in traditional production-oriented businesses (Freeman and Perez 1988). Interactive service work implies close interaction with customers, and thus seems to resist routinization. For obvious reasons, a globally operating organization will necessarily need to establish a minimum of uniformity in its products, services, internal routines and reporting simply to be recognized as one and the same entity by its surroundings, and to be able to coordinate and communicate internally. Yet, the exact *extent, level, type* and *location* of this uniformity are anything but obvious. In a thoughtful exploration of this dilemma, Leidner (1993: 30) consciously chooses the extreme case of interactive service work at McDonald's, an organization obsessed with and recognized for uniformity. The dilemma is that: 'uniformity of output, a major goal of routinization, seems to be a poor strategy for maintaining quality ... since customers often perceive rigid uniformity as incompatible with quality'.

Much of the commercial success of McDonald's, contrary to more popular representations (Ritzer 2000), Leidner argues, hinges on the way uniformity is simultaneously *superimposed* by 'personalized' interaction, including friendly greetings ('how are you?'), smiles, gestures and even scripted jokes. Hence, the issue of what constitutes high quality for the customer cuts across simplistic dichotomies like uniform versus customized. It points to a conceptualization of standardization of work that avoids the perceptions of standardization as something imposed on docile subjects (Timmermans and Berg 2003).

As pointed out by Jones et al. (1998), the challenge when providing global services is to bridge the gap and get close by establishing 'authentic' relationships. These relationships are not singular links but rather need to be more broadly embedded and meshed: 'The new customer–supplier relationships involve longer-term, closer relationships based upon a high level of mutual trust; they are deeply socially, as well as economically, embedded' (Dicken et al. 1994: 39).

The notion of *embeddedness* underscores how action in general, and organizations more specifically, are bound up or embedded in local culture, social relations and networks. In his article, Granovetter (1989: 484) criticizes the 'under-socialized' conception of economic behaviour found in neo-classical economic theory as it: 'disallow[s] by hypothesis any impact of social structure and social relations on production, distribution, or consumption. In competitive markets, no producer or consumer noticeably influences aggregate supply or demand, or, therefore, prices or other terms of trade.'

Elaborating this point, Amin and Thrift (1994: 5) argue that part of the flows in a global world of interconnections, a world ruled by global-scale capitalist imperatives, continues to be constructed in and through 'territorially bound communities', thus making the notions of 'global village' or 'one world' deeply contradictory. In elaborating the relations between global 'forces' and local embeddedness, they view globalization as 'above all, a greater tying-in and subjugation of localities (cities and regions) to the global forces' (ibid.: 8). Even though the local is presented as a relational and relative concept which is fluid and constructed through its relation to global forces, Amin and Thrift maintain the importance of 'real' space in the sense of being 'constructed out of the juxtaposition, the intersection, the articulation, of multiple social relations' (p. 9). Places become shared spaces where the local meets globally distributed concepts, structures and impulses in an ongoing process.

Other scholars on globalization, especially Giddens (1990), emphasize how such close relationships are exactly what is under pressure. The disembedding of social relationships undermines the closeness, since: 'The advent of modernity increasingly tears space away from place by fostering relations between "absent" others, locationally distant from any given situation of face-to-face interaction' (ibid.: 18).

In this process, place gets 'increasingly *phantasmagoric*', a notion Giddens uses to denote the penetration of place by social influences distant from them. A local phenomenon is not solely structured by the things present there, but also by distanciated relations implying: 'the *disembedding* of social institutions ... the "lifting out" of social relations from local contexts and their rearticulating across indefinite tracts of time-space. This "lifting out" is exactly what I mean by disembedding, which is the key to the tremendous acceleration in time–space distanciation which modernity introduces' (italics added) (p. 21).

To compensate, bridge or mend the disembedded relations, they have to be re-embedded. This is a process that Giddens programmatically outlines as involving abstract trust, that is, going beyond traditional, interpersonal, face-to-face trust relations:

> *Reembedding* refers to processes by means of which faceless commitments are sustained or transformed by facework [face-to-face interaction]. (p. 88)

> My overall theses will be that all disembedding mechanisms interact with reembedding contexts of action, which may act either to support or to undermine them, and that faceless commitments are similarly linked in an ambiguous way with those demanding facework. (p. 80) (italics added)

The mediated character (telephone, fax, e-mail and other information systems) of the largely faceless interaction between the globally dispersed GSN network of RRM and the headquarters will necessarily imply abstract, not face-to-face, trust. As Knights et al. (2001: 316) point out, 'working for a company entails "interpersonal" *and* "institutional" dimensions of both trust and control'. Yet, combining a focus on local sites in global organizations with perceptions at the headquarters, highlights the abstract or institutional dimensions of trust. We aim to flesh out the programmatically stipulated role of abstract trust as it unfolds dynamically within a global organization.

The issue of trust in organizations has attracted a considerable interest recently (Ring and Van der Ven 1992; Fukuyama 1995; Lane 1998; Sako 1998; see also special issue of *Organization Studies*: 2001, **22** (2). This focus on the role of trust has several motivations. One strand attempts to ascribe decisive importance to the role that trust plays in facilitating regional networks of collaboration, thus accounting for their economic competitiveness (Piore and Sabel 1984). A second thread circles around basic principles of organizational behaviour and the extent to which trust does (or does not) function as an alternative mechanism for control (Lane 1998). As Knights et al. (2001: 313) point out, 'trust has commonly been identified as a feature of systems that posit an alternative to Taylorist and Fordist systems of control'. A third, and for our purposes most relevant entry into the debate, is the way that trust in institutions and abstract systems is deeply implicated in the set of transformation processes for which globalization acts as a convenient short-hand. The disembedding of social interaction through time–space separation presupposes trust in abstract systems (Giddens 1990: 87).

Given that trust does not materialize out of nowhere, the key issue for our purposes is to analyse the dynamics, that is, the process whereby trust in abstract systems is produced. Lane (1998) outlines three notions of trust: (i) 'calculative' trust based on a rational choice approach which 'does not stand up to sociological scrutiny' (ibid.: 7; compare Granovetter 1989); (ii) 'value- or norm-based' trust founded on the assumption that trust cannot develop without common values, thus side-stepping the issue of how these values come into being; and (iii) 'cognition- or expectation-based' trust which encompass a variety of strands that share the socially constructed basis of trust. With our ambition of analysing the dynamics of how abstract trust and hence re-embedding unfold, we employ the last of Lane's perspectives. From the general insights of science studies (Law 1991; Latour 1999), this implies treating trust methodologically as a process-oriented notion. In the same (methodological) manner as social arrangements, concepts, 'truth' and decisions, abstract trust is seen as the *performed* achievement involving enrolling allies, building coalitions and translating interests (Law 1991). An interesting aspect of this performative or process-oriented perspective on trust is the affinity with issues of control and power as 'power can be hidden behind the façade of "trust" and the rhetoric of "collaboration", and used to promote vested interests through the manipulation of and capitulation by weaker partners' (Clegg and Hardy 1996: 679) and as one 'seeks to construct, "enrol", and "mobilize" ... a compliant [relationship]' (Knights et al. 2001: 315). This avoids the dichotomy, pointed out by Knights et al., between trust and control.

In his analysis on the dynamics of modernity, Beck (1994) makes the relevant observation that despite the disembeddedness of social interaction, local action can – and indeed does – have 'global' implications. This underscores the point about trust made by several writers, namely its fragile nature (McAllister 1995; Lane 1998). Even 'small' events can have 'large', potentially unanticipated, effects. Hence, a too strict adherence to a specific level of analysis is problematic as 'the words "local" and "global" offer points of view on networks that are by nature neither local nor global, but more or less long and more or less connected' (Latour 1993: 122).

The fragility of trust implies that reaffirmation goes beyond mere repetitions. It is rather a necessary prerequisite for maintaining the relationship. Without reaffirmation it would fall apart: 'no institution can remain trusted without the continual reproduction of trust through interpersonal relations' (Knights et al. 2001: 314). Yet, as Beck (1994: 9) insists, the pursuit of it becomes increasingly futile in our age of reflexive modernity as: 'The expansion and heightening of the intention of control ultimately ends up producing the opposite'.

A salient aspect of trust is the emotional elements of it (McAllister 1995; Jones and George 1998). Emotions, Fineman (2000: 1) emphasizes, are not merely appended to the relations as 'boredom, envy, fear, love, anger, guilt, infatuation, embarrassment, nostalgia, anxiety – [they] are deeply woven into the way roles are enacted and learned, power is exercised, trust is held, commitment formed and decisions made'. This implies that attempts to factor out emotions are problematic. McAllister (1995: 25) represents such an attempt when distinguishing between affect- and cognition-based trust, the former of these 'grounded in reciprocated interpersonal care and concern'. McAllister's focus is exclusively on interpersonal trust between managers and employees, thus disregarding issues of abstract trust altogether. Jones and George (1998) also analyse emotional aspects of trust in their modelling of the experience and evolution of trust. Distinguishing between emotions (intense, instantaneous) and moods (less intense, generalized affective states), they present a three-phased model for the establishment of trust. Such a model with identifiable states and phases through which trust evolves breaks with the perspectives outlined above, which emphasize the ongoing, contingent and fragile aspects of trust.

Furthermore, by focusing exclusively on the experience of trust, Jones and George fail to link the emotional aspects of trust with the formation of identities as emphasized by scholars on the subject of globalization (Giddens 1990; Lane 1998; Castells 2001). The relevance of the link between identity formation and trust relations is that it serves to underpin the importance of trust to more than merely an issue of how well communication between units or individuals functions, and accordingly, how trust can either enhance or reduce job efficiency. In our case, it is fair to say that the emotional and identity-related experiences associated with trust are as important as the local GSN representatives' ability to do their job.

As Lane (1998: 23) explains, citing Luhmann (1979), the fragility and emotional aspects of trust are intimately tied up with the self-development of identity, a project radically different in a globalized world. Identity formation, according to Giddens (1990: 5; see also Castells 2001), takes the form of an individual trajectory in the modern society, a project disembedded from its traditional ties with family, background and culture as 'self-identity becomes a reflexively organised endeavour'.

Self-identity, lifted out of tradition, presupposes self-construction and revision, thus urging individuals into more consciously 'choosing' their own identity. Obviously this does not imply that traditions are irrelevant, only that they are delegated a less central role (Giddens 1990: 5).

Still, the basis for self-identity in the late modern world is risky, since it is open to reflexive, dynamic treatment, hence it is unstable. The lack of 'ontological security' (Giddens 1990), that is, the ground for acting and understanding the world forged by the de-traditionalization or disembedding dynamisms of late modernity, may accordingly lead to increasing 'existential anxiety'. This does not imply a total chaos and breakdown of self-identity, but indicates a more flexible and fluid construction of identity.

Thus professional life links closely with the broader handling of self-identity, implying that changes in work conditions become part of the project of self-identity. In this way, the question of trust relations concerning work can lead to deep and emotional reactions, as it is tied to the self-identity of individuals, not 'merely' their work.

Summing up, we have analysed empirically how the re-embedding of relationships hinges on the construction of abstract trust through processes characterized as (i) provisional (ongoing, performed), (ii) fragile (contingent, small events – large consequences, requiring reaffirmation) and (iii) emotional (tied up with identity formation as a trajectory).

**Background and setting of the study**

With Norway's long and winding coastline, Norwegians have always been a people concerned with fishing, trading and ship building. Over the last century, the maritime clusters of ship building have travelled from the south, then to the Oslo fjord area before ending up in their current stronghold in the northwest off Trondheim. An area dominated by very small, family-owned workshops and handcraft enterprises, the northwestern corner of Norway has during the last couple of decades developed into an extensive network of suppliers, subcontractors and customers of ships and ship equipment.

A major hub in this network has been the 80-year old business of the Ulstein family. During the 1980s, Ulstein gradually grew through smaller aquisitions and mergers in Norway, Sweden and Finland. Priding themselves on producing high-quality, handcrafted products – including 'the Rolls-Royce of propellers' – Ulstein grew into a substantial maritime conglomerate, whose constituent sites enjoyed extensive autonomy.

Thriving on the offshore boom following the Norwegian build-up of oil production in the North Sea, Ulstein was simultaneously exposed to the significant fluctuations within this sector. In 1998, in a bold move to escape from this vulnerable position and to the surprise of most of the maritime cluster, family owner Morten Ulstein decided to specialize and differentiate by splitting Ulstein into the (still family-owned) Ulstein Shipyards and selling off Ulstein Industrier, the distributed network of largely autonomous production sites for ship equipment such as propellers, gears, bearings, winches, rudders, diesel engines, thrusters and automation in a NOK 3.9 billion ($500m) sale. In an effort to secure a firm footing, Ulstein Industrier merged a year later with the London-based Vickers to form Vickers-Ulstein with 5000 employees. This set off a series of major reorganizing efforts aimed at 'realizing the synergies', a challenge that had to overcome the traditional competition between the former Ulstein and elements of Vickers. The formative stages of this process were the period following the Vickers-Ulstein merger.

In essence, the commercial logic underlying the merger was to exploit the potential for a wider product range, moving towards complete, systems solutions rather than singular installations and 'local support provided globally'. A vital element in achieving this was the GSN, which is the globally distributed sales and service function. Far from completion, these reorganization processes were interrupted by an acquisition: the whole of Vickers-Ulstein with its 50 000 employees was acquired by Rolls-Royce less than a year later. In an effort to expand into areas outside its traditional (and stagnating) bias towards military aspects of the maritime sector, what was to be called Rolls-Royce Marine was established to gain a footing in the potentially expanding commercial marine area. Although modified, the basic thrust and direction of the reorganization process initiated with Vickers-Ulstein was continued by RRM. In a gesture to underscore its willingness to decentralize, Rolls-Royce decided to locate the new RRM headquarters in Ulsteinvik, the traditional homeground of Ulstein.

Our data collection relies primarily on a total of 31 semi-structured interviews conducted in eight rounds during 1999–2002. The early ones were relatively open-ended, exploring the issues and tensions embedded in the reorganization efforts. This led to a gradual focus on the relationship between GSN and the suppliers as a core theme. The interviews were conducted at five sites: the two largest GSN sites, the two largest supplier sites within RRM (called the 'principals' by employees, and located in Scandinavia) and the headquarters. Table 17.1 summarizes the interviews.

*Table 17.1    Interview categories and number of informants*

|  | GSN representatives | Suppliers' representatives |
| --- | --- | --- |
| Senior management | 2 | 4 |
| Middle management | 5 | 4 |
| Sales | 4 | 5 |
| Service | 3 | 4 |
| Total | 14 | 17 |

In addition, there were four meetings aimed at validating preliminary interpretations by discussing observations with stakeholders in RRM. In total, 16 people participated in these meetings, providing objections to, comments on and elaborations of our observations. We have also had access to internal newsletters (*In-depth, Marine Info*), memos, reports, contracts and electronic archives.

## Managing over distance

### Getting close to the customers
As outlined earlier, much attention has been focused on the 'sovereign' customer and the need for organizations to be more responsive and flexible

to customer demands. The ongoing reorganization in RRM, starting with the Vickers-Ulstein merger, is heralded under the banner of 'customer facing'. In part, this is but a mirror image of the more general trend, yet the specifics of the history and configuration of RRM provide crucial, additional weight to the general trends. In the case of RRM, the form this takes is shaped by a number of parallel, superimposed processes and agendas.

Managerial strategies promoting the importance of closeness to customers should not be shrugged off as mere espoused theories (du Gay and Salaman 1992). Managerial representations, social constructivist thinking instructs us, are 'real' in the sense of having (potential) influence on the organization and contents of work. Hence, there is but a modest element of innovation when RRM proclaims its 'global but local' strategy:

> The basic 'global but local' strategy was initiated last year [in 1999] following the forging of Vickers Marine with Ulstein ... It has now been embraced by Rolls-Royce in its new marine business ... Rolls-Royce is increasingly moving towards a higher level of local competence, a greater level of locally-stocked spare parts, and an expanded logistics planning system. Overall the company is moving closer to the customer, cutting delays and improving response times to calls for assistance. (*In-depth*, Autumn 2000: 5)

Indeed, most global companies are under pressure to 'think globally, and act locally' (Ger 1999: 75). The interesting aspect of such a strategy is how it is construed, negotiated and translated, that is, how this hybrid is worked out in practice.

From a managerial point of view, a key strategic objective was to integrate the different producers in order to construct 'one' RRM. Still struggling to smooth out the wrinkles, not to say distrust or mutual ignorance, between the former production units and brands, customer facing was intimately tied up with presenting a more uniform, non-fragmented and integrated image to the outside world. In reality, the task of coordinating the contacts with the customers in RRM has been delegated to a so-called 'account manager'. The intention was that the account manager would establish a seamless link between the customers and the whole range of RRM's products and services. Parallel to this, the company also switched from a product-based organization to a market segment-based organization, by organizing its activities according to four different market segments, each responsible for marketing the whole range of products in its segment. The strategic effect of this is that the initiative and resources are taken from the factory's staff of engineers and their focus on technical solutions, and transferred to the account managers, as explained by a GSN representative:

GSN crosses all boundaries; you could almost say that we're not interested in the segments, we're not interested in which principal [supplier, Scandinavian based] is supplying the equipment. Our focus is on the customer. The customer has a product, and he has a problem where he is. We provide the skills, we liaise with the principals to get the information required and the spare parts and the service support necessary to support our customer.

Hence, one element in the RRM's strategy was to tie the different producers together. For our purposes, however, a more relevant aspect of the intention to get close is related to the transformation – perceived or for real – of the very business of RRM. Scholars have for some time pointed out the deficiencies of Fordist ideals of production and the corresponding importance of flexibility, responsiveness and decreasing vertical integration (Piore and Sabel 1984; Womack 1990). Alongside and beyond this, RRM is in the midst of a transformation whereby their services (repair, maintenance and spare part delivery and installation) are growing in importance. As one local representative, half-jokingly, half-seriously, explained:

Gillette realized a long time ago that they were only going to sell you one razor every 5 years or so. But once a month they would sell you new blades [saying]: 'let's give away the razors, and let's charge an arm and a leg for a very specialized little blade that you can't buy anywhere else' ... It's an analogy that fits here; it's the same approach ... basically a philosophy where you want the customer over the full lifetime of the product ... We should absolutely be taking the same approach ... Let's bundle it all together: maintenance, finance, insurance, the lot.

This emphasis on (locally embedded) service delivery gives the 'closeness' to the customer a different meaning. To the extent that service work is increasing, the importance of local presence, local competence and embeddedness is growing. As a senior manager of GSN points out:[1] 'Local presence is the company's greatest differentiator in the market. The fact that we have the largest ground force in the market is one of our key strategic advantages ... a key objective is to ... build local customer relationships.' Similarly, as pointed out in the information material of RRM:

With offices in 33 countries, Rolls-Royce offers an unequalled global marine support capability. This international presence is strengthened by a team of more than 500 personnel, of whom over 300 are service engineers. *Such an organisation is unique in the world today* ... [RRM's] strategy is to get closer to the customer, beginning with a commitment to embrace local languages and cultures wherever practical. (*In-depth*, Autumn 2000: 5, emphasis added)

For a company with the prevailing identity very much tied up with production-oriented images and symbols, clearly this transformation is not without friction. Priding themselves in, and identifying with, 'manufacturing the Rolls-Royce of propellers', it involves issues of power as well as identity.

What, then, does the local embeddedness amount to and how is it performed (Amin and Thrift 1994; Ger 1999)? Leidner (1993) discusses how service work, when delivered globally, seeks to superimpose scripted and uniform procedures with closer, more personalized features. One local representative explains:

> Every customer is different and as I said before, it's knowing when to push towards the customer, and knowing when not to, when to fall back. You have to be able to relate to people from all different levels in the client company and through that develop a sort of sense of or a 'feel' for the customer.

This personal feeling is required as 'customers increasingly demand that [service work] is "authentic", [hence] cannot easily be standardised' (Jones et al. 1998: 1049).

The closeness argument is driven by two agendas. It is in part a vehicle for realizing the merger by presenting a uniform front stage that purges the former distinctions between the different suppliers (and their networks). Simultaneously there is an emphasis on the locally embedded, 'authentic' relationships with the customers.

### Global uniformity and local autonomy

The emphasis on closeness and service is, at least on an espoused level, accomplished by a delegation or 'empowerment' of the local representatives, as voiced by a senior RRM manager:[2]

> In other words, we are empowering the local [representative] ... to represent the entire company. Previously, there was the propeller man or the water jet man working for the Ulstein propeller network, the Bergen network, the Kamewa network, and so on. *Now the account manager can 'own' the customer relationship* and represent the entire group instead of being restricted to promoting one type of product. (emphasis added)

The literature on empowerment is, of course, systematically ambiguous as to whether this is due to functionalist reasons, as illustrated by a senior GSN manager:[3] 'The establishment of such a capability [local service and sales through GSN] is in direct response to customer requests: they want to be able to talk to personnel in their time zone, and not have to wait days while specialists are flown in from European-based factories', or whether this indeed implies empowerment in a 'true' sense (Clegg and Hardy 1996). Despite the dangers of slipping into an essentialist vocabulary, separating 'true' from 'façade' versions, claims about empowerment need to be approached with critical awareness (Knights et al. 2001).

A key, regulating and disciplining vehicle in this is the formal, contractual agreement between the suppliers (the production sites largely located at 'home' in Scandinavia) and the globally distributed local representatives of GSN ('away' across 33 countries). The agreement defines how cooperation between local representatives of the company (within the GSN) and the suppliers operates; describes the duties and obligations that the respective parties have towards one another; regulates responsibilities, standards for payments and procedures in the event of disputes between them; and regulates the activities of local representatives by specifying their responsibility to inform and obtain acceptance from the suppliers, about how to market products, and what information to distribute to customers. More specifically, with the agreement, the suppliers retain control over all contracts, and the responsibility for negotiating and accepting them, and forwarding offers to customers, direct or via local representatives.

The suppliers specify and regulate, on a fairly detailed level, what the local representatives can do with regard to marketing and sales of new equipment. The service work is more autonomously organized. Nevertheless, the local representatives may neither manufacture nor purchase spare parts from anyone other than the suppliers, except with the approval of the latter.[4] The master agreement is a key disembedding mechanism (Giddens 1990: 18).

In as much as it is purged of interpersonal relations, the agreement is phrased entirely in terms of specifying roles, obligations and duties. As a consequence of this, the control and distribution of product knowledge and information is strictly maintained by the suppliers, leading to friction and frustration at the local sites, as one GSN representative declared:

> The production sites are reluctant to share the information with us, even when this had made life a lot easier for us – and for them. This is how it's always been. Some of the sites are good at sending updated information while this [pointing on the screen] is a list from 1998. ... Internally at the production sites they have electronic access to all information, also the drawings. But we are cut off from this.

The agreement produces – largely unintentionally (Giddens 1990; Beck 1994) – effects that are perceived as the opposite of those embedded in the ideals of 'customer facing'. This disembedding does not imply that work and work routines disintegrate. It is rather the case that re-embedding takes the form of additional, often 'invisible' work that serves to fill the glitches and bridge the gaps (Bowker and Star 1999). The disembedded nature of the work at the local sites, without close links with 'home', gives rise to an extensive set of work-arounds to collect necessary information (Gasser 1986) as one GSN representative explains, referring to his ICT system: 'Now we have to go back and forth continually, both to get the right article numbers and the right parts prices. To work around the problems, we make use of old orders to look up prices, possibly updating these from our private archives'.

Thus, the detailed controlling and regulation of local autonomy, intended to ensure high-quality service, risks producing the opposite effect. This underscores an important and darker aspect of the discourse on globalization (Beck 1994: 9), whereby pursuing control – may in itself produce the opposite effect. As the meshing and interleaving of local and global action increase, traditional means of control are countereffective in so far as the side-effects are as important as the intended ones (Giddens 1990; Beck 1994; Ciborra 2000). As one of the GSN representatives complained, attempts at customer facing seem to produce the opposite effects: 'RRM has decided that GSN should buy everything through the production units. This causes problems, especially when the customer knows that they can buy it locally at a better price. *Is that customer focus*?! It's disastrous for our reputation'. This was reiterated by another GSN spare parts manager:

> I am forced to order spare parts from the factory. Even when it comes to parts that they don't produce there. For instance, a bearing: the customer needs this and I say OK, I can get that and it will cost you, for example, $500. But the customer knows he can get this part from a local supplier for half the price! And I will never sell another part like that again ... and what's the value of our organization? The value is our reputation.

The reason for withholding this information from the local representatives, and for the centralized control of spare parts, is because the suppliers have to maintain control over these things, as laid out in the agreement. The suppliers want to prevent sensitive information from getting out, and therefore they restrict access to central ICT resources. They need to ensure that the local representatives follow standards on prices and what spare parts to use in equipment supplied by the company.

The design, production and servicing of high-quality equipment such as that in the RRM portfolio invariably involve a substantial amount of highly competent work. The booming literature on knowledge-intensive work, despite its distinctly rhetorical slant (Alvesson 2001), reinforces many of the arguments about the local, contextual and situated nature of service work (Blackler 1995). In her comparative study of knowledge work in a British and Japanese engineering company, Lam (1997) demonstrates the locally (culturally) embedded character of the work routines in the British and Japanese teams. Similarly, the locally embedded knowledge about the market and the customers was challenged when Rolls-Royce initially attempted to promote their traditional mode of operating. Yet, the input of the British Rolls-Royce work routines is largely sidelined, as a senior RRM manager explains: 'they show up in ties and black suits demonstrating a total lack of insight into the business ... accustomed to military projects with time-spans of decades and enormous amounts of bureaucratic documentation overhead, the work routines of Rolls-Royce are of little value to us'. As argued by Jones et al. (1998), the recruitment policy is typically the acid test for assessing the commitment of global organizations to cultural heterogeneity. The pattern they describe, where employees from the 'home' country are favoured, is also evident in RRM. The pivotal role of the former, Norwegian-based Ulstein group caused substantial frustration within the GSN as several interviewees complained about 'Norwegians showing up everywhere'. This was reinforced, one GSN representative explained, by the fact that it 'comes together with talk about Scandinavian egalitarism'.

Part of the major reorganization is also to enable more synergies between compatible and possible connected products and services. On sales and production this is pursued by configuring products into packages or 'total solutions' to paraphrase RRM's strategy. But this global ambition also concerns the way customers will be equipped, and thus affects the work of local service personnel:

> You're talking about the impossible here; these are the silly guys in an office who say 'well, let's throw these guys together'. It doesn't work that way. We have got, let's say, about 30 different products, Ulstein has got just as many ... And you can't mix your products with somebody else's products, because that weakens his position. Instead of making him strong, you are spreading his expertise too thinly across many products.

Finally, the formal agreement also structures the division of labour between the local sales personnel (account managers), and the sales and marketing representative of the head office at the production sites. A further narrowing of the 'empowerment' of local representatives is due to splitting the actual pre-sales work and the final responsibility for contracts. The locals must in this final phase 'hand over' the customer to the head office representative – disembedding the relationship – and potentially upsetting the customers. As a UK-based GSN representative explains:

> A lot of UK customers want to deal with the UK company. The fact that the products are made somewhere else is not really relevant; they still would like to deal with the UK company – with the thought that if anything goes wrong, it's Rolls-Royce UK that is responsible.

This also has a more practical side, since the relationship between local representatives and customers evolves over time in a project, and thereby makes it difficult for the customers to deal with the suppliers in the final phase of a project:

> This happened recently, on a couple of projects, we had done all the work with the company, and they come to place the order, and we say 'oh no, don't send it to us, send it to Sweden or something'. And they go 'but we can't do that, we've dealt with you, all our correspondence is with you, and you're telling me I have got to deal with somebody else?'.

Also, the switch implies that customers will have to communicate with various units and people, since each of the suppliers will have to make their own contracts on the equipment they provide:

> And we've got a UK shipyard. They want to buy steering gear for one project, and a propeller for another project. They don't want to go to RR Norway for one, and RR Sweden for another. They want to deal with one company, not the whole range. And they come to us then, if they've got a problem; who is going to sort it out? And I think from a customer's point of view, this makes a lot of sense. Of course, that should be why we're here. We are the local office.

A more general way of viewing this problem is that local contact with customers presupposes a deep interest and knowledge of who they are, of how to communicate and approach them, and last but not least, when to contact them. As one GSN representative explains:

> You get a sort of a feel for when the customer would like a visit ... Every customer is different, I mean we even find some of the shipyards are only too pleased for us to help with design and that sort of thing because they haven't got their own design, whereas other shipyards have got a design department and are not interested in that aspect of what we can sell. So you have to treat each customer, you know, have to give them what they want, and sometimes we have to say to the principals [production sites, in Scandinavia]: 'you know, hold back a little bit, this customer doesn't at this stage want that aspect'.

The key, regulatory device, the agreement between GSN and the suppliers, is a disembedding mechanism that also produces effects exactly opposite to those intended. The lack of local appropriation of the agreement by drawing on local resources implies, at times, anything but closeness to the customer. The locally embedded knowledge about acquiring a 'feel' for the customer tends to become invisible and downplayed (Bowker and Star 1999). Although the formal agreements and prescripts are tools the company uses to regulate the way work is done by local representatives and the suppliers, there will still be situations where locals have to make decisions based on their own experiences and knowledge. The local representatives, embedded in their local contexts, will have competence and experience which makes them able to adapt to the local customers and their specific needs in ways that could, as we have seen, be different from the more globally standardized designs of the head office.

### Trust and (ICT-)mediated communication

At heart, RRM's reorganization efforts involve transformation along two dimensions. First, it necessarily involves eroding the previous boundaries defined by the production sites to emerge as a 'seamlessly integrated' collective for production. In short, the internal organization should move away from functional units to a more process-oriented one. Second, and the focus of this chapter, it implies viewing the whole value chain – production, logistics, sales and service – in total rather than as disturbingly independent entities with bounded responsibility and accountability. An essential mechanism in this, then, is to tie in and integrate the activities 'abroad' in the GSN with the (production) activities 'at home'. This implies carving out roles and responsibilities, but more importantly, it requires establishing a sense of trust that *facilitates* this communication and cooperation. Establishing, maintaining and expanding the trust between GSN and 'home' acts as a key element in re-embedding this relationship. As outlined earlier, we employ a process-oriented perspective that underscores the performative nature of the construction of trust.

The construction of abstract trust relations between the local sites and the head office is tied to how the actors perceive the process. In our case, ongoing and provisional aspects of trust are displayed in the need for the local representatives to be *reassured and reaffirmed.* This illustrates how power issues intertwine with establishing trust (Knights et al. 2001). Being part of, and not excluded from, the whole of the company is of course one way to ensure that the relation is important both for the (Scandinavian) 'home' office, and the 'local' office abroad. Much of the communication between home and the GSN is about offering information, responding to inquiries from the GSN on prices, availability of parts and delivery time. One of the perceived problems at the local level is the significance of the time span from when inquiries are sent until an answer is received, as one interviewee illustrates:

> There was this oil rig off the coast of Texas, and we had delivered 8 rotating azimuth thrusters, each of 40 tons. They were prepared and overhauled at the factory and sent over. A month ago, we got a message that there were some problems. I sent a letter to the principals describing what the problems were, the need for equipment, and the price of having the job done. We also needed drawings and technical specifications to sort things out for the service engineer.

> It took 4 weeks to get an answer! If I had been a local guy, this wouldn't happen. They have no respect for the things we're trying to do, and I have no-one up in the system to go to. It hits a black hole!

Building on Harold Garfinkel, process-based trust focus on how expectations are formed over time by the accumulated trust experiences (Lane 1998: 11). Expectations differ in the way they assume unity of expectation either to be present and taken for granted, or, alternatively, to have to be produced. Process-based trust entails the incremental process of building trust through the gradual accumulation of either direct or indirect knowledge of the social relation present. Typically, the way these trust relations can be developed and maintained, is through various forms of feedback among the participants, or to what extent they give confirmation on each other's initiatives, or approvals of the way the work is conducted. In the episode quoted above, the lack of feedback ('it hits a black hole') undermines the possibility of building and maintaining trust relations. The experienced silence ('black hole') gives little reassurance of the commitment from head office. Confirmation from 'home', even without a fully-fledged answer to the query, functions reassuringly and soothingly, re-establishing the ties that could otherwise be disembedded.

This lack of confirmation was not a unique episode, as one GSN representative explains:

> When I send an inquiry to the factory for some parts and prices, they sometimes send me a confirmation, but many of them don't, and then I am not sure whether they've got it or not, if it's lost, disappeared or something. I even get some answers that it's the first time they've seen it. It would be a tremendous benefit if they could just tell me they've got it, and if they could keep me informed of the progress as to when I could get a proper answer. Instead I have to call up every now and then, pushing so that I can have something to feed to the customers.

The local representatives experience the lack of feedback through long response times without any periodic updates. Further, the lack of technical data, handbooks, diagrams and so on intensifies the disembedding of locals from their head office in matters of knowledge and the ability to influence their own work. An employee working with ordering and handling spare parts commented:

> Because we have no diagrams or handbooks, we don't know what we're offering. And it's a big problem. Sometimes we can have a handbook, and we can look at the diagrams and say 'oh yeah, that O-ring goes there', but we wouldn't necessarily know where the items should go. If the customer finds out that he is probably a couple of O-rings short, we wouldn't know.

Since RRM maintains what we may call 'double' functions on both sales and service, in the sense that both suppliers and local representatives are capable of doing the work, this causes situations where they might cross each other's 'borders', as the following statement from one GSN representative illustrates:

From time to time, the suppliers send people over to our territory that we don't know about before they're actually here, and this is not good for us, and it doesn't look good in front of the customers. And it is not a good way of using our resources. Someone can suddenly come into our office here and ask for help with something, without us knowing that they were here.

Similarly, another GSN representative commented:

When [the after-sales] was identified as the biggest cash generator, everyone wanted to be engaged in the after-sales. There is no clear organization to it. For example: we have people who come from Finland to our sales territory to deal in the after-sales market, and we have no idea what they're doing.

The negotiated border between local representatives and the suppliers regarding these double functions, threatens to damage or disrupt any potential establishment and maintenance of trust relations, and thereby makes the empowering of the locals a difficult ambition to fulfil. This underscores the fragile aspect of trust, making it difficult to maintain, but easy to disturb. The locals express their insecurity towards the suppliers' motives and their practice of bypassing the locals.

RRM's strategy of getting closer to the customer is – both by empowering the local representatives and through improved internal coordination – to secure sales across the whole product range of the company. But this clashes with established routines for ensuring the suppliers' control over how the local representatives do their work. The tensions between the need for uniformity in a global product, and service range and local autonomy surface as problems of sharing information, different modes of trust/distrust relations, and finally through negotiated borders concerning the way the company coordinates the double functions of both suppliers and local representatives on sales and services.

The issue of trust also concerns the way in which these actors view each other's knowledge and competence. Given that identity formation is increasingly influenced by professional trajectories (Giddens 1990; Castells 2001), this underscores how trust is linked to existential anxiety. Lack of trust in local competence thus translates into an issue of identity. As one GSN representative states:

Once a brand new man was set to work with two senior service engineers [from the suppliers]. It was a major overhaul and the seniors took the dayshift, and left him alone on the nightshift, to supervise the nightwork. And he made a mistake, and damaged a bearing, and they said: 'Ahaa! This is what we've been talking about; they don't know what they're doing here. These Americans don't know what they're doing, they're sledgehammer mechanics!' They were prejudiced against Americans.

The newly designed agreement, described earlier, specifies that warranty work is the responsibility of the suppliers. However, the coordination between local representatives and suppliers is not a straightforward matter, and has been a source of insecurity and distrust. Further, with regard to more complex cases concerning warranty claims, a GSN representative complains that the suppliers question the local competence:

When a customer claims a warranty case, this always happens after having received an invoice, with a service report. The claim from the customer is forwarded to the supplier, but in nearly all cases these are rejected. They don't acknowledge our competence or the serviceman's competence, and blame the customer. We get the impression that no matter what, our reports don't matter. The suppliers see us as acting on behalf of the customer. It's very frustrating!

This insecurity stems from the way the local, GSN representatives get caught in the middle between the customers and the suppliers. The actions and reactions of the suppliers on warranty claims from customers are interpreted as more or less open distrust and a questioning of their (the locals) integrity, loyalty and competence.

The link between trust and identity formation accounts for the deeply emotional aspects (Lane 1998). Disrespecting local competence in the GSN network becomes not merely an issue of additional work and unnecessary hassles (as described above; see also Gasser 1986). More importantly, it undermines the local GSN representatives' identity within RRM by transforming it into a question of whether they are part of the family or not. Or, as expressed by one local GSN representative, whether they are 'real' children or only 'stepchildren':

I got the feeling that they feel like, and I hate to say this, that we would misuse it. And I therefore feel like, you know, I hate to say, *feel like a stepchild*, but in that sense basically I have been here for 10 years, and I don't think I have misused too much of any information.

Confronted with this, management at the suppliers and head office replied: 'Well, they're right. To our knowledge and in our experience, local representatives have in cases acted more as representatives of the customers than the company.' They also add that 'it's a jungle out there, that's a well-known fact in this business', so customers use confidential information from suppliers in a game to win favourable deals. The culture of this business does not invite trust, unless there is the danger of becoming vulnerable.

Luhmann (1979) views trust and distrust as mutual and connected qualities. The connection between them explains the fragility and highly *emotional reactions* when trust is betrayed. Trust is a learned experience, in a process of generalizing from isolated experiences, closely tied up with identity formation ('stepchildren' versus 'real' children). This is because the choice of trusting or distrusting is an inner process of the individual. One falsehood may therefore cause great emotional intensity and undermine trust in the future (McAllister 1995; Lane 1998). In this way, trust may be transformed into distrust, and therefore, to prevent this from happening, trust must be sustained through appropriate actions. The reactions and frustrations of the local representatives can also be interpreted as reactions to more fundamental attacks on their personal identity or character according to the more individualized 'responsibility' of reflexive identity construction (Giddens 1990).

## Conclusion

We have analysed the dilemmas of a global company struggling to forge hybrid solutions, combining the need for control and uniformity while at the same time responding to the increasing pressure for more locally embedded customer focus in service work. Based on an empirical analysis of how local sales and service offices negotiate and perceive the 'gap' between these demands, we argue that this dilemma goes beyond questions of managerial models and organizational structures.

Building on the tensions in the 'late modernity' of Giddens, between disembedding mechanisms and re-embedding local actions, the issue of abstract trust becomes salient in our analysis. The role of ICT-mediated communication is deeply implicated here. We argue that the notion of trust in previous research on global organizations has had a tendency to neglect the importance of emotional aspects of abstract trust, and the connection between identity formations and constructions in late modernity on the one hand, and trust relations on the other.

We propose three distinctive characteristics of abstract trust relations within global organizations: (i) the process-based, ongoing perspective emphasizing the dynamic need to assure and reaffirm trust relations, due to (ii) the fragile aspects of trust which makes it hard to establish and maintain, but easy to disturb, and finally (iii) the emotional aspects of trust, connecting trust to the reflexive 'project' of self-identity constructions in late modernity.

**Acknowledgement**

We are grateful to Michael Barratt, Stefan Hoffmann, Matthew Jones, Morten Levin, Knut H. Rolland, Susan Scott, Knut H. Sørensen and Geoff Walsham for comments on earlier versions of our chapter. We have also benefited from comments from the reviewers of the Handbook. This work has in part been sponsored by the project 'Business Prospects' NTNU.

**Notes**

1. Interview in *Marine Info*, November 1999: 6.
2. Interview in *Marine Info*, November 1999: 6.
3. Interview in *In-depth*, Spring 2001: 17.
4. The exact details of this agreement, which have been continuously negotiated, are confidential, so we are obliged to describe it in fairly general terms. The most recent version, stemming from spring 2001, spells out the autonomy of the local sites, together with regulations concerning internal pricing and the settling of disputes.

**References**

Alvesson, M. (2001), 'Knowledge work: ambiguity, image and identity', *Human Relations*, **54** (7): 863–86.
Amin, A. and Thrift, N. (1994), 'Living in the global', in Amin and Thrift (eds), *Globalization, Institutions, and Regional Development in Europe*, Oxford: Oxford University Press, pp. 1–23.
Beck, U. (1994), 'The reinvention of politics', in Ulrich Beck, Anthony Giddens and Scott Lash (eds), *Reflexive Modernity*, Cambridge: Polity, pp. 1–55.
Blackler, F. (1995), 'Knowledge, knowledge work and organizations: an overview and interpretation', *Organization Studies*, **16** (6): 1021–46.
Bowker, G. and Star, S.L. (1999), *Sorting Things Out: Classification and Its Consequences*, Cambridge, MA: MIT Press.
Castells, Manuel (2001), *The Power of Identity*, 2nd edn, Oxford: Blackwell.
Ciborra, C. (ed.) (2000), *From Control to Drift: The Dynamics of Global, Corporate Infrastructure*, Oxford: Oxford University Press.
Clegg, S. and Hardy, C. (1996), 'Conclusions: representations', in S.R. Clegg, C. Hardy and W.R. Nord (eds), *Handbook of Organization Studies*, London: Sage, pp. 676–708.
Dicken, P., Forsgren, M. and Malmgren, A. (1994), 'The local embeddedness of transnational corporations', in A. Amin and N. Thrift (eds), *Globalization, Institutions, and Regional Development in Europe*, Oxford: Oxford University Press, pp. 23–45.
du Gay, P. and Salaman, G. (1992), 'The cult[ure] of the customer', *Journal of Management Studies*, **29** (5): 615–33.
Fineman, Stephen (2000), 'Emotional arenas revisited', in Fineman (ed.), *Emotions in Organizations*, London: Sage, pp. 1–24.
Freeman, C. and Perez, C. (1988), 'Structural crisis of adjustment, business cycles and investment behaviour', in G. Dosi, C. Freeman, R. Nelson, G. Silverberg and L. Soete (eds), *Technological Change and Economical Theory*, London: Pinter.
Fukuyama, F. (1995), *Trust: The Social Virtues and the Creation of Prosperity*, London: Hamish Hamilton.
Gasser, L. (1986), 'The integration of computing and routine work', *Association of Computing Machinery (ACM) Transactions on Office Information Systems*, **4**: 205–25.
Ger, G. (1999), 'Localizing in the global village: local firms competing in global markets', *California Management Review*, **41** (4): 64–83.
Ghoshal, S. and Barlett, C. (1989), *Managing Across Borders: The Transnational Solution*, Boston, MA: Harvard Business School Press.
Giddens, Anthony (1990), *The Consequences of Modernity*, Cambridge: Polity.

Granovetter, M. (1989), 'Economic action and social structure: a theory of embeddedness', *American Journal of Sociology*, **91**: 481–510.

Jones, C., Thompson, P. and Nickson, D. (1998), 'Not part of the family? The limits to managing the corporate way in international hotel chains', *International Journal of Human Resource Management*, **9** (6): 1048–63.

Jones, G. and George, J. (1998), 'The experience and evolution of trust: implications for cooperation and teamwork', *Academy of Management Review*, **23** (3): 531–46.

Keat, R. (1990), 'Introduction', in R. Keat and N. Abercrombie (eds), *Enterprise Culture*, London: Routledge.

Knights, D., Noble, F., Vurdubakis, T. and Willmott, H. (2001), 'Chasing shadows: control, virtuality and the production of trust', *Organization Studies*, **22** (2): 311–36.

Lam, A. (1997), 'Embedded firms, embedded knowledge: problems of collaboration and knowledge transfer in global cooperative ventures', *Organization Studies*, **18** (6): 973–96.

Lane, Christel (1998), 'Introduction: theories and issues in the study of trust', in C. Lane and R. Bachmann (eds), *Trust Within and Between Organisations*, Oxford: Oxford University Press (2000 edn), pp. 1–30.

Latour, B. (1993), *We Have Never Been Modern*, Brighton: Harvester Wheatsheaf.

Latour, B. (1999), *Pandora's Hope: Essays on the Reality of Science Studies*, Cambridge, MA: Harvard University Press.

Law, J. (1991), *A Sociology of Monsters: Essays on Power, Technology and Domination*, John Law (ed.), Sociological Review Monograph 38, London: Routledge.

Leidner, R. (1993), *Fast Food, Fast Talk: Service Work and the Routinization of Everyday Life*, Berkeley, CA: University of California Press.

Luhmann, N. (1979), *Trust and Power*, Chichester: John Wiley.

McAllister, D.J. (1995), 'Affect- and cognition-based trust as foundation for interpersonal cooperation in organizations', *Academy of Management Journal*, **38** (1): 24–59.

Nohria, N. and Ghoshal, S. (1997), *The Differentiated Network: Organizing Multinational Corporations for Value Creation*, San Francisco, CA: Jossey-Bass.

Piore, M. and Sabel, C. (1984), *The Second Industrial Divide*, New York: Basic Books.

Ring, P.S. and Van der Ven, A.H. (1992), 'Structuring cooperative relationships between organizations', *Strategic Management Journal*, **13**: 483–98.

Ritzer, George (2000), *The McDonaldization of Society*, Thousand Oaks, CA: Pine Forge Press.

Sako, M. (1998), *Prices, Quality and Trust: Inter-firm Relations in Britain and Japan*, Cambridge: Cambridge University Press.

Timmermans, S. and Berg, M. (2003), *The Gold Standard: The Challenge of Evidence-based Medicine and Standardization in Health Care*, Philadelphia, PA: Temple University Press.

Womack, J.P. (1990), *The Machine that Changed the World*, New York: Rawson Associates.

# 18 Competing rationalities: a critical study of telehealth in the UK

*Ela Klecun*

## Introduction

Telehealth offers an interesting, rapidly changing field to study that encompasses a wide range of health services delivered at a distance and, more specifically, over various telecommunication networks. The history of telehealth is chequered, with the majority of early projects failing to survive the end of funding and being unable to move from projects to sustainable services. Yet, increased pressure on the health services in many countries and advances in technology brought renewed interest in telehealth in the 1980s and 1990s (Perednia and Allen 1995; Darkins and Cary 2000). So far, in the UK, the majority of telehealth services are provided by pilot, small scale projects (May et al. 2001; Klecun-Dabrowska and Cornford 2002). These tend to be funded as research as much as operational systems. They differ in scale, type of services offered and application area (in terms of medical speciality and geographical scope), and they employ different technologies and target diverse users, reflecting the heterogeneous nature of telehealth (Klecun-Dabrowska 2002). Nevertheless, large government initiatives, which could be classified under a broad umbrella of telehealth, are gaining momentum. For example, a nurse-led triage telephone system (NHS Direct) is in operation throughout the country, electronic bookings systems are being piloted, and the Integrated Care Records Service (ICRS), a portfolio of services covering the generation, movement and access to health records, is one of the four key deliverables set out in the new National Health Service (NHS) information technology (IT) procurement strategy (DOH 2002). Health organizations are being encouraged to consider telemedicine for all new initiatives undertaken (DOH 1997, 1999, 2002; HMSO 1999).

The research into telehealth has been primarily concerned with the technology and its performance, and – to a lesser extent – the economic and organizational feasibility of telehealth services, legal considerations and ways of evaluating telehealth. Most of the literature on telehealth reports on individual projects and often on this limited basis makes claims regarding benefits of telehealth. Alternatively, 'visionary' works make sweeping statements about telehealth and its potential for solving all shortcomings of current healthcare systems, particularly in terms of immediate access to specialists and medical knowledge. There are some works, however, which discuss the many problems faced by telehealth services, not least organizational and social aspects, and challenges their evaluation (Wootton and Craig 1999; May and Ellis 2001; May et al. 2003). Although sharing many of these concerns, the research reported in this chapter aims to address fundamental assumptions about the nature and role of telehealth in the UK. To this end, critical theory has been used to draw out key *rationalities*, the identification of which forms a contribution to the understanding of social, organizational and technological change in healthcare.

In the field of information systems (IS), the call to study problems from a critical theory perspective has been explicitly voiced by a growing number of researchers (Lyytinen and Klein 1985; Hirschheim and Klein 1989, 1994; Jonsson 1991; Ngwenyama 1991; Lyytinen 1992; Myers and Young 1997; Wilson 1997; Saravanamuthu and Wood-Harper 2001; Doolin and Lowe 2002). Most of this research tends to be theoretical in nature and the majority of papers draw on Jürgen Habermas's theories, although there are calls for broadening this interest (Brooke 2002). This research is an example of such a broader critical research, drawing on the Frankfurt school, Herbert Marcuse, Andrew Feenberg and more recent insights of information society theories.

The central idea in critical theory is that all social phenomena are historically created and conditioned (Horkheimer and Adorno [1944] 1972; Horkheimer 1972). This suggests that to understand telehealth we need to study particular contexts within which it has been developed. Thus, my research has aimed to combine a local, situated study with a wider societal perspective. To this end, a three-layer approach, spanning the UK's policy and strategy issues (macro layer), local strategies (community perspective – mezzo layer) and individual projects (micro layer), was adopted.

To contribute to the understanding of telehealth and wider social, organizational and technological change in healthcare, and to the body of critical empirical research, this chapter aims, first, to present a critical analysis of telehealth in the UK, by focusing on different rationalities underpinning telehealth. Second, by drawing on this analysis, it aims to consider potential implications of telehealth for healthcare. Third, it provides an example of a critical study and through this example it seeks to illustrate what critical theory might add to the research into telehealth. In pursuit of these aims, the structure of this chapter is as follows. In the following section, the concept of rationality is introduced. The next section describes the research approach used in this study, followed by a section that discusses the context in which telehealth is developed and legitimized. The main findings of this work are then presented in the next three sections, where the rationalities underpinning telehealth at national (policy), local and project levels are shown. This work is discussed in the penultimate section, where the implications of telehealth to healthcare are considered, and the contributions of the research approach in developing a greater understanding of telehealth are discussed. The final section closes this chapter with a summary and a brief overview of further work.

**Introducing the notions of rationality**

The study focused on the rationalities in the field on telehealth. But what is rationality? Words like rational or irrational are often used in our daily language to describe actions or people. Those who can logically explain their beliefs and actions are considered rational. Similarly, rational actions are those which enable actors to achieve desired ends. The concept of rationality is more complex than its everyday meaning may imply and thus it is discussed further in the following section. The starting point of this chapter is that there is no single rationality that drives innovations (although one can be dominant) and that rationality is embedded in the history of different societies rather than being universal (Avgerou 2002).

The concept of rationality has been developed by a number of critical theorists, mainly Horkheimer and Adorno ([1944] 1972), Marcuse (1970) and Habermas (1984, 1987), but earlier works of Max Weber (1978) are acknowledged as seminal in this area. Thus, we start by very briefly outlining Weber's position. Weber was interested in understanding modern bureaucratic organizations and how they are sustained, and he developed the concept of rationality in relation to such collectives. He distinguished between formal and substantive rationality. Formal rationality refers to the calculable means and procedures taken to achieve given ends. Substantive rationality is concerned with the relationship between an action and its ultimate, substantive end. By considering an action's end we can make sense of or judge its appropriateness. Thus, the same actions and outcomes can be judged differently according to different substantive rationalities. For example, under economic rationality in the modern capitalist system directed towards maximizing efficiency, management action to undertake business process re-engineering and lay off many employees may be considered rational. The same action – if judged against the substantive end of social justice and employee empowerment – may appear misguided. Furthermore, this action, even if judged under economic rationality but from a perspective of society, may be considered unsatisfactory, as the burden of unemployment and related social costs will have to be carried by society. Thus, different rational systems of ideas may be legitimate for different groups of people in different situations.

Weber was concerned with a process of technically enabled rationalization that supports ever-efficient means of achieving ends, without questioning their substantive rationality. He demonstrated that bureaucracies and administrative systems are governed by formal rationality. This concern is also present in the works of different critical theorists, including Horkheimer and Adorno ([1944] 1972), Marcuse (1970) and Feenberg (1991, 2003).

Horkheimer and Adorno introduced the concept of instrumental rationality, that is, the spread of rationalization (scientific rationality) to life itself and the extension of means–end (formal) rationality, implying increasing control, calculability and formalization of different processes. An example of such a process would be *scientific management*, popularized by Taylor (1911). Pursuing a goal of the most efficient ways of production, Taylor undertook time and motion studies, the result of which provided foundations for the management of labour based on the division of work into smaller tasks, and then into individual steps repetitively performed by workers. This has led to a shift from craftwork into piecework, and resulted in the deskilling of workers and their disengagement from the final product of their work. However, the process of rationalization may be subtler than the example just given. For example, it may manifest itself in standardized teaching methods and guidelines, in the way local authorities deal with people who have a variety of problems, and in the way medicine is administered.

Marcuse (1970) has taken Horkheimer and Adorno's ideas further. He was concerned with a particular facet of instrumental rationality, that is, scientific–technical rationality or *technological* rationality. He claims that although science and technology may appear neutral '[i]n the construction of the technological reality, there is no such thing as a purely rational scientific order; the process of technological rationality is a political process' (p. 137). He suggests that technological rationality collapses the social and technical into one and not only limits actions to solving technical problems but also restricts the 'rational' discourse to technological rationality. According to Marcuse, technological rationality ceases to be the means to (capitalist) goals and becomes dominant in its own right, serving its own goals.

In our discussion of rationality we must acknowledge Habermas's contributions, particularly given that out of all the critical theorists, he has had the most influence on the IS discipline. Habermas (1984, 1987) builds on the works of Weber. For example, his conceptualization of instrumental and strategic rationality is based on Weber's idea of formal rationality. According to Habermas, instrumental and strategic rationality are directed towards success. Thus, instrumental actions are performed according to technical rules and are judged in terms of their effectiveness in a physical world. Strategic actions aim to achieve success through influencing other people. In addition to instrumental and strategic rationality, Habermas theorized a distinct type of rationality, which he called 'communicative rationality'. People motivated by this rationality aim to achieve mutual understanding based on communication. In contrast to the other critical theorists, Habermas does not consider rationalization as an inherently negative process but rather as ambivalent. That is, as a positive process when limited to work (making work efficient and productive), but troubling when expanded to the domain of human interaction (*lifeworld*).

Building on the work of the Frankfurt school (including Marcuse), Martin Heidegger and postmodernist thinkers, Feenberg (1991) revisits the concepts of reason and rationality, and develops a critical theory of technology. He considers technological rationality as a condensation of capitalist social and technical requirements, and sees technologies such as computers as serving to sustain it. Thus, the construction and interpretation of technological systems is conforming to requirements of a system of domination. Focusing on the issue of neutrality or bias of technology, Feenberg proposes that the decontextualized elements from which the biased system is built are indeed neutral in their abstract form. But such elements should not be seen as decontextualized or separate. Essentially, Feenberg's argument is that although a rock may be neutral (and the bias is only in its use), formal systems like technology are created for a purpose in specific social contexts. For example, elements of an information system abstracted from their context may appear to be neutral, but when they are put back in a particular time and context they become value-laden. Yet, Feenberg does not claim that the bias of technology has to be always negative. Giving an example of online education systems, he argues that the technology of the internet may be deployed to make education into a technocratic commodity, or, on the contrary, allow much greater access to valuable information and democratize education.

This brief review illustrates how Weber's ideas on rationality have been further developed by critical theorists. Although each thinker's contribution is unique, their ideas are complementary. They illustrate the limitations of economic and techno-scientific rationality and the dangers of rationalization, where other options and ways of understanding the world are closed off or at least banished from what is considered to be a 'rational' discourse.

The IS literature, drawing primarily on Habermas (but also Weber and different critical theorists), has set out to examine the roles that IS play in the rationalization of organizations and the implications of these processes (Lyytinen and Hirschheim 1988; Klein and Hirschheim 1991; Cecez-Kecmanovic et al. 2002), to explore the intellectual structures permeating the field of information systems development (ISD), revealing conventional thinking in the IS field about communication, information and knowledge, in order to inform practices and theories of ISD (Klein and Hirschheim 1991; Hirschheim et al. 1996; Cecez-Kecmanovic et al. 2002; Varey et al. 2002). These works are concerned with the ways that IS may contribute to increasing formal rationality, formalization and depersonalization of the workplace, with an emphasis on control and alienation. They also propose that IS development and implementation in organizations can be driven by different types of rationality, including communicative, and contribute to IS that best serve all project stakeholders. This is, for example, to be achieved through identification of different options (or 'design ideals' as put forward by Klein and Hirschheim 2001), the trade-offs between them, and making the choice based on a construction of arguments and evidence (as presented by different stakeholders). These works play an important role in IS literature, questioning the underlying assumptions behind ISD and proposing alternatives.

However, calls for IS to be developed to serve communicative rationality draw on Habermas's concept of the 'ideal speech situation' referring to the goal of freeing communication from distortion and power. This chapter agrees with Giddens's (1984) criticism of this notion and an assertion that power is endemic to all forms of communication. Thus, rationality and communication should be studied together (Walsham 1996).

Building primarily on the ideas of Weber, Adorno, Horkheimer and Marcuse and institutional theorists, Avgerou (2000, 2002) discusses the deployment of IS in developing countries. She suggests that rationality should be considered as a system of reasoning constituted by historical experiences and related to culture. This statement finds particular resonance in the field of healthcare, even if, as in this chapter, we focus on healthcare in a Western country (UK). Avgerou also suggests that there is no one overreaching rationality but that IS innovations arise from context-specific substantive rationalities (see also Chapter 14 by Avgerou and McGrath, this volume).

The position taken in this chapter is that rationality is not unified and monolithic, but as argued by Bruno Latour (discussed in Feenberg 2003), various forms of modern rationality should be seen in terms of a continuum, and as embedded in daily practice rather than as distinct realms. It is the daily practice of telehealth initiatives and 'actual instances of rationality' (ibid., p. 83), rather than their abstracted forms, that this chapter is concerned with. At the same time it remains sensitive to Marcuse's and Feenberg's warnings about the increasing dominance of formal rationality and limiting rational discourse to technological discourse.

Technological developments are fuelled by technological rationality and in turn they potentially re-enforce it. The assumption here is that technology is not autonomous but an instrument of social control placed in the hands of the 'vested interests' which control society (Marcuse 1970; Feenberg 1991). However, this does not mean that technology is destined to serve (capitalist) interests or that the interests it serves are always homogeneous. Indeed, this chapter illustrates how different interests and rationalities might influence the use (or non-use) of technology. Nor does it mean that technology is neutral, but rather it is 'an "ambivalent" process of development suspended between different possibilities' (ibid., p. 14).

The ideas presented here are utilized in the following sections to explore the notions of rationalities underlying telehealth, and from this point of departure to make comments about the potential implications of telehealth for healthcare. First, the research undertaken is described.

**Research approach**
The research reported here was undertaken between 1996 and 2001. The choice of research methods was guided by the theoretical underpinnings of the research, although it must be emphasized that critical theory is not prescriptive with regard to techniques of investigation (Morrow and Brown 1994). The study was designed to span three levels, macro, mezzo and micro. Within these levels it was impossible to explore all phenomena in-depth. Thus, from the macro perspective we concentrated on the analysis of the UK national health policy and IS management strategy papers. At the mezzo level, local strategies and initiatives of the health and local authority organizations serving the London Borough of Lewisham were investigated. The micro level comprised the study of a few individual projects. The research findings at these different levels are reported below. These are necessarily general and a more detailed description can be found in Klecun-Dabrowska (2002).

Qualitative research methods were used, including largely unstructured interviews and, whenever possible, direct observation. The researcher attended two public forums (discussing issues around health, information and communication technologies (ICTs) and the local population's needs), five local and national workshops and project-specific meetings. These lasted between four and six hours. Notes were taken during these events, focusing on ideas put forward by different people and interactions between them. In addition, a total of 43 people were interviewed, mainly healthcare professionals and researchers, those involved in telehealth projects, representatives of local government and the Telemedicine Policy Team (a small advisory body). Interviewees were chosen because of the positions they held in organizations or their interest and involvement in telehealth. The majority of interviews were recorded and transcribed.

Data analysis was guided by critical theory insights and a hermeneutic mode of enquiry. The researcher followed the hermeneutic circle of understanding (Gadamer 1976) when conducting the analysis of UK policy and strategy documents and empirical research. The hermeneutic circle expresses the need to understand the parts of a text through the understanding of the whole, while the understanding of the whole is determined by our understanding of its parts. The process of reading and interpreting is not finite; there is no definite point at which our understanding becomes complete. Thus, a number of readings were conducted within different circles. The documents (including interview transcripts as well as project documentations, policy and strategy papers) were coded into themes at a paragraph rather than sentence level, so as not to lose the context in which they were said or written. This was done manually and essentially relied on the researcher's intuition. Moreover, each document was considered as a whole and its sections as parts, that is, its parts and themes identified were interpreted in the context of the whole document. However, the 'whole' was also understood as something much bigger. The policies, local initiatives and projects themselves were considered in the light of the health and medicine debate, national and international policies, political discourse and general trends in society.

**Organizational context and legitimization of telehealth**
This section outlines the environment in which telehealth services are often conceived and delivered in the UK, that is, the National Health Service. Then, it discusses the rationalities guiding the practice of medicine and thus potentially telehealth, and the legitimization practices of telehealth.

In the UK, the NHS is the largest healthcare provider, having about 95 per cent of the market (Atkinson et al. 2001). Therefore, the study focused on the NHS rather than on private healthcare organizations. From its conception in 1948, the NHS has been funded through general taxation and offered free (at the point of delivery and with some exceptions) healthcare to the population. The NHS has been strongly influenced by government policies and medical professions, which enjoy a great degree of autonomy. In the last two decades, rising costs of healthcare, fuelled by the availability of expensive treatments and technologies, an ageing population and the raising of expectations, increased the financial strain on the NHS. This gave rise to the consecutive governments' efforts to increase efficiency and effectiveness. Economic rationality in the NHS gained a stronger foothold with the introduction of fundamental administrative reforms in the early 1990s, primarily the establishment of an 'internal market' (DOH 1989). This involved the separation of the service into purchasers and providers of care. Later on, the Labour government oversaw the replacement of the internal market with a model of integrated care (DOH 1997). Yet, these changes did not undermine the economic rationality, particularly with the introduction of primary care groups and trusts, responsible for managing their budgets and purchasing services.

These reforms brought with them a rising number of professional managers in the NHS and managerialist rationalization. This process has permeated healthcare provision in the Western world in the past half-century and is on the increase in the UK (Hillier 1987). These reforms also fuelled a demand for administrative and managerial IS, to deliver information on potential purchasers and providers of healthcare, and to monitor and plan the provision of care (Mackintosh and Shakespeare 1995).

Despite these changes, as our ongoing research into healthcare indicates, medical professions (particularly clinicians) continue to have great influence over the way healthcare is delivered (Plamping 1998). They also have a very strong identity enforced by, for example, education (medical schools) and professional associations.

Within this tradition, ethics have a particularly strong formal position based on patients' rights and doctors' duties to a patient. The practice of medicine is predominantly based on the scientific view of the human body as separated from the mind and understood through 'scientific' (systematic, rule-governed and quantitative) studies (Sosa-Iudicissa et al. 1997). This view has led to a shifting of focus from a human being to the body and from caring for the person to curing the disease. Cribb and Barber (1997, p. 298), when discussing drug-prescribing practices, suggest that 'The biomedical paradigm does not only dominate in research, but is also employed to frame policies and guidelines.' Thus, problems, which may have different causes, are often seen and treated in bio-medical terms (in accordance with scientific rationality).

Within the last two decades, scientific rationality has been challenged by a changing understanding of health and illness (Gott 1995). The debates about new models of care, based on notions of health, wellness and a holistic model of care have permeated societal and policy discourse (DOH 1999). Grassroots movements challenging the established ways have become increasingly popular. For example, a successful movement to de-technicalize childbirth resulted in having the option of a home birth, use of midwives, and allowing partners to be present during birth (Feenberg 1991). Currently, mental health patients' groups are very vocal in fighting for a different approach to mental health problems that takes into account patients' experiences and knowledge, and as our research indicates, their concerns have been recognized (at least to some extent) by the mental health trust in South London. Some alternative forms of medicine, for example, acupuncture, have also gained recognition within the field and are even provided free on the NHS.

This brief introduction indicates that at least two, often competing, rationalities come to play in the NHS organizations: scientific (medical) and economic–managerialist. Yet these, at least to some extent, are being challenged by ideas of holistic medicine. This suggests that developments in telehealth could potentially be guided by different rationalities.

These different rationalities are also manifested in the way that legitimization of telehealth is sought. Seeing telehealth as a medical intervention or medical technology means that legitimization is sought through the strongest medical approaches, including randomized-controlled trials (RCTs). One of our interviewees saw RCTs as a way of protecting the public against techno-managerialist rationality and the vested interests of commercial suppliers:

> Randomised trials are used by the scientific community as a way of settling arguments. They are the 'golden standard'. … I think that the way telemedicine is legitimised in this country and how it gains credibility is via scientific trials, not commercial interests. Scientific legitimisation is indeed what we would like. What many of us worry about is that driven by commercial interests telemedicine might be put to use untested, or when it is unnecessary, with unproven benefits. (Senior Research Fellow in Telemedicine, Medical School)

However, RCTs have their opponents too. Some researchers suggest undertaking evaluation of telehealth projects in their normal settings (rather than under laboratory conditions), using qualitative methods, and focusing not only on the clinical or therapeutic outcomes but also on changes to work processes, institutional structures, and the doctor/patient relationship (McDonald et al. 1998; Heathfield et al. 1998; May and Ellis 2001; Klecun and Cornford 2003; May et al. 2003). This is because it is difficult to evaluate telehealth as you would assess a drug. Not only is technology changing very quickly but also telehealth is embedded in complex organizational practices from which it cannot be divorced.

Interestingly, our interviews revealed that the attempt to conduct RCTs is, in some cases, motivated more by a desire to achieve credibility, as RCTs are still seen as the established, 'scientific' method in a medical community. This would confirm research results in other IS domains that suggest the use of formal methods of evaluation for the purpose of legitimization (Introna 1997).

In the UK, some telehealth projects are considered as a 'political imperative' and evaluation is not seen as a priority. For example, NHS Direct was not formally evaluated before being rolled out to other areas. The policy documents claim a societal legitimacy for telehealth through an image of an empowered population, served by informational resources, and making decisions about their own health and participating in the process of setting healthcare policy (Milio 1992; Gann 1998). Telehealth is identified as one of the services offered in an information society, often in the context of the 'online' community, and in the healthcare setting (within and beyond NHS structures) as an extension of healthcare IS. Thus, telehealth is seen as a 'right'.

Yet, for other projects there is a perceived need to demonstrate economic viability. As the clinician involved in the telepsychiatry project articulated: 'Well, it is essentially for political reasons with a small p. It is for reassuring sceptical colleagues, insurers and our legal people. It means accruing evidence that suggests this is not the off-the-wall thing to do, that it is a reasonable activity.'

Nevertheless, our research and the literature review indicates that formal evaluation of telehealth projects is seldom done (Wyatt and Wyatt 2003). Only a few researchers attempt to conduct cost analysis taking into account the social costs and benefits of telehealth services and considering other alternatives to telehealth. These show that the results are not necessarily favourable to telehealth (Halvorsen and Kristiansen 1996; Wootton et al. 2000). Moreover, research on telehealth suffers from methodological shortcomings and weaknesses in data, making it difficult to substantiate claims of its proponents (Hakansson and Gavelin 2000; Whitten et al. 2000; Roine et al. 2001). As Williams et al. (2003) suggest, the criteria for evaluation are often developed to demonstrate the technology promise as a clinical resource rather than its actual deployment. Thus, legitimization of telehealth, beyond certain areas or individual projects, has not been accomplished.

Legitimization of telehealth is an area where different rationalities compete but also converge. Scientific rationality – represented by RCT-based evaluation – is seen as guarding against techno-economic rationality. However, both of these rationalities might be supporting a similar model of healthcare and potentially telehealth, based on a scientific model of medicine. They are challenged by a holistic model of care and a view that telehealth is a social technology that demands different evaluation techniques. Thus, as this brief review indicates, rationalities influencing telehealth are diverse.

**Roles and meanings of telehealth in health policy and strategy documents**
To begin the presentation of the main findings of this work, this section discusses the different roles and meanings that telehealth acquires in national policy and strategy papers, highlighting the underlying rationalities. It is argued here that health policy and strategy constitute one of the main factors shaping telehealth in the UK.

The recent UK government's policy and strategy papers tend to present a technologically deterministic view, that is, that ICTs are beneficial and benevolent. Their benefits are assumed and people just need to realize them. For example, the provision of information is often equated with knowledge or power, as noted in *The New NHS: Modern, Dependable* (DOH 1997): 'Providing knowledge about health, illness and best treatment practice to the public through the Internet and emerging public access media (e.g. digital TV). ... The aim will be to create a powerful alliance between knowledgeable patients advised by knowledgeable professionals as a means of improving health and health care' (p. 20).

Technologies are portrayed as just having 'impacts', for example, as depicted in the following extracts from the web version of *Information for Health* (NHS Executive 1998):

Electronic Health Records and secure networks will improve confidence in the accuracy and confidentiality of medical records.

NHS staff will share the benefits enjoyed by patients because much of the frustration felt through poor clinical records and co-ordination of services will be eliminated. But the new information technology will bring other benefits to the NHS.

It will give medical and nursing staff instant access, at their desks or at the bedside, to the most recent medical research and to treatment best practice.

In these documents, the role of ICTs is often seen as transforming rather than simply supporting existing practices. Thus, telehealth is increasingly understood and projected as being able to reshape the way healthcare is delivered; remotely instead of person to person, in home rather than in hospital, to groups rather than to individuals, and across traditional institutional boundaries (DOH 1997, 1999, 2000).

The focus on creating new and exciting technologies and a belief that these lead to better care is noticeable in these documents, and even more so in public statements (for example, see Prime Minister Tony Blair's speech in 2 July 1998 marking the 50th anniversary of the NHS). This focus coexists with a medical dimension that seeks medical solutions to health problems. Both culminate in attention to high-tech telehealth applications in highly specialized medical fields, for example, teleradiology and tele-operations. This approach is criticized by one of our interviewees:

In the policy paper part of the telemedicine vision is about fancy, sexy stuff, for example, an idea of a camera mounted on paramedics' helmets. The sort of thing that looks good on the news but might not in fact actually deliver that much more real business benefit than some of the other things. (Associate Director, Information Systems, Health Authority)

From this, it appears that the developments in telehealth are driven by technological rationality. Yet, the role of telehealth, and more generally of ICT, is perceived firmly within the boundaries of long-established goals for the NHS, particularly of providing care regardless of people's social class or geographical location. Understood in this way, this role fits in well within the overall discourse of social responsibility and community values present in the health policy documents. Thus, although policy papers may reflect technological rationality, they also make an appeal to different substantial rationality, for example, of social justice.

Such a discourse, then, implies that telehealth can develop within a framework of actions aimed at combating social exclusion, increasing social cohesion and bringing better healthcare to the worst off. In policy documents, ICT is explicitly depicted as a means of (positive) social control. Telehealth is then not only seen as medicine or a medical technology or even as a clinical practice, but as a societal and community service. Yet, the policy documents give rise to other expectations too. The intertwined managerial discourse directs attention to efficiency and effectiveness. Information systems are identified as enabling and supporting such aims (Klecun-Dabrowska and Cornford 2000). This means that the role of telehealth is seen additionally, or perhaps most importantly, as helping to contain the cost of healthcare.

The policy papers imply that these different roles can be reconciled and that telehealth can provide better and, at the same time, more cost-efficient services. Yet, this may not be so easily achievable and one of the discourses (probably the managerial) may exert a dominant influence on the developments in telehealth. Table 18.1 summarizes, in very simple terms, the different meanings of telehealth that arise from these different trends.

**Telehealth and local implementations**
Policy and strategy papers are only one of the factors, albeit an important one, that are shaping telehealth services. Telehealth is also constructed and enacted through local strategies, their implementation and autonomous, bottom-up initiatives. To continue the presentation of the findings of this work, this section briefly considers such construction of telehealth in one locality – South London.

Between 1998–2001, local health authorities (purchasers of care for different geographical areas) were required to produce a local implementation strategy (LIS) to show how they, together with other provider institutions (for example, hospitals), would meet the government's targets. These documents

Table 18.1   *Meanings of telehealth*

|  | Concordist | Antagonist |
|---|---|---|
| Trends | Discourse of social responsibility & community values; health prevention, primary care-based & patient-centred services; patient empowerment | Managerialist discourse; 'reform' agenda with focus on efficiency & effectiveness; limited resources |
| Meanings (roles) of telehealth | Improving healthcare & making it more equitable (fighting geographical & social exclusion) Empowering patients & professionals Supporting communication & cooperation between different groups & organizations | Enabling financial control (e.g. monitoring budgets) Enabling clinical governance (e.g. enforcing standardization) Shifting power relations and responsibilities Technical solutions to save money |

offer a view of rationalities behind local strategies for the deployment of ICT in the delivery of health and social care. However, the view afforded through a LIS is only partial, that is, limited to what can be included in official documents. Thus, this section also gives voice to those involved in the setting of the strategies or affected by them.

LIS documents reviewed in the course of this study, tend to (understandably) echo the national policy papers' thrust towards modernization and seldom question the spirit of *'Information for Health'*. Although uncovering many complex issues that surround the implementation of IS and telehealth in such a complex institutional environment, they often reveal a simple understanding of the consequences of technologies, suggesting underlying technological rationality, as illustrated below:

> *Information for Health* is a principal vehicle for transforming the delivery of services within the NHS. Its implementation will:
>
> Empower people though information
> Open up access to services and change the way care is delivered through technology
> Reduce inequalities through easier access to comparable data. (LIS 2000: 1)

A more extensive analysis of national and local strategy documents can be found in Klecun-Dabrowska and Cornford (2000) and Cornford and Klecun-Dabrowska (2003).

The local service providers and health authority representatives whom we interviewed saw the implementation process as highly questionable and the official documents as underestimating problems. For example, as the following quotations indicate, concern was expressed about the amount of change they were required to absorb, the availability of resources, the subtle power shifts that such reforms might bring, and the organizations' (understandable) drive to protect their own interests and budgets:

> The government and the NHS have been pushing technical solutions on us very quickly and we are not ready. (Clinical Development Manager, Hospital)

> There is a big gap between what LIS promised and what we have funds to deliver. (Head of IT, Health Care Trust)

> The LIS investment plan will undoubtedly exceed available resources, which will make the prioritizing a difficult and political task. Pooling resources from organizations for the greater good of the community are noble words, but will organizations give up their budgets for the benefit of others? (Manager of Information Services, Local Authority)

> We need organizational change, breaking down barriers between social services and health, but existing legislation is obstructing this process. (Associate Director, Information Services, Health Authority)

Although in general agreement with the concept of a more open local government and ideas of close cooperation between different agencies (for example, health sector and social services), social workers remained sceptical about the feasibility of modernization plans, or they were frightened by the pace of change which could lead to some people 'being left behind'.

Others pointed out problems not only with the way the government's vision is to be implemented, but also with the vision itself (or rather with some aspects of the vision). For example, a clinician voiced concerns about telecare (for example, technologies monitoring infirm people in their home environment) in terms of privacy and the right to self-determination. A social worker pointed out that sharing customer data between different agencies is not only a matter of security (and thus having a technical solution), but also about preserving the trust of clients, who may not wish social services, for example, to have their health data. A couple of interviewees complained that telehealth and modernization in general is being 'pushed onto them' (that is, that the central government puts pressure on organizations to implement telehealth solutions, and the organization then may force workers to embrace them). This raises concerns that those who may have genuine and legitimate misgivings would be branded as Luddites. As some interviewees suggested, IT may have potentially alienating effects on staff, and the financial costs of providing online services are expected to lead to cutbacks in some conventional services (and thus privileging people with skills and access to the internet).

Such negative views are not shared by everyone. Proponents of telehealth construct a vision of telehealth as helping the delivery and management of healthcare. For example, they see it as (potentially) supporting existing services (for example, email used to contact patients), altering the delivery of current services (for example, widening access to specialist services in distant areas), by introducing new means of consultations (e.g. in telepsychiatry) and providing new services (for example, web-based information, facilitating self-management of chronic diseases and creation of self-support groups not limited by geographical boundaries). This belief in the potential of telehealth is vocalized by a corporate development manager in a mental health trust:

> We are hoping that telemedicine will be one way of releasing some clinical time so therapeutic work can be done to stop patients almost constantly being on the revolving door of getting well but not quite addressing the problems, then relapsing and coming back again. So this is a way of intervening earlier in an illness or doing a follow-up. ... We feel that we have a way of revolutionizing the delivery of healthcare, making it more accessible and immediate. And particularly for disadvantaged communities, they may not have access to expert care – a way of bringing it to them. Perhaps in 20 years it will be happening everywhere, as e-mail, computers and internet are now. But for now it feels like an uphill struggle with funding

Telehealth is also seen as a way of enhancing organizational status (becoming a centre for excellence) and increasing organizational income (when hospitals can enlarge their catchment areas and sell services abroad):

> We think we have a real opportunity to be identified as a centre for excellence, to almost pilot telepsychiatry in the mental health field for the Southeast of England, given that this is one of the priorities in the Labour party's manifesto; Tony Blair has spoken about it in various speeches, and it is one of the key plans in the *Information for Health* strategy. (Corporate Development Manager, Mental Health Trust)

> There is an opportunity for the Trust to get more customers, to make more money through the use of telemedicine. (Telemedicine Manager, Hospital)

> I suppose if we don't do it [telemedicine], somebody else will. So, it could also be a threat to us if we didn't do it. ... Someone could take patients from us. (Telemedicine Manager, Hospital)

These quotations suggest that the developments in telehealth may follow technological-economic rationality. However, economic concerns are tempered by ethical considerations. Thus, although the business site of telehealth is readily identified and explored by the telemedicine manager, the research activities are clinically driven:

> We are a medical school hospital. We need to be conducting R&D into these new technologies from a clinical point of view. Our role here is clinical services; we are not an IT or telecommunications company. Our business is medicine. ... The main aim of telemedicine initiatives here is to improve the delivery of healthcare through the use of modern telecommunications and IT – that's the overriding thing.

This section has illustrated some of the problems experienced by those who are affected by the government's policies. Telehealth is perceived either as a threat or as having a great potential for 'revolutionizing' healthcare – or as both. Some acknowledge that telehealth, even if improving some of the aspects of healthcare, may bring its own set of problems. As Feenberg (1991) notes, even relatively neutral systems are biased because of the prejudicial choice of the *time, place and manner of their introduction.* But telehealth systems are not simple, relatively neutral tools; rather, they are complex systems with many biases. This is not acknowledged in policy and strategy papers, but it is experienced by those being affected by such systems.

### Telehealth projects and situated rationalities
To conclude the presentation of the main findings of this work, this section examines how the potential of telehealth, as outlined in the previous sections, is enacted in actual projects. It also discusses manifestations of rationalities underlying these projects. It considers the projects' formal aims, as they are presented in documents and articulated by the interviewees. This constitutes the initial 'reading' of the projects. In subsequent readings these aims and the rationalities they represent are questioned.

In the course of this study a number of different projects in London were investigated; for the purpose of this chapter, four will be considered in greater depth:

1. a telepsychiatry service allowing consultations to take place in a family doctor's practice linked to a hospital-based consultant via teleconferencing equipment;
2. an early pregnancy assessment unit based at a local centre with a telemedicine link for ultrasound scans and teleconferencing to hospital consultants;

3. EmpowerNet, a web-based information and limited interactive service for people with mental health problems; and
4. the SeaHorse project, utilizing the potential of ICT (for example, the internet, CD-ROM) for supporting people with HIV/AIDS and facilitating collaboration between carers.

Interviewing people leading the first project and reading academic papers written by them revealed that they wanted to address perceived clinical need and to explore new technologies (McLaren et al. 1999). The broader aims were to move towards more local, primary care-based services and to increase cooperation among different organizations within the NHS, and thus improving patient care and making it more accessible.

The second project took place in a women and children's centre in Deptford. The centre was promoted as an integral part of a local hospital's larger strategy of continuation of care. As there is no permanent consultant on the premises, it was intended that the Early Pregnancy Assessment Unit at the centre would be supported by a telemedicine link to the hospital. When a doctor's opinion is required immediately the ultrasound image, together with key patient data, could be viewed live from the hospital, with video conferencing facilities also available. Alternatively, a store-and-forward technology could be used. The nurse at the centre considered the provision of new services and increased access to appropriate healthcare for women in a very deprived area, as the main aim of the centre.

The next project, EmpowerNet, offered a web-based service for mental health patients. It was low key and low budget. However, it was linked to other initiatives in the local area, aiming at empowering mental health sufferers. It encouraged participation from patients (referred to as 'service users'). Our interviewees (service managers at the mental health community Trust) saw the internet as a convenient means of delivering information to the public and to service users, for example, to facilitate peer support activities, and for opening new channels of communication between the Trust and its patients. The project arose as follows:

> We thought: wouldn't it be good if it wasn't just staff that could get access to up-to-date information on the internet. Service users would make it available to a wider group of people through informal advocacy and support work. Also, in another breath, it is interesting how these things come together, locally we had projects developing vocational and employment services for services users. ... There was a small project about getting those projects in touch with each other online. ... And the notion was then that this would be quite empowering because they could be using the technology but at the same time also be in contact with peers. So putting those all together, we suddenly thought, what about if we took it one step further and bring these folks together by setting up a website that would be specifically of interest to local service users, and getting them to really

contribute to the site's content and looks and to managing it. And it just happens that at the time there was a bit of slippage money from joint finance (local authority and health money). So, we just got five thousand pounds, a very small amount of money, but that would help to take this project forward. (Borough Director, Mental Health Trust)

The final project had a number of partners from different countries. Its full name explains its purpose: Support and Empowerment for AIDS and HIV: the On-Line Research and Self-help Exchange (SeaHorse) (Cullen 1996, 1997). The services provided largely consist of websites offering relevant, up-to-date and localized information and interactive services, for example, bulletin boards, users rating existing material and adding new information. A program allowing the users to keep track of their symptoms and drugs taken was also available online.

The first reading of the projects indicates that they did not follow exclusively or narrowly a techno-economic or managerialist rationality. They did not focus on cost efficiency, managerial control or even techno-medical solutions. Rather, they seemed to follow substantive rationality of providing care based on a holistic understanding of 'wellness', framed in social rather than purely medical terms, aimed at serving socially excluded groups.

Subsequent interpretations or 'readings' of the projects hint at the existence of other rationalities. For example, the first project provides a technical solution (a teleconferencing system) when the distance perhaps does not necessitate it and travelling for patients, or indeed the consultant, would not be difficult. Is this project, then, driven by technological rationality and motivated by political or purely research aims? This seems to be so, at least to some extent. As one of the project initiators admitted: 'our interests, were very much technology driven'. But he then argued that the aim was to explore how new technologies mediate clinical practice, so that they might be applied in areas where distances are far greater and thus where clinical need might be stronger. He added:

It will be wrong if they [government] decided that telemedicine is the way forward and invested a billion or more to upgrade technology and put everyone on ISDN and made sure that everyone does video conferencing. Because that seems to be a sexy thing to do. When the evidence is not there and when there are many other alternative ways in which one can spend that money in a circumstance when one is undoubtedly struggling ... I stand on the other side of the argument sometimes.

In the second project, the ultrasound telemedicine link was never used and was discontinued. The nurse at the centre told us that serious problems with the technology, aggravated by the lack of support from the suppliers, made the system difficult to use. She then gave more reasons for the non-use of the technology:

> We haven't referred any pictures via the link. The guidelines are such that it is easy to make a diagnosis. But if reviewing is needed, I feel that patients need someone actually physically examining them rather than looking at pictures. I feel that I should have a recognized scanning qualification if I'm to scan the pictures. There are more issues around using the machine, not just technical, i.e. what pictures to take, how to judge it, what if I omit something at the scanning phase? I'm not happy to scan without the course. And if you actually have the course in scanning then you don't need your pictures reviewed.

Thus, we might ask: why did this pilot take place? Was the technology seen as a solution to a problem that did not exist? Was it politically motivated, initiated to demonstrate that the government policy on telehealth is being implemented? The interview with the clinical development manager at the hospital confirmed that the aim was to better serve a deprived area: 'So the manager at the hospital decided that if women can't get here we will go to them.' But she also revealed: 'The telemedicine aspect happened, in the way a lot of them happen, partly because the manager involved had a particular interest in technology. It would not be cost effective to send consultants down there [to the centre] in person.'

Interestingly, the centre itself, although not cost effective in simple monetary terms, proved popular with the staff and the local population (CORU 2000). In the words of the nurse from the centre: 'Customers like the centre, they like the fact they are seen quicker than in the hospital. I think the actual clinic is very useful to have it here. It is just telemedicine that isn't.' Yet, the service was not dismissed altogether, but it is being considered for an application in another speciality. Even the nurse asserted: 'I think telemedicine has a great potential and it might be used in other locations.'

Both SeaHorse and EmpowerNet relied on more-established technologies and did not necessitate significant rearrangement of clinicians' working practices (although, of course, the projects might have implicit implications for working practices). Yet, the projects were not without problems. During their implementation, conflicts and problems arose, as different stakeholders tried to overcome constraining structures (for example, the organizational culture, legal matters or lack of funds and skills), and struggled to find common meanings (for example, different ways in which the notions of empowerment and social exclusion are perceived and acted upon). Moreover, although providing an important service, SeaHorse has been allocated limited funds and may not be supported in the future, as one of the project coordinators bemoaned:

The people were supposed to use it only for 2–3 months and then however good it is, unless you can get some money, it is going to be turned off. ... The SeaHorse project really does offer a valuable tool for accessing information. And it would be very good if it was maintained and made more widely available.

Overall, the projects studied achieved limited social aims, primarily in providing better access to information or services, and to a lesser extent, opening new communication channels, and facilitating self-support groups beyond geographical boundaries. They appear to belong to the concordist column in Table 18.1. But the projects' claims regarding empowerment of patients/citizens seemed to be overstated. Furthermore, as the Deptford centre illustrates, reorganizing work practices might be more beneficial than the introduction of technical systems.

Furthermore, the interpretation of the projects in the context of financial pressures faced by the NHS and the social services implies that eventually such services may be seen in terms of 'saving costs', and that this can only be achieved if traditional services are reduced. This would shift such services to the antagonist column in Table 18.1. For example, the SeaHorse report (Cullen 1997, p. 13) states that 'the project is concerned with contributing to a better understanding of how to empower and support users in effective management of their health – to ultimately reduce their use of healthcare'. However, during the interview the project coordinator clarified: 'I have to say that it is the sort of rhetoric that the Commission [European funding body] wants to hear.' In EmpowerNet, electronic channels of communication between the Trust and mental health patients were seen as enabling more contact with patients; but would they be deployed in addition to personal visits and telephone calls or instead of them? Answers to such questions need to be sought through longitudinal studies.

Having discussed the various findings resulting from the research, the implications of this work are now considered.

**Discussion**
To discuss the implications of telehealth for healthcare, and the contributions of the research approach in developing a greater understanding of telehealth, this section brings together this research into policy and strategy on the use of ICT in health and the empirical study of telehealth projects.

This research suggests that telehealth is influenced by different rationalities that people draw on, as illustrated by the projects described, but also that these rationalities are constructed within wider discourses, for example, political, academic, and practice and profession based. The research suggests that these discourses are, to some extent, limited by technological rationality.

For example, technological rationality is embedded in national and organizational policy and strategies, and in decisions of funding bodies.

It appears that telehealth is being employed to serve a political imperative of improving healthcare and containing (if not reducing) costs, but that its application is understood in somewhat simplistic and unproblematic terms. It seems that the overriding message of such policies is that ICTs *work* and will *make things work*, and the only problem is their 'correct' employment. In many cases developments in telehealth services are bottom-up, initiated by health professionals. These projects, too, are often driven, at least to some extent, by technological rationality (for example, by a research-driven interest in technology and by a belief in the technology's potential).

Yet, it would be unfair to assert that telehealth is employed to serve formal rationality and that its ends are not questioned. National policy and strategies, although revealing thinking driven by technological rationality, appeal to different substantial rationalities. The projects' goals are often expressed as social or health aspirations. These reflect the movement towards holistic medicine and patient empowerment. Although some of the statements made by our interviewees could be seen as a reflection of technological rationality, it does not mean that they see technology purely in terms of reified decontextualization. On the contrary, they all acknowledge the importance of the organizational and societal context.

We also see that legitimizing practices are open to question about the value of telehealth in societal terms, and that evaluation frameworks go beyond questions about the safety of the technology. At the same time, it seems that telehealth services are seldom evaluated against other potential services or improvements to current ones and that criteria for evaluation tend to be developed in such a way as to demonstrate the technology promise as a clinical resource rather than its actual deployment. This leads us to conclude that technological rationality plays a significant role in influencing developments in telehealth, but it does not achieve a total dominance as it is challenged by other rationalities.

This indicates that telehealth's implications for the provision of healthcare, the 'art' of medicine and for different communities are ambiguous. The policy documents proclaim that telehealth will facilitate changing work practices, cooperation between different services (for example, healthcare and social services) and a more active role for patients, resulting in better and more accessible healthcare. The projects suggest that indeed telehealth might facilitate the attainment of some of these goals, but technology *per se* achieves little, and changing attitudes, work practices and organizational arrangements must come first. We need to contextualize telehealth and place it within people's and communities' working practices and daily lives, as well as within wider reforms striving towards (some form of) emancipation.

Even then, achieving change is not a foregone conclusion. For example, a study by Greenhill and Rooney (2003) illustrates that the existence of a strong alliance between scientific management, technological determinism and clinical science helps to preserve the status quo. As Feenberg (1991) asserts, technology is conceived within the prevailing rationality and thus helps to sustain it. The literature suggests that information systems not only acquire meanings within a managerialist discourse, but may also in turn reinforce the trend towards managerialization (Bloomfield 1991; Ferns and Mowshowitz 1995; Doolin 1999a, 1999b; Varey et al. 2002).

The concern is that telehealth may re-enforce techno-scientific rationality and the rationalization of healthcare, for example, by undermining local knowledge and experience (for example, through enabling remote consultations and training) and facilitating the practice of evidence-based medicine through access to online information resources and the introduction of protocols. We could imagine rationalization of healthcare expanding towards rationalization of our *lifeworld*, for example, in the way the elderly and vulnerable are being cared for. However, in addition to the managerialist discourse there are other potentially counteractive powers, for example, of healthcare professionals. Thus, managerialist-driven applications of information systems are resisted by the medical profession and often fail or are reinterpreted (Doolin 1998, 1999a).

Nevertheless, we cannot stop asking: what sort of health service and, more generally, society would telehealth encourage and re-enforce? Would it support the view that healthcare is a public good or alternatively a private commodity? Ultimately, will it support a caring society, based on human contact and social inclusion, as well as individual and community empowerment, or will it further extend the hold of instrumental reason, increasing alienation, and distorting the concept of individual choice and empowerment to mean commodification of health and information?

The above insights into telehealth lead us to make some observations about the concepts of rationality. This study tentatively supports Marcuse's assertion about the domination of technological rationality in Western culture. The field of telehealth, often looking for technological solutions to healthcare problems, might be considered as a reflection of this rationality. However, technological rationality is challenged by other forms of rationality. This supports Avgerou's (2002: 239) conclusion that '[m]odern societies have not become single-dimensional in terms of the values they foster'. This study illustrates how different rationalities are intertwined and reconstituted at different levels. These are enacted in daily practice and might be seen as resources on which actors draw in their everyday actions and sense-making of them (Shoib and Nandhakumar 2003).

Having discussed the findings of this study, the remainder of this section considers what critical theory brings to the research of telehealth. A critical approach makes the critique of existing knowledge claims an explicit requirement and focuses the researcher on this task, and thus it *may* lead to insightful results, that is, insights that question taken-for-granted assumptions (held by others and the researcher). For example, this research questions the simplistic notion of telehealth as a 'saviour', particularly in relation to claims about empowering and socially inclusive potentials of telehealth. It also shows how evaluation was used as a way of legitimizing telehealth, for example, in some cases it was primarily done for legitimization reasons, and how it can be used as an argument/weapon in a battle of different vested interests and rationalities (for example, 'scientific' evaluation was seen by some as guarding the interests of patients and opposing decisions driven by managerialist rationality or commercial interests).

Within the area of telehealth, the critical theory tradition encourages the investigation of dominant rationalities, for example, scientific, medical and managerial and presumptions that the IS discipline is based on. Thus it inspires us to look for alternative understandings of health, well-being and how technology could support those, rather than seeing the development of 'scientific' or technological solutions as the only option. It encourages the consideration of alienating features of technology and more broadly technological systems.

Critical theory contests the notion of inevitability and illustrates how we are conditioned to accept a techno-economic regime and believe alternatives to be unrealistic. In depicting the existence of different rationalities, we have hoped to show that alternatives do exist. Telehealth technologies are not simply autonomous but they are socially constructed (through often interrelated actions on macro and micro levels), and thus can be potentially directed in their development and use towards emancipatory aims.

**Conclusions**

To contribute to the understanding of telehealth and social, organizational and technological change in healthcare, and to the body of critical empirical research, this chapter has aimed: first, to present a critical analysis of telehealth in the UK, by focusing on different rationalities underpinning telehealth; second, to consider the potential implications of telehealth for healthcare; and third, to illustrate what critical theory might add to research into telehealth.

In pursuit of these aims, we have met the concept of rationality and the research approach used in this study. We have seen the context in which telehealth is developed and legitimized and have considered the main findings of this work with regard to the rationalities underpinning telehealth at national (policy), local and project levels. Finally, we have discussed this work in terms of the implications of telehealth to healthcare, and the contributions of the research approach in developing a greater understanding of telehealth.

The field of telehealth and more generally health informatics is exciting, ever-changing and driven by many competing rationalities and thus, I would argue, particularly suitable to conducting critical applied research. The study reported here was very broad and did not include all aspects concerning telehealth developments. For example, there was no discussion of how such technologies are actually developed or consideration of the role of the private sector. Furthermore, although some insights into the expectations and experiences of different people were gained, there is a need for a more comprehensive study from the point of view of patients and citizens. Moreover, the questions we posed regarding the potential influences of telehealth indicate a need for more theoretical and empirical research into telehealth, particularly in terms of the relationship between such technologies/services and society, focusing perhaps on the long-term influence of the implementation of such technologies on the health services and the practice of medicine. Further analysis of telehealth through the notion of power may lead to additional insights and complement this study. This is because, knowledge, as Foucault (1980) would argue, is interlaced with power. Similarly, different rationalities are built and sustained through power relations.

**References**

Atkinson, C., Eldabi, T., Paul, R.J. and Pouloudi, A. (2001), 'Investigating integrated approaches to health informatics', in Sprague, R.H., Jr. (ed.), *Thirty-Fourth Hawaiian International Conference on Systems Sciences* (HICSS-34), Maui, Hawaii: IEEE Computer.

Avgerou, C. (2000), 'Recognising alternative rationalities in the development of information systems', *The Electronic Journal on Information Systems in Developing Countries*, 3 (7), 1–15.

Avgerou, C. (2002), *Information Systems and Organizational Diversity: The Articulation of Local and Global Rationalities*, Oxford: Oxford University Press.

Bloomfield, B.P. (1991), 'The role of information systems in the UK National Health Service: action at a distance and the fetish of calculation', *Social Studies of Science*, 21, 701–34.

Brooke, C. (2002), 'What does it mean to be "critical" in IS research', *Journal of Information Technology*, 17, 49–57.

Cecez-Kecmanovic, D., Janson, M. and Brown, A. (2002), 'The rationality framework for a critical study of information systems', *Journal of Information Technology*, 17 (4), 215–27.

Clinical Operational Research Unit (CORU) (2000), 'Evaluation of telelinked women's health services in the community Deptford Centre', CORU, Department of Mathematics, University College London.

Cornford, T. and Klecun-Dabrowska, E. (2003), 'Studying structural aspects of telehealth technology: towards a concept of consequence', *Methods of Information in Medicine*, 4, 353–9.

Cribb, A. and Barber, N. (1997), 'Prescibers, patients and policy: towards the limits of technique', *Health Care Analysis*, 5 (4), 292–8.

Cullen, J. (1996), 'SEAHORSE: support and empowerment for AIDS and HIV: the on-line research and self-help exchange', Unpublished report, 'Deliverable 1.1', The Tavistock Institute, London.

Cullen, J. (1997), 'Final report on the feasibility of SEAHORSE', Unpublished report, 'Deliverable 1.2', The Tavistock Institute, London.

Darkins, A.W. and Cary, M.A. (2000), *Telemedicine and Telehealth: Principles, Policies, Performance, and Pitfalls*, London: Free Association Books.

Department of Health (DOH) (1989), *Working for Patients*, London: HMSO.

Department of Health (DOH) (1997), *The New NHS: Modern, Dependable*, London: HMSO.

Department of Health (DOH) (1999), *Saving Lives: Our Healthier Nation*, London: HMSO.

Department of Health (DOH) (2000), *The NHS Plan: Command Paper 4818–1*, London: HMSO.

Department of Health (DOH) (2002), *Delivering the 21st-Century IT Support for the NHS: National Strategic Programme*, London: HMSO.

Doolin, B. (1998), 'Information technology as disciplinary technology: being critical interpretive research on information systems', *Journal of Information Technology*, **13**, 301–11.

Doolin, B. (1999a), 'Sociotechnical networks and information management in health care', *Accounting, Management and Information Technologies*, **9**, 95–114.

Doolin, B. (1999b), 'Information systems, power, and organizational relations: a case study', *Proceedings of the 20th International Conference on Information Systems*, Charlotte, NC: ICIS, pp. 286–90.

Doolin, B. and Lowe, A. (2002), 'To reveal is to critique: actor-network theory and performativity in critical information systems research', *Journal of Information Technology*, **17** (2), 69–78.

Feenberg, A. (1991), *Critical Theory of Technology*, New York: Oxford University Press.

Feenberg, A. (2003), 'Modernity theory and technology studies: reflections on bridging the gap', in T.J. Misa, P. Brey and A. Feenberg (eds), *Modernity and Technology*, Cambridge, MA and London: MIT Press, pp. 73–104.

Ferns, W.J., and Mowshowitz, A. (1995), 'Knowledge-intensive systems in the social service agency: anticipated impacts on the organisation', *AI and Society*, **9**, 161–83.

Foucault, M. (1980), *Power/Knowledge: Selected Interviews and Other Writings 1972–77*, Brighton: Harvester.

Gadamer, H.-G. (1976), *Philosophical Hermeneutics*, Berkeley, CA: University of California Press.

Gann, B. (1998), 'Empowering the patient and public through information technology', in J. Lenaghan (ed.), *Rethinking IT and Health*, London: Institute for Public Policy Research, pp. 123–38.

Giddens, A. (1984), *The Constitution of Society: Outline of the Theory of Structure*, Berkeley, CA: University of California Press.

Gott, M. (1995), *Telematics for Health: the Role of Telehealth and Telemedicine in Home and Communities*, Oxford, New York: Radcliffe Medical Press.

Greenhill, J. and Rooney, D. (2003), 'Technology drives organisational change in health services: artifice or actuality?', Paper presented at Critical Management Studies Conference, Lancaster, UK, 7–9 July.

Habermas, J. (1984), *The Theory of Communicative Action: Reason and the Rationalisation of Society*, Boston, MA: Beacon.

Habermas, J. (1987), *The Theory of Communicative Action: The Critique of Functionalist Reason*, Boston, MA: Beacon.

Hakansson, S. and Gavelin, C. (2000), 'What do we *really* know about the cost-effectiveness of telemedicine?', *Journal of Telemedicine and Telecare*, **6** (Supplement 1), S1: 133–6.

Halvorsen, A. and Kristiansen, I.S. (1996), 'Radiology services for remote communities: cost minimisation study of telemedicine', *British Medical Journal*, **312**, 1333–6.

Heathfield, H., Pitty, D. and Hanka, R. (1998), 'Evaluating information technology in health care: barriers and challenges', *British Medical Journal*, **316**, 1959–61.

Hillier, S. (1987), 'Rationalism, bureaucracy, and the organization of the health services: Max Weber's contribution to understanding modern health care systems', in G. Scambler (ed.), *Sociological Theory and Medical Sociology*, London: Tavistock, pp. 194–220.

Hirschheim, R. and Klein, H.K. (1989), 'Four paradigms of information systems development', *Communications of the ACM*, **32** (10), 1199–216.

Hirschheim, R. and Klein, H.K. (1994), 'Realizing emancipatory principles in information systems development: the case for ETHICS', *MIS Quarterly*, March, 83–109.

Hirschheim, R., Klein, H.K. and Lyytinen, K. (1996), 'Exploring the intellectual structure of information systems development: a social action theoretic analysis', *Accounting, Management and Information Technology*, **6** (1/2), 1–64.

HMSO (1999), *Modernising government*, London: HMSO, http://www.archive.official-documents.co.uk/document/cm43/4310.htm.

Horkheimer, M. (1972), 'Traditional and critical theory', *Critical Theory: Max Horkheimer*, New York: Herder & Herder, pp. 188–243.

Horkheimer, M. and Adorno, T.W. ([1944] 1972), *Dialectic of Enlightenment*, New York: Herder.

Introna, L.D. (1997), *Management, Information and Power: A Narrative of the Involved Manager*, Basingstoke: Macmillan.

Jonsson, S. (1991), 'Action research', in H.-E. Nissen, H.K. Klein and R. Hirschheim (eds), *Information Systems Research: Contemporary Approaches and Emergent Traditions*, Amsterdam: North-Holland, pp. 371–96.

Klecun, E. and Cornford, T. (2003), 'An interpretative evaluation of a health care intranet', *International Journal of Healthcare Technology and Management*, **5** (6), 407–21.

Klecun-Dabrowska, E. (2002), 'Telehealth and information society: a critical study of emerging concepts in policy and practice', Unpublished PhD thesis, Department of Information Systems, London School of Economics and Political Science, London.

Klecun-Dabrowska, E. and Cornford, T. (2000), 'Telehealth acquires meanings: information and communication technologies within health policy', *Information Systems Journal*, **10** (1), 41–63.

Klecun-Dabrowska, E. and Cornford, T. (2002), 'The organising vision of telehealth', in S. Wrycza (ed.), *Proceedings of the 10th European Conference on Information Systems*, Gdansk, Poland: Wydawnictwo Uniwersytetu Gdańskiego (Gdansk University Press), pp. 1206–17.

Klein, H.K. and Hirschheim, R. (1991), 'Rationality concepts in information systems development methodologies', *Accounting, Management and Information Technology*, **1** (2), 157–87.

Klein, H.K. and Hirschheim, R. (2001), 'Choosing between competing design ideals in information systems development', *Information Systems Frontiers*, **3** (1), 75–90.

Local Implementation Strategy (LIS) (2000), 'Full local implementation strategy', Cut 1 Draft 2, Lambeth, Southwark and Lewisham Health and Social Care Community.

Lyytinen, K. (1992), 'Information systems and critical theory', in M. Alvesson and H. Willmott (eds), *Critical Management Studies*, London: Sage, pp. 159–80.

Lyytinen, K. and Hirschheim, R. (1988), 'Information systems as rational discourse: an application of Habermas' theory of communicative action', *Scandinavian Journal of Information Systems*, **4** (1/2), 19–30.

Lyytinen, K.J. and Klein, H.K. (1985), 'The critical theory of Jürgen Habermas as basis for a theory of information systems', in E. Mumford, R. Hirschheim, G. Fitzgerald and T. Wood-Harper (eds), *Research Methods in Information Systems*, Amsterdam: North-Holland, pp. 219–36.

Mackintosh, C. and Shakespeare, C. (1995), 'Primary healthcare and general practice', in R. Sheaff and V. Peel (eds), *Managing Health Service Information Systems: An Introduction*, Buckingham, UK and Philadelphia, PA: Open University Press, pp. 47–65.

Marcuse, H. (1970), *One-Dimensional Man*, London: Sphere Books.

May, C. and Ellis, N.T. (2001), 'When protocols fail: technical evaluation, biomedical knowledge, and a social production of "facts" about a telemedicine clinic', *Social Science and Medicine*, **53**, 989–1002.

May, C., Gask, L., Atkinson, T., Ellis, N., Mair, F. and Esmail, A. (2001), 'Resisting and promoting new technologies in clinical practice: the case of telepsychiatry', *Social Science and Medicine*, **52**, 1889–901.

May, C., Mort, M., Williams, T., Mair, F. and Gask, L. (2003), 'Health technology assessment in its local contexts: studies of telehealthcare', *Social Science and Medicine*, **57**, 697–710.

McDonald, I., Hill, S., Daly, J. and Crowe, B. (1998), 'Evaluating telemedicine in Victoria: a generic framework', Victorian Government Department of Human Services, Melbourne.

McLaren, P., Mohammedali, A., Riley, A. and Gaughran, F. (1999), 'Integrating interactive television-based psychiatric consultation into an urban community mental health service', *Journal of Telemedicine and Telecare*, **5** (Supplement 1), S1: 100–102.

Milio, N. (1992), 'New tools for community involvement in health', *Health Promotion International*, **7** (3), 209–17.

Morrow, R.D. and Brown, D.D. (1994), *Critical Theory and Methodology*, London: Sage.

Myers, M.D. and Young, L.W. (1997), 'Hidden agendas, power and managerial assumptions in information systems development: an ethnographic study', *Information Technology and People*, **10** (3), 224–40.

Ngwenyama, O.K. (1991), 'The critical social theory approach to information systems: problems and challenges', in H.-E. Nissen, H.K. Klein and R. Hirschheim (eds), *Information Systems Research: Contemporary Approaches and Emergent Traditions*, Amsterdam: North-Holland and London: Elsevier Science, pp. 267–80.

NHS Executive (1998), *Information for Health: An Information Strategy for the Modern NHS 1998–2005*, Leeds.

Perednia, D.A. and Allen, A. (1995), 'Telemedicine technology and clinical applications', *Journal of the American Medical Association (JAMA)*, **273** (6), 483–8.

Plamping, D. (1998), 'Change and resistance to change in the NHS', *British Medical Journal*, **317**, 69–71.

Roine, R., Ohinmaa, A. and Hailey, D. (2001), 'Assessing telemedicine: a systematic review of the literature', *Canadian Medical Association Journal*, **165** (6), 765–71.

Saravanamuthu, K. and Wood-Harper, T. (2001), 'Developing emancipatory information systems', in A. Adam, D. Howcroft, H. Richardson and B. Robinson (eds), *Proceedings of (Re-)Defining Critical Research in Information Systems: An International Workshop*, University of Salford, pp. 91–109.

Shoib, G. and Nandhakumar, J. (2003), 'Cross-cultural IS adoption in multinational corporations: a study of rationality', in M. Korpela, R. Montealegre and A. Poulymenakov (eds), *Organizational Information Systems in the Context of Globalization*, Greece, Boston, MA: Kluwer Academic, pp. 435–51.

Sosa-Iudicissa, M., Oliveri, N., Gamboa, C.A. and Roberts, J. (eds) (1997), *Internet, Telematics and Health*, Amsterdam, Berlin, Oxford, Tokyo, Washington, DC: IOS Press.

Taylor, F.W. ([1911] 1998), *The Principles of Scientific Management*, Norcross, GA: Engineering and Management Press, New York and London.

Varey, R.J., Wood-Harper, T. and Wood, B. (2002), 'A theoretical review of management and information systems using a critical communications theory', *Journal of Information Technology*, **17**, 229–39.

Walsham, G. (1996), 'Exploring the intellectual structure of information systems development: a short critique', *Accounting, Management and Information Technology*, **6** (1/2), 133–8.

Weber, M. (1978), *Economy and Society*, Berkeley, CA: University of California Press.

Whitten, P., Kingsely, C. and Grigsby, H. (2000), 'Results of a meta-analysis of cost–benefit research: is this a question worth asking?', *Journal of Telemedicine and Telecare*, **6** (Supplement 1), S1: 4–S1: 7.

Williams, S., May, C., Mair, F., Mort, M. and Gask, L. (2003), 'Normative models of health technology assessment and the social production of evidence about telehealth care', *Health Policy*, **64**, 1–16.

Wilson, F.A. (1997), 'The truth is out there: the search for emancipatory principles in information systems design', *Information Technology and People*, **10** (3), 187–204.

Wootton, R., Bloomer, S.E., Corbett, R., Eedy, D.J., Hicks, N., Lotery, H.E., Mathews, C., Paisley, J., Steele, K. and Loane, M.A. (2000), 'Multicentre randomised control trials comparing real time teledermatology with conventional outpatient dermatological care: societal cost–benefit analysis', *British Medical Journal*, **320**, 1252–6.

Wootton, R. and Craig, J. (eds) (1999), *Introduction to Telemedicine*, London: Royal Society of Medicine Press.

Wyatt, J.C. and Wyatt, S.M. (2003), 'When and how to evaluate health information systems?', *International Journal of Medical Informatics*, **69**, 251–9.

# Index

mild constructionism 72
Miller, P. 250
Mintzberg, H. 64
Moore, K. 293–4
morality 309–11, 320
Morgan, G. 20, 253
Morrow, R.A. 40, 41
Muers, S. 331–2
Mumby, D.K. 115
Mumford, E. 104
Murray, F. 53, 56, 85, 94
Myers, M.D. 3, 34–5, 76, 86

narrative analysis 115–16
nation-states 276
National Health Service (NHS)
  reforms 311, 395–6, 399–404
  London Ambulance Service (LAS)
    case study 311–21
  *see also* telehealth
natural world, and social world,
  differences between 27–8
Neuman, W.L. 25, 26, 37
Neumann, P.G. 80
neutrality, social and political,
  assumptions of 30
New Zealand
  casemix information system case
    study 251–3
  executive information system (EIS)
    case study 256–9
  intranet case study 262–5
Newman, M. 87, 92, 246, 312
Nicoll, D.W. 208
Noble, D. 196, 200
non-performative intent 4
Novick, D. 106

objectivity 4–5, 25–6, 27, 38–9, 76
organizational behaviour studies
  302–3
organizational configurations, types of
  366–7
Orlikowski, W.J. 27, 38, 74, 75, 85, 225,
  251, 261–2, 264–5, 300
Ormrod, S. 255, 256
Oudshoorn, N. 201, 214

panopticon metaphor 49–50, 57, 58,
  59, 250

Parker, M. 192
participatory action research 40
patriarchy theory 158
performativity 181
Perrow, C. 81
Peters, T. 137
Pettigrew, A.M. 56–7, 61
Pickering, A. 72
Pinch, T. 201
Pinto, J.K. 81
Popular Front 189
positivist IS research
  assumptions 27, 38–9
  criticisms of 22
  methodology 38–9
  purpose of 21
  values 25, 26
positivist research, and theory 33
post-industrial society 274, 275
post-positivism 25
postmodernism 278–9, 280
Poulymenakou, A. 82–3
poverty 226
  rates, USA 351
  *see also* urban poverty
power 47–8, 112, 249–51
  actor-network theory (ANT) 63–5,
    94, 95–6
  and capital 284–5
  casemix information system case
    study (New Zealand) 251–3
  centralization of 32
  'circuits of power' 62–3, 65
  and communication 393
  confession 108–9
  critical discourse analysis 106, 107,
    112, 118–19
  emancipation 3, 51, 58, 59
  'episodic' 63
  and ethics 129
  and evaluation 329
  and ideology 111
  integrative framework for study of
    62–3, 65
  and knowledge 277, 320
  and morality 309–10
  'power discretion' 56–7, 58, 61–2
  'power over' 51–4, 58, 60
  'power storage' 54–6, 58, 60–61
  'power to' 49–51, 57–9